WITH THE
JOCKS

Peter White in the uniform of the King's Own Scottish Borderers at his parents' home in Sussex.

WITH THE
JOCKS

PETER WHITE

FOREWORD BY
SIR JOHN KEEGAN

SUTTON PUBLISHING

This book was first published in 2001 by
Sutton Publishing Limited · Phoenix Mill
Stroud · Gloucestershire · GL5 2BU

This paperback edition first published in 2002

British Library Cataloguing in Publication Data
A catalogue record for this book is available from the British
Library

ISBN 0 7509 3057 8

Typeset in 10.5/12pt Times.
Typesetting and origination by
Sutton Publishing Limited.
Printed and bound in Great Britian by
J.H. Haynes & Co. Ltd, Sparkford.

CONTENTS

FOREWORD

by SIR JOHN KEEGAN

This awful winter of 2000/2001, alternately sodden and freezing, sometimes both together, has reminded the survivors of the campaign of 1944–5 in the flatlands of north-west Europe of the terrible conditions in which they fought to bring the Second World War to an end.

Peter White, author of this unforgettable memoir of the British Liberation Army's ordeal, was a platoon commander in the 4th King's Own Scottish Borderers, a Territorial battalion of that famous regiment which joined the battle soon after the failure of the airborne descent on Arnhem in September 1944. It belonged to 52nd Lowland Division which was tasked to take the island of Walcheren and open the mouth of the Scheldt estuary, so that the port of Antwerp could be cleared to supply the Allied armies in their final offensive against the western defences of the Reich.

By the time Peter White's platoon became engaged, the fine summer and autumn in which the British and Americans had liberated France and Belgium was over. Temperatures had fallen, rain, succeeded by snow, had set in and the waterlogged ground resisted efforts at digging in. No one who reads Peter White's account of striking the water table fourteen inches below the surface of a frost-hardened crust of soil, and pressing harder into the mixture of slush and mush at the bottom of his uncompleted slit trench in an effort to shelter from accurate German artillery and small-arms fire, is likely to forget the description.

Whole nights were spent in such conditions, which combined disabling physical hardship with acute danger. Peter White was not hit throughout the eight months his narrative relates. All but two of the Jocks in his platoon of thirty were hit, the number of dead equalling that of the wounded, and together exceeding the platoon's strength when it began its advance into Germany. His Jocks were shot, burnt, blown up, dismembered. Some of their worst experiences were suffered at the hands of their own side, gunners who dropped shells short, tank crews who mistook their positions for those of the enemy.

The willingness of the Jocks to suppress the horror of yesterday and go forward on the morrow at times beggars belief. It clearly astounded Peter White, who was not only an amateur soldier but a pre-war pacifist whose aversion to killing was founded on deep Christian belief.

It is entirely appropriate that his memoir of these terrible months should be called 'With the Jocks', for ultimately the subject of his story is not the bleak winter of 1944/5, nor the miserable terrain of the advance into Germany, nor the battles the 4th KOSB fought in those conditions, but the endurance and bravery of the soldiers he commanded. As his narrative unfolds, with its relentless emphasis on cold, casualties and the impersonal cruelty of war, the reader becomes almost consumed with disbelief that men could endure what they did. To get up each morning, after a day which had been itself an escape from death, to swallow tinned bacon, hard tack and chlorine-flavoured tea, to plod forward across soaked fields in which every footstep might set off a lethal explosive charge, to lie for hours in freezing water while shells raked the landscape, to rise as darkness fell in the hope of finding a dry spot to shelter for the night after a mouthful of bully beef and hard biscuit: what comfortable reader, congratulating himself or herself on belonging to a nation that beat Hitler, cannot be subdued by the thought that Peter White's Jocks incarnated an exceptional generation?

War is often narrated as an adventure story. War may be an adventure. Peter White's war was not so, nothing but a grim passage of duty, dedicated to destroying tyranny in the hope that it would not recur. His account of the courage and imperturbability of his Jocks should inspire all who read it to guard the liberty they won for us as a precious treasure.

ACKNOWLEDGEMENTS

The publication of *With the Jocks* would not have been possible without the support and kindness of many people, but the greatest thanks must go to Peter White's widow, Elizabeth, Harry Prince, whose enthusiasm and tireless efforts brought the book to print, and the members of the King's Own Scottish Borderers (KOSB). The publishers also wish to thank Jenny Shaw, who helped prepare the manuscript for publication, and Lt Col C.G.O. Hogg, DL, from the KOSB Museum at Regimental Headquarters, Berwick-upon-Tweed, who provided much of the background information included in the introduction and epilogue. Thanks are due also to Sir John Keegan for kindly agreeing to write the foreword.

The illustrations are all either Peter White's drawings or photographs from his own collection that he pasted into his diary. As far as can be ascertained, no photographs survive of the KOSB in action in north-west Europe during the period covered by the book and White's pictures are, therefore, a doubly significant record of the Jocks at war.

EDITOR'S NOTE: Peter White's text remains as he wrote it, with the exception of minor changes for clarity and consistency. Editor's additions are indicated by square brackets.

THE JOCKS

PUBLISHER'S INTRODUCTION

For the millions of ordinary men who fought the Second World War on front lines drawn across Europe, Africa and the East, the conflict was a day-to-day, human battle against almost impossible conditions. Fear, uncertainty and doubt were constant companions in a war fought out in small, muddy pockets of attrition that were part of a 'bigger picture' known only to those in remote headquarters. Yet in dugouts and trenches they also experienced powerful comradeship, discovered self-belief, and shared moments of exhilaration and triumph. *With the Jocks* is a personal and vivid first-hand account of these experiences. It is the diary of Peter White, a quiet, intelligent, thoughtful young man with deeply held religious convictions about the sanctity of life, who found himself in charge of a group of robust Scottish soldiers in north-west Europe from October 1944 to VE Day. His talent as writer, together with his artistic flair, combined to produce a moving record of his experiences. This is, in his own words, an honest, 'warts and all' account of life in battle conditions.

White was born into an upper-middle-class family in 1921. His father, an engineer, and his mother, an artist, were living in South Africa at the time, but returned to Surrey, England in the early 1930s, partly for the sake of their three boys' education. Peter attended Ottershaw College where his artistic abilities soon became apparent. He started keeping a diary in 1938, noting down the activities of the day and also items of significance off the 'wireless' and from newspapers, illustrating his entries with drawings or sketches.

When the Second World War began in 1939, his father and elder brother, John, went into the Army and received commissions. White was too young at seventeen and was accepted as a student at the Royal Academy of Arts in October 1939. The war gave him much cause for thought. The Whites were a religious family and Peter, a pacifist at heart, found the idea of killing any living creature repugnant. However, he could see the need for men to fight in this conflict clearly enough, and in his own words '. . . could see no logical reason why it should not be me'. He joined the Royal Artillery in May 1942 and was commissioned as a lieutenant in May 1943. His long-range, impersonal war did not last for long, however, and in April 1944, as the Luftwaffe's threat to the skies over London receded, he was among a group of young gunners transferred to the infantry.

Initially White was horrified at what might be expected of him as an infantryman in the days ahead. The thought of killing human beings at close quarters seemed beyond comprehension. However, his faith sustained him. His diary makes it clear that he determined at the outset to do his best and hoped that he had learned enough during his infantry conversion course to be entrusted with men's lives in action.

As his father was a Border man, White chose a Border Regiment – the King's Own Scottish Borderers (KOSB). He was attracted to the 4th Battalion which was listed as being in a mountain division and seemed therefore to offer the opportunity of winter sports at the Army's expense. White was posted to 10 Platoon, B Company, and his transformation to an infantryman completed by the tartan flashes he now wore on his shoulders and the silver-badged tam-o'-shanter on his head.

The KOSB (25th Foot) has a fine history. Raised in Edinburgh in 1689, its battle honours include Minden (1759) and South Africa (1900–02). During the First World War, the Regiment comprised two Regular Army Battalions (1st and 2nd), two Territorial Battalions (4th and 5th), three 'New Army' Battalions (6th, 7th and 8th), a 9th Battalion, which provided reinforcements for the others, and a 10th (Garrison) Battalion. The 4th and 5th Battalions fought at Gallipoli in the 52nd (Lowland) Division, and with distinction in Palestine and France. The civilian soldiers who fought in the Territorial Battalions returned to their peacetime occupations after 1918 and the Regiment reverted to its peacetime role. Many Border men, however, carried on soldiering in the

Territorial Army even when their contribution was unfashionable and poorly paid. When the Territorials launched an appeal for recruits on the eve of the Second World War, men from the Borders (Berwickshire, Roxburgh and Selkirk), Berwick-upon-Tweed, Dumfries and Galloway flocked to join the KOSB. The 4th (Border) Battalion, the TA Battalion of the Borders, which had been reformed in the inter-war years, received its share of recruits and was soon up to battle strength. Men of the Borders had a particular character, living nearer to nature than their comrades from industrial Clydeside or the more academic Edinburgh, and the TA battalions reflected the society from whence their recruits came. In 1939, the KOSB order of battle was 1st and 2nd Battalions in the Regular Army, with 4th, 5th, 6th and 7th Battalions in the Territorial Army. (There was no 3rd Battalion.)

Soldiers of the KOSB were engaged in the action from the beginning. 1st Battalion was sent to France in 1939 with the British Expeditionary Force and was among those evacuated from Dunkirk in May 1940. 4th and 5th Battalions, part of 155 Infantry Brigade with 7th/9th Royal Scots Territorial Battalion in 52nd (Lowland) Division, were part of the 2nd British Expeditionary Force. They were evacuated from Cherbourg on 18 June 1940. From October 1944 until May 1945, the period covered by the diary, 52nd (Lowland) Division was part of 21st Army Group, commanded by Field Marshal Bernard Montgomery, which comprised the British Second Army and the First Canadian Army.

On arrival back in Britain in 1940, the Lowland Division had begun training for mountain warfare, and White joined the 4th Battalion at Banchory on Deeside in 1944 for exercises in the Cairngorms. The Division expected to be deployed to Norway, but in early summer 1944 moved to Stonehaven, where a new role awaited them. They were to take to the air, and be transported in Dakotas to an active battlefield. Complicated tables had to be prepared, setting out the Battalion in plane loads and showing, to the exact pound, the number of troops and amount of equipment each plane could accommodate. The men were fit from mountain training, but as airborne soldiers, each had to be turned into a self-reliant machine. He had to carry more ammunition, food and clothes. Route marches with fully loaded rucksacks were compulsory.

The exercises gave White the opportunity to get to know the Jocks and his fellow officers – he was delighted to realise that he was beginning to understand even the densest Scottish accent! At first, however, he found integration into the Battalion difficult, joining it as a 'Sassenach outsider' when the mess members were already a tightly knit group, many of whom had known each other as Territorials for years. For its part, the Battalion initially had doubts about White's suitability for his new role and two successive Battalion commanders considered him 'too quiet and reserved for an infantry officer'. This view was to change: White developed his own, highly effective form of leadership and made a conscious effort to make more noise. While at Stonehaven, White was given responsibility for two 20mm Polsten anti-aircraft guns and the training of their crews. As a result, from summer to December 1944, he was attached to the Carrier Platoon in Support (S) Company.

On 3 August 1944 the units mustered to leave Stonehaven for Piper's Wood, near Amersham, Buckinghamshire. This was a first trip across the border for many of the Jocks and, perhaps, their first brush with the war. Lancaster and Halifax bombers could be seen overhead on their way to operations over Germany on clear evenings.

The Jocks waited at Amersham for several weeks, almost daily expecting the order to fly off to the continent. There were several false alarms followed by a period of anti-climax during which training and preparation continued unabated, adding to the tension. To counter the German habit of rendering the Jocks leaderless by targeting their officers and NCOs first, officers were advised to hide all badges of rank and those with moustaches (a tell-tale sign of a British officer) either trimmed them drastically or shaved them off. All platoon commanders were instructed to draw up a list of the next-of-kin of their men so a note 'could be sent as a personal touch in the event of a casualty'. Censoring of letters also took up much of their time. Lectures covered security, how to kill someone with bare hands, what to do if a plane crash landed, how to organise a dropping zone, what to do if captured and tortured and how to escape. It was expected that the Battalion would serve in Europe alongside the US 101st Airborne Division, so American paratroopers went to Piper's Wood to acquaint their allies with the appearance, procedures and weapons of the US forces in the hope of avoiding 'friendly fire' incidents. Refresher courses were held to ensure each man was familiar with his own range of weapons, transport, radio, explosives, fieldcraft and tactics.

After about half a dozen 'flaps', the Commander of 52nd (Lowland) Division, Major-General Hakewell-Smith, spoke to all the officers. He had just returned from battlegrounds in France and was therefore in a position to explain the current situation and give a good idea of the conditions the Division would meet on the continent. The proposed operations had fallen through as the speed of the Allied advance rendered them unnecessary. The facilities of the ports on the continent available to the allies were now overstretched, with fuel and supplies running low. Therefore, time was needed now to build up supplies, reopen railways and free more ports to allow the advance to continue. The Jocks would have to wait again, scanning news reports for any clue about where and when they would join the war.

On 4 September 1944 the order 'prepare to move' finally came. The Division set off for Woodhall Spa in Lincolnshire so that they would be near to airfields for immediate take-off when required. Everyone sensed that something was brewing, but the days passed with no call to action and another period of uncertainty began with yet more intensive training. Captured enemy equipment was displayed and handled and the inhabitants of Woodhall Spa were treated to mock street fighting. Men were taken for familiarisation trips in aircraft, White in a Lancaster of the elite 617 'Dambusters' bomber squadron based at Woodhall Spa aerodrome. Practice moves were made to a dummy airfield, where each unit deployed with all its equipment separated into aircraft loads.

Tension mounted in the camp as the pace of activities was stepped up and censorship became stricter. On 17 September, the air armada to Arnhem was announced on the radio and it seemed certain that the Division would take part. Each unit waited expectantly. Polish paratroopers, scheduled for departure before the 4th Battalion, sat in their aircraft waiting to go, took off, were recalled, and took off again only to be badly mauled on arrival at Arnhem. White and his Jocks realised that the operation was not working out as planned. An emergency change of plan was announced: it was far too dangerous to fly the troops over in Dakota aircraft, so as a desperate measure to keep the Arnhem pocket open and to give the armour time to link up (or at least to support the troops already committed to the operation), it was decided to fly rifle companies over in Waco gliders. Consequently, company commanders sat up all night working out new loading tables and learning about gliders. As all the preparations were completed, this operation, too, was cancelled to great relief all round. However, waiting for weeks on end to leave at a few hours' notice had wracked the Jocks' nerves; one summed up the company's sentiments with the thought that even a condemned man would feel more settled with a definite execution date.

During the enforced wait at Woodhall, White's feelings of being isolated faded as teamwork developed and friendships formed. Battalion pride was bolstered.

The order to move finally came on 12 October 1944 and on the 16th, the Jocks departed by train for Southampton. There they were taken by truck to a rain-sodden tented transit camp. Next day, a sense of adventure was in the air: the men were taken to the docks where they waited in company groups to board the ferry-boat *Lady of Man* bound for Ostend, Belgium. Each boarded armed with blanket and seasickness pills in addition to his kit. White and his men knew that finally 'this was it', and thoughts turned inevitably to loved ones at home and to what might lie ahead. Against orders, it was decided to take the full Battalion pipe band kit and drums. The drums would be stored in Belgium until needed.

The Channel crossing was rough and uncomfortable. *Lady of Man* was packed with men attempting to sleep on every available inch of floor space. Many men suffered sea sickness. Next morning, the Belgian coast was sighted, and with it came the thought that the Germans were not very far inland. The gale and the swell were too violent for the ship to enter the harbour, so *Lady of Man* headed back to shelter off Dover. Yet again the Jocks had to wait.

On the morning of 19 October *Lady of Man* sailed back across the Channel, docked without incident at Ostend, and the troops disembarked. Evidence of the recent German occupation was all around – buildings demolished, massive, sinister concrete bunkers, shrapnel scars. The local people were badly clothed, preoccupied and under-nourished, but many of them waved or shouted greetings to the Jocks who responded with enthusiasm. White noted that language barriers never seemed to bother a Jock. The night was spent in a former German barracks and next morning, a nose-to-tail stream of mechanised equipment, tanks, Jeeps with trailers and trucks carrying the troops trundled down roads rutted with shrapnel rips and rubble-filled craters, past houses blown apart to reveal their smashed up interiors.

The Jocks were finally on Belgian soil but still did not know when, where or how they would go into action. They were pleasantly surprised to arrive in Vive St Eloi where they were greeted warmly by the villagers. Battalion headquarters was in a farm owned by the Duhamel family and it was here that the drums were stored for safety. Jan Duhamel, a son of the farmer, had evaded capture by the Germans and was head of the local resistance movement. He spoke fluent German, so the Battalion Commander, Lieutenant-Colonel Chris Melville, appointed him interpreter and gave him the honorary rank of 2nd lieutenant.

Now the Battalion waited for several more days, although some units, including 'S' Company and Peter White, moved to the next village of Vive St BaVon. Each man was found an excellent billet and friendships formed at this time which still survive. M Lambrecht, whose home became the officers' mess, told White he was impressed by the demeanour of the British troops compared to the glum Germans, and he was sure that the quality of British equipment was superior to Germans'. Peter White and the Jocks were about to find out whether this was true.

PREFACE

For seven years prior to these events I had kept a diary day by day, illustrating it whenever possible. The realisation that the current volume would have to be sent home for storage on our unit going into action was a great disappointment. 'I'm afraid old boy, you will have to knock that off when we go overseas', said the CO one night as I illustrated my current diary in the mess as he peered over my shoulder. He took quite an interest and was the recipient of several sketches later in Belgium and Germany, one of him writing home as we crossed the Channel in the ferry.

However, the habit I had formed during these years of absorbing the events of each day with a view to writing and illustrating them at nightfall became too much a part of me to be easily put aside. As a result I became aware after a short while that I was amassing this same information, but by other methods. These took the form of copious notes in order books, the orders themselves, sketches and odd details on scraps of paper which I stored with my kit from time to time in 'B' Echelon, in letters written home after the appropriate time lapse following various actions and by cross-checking with others of the Battalion when collecting all this material together.

The life in infantry action which fell to my lot and which is recorded here as a continuation of my diary was, I think, fairly typical of the experience of any infantryman in the campaign. It traces but one thread among the many thousands forming the intricate fabric of the Allied armies' struggles. Many threads must have been put to far fiercer tensions than mine in the skein that wove towards victory. The variety of battle circumstances was infinite.

If the thread of my experience was not typical in one respect of the average Infantry Platoon Commander, it was that by the grace of God it was not snapped short after only a few actions, or interrupted by injury or battle-exhaustion, but ran right through to the end despite continual replacement which sadly renewed the weave about me.

To my increasing gratitude and perhaps amazement, I became aware that to trust God as the only real and wholly good power and cause, despite all appearance to the contrary in the material evidence of battle, gave one a sure path on which to tread even if, as so often, one trod it in fear and trembling.

No words, however set together, can convey even a minute concept of the searing mental and physical impact of the shambles of infantry action unless one has personally experienced it. Nevertheless, I have attempted to do this in its personal impact, day succeeding day, however inadequately; and also to sketch in the ordinary detail of our lives, hopes and fears, between our periods of passing through the furnace.

If no words can convey the 'action', it would be an even harder task to express my appreciation, admiration and high regard for the wonderful qualities of humour, compassion and 'guts' displayed by those with whom I had the privilege to serve.

THE ATTACK ON
WALCHEREN ISLAND

A route march or two of intense interest in our new surroundings and various other training filled in our time for a few unexpected days' respite. On October 27 1944 the whole village turned out to wave a tearful departure, displaying a depth of emotion which touched us deeply. Our convoy bumped and splashed over roads breaking up under excessive war traffic until we pulled up in the village of Kleit, 10 miles due east of Bruges. The Germans had pulled out about three weeks before. It was a poor village and conditions were rough, though happily we still had civilian billets, of a rather squalid type in most cases. As an officer billeting men one made a note of each address, owner's name, how many men they could take and whether they would have beds of straw. The householder was then eventually compensated by the Burgomeister. Not all householders would take payment however. Some explained that they were making a small return for their liberation.

My billet was a garage run by a rough walrus-whiskered peasant. His small son delighted in playing football about the cobbled street, kicking a clanking German helmet. His usual opponent was a scraggy 13-year-old youth who sported an imposing pair of German officer's jack-boots. He boasted: 'I haf shot de schwein ven he leef dis fillage!' So saying he attempted to borrow my rifle to demonstrate his claimed feat: 'Here, I will make you see how vos done, yes.'

The Jocks were intrigued with the churchyard. 'Each tombstone has a *** photey of the poor devil inside Surr!' The sanitation and hygiene in these small Flemish villages was really primitive and still probably as it was centuries before. Perhaps a need to provide fertiliser for the overpopulated land dictated this in part. The village public convenience was initially rather a shock. Its position was blatantly indicated merely by villagers using a particular spot in the village which was entirely devoid of any surrounding structure. The adaptable Jock accepted this and other aspects of Flemish village life with little comment and without batting an eyelid. The church was the most popular building in the village and people shuffled to and from it from dawn till dusk.

That we were much closer to the enemy now we gathered from several indications. Two of these puzzled us a lot until we heard that V2 rockets were falling on London. In the daytime, to our north, the sky sometimes displayed a thin vertical vapour trail which rose from a slow start with unbelievable acceleration until within seconds it had passed straight up out of sight. At night, a star-like light replaced the vapour trail to indicate the rocket's course.

Tangible evidence of the fact that our first action was soon to come and that it was going to be an unusual one was provided by the arrival of a convoy of fourteen tank transporters in our village carrying strange cargo. These Weasels which they unloaded were small brothers of the amphibious Buffaloes.

Swiftly following this, word went about that we were to attack the port of Flushing on Walcheren Island. The assault was to be carried out from the wrecked shell of a small port called Breskens opposite Flushing and on our side of the Scheldt estuary. It was to be a combined land, sea and air operation. A miniature 'D' Day. On this attack rested the clearing of the approaches to the vital supply port of Antwerp, the key to any further effort to break through into the north German plain. For this operation, we were to be under command of the Canadian 1st Army, to the delight of our own attached Canadian officers. Opposing us on the island were 15,000 German troops, a mixture of Wehrmacht, marines, SS and AA men, backed by masses of guns, interconnecting massive fortifications, mines and torpedoes. The island dominated the estuary and even the loading up of our assault craft would be under enemy observation and fire. That the Germans were grimly determined to hold on, we soon realised. If confirmation were needed, a captured proclamation read: 'The defence of the approaches to Antwerp represents a task which is decisive for the future conduct of the war. After overrunning the Scheldt fortifications the British would finally be in a position to land great masses of material in a large and completely protected harbour. With the material they might deliver a death blow at the north German Plateau and Berlin. For this reason we must hold the Scheldt fortifications to the end. The German people are watching us. In this hour the fortifications along the Scheldt occupy a role which is decisive for the future of our people.'

The Sunday before the attack the Padre held a Battalion church service on the Kleit village green. Because of the circumstances it proved a solemn and moving occasion. I think we were all much more thoughtful than usual and sincere in prayer. Though we were all trained nearly to the pitch of overtraining in all that human ingenuity could devise to condition us to what we were likely to meet in battle, including training with live ammunition to 'Battle inoculate' us, and endless schemes to physically and perhaps mentally exhaust us; we all realised thus far that we had met only molehills as compared with a possible Everest. The biggest unknown factor was the mental reaction of the individual, especially of those in responsibility. What part would fear play? How well could it be overcome, or hidden? The tense realisation dawned ever larger that the lives of one's friends and one's own life would depend on split-second decisions in an unknown world of utter chaos.

Before in life one had been accustomed to planning and looking ahead in terms of days, weeks or even years of fair certainty. Now, we realised squarely, for the first time perhaps, that one's future appeared to take a dip out of sight into the unknown only a matter of hours ahead. At this point in thought it became very clear that for any faith in continuity at all, one had to search for something outside of human structure and organisation on which to rely; something which would not change; where the future was not a human responsibility.

The service over, the CO gave a short talk to 'put us all in the picture'; to give an idea of what was expected of the Battalion, the

Brigade and the Division in this formidable task. As he spoke, I glanced round at all the rugged friendly faces and felt reassured. We were all in the same boat, but it was difficult not to wonder a bit, to think of the families of each at home. Where would each be in a couple of days, a week hence?

In view of the difficulties of getting vehicles over to Flushing it was decided to leave the carriers and anti-tank platoon out of the initial attack. This at first seemed to mean that Jimmy and I and our men would not take part, but we found within a few hours that we were assigned to a job on the beach. There we would have to cope with every scrap of food, ammunition and stores needed for the battle. We were pleased to find that Capt Tammy Youngson and Frank Clark were also assigned to this. 'Uncle Beach', at which the landings would take place, and the only spot available, was only 85 yards wide! If Jerry was accurate with any guns and mortars, to survive the initial assault it seemed we would be in for a thin time. In case casualties were steep, it was decided to institute a system called LOB – Left out of Battle. One or two officers, a few NCOs and a handful of men would take a turn out of battle from each company, to form a nucleus round which a unit could be more easily rebuilt with replacements. However, after this, our first attack, we were to find ourselves so continually short of men that the idea never could operate properly. A pocket of Germans holding out near Blankenberghe on the coast had to be eliminated before the attack. To this end a large artillery programme was laid on to fire all night at these Boche, before swinging on to Flushing. This barrage was to lift off the beaches and into the town as No. 4 Commando, the first wave, went in to secure a bridgehead before dawn. 4th KOSB were to pass through if possible before first light to secure the northern part of the town, followed by 7th/9th Royal Scots and the 5th KOSB. Some of 4th Commando were free Dutch.

At the same time another force would be landing farther up the coast at Westkapelle. The Canadians with 156 and 157 Brigades were already on the go attacking along the Walcheren causeway to the back door and on 28 October had secured the north by an attack on South Beveland. Once Flushing had fallen we were to work up the banks of the Middleburg canal and the railway track to link with the other two Brigades. Just before the assault the RAF were to breach the Walcheren Dykes, letting the sea through to isolate the blockhouses with which the island was peppered and to isolate the fortifications round the rim of the island. As this took place HMS *Warspite* would be pumping in 16-inch shells onto the German coastal batteries and other strong points on Walcheren.

The RAF promised a 'Stonk' on the town just before the attack. Flares were dropped, but the weather must have been unsuitable for bombing for the raid never came off. The Typhoons, though, gave wonderful close support with their rockets and cannon on obstinate strong points. The operation was to be an intensive small-scale repeat of the Normandy landings.

Detailed preparation and planning was rushed ahead. The final Battalion briefing conference took place in a little *estaminet* in Kleit just as the 284-gun barrage opened up at 10 pm on 31 October, like a thunderstorm to the west, lighting the sky with a fitful pale light and sharply silhouetting the roofs of the village houses from which the Flemish villagers spilled to watch and wonder.

Inside, in the warmth of the *estaminet*, briefing dragged on until about one in the morning. At the end one or two of the officers slipped sealed envelopes to the 2i/c, who would be 'left out of battle', in case they should not survive.

It was a pretty miserable wait for the Battalion up in Breskens. The orchestra of battle noises, still evilly new to our ears, crashed and shrieked in preparation for the performers to appear, the first-night effect on nerves and stomach being felt in proportion to the scale and importance of the performance. All were new actors.

Breskens turned out to be a smashed heap of bricks and matchwood, reeking with a sickly smell of burning and of bodies trapped under the rubble, with which we were to become so familiar. Our objective over the water, Flushing, stood out clearly in the daytime as a row of buildings, crane gantries and chimneys about 2 miles over the estuary. That night the buildings showed only as burning husks shimmering amid a sequin-twinkle of explosions. So far, very few shells had been reported coming in return. At 4.30 am the time to load the assault craft had come. Down at the wrecked Breskens jetty, the first of the five waves of troops to go boarded the twenty-six bobbing camouflaged assault craft which slid rumbling softly to dissolve in the inky waters of the estuary. Inside each frail craft silent tense men crouched, gripping their weapons with pounding hearts; for each the first battle had already started mentally. The moorings with the known were slipped; ahead, in a few minutes they would be tipped from the flimsy eggshell protection of their vessels into the fear-fringed unknown . . . if they got that far.

The Commandos had crossed in darkness to jump on the beach at high tide while to a large extent the Germans' heads were pinned down with the gunfire. C Company, led by Capt David Colville sounding his hunting horn, as also did Charles Marrow with D Company later, were able to get ashore without too much opposition. However, as time went on and the tide out, the following companies fell into water and deep mud under heavy sniping, mortaring and bursts of 20mm cannon and 37 and 88mm airburst shells which plumed the sky and the water about the assault craft and the Jocks. In spite of this, the Battalion was far more fortunate than those landing up the coast at Westkappelle who lost two out of every three landing and assault craft before getting as far as the beaches.

Capt Jim Bennet, our Company commander, was the first casualty among the officers. When on a reconnaisance to Commando HQ in the first wave, he was hit in the spine by a sniper. His batman-runner dragged him out of fire into a shop. Later, Malcolm Nisbet was hit (on the 2nd) and died trying to bring in one of his men under fire.

Communication was very difficult initially as sniping and mortaring had smashed several radios. Next night, Jimmy Wannop, Tammy Youngson, Frank Clark and I rumbled over the inky waters with a group of S Company men in Navy-manned assault craft. As we got close in towards Flushing we began to hear above the noise of shells shrieking in and the throb of engines and lap of water on the hull, the pounding of mortars and shell exploding amid the buildings, the desolate crashing of tiles as the fires spread and rattling bursts of small-arms fire. Spilling out onto the cold and wet of the beach we set straight to work like madmen, all night in unloading ammunition from the assault craft.

Despite the Battalion being well established, the occasional crack and sing of a sniper's bullet twanged the darkness. Towards dawn the whole of 'Uncle Beach' and for 50 yards inland was a solid stack of ammunition. We had been worried at about midnight by some of our own artillery screaming in to erupt in flame very 'short' and dangerously close to the many tons of explosive with which we were surrounded. One shell among this and we realised our hours of frantic labour, all the reserve ammunition on which the attack depended, and ourselves, would all go up in one gigantic explosion. As each landing craft was emptied, the steady trickle of casualties brought through the town wreckage to the beach by Weasels were loaded and sent back over the water to Breskens. Serious cases were flown back to the UK within a few hours. Meanwhile, the Weasels had loaded up with supplies and ammunition and had lurched back to wherever the fighting had by then reached.

Our HQ was established in a large coal cellar beneath a tall building near the beach. We retired there for a short rest and to eat in shifts before returning to supervise operations on the beach towards daylight. Several times more there had been the rip of a machine-gun quite close, but it was not until it grew light that we began to realise that we were visible to stray German snipers and that the Commandos had not been able to winkle out all opposition near the beach. A shower of bullets crackled and whined off the pebbles, spattering the woodwork of a breakwater behind us as a chap I was working with carrying a crate of mortar bombs rolled over grovelling erratically in the sand doubled up beside a second Jock who had been hit. We dropped flat, trying to locate the source of fire while noting with apprehension that the spray of bullets had nicked chips off some of the ammunition crates. Neither Jock turned out to be badly wounded. Meanwhile, to continue unloading seemed out of the question, so we fired back heavily at all points from which we suspected the fire might have come: the control cab in a tall crane and a big warehouse with gaping windows in the dock area. Jimmy and I later painfully stalked this building when fresh fire swept the beach, but after several hundred yards of effort we found nothing. A figure appeared for a few seconds at a window to the centre of a row of houses looking on the beach. At the same instant a crackle of fire from the Jocks passed overhead and twanged brickdust around the window frame and the figure, which I was shocked to realise was that of a woman civilian, fell, striking the frame, hit by one or more shots. Some mountain artillery had now joined us on the beach and set out to eliminate one source of the fire while we continued unloading. This particular sniper, with an MG34 machine-gun, had been located, as we suspected, in a crane control cabin amid the gantries. The cabin had been armoured and our small-arms fire could do nothing with it. However, the mountain gunners scored a direct hit over open sights and knocked this pest out of existence. It was ironical that we should, as a Division trained in mountain warfare, be chosen to attack on land actually situated below sea level! No doubt the Germans thought it was some devilish-cunning British scheme. The Jocks summed it up otherwise as the flood waters started to rise.

These mountain guns, being detachable into loads which could be carried by men, were invaluable in winkling the Germans out of the dock area and around the hulk of a 20,000-ton ship under construction there. In one instance, we heard later, an artillery officer spotted twenty Germans rush for cover in a concrete fort and indicated this by radio to one of the gun teams. The gunners took the gun to bits out of sight of the enemy, carried it upstairs into a house overlooking the German bunker where the gun was re-assembled and had within twenty minutes fired the first shot. This brought the ceiling in part down on their heads with the blast, but it also got the Germans on the move. Two appeared at the doorway just in time to coincide with a direct hit from the second shot which completely dissolved them. Six more shots accounted for the rest, by which time the house from which the gun was being fired was in a state of collapse, the recoil having driven the gun-trail through the floor. One of the Weasels driven by a small nervous Jock who looked 'all in', arrived from time to time for ammunition, usually with two or three casualties on stretchers aboard. His vehicle had been peppered with shrapnel from a mortar burst and bullets from a sniper who riddled it on his every trip through the town. The last time I saw him he told me with heated feeling that he had finally located and shot the sniper, a woman. She was either a German or a collaborator.

The scream of shells ploughing into the town had nearly ceased by now. A frightening noise we never really got used to, though we were now getting experienced enough to guess more or less where they would land from the sound of their trajectory. The brittle crackling of small-arms and deeper artillery explosions continued unabated in the town. As darkness fell on the second night's fighting unchecked fires blazed furiously.

Though occasionally during the hours of darkness the noise died down to some semblance of no shooting or explosions, this 'silence' was fitful. A lone shot usually triggered off quite an outburst as though in nervous reaction beneath the lurid glow of the flames and the lazily coiling re-tinted smoke canopy. Always there was the distant erratic clatter of falling tiles and smashing woodwork as some roof collapsed into the fire. Once or twice voices could be heard shouting distantly, a dog barked hysterically and somewhere an engine revved intermittently as a vehicle laboured on some task through the rubble and craters. In this atmosphere, Jimmy and I, our assignment just about done and feeling 'done' ourselves, joined Frank Clark in entering a small battered house for a sleep on the bare boards, over which the wind played through the broken windows. We dozed fitfully with restless thoughts, getting steadily colder. For a while the artillery opened up, perhaps on a counter-attack somewhere in the early hours. Occasionally a sniper's bullet cracked outside or some other sound disturbed us. In the cold light of dawn I was disconcerted to find we had not been alone in the house. Through an open door of a back room lay six of our dead, rigid in the frosted air amid the dust and plaster. Recognition of their faces added a haunting chill to the shock and to cheerless daybreak.

From time to time Typhoons circled high over Flushing in response to some radio appeal, suddenly to slip swiftly down at an angle. The harsh engine note became more insistent, then whoosh, the rockets streaked ahead to blast heavily against some strong point while the planes dipped momentarily behind a shattered house and soared away, leaving a leisurely pall of smoke to rise and mix with that of the fires. It was at first difficult to realise that these jagged, unreal sounds of war generally meant death or maiming for someone.

Back on the beach, some of the casualties looked in a very bad way, grey-green in the face and lying still in the cold as though already dead, while waiting for a landing craft. It may have taken several hours for some to be brought thus far from some distant part of Flushing. The sea had grown rougher and landing craft were being driven broadside on to the beach and battered. To get them off it was necessary to wade into the icy sea, knowing that the clothes would then have to dry on one during the rest of the freezing days and nights which lay ahead. Casualties were difficult to get aboard, especially at low tide, when acres of mud were exposed. To help in this the Weasels and Buffaloes were invaluable. If the waves were not too severe a Buffalo could swim right over to Breskens and back under its own power, then churn up out of the water, over the beach and into the town with its load.

We soon had a steadily increasing preoccupation in the form of a trickle, then a flood of German wounded and prisoners. For so much of the war the 'Germans' had seemed rather an abstract word from which bad results had sprung as though at second hand or by remote control: by bombs from aircraft, or through the news. Now, here they were. We could properly examine them. There seemed a much greater variety of type than among our chaps. Very old, very young, massive and brutish – the type one expected – or frail, wheezing, cold and frightened parodies, small and almost pitiful in jumbled ill-fitting uniform. Most carried lots of belongings and had discarded their steel helmets, almost invariably wearing instead their peaked-caps which so called to my mind a group of vultures with their beaks twiddling this way and that as their heads swung. Also popular were cooking pots, mess tins, rye black bread, water bottles full of alcoholic drink, and evil looking heavy sausages. Their tin-shaped respirators were always in evidence. This latter point used to cause me thought at times for our gas-masks were nearly always with 'B' Echelon some miles to the rear. It seemed to me that the enemy always had theirs handy in case their command should at any time resort to gas in desperation under the Fuehrer's mad direction.

We learned that the Hotel Britannia, centre of a network of

fortifications, was still holding out and that it housed the enemy HQ. The shelling during the night had been the preliminary to a Royal Scots attack, a very fierce engagement in which large numbers of the enemy were killed and captured. By the evening of November 3 the whole town was in our hands. The Royal Scots unfortunately lost their CO in this attack, though they captured the German local garrison commander who, with a swarm of shell-dazed prisoners, created quite a problem for Tammy, Frank, Jimmy and me.

To find some immediate solution to guarding these hosts of prisoners with our handful of men, we marched them all into a wired-up orchard. The Jocks took a delight in solving the luggage problem of the prisoners, who had enough odds and ends, a lot probably looted, to fill a landing craft. I was interested to notice that nearly all of them had their waterbottles filled with cognac, wine or some other spirits to form a 'Dutch courage' reservoir in an emergency. One or two had obviously partaken of it too. Some were genuinely shell-shocked, but others' unsteady condition, as given away by alcoholic-fumed breath, was due to mental escapism in drink. They stood among the autumn stark apple trees, or sat with exhaustion and dejection, a grey-green silent mass from which a peculiar sour 'German' reeking odour issued reminiscent of a Kaffir kraal. I suppose some of this came from their evil-looking sausages. We fed them on our rations and handed their surplus bread and meat over the wire to a collection of delighted though poorly dressed and ill-fed Dutch civilians who lined the wire, gloating in silence and sometimes verbally, immensely enjoying the spectacle of the 'Master Race' who had so recently lorded it over them and were now stripped of their power. Many of the Germans were really blast shocked and some miserably and rather surprisingly fearful. All looked dejected, grey in the face with dirt and tiredness and many if spoken to could only utter 'Allus Kaput . . . Hitler no good.' The officers were quite different to the sheep-like other ranks who came in long crocodiles under the escort of some casual Jock. We locked up these arrogant blighters in a concrete shed. They were eternally complaining about something or other, talking about 'their rights' and quoting the Geneva Convention. What riled them most was that as our Jocks and officers were dressed alike, often carrying the same weapons and with no visible badges of rank, they were never sure whether they were being dealt with by an officer or a private. The garrison commander gave every appearance of being a particularly nasty type and the last word in arrogance. Tammy's batman took him down a peg or two when to his white rage he told him in rich language just what he thought of him as a fellow human creature, then calmly relieved him of his fur-lined gloves before he was made to wade out over the mud with other prisoners to board assault craft for evacuation to Breskens. About 3,000 of the 5,000 prisoners taken by the Brigade eventually passed through our hands. One German had been captured, sitting dazed in his slit trench beside his Dutch girlfriend who had been killed the night before.

Rubber ankle boots had been issued early on during the attack and these, together with the amphibious vehicles, became more and more invaluable as the flood water caused by the breached sea walls steadily rose in the lower parts of the town. There were very few civilians in Flushing as these had mostly evacuated to Middleburg in the centre of the island in anticipation of the shelling and fighting. Those still there did great work dashing here and there under fire, wearing white arm bands and carrying a satchel, tending the wounded – surprisingly the Germans too with equal care and gentleness; making a note of the dead and their identity discs for records. This amazed me.

All this while the German commander of Walcheren in the crowded historic town of Middleburg steadfastly refused to surrender. The forward companies had very heavy, difficult fighting through the dock area and the strongly fortified northern rim of the town where flood water driven by the wind and tide swirled fiercely round the wading Jocks who were brought to a standstill by running into Schu minefields and fire. Both took steady toll. These wooden mines foiled detectors. The presence of so many civilians in Middleburg made it very difficult for the artillery and the RAF, who had to try to confine their fire to strong points and leave doubtful targets.

Eventually resistance was overcome with Buffaloes loaded with Jocks paddling cross-country in the floods and up the canal past the strong point in the darkness. Some of these vehicles carried mountain guns ready to fire as they paddled. These big clanging vehicles unloaded the Jocks right in Middleburg. The garrison commander insisted on an officer of suitable rank not to offend his dignity to surrender to in the town square. There was not one available, so one of our officers with borrowed insignia promoted himself on the spot to the required exalted rank. Honour codes thus being met, Lt Gen Daser formally capitulated on the fifth day of the fight. For three more days the Battalion stopped on in Middleburg amid the wildly grateful civilians, sorting out prisoners, collaborators and guarding food dumps.

The Divisional Commander in a letter to the Colonel of our Regiment summed up: 'You will be pleased to know that both your Battalions in the Division did very well indeed. The 4th Battalion successfully carried out a most difficult assault landing right on the front door-step of what I believe to be the world's most strongly defended place. The 5th Bn completed that operation by mopping up a large area riddled with enormous pillboxes inter-connected by underground passages. According to all the rules of war, neither task should have been successful, but both Bns went in with such determination and sheer guts that nothing could have stopped them. I am glad to be able to tell you that their losses were extremely light in relation to the strength of their objectives.' (137 men, of whom 19 were killed or died of wounds.)

Flushing was in an awful mess, nearly every house shattered, streets and drains cratered, flooded and scattered with dead, including quite a few emaciated horses. There was almost no food and drinking water. The spirit of the few people who remained in their smashed homes was wonderful. One old lady dressed in peasant costume with a white Dutch cap twirled with gold wire ornaments said to me: 'What does it matter! We are free.'

As swiftly as possible the prisoners were sent off the island, 300 German forces women being in one batch and some AA troops who had been firing the V2s on London. They were very interested in our equipment, especially the amphibious vehicles. We found the prisoners of equal interest, being so new an experience.

One evening Jimmy and I took back an English-speaking Jerry medical officer to supper in our cosy HQ house. The top floor was smashed and water lapped against a flood barrier of wood sealed with grease which I had built in the front doorway. Two naval officers from a landing craft joined us, and together we ate an interesting mixture of chips and German and British rations cooked by Jimmy on the Dutch stove; our first proper meal for some days. The German MO, a slight, dark-haired, pale fellow seemed a decent enough chap. He was responsive, professed to dislike the Gestapo and was really obsessed with a fear of the Russians. 'In a year from now you will be asking us Germans to help you drive the Russians back. I tell you they are devils, evil. You cannot know what they are like or you would be fighting them, not us.' He was puzzled as to how the British Empire held together as well as it did and said, out of the blue: 'England is the only nation on Earth capable of handling the Indian problem.' Talk on the war and politics soon revealed that Nazi propaganda had done a thorough job on him. His ideas of right and wrong were set lopsided in a rigid mould and he could not or would not let his thoughts free to reach a conclusion independent of those laid down for him. We had been interested in glimpsing the German attitude to varied topics, but soon tired of this fanaticism which flowed from him with surprising and unexpected fervour, and so locked him up again with the other officers. Among the other-rank prisoners we met a wider range of feelings which ranged from a young Nazi thug – who boasted with pompous arrogance: 'In a year from now, the boot, as you say, will be on the other foot. We will be top dog' – to an old wizened cook who had served in the first war, and who said: 'Hitler is a devil, he has taken both my sons, but what can one do?' Then he continued, 'In three months Germany is Kaput.' Others hated the Japs: 'But they have their uses now.'

The prisoners disposed of, we received orders to collect up all ammunition, weapons and dead. Jimmy, Frank Clark and I each had a section of the town to deal with and a squad of men. These included a few prisoners to see to the German dead who were in an awful mess and quite often scattered in bits and pieces which meant collecting them in buckets and sacks at times. There was so little transport on the island that we had to rely on carts and skeleton horses left by the Germans. The numerous German dead were buried in big communal graves and as we worked Dutch resistance men in armbands and white coats helped us note identity disc details for the records. One or two of the horses collapsed in the shafts and were so far gone we were forced to shoot them. Rather than use the remainder of these poor animals whom the Jocks tried to feed up well again, we cut them loose and pulled the carts ourselves. This was our first experience at dealing with the dead and debris of battle, and though our thoughts were dulled in sensitivity by the sights and sounds of the last few days, I felt terribly what a complete shocking waste war was and great sorrow at the realisation that somewhere each of these men, friend or foe, was loved by a family as yet in ignorance of their death. I tried to think that the heavy impersonal bundles we lifted were just sacks, but the waxlike hands, forlorn feet and mask-like haunting faces made this escapism difficult. We were very glad when this task was done, particularly as some of the earlier ones had been buried unrecorded and realising that these would be listed as missing we forced ourselves to the unwelcome task of digging them out again. The bodies of our own men were taken back to the mainland, a few being temporarily buried beside the beach.

My section of the town included a large slice of the fortifications along the front and took a long time to cover. We worked warily after nearly bumping into one of the seven boobytraps we eventually found, wired up, I supposed, in anticipation of just this task. These were generally placed amid the dark labyrinth of communication tunnels with which the seafront fortifications were honeycombed. They consisted of a stick grenade to which five egg grenades were wired, the whole to be touched off by means of a pull igniter and trip-wire. In this search we unearthed masses of ammunition, gun positions, an underground naval torpedo storage chamber and a barracks eloquent of the initial alarm in the half-finished meals and scattered clothing and equipment. Similarly in the officers' mess hurriedly scattered clothing and bedclothes conjured up the frantic scene as the first shells crashed in, spattering the place with broken glass, plaster, pictures of wives, children and sweethearts, souvenirs of Holland, Belgium and possibly also panic.

All over Flushing, at key points, were the typically German massive, camouflaged, concrete bunkers also scattered with equipment and weapons. We moved everywhere armed and warily in case there might be a few fanatical Germans like the ones in the bunkers along the Middleburg canal banks still lurking about. Several times we stalked furtive sounds only to find some ill-fed Dutch chap helping himself to food, clothing and no doubt to any of the other things of every conceivable type which lay in profusion on every inch of the floors of the buildings. These included pay-chests stuffed with notes, cine-cameras, clocks, watches, jewellery and drink. I eventually took a party of Jocks to clean up these seaside hotels, which had formerly been used as barracks, to make way for the rest of the Battalion who were on their way back from Middleburg. While engaged in this task we found the remains of yet another German, just the top half: a direct shell hit had dissolved the rest of him. We buried him in a shellhole. Before we left for the mainland I took a last look round Flushing with Jimmy and we looked round the hull of the big ship being built in the shipyards and which the snipers had so made use of. As we wandered about, civilians were gradually reappearing from nowhere.

The Brigadier and his staff had stopped over in Breskens in a big concrete bunker, directing the battle, and had now come over for a look round too. How different our return trip to Breskens was to the outward one. Sun was beating down on the deck of the LCT [Landing Craft Tank] and prisoners were crowded in. Our tenseness and uncertainty were replaced by a little more confidence and the guns were silent. Already minesweepers were busily clearing the Scheldt in preparation for the mighty flow of power up this artery. Within a few months it would reach right through Germany.

DEFENSIVE WARFARE ON THE RIVER MAAS

On 11 November 1944 we returned to Kleit where another memorable church service was our first activity. A sad occasion, it was held in the dimly lit, incense-fumed and stained-glass-windowed setting of the village church which was loaned to us 'In gratitude and in memory of those who were lost in the attack.' It took a long time for the Battalion to become reconciled to these first losses. To prepare one's mind to accept the sudden elimination of friends all in the prime of life and as a continuous process seemed too foreign a thought to be real. Neither did the repeated occurrence of these blows or the passage of time make this madness easier to accept.

156 Brigade had stopped on in Walcheren to complete the clearing up and to help in the restoration of civilian life on the island. Jock Milne Home took over as our Company commander in place of poor Jim Bennett who survived, but was paralysed.

An opportunity occurred for a party of us to pay a visit to inspect the 'West Wall' fortifications near Ostend – massive inter-connected strong points in the sand dunes, with remote-controlled mines and obstacles offshore. These were very similar to those on Walcheren and had we seen them before our attack I think the seemingly impossible prospect might have almost induced failure.

This trip was our first chance of spending our new foreign currency and the Jocks made a beeline for the shops. In most there was pathetically little to choose from, especially food, which in any case we were instructed not to buy for this very reason. There were, however, quite plentiful and cheap peaches and grapes and on these the Jocks concentrated. They quickly picked up the semi-

Anglicised phrase: 'Nix in the Winkle' (nothing in the shop). The hospitality of the villagers of Kleit, with this situation in mind, was touching and embarrassing for it was frequently difficult to evade pressing offers of ersatz coffee and equally synthetic cake. Both in any case tasted really awful, so our attempted refusal was genuine enough. One could not always succeed though and then the shock of the awful taste of both coffee and cake took some concealing facially. The locals seemed quite hardened to it and, indeed, evidently thought it quite good.

Just on the edge of Kleit was a very active airfield from which Typhoon patrols were constantly setting off in missions of four to give close support with cannon and rocket fire at the front. Exactly how far off this line was we were not too sure at our level. We could hear no sound of gunfire. Several truckloads of us at a time set off for the public bath house in Bruges, to soak an accumulation of dirt off and put on a change of under-clothes, shirt and socks. I never saw a bath in our village and I think only fairly wealthy homes could boast of such a novelty outside the towns and cities.

Writing home took on a new urgency and importance for all, but this was a particularly difficult task for no word could be told of our activities or whereabouts until either the OK was given or ten days or more had passed. If any action was close at hand or if we were actually involved only a printed card could be used on which one crossed off the bits which did not apply – 'I am well', 'I am getting your mail', etc. Anything else led to the destruction of the card. As officers, letter censoring had now assumed quite a weighty task.

The Belgian and Dutch Catholics amazed the Jocks in their tremendous church-going. The urgent patter of feet at the crack of dawn revealed quite a procession of darkly clad women in enormous felt hats, the younger ones and children in short white cotton stockings, and the boys in a version of Oxford bags and with a beret on their heads. Other features of Belgian life which struck us in their novelty were the clip-clopping in an infinite variety of sound of the clogs of the villagers on the cobbles. One or two Jocks who wore these in the evenings said that with their felt inner-linings they were dry and warm compared with boots.

Many of the homes had enormous sliding plate-glass windows covered with 'roll-top desk' shutters. Fresh air was frowned on. Each billet seemed its own pub. Each evening the family would offer us an apple 'night-cap' which was peeled and eaten in unison as we sat round the Dutch oven and stove which stood out from the wall on a tiled floor.

Dogs seemed to play quite a part in village transportation, and when they were not pulling little carts of milk churns, or assisting to pull ice-cream wagons, they were to be seen pulling some lazy cyclist. The Dutch and Belgians, we supposed partly because of recent liberation, showed their flags and national colours on all possible occasions. Often this display of colour was added to in numerous fairs and festivals at which bunting over the streets, and the sound of barrel organ music swelled the air of rejoicing. The black market, and general traffic round the rim of the law, we concluded, must have been also at least in part a result of occupation for so long. An example of this, quite apart from Jocks being offered NAAFI cigarettes by locals before long, was the following true tale.

Soon after arriving in one particular billet we became rather mystified by the frequency with which a civilian car was being run in such a petrol-starved country. The reply given with pride of achievement, and not the slightest hint of it being illegal or dishonest in any way was 'But didn't you know that PLUTO (the forces petrol pipeline) runs through our land?' The thriving black market seemed to be tied up with the natural commercial astuteness of the Belgians.

On 14 November after more farewells, we were again sitting crammed in our 3-ton TCVs [troop carrying vehicles] and enveloped in the uncertainty and lack of information to which we at our level were becoming so familiar. However, the scenery was new and the ride, a long one of 300 kilometres, was full of interest. Each long, straggling, flag-decked village had its quota of waves and cheers from the children. The signs of war were erratic, and often caused by the attacks of Typhoons – a row of saucer-shaped holes in the road, gashed trees, then a wrecked and burned out German vehicle already rust streaked and stripped of any useful items by villagers. A smashed locomotive on rusting tracks.

A blown up bridge temporarily patched by the Royal Engineers with Bailey bridging. Here and there tank shells had splashed through house walls. We were heading by way of Ecloo towards Antwerp, on to which the Germans had already turned their V1s and V2s.

The trees along the roadside were strung with yellow signal cable looped round cotton reel insulation, and frequently decked with unit signs and code route signs 'Moon up', 'Moon down', 'Maple leaf up' and 'London down' and so on, and with these a driver could find his way with ease when familiar with the base at the 'down' end and the front at the 'up' end. Quite often white mine tape and notices of mines adorned the roadside, to warn the unwary to keep on the highway. Once or twice we were later to see the result of careless drivers ignoring these. This could only be done once by driver or truck.

Soon we were rumbling under the River Scheldt by way of the fine white-tiled Antwerp tunnel, lit by orange-coloured sodium lamps, then north along a tram route towards Holland. Occasionally we passed two-or-three-coached, cream-coloured trams which had a distinctive many noted claxon horn. These were the first form of public transport in use that we had so far met.

Meanwhile, 50 kilometres ahead of us the advance party with one or two representatives from each company were busily engaged in finding billets for us in and around the village of Berendrecht.

Nearing the end of our trip we passed a farm which had just got a direct buzzbomb hit, and was still smoking as people dug in the wreckage. Not all the air traffic was going the wrong way, however, and the next morning the villagers ran out into the streets to cheer a swarm of very low flying Lancasters on their way towards Germany.

The advance party met us at the entrance to the village of Berendrecht, a pleasant, quiet place with friendly occupants who welcomed us warmly. Battalion HQ was billeted in a school, and the rest of us round about in snug homes. Jimmy and I were in the home of Hendrix Ots, the local butcher, and were soon busy trying to talk to the family in broken English and equally broken

French. We had a nice room over the 'Fleisherie' and were shown round the stables and piggery by the children. I was interested to so often see in these Flemish people the identical types one meets in Rubens and Van Dyck paintings.

Twenty-six men and two officer replacements joined us here – 'Pip' Powell and 'Wee-Mac' McColl. We were soon reorganised, though a little below strength, for whatever lay in store. A fortunate few of us managed to get a 'Liberty truck' trip down to Antwerp to look round and buy a few things at inflated prices. Despite the buzzbombs and rockets, the crowds and neon-lit shops were a treat to see, and apart from the military traffic there was quite a peacetime atmosphere we had not expected.

17 November saw a very early start to another move. The Ots family insisted on giving us a tremendous pork chop breakfast as they had just killed a pig. It was served by the Rubensy-blond and fizzy-haired daughters, who with the rest of the family had got up extra early to supervise our shaving under the pump in the yard, see us fed – we could not refuse – to bursting point, and finally to see us off.

The tree-lined, straight, cobbled roads were teeming with military traffic, mostly supply vehicles with ammunition and food. As the kilometres reeled past, we noticed the gold, red and black Belgian flags had been superseded by the red, white and blue of the Dutch. This told us we were in Holland again and in the absence of other news we relied on our eyes for further clues to the future.

It did not take us long to guess we were getting nearer to the front. Towards Tilburg we saw blown rail bridges, then smashed villages. Not all this was caused by bombing and shelling. There had evidently been heavy fighting. Houses sagged, tileless with holes punched through them by solid shot from tanks, or the bricks splashed with HE [high explosive] shells. Gutters were strewn with smashed tiles, glass, rubble and telephone wire. We rolled and bumped painfully over hastily filled mortar and shell craters in the roads, and occasionally passed a burned out truck or tank with a hasty grave or two by the grass verge. One could often tell the unit, or whether it was friend or foe, from the headdress hung on the rough stick cross.

The roadside trees, now often shattered or demolished by the Germans to provide a clear field of fire, were linked by white mine tape. Beyond in the fields, rutted with the spewed earth of tank tracks or pock-marked with craters, was a sad sight: dead cattle. They lay, black and white Friesians, grotesque and ballooning with legs sticking out, like tipped up beetles. An airfield and adjoining village were bombed to obliteration. The acrid sickly smell of death in the rubble told us of buried casualties. Peering out of the truck towards the north disclosed the front was only a matter of 3 miles or so off now, for wheeling like vultures above a column of smoke were the 'Tiffys' or Typhoons. Then, as though in confirmation, we passed through the guns deployed in the fields, and turned off the main road. The now familiar quickening of the pulse, and reaction of the stomach, crept upon us. One became more alive to everything around, and aware of life as though boosted with a supercharger. It was not altogether an unpleasant feeling, surprisingly.

The village we had arrived at was Vught, just south of s'Hertogenbosch. Our billets were mostly in a large incomplete German barracks consisting of pleasant red-brick buildings sprinkled in a pine wood on sandy soil beside a lake. These SS barracks struck us as delightful in their appearance and surroundings. They were modern, spacious, airy and only marred by harsh war-theme mural paintings. We had not, however, yet seen the whole camp. The beauty and birdsong, the lake and the pinewoods were but a façade to a hidden horror which really staggered us. Vught, we soon found, included a notorious concentration camp. Pitifully few of the original inhabitants had survived to be liberated and the buildings now housed Dutch Quislings and German civilians bombed out from Aachen. Tammy, Charles and I strolled over to have a look. When we arrived these new inmates were being stripped and sprinkled with DDT powder to de-louse them. It all looked very peaceful and orderly. The same careful planning and construction had been lavished here as in the barracks, but in this case on scientific, modern, chromium-plated torture and methods of lingering and mass death as applied by painstaking Teutonic minds. We walked as in a daze from one monstrous site to another. Here were chambers where people were gassed to death, then for experimental variety others where they were locked in and steamed to death. A guard was reported to have said: 'You can tell when they are dead when the screaming stops.' Near this was a vivisection room where people were trussed on marble slab operating tables thoughtfully provided with grooves to drain off the blood. Six-inch iron spikes formed a carpet with a possible use we shuddered to think about. Then there were the more orthodox and classical tortures of thumb-screws, racks for stretching and solitary-confinement cells and other horrors we could only guess the use of. Some of the confinement cells were small brick structures the size of dog-kennels in which the victim was locked doubled-up to fit in. Outside stood a gibbet with a well-worn noose. Under this structure were two wooden blocks that tapered to a tiny base. The purpose was to string the victim up by the neck precariously balancing on tip-toe on the wobbling blocks. Here we were told the agonised victim might sway for hours until either fatigue or desperation caused the slight movement necessary to topple the blocks and complete the execution.

Beside the gibbet stood a triple crematorium, one unit being mobile. The walls of this building were shelved with little earthenware jars for the ash. This ash lay like thick grey flour all over the floor and on our boots while another pathetic little scattering of it dusted a well-worn metal stretcher which was used for the cremation. The remains of 13,000 other victims, who had arrived too swiftly for the crematoria to cope, had been buried in a part open lime pit at the door. We had started to get a clearer idea not only of our enemy, but more important to us, the reason for our presence in Europe. Tammy, Charles and I were far more thoughtful as we returned past the watch towers, electric and barbed-wire fences and ditches which surrounded the camp than we had been on our way in. We were staggered to think that such monsters could exist to staff and run such a place, yet some news from the front showed that apparently any German unit with a stiffening of SS troops was capable of this. Just down river from our arc of front, west of the blown rail-bridge, the Canadians whom we were taking over from reported that German troops had

herded men women and children into Heusden church and there
burned them to death.

The Canadians had more men, transport and greater firepower
per battalion than we did, and all their communication was by
radio. In consequence, we, in taking over a 5,000 yard wide river
front, would have very scattered and isolated positions. The
distance, floodwater and heavy mortar fire played havoc with
contact by field telephone. We were soon to find too that some of
the civilians were hostile collaborators. More than once the signal
wire was found cut and tied back onto the posts by such persons
to make the break harder to find. The radio distance was a bit far
for our 38 and 18 sets to be effective. Beyond s'Hertogenbosch
the ground sloped down towards the Maas and the front with a
good view over a mile of partly flooded flat pasture. The town
received very little shelling from the enemy except for a bit at a
later date to coincide with the arrival of a train in the station.

From the town one had a view of the dyke on which stood the
ruined and deserted Dutch villages of Empel and Gewande,
backed by another village a bit up from the river banks:
Rosmalen. The takeover had to be done in the cover of night as
the enemy could see any movement made during daylight.

I considered myself very fortunate in these early days in still
being with the Carrier Platoon. While so engaged I only went
forward to the front for a few hours at a time to take supplies,
evacuate casualties after dark or to join Frank Coutts in
shooting up specific targets with my 20mm guns and his
6-pounders.

Just as I was resigning myself to this cold routine, Jimmy
Wannop and I were granted an unexpected 48-hour pass to visit
Brussels, now a large leave centre. We had a wonderful time,
much of it asleep in the warmth of comfortable beds in a
centrally heated room in the Atlanta Hotel, or revelling in
proper meals. The millionaire American troops had already
inflated the prices of goods in the shops which ruled out
sending some presents of lace home. All too soon the leave was
over and we were back on the Maas.

Soon after my return, Cpl Oliver, one of my gun crew,
accidentally shot and killed one of his greatest friends and he

never seemed to quite get over the shock of it. He was himself badly wounded with a mortar bomb soon afterwards on one of our visits to the front. This mortaring by both sides was, with patrolling of the 800 yard wide flooded river in rubber boats at night and along the banks, the main activity. The enemy mortaring was sudden, intensive and disconcertingly accurate. Occasionally word was passed round to look out for and help back a spy or two of ours from enemy territory. This included a description, password and possible time of appearance.

When we joined the anti-tank guns in shoots at the front, the aim was usually to knock the spires off churches and the lids off windmills and drill holes in any other tall landmarks the other side of the river. These were invariably used by the enemy as observation posts to spot for his mortaring. Twice we also took the guns up to use in a ground role to shoot at a suspected OP [observation post] dug in the opposite river bank.

To reach the front was an eerie experience. One could only move in the dark (in a Jeep or carrier). No lights could be used. One had to peer intently to make out the dim trace of a meandering mud track which wandered in and out of the flood water. Where the track was quite submerged one had to rely on trying to follow dimly seen white mine tape linking a series of posts which protruded above the swirling water. If one missed the track, as happened with one gun and carrier, both vehicle and gun were submerged in the roadside ditch. Part way through the floods on our first trip my carrier stopped with a jammed track. Sgt Leslie was driving. As the engine stalled we became oppressed for the first time by the expectant silence of the front at night. The only sound was the rippling of the sea of water which swirled about us as far as the eye could see in the gloom, and occasional distant explosions and flashes of light. We managed to free the track, climbing about on the bogies to keep our feet dry for the icy night ahead. Several times we stopped our work to look and listen hard about us, thinking we had heard what might be an enemy patrol in a rubber boat. Several times already our patrols on this side of the river had sustained casualties from such intruders.

As we approached the battered village of Empel silhouetted against the night sky on the dyke wall, we pulled up again to see that all looked quiet and normal, then tensely we lurched forward again, very conscious of the awful whine of loud carrier gears in the silence. Our fears concerning the noise proved justified. We had not covered many yards more before we crouched deeper in our seats at the awful crash of a batch of very accurate mortar bombs which flashed in succession on the track we had just come along to our rear, the flame of explosion lighting up the battered houses just ahead of us. The enemy had as usual heard any vehicle approaching and always dropped his bombs just where the flooded road entered the village. Having parked the carriers and guns in as safe a place as possible, we selected a tiny house in which to cook up a supper of some Spam and Compo tea (ready mixed milk powder, tea and sugar).

These farms and houses were used as billets by the platoons and standing patrols of the forward companies. Battered though some of them were, there was still the odd head of livestock about which had so far survived the cooking pot and the efforts of the enemy; a few goats and chickens and even furniture of a sort to make life more bearable. To look in on a standing patrol could provide quite a cosy scene: a blacked-out room in which those off duty relaxed and slept beside a red-hot stove on which a chicken was boiling and filling the air with an appetising aroma. Sometimes a ham would be unearthed to provide bacon to accompany the eggs and pint mugs of Compo tea.

The few goats left were, I think, spared the pot because they seemed to have developed an uncanny sense of when mortar bombs were due to arrive and would scutter in over the broken tiles in the road, to take cover in some battered house: a most useful danger signal. Their hearing must have been more acute than ours and experience had possibly led them to connect the plop of distant mortar discharge with the unpleasant swift results. If there was not too much immediate noise and the wind was right we could plainly hear the muffled plopping of the mortars' discharge over the river ourselves and took cover to wait tensely in the stillness for the faint whisper of their descent, which if they were coming close, could be heard a fraction of a second before the frighteningly decisive 'crump' and whine of shrapnel on their arrival. Satisfaction could to some extent be derived if one counted the tantalisingly casual succession of plops of discharge, then counted the number of explosions on arrival. The proportion of dud bombs was sometimes pleasantly numerous.

Every possible step was taken to locate these mortars by cross-bearings and by means of spotter planes. Whenever it seemed likely they had been located, our own 3-inch mortars under Capt Viney Scott and the artillery put down a heavy concentration of fire which usually put the German effort to shame.

On this particular trip forward to Empel, Frank Coutts and I had to get the guns ready for firing early in the morning. Frank hid one of his between two houses looking out over the river and the other beside a couple of haystacks on the dyke wall. My two long, sleek, black cannon rejoiced in the names Cecil and Claude and were named after a pair of sleek, black, half-Siamese cats at home. For this particular shoot only Cecil had been brought. Cecil was taken to pieces and re-assembled in the ground floor room of a farm overlooking the river, where we set it well back facing an open window so that deep in the room our muzzle flash would be hidden and smoke concealed. We would have to take great care though that none of the explosive shells hit the window frame when we fired. We had located the target on an earlier afternoon with the aid of the sniper section and their telescope situated in the attic of a house. We were up there a considerable time, peering through a hole in the tiles. Unfortunately, soon after we had spotted some enemy movement on the opposite bank over the swirling muddy waters of the Maas, they must have seen some movement of ours. Five mortar bombs straddled our hideout with amazing accuracy, one landing with a crash of tiles and clouds of dust right on our attic roof. Nobody was hit, but we all made a dash for the ladder. Frank Coutts' massive frame shook the attic as he thundered down the flimsy ladder and he had nearly reached the bottom when he yelled out 'Christ!' in pain as he was stunned by a heavy crack on the head. A sniper's voice from above remarked: 'You couldn't be righter Sir! Christ it is.' The heavy vibration had dislodged a painted plaster effigy of Christ, so common in this Catholic part of Holland, which had been balancing near the head of the ladder.

The average German mortar bomb fortunately seemed to have

a more sensitive nose than our ones and usually did not penetrate far into a house before exploding, which I think spared us a few casualties. We spent that night in another small house, several of us lying complete with boots on one bed, kept awake by almost incessant mortaring. This was a particularly lonely and cheerless sound: the crash, whine and tinkle of shrapnel echoing up and down the deserted village street, occasionally clattering down a melody of tiles. To be woken up by a shower of mortar bombs at 3 am on an icy night with teeth already chattering with the cold seemed to me to know morale at its lowest ebb. One's mind woke out of partial sleep with an unpleasant jerk to the significance of this singularly decisive sound. It required a major mental adjustment and a complete overhaul of values to feel in any way used to them. I found a similar process of thought necessary later each time we went into action, one which came no more easily through repetition, perhaps largely because of constant lack of sleep. We did not envy the chaps on 'stag' [watch], peering out over the inky night floodwaters towards the enemy or stumbling along the slippery dyke wall on patrol. Not infrequently a burst of firing at night indicated a sharp clash with an enemy patrol which usually resulted in several casualties on each side. It was on one such patrol that cheerful Sgt Willy Lees was killed.

Sometimes imagination caused a tired sentry to fire. Once or twice during the night a Bren gun in B Company positions farther up in the village chattered and echoed to emphasise the silence, or a mortar flare fizzled its white light momentarily through the smashed shutters and windows of our little freezing room.

Eventually the icy dawn arrived. With it the punctual Jerries knocked off pestering us to take their breakfast while we made our way to our guns to get our own back. Between us flowed the broad placid Maas, reflecting the radiant dawn sky like a shimmering sheet of mother-of-pearl.

Frank fired first with his 6-pounders. The concussion brought down a minor avalanche of rubble and tiles while over the river the bank erupted with flame, smoke and spinning clods of dark earth just where we had spotted some figures moving in a cleverly concealed dugout the day before. Meanwhile, we with the Polsten cannon slowly moved the boards covering the doorway to reveal the bleak expanse of river and the distant German-held village of Veld Driel 2 miles beyond. Sgt Leslie and I took turns at laying and firing the gun while Lennox slammed on new magazines as each was emptied. As the gun had AA mounting and sights it was difficult to keep the rapid bursts of fire consistently on target for we had purposely loaded with HE and solid shot shells, having left the tracer out which would otherwise have immediately given away where we had concealed the gun. We were most anxious, out of respect for the enemy prowess with his mortars, to keep our positions undetected. This, to my surprise, we succeeded in doing after emptying all our thirty-round magazines. Frank's guns had already gashed a dark smoking wound into the green bank opposite as our shells joined in, exploding like glittering diamonds on the velvet of the grass. It was difficult to realise such a pretty result was lethal. Only one German showed himself scampering desperately for cover during the performance. Anyone in the observation post must have 'had it' for the high-velocity solid shot would have penetrated many feet of earth. We ceased fire after 150 rounds. Meanwhile, we became aware of two things happening outside. The Germans had quickly spotted Frank's guns and had within about one and a half minutes put down a heavy retaliation of mortaring, one gun's crew nearly sustaining a direct hit. The second new factor was that Frank's other gun, which was situated against a haystack, had set fire to it with the blaze of muzzle-flash. This haystack continued to burn for several days much to our disadvantage for at night the enemy could see our movement along the dyke wall road between the houses in the glare of the fire. Our second attempt at the same shoot was terminated rather abruptly. We decided to join Frank in firing from the open as on the last shoot we had to expose ourselves to enemy mortar fire to reassemble the gun outside at the end. This time we had hoped to fire and clear out fast before the enemy had had time to pinpoint and range on us. We opened fire together, but after forty-five rounds the gun jammed. Before we could clear the gun and after about 90 seconds from starting, the Jerries brought down a heavy 'stonk' of bombs which straddled us with the very first salvo. Before we could begin to move for shelter, wicked black splodges of smoke blossomed with jagged crumps round us on the cobbles and houses. These explosions initially looked quite harmless as puffs of oily dark smoke; however, the lethal twang of shrapnel soon had the greenest to battle of us scampering fast for the nearest doorway. One of a cascade of bombs which straddled us jolted me as it exploded six yards off. At the same instant Pte Nealie, who was standing some way off near the gun, spun round swearing as he dropped a magazine to grasp a hit in the shoulder. He was fortunately only nicked. There seemed no future in this pastime in the absence of cover from which to fire so in the first respite we packed up fast. Frank also had a close shave in this shoot when a bomb had apparently burst on the tiles above one of his guns.

At this period the 4th Battalion and the 7th/9th Royal Scots were in the line, with the 5th KOSB in reserve. Between turns at the front the Jocks went back to the comfort of private billets and family life in s'Hertogenbosch about 2 miles from the forward positions. The civilians were an amazing lot and went around as though the front was many miles away. Christmas was near at hand and children dressed as darkies toured the streets acting some traditional mummers play. The Canadians with similar nonchalance held dances within rifleshot of the front. Often those civilians who had lived in the front line villages tried to return to feed their animals or save possessions. As each might have been a collaborator or spy, a system of checkpoints and passes had to be instituted which caused us much extra work. I spent quite a lot of my time back at 'B' Echelon at Vught, censoring mountains of mail at our lakeside café HQ. Frequently my companion was the post corporal who worked at the sad task of parcelling up the personal possessions of casualties which were then sent to be held in a central depot to wait long enough for official notification to reach the next of kin. Among these bundles were some letters and parcels sent in anticipation of Christmas to men who had been killed since last they had written home. At the request of the pioneers I cut a stencil of the KOSB badge to paint onto the temporary crosses which they had made.

For a few days my billet was with an old Dutch couple who every evening sat listening to the BBC news in Dutch on a hesitant radio which had been hidden under the damp floor for some years. As the old chap listened, he peered at an atlas under the dim flickering electric light. On it he pointed out the tidemarks of the Allied advances which he had squiggled there in pencil since D-Day. They could talk no English so we only smiled at each other from time to time for conversation, or watched their poodle dog Meersa munch its supper: an apple. Usually we too ate this Dutch night-cap in champing unison to the accompaniment of the wheezy radio.

We later found that planning had been in progress at this period in Div. HQ at Sittard for an operation called 'Shears' – a full-scale attack to drive the Germans over the line of the River Roer, sweeping sideways along the line of the Siegfried defences – but on 13 December this stunt was cancelled. A little before this some of our officers had had an opportunity of hearing Montgomery speak on some other job of work which was waiting for us, but on which he did not elaborate at our level. Meanwhile, on the cancellation of 'Shears' we heard that we were to spend another period on the defensive in the Gangelt-Geilenkirchen sector, holding the villages of Birgden and Kreuzrath in the icy white grip of approaching midwinter. This time there would be no river as a buffer between ourselves and the enemy.

A QUEER CHRISTMAS

An icy, tedious journey of eighteen hours over terrible roads and through scenes of desolation, brought us on 7 December 1944 to the Dutch village of Stein alongside the Juliana Canal, north of Maastricht. From dusk onwards the drivers had struggled with no lights in pitch blackness as we again neared the enemy who were very active in the air. We had expected to be sent straight into some fresh task at our level for we did not yet know of the cancellation of 'Shears'. Instead we found ourselves in civilian billets enjoying a very welcome and unexpected respite.

These few days I spent in the cottage of a Dutch miner who worked in the state-owned Brunsum colliery. It was a most enjoyable interlude. Capt Tammy Youngson, OC HQ Company, and Usher, his batman, were also in the house with me. Usher, a comical bald-headed fellow, had been a miner in Durham himself and though he must have been well over age for infantry service had been persuaded by 'Tammy' to stay on as his batman: 'I could not soldier without him!', Tammy explained. Usher, I think, really appreciated his relationship with his boss. They both had an impish sense of humour and though Usher was always respectful, he loved to fuss over his OC as though he were a shadow company commander. Usher made an instant friendship with our Dutch miner host and went with him on a visit down the Brunsum mine. He returned enormously impressed with the technical efficiency, the tiled galleries and the conditions as compared with his own colliery.

In the evenings Usher delighted in many a game of draughts with the miner or his teenaged daughter. With the latter, a substantial girl with mousey hair, he kept up a stream of one-sided conversational leg-pull in English. Fortunately she knew no

English, for much of what was said would have embarrassed her exceedingly could she have understood it. To the delight of onlookers she politely replied 'Ja' at intervals and giggled uncertainly, occasionally blushing deeply at the roars of mirth which followed. These people were exceptionally hard working. Their cottage, much of which was walled and floored in tiles, seemed constantly to be being washed. In the corner of the sitting room was a small plaster figure of Christ which was lit day and night by a low powered lamp with the filament in the form of a cross. The family retired into this room at night for long, audible prayers.

My batman, Pte Stein, who to the delight and amazement of the household had the same name as the town, spent a part of each day equipped with my cigarette ration in trying his skill at barter at local farms in an effort to vary our food a bit. It was amazing how easily he ploughed through the language barrier.

One day I paid a visit with Frank Clark, another officer, to an island between the Maas and the Juliana Canal. We rowed over on a ferry boat, each carrying our constant companions, a rifle and revolver. The reception that the wide-eyed children and delighted, waving and cheering villagers gave us was startling. It certainly seemed we must have been among the first British troops they had had on the island. In addition to those who turned out to welcome us, we were aware of other faces peeping at us from almost every window. The same enthusiastic delight was always accorded to the appearance of our kilted pipers, especially when playing on a route march to exercise the Jocks.

My own stay in Stein was a short one for much of this lull was spent in unexpected surroundings and hectic activity. The Division had set up a battle school in Bergen-op-Zoom some miles to the north-west of Antwerp. There officers and NCOs from the various battalions took turns in the study and practice of the latest lessons learned in patrolling methods, attack, mines, enemy weapons and so on. I was fortunate to get this early in my battle experience. It was a ten-day course and to get to the battle school, which rather fittingly, I thought, turned out to be located in a lunatic asylum called Vrederust, involved another very long drive over treacherous roads glazed with ice.

Those of us on the course, realising it would extend over the Christmas period, had expected at least some sort of a Christmas dinner other than the usual army rations. Our chief memory, I think, was that this did not turn out to be the case. A dance had, however, been held on Christmas Eve to which a few local girls had been invited to provide partners. Our lack of turkey and plum pudding the next day may have been due to the fact that one of the Scots officers from another Battalion, who was on the course, had got a bit tight and thinking the Commandant had pinched his partner for one dance he had promptly 'bashed him good and hard'. He was instantly placed under close arrest and hustled back to his unit with an officer escort.

We had a lot of very enjoyable exercise in sandy pinewoods, on heathland and on the seafront, expending large quantities of ammunition and explosives on varied schemes, some of it German. One officer got badly burned when an overkeen type threw a phosphorus grenade at him so that he took fire like a candle. Each time the water in which we soaked him drained off he took fire afresh. On 28 December the course was interrupted for forty-eight hours when to our surprise some German paratroops were reported as trying to blow up some dyke walls near the sea. This caused us to spend a whole night cold and soaked through, stalking and crawling over mud-flats and wading ditches of icy water in search of the enemy. Finally, quite fed up, we spotted a group of distant figures up to something at the base of a dyke wall in the morning half-light. We were just preparing to mow them down when in the nick of time it was realised that they were Dutch farmworkers on legitimate business. They never knew how close they had been to a sudden demise.

The Dutch girl who had been my dancing partner asked me to her home one day for tea with another officer. The Van Hemels were a very large family of over a dozen of whom I only mastered four names: Joy, my partner, Freda, William and Oda aged three, the youngest. The father, a Belgian, was a composer and several of the children were talented at the piano and violin, while even the youngest had mastered a couple of words of English to greet us. Several spoke fluently and were most interesting to listen to as they talked about the Germans, their trials and liberation.

Holland seemed to have been hit by far the hardest in occupation. The shops were almost empty of all but a few goods of very shoddy quality. The mother must have had a terrible time in trying to feed her large family. At times tulip bulbs had been eaten in place of potatoes while crushed turnip and other seeds had been used to provide cooking fat. Meat was almost unknown.

So keen were the Dutch to get hold of Belgian money with which to buy food and smuggle it back over the border, that the Jocks had found it possible to buy themselves drinks in a Dutch café with a Belgian note and still get more Dutch guilders back in change than they had in actual money terms handed in. Until stopped, this led to a vicious circle racket whereby the astute few changed their guilders back again into Belgian francs via the army paymaster. This racket had another variation in which cigarettes and other NAAFI supplies featured. Some troops were in possession of an acute business sense. This, allied to liberating German pay chests containing low denomination currency and various other precious articles which as we saw in later attacks could be so easily secured by front-line troops, led to the strong rumour later that a certain batman in the Battalion had secured sufficient assets to convert these into an *estaminet* to which he intended to retire after the war! Later I gradually became aware that one of my men was transforming himself into a mobile jewellers shop, but he did not survive to make use of it.

The cold had become intense and with it a civilian fuel shortage which was partly the result of the war-torn, disrupted transport. The local children took full advantage of the freeze-up and were out in strength with their skates and toboggans. They propelled themselves over the ice on these latter vehicles by means of metal-tipped sticks so that they shot along like giant water-beetles. Enemy aircraft continued unusually active and a Fw190 fighter plane had the cheek to knock a headlamp off one of the battle school officers' cars with a burst of fire. An even more frequent sound overhead by day or night was our old friend the buzzbomb as it rumbled harshly towards the supply port of Antwerp. Occasionally one exploded in the neighbourhood or got out of control and went roaring out to sea or in immense circles, getting a cheer from those below if it headed back towards the enemy. The locals had a theory that the British had evolved a device which upset the gyro-compass and put the bombs off their target. This, as far as I knew, was only wishful thinking, but we just nodded wisely and said nothing to queries.

Our time at Vrederust was all too soon over and with our bedrolls and other equipment aboard a 3-tonner we set out southwards for a long, really arctic trip over iced roads to rejoin the Battalion. We travelled at fair speed, nevertheless, over the long straight cobbled roads to begin with, only slowing down to negotiate rubble-filled craters and blown bridges patched up with Bailey sections. All went well until just near Maastricht our heavily loaded truck got into a bad skid on the glazed cobbles and spun three complete circles at 45mph. We narrowly missed vehicles coming the other way and fortunately neither hit the wayside trees nor the mine-taped border of the road. I was amazed to realise afterwards that our recent past experiences and future prospects had so conditioned or dulled my reactions that I could recall only a slight excitement at this episode. Soon snowfall added to our difficulties, clogging the windscreen and obscuring the route signs.

Hours of crawling without lights over the snow-packed roads followed as we wearily tracked down the Brigade and then the Battalion signs nailed to telegraph poles and trees until late that night we found ourselves in the Dutch town of Oirsbeek. The aspect of our trip which had most impressed us had been the amazing amount of material that had flowed through Antwerp in so short a time and now was stacked in enormous wayside dumps. The PLUTO petrol pipeline too had extended its branches like some monstrous creeper with tendrils feeling their way towards the front. The Battalion had moved a short distance since last we were with them, hence our need to track down their present unfamiliar location by means of unit signs. I found, on reporting back at HQ, that this was 'B' Echelon area and that the companies were again holding the line a few miles away.

HOLDING THE LINE
IN WINTER

TRIPSRATH WOODS

My immediate information was that I had been allotted a very nice billet with a family called Hennes for a few days in 'B' Echelon. The young couple, who lived in a very English-looking suburban home, gave me a fine room and were very kind and keen to talk. Their chief delight was to get their school-girl daughter to practice her English on me. She rejoiced in the name of Joke and when she learned its English significance presented me with a photograph of herself saying 'Ze joke is on me, yes?' I think she must have been primed in this by my batman.

I had just settled in that first evening to sleep in my new home when I realised from the melancholy out of tune noise of bagpipes in the hands of a tipsy piper that it was New Year's Eve. The Jocks had been celebrating with a 'booze-up'. The drone of this piper could be heard continuing his celebrations in various parts of the village stolidly until about 3 am. This continued despite the interruptions of first some low-flying and machine-gunning enemy aircraft chased by searchlights and furious AA fire, then two buzzbombs. One of these cut out its motor over the village and exploded unpleasantly close, breaking windows. Through the ensuing noise and blast the drunken pipe music emerged bleating but unstopped. I had thought this piper's performance up till then rather a disgrace in the ears of the locals but had put up with it, realising they would get no sleep with the enemy action anyway. However, perhaps his unshaken playing through the buzzbomb explosion had slightly retrieved the situation. The next morning proved no more peaceful for several very low-flying Me109s skimmed over the village, machine gunning the roads, chased by pleasingly accurate AA fire and the small-arms fire of numerous Jocks blazing away from doorways with Bren guns and rifles. Several of these aircraft were brought down. One crashed at the front while trying to get back after being hit. From the pilot of this plane the CO secured a fine pair of fur-lined boots for himself.

The enemy seemed to be putting forth a supreme effort, and their last on this scale we met, to gain some semblance of air supremacy at the front with the evident intention of smashing the Maas bridges. We had noticed a wrecked German Fw190 the day before which had smashed right up against one of these bridges while attacking it. Much of their effort was in low-level, fast, night attacks. The resultant fireworks from the light AA guns and searchlights was well worth watching. Only one casualty resulted to our chaps in the village as far as I was aware when the post Corporal was nicked by a chunk of shrapnel as he peered from a village doorway at a strafing plane.

Though 'B' Echelon was in Holland, the German border was very close. Over the Christmas period the Jocks had been well established on German soil in a group of villages named Birgden, Kreuzrath and Stahe which had been taken over from the 43rd Wessex Division and the infantry elements of the Guards Armoured Division. The German 15th Panzer Division opposed us from a high ridge overlooking 1,000 yards of snow-carpeted and mine-strewn 'No man's land'. Neither side had taken any major offensive action, but had contented themselves with patrolling, mortaring, shelling and bursts of occasional machine gun fire until one foggy morning, after heavy shelling, the enemy attacked on the 5th KOSB front alongside the Battalion. They were repulsed after losing 30 dead and 100 prisoners. However, the weather and sleepless nights were proving the greater enemy. In spite of the appalling conditions of cold and exposure the Jocks had for the most part been in great spirits and were making the most of the enemy pig and poultry supplies left over from the Christmas feasting.

On these clear frosty nights of silent, tense waiting, 'D' Company had night after night become familiar with the sound of a horse clip-clopping over the frozen roads behind the enemy lines. It became evident that its occupation was in bringing up rations and supplies at always, German fashion, the exact same time. This horse came to be known as 'Pinkie' by the Jocks. The meticulous exactness of the German routine put a great strain on the horse-loving OC of D Company. Finally, the claims of war could be set aside no longer and with reluctance poor old Pinkie and his German masters for the last time exactly on schedule coincided with a prearranged shattering of the silence with a hail of high explosive. We never knew of the exact result as far as the ration party was concerned, but sadly Pinkie's leisurely walk never again sounded over the frozen night landscape.

I was personally rather sorry to hear that a similar fate had overcome a lusty choir of 'Stille Nacht' accompanied by an harmonium, which melodious and haunting sound had floated from the German lines on Christmas Eve. However, the Germans were not to be put off their carol singing so easily. Despite the efforts of the forward observation officer of the artillery and the sustained efforts of the guns, singing continued at intervals with such persistence that it was concluded that there must have been quite a heavy consumption of schnapps as well as the harmonium as the accompaniment!

The CO and the Padre had succeeded, I heard, in visiting all companies on Christmas Day, the Padre to hold a service and 'Chris', as he was known by all, to toast victory with the rum ration. Thereby it was hoped all needs of 'the spirit' were met.

On 28 December the Battalion were relieved in the line by the 4th/5th Royal Scots Fusiliers. However, there was a sudden stepping up all round in enemy activity and pressure and we heard that we would have to go straight back into the line again at Tripsrath, scattered along the line of woods and villages, taking over from the 1st Gordon Highlanders and the 5th Highland Light Infantry. This activity we later realised, together with their air action, was the build-up for the tremendous German attack on the right flank of our Division into the Americans in the nearby Ardennes.

With this news [of our new orders], I was instructed to hand in the Polsten guns to a base ordnance dump and rejoin my old platoon, 10 platoon of B Company. That afternoon I bumped my way forward over ice-sheeted roads and through a shell-ripped landscape of snow and desolation into Germany. Battalion HQ I found to be in a wrecked farm situated ¾ of a mile from the forward positions. In the stable yard the frozen, bony remnants of dead and mutilated horses littered a sea of frosted mud like some ghastly statuary.

B Company Jeep drew up at dusk and I slung my bedroll of three blankets and my rifle and small pack in, followed by the four boxes of Compo rations, a bag of mail, a few jerrycans of water, a tin of paraffin and the rum ration and off we moved. The cold heaviness of the stone rum jar which I carried on my lap seemed to echo the sentiments of my heart as we neared the forward positions. I reflected that a green actor with a responsible role to get through might feel as I did then just before the rise of the curtain of my return to commanding a platoon in a rifle company; he at least had the advantage of knowing the course of the plot.

A few days earlier Donald Urquart, one of our Canadian officers who had been with B Company, had tried to stalk a party of Germans on his own armed only with a 2-inch mortar. He had been shot at by the enemy and wounded in the arm himself as he fired and returned to his Platoon HQ angrily exclaiming: 'That Goddam got me one!' As Pip Powell and Tommy Gray, the other two Platoon commanders and Colin Hogg, the OC, were already out of action for one reason or another I found I had joined Capt John Elliot as the only other officer. We were fortunate to have had our Company Sergeant Major, Frankie Pook, still with us too for not long before I arrived a dud German 75mm shell had crashed into Company HQ and come to rest right beside him without exploding.

The Company position, reached after a tedious bumpy journey in low gear over log-lined mud tracks through a thick wood called Hoverbusch, was on the right of the Battalion line. My Platoon I found to be on the right of the Company line on the rim of our block of forest. The nearest enemy were about 600 yards off over a snow-covered field towards another wood, I learned at Company HQ. I was very sorry to also hear that Driver Hogg of S Company who had come home to tea with me in England had been killed when his carrier blew up on a mine, and that CSM

McTurk had been very badly wounded in the stomach when he had been hit by a mortar.

We ran the Jeep into a hole in the ground to protect it from shrapnel. Then after I had found out all I could from John Elliot about the 'Form', which was really a sort of briefing, I made my way warily through the trees towards my Platoon positions. En route in the dark snowbound silence under the gloom of the trees I passed through 11 Platoon positions, only distinguishable by a few windproof-headed, breath-steaming figures of Jocks poking out of their slit trenches, some sipping tea and munching supper as they peered from behind their weapons lying on the parapets towards the invisible enemy over the snow. The pungent smell of burning Hexamine solid fuel tablets from other dugouts told of some tins being warmed for supper or 'char' being brewed. These men were engaged on the routine 100 per cent 'stand to', which took place during the period of half-light for an hour every dawn and dusk to be prepared for this most likely time for an enemy attack. 'Stand down' was given as I reached my new home in the dark. It was a twig and earth covered 5 foot square hole in the ground with an outside slit trench to fire from. Crawling inside I was delighted to find that I had Sgt Dickinson as my Platoon sergeant (later MM). He was curled in a blanket in a patch of straw on a mud shelf reading a book by the light of a candle propped in a hole scooped into the frozen earth wall, and sipping tea. His jovial, round, stubbly face creased into a grin of welcome.

Before setting off on my rounds with him to familiarise myself with the layout of the section positions, I set to work to warm a tin of stew to add to some biscuits for supper. Outside the freezing silence had been broken by the monotonous steady crashing of mortar fire lobbed into our wood by the enemy. It sounded like an angry giant crashing backwards and forwards on heavy-booted sentry duty. This stopped as suddenly as it had started and life again moved uneasily in our section of the wood. The ration party staggered hurriedly back from Company HQ, dumped their load and commenced to break open the box of Compo and to divide it into four little heaps of rations for Platoon HQ and the three sections. Soon section commanders had arrived to collect this, the new password, a few candles, their share of the rum ration to ward off the bitter cold for those on 'stags' and those that needed it renewed their supply of paraffin. Each gave a statement of ammunition and a report on their men, all the while with senses straining to catch any hint of descending mortar bombs or shells. Their dispersal was as rapid and furtive as their arrival with muffled footsteps in the snow. This over, I set out with Sgt Dickinson to look round the section positions. Breathing the freezing air nearly froze one's nostrils. To stand still in the dark tracery of trees mapped against the starlit sky gave one an oppressive feeling of isolation. We were now in the forward section, 20 yards from our HQ dugout. Here the trees ended on the eerie waste of snow. Within calling distance out there in the black rim of another wood over the field of snow and stubble were the German forward positions, fellow beings cut off by the mysterious vacuum of no man's land.

Here we were in the middle of the twentieth century looking towards our nearest neighbours and trying hard to realise that if either paid the other a visit or saw the least sign of life, it was his sworn duty to do his utmost to exterminate these complete strangers. No mercy was expected or likely to be given in this task which was bolstered with every modern and efficient method of killing money and 'science' could supply. Here we were ordered to be and here we stopped if we survived, until ordered somewhere else. If we were overrun or went to sleep we had only ourselves to blame and largely to rely on. If a full-scale attack chanced on our front a decision one way or the other as far as we were concerned would be swiftly over. What we could not hold with our limited Platoon weapons we could in desperation try and stop by using a code word which would call down our own artillery onto our positions in what was called an 'SOS' task.

It must take about seven years, I reflected, to make a being feel really like a soldier and not just a civilian dressed up. The situation still all seemed so ludicrously unreal and yet grimly real at the same time. We could at least comfort ourselves with the knowledge that the poor blighters opposite us were in the same boat even though it was a boat of their seeking. There were about thirty of us in our immediate outpost in the wood and about another seventy-five of the rest of the Company within 250 yards to our left. The nearest troops to back us up behind in reserve were several hundred yards through the woods somewhere. The 7th/9th Royal Scots, the next unit to our right, were about 500 to 800 yards away, we judged from the distant chatter of their firing on occasion the other side of the wood, so we knew with discomfort that there was a big gap in the front beside us through which the enemy could filter to our rear after dark. It was nevertheless peculiarly satisfying, if disconcerting, to realise that in whatever decisions one made here as an officer, the choice was one's own. There was no other mortal to rely on. No red tape or instructing 'brass hats' to blame. These were all miles to the rear. I was finding my reactions most interesting to compare with expectations in the still novel situation. One of the most unexpected and odd reactions I had begun to notice, and for which I was most grateful on my later occasions in attack, was, firstly, how much responsibility kept one's mind off oneself and next, however afraid one was – which for hours at a time might be intense – I found the fear of showing it to one's men (which would have been fatal) was always so much stronger that in effect it cancelled the primary fear out. This discovery at times so intrigued me as to cause a paradoxical feeling almost of elation.

To move in the Platoon forward areas was a very tricky job and a real nightmare after dark as the ground between the trees in a 40 yard deep belt was criss-crossed with numerous thin steel wires attached to hand grenades and magnesium flares bound to the trees. If any person was careless or unfamiliar with the traps a touch on a wire set off a glare of light or an explosion, sometimes both, by means of pull-igniters. To add to this menace one often had to contend with a blanket of snow covering the wires, darkness and a batch of falling mortar bombs to speed one's steps to comparative shelter. These trip-wires and a belt of anti-tank and anti-personnel mines out in the field were, together with the tired eyes of underslept Jocks, the only way of being warned in time of an attack or patrol coming on top of us. As the enemy patrols usually wore white smocks as snow camouflage they were hard enough to detect visually even in daylight. Many a time the weight of snow on the wires or an overtired Jock whose eyes had started to play tricks with him set off a burst of firing, a blast of explosion or a glare of brilliant light. Frantic activity ensued until the cause was established and then a message was sent back to a worried Company HQ to explain the alarm. The wide gap between ourselves and the Royal Scots caused me continued uneasiness. I was amazed at the way the Jocks took to and stuck the appalling conditions day after day in the cold and night after night with up to seventeen hours of darkness to anxiously watch through. Each slit trench had two Jocks who shared the duty in two-hour shifts of watching and attempted sleep in the frozen mud and straw of the trench bottom in hoar-frosted clothes. Cpl Beal, one of my Section Commanders in the most isolated of the Platoon positions overlooking a snow-covered track into the woods, set up notoriety for seeing things during his spells on stag. Almost every night we heard the lonely chatter and echo of his Sten gun at some time or other. He was killed a few weeks later.

It was becoming steadily more difficult to keep properly awake or anywhere near warm, both problems being linked into one as a vicious circle: it was nearly impossible to get warm enough to get to sleep and the less sleep we had the colder we felt. Our cold or tepid scratch meals of tins and biscuits, sweets, chocolate and bread probably did not help. Each plop of snow slipping off a tree somewhere or a twig cracking in the frost sounded to our taut senses like stealthy footfalls and brought one with a jerk out of chilled tired-eyed fatigue on stage to peer with anxious intensity and quickened pulse into the monochrome of snow-blanketed monotony.

Our daily activities grew into a general routine. An hour before first light if it was not then my turn for stag while Dickinson slept, I crawled out of what warmth I had managed to generate over the last two hours in my blankets and little heap of straw. Being always fully dressed complete with boots and equipment, it was only necessary to pick up my rifle and pull on the tin hat in creeping to the entrance.

At this time the enemy usually sent a few dozen mortar bombs over in case we 'overslept', so one would pause at the entrance to try to detect the plop of their discharge or any sign of other dangers in the frost-crisped darkness. To all appearances one might have been entirely alone in the incredible silence of the snow-carpeted woods. By contrast the jerky crunching of it underfoot and the inevitable snapping of an occasional twig in going the rounds of the section positions to see all was well seemed to make a noise which one felt even the enemy could hear. After 'standing the men to' in each trench to cover the period of half-light and collecting any information on overnight activity to pass on to Company HQ, I made my way to the next dark gash in the snow, keeping a wary eye open for trip-wires.

Usually Jocks would recognise one coming or call 'Halt' softly and ask for the password. Occasionally a semi-dozing Jock would be come upon who started out of partial sleep on being spoken to and who had to be reminded sharply of what he was up to. As I went these rounds two or three times a night to be sure all was well I occasionally had an uneasy feeling that some 'trigger-happy' half-asleep Jock might some time mistake me for the enemy. This mistake did twice happen later in similar circumstances and once nearly proved fatal as the offender gave a lengthy burst of machine-gun fire which in bad light was fortunately not accurate.

I had great regard for the average Jock huddled on his own peering towards the unknown over the parapet with his 'mate' asleep at his feet in the trench bottom. The way they stuck the continuous physical misery as though they had always been at it while so often holding only a vague half-thought-out idea as to why it should be their lot anyway, struck me as remarkable.

Ever since my arrival the mortaring had been coming over at irregular intervals in batches of five or six bombs in quick succession. This usually caused retaliation by our own 3-inch and sometimes 4.2-inch mortars and artillery which invariably put up a more impressive display, sweeping a heavy blasting ripple of detonations to our ears over the snow. Our own artillery for their part flung batches of shells at intervals to waffle their thin, weird sound across the sky ending in a crump-crump-crumping in the distance. It was our routine also, while 'standing to', to pour a little of the water, which arrived each day in jerrycans, from our waterbottles into a mess tin propped over sticks pushed into the earth surrounding a little heap of Hexamine tablets in the trench bottom. This resultant compo tea was looked forward to all of each icy night for its scalding warmth. A whole pint of fire which trickled into one's frozen body. Some Jocks delighted to add some rum if they could secrete it, to give an added kick to the brew.

When the tea was finished, 'standing to', a few soya-link sausages or some tinned bully beef was dropped into the same mess-tin to heat up after the tea leaves had been shaken out. As there was on most occasions not enough surplus water to wash, shave or to clean the mess tins properly, the tea's main virtue lay in its heat. It tasted awful and not infrequently had gathered chemical-smelling fumes from the Hexamine. This meal was usually finished by thick blocks of bread piled with plum jam or some iron-hard army biscuits. If one ever got a square meal out of them it was solely by virtue of their shape.

Often sections preferred to cook their 'meals' centrally using the section paraffin pressure stove but this depended on the intensity of enemy activity which might keep us pinned for two- or three-hour stretches to our holes. If things were quiet I occasionally rejoiced in the luxury of my batman bringing me my meals, his only and very rare job for me in action as he then reverted to his other role of Platoon HQ runner.

By now it would be light and perhaps a pale wintry sun cast weak patterns over the snow in the trees after 'stand down'. Once daylight had come, a rash move by the enemy, except for a major attack, was far less likely. It was time to go round positions again, to inspect weapons and talk about things in general with the men. Usually the Jocks would ask if there was any news, by which they meant news of the front. If they had had any mail from home it was an opportunity to get to know a bit about their families. How those chaps with a wife and children depending on them at home stuck it so well I never could fathom.

As movement on the forward edge of the wood could be seen by the enemy on these visits, the sections right on the rim were difficult to reach without drawing a burst of fire or mortaring which could be very trying with no surplus holes available in which to take cover and trip-wires to keep clear of. We had no proper latrines as this was only a temporary position and the weather being so bitterly cold helped keep things more sanitary than would have been tolerable in the warm weather. In consequence, a short walk back into the woods, praying the enemy would not bomb or shell for a while, had to suffice. How often he did not hold his fire on these occasions. It did have its funny side though and many a laugh was raised by some desperate, partly clad apparition tripping and diving for cover to the accompaniment of 'choice language' . . . and twanging shrapnel.

The casualties, though a steady drain, were not heavy or often fatal during our tenancy of this position. One chap lost a hand to a mortar burst and others had varied flesh wounds. One or two were got the better of by the cold, exhaustion and wet clothing due to lying in part-waterlogged holes in sopping straw night after night. A few also were tensed up to the degree which required a visible effort on their part to withstand a shower of mortar bombs. Occasionally a heavy shell thundered somewhere in the woods, evidently from the Siegfried Line guns. On 7 January we were staggered by a really enormous blast of explosion which ripped heavily through our positions from behind in a long wave of pressure. No gun or shell we had yet heard had made a fraction of such an explosion and we fervently hoped Jerry had not brought up some new weapon. The colossal blast must have shaken him even as much as it did us. Puzzled heads looked with alarm from every hole, disturbed from sleeping, writing, eating or being on stag. Soon we heard what had happened. Forty-seven men, seventeen of ours and thirty attached engineers had been engaged in carrying and arming 2,400 anti-tank grenades a few hundred yards away which were to have been laid that night forward of our positions between Tripsrath village and our wood. The CO and the CRE were watching the unloading from a short distance when suddenly there was an explosion at the head of the carrying party. This spread by sympathetic detonation right along the 120-yard line of men, each carrying a sack full of the grenades, and exploded the main dump. 2,350 of them went off altogether. According to rumour, one man alone in the line survived the explosion. The CO later stated: 'How the CRE and myself escaped I don't know . . . The scene on the ground was one I will never forget. At first one's natural reaction was to send for stretcher bearers and the doctor to deal with the wounded, but a quick walk round the area soon established the fact that all who had been there had perished and that there were no wounded. For the sake of morale, both of the Battalion and the Sapper Company, fresh mines and fresh personnel were ordered up at once and the minefield was laid that night in a snow blizzard as had been originally planned.' Two-thirds of my Platoon were borrowed as a result to carry up some of the new mines for laying, a job which under the circumstances they did not relish.

Only ten minutes later there was another explosion in Tripsrath itself which brought the casualties up to fifty-one. The Pioneer, Sgt McAllan, and three other chaps were killed in trying to neutralise a small German 'Regal' minefield. This was a sad loss to the Battalion. Ironically, among those that had been killed were many of the men who held what usually were the 'safest' jobs in the Battalion: the Quartermaster's staff, the CO's and the Padre's batmen and cheerful and efficient 6-foot Provost Sgt Howie.

The usual day's routine was completed with trying to catch up on sleep, in cleaning weapons, improving the trenches or in making the odd 'Fly cuppie' tea. Lunch was really no different from the other meals. We just warmed up whatever tins there were, plum-duff, meat and veg and so on, then filled up with bread and jam. I always swapped my free cigarette issue for extra chocolate or sweets. A Jock who normally smoked became very miserable with no cigarettes, especially if things 'got rough'. After tea the rations and water came again, the rum issue being stored up until it was really needed in Sgt Dickinson's water bottle. The only time I partook of this was a touch on plum-duff which in retrospect gave it the illusion of having been warm.

About this time I always made my way to Company HQ about 250 yards off through the trees to have a chat with John Elliot or Major Colin Hogg, when he got back from LOB, to get any news, orders or briefing for any patrols. As we talked the signallers were busy crouched over their 18 set radio in a corner. Having collected the new password for the night I returned before dark so that I could hold a section commanders' briefing and split the rations before 'stand to' again at dusk.

Sometimes I took my rifle and a couple of chaps and scouted round several hundreds of yards into the trees to see if any unexplained tell-tale footprints of enemy patrols had been left in the snow overnight or since we last scouted. On one of these patrols we did find tracks faintly shown. How old they were it was difficult to decide as they were in parts obscured by new snow. They led us towards the enemy lines in a strip of wood which jutted forward between ourselves and the Royal Scots. As we got gradually closer to the enemy lines and about 600 yards from our own we went very warily until, half-concealed in the snow, we located weapons and equipment and scenes of recent heavy fighting. Next a group of dead Germans, frozen and snow covered and lying towards two solitary bodies, one beside a smashed radio. These two we found were a forward observation officer of the RA and his radio operator who had been overrun by a German fighting patrol. They had given good account of themselves before being killed. We should not really have come as far out as this without notifying Company HQ, so we made our way back carefully, stopping many times to peer after some unexplained sound, lying in the snow, then on again until we were challenged by Cpl Beal. I took a patrol of Beal's section and some stretcher bearers to recover the bodies in the half-light and a snowstorm that evening. It was a dismal task. On the way out we spotted two figures dimly picking their way towards us. We spread apart and lay low, covering them with our weapons as they approached. It was difficult to make out any more than two indistinct shapes moving in the swirling whiteness. Anxiously we searched to see if there were other figures behind or to either side. To our relief they turned out to be two of our snipers; one Sgt Scott. They had been out to see if they could stir up the enemy a bit, but had themselves been persistently sniped at a bit deeper in the woods. Neither they, nor the Alsatian war dog with them, (who had early told them of our presence) could locate the source of fire, which was too close to the enemy lines to press far. Soon we had the bodies on the stretchers, frozen as they had fallen, and were on our way home. Cold caressing snowflakes softly feathered our faces and chased with mute rustling through the black-ribbed tracery of the trees – each dark trunk a silent bridesmaid, expectant, white veiled, gently mantled – then swirled about the feet by chill confetti. A crisp, compressing crunch of

snow jerked muffled protests to our every step. It was a mournful
return, in many ways more worrying than the trip out. With one's
back to the enemy in this eerie snow-filmed half light, I had an
uneasy feeling we were being followed. One sensed and
restrained that same sensation felt by a child going home in the
dark – the urge to run and quickly reach familiar surroundings.

After taking out their personal possessions, and one of the
identity discs, we buried the two gunners as it grew dark next to a
wrecked 43rd Division carrier in the Platoon positions. While we
were digging the hole in the iron-hard earth, a shower of mortar
bombs crashed into the wood, and for a while we lay flat in the
snow beside the pale-faced, blue-lipped young gunners. Looking
at the digging party hugged flat beside me, with the black
splodges of smoke drifting beyond, it was most depressing to
reflect that of our six silent forms round the open grave, it seemed
merely a matter of speculation as to how many might complete
the ceremony in a different role. Life seemed to have so
completely departed from familiar values, I found my mind just
refused to react more deeply than to try to follow the best human
course available from minute to minute. As we shovelled back the
earth with anaesthetised thought, I paused to wonder anew at the
detailed functional beauty of form of a hand still showing; now so
expressive in death of stilled perfection, wasted.

Next day, John briefed me to take a patrol out to the end of our
wood, some distance to the right of where the gunners had been
found. Our task was, with the aid of a sapper, to get hold of what
was suspected to be a new type of mine which Jerry had recently
laid in a clearing between our wood and himself. It was an anti-
personnel mine, we knew; but exactly where the enemy positions
were in the area, or how far the mines extended into our wood, we
did not know. I took five chaps, two Brens, two Sten guns, some
grenades and my rifle in case we ran into trouble. To get there was
a slow, freezing job. Eventually the wood thinned out, and in the
distance I was surprised to see the mines showing unexpectedly
obviously in the white of the field, so much so that I suspected a
trap of some sort, and we took 30 minutes carefully approaching
them, feeling forward each inch of the way with bayonets into the
snow for trip-wires and Schu mines, expecting every second

might be our last. However, we got right up to them with no mistakes, and out into the field without attracting enemy fire. This also surprised me as seldom are minefields laid where not covered by fire, but perhaps the dusk had cloaked us. Another surprise awaited me: these were concrete stock mines, a type already well known, and, to the evident relief of the sapper with the recent mine accidents in mind, I decided it was not worth lifting one as a souvenir in case they had an anti-lifting device.

Another fall of snow started on the return trip, and we stopped in our tracks several times, having imagined movement ahead in the white scurrying murk. The snipers had been just about invisible the day before whenever they had stopped, for like the German patrols, they had worn white hooded snow clothing. The crisp, eddying snowflakes sifting through the woods had obliterated our outward tracks and returning slightly off course, we stumbled into some abandoned 43 Div positions. The white blanketed trenches were scattered about thickly with weapons and equipment, telling of either heavy casualties, or an outpost overrun and captured; perhaps both.

One afternoon a runner arrived from Company HQ with a message that we were to 'stand to' 100 per cent to cover an attack to be put in by the Royal Scots on our right with the object of straightening the line a bit. In support they were to have the 3-inch mortars of both Battalions, the demoralising 4.2-inch mortars, the mountain artillery, 25-pounders and 4.5-inch howitzers.

As we stood by in our holes in the ground, waiting as the minutes slipped by towards H-hour, with our thoughts on the Royal Scots somewhere over the wood where we had inspected the minefield, to a degree we shared in their mental ordeal of waiting for the word 'advance' and all that went with it. Suddenly, from far to the rear came the multiple thudding thunder of guns and mortars discharging by the score and the air overhead was rent with the shriek like panicking wildfowl of varied calibre shells. Then came the third wave of noise to merge with the other two: the dull insistent drumming throb of explosion and blast from the enemy positions. On top of these deep noises we became aware of the brittle, fast rattle of small-arms fire and the calico-tearing speed of Spandau machine guns being fired at the advancing Royal Scots by the Germans. The Bren guns kept up a steady undertone of more leisurely chatter in bursts. Much more eloquent to our ears of the turmoil and shambles of attack were the faint occasional sounds of shouting.

These sounds had been in progress only a very short while before a new and frightening factor gripped our attention which caused us as one man to duck our heads below ground level. A piercing triple or quadruple shriek grew swiftly in insistence and volume to terminate with heavy concussion in showers of black earth vomiting among us. To these were added a steady shower of mortar bombs which crashed into our positions from the enemy. At first it appeared that some of our own guns were firing very short, but the addition of the mortar bombs indicated the enemy may have thought we were in the process of joining in the attack. One of these mortar bombs burst on the roof of our dugout, spilling earth inside. Though the layer of earth over the logs of the roof was only a few inches thick it was frozen to the hardness of concrete and so stopped penetration. But for this fortunate circumstance we would, as Sgt Dickinson put it, have '. . . bought our ruddy packet!'

After each period of mortaring it was as well to glance round the sections to see the heads reappear and so signify all was well. I was particularly worried at night after exceptionally heavy mortaring, being driven by uncertainty as to whether a bomb or two might have fallen into a slit trench or shrapnel have wounded someone to climb out yet again into the cold to make sure. The nightly average of bombs into our 25 yard by 70 yard area of wood which the Platoon occupied was 25–30. It was incredible that no one bomb got a hit right inside the fifteen slit trenches. Many burst in the trees, which were getting starkly whittled away, and others ripped equipment which had been left on the edge of holes. Each missile landing overnight if it did not explode until it hit the ground and if it did not snow afresh could easily be located in the morning by freshly scattered earth about a black-rimmed crater. I was uneasy about the number of dud bombs with which the area was scattered and hoped they all remained inactive. When quietness again returned, Dickinson and I retired into our dugout, after stand down, with the section commanders for a chat and to get warm round a cluster of candles in the mud. Unhappily we had news that the Royal Scots attack was not entirely a success due to the fact that the assaulting platoons had run into a thick belt of Schu mines which both caused casualties and slowed them down to make better targets for the machine gunners. Reports indicated it had been 'Expensive'.

Of all my NCOs at that time I am surprised to see that Sgt Dickinson is the only one who got to the end of the road untouched and there were many subsequent replacements who came and went. My NCOs were: Cpl Beal (Killed, Heinsberg), Cpl Finney (Wounded, Waldfeucht); Cpl Allan (Wounded, Ibbenburen); L/Cpl Duncan (Killed, Ibbenburen); L/Cpl Wilson (Wounded second time, Ibbenburen); Cpl Parry (Killed, Allenwahlingen); Cpl Hepburn (Nicked at Afferden). As time and various actions passed and with them the replacement NCOs and men, the prospect, viewed humanly, seemed not over cheerful.

Jimmy Wannop used to occasionally come and see us while visiting one of his 6-pounder anti-tank guns dug deep into a corner of our wood. This gun made us feel a little happier about the possible appearance of enemy tanks over the snow to our front. The Jocks of the gun-crew had built themselves a wonderful home at the rear of their gun-pit, and to visit them was well worth it, if only to sit and get warm for a while in its straw-lined depths.

As the day dragged by, our constant lack of sleep and the nagging arctic cold began to tell on us in jumpiness, difficulty in keeping sufficiently alert and in a noticeable lack of resilience. On 9 January 1945 we heard with great relief that we were to get a short spell out of the line and were to hand our positions over to the Royal Scots Fusiliers.

OPERATION 'BLACKCOCK'

THE PREPARATION AND FIRST PHASE, OPERATION 'BEAR'

With infinite relief we handed over our positions and it was only as our long, dark column of kit-laden men had threaded its way back through the snow-clad pine and larch woods, and our opposite numbers to whom we had handed the line were many hundreds of yards behind us, that we began to feel relaxed again. One began to realise just how taut and intent one had subconsciously been in listening for the first hint of approaching danger every passing second. Above all we looked forward to the promise of a long, unworried sleep and a proper hot meal. The sleep took precedence by far in our anticipation. I was astonished in looking at the chaps walking in section files on either side of the road to realise that I must look as fearsomely unshaven, bleary-eyed and grey in the face with dirt and tiredness as my companions.

My thoughts went back to the officer I had handed over to. I wondered if he would remember where all the trip-wires, mines and numerous other detail I had pointed out to him were, and the habits of the enemy as we had got to know them. He was a very young chap, probably a replacement on his first time in the line, and I suddenly felt very sorry for him. Somehow, although we had been at it such a short time ourselves, this period seemed a lifetime. We had grown to know more or less what to expect of various signs and sounds and of the enemy in a few of his reactions. Most important of all, we were having an experience few people properly have, and a novel one; of beginning really to get to know ourselves, our real selves to whom we now knew we were strangers a short time ago.

Perhaps if an aircraft in the hands of a test pilot could think before and after its first few power dives and tests of structural strength and reliability, it would have that same feeling of relief and perhaps puzzled wonderment at the realisation that so far the wings and tailplane had not shown signs of coming adrift. There was still however very much the feeling of facing the unknown. We had hardly started and were still very green. What would happen when the stress was doubled, trebled and carried on over the months ahead? As for visualising what one might be involved in or where one might be in the near future, or, incredible thought, when the war was over, this was quite useless. Each passing moment, it seemed, had to be dealt with as best one could as it came. I found the thought of enormous help and comfort though: that a candle in the face of immense blackness need only concentrate on expressing light to keep the darkness, however intense, at bay. The candle itself could do no more, but it was comforting to realise that the light was positive and could hold the initiative, while the darkness was negative and depended for its advancement on the light first failing. That light I took to be the adherence in consciousness that God was the only real cause and that no effect could stem from any other cause if this anchor was clung to.

On either side of the road as we marched, lay white silent wastes of snow which stretched to distant trees and deserted villages, with everywhere an air of desolate lifeless solitude. The only sounds, other than metallic clinks and the hard scuffle of our boots on the compressed snow caked roads, were the now comfortingly faint and occasional explosions way behind us, and at intervals the moan of carrier gears and the crack of their skidding tracks as they passed, fighting to keep to the crest of the glazed road.

As usual we had no concrete news of what was going on other than that we were marching due south towards Geilenkirchen, which we had soon by-passed. The little black figures straggled out ahead, sprinkled towards an indeterminate horizon which faded into a sky the same sombre coldness as the snow.

The only civilian so far seen was an old man, who with sullen dejected face struggled, a lone, conspicuous figure behind a battered perambulator loaded with household goods, against the tide of Jocks. All other civilians seemed to have been evacuated over the River Roer just beyond the front. How strange, I thought, that this old German, who was no different except for the immunity of his tattered civilian clothes and age to those whom dressed differently we would have shot to kill on distant sight not many minutes earlier, should here toil defenceless and safe through our midst by virtue of his rags and close proximity! Yet to kill a fellow individual was about the last possible thing the average kindly Jock would ever contemplate. How senseless war is that two complete strangers, both possibly friendly, timid people who in different circumstances might be bosom friends, should slaughter each other for the sake of evil ideas remotely imposed. At the front, however, the individual was lost as the 'Jerries' or 'them', a killable or be-killed entity at the apex of concentrated training, skill and immense expenditure. At least we had a right cause.

At last the damaged and snow-covered village of Teveren was in sight. We would soon be asleep, a wonderful thought. What a precious thing sleep is! How blissfully ignorant we were that it was going to amount to only a few hours of precious oblivion in the next shattering two weeks, during which we came to look back on our duty in the woods, at times, as a rest cure. My three sections were soon established in as many homes, with Platoon HQ in another over the road, and the very minimum of 'stage set'. With the delightful prospect of a proper hot meal in a few hours, prepared by the company cooks now up from 'B' Echelon and established with their 'blowers' in a barn, we soon snuggled free of equipment, and toes waggled bootless at last in a heap on the floor and on a battered bed. We lay in a tiny room in the centre of which a tubular stove with pipe roared, red hot, as though blushing at the snoring blissful confusion scattered about it.

Some hours later, after queuing for a while in the biting cold, we returned to our little room triumphant with two steaming mess tins of food: stew, with big blocks of bread, a heap of jam, spotted dog steam pudding with custard, and a scalding pint of thick tea. Having consumed this with relish, we instantly returned to sleep with renewed appreciation.

Next morning, a basinful of snow was stood on top of the stove to produce enough hot water for six of us at a time to wash our filthy faces, and shave off the stubble from our chins. At the end of each batch, the water was almost as thick as mud. I thoroughly enjoyed this, and with the sleep, felt fresh and a new being. The world seemed a different place, and certainly the Platoon looked quite another set of men.

We were becoming accustomed now to the fact that towns and villages near the front, or through which fighting had taken place, had no public services working in them. No electricity, water sanitation; life had ebbed out of them. Taps, electric switches and WCs were just so many empty symbols of saner days. The abandoned animals were the most heart-rending aspect of these deserted places; often just skeletons chained in their stalls or roaming the streets. Sometimes the Jocks, having set loose and done all they could for the bigger animals, would be seen walking about with the head of a puppy or kitten poking out of the warmth of their windproof smocks: something to protect instead of destroy.

As I walked towards Coy HQ to get orders, I noticed for the first time the new beauty of the sounds of melody and concord coming on this occasion from a Jock's mouth organ, which following the recent discordant destructive noises of battle. It soothed my surprised senses with a wealth of new enjoyment.

Later in the day an 'MBU' – mobile bath unit – arrived and set up shop. Where they got the water from I'm not sure, but with blowers going they soon produced clouds of steam and a spray of reasonably hot water from a system of overhead pipes. I feel sure the inhabitants of Teveren, had they been there, would have been surprised to witness this new winter scene in their staid Catholic village. A host of naked Jocks and officers, singing, shouting, and popping in and out of sight in a cloud come down to earth. One might almost have expected to see haloes, harps and wings attached to these pink apparitions were the show not given away by the exclamations and 'language' induced by the cold.

Soon the whole Battalion, rejuvenated, glowing, and reclothed with fresh socks, shirts and underwear, was busily engaged on generally smartening up, cleaning weapons, renewing damaged stores and equipment, drawing ammunition up to scale and, where necessary due to casualties, re-organising.

This finished, a period of feverish letter writing set in. Everyone seemed to be writing; all faced with the same tantalising difficulty that we could write about nothing more recent than a period named, two weeks before. This of course was for security, and to make sure about it each officer had to read and check his men's letters handed in unsealed for this purpose, then affix signature and rank at the end, and seal.

A surprising number, either from a disinclination to express their feelings on paper due to it being read later or through an inability to do so, wrote letters which might have come from some other town in Britain. Some talked about the countryside, the people and human things. Others entirely referred to details in letters received – about the kids and home. Usually the finish was a row of Xs, and often the envelope bore SWALK on the back – 'sealed with a loving kiss', I took this to mean; in which case the loving kiss was from me! No stamp was needed, but in lieu of this the words 'ON ACTIVE SERVICE' had to appear. Quite a few married chaps managed to write some sort of a letter almost every day wherever they were.

After tea, there was just time to call in at some of the other platoons and Company Headquarters to see one's friends, whom, of course, one could not see except some perhaps very occasionally in action. If one did not see a well-known face of a friend immediately at another Company, one became, as action succeeded action, almost fearful to ask as later all too often the reply was reduced to one of two, possibly three alternatives. Killed. Wounded. Missing. Happily there had been few fatal casualties this time other than those in HQ company, one of whom I realised I had lent some money to, a symbol that had no value now though . . . my friend the post corporal.

Our 'period of rest', we were startled to hear after our second night's sleep in our hot little room, was over. We were to move back to Bunde, 4 miles north of Maastricht on the east bank of the Maas, to form up in our concentration area for an operation we were told was to be called 'Blackcock'.

Once more we found ourselves (a few miles off) back in

Holland, and we unloaded outside a windswept open barn on a bleak hillside. Here we were scheduled to stay. Fortunately, someone objected to the situation strongly enough and we moved again 2 miles south to Meersum after one more sleepless night in temperatures far below freezing; and we did not have our greatcoats with us. Some idiot at Brigade seemed to have organised this.

At Meersum the company had fine billets in a centrally heated school, and the officers in houses over the road. My one was with two fine old Dutch people called Matthew, or the Dutch equivalent. Outside their house, and up and down the road were stacked mountains of crated 17-pounder anti-tank shells. We were to work with tanks in a big way, we speculated – and correctly!

The object of this operation, under the command of Gen Ritchie, was to destroy the enemy in an extensive triangle between Roermond at the apex, and a base line from Sittart to Heinsberg, with the Dutch–German frontier squiggling through from side to side. These sides were bounded by the River Maas, and to the east the River Roer. This strong position was backed by the guns of the Siegfried Line, some of them unpleasantly heavy as we were to see, and constituted a threat to the right flank of the British 2nd Army.

Opposing us were two German divisions, some fusilier battalions, a parachute regiment, and an unusually large concentration of mortars, artillery, self propelled 88mm guns, and finally an unexpected number of Heavy Tiger tanks and some Mark IVs. Some of his infantry had been mauled quite heavily, but was exceptionally well backed up with heavy weapons.

We could not, however, complain about lack of strength ourselves for this important attack which was designed to be the break out from the static period of winter build up. It was the 'curtain up' to the 1945 British 2nd Army offensives, which were to carry us right up to the Russians on the Elbe. 'Our team' consisted of the 7th Armoured Division ('Desert Rats'), the 8th Armoured Brigade, elements of the 79th Armoured Division with their 'Crocodile' flame-throwers, 'Kangaroo' turretless tank troop-carriers, 'flail' mine destroying tanks. There were also 'AVRE' tanks, which threw a bomb the size of a dustbin at blockhouses and carried fascines to cross A/Tk [anti-tank] ditches. Also with the rest of our 52nd Division, we were to have the infantry of the 43rd (Wessex) Division. Behind all this was the massive artillery we came to always expect as a part of a Montgomery operation. We had not, however, expected a personal visit from 'Monty', who one day as we waited on the start line, staggered the Anti-Tank Platoon by visiting them with a present of newspapers and cigarettes!

The whole operation, it was thought, would last about ten days to two weeks, on the go night and day 'to give the enemy no rest' – nor ourselves as we later fully found. Due to the positions having been static for some time, both sides had become well dug in, with heavily mined forward areas. This ruled out the chances of a broad frontal attack. The plan therefore was for the 7th Armoured Division, the 8th Armoured Brigade and our own 155 Brigade working with Kangaroos to punch a hole through at one point, at Susteren, and move fast in a curve, way behind the main enemy positions. This was operation 'Bear'.

With the enemy attention distracted from behind by us, operation 'Crown' – the rest of 52 Div were to move forward over our old defence line. When this was completed, the final 'Eagle' operation was scheduled – a sweep by us down onto Heinsberg, while 43 Division who would by then have punched another hole in the south and sweep up north to meet us.

The weather took sides with the enemy, and we were in for nine days of the coldest weather of the winter, plus blizzards and 20 degrees of frost. Yet as we were going to work with Kangaroos we were to travel as lightly as possible. This meant no blankets, no greatcoats; just what we had on, and a gas-cape! We were soon to find what this meant at 3 am in midwinter with sleep and proper meals only a memory, a wet hole in the ground to lie in, and a very active enemy on three sides of us!

We had not worked in action with armour before, and we were told that the short stop of three days here would be spent in getting as much rest as possible, and in getting thoroughly acquainted with the turretless Grant or Sherman tanks known as Kangaroos, in which we were to operate. These tanks took twelve men in each. They were to take us right onto, or as far as possible towards, our objectives where we were to roll out over the sides (a method of getting out quickly without showing ourselves as targets needlessly). As we were to unload right among the enemy we would have to both think and act swiftly in the confusion, and try to get ourselves sorted out and into action before their recovery. Having been 'blind' inside the tank, we would roll out into strange surroundings, and possibly under close enemy fire. Our only line seemed to be to realise this and to get a grip on the situation and act more swiftly than they.

There were many problems to solve. How best to load the men so that they would unload in the right order to be of maximum use. What weapons, ammunition and rations in view of the confined space. (Hence no greatcoats.) What radio communication at various levels, and so on.

Once we were unloaded, the Kangaroos were to clear out of it as fast as possible. With no guns other than a machine gun they were fairly helpless and could only harm the enemy by churning his trenches in with their tracks. We were to be escorted in by armed tanks, but these would only stay on the objective for as long as it took our anti-tank guns to get up. Otherwise, unless the tanks could find a 'hull down' position they might be 'sitting birds' to 88mm guns or *panzerfausts*.

Two visits were paid to the Kangaroos, which were manned by Canadian crews, and we did everything we could to become familiar not only with these big thundering sardine tins, but also with the friendly informal Canadians, who rolled cheerfully into war armed with frightful, nasal-twanging swear words, whisky and an amazing careless nonchalance. I thought later, could the enemy have seen this they would have been so shocked at the apparent lack of respect for them that they would have given up in puzzled helplessness on the spot.

As always, the order to move came in the middle of the night, on 16 January 1945, and the old Dutch couple whom we earlier had had a cosy evening with round the fire were up to see us off. We were touched with their concern on our behalf: that we were to miss the rest of the night's sleep, and that we should take care of ourselves. We might have been their sons from the concern shown. They, of course, knew nothing of what we were up to, but guessed. We at that time did not yet know much more than the bare outline ourselves, and many times in the coming day I looked back rather nostalgically on their warm little home and the irony of their concern that we should be warm, take care of ourselves and be well slept!

The cold outside was bitingly intense, so much so that later a Brigade signaller had to be disentangled from his radio and evacuated with frostbite. Underfoot, if we stood still for a few seconds, one could feel the metal studs and heels of the boots suddenly grip and freeze to the road.

Having struggled once more into the weight and harness of equipment – small pack and gas cape, waterbottle, short-handled assault shovel, rifle, bayonet, 50 rounds, .303 revolver, compass, 48-hour ration pack, first aid kit, tin hat, mess tin, mug etc – we were ready to go. Section commanders were briefed, weapons and ammunition checked. I was most grateful for the hood of the windproof smock which we wore together with a balaclava helmet. On my hands I wore mittens with gloves over them which were taken off in action as mittens alone were less clumsy for firing and loading.

It was getting on for 3.45 am when at last the figures ahead started to move on an unexpectedly long trudge over slippery roads to the forming-up point, where we would meet the Canadians waiting with the Kangaroos.

We were not exactly in overcheerful spirits, each one tramping silently in the chill darkness to the clink of metal and crunch of snow in the company of his own thoughts on the rapidly approaching unknown, and adjusting his mental outlook and values just as one braces muscles to take a sudden strain. I looked at the four little groups of my men plodding along in file on alternate sides of the road, and at the men of Company HQ ahead, and wondered what they were thinking. For some the action was to result in the award of medals, for many it was the last; for myself later the unexpected task of commanding the company as the only officer left.

Eventually my wandering thoughts came down to earth again, and centred on a few shielded lights among some dark massive shapes in an orchard. The booming rumble of many tank engines warming up told us that we had arrived. We were pleased in this knowledge only in as much as it promised a rest from the cutting weight of equipment and cross stays. The cramp-like numbness in one's shoulders was eased.

Once seated, shivering and doubled up on the driving shaft cover or floor of icy steel in the Kangaroos, we were soon wishing ourselves marching again as the cold was intense. To touch the metal of these giant ice-boxes stung, and gloves slightly damp with perspiration from our recent exertions froze and clung to the metal and weapons. Each Kangaroo had a girl's name painted on the side, and my Platoon HQ tank was called 'Lucy'. One of our Canadian officers was heard to remark that his particular Kangaroo, 'Esther', was 'the coldest b*** woman I have met'. There was one thing about these ladies though – their breath was wonderfully hot! At every opportunity when the column slowed to a stop we took turns to nip out and stand against the flame-spitting engine cover at the rear of the tank as it belched a vibrant blast of hot exhaust.

Once under way at 5 am and out of the shelter of the orchard, it got even colder. We soon found that a tank, in spite of its broad tracks, is, due to the enormous weight, a most difficult vehicle to control on a road with a camber of snow pressed into a sheet of ice. Several loud crashes at regular intervals, with no appreciable jolt to the tank, informed us to our amazement on looking out to the rear that we had just skidded off the road and bashed down a line of telegraph poles like matchsticks. Back on the road again we had the opportunity of seeing the tank ahead skid helplessly sideways off the road and do likewise.

We rumbled through Dutch villages in the dark, several times narrowly missing the wall of some old house or shop. The occupants, woken from their sleep by the long column of noisy monsters, which must have shaken the buildings heavily thundering past at fair speed, little realised as they leaned out of the warm bedrooms to wave us on towards Sittard, how close they were to being tumbled into the street in a shower of rubble. 'Lucky b***s in their homes', a Jock grumbled to himself.

In the small village of Schinnen on the route north we joined forces with the tanks of the 8th Armoured Brigade, and this massive display of armoured might pulled up for a while to let more tanks pass up the column. Seizing our opportunity – we had scented the smell of baking bread nearby – we climbed out of 'Lucy' and into a baker's premises. In no time the Platoon had some water on his oven for tea, and bread toasted and spread with tinned butter and jam as we sprawled thawing in the warmth and glorious scent of baking bread. We had moved from hell to heaven. The baker, who took this invasion very well, showed great interest in our white bread.

We were due to come into action some time in the middle of the afternoon if all went well. However, no sooner had we reached the Brigade start point than the news came that the 7th Armoured Division had struck trouble and that the attack from the west had also met violent opposition and was now halted at a blown bridge. Twice the sappers, suffering heavy casualties, had to rebuild the bridge. The first time it was smashed again by the enemy, but finally 15 hours later, the 1st/5th Queens cleared Susteren.

Our start point, Geleen, was fortunately quite a nice village and it was here that we found ourselves at dawn. The armoured column had drawn up alongside a row of suburban houses and as it appeared to be a prolonged halt, we hopped out to jump about a bit and try to regain some warmth. At this time we at Platoon level did not know what had caused the hold up but had gathered that the wait would be long enough to prepare some breakfast. Typical of infantry life, we were to find three days of unexplained waiting pass, all the while expecting from hour to hour that we would roll into action: a most wearying process on nerves.

Within a few hours each tank-load had made friends with one or more of the families in the wayside houses. The family that 'adopted' 'Lucy' consisted of a tough, likeable miner, his good-humoured wife, a daughter of sixteen or so and a little boy and a girl of five and three. Somehow the whole Platoon managed to sleep in this modest little home on the lounge and dining-room floor in warmth and therefore, to us, fair comfort. The kindly families seemed anxious to do all they could for us. Here we ate all our meals and used their kitchen to wash and shave on a roster basis. In return we washed up for the wife and cooked their food for them, strongly bolstered up with our army rations containing things they had not eaten for years. They seemed to greatly enjoy our speciality of bully beef stew with thick slabs of white bread and tinned butter, followed by tinned fruit or plum-duff with a dash of rum.

The chocolates and sweets as usual went to the children: the first they had ever eaten in the case of the youngest. The mouths of the toddlers were soon spattered with chocolate as they crawled over the sprawling Jocks on the floor. Both Jocks and children were enjoying themselves thoroughly, playing toy soldiers with lines of upturned cartridges. Several of the chaps with youngsters of their own at home I think imagined themselves playing with their own toddlers. How mad that these same bullets, clutched and cooed over with delight in tiny chubby hands should so soon after be fired with the intention of depriving men of life. Some of the youngest of the Jocks delighted more in palling up with and pulling the leg of the blushing sixteen year old 'wee bit 'fluff'. By the time we had to depart I had sketched all the family by way of some small return for their kindness. They loved to join us, cramped though it was, to listen to Cpl Parry trilling happily away on his mouth organ, usually with an enraptured child on his knee. At times I found it difficult not to feel a touch of envy at the contemplation of the cosy certainty of the civilians' family life and a warm bed to go to each night. During this period we also made great friends with crews of the three tanks which carried the Platoon; six lively likeable Canadians. Eventually a slight thaw, which slushed the roads, and the order 'prepare to move' came together. To the delight of the children and together with the tank crews we tested each automatic weapon with a burst into the air in front of the houses. At dusk on the 18th January we roared off into the gathering darkness after a tearful farewell from the womenfolk. We clustered tightly together for warmth in each tank. I sat beside the gunner/radio operator, astride the transmission shaft, listening to the crackling chatter of the other Kangaroos coming in over the radio, the squeak and crunch of the tracks, the roar of the engine and the cursing of the Jocks. The temperature again dropped steadily and sleet swept in the open top which we eventually covered with a tarpaulin. Finally, at ten that night we lurched to a stop in the village of Heide. As the engines cut out we were aware with a quickening of the pulse and an empty feeling inside that we were once more among the sound of shells in flight and explosion and that not all of them were going the right way. This village, just through Susteren and to the east, had only been captured earlier in the day, as we could easily see from the surroundings of glowing rubble and flaming timber and the acrid, smoking ruins.

At the call of a Company HQ runner for 'Orders Group', or 'O' Group as we knew it, I tumbled out of 'Lucy' and joined the other two platoon commanders, and Maj Colin Hogg, now back with us, and gathered with Capt John Elliot and CSM Pook in the cellar of a small, smashed house. We knelt on the straw-littered floor round a map illuminated by a hooded flashlamp. The position and information were not at all clear as things were in a state of flux. The enemy were suspected to be in the next village of Slek, just up the track ahead, and D Company with some armour had gone up to investigate. Somewhere 3¼ miles to the east of us an armoured force had driven a wedge and we were to catch them up on foot, leaving the Kangaroos, which would be helpless against enemy infantry anti-tank weapons, in the dark. Exactly where else the enemy were we did not know.

My job was to memorise the three-odd miles of twisting branching tracks and to lead the Company forward to contact the tanks. Outside the sleet continued, lit by 'Monty's Moonlight' – our searchlights shining low across the sky, silhouetting the tileless skeletons of the ruined houses and lighting everything with a greeny-blue glow.

The Jocks, cursing, de-bussed from the Kangaroos and in single file we staggered forward in the half-light and blizzard, stumbling over the spewed up ribs of earth and broken ice of the tank tracks which criss-crossed, wandering out into the fields, breaking the fences on either side. This mess would have rendered my task difficult enough in the daytime, but now not only the tracks had vanished, but the wayside houses too had been blasted flat by the AVREs with D Company. That some had been there at all I could only tell from occasional heaps of still smouldering rubble with embers glowing in the dark. The map was pretty well useless now. To make it trickier, possible enemy infiltration back between ourselves and the now isolated armour was likely. For two hours we slowly picked our way. I paused many times to puzzle out the route, then on again. In case we met trouble I had Cpl Allan and a couple of chaps with Stens; and we kept a bit ahead of the Company.

A large object glowing a faint pink in a field beside the track south-east of Slek, which was sizzling in the sleet and giving off tremendous heat, told us the Germans had been here a short time before – it was the hulk of a burnt out and still completely red-hot Sherman tank. As we passed, much more on the alert, we wondered if the crew had managed to get out.

John was now up with me helping to find the way. We debated which of two tracks to take for some time before we moved on, as we had by now expected to contact our tanks, and had no further clues to go on. Eventually we both decided on the more southerly of the two as we knew they would swing more south than east. The tanks must have crossed the fields to get ahead for there were no clues on the track on which frost and sleet had formed a cover. How very fortunate this choice was for us we did not know, strangely enough, until three and a half months later as will unfold in the story, for 300 yards up the track, and closer than our tanks turned out to be, a complete German battalion was sitting, as unaware of us as we were of them!

Finally, in the darkness and stillness ahead we could just make out the idling throb of a tank engine. Whether it was one of ours or theirs we were not sure, so we crept very gingerly the remaining 100 yards until we could make out several massive dark shapes, from which the noise emanated, drawn up on the track. Being endways on, we could not make out the shape clearly enough to recognise them, so we closed in a bit more, ready to dive for a ditch if given a wrong challenge. A little further and we were relieved to see the tanks were Shermans, and we got right up to them without a challenge or the sight of a soul: I think they must have been brewing tea inside!

These were the right people, and at the head of the column another 'O' Group was held. We were to dig in on the edge and corner of a wood called Echter Bosch just in Holland; and cover the armour for the night. At dawn there was to be a two-company and armoured assault on what appeared to be a strongly held village called Koningsbosch, towards which the head of the armour had penetrated and started to meet resistance in blizzard conditions earlier in the evening.

So far resistance had been fierce, but in pockets behind blown bridges and in villages. The Dutch–German border kinked in about 3 miles here, and Koningsbosch was still just in Holland. We were wondering just what difference the next battles would reveal with the Germans fighting to defend their own villages.

I sited the Platoon positions closely in the dense wood of small pine trees, and along the rim of the wood. The trees were so tightly packed and webbed with undergrowth that contact with men dug in only a few feet off was difficult. As we were blind towards the most probable position of the enemy in the wood ahead, I sent out a listening post of two men, connected by means of a cord to the wrist of a chap in Platoon HQ beside me, to give an early alarm silently.

Once dug in to the frozen earth, and with stags fixed, I went to Coy HQ but could get no further news of the enemy and returned to dig my own slit trench, rejoicing in the opportunity of getting some warmth. Soon I had a respectable hole 5 feet deep, and covered with sticks at one end over which I put my gas cape and some earth to slow down any shrapnel bursting in the tree tops if trouble started. Then the freezing, all-night vigil commenced, alternately crouching tight with cold in the trench bottom, and paying visits to sections. This I did warily, as a Jock was likely to shoot first and challenge afterwards with visibility almost nil in the trees. This was one of the coldest nights we ever spent. Our clothes were already wet with sleet and the sweat of digging, we only had what we stood in with no covering, and we heard from the tank chaps next morning there had been 20 degrees of frost.

Towards 3 am I slowly started to dig my trench again to generate warmth, munching what biscuits I had left. Faint scrapings nearby told of someone else also doing this. However, I felt tired and was getting no warmer and gave it up. I was surprised to find when I put a block of chocolate in my mouth that it crunched to powder but did not get enough warmth there to melt! I could no longer feel my feet, and there did not seem the necessary energy left to shiver and get even what warmth that provided.

At first light I creaked out of the hole and round sections again for 'stand to', then returned to boil some water in my mug in the trench bottom for tea, wishing I had had enough Hexamine and water to do this during the night. Next I put on some Spam to thaw out and eat with biscuits as breakfast.

Up to now, except for distant explosions and a stray shell or two, it had been peaceful, but suddenly the crump, echo and whine of fragments told of mortar bombs about 75 yards farther in the wood. Immediately this was joined by the furious whiplash crash of tanks firing on two sides of us and shots passing overhead and behind, the solid shot nicking off the treetops, and the HE shells bursting short and spraying the trees with shrapnel.

Breakfast would have to wait. Within seconds three Sherman tanks had been knocked out on the track just behind us either by a German SP [self-propelled] gun or a Tiger tank well concealed to our left. A Cromwell and Sherman firing on our right told of more enemy in that direction. They were, in fact, on three sides of our wood.

As part of this disturbance, a German patrol had filtered into C Company area alongside us by creeping through the trees. They had run into two of our Jocks and an NCO, who were apparently out egg hunting to boost their breakfast and, stupidly, these Jocks were not properly armed. Some firing ensued and one of the Jerries, hit badly, fell screaming to the ground. With commendable presence of mind the NCO sized up the hopelessness of his situation and also fell in such lively imitation of the wounded German that he was left as finished by the rapidly withdrawing patrol and so got back. Some swift work by someone in C Company resulted in an opposing patrol cutting off and capturing two of the by now nearly unnerved Germans who marched back, hands as high as they could go. It was from the two Jocks who had just been captured and whom we recaptured when we overran Fallingbostel POW camp three and a half months later that we learned with astonishment that they had been led back to a complete German battalion only a few hundred yards away. Our two forces had spent the night peacefully in calling distance, each totally unaware of the other's presence.

With the return of comparative peace, I finished my breakfast just as a runner called me to Company HQ. Colin asked me to take a patrol in a circuit to the high ground at the far rim of our block of wood, where we felt the enemy most probably would be as it dominated the approach to Koningsbosch. I felt a number of us would be too conspicuous as it was now broad daylight, so I picked out Sgt Johnny Manson to come with me. He, a large, keen, redfaced fellow, was sporting a pair of wellington boots he had picked up that morning from the Jerries. We took a rifle, a Sten, some smoke and some Mills grenades and, keeping close in against the cover of the trees, set off to subdued exclamations of 'Good Luck' and 'Take it easy'.

We kept well apart in case of trouble, Manson moving 25 yards to my rear, so that both of us should not be put out of action at one go. After skirting the wood on low ground, moving to the east, I cut up the hill on the edge of a clearing, climbing warily for some hundreds of yards towards the crest. I felt conscious of a mingled intensity of fear, excitement and extreme alertness. If the enemy were up there in force, I hoped Manson would be able to extricate himself behind and get back with this information. That the enemy had been here within the last hour and a half we were certain because of the mortar bombs which had sailed down onto us at daybreak. I felt as though I were deliberately walking up a scaffold to some sort of execution which at best would entail being taken prisoner. Repeatedly we crouched to look and listen. Our dark forms were awfully conspicuous against the snow. The tension as we neared the top was really almost unbearable. Each second carried the expectancy of being ripped through with bullets as we went over the crest, the most likely place for the enemy to be.

Still no fire came at us, nor could we see signs of the enemy positions. Ahead lay more woods and thick patches of snow. We felt queerly alone. I turned to the west along the ridge and saw with a jolt some newly cut tree stumps – a likely sign of dugouts having been built nearby recently. Next our hearts thudded even more at the discovery of newly made heavy footprints leading down through a slight clearing towards our positions below. These, we realised, must have been made some time since 3.30 am when the last snow shower had fallen.

Moving in the trees on each side of these tracks, we trailed them carefully down. Suddenly, just ahead in the trees our eyes were startled by the closeness of a group of stout German log-bunker dugouts. We both dropped flat into the snow, to lie for what seemed a lifetime, listening intently with many a quick glance to our rear up the track. What should we do? If there were Germans there we could get no sound of them or idea of how many. Creeping silently to the closest one, we saw that the ground was fouled and ration tins scattered about.

We had approached these positions from the rear. Our forces lay the other side at the foot of the trees. 'Keep me covered', I whispered over to Manson as I crept towards the door of this first bunker and pushing it slightly back, I peered in. About two seconds passed before my eyes adjusted to the darker interior, but somehow I knew even before then that it was empty of Germans. Quickly we searched the others, but with no less care not to make a sound. To our immense relief, they also were unoccupied but there was ample evidence to show that they had been very recently. Each dugout had its own table, bunks, chairs, stove, lamp, coal and utensils of every kind. One had a radio, a clock, a pushbike and the remnants of a meal on the still hot stove. No doubt most of this stuff was looted from the Dutch for in the enemy's evident hurry of departure they had not seemed concerned to take much away. Perhaps the realisation at daybreak that we were so close with armour had made Jerry pull out fast after firing off surplus stocks of mortar bombs at us.

Down at the bottom once more, the two of us attempted and succeeded in getting right into our Company positions without being challenged to see if this could be done. Meeting no enemy on the patrol had given an elation which had made us a bit reckless, I reflected afterwards, for moving through the dense thickets silently into our own lines might have led to a sticky finish to the patrol. I reported back to Colin on our trip.

While we had been thus engaged, the assault by A and D Companies had already gone in on the closest part of the long village of Koningsbosch in Kangaroos and word came that we were to follow on foot. So rapid was the action by A Company that Sgt Barton with some men overran two 88mm SP guns and forty surprised Germans who were captured after little more than a couple of bursts with a Sten gun. A blizzard was again blowing a freezing haze of snow off the desolate landscape, and with it the news that more of our forces were successfully pushing towards us in operation 'Crown'. Major Rae, with D Company, having just heard this, spotted a large white tank in the village, but no one was quite sure to which side this massive vehicle belonged. To determine this, Major Rae put out a yellow recognition smoke signal. The response was immediate. The long gun barrel swung round and crashed a solid-shot shell through a wall a yard above his head.

Our job was to pass through D and S Companies to consolidate the attack on Koningsbosch. A lot of our armour had joined us in a clearing in the woods by the time we moved forward in the swirling sleet. To get to the village involved covering a mile of track in the open under enemy observation from the left flank. 'Peter, take your Platoon up to the head of the column, will you', Colin ordered. Immediately we came into view clear of the trees the mortaring started. There was nothing for it but to keep doggedly going over the frozen white waste of country. We were moving in single file in section groups. How no one got hit, which as far as I know was the case, was astonishing, for the black smoke puffs were crashing on, over and short of the track, and blowing off over the fields. The blast from one knocked over the chap next in file behind me, just shaking him, while fragments cracked past from close bombs or buzzed past like a bumblebee from more distant ones. 'Lord, man! 'tis plain murder, there's no future in this: no cover for miles', Taffy grumbled unhappily.

Nearing the end of the track, after 1½ miles, the range for the mortars which were firing parallel to our path from the north began to get just too great for them to quite reach us. Our elation, however, was short lived: as we rounded the next bend on reaching the village, the awful distinctive crash of an 88mm dissolved the front of a cottage ahead in a shower of dust and smoke. Near it were two Kangaroos which had been knocked out.

I was shaken to notice that the leading one was our 'Lucy' and that the Canadian sergeant lay by her side with a leg missing. He was surprisingly cheerful, though, and recognised us as we passed, calling 'I'll soon be home now!' His radio operator knelt by his side and waved us on, shouting 'Give the b***s hell!' as he tended him. How fortunate we were not in 'Lucy' after all. Two more crashes from the 88s scored direct hits on one of the captured SP guns and a German motorcycle taken by Sgt Barton. To these the renewed crash of enemy mortars joined. Capt Viney Scott, who was talking to Jimmy Wannop ahead of us down the road, was killed by a direct hit. This was a great loss to the Battalion and especially to Frank Coutts, Bill Halliburton and 'Ally' Ross who collectively used to refer to themselves as the 'The Soviet', due to the Canadian-pattern assault tin hats they wore, and who were bosom pals.

Sgt 'Dodd' Oliver emerged from a bunker with about seventy more Germans whom he had captured 'Nattering to each other' and seemingly unaware of our close proximity. The cause of the 88 fire was, I was astonished to see, only too clearly a Tiger tank drawn up alongside a farm called Swaantjeshof 500 yards off on another track over the fields. It gradually became evident that there were four other Tiger tanks operating with this one, but for the moment otherwise occupied. 'What are ye waiting for? Can ye no' see the b***s?', an exasperated Scots voice called up at one of our tank crews. Several of our Shermans with their much lighter armour and guns had had a shot at it but had either missed or done no damage: their excuse, 'Frost on the telescope lens'. However, I don't blame them for their discretion. The road we had just covered had a fair sprinkling of knocked out Shermans and Kangaroos.

The village street, open on the side towards the Tiger tank, was becoming increasingly unhealthy with mortar and MG [machine gun] fire and an occasional HE shell from the Tiger, to whom we were now in clear view. Some minutes passed while we worked our way half of the distance towards our objective, the 'T' junction of the village. We had been getting closer to the tank all the time and I think the only reason we had got so far without casualties in the Platoon was that he must have been conserving his MG ammunition. The few HE shells he fired passed between our advancing figures, missing the Jocks perhaps only by inches, with an awful supersonic crash, louder even than the explosion of hitting the nearest object behind us. I decided not to tempt providence too far and for a while we took to the earth, a gutter, a ditch and beside a small house to wait and regain our breath for about three minutes. Finally we got up and sprinted doubled-up, as fast as we could scurry, the remaining 200 yards to the objective, fearful that at any moment we would run into a hail of fire from concealed enemy infantry.

The Platoon quickly deployed in houses astride the 'T' junction while the rest of the Battalion crept through to complete the consolidation. So far no more enemy infantry had been sighted, but we felt great apprehension of the outcome of one or more of the Tigers starting to roll forward, for the Battalion's anti-tank guns were not yet up, neither were any of our tanks. I don't think our PIAT anti-tank projector, with which each infantry Platoon was equipped to throw a small but powerful bomb against tanks, would have done much more than shake the massive frontal armour of a Tiger.

It was already getting on for mid-afternoon! The forces of operation 'Crown', pushing towards us from the south-west, had not yet linked up. Our force had swung in a 7½ mile arc leaving us at the point of this drive into enemy territory, an isolated position to be with dusk rapidly approaching. I realised that at best we would probably have another sleepless night, for we now lay astride the escape route of any enemy who might be pushed onto us by operation 'Crown' and who possibly would not be aware of us being there. We had a definite threat from one side and a possible one from the three other sides to beware of overnight. Having established my HQ in a small cellar, I called at Coy HQ to seek information, get the password and find out as usual whether Colin wanted us to maintain radio contact with him for quick warning overnight. I decided to keep two-thirds of the Platoon at a time on stag and try to make up sleep if a chance occurred next day (which it did not). The village seemed completely deserted of civilians. We only saw one stray figure, probably a cut off German, flit across the road to our rear at dusk. It was bitterly cold. To make up for our lack of food since the so-called breakfast, the remaining rations we could muster were heated over piles of Hexamine in the cellar, the fumes almost putting us off eating it in the confined space. The tea was fine. The water we used was at times a bit questionable, and for such occasions we carried water sterilising tablets, making it taste even odder. Just before dark we were delighted to see a few of our tanks had taken advantage of the failing light to run the Tigers' gauntlet and reach the village. However, to our intense regret, they pulled back a bit at nightfall. I think we all inwardly prayed that the Tigers would not prowl that night.

Towards the early hours it seemed so quiet outside in the frozen monochrome of snow, that I retired, fagged-out, to attempt some sleep with those off stag in a pile of straw in the cellar. Though I eventually got warm, I just could not sleep, being either over-tired or too mentally alert to surprise from above and the lone and unexplained sounds of isolated violence in the night. Strangely the silences between seemed more pregnant imaginatively than the violence of the punctuations.

I had hoped to get more rest but Sgt Dickinson was LOB for this action. Before first light I got up to check round section positions in preparation for 'stand to' at dawn. The silence and cold now rivalled each other in intensity in the white, deserted streets of this smashed, dead village. The muffled chaps on stag seemed glad of the chance to talk a while, softly through their breath-frosted woollens which, with the windproof hood, covered all but a slit for the eyes.

At 'stand to' word came that 'Crown' force had made contact overnight and we had again come under command of 52nd Division. At sunrise, after 'stand down' a runner from Company HQ called me to an 'O' Group. This turned out to be a briefing by Major Harcourt-Rae at Battalion HQ. 'White, the CO wants a patrol taken out at Platoon strength immediately you have had a bite to eat. You are to penetrate up the road towards the village of Aandeschool about a mile north-east of Koningsbosch, checking past the position from which the Tiger shot us up yesterday. Don't go into Aandeschool, but I want you to observe it for enemy occupation. If you meet any enemy I want you to draw his fire and estimate his likely strength. C Company will later want to get to this village to secure the flank of a 5th Battalion attack on Waldfeucht just over the border into Germany. Right? Well, off you go and let's hear how you got on when you return.'

I scrambled back to the Platoon area to get breakfast and to brief section commanders and the Platoon. Smoke was pouring out of my HQ when I arrived. Some Jock had filled a German methylated stove with petrol to cook his breakfast. Instead, it had nearly cooked several Jocks. The stove had two small tanks. One had just exploded, setting one room on fire. I was most anxious to quell this fire, not to save the house but to prevent drawing enemy attention to ourselves, especially in view of the forthcoming daylight patrol. To this end I succeeded in throwing the remnants of the flaming stove out of the window, searing my hands as I ran, spilling burning petrol over them. Just as I let the stove go, the second drum blew up in my face. Fortunately, none of the buzzing metal hit me, but the blast of flame clean removed every hair on my unshaven face, eyebrows included, that part of my head of hair not covered by my tin hat and even my eyelashes. I was certainly the best trimmed man in miles! After a bit of a tussle the rest of the fire was put out with sand and some stagnant water. Really warm at last, we cooked breakfast on Hexamine tablets: hot soya-link sausages between thick blocks of bread, and a pint of tea apiece scalding our lips. After an inspection of weapons, equipment and ammunition, we loaded, fixed bayonets and set off for the start line. The air was crisp and clear, a lovely day. Perhaps one appreciates things most when there seems the possibility of their being taken away: the sun, the sky, the glinting snow, the beauty of the winter landscape and the faces and voices of friends.

The start point was the main crossroads and dominating it, a Canadian-manned Sherman tank, one of several, poked its gun through a hedge towards the enemy. I contacted the tank commander and crew before setting off and told them what we were up to. 'I'll let you know when we get in again', I said. Finally, and fortunately, I fixed the firing of a 'red over green' verey light as a recognition signal if any doubt arose as to our identity on the return trip. 'Sure Scottie, we'll keep an eye peeled. Mind those Tigers and have a nice walk boys, the weather's dandy', the Troop Commander called.

It was now broad daylight and with a straight road of virgin snow stretching up to Aandeschool village in the distance, there was precious little cover with which to conceal our thirty dark figures silhouetted against the snow. If the Germans were lying in wait for us in any of the numerous little smallholdings set each in its orchard 25 yards from the road, or in the village itself at the end, we were in for a sticky time. I decided to let only one section advance at a time, covered in turn by the rest of us. 'Keep off the road and work along the ditches. If you are fired on shoot back as hard as you can even if you can't see Jerry.' This sort of patrol had a queerly fascinating fear-packed exhilaration about it. Anything, or nothing, might happen.

It was a slow exhausting job forcing forward through the thick drift snow of the ditches and covering and searching each of the farms in turn to make sure we were not shot up or cut-off from the rear. The first few farms were deserted and after half a mile or so we rested, panting and pouring with sweat, sprawled in the snow while I surveyed forward with my glasses. I noted with satisfaction that though we could see the broad track-prints of the Tiger that had fired at us the day before, there was no sign to indicate that this particular monster lay in ambush ahead.

'By God Surr! There's something moving in the doorway of the far farm on the right!', Cpl Finney puffed. This building was situated at about the limit of our expected patrol and we set out to stalk it with infinite stealth. 'Don't fire, it's onny a b*** civilian johnny,' a Jock stage-whispered back from the point-section. Behind this chap, a farmer who had been recognised for what he was only just in time to prevent tragedy, we could now see the heads of several children peeping timidly at us. This Dutch family were the first civilians we had so far met in this operation. Their land ran back to the German border a few hundred yards to our right front. 'Keep a sharp watch a bit!' I ordered and went in to the warm earthy interior of the farm into which the scared family had vanished. It transpired they had thought we were Germans, and in spite of our dress and speech eyed us with nervous uncertainty which gradually gave way to hesitant smiles and exclamations of joy. When at last convinced, they were anxious to help all they could. The mother, followed by her wide-eyed, thumb-sucking, dirty brood, hastily poured out some mugs of hot milk which had been simmering on the oven. While the Jocks with me gratefully gulped this down, I tried to get sufficiently through the language barrier to learn what they might know of the movements of the enemy, particularly the 'Panzer'. This had apparently withdrawn with some enemy infantry, as far as they knew, towards Aandeschool the previous evening. This made things difficult. To try to get more definite news of the enemy we would now have to go quite a way beyond our expected patrol.

Watched sympathetically by these kindly Dutch folk, we gingerly edged forward to the outskirts of the village, but keeping out of it as instructed. Still no sign of the enemy could be seen either in the village or beyond when looking through the glasses. With a hammering heart and very unwillingly I stood up and walked backwards and forwards over the road to see if this would draw fire and give some definite information with which to return. With a deep sense of gratitude and relief for our good fortune, I set our course for 'home'. Caution now seemed needless but just to be sure, I instructed section commanders to return in bounds, one section at a time, as we had come. When about 800 yards from Koningsbosch, hell broke loose about us. 'Blast it! Get off the road! Anyone see where it's coming from?' A violent, fast crackling filled the air about us, ripping the snow, spinning debris and flicking a shower of tiles off the roof of a house behind us with melodic clatter and whine of mutilated bullets which continued to race a devastating pattern of chips and holes out of the side of the house. We frantically flung ourselves towards any cover in a volley of obscenity which filled the air as viciously as a second long burst of fire. My first feeling was that a German patrol had got in behind us, or that we had overlooked some enemy in one of the farms. I lay, heart and lungs pounding, next to sweat-streaming and swearing Cpl Finney against a low mud bank trying to locate the source of fire. It was a very rapid rate, but not fast enough to be a Spandau; more like a Besa. 'Hell Surr! It's our own b*** tanks!' This was confirmed by yet another burst, one or two bullets whacking the bank with a loud hollow clump ahead, thus placing the fire as from our own lines. From the thicket which concealed one of the Canadian tanks – the very one we had informed of our patrol – I noticed a tell-tale blue smoke haze blowing. A 'red over green' verey from my pistol stopped this. Miraculously no one had been hit, though several of us had been spattered with torn earth and snow. The bitter horrible language which accompanied us on the rest of the journey back built up to a scathing crescendo as we drew level with the apologetic 'trigger happy' tank gunner responsible. 'Whose *** side do you b*** well think you're on, you ***!' was about the politest of the phrases which greeted the white-faced, appalled and speechless Canadian. In his intense excitement at seeing figures approaching from the enemy lines, he had fired immediately and automatically, to think afterwards. 'Well, I'm darned grateful you didn't use your damned 17-pounder on us anyway', I said in mitigation of the horrible language with which he had been stunned. I reported back to Battalion HQ on my return. In talking afterwards I was saddened to hear that among the casualties sustained on our entry originally into Koningsbosch, the young sniper I had met in Tripsrath woods with Sgt Scott and who had been the CO's bodyguard had been killed in a carrier hit near where 'Lucy' had been knocked out. He was a keen young chap, always questing to snipe the enemy from some forward position. A second carrier had been also hit there, wounding the control-set radio operator.

COUNTER-ATTACK IN KANGAROOS

Shortly following our patrol, C Company safely established themselves in Aandeschool and at the same time a couple of squadrons of Churchill tanks with flame-throwing attachment and trailers, as well as some Sherman tanks, drew up in our village. In doing so one tank accidentally flattened out a 6-pounder anti-tank gun of Jimmy's. It said a lot for the sturdy construction of the gun's mechanism that it still worked afterwards! All this strength beside us enabled us to relax. We lit a stove for warmth and to cook a lunch of tinned meat and vegetables followed by plum-duff; then we settled on the floor to get a sleep. The enemy had obviously observed this build-up of strength, sure sign of our preparing another attack, for our peace was immediately shattered. Jerry had rigged up a heavy mortar somewhere. The most appalling crashes and blast swept dust and glass through smashed windows on to us. Those of us who were not already on the floor trying to sleep, dropped flat. I crept to the door to investigate and was staggered to see that the house just beside us and containing Cpl Finney and his section had had a direct hit, taking away the side wall and exposing the stairs only 14 feet from the room in which we had been sleeping. A couple of dust-covered but unhurt Jocks materialised, coughing and blaspheming, through the side of the house. 'We're OK Surr, no yin hit, but that was *** close!' Another faint swish of a descending bomb impelled me to throw myself back through my doorway. At the same moment I caught a glimpse of an ambulance slither to a stop outside I Section billet opposite. The crew frantically scattered for shelter just too late, apparently having seen my crash-dive. The road erupted with ear-shattering blast, rippling an avalanched cascade of tiles from our billets. For several seconds I could see nothing but tumbling smoke and powdered snow through which debris clattered. Gradually the crater materialised and on its lip lay what was left of one of the stretcher bearers. Next to him and nearer the apparently unharmed ambulance another lay groaning and doubled up. With amazing agility the remaining crew of the ambulance recovered, put the two casualties back into the still functioning ambulance and drove off fast. They were well advised to for the village was heavily mortared for quite a while. I felt uneasy that a bomb might land on one of the flamethrower trailers with its hundreds of gallons of fuel which lay against our billet. I did not relish being burnt again that day and in so wholesale a way. When eventually the enemy seemed to have grown weary of mortaring us we resumed our disturbed rest for a while before scouting about outside to see what clues might be picked up concerning our future.

Just outside Cpl Finney's billet, which included a corner café, I paused in amazement to listen to the most incredible blare and rasp of raucous music which issued from within, accompanied by shrieks of laughter. Drums rolled, symbols clashed, bugles blasted and castanets clattered above the background of some tortured tune which blared, boomed, crashed and tapped from an automatic organ. The volume of noise was staggering. The music was far from being consistent or in tune for some of the notes had been shot away or seared with shrapnel and the controls blasted. At the pump handle working this machine, with a speed and force it could never have experienced before, were two semi-convulsed, sweating Jocks. Their audience of about ten more of my men were doubled up, leaning against the walls and almost rolling on the floor in the weakness of nearly hysterical mirth. The stampeding contrast of this extraordinary interlude soon had me wiping tears of laughter from my own eyes with my cuffs while my ribs and tummy muscles ached with laughing. I sincerely hoped the enemy did not hear us and, knowing where the organ was, start mortaring us again.

It was clear some sort of attack was soon to be resumed and we were not surprised when an 'O' Group was called and details were worked out for our attack with C Company on the town of Bocket. Just before this 5th KOSB would attack Waldfeucht, a small town a mile or two to our north. We were to get into position overnight for a dawn attack supported by artillery fire coming in at right angles to our advance up till the last moment.

5th KOSB got into Waldfeucht on the night of 20/21 January 1945 with surprising ease but this was rapidly to prove a far from bloodless victory. German infantry supported by a strong group of Tiger tanks immediately counter-attacked and burst through the streets taking a heavy toll both of 5th KOSB and our tanks, which had much lighter armour and guns. They rapidly worked round the town until a large part of our sister Battalion was cut off. Their Battalion HQ itself was under fire from at least three Tigers from our side of the town. We later found that the 5th anti-tank platoon commander, with his gun-crews out of action, made a wonderful stand with his sergeant for which he won an MC. Manhandling a 6-pounder in the open street in spite of wounds, he engaged two of these monsters with his puny weapon and knocked them both out.

As a result of this news our own attack on Bocket was immediately cancelled while the position of the 5th deteriorated further. Meanwhile, we spent another restive night listening to this activity as we lay in Koningsbosch. We had a quick breakfast as the order prepare to move came. A hurried briefing followed in BHQ [Battalion Headquarters]. We in B Company were to put in an attack in Kangaroos at 11 am to relieve pressure on the 5th in Waldfeucht while the rest of our Battalion worked round to the south-east to attack the town from the other side, probably in the early hours of the next morning, coming in by way of Bocket which had just been captured by the 6th HLI [Highland Light Infantry]. We were immediately ordered to board a group of Kangaroos drawn up in Koningsbosch while an appeal was sent to the gunners to put down a hurried 25-pounder smokescreen to give us a sporting chance of cover from the Tigers on our side of the town as we roared in to attack. Once the Kangaroos had got us on to our objectives, they were to clear out of the Tigers' range as fast as they could before the smoke blew away. We did not feel particularly happy as we moved off. Quite apart from the prospect of being hit on the way like a can full of sardines by a Tiger's 88mm, we were ploughing cross-country at full throttle over a possible minefield; further, we had no information at all as to what hellish situation we would be tipped out into at the end of our desperate run. All plans would have to be improvised in split seconds on our arrival as we fell out among the enemy.

My new Kangaroo was named 'Annie'. I hoped she had a thicker hide than poor 'Lucy' if things got out of hand. The driver got an early scare over the radio of a Tiger somewhere to our left so we took immediately to the fields, the engine racing a power-packed roar as we ploughed lurching sluggishly like a ship in a swell. The complaining engine drowned all sound other than the frightening oscillating shriek of 25-pounder smoke canisters which plumed veils of billowy smoke to merge with the snow.

Soon this lung-biting fog of war, together with the snow, had us enveloped in a swirling world of whiteness, above, below and all around. Because of it we could not see where we were going; wherever that was, we were ploughing and bucking at top speed, crouched tense with racing hearts and the cold forgotten. We were rolling like so many tin cans through the smoke towards the fire. Somehow we hit neither another Kangaroo, a haystack, nor a house.

A sudden spin turn, and we crunched to a stop. Immediately over the radio from the Company HQ tank came the order to 'De-bus!' All in the same instant above the rumbling of the idling engine, we looked uneasily at each other with a sinking of the stomach as the fierce rip of an enemy machine gun and the most almighty crash of explosion enveloped all our senses. Once our heads appeared over the steel rim of the tank anything might happen. I yelled 'De-bus! Take up all round positions.' There was fortunately no time to think as we desperately tumbled and scutttled to get clear of the tracks and flung ourselves flat, facing outwards. Already the Kangaroo, revving madly, slung earth off the spinning tracks as it lurched swiftly into the swirling, spark-jewelled smoke. Everywhere were crouched scattering figures, dimly seen in the thinning, flame-reddened smokescreen, yelling voices, the cry of wounded, complete ear shattering pandemonium.

Immediately against us on the left were a row of Jeeps, trailers, kit, an ambulance and a house, all burning furiously with a billowy roar of sheets of petrol-fed flame, and dense coiling smoke. Another hideous crash of flame and swift loud rip of machine gun fire through the wall of smoke drew my eyes to fix with amazed horror on the source of all this hell-like confusion. Twenty-five yards away, wedged in the archway of the town wall and just too broad to get through, was a Tiger tank. A venomous spitting wall of steel itself, it was pointing right at the flaming inferno of the road and ourselves! The smoke had just lasted thick enough to save us, and 'Annie', from a far worse fate than 'Lucy's' long-range hit.

A swift painful scramble found us panting with pounding hearts against a low garden wall, and out of the immediate line of fire unless the tank chose to blow this protection to dust. My throat seemed like dried leather, and I felt sure it was not just the smoke. Any paralysis of fear seemed mercifully drowned in the flood-tide of noise, movement and excitement. No stretcher bearers could for the moment get at the casualties farther down the road. Miraculously some semblance of order had emerged and I could see my three section commanders sprawled amid the rubble and along the wall together with men of Company HQ, and these chaps signed that they were in contact with their men, though I could not see them all myself.

Sgt Johnny Manson grasping a PIAT just ahead of me at the end of the wall on the road started to move forward with the evident intention of crossing the road to outflank the tank and shoot it from the side or rear. He had just emerged from behind the wall when he coincided with a burst of fire and staggered back, crouched, stunned and splashing blood with his hand to his face covering a gaping wound where his jaw should have been.

Colin crawled up to join us, and we crouched below the wall next to Manson who now knelt in silent agony. We obviously had to try to outflank the tank somehow, but it did not seem possible from this side. Colin asked me to take 10 Platoon over the road to work through the houses behind the arch and try at the Tiger from there. Having seen what happened to Manson when he showed himself, I decided not to throw a '77' smoke grenade into the road, as this, though it would obscure us, would most probably draw a steady hail of fire. Instead I had section commanders line their men up four abreast to run flat out across the road at odd intervals. I shall never forget the desperate tension in running over in the first batch. It seemed deliberate suicide, yet incredibly the whole platoon got over without a scratch within about three minutes. It seemed impossible that the deafening, crackling bursts of point-blank fire had been real, for we had literally acted as figures in a shooting gallery. I think what had saved us was the very closeness of the fire, and the consequent inability of the gunner to traverse the gun with each crossing group. Fortunately the Tiger was too broad to either get through the arch, or traverse the long telegraph pole-like 88mm barrel of the gun far without hitting the sides of the arch, or he might have chased us by blowing down the walls of the lane. Just over the road we noticed for the first time a burned out 17-pounder gunned Sherman tank, the crew, it seemed, still in it. A little beyond, frozen dead in its tracks and also burned out, was one of the two Tiger tanks knocked out by Capt Hunter of the 5th – hit in swift retribution following its victory over the Sherman which had been hit at 35 yards range. We later found other Shermans trapped and smashed deeper in the town.

Crossing the back gardens of several houses warily to get level with the arch, we found the tumbled grey-green-clad forms of numerous German dead, most of them very young, sprawling in and about trenches, tangled in fence wire, weapons and equipment. As we moved forward, Coy HQ and the other two platoons remained on the far side to break their way through the houses parallel to us.

Some figures moving ahead turned out to our mutual relief to be the battered remnants of a 5th Bn platoon. The platoon Commander, a begrimed, sandy-haired chap of my age, came forward to meet me with 'Thank God you've got here'. I noticed with surprise that though he had lost all his fingers except thumb and index finger on both blood-streaked hands, he still brandished a captured Luger pistol in greeting, held precariously in the stumps of his right hand. He explained his PIAT and team were both put out of action, when after several attempts to fire down onto the rear of the Tiger from an overhanging window, a bomb had exploded against the window-sill from which they were shooting. I crawled up the rubble strewn stairs of this corner café with him after my Platoon had taken over positions from his remaining weary men. This should have enabled us to try our skill down onto the Tiger too if it was still in the same position. The tank commander must have been getting a bit restive in wondering what we were up to for we found the archway empty, and glancing up the road we were just in time to see the tank pulling slowly round a corner out of sight, in reverse.

As we looked from well back in the shadow of the smashed room, two German soldiers with rifles appeared unconcernedly in a doorway 100 yards off and looking in our direction. It seemed these two had been ordered to show themselves to draw fire, thus disclosing our whereabouts either for snipers or for the tank to come forward again. We could see from the smashed state of the house that the Tiger had put several shells through it. Perhaps he was collecting more ammunition. The young 5th chap, seeing I had a rifle, suggested we had a go at them well back to conceal the source of fire. I can still feel the heavy reluctance with which I slowly raised the rifle, realising that later it might be them or us if we let them go now. Next came the awful choice – which one should it be? How mad the values of war that I should feel such shame at the thought 'fire between them, no one will ever know'. Was the CO right, did this mean I was not 'suitable' for this sort of thing? The sight was steady on the left-hand German still looking peacefully our way as I squeezed the trigger slowly. Even as I did so, the full realisation that a human life hung on the minute pressure left to my finger made me dip the sights a shade to wound and not kill him if I could. As the rifle kicked in my shoulder and we ducked from sight to avoid being seen, I wondered if he was a married chap, with children at home. Peeping up slowly again, in case we had been seen by a sniper, we just caught a glimpse of two legs and feet trail out of sight, apparently being pulled by his pal.

The tank must have taken this in, for we heard the roar of its engine as it pulled forwards. I realised then that it must have just been the fact that these two men were such sitting ducks which had swayed my thoughts, for I felt no pity for this monster and dashed down to collect the PIAT team, McKenzie, and Syd

Brown, to have a shot at it. Clattering down the rubble strewn stairs I found these two and we dashed across a little side alley after peering up and down it swiftly. First, to make sure we were not sniped at by the next house up, I had a quick look over it. It was empty, but revealed no suitable spot from which to fire at the side of the tank as it went past for we would be so close to it that the back-blast from the PIAT bomb would most probably have harmed us more than it would the Tiger. We dashed back to the small alley which let at right angles onto the main road down which the Tiger would come and dropped into the gutter.

The three of us lay side by side, McKenzie in the centre with the projector and Brown his number two, with spare bombs to reload on his other side. Our hearts were pounding furiously. I trained my rifle on the corner 15 yards distant where the tank would pass broadside on to us, intending to hit at least the first of any infantry screen who might advance with the Tiger and peer round the corner. The situation still held a queer cinema unreality to it, but I knew this time that I would not hesitate. It would be them or us. The suspense was terrible. I was conscious of a tense quivering of mingled excitement and fear as our ears detected the distant revving of the Tiger's engine getting louder, then the clink-clink and squeak of slowly approaching tank tracks, still distant but coming steadily. I glanced behind to see if by chance any enemy infantry might have broken through our rear and was reassured to see we were covered as we lay by several automatics and rifles of others of the Platoon, poking from doors and windows, waiting silent and intent.

Suddenly, in an unexpected flash of blood-chilling sound, our ears tuned from the noise of the approaching tank to a new menace. A faint, whispered moan of a salvo of artillery shells mounted in a split second to an all-embracing hypnotic shriek which we just had time to appreciate was coming directly on us before the whole structure of our surroundings erupted and vomited with appalling blast and indescribable noise as though a brace of super-fast express locomotives with whistles jammed had coincided in one gigantic crash in our midst. The air was swirling with brick dust, powdered snow, smoky acrid yellow-black fumes and bits of heavy rubble and tiles thudding and pattering everywhere, hitting us painfully and whacking with metallic clatter on our tin hats. This sudden switch in climax from our ear-straining tension and concentration on the approaching Tiger had nearly wrought paralysis on our ability to react. 'By God Surr! Were those no' our ane b*** shells, the ***ers!' They were indeed our own 25-pounders. Another couple of salvos followed as unrepeatable words of obscenity and blasphemy also exploded about me. As the dust settled in a pinkish-grey film over the snow, I was staggered to notice that the cause of our being so heavily pounded with blast and rubble was a new shell hole 5 feet above us in a wall beside our gutter. The shell had just penetrated far enough through the wall before exploding for the main blast and fragments to smash into the yard beyond. Whoever had asked for these gunners to fire, most probably Colin at Company HQ somewhere behind us over the road, could have had no idea we were so far forward. Perhaps this was a blessing in disguise. The renewed revving of the Tiger showed him to be coming forwards again; this time, as we later realised, without an infantry screen, it having, I supposed, been decided by the Germans that we would have no infantry either where our own shells were landing. I was not at all sure that our PIAT would do more than annoy the Tiger if we got a direct hit, but was counting on the fact that the entrance to our alley was rather too narrow for him to swing either his long gun barrel or machine guns onto us without first swinging the body of the tank, which I hoped would expose the thinner side armour to any heavier anti-tank weapon back near the burning vehicles through the arch at the 5th Bn HQ.

The clink and squeak was almost on us now as the Tiger drew up to the corner. Slowly the muzzle-brake at the end of the slim lengthy green barrel came into view, inch by inch, then stopped. Two thoughts were worrying me. First, if the tank was not going to come far enough forward to expose the side properly, we would have to move to the other side of the alley to our right. Secondly, I still feared we were so close to our target that we would harm ourselves more than the tank. I saw a convenient doorway a few feet farther back on the better side. The gun barrel was still stationary, so with these thoughts in mind I signed to Mac and Brown and we scrambled into the doorway. Before showing the

PIAT I decided to remain hidden and see what it was that had caused the Tiger to pause. Peering through the yard doorpost crack from our new position, we could see both the gun barrel and huge front sprocket. Suddenly two Germans in dark tank overalls, evidently some of the tank crew, dismounted, looked round the corner against the tank, then vanished. I was thankful we had moved for we had not been seen. A few more seconds of tension, then the Tiger revved loudly and clinked back a couple of links, engaging gear, then lurched forwards exposing three-quarters of its flank. 'Right Mac!' I whispered. He pushed out the PIAT, the three of us crouched at the door, Brown with a second bomb, and I gave the word 'Fire!' 'Got the b***! Good shot Mac!' Someone exclaimed behind. The flash of flame had been followed by a billow of blast and oily black smoke which swept back from the top of the alley. For a few moments, during which Mac and Brown excited by the success bungled the reloading, the tank was obscured by thinning smoke. I think we were all three distracted by our success and trying to see where we had hit. The flash had been high near the turret. Three or four precious seconds slipped by while the stunned German crew recovered. Gears grated, there was a frantic unexpected revving roar and the Tiger withdrew slowly in a lingering trail of smoke to our distress and disgust. Left lying in the road was a massive chunk of metal which could have come from the gun mantle. Just what damage we had done was difficult to decide. We gradually concluded, in view of the fact that the Tiger never again came forward or fired the 88mm gun, that we must either have holed the barrel – which if fired again would have split or exploded – or we had wedged the mantle or turret.

The Germans' reaction was immediate. Within a couple of minutes I was startled to see a group of Jerry infantry moving through the yard of the house on the corner to clean us out. They were near the shell-holed wall. Mac had reloaded the PIAT now so I whispered: 'D'you see them Mac? Have a go.' Mac, crouched ahead of me, fired from the hip at the same instant as the Germans saw us, to be immediately enveloped in a blinding explosion as Mac crashed back heavily into me with the recoil. The recoil fortunately threw the bomb high enough to clear the wall. No

Germans remained when the smoke cleared. The terrific blast must have accounted for all of this bunch. However, it swiftly became apparent that there were quite a few others. Those left decided on a similar line of attack. As we anxiously watched, a much closer German showed for a moment throwing something towards us. 'Look out!' someone yelled. A stick grenade was spinning slowly to drop right on us, thrown from less than the length of a cricket pitch. We dropped frantically for the earth. There was no explosion as four, five, six seconds sped by. 'It's wedged in the tree just above us Sir . . . seems to be a dud!' It was 10 feet up directly overhead, held in a branch fork by its stick handle. We had to explode it with a Sten burst for safety in case it slipped later. 'B*** me that was close!' said Brown.

'More Jerries coming', a Jock shouted. We were at a great disadvantage in firing to the right along the alley being all right handed, so with Cpl Finney I stepped out into the alley to fire. My rifle was still in my left hand when Cpl Finney yelled from behind: 'Watch out Sir.' At the same moment I saw more Germans, three of them with Schmeisser automatics raised to the hip rushing the 15 yards which separated us. Everything happened in a flash of desperation. Realising I could not hope to get my rifle even part way onto the Germans and into my right hand to fire properly, I shot it as it was from my left hand into the cobbles just ahead of the three in the hope that at least it might disturb their aim. As the bullet whined off the cobbles I threw myself back to try to get through the doorway before the Germans fired. Even as I fell, Cpl Finney with his Sten tried to beat them to it. His bullets crashed past my cheek and at the same moment a hail of Schmeisser fire swept back the other way. They had evidently withheld to close the gap, realising our disadvantage. The fire, aimed at me, crackled fiercely past, smashing Finney's right hand off his Sten. Several bullets passed up his arm longways from wrist to elbow ripping his arm and his hand to shreds. He reeled back through the door, groaning and streaming blood, while in desperation I fired back as fast as I could work the bolt round the doorpost to the right. I could not get a proper look at where the enemy had got to without showing my head momentarily. I had the oppressive anticipation that my face would at any moment suffer a similar smashing to Cpl Finney's arm. I dared not look even long enough to see if my shots had found their mark and knew with a ghastly sense of approaching climax that unless a miracle happened Finney and I had had it, for my rifle could not hope to compete with three automatics from what I knew must be 3 or 4 yards range by now if they were still coming. My heart was hammering so fiercely I felt it would give out, at the realisation that I had reached the last round in my magazine. How this wild firing had intimidated the enemy I never would make out afterwards, but as I fired the last shot I glimpsed hesitation change to retreat among the Germans who had faltered 8 feet away. While still concealed I desperately fumbled to reload another clip. At that moment Brown reached my side with a Bren gun which he had grabbed and pushing it round the corner he fired several bursts which whined and crashed deafeningly off the cobbles. The Germans' boots clattered in retreat. Cpl Finney still stood, numb with pain and ashen in the face, his Sten in his left hand and repeating wildly: 'The b***s got me!' I put a tourniquet on with a web strap but despite his screwing it tight he was losing blood fast and as he was useless for further fighting, I put his arm in a sling and sent him to find his way back to the regimental aid post.

'Well I'm ***! We've scared the ***s off Surr!' Brown reported with a relief which I heartily shared. 'God! I thought that was our b*** lot, Surr.' We waited with fearful tension, watching for any renewal of the attack by the Tiger or the infantry, but moment followed moment and no sight or sound of further trouble materialised. I didn't know then what casualties the enemy had sustained from us. 'Keep watching, Brown,' I whispered. 'I'm going to crawl up the stairs and see if I can locate them again.' I scrounged a grenade from another section on my way, but could see no sign of movement up the main street.

Ever since we had taken over from the 5th Battalion chaps at midday we had been entirely out of touch, without sight or sound of the rest of our Company, and I could not get a squeak out of the radio to contact them. It was rapidly getting dark and all this time I had been expecting an order for us to attack forward into the town to try to regain closer contact with the 5th KOSB who were still surrounded. The situation was getting rather worrying. It would be dark in half an hour and perhaps the rest of our company had met serious trouble or surely Colin would have sent a runner. A reaction of cold, desperate fatigue and hunger set in as we shivered, watching the sinister glassless windows over the road and up the street, each one of which might contain a watching and waiting enemy. We knew they were still there for the 5th were still cut off 300 to 400 yards beyond. With the stimulus of danger and excitement less evident to the Jocks, we were left in a very tricky situation for the night. Any renewed attack on us, if we were not outflanked by more infantry and Tigers working round the town to our rear, would originate from cover only 12 to 14 feet away from us in the houses lining the opposite side of the alleyway.

I'd sent back a runner earlier with our news and at last as darkness fell I had word back from Colin: 'Hold your present positions overnight while the rest of our Battalion attack from the other side of Waldfeucht.' All this time there had been considerable shelling by both sides scattered about the town. The runner brought news that while 'our' Tiger had been operating, it had shot up the clearly red-cross-marked aid post the other side of our archway and some of the wounded had been hit a second time. The Jocks were really wild at this.

In order to ensure no move was made by the Tiger tank up the road during the night, I collected all the '75'-type anti-tank grenades carried one per man by the Platoon. These I primed with the aid of Cpl Allan and then I tied them onto a long piece of binder twine to form an unwieldy necklace. As soon as it was dark I carried these numerous grenades over the main road and laid them down, then dashed back trailing the surplus twine. 'Allan, see that one of your Jocks is on stag here during the rest of the night. If a Jerry tank comes forward I want him to wait until the last moment and pull the string of grenades under the tracks. That should stop even a Tiger for a bit as they will probably all detonate being so close', I instructed. 'He'd better use the full length of cord or he'll blow himself up too', I added on reflection.

The last enemy movement just as the light failed had revealed him to still be in the adjoining house at the corner. A few chaps at a time were now opening tins to have their first bite to eat since breakfast time, while the rest of us kept watch and improved our positions for the night. We barricaded all doorways and windows with furniture weighed down with rubble where not required for a weapon to poke through. The lane was well covered with cross-fire by all the automatic weapons we could muster and the PIAT with its crew was established at a ground-floor window in the café, looking up the main road. I was worried that the enemy might try to sneak attack if it got dark enough and so spent some time in collecting all the old tins and bits of scrap I could find then with infinite apprehension that we might get shot up in so doing. I sneaked out with a couple of Jocks and we scattered all this clanking junk about the alley in the hope that the enemy would trip and rattle them with their feet. At about 6 pm the fitful silence which had settled over Waldfeucht was again shattered by a concentrated 25-pounder barrage. This shelling was joined by a few salvos of a different calibre coming from what seemed to be the direction of the enemy. For the second time that day our billet got a direct hit, smashing the roof and adding to the mess caused by the Tiger which had earlier put several solid shot and HE shells clean through both floors. The strain of watching and listening proved very great with the enemy so close, though so far he seemed content to call a truce. I instructed section commanders to change stags every half hour in a few of the vital spots to a 'rest' in a less essential one. I had been pleased to discover at last light that we were now backed up by 12 Platoon who crouched in the garden among the numerous dead Germans, which seemed to me the most depressing pastime for 'a night out'. Some of 12 Platoon were also in a building near the town gate.

The barrage, I suspected, must have been in connection with the attack by the rest of our Battalion, which, if all went well, was due about an hour later. The weird sound of these droves of shells quite filled the dark sky. It was tinged here and there with columns of fire – lit smoke and tongues of flame from which sparks soared high. Again we heard the dismal musical avalanches of tiled roofs collapsing as in Flushing. There was a fairly continuous crash-crump-crump thudding of shells which sometimes fell unpleasantly close as the already shattered houses were further pounded. Every now and then a shell stoked up a burning house like a giant poker and sparks and an orange-tinted blazing snowstorm swirled for a bit. We watched intently the while in case the attack drove the enemy back onto us.

Our searchlights shining low towards the enemy (Monty's Moonlight) lit the snow-ribbed, shattered streets and roofs with a greeny-blue glow, but we couldn't detect any human movement in the frosted scene or the dark cavernous window sockets of the houses which brooded opposite as though trying to hypnotise us. The noise died down quite suddenly and gradually the fires too. An uneasy silence and complete lack of information concerning the attack kept us restive and alert for the remaining freezing hours of darkness. I dared not retire for long to the Platoon HQ cellar for a sleep, though I did manage half an hour. The lack of news worried me. So far as we knew the enemy were still only 14 feet away over the lane. At about midnight Phil Carruthers, one of our Canadian officers, passed through my positions leading a contact patrol. He paused to swap information for a while, but had very little news. He intended to try to contact Lt Col W.F.R. Turner of the hitherto cut-off portion of the 5th Battalion in the centre of the town and escort him back. 'Watcha, Pete!' he called in greeting. 'It's as *** cold as the *** Yukon; *** it! What's Jerry up to? Have you seen him recently?' We gave him all the information we could on the enemy and wished him a safe mission as he flitted off into the street from shadow to shadow with his men. He had soon vanished from our sight towards where we had last seen the Tiger by the smashed church. No sounds of trouble came back in the stillness; perhaps, as we had suspected, the enemy had withdrawn a little.

For some while before Phil had arrived, we had been kept very much on the alert by the brittle sounds of tiles and broken glass being walked on from time to time somewhere ahead of us in the cold blue stillness. Finally, these sounds passed noisily right against our café and not a sign was visible of any dark form to answer the hoarse and worried challenge of Cpl Beal, who called me over. I could certainly hear the noise, but could not see anything with which to connect it. It seemed about an hour since first these sounds had disturbed us. 'If it's a ghost it's a *** clumsy and solid one!' he remarked. I crept out to have a look round, very puzzled. I had half expected to find a shell-dazed civilian wandering about, but could not understand why all our eyes had seen nothing. It seemed to me though that whatever it was, a bullet would be able to stop it. Suddenly, round the corner of our billet amid the dark patches of debris, a heap of snow seemed noisily mobile and my blood ran cold. 'What on earth could it be?' I wondered as I took a step backwards. At the same moment an unhappy, shell-shocked and half-frozen white goat pushed its head against me! No wonder we had not easily seen it against the snow and rubble and darkness.

A few minutes later, as we relaxed a bit inside, it appeared that the goat was making far too scattered and heavy a noise for so small an animal. 'A group of figures comin' doon the *** road Surr, in the shadow!' a hoarse whispering Bren gunner gasped with intensity. Yes, I could see them moving steadily our way 50 yards off towards the church in the blue snow shadows. Covering them with all the weapons we could train down the main street, I challenged them, to get a cheery Scots voice in reply. It was a patrol from the cut-off section of the 5th Battalion. From them we learned that the rest of our Battalion had walked in overnight in their attack without having to fire a shot. As far as they knew the Enemy had pulled out. With this welcome news I stood down two-thirds of my men and we rested all we could until the biting cold and a pearly glow in the sky told us that another day was dawning. What would this one hold? We felt too fagged-out to care.

At this first sign of light came the order 'prepare to move'. Hurriedly munching a soya-link sausage I worked with Cpl Allan in retrieving and removing the igniters from the string of '75' grenades. Next we buried a few of the Germans nearest us temporarily in their slit trenches against our billet, taking one of each of their metal identity tags to hand in at Company HQ and marking each grave with a rifle stuck in at the head on which we hung a tin hat. One German, a fair-haired boy, did not look more than seventeen. Some photographs of his family spilled out of one of his pockets as we laid him to rest, face peacefully upturned and we could not shovel in the earth until we had found something to cover it with; a piece of lino. 'God Surr! What a b*** useless muck-up this war is, yon bairn should still ha' been at school' remarked the dejected Jock I was working with.

We had not time to bury more than half a dozen before Colin ordered me to move forward ahead of the Company with my men through the town to the south-eastern gate about 700 yards away. It was still not quite light, and as we had no certain information that the town centre was all clear of enemy we took things slowly making from cover to cover against the walls. I had put L/Cpl Wilson in charge of Cpl Finney's section. Rubble, craters and tangled wires made movement very difficult. The place was in an awful mess. To glance back from the scene of our earlier fight and see the enemy's viewpoint I found intensely interesting. Passing the spot where I had sniped the German, I saw another burned-out Sherman tank where the road opened into the town square at the foot of the church. On the right, down a side road, were two more of our tanks smashed, one still smoking. The day before, during the fighting a keen but ignorant Jock had stalked a tank standing by the roadside with its engine running. He had clambered onto it to sling a Mills hand grenade down through the hatch. Fortunately the tank contained no one . . . it was one of our own! Ironically, had the tank actually been German, no doubt the well-meaning Jock might have collected a medal instead of a rocket. That the tank was empty was due to its having had one track partly blown off by the enemy a few minutes earlier. It was just hereabouts too we heard later that a shell from one of the German tanks which had been cruising round the streets had smashed the 5th Bn radio link to Brigade, putting them out of touch. Two companies of 5 KOSB had also been isolated from their own HQ by radio and runner for long periods during the action.

The Germans had proved to one Jock at least that they had some deadly shots in opposition. While reinforcements were approaching, one of the cut-off companies, the Jock in question, realising their danger had put his hand out of a window to signal the proximity of the enemy: he immediately withdrew it shattered by five bullets.

The enemy resistance in this action was, we were to find, repeated in similar aspects on many later occasions. Sometimes he fought more fiercely, at others less, and for various periods of time. Nearly always, though, he seemed to show a complete disregard for the suffering and destruction he caused to his own civilian countrymen and property if they happened to get in the way. One hour he would seem to be stubbornly dug in and determined to fight it out fiercely to the last man, then swiftly and quietly he would pull back to another defence position perhaps miles to the rear, leaving a trail of mined roads, blown bridges and sometimes booby traps. We were perhaps singularly fortunate as a battalion in freedom from becoming victims to these devices. Rumour had it, though, that the enemy occasionally secreted these with devilish cunning in a wide variety of positions which ranged from explosives with an anti-lifting device under his own or our dead or even wounded men, to booby trapped vehicles, door-handles, stoves, WC chains and so on. Battalion HQ were later fortunate to evacuate a building in Bremen which had been mined and which subsequently blew up. The continual possibilities of being 'had' in this connection in recently overrun territory kept one ever restive and suspicious.

It was sad to contemplate Waldfeucht even though it was our first experience of helping to smash an enemy town instead of an Allied one. A few hours before it must have been a pretty little place with medieval-walled, compact picturesqueness. Now there were few houses anywhere near intact. Those that were not smouldering heaps of hot rubble were gutted, smoking shells or shattered by the artillery and tank activity. We picked our way with tense alertness through this depressing, acrid shambles, tripping and clattering over the broken tiles and glass. We moved uneasily, weapons at the alert. Had Jerry really pulled out or was he re-organising somewhere for another breakthrough with his tanks?

How many cellars full of trapped men, women and children or animals caught in smashed stables were there, I wondered. No one seemed to be doing any rescue work or firefighting and it seemed unlikely we would find time to help. The snow was dirty with a red or grey film of brick dust and eddying ash from the fires. The air reeked with a smouldering sickly smell.

As we came within sight of the far arch of the town, we spotted some of the Jocks, Jeeps and carriers of the rest of our Battalion and some of the 5th chaps. The men called cheerful greetings and banter to each other as we passed, recognising, perhaps, with mutual surprise and certainly pleasure familiar faces grinning in confident, if weary, intactness.

Ahead, through the arch of the town gate, we caught a refreshing glimpse of clean, glistening virgin snow in the country beyond. Just outside the gate I halted my chaps to await orders while we rejoiced in the crisp, clear freshness of the morning air after hours of breathing the acrid stench of burning and explosives. The road, stretching towards the sunrise, glowed and sparkled under its mantle of snow like a pink ribbon, the reflected light adding a blush to our sallow faces. On either side were a few houses with beyond, some farms stretching into the bluish distance where the sun had not yet caught the snow. Well might we and the beauty of God's creation ahead blush at the madness of man's handiwork behind, I thought.

Colin, who had joined me, ordered the taking up of defence positions in some houses just outside the town gate on either side of the road. This was welcome news and promised possible rest, warmth and perhaps a good hot meal, provided the enemy behaved himself. After a quick recce, I chose two buildings on the right of the road for Platoon HQ and two sections, with the third section in a big, red-brick school building over the road. My Platoon HQ turned out to be an 'Apotheek', or chemists shop, as well as a home. It was not too badly smashed, though well looted by the retreating Germans. Down in the basement we found a deserted, improvised hospital of eight white-painted iron beds. These would serve us well for the night I hoped.

Over the road Cpl Allan had his section well established in the school and trenches were being sited and dug. The men and section commanders had picked up a very good idea of how and where to site positions by now and these seldom had to be altered when I came round to check them. So far we had no news as to the whereabouts of the enemy. The countryside was quite silent and seemingly deserted, but we were working to get securely dug in as swiftly as possible: the Jocks had already learned that silent peace could be transformed into hell in a split second.

In the playground of the school, either a bomb or a very large shell had fallen. On going inside we found the pathetic, huddled, frozen body of a young chestnut-haired German girl in a blast-ripped, grey-green woollen dress, lying on the floor of the classroom amid sprinkled glass from the windows. The blast of this missile had apparently killed her, as she was seemingly unmarked by wounds. She looked up at us through half-open, dark blue-grey eyes and with lips parted, showing her teeth as though gasping some reproach tinged with pain. The intense cold had given her flesh, face and hands the delicately unreal and semi-transparent look of a wax figure. We had by now just about got used to the sight of dead soldiers, beings who seemed designed for the part, but I don't think we ever did become used to the sight or sound of women, children, old people and animals who were killed or hurt in this senseless business in which they seemed to play little part but as sufferers. She had evidently been the schoolmistress. The Jocks who had been standing round her in a silent, almost reverent group, tenderly covered her with a curtain from the smashed windows of her classroom, with a last lingering look at her face. One of the feet still showing was shoeless. Cpl Parry picked up and shook the glass and dust from the separated shoe and moved as though to put it on her frozen foot, then dropped it again as he turned suddenly away and blurted out with a fierceness in his voice: 'Poor wee lassie, she's o'er young frae such a hellish end.' As she was a civilian, with no identity discs as a record for relatives, it was best for the local people to do the burying. In searching a farm alongside we found an old farmer and attempted, despite the language difficulty, to instruct him to do this task. We then spent two hours at section strength searching all the scattered farm buildings, barns and a few farms within about 600 yards of our positions to make sure there were no German stragglers about.

We found plenty of civilians: women, children and older men of peasant stock. They were sometimes frightened but always curious in an indirect, stolid way and not infrequently seemed to fear the worst of us. Some reappearing from forty-eight hours or so of sheltering in the cellars during the fighting gazed in mute horror up the road at the changed appearance of the town since last they saw it intact and alive such a short while before.

Everywhere we went I became aware of the eyes of these people following us, especially the sturdy, blue-eyed and often blond children, who peeped wide-eyed from their mother's skirts. This made me remember we were no longer among joyous liberated Allies, but over the border. Though their faces were stolid and so often expressionless, some did appear relieved the war had passed them by unharmed, though not without bitter cost as we realised frequently from a black-banded photograph in a place of honour depicting some uniformed German. These people had had a long schooling of Nazi propaganda and I sensed we might be being matched up to the possible brutal monsters they had been led to expect. The sad sight of Waldfeucht had evidently not reassured them. Had the Jerries not counter-attacked, the town would still have been almost untouched.

As we covered the last few farm buildings our hunger of several days' accumulation began to become insistent in the thoughts of a proper breakfast, and so we levied a toll of some eggs and some milk before returning to the Platoon positions. Although we were so close to the Dutch border, only half a mile away, the people seemed thoroughly German.

Nearing the section positions, we could see down the road into the town where a few civilians wandered aimlessly, stunned by the condition of the place on their plucking up courage to come out into the streets again from their shelter. Looking up out of the ground and from fences on either side I passed the heads and shoulders of muffled Jocks on stag behind their weapons, and was greeted by a sing-song Scots accented voice: 'Any news Mr White, Surr?' Then on seeing the eggs and milk: 'You'll be having a right guid tuck in the-noo-Surr, there's a muckle hen in th' pot an all.' In my absence some of the chaps from each section had got down to work on breakfast in a big way on stoves which had been worked up to red heat on finely chipped wood to keep down smoke to a minimum, then gently fed with small bits of coke and coal ovoids; but it was something else that took my attention.

One of the Jocks was playing the piano surprisingly well, looking very out of place in his grimy windproof, unshaven and muffled up at a grand piano amid plaster and broken glass from the windows scattered over the blue drawing-room carpet. He seemed quite lost in the music, tin hat on the back of his head, and rifle leaning against the keyboard. Out of the window into the surrounding snow the harmony of this melodious sound soothed us like sunshine after the discordant and shattering noises of the last few days. It was only the delightful smell floating up the stairs from the kitchen that finally broke the spell.

The rumbling of powerful engines outside informed us that a couple of the 'Recce Regiment' armoured cars had gone to see if they could locate the enemy towards Frilinghoven village, so we relaxed to the more complete enjoyment of the meal. I was rather shocked to think how out of normal perspective the importance of food, sleep and warmth were to us now. We were living like animals.

While I had been out with the one section searching houses, some of my Jocks had had a more fruitful search returning with about eight Jerry NCOs and men, and we did not find ourselves hard-hearted enough to 'tuck in' without giving them something as they huddled in a dejected group among the Jocks. One of them was wounded, and had been patched up by one of the chaps sufficiently until we got instructions regarding their disposal. After breakfast I tried out firing some of the weapons (a Schmeisser automatic and some rifles) which belonged to these Jerries, before smashing them to bits against the doorstep in the yard. I was surprised at the ease with which one could bend the barrels once the wooden stock had been broken. I found I had been rather thoughtless, unwittingly, when I got back inside. The Germans having heard the bursts of fire in the yard, and knowing their compatriots had pulled out, looked searchingly at the faces of the Jocks, distinctly uneasily. Somehow prisoners captured in an action to my mind always seemed to have no connection with those beings, 'the Jerries', actively engaged and opposing us with weapons; yet they were, we knew, the same people – perhaps the chap wounded in the leg was the one I sniped – perhaps the surly NCO from whom we had taken the Schmeisser was the same one who had aimed to finish me off, and had hit Cpl Finney instead? I wished I had asked them what they had been up to. We really felt no more ani-mosity towards them as ordered-around individuals than I expect we would have towards an opposing football team, though we felt wild with the tank chaps for having shot up the clearly marked Regt Aid Post.

While the Jocks had been giving the Jerries their meal, which they ate heartily, an attempt was made to bridge the barriers of language in pointing out to them with a Jock's directness of manner, that, had the boot been on the other foot, the Jocks had more than serious doubts that they would have been treated as well. I think, however, they were too worried about their immediate future to follow this deeply. What did obviously take their deep and even voluble attention was the opening of a Compo ration crate in front of them to split the rations for sections. I was never too clear on exactly how the German rationing and supply system worked. It was evident, however, that they had seen nothing like this before for exclamations greeted the sight of the chocolates, the sweets, the cigarettes, the white bread, and the tins of butter, and so on. I could understand their interest in the white bread; theirs had the appearance, texture and weight of a brick. It seems more than probable the Germans lived far more off the unfortunate people they happened to be among. We were self-sufficient; but the Jock was always keen to learn as I could tell from the delicious smell of more chicken cooking for lunch.

Upstairs I had a look over the chemists shop, which seemed well stocked, and sealed it up for the field ambulance chaps to come and look over. A lot of things would probably be needed for civilian casualties in the town. No public services were working, of course, and I saw no civilian officials trying to do any rescue work, fire-fighting, treatment of casualties, or police work to stop looting. A large part of the population had, I think, fled or been cleared out over the River Roer before we arrived.

This pause meant all the usual reorganising: collection of fresh ammunition up to scale, weapon cleaning and inspection, and replacement of such things as field dressings which might have been used on casualties. We each carried two of these; one in a little pocket in the top of the battledress trousers, and the other under the 'scrim' netting on the tin hat. It was staggering how careless a Jock could be in losing bits and pieces of kit, even as large as a 2-inch mortar or the bolt from his rifle, unless eternally checked and chased by section commanders, the Platoon Sergeant and myself.

I had not thought a shave with hot water and a good wash could be quite such a pleasant experience. Soon we all looked reasonably clean, if not smart – the clothes were beginning to show definite signs of their rough usage day and night in tears and dirt. We all felt excessively tired and to sit near a stove in the warmth with a good helping of chicken inside gave one the feeling of being smothered in chloroform. To concentrate was difficult, and to prop one's eyes open and keep them focused was more so. Uppermost in our minds was the prayer that we might spend a peaceful night here.

As it happened we were to spend that night there, and the best part of the next day in and around this side of the town keeping alert with plenty of 'stags', and acting as a firm base while part of 156 Brigade moved through. Blankets seemed to be unknown in this part of the world and at nightfall we each managed to get a period of sleep, or at least rest, in tight heaps on each groaning bed covered by huge, thick, red-coloured eiderdown quilts. How fortunate for the Hausfrau's peace of mind that she was not there to witness these grimy snoring heaps of equipment-cluttered Jocks. To go out round section positions from time to time from this comparative comfort seemed far more of a hardship than from a slit trench.

Operation 'Blackcock'

THE FINAL PHASE – 'EAGLE' – AND THE
ATTACK ON HEINSBERG

By the middle of our second day at the 'Apotheek', the Jocks were about ready for another move – all the chickens were eaten. It was perhaps as well they had been made use of because in their flight the civilians had left them without water or food, and they could not have found any in the snow and iron-hard ground.

Towards dusk on the second evening we threaded our way north round the rim of Waldfeucht through thickening snow, and out off the main road to a lonely farm called Erdbruggerhof. The rest of the Battalion were in Bruggelchen, a little village about 700 yards to the north-west. Our new Company position was in a spinney containing some straggling farm buildings and some very well-constructed light AA gun-pits and bunkers. The bunkers (dugouts) were wonderfully made, room-sized holes in the ground, lined with massive logs and a hessian cover. Each was very well furnished.

After we had been there a while the news filtered down to our level that we were to remain there, acting as firm base for an attack passing through us, to be put in by the 7th/9th Royal Scots and 6th HLI on the village of Obspringen to the north-east, a mile off over the snow. This attack in its turn was to secure a line of villages to act as a springboard for our attack on the final objective: Heinsberg.

Before settling into our positions we carefully searched all the farm buildings. The only Germans this brought to light were a very old farmer and his wife. We entered the Jerry bunkers very cautiously in case of booby traps in the dark. After descending a few steps into the first one, a smooth surface underfoot creaked ominously – this time nature had done the booby-trapping in the form of flooding and ice. The next one was dry, but also disclosed a sinister sound, the ticking of an alarm clock. However, this proved quite innocent of any attached explosive, and also suggested the Jerries had only pulled out about twenty-four hours earlier at the most as it appeared not to be an eight-day one. The furniture included a tubular stove (which we dared not light in case our tenancy of this site was given away by sparks), a stout table and tiered bunks.

The Jocks gradually blasted their way into the frozen ground with crashing spades and swear words, both of which had to be discouraged from time to time, not so much because of the 'language' as the fact that we did not know how close the enemy might be. The wastes of snow gleamed all around under the glow of Monty's Moonlight like sheets of newly cut lead.

Once the trenches were finished, those of us on stag stood peering out over the silent, unreal, arctic scene, getting steadily colder as the warmth from the digging was sucked and scraped from us by the razor-edged north-east wind. Quite early in the evening the silence was slashed by the crash and echo of a burst of firing from Cpl Beal's Sten gun. He swore he could see a white-smocked Jerry patrol moving and crouching in the wind-wisped, white wilderness ahead of his section. I wondered if he was just 'trigger happy' with tired eyes and nerves playing tricks on him. The only way to be sure was for a small patrol to go out, as a flare would draw attention. In the north-west corner of the spinney I had a section hidden in and around a haystack which the Germans had hollowed out as a strong point, and three of these chaps went out, but returned with nothing to report. Fortunately Beal had not fired the Bren which, with its greater range, would have shot up the rest of the Battalion in Bruggelchen and probably started a shooting match in error.

The Jocks were getting so icy in their exposed positions that after a few hours of bone cracking cold, I set them to work in turns, 'silently' digging extensions to the trenches which would prove useful if trouble came. While we were employed on this, word came to 'stand to' 100 per cent. Almost at the same moment, a flicking succession of red lights reflected off the snow, matched by loud, hollow, echoing 'cracks' overhead which drew our eyes to follow the ruby-red strings of Bofors 40mm tracer shells. These fired at intervals low overhead, about five jewels to each burst. This beautiful sight was used to keep the attacking infantry on course in the dark as they approached cross-country. Each glowing set of shells ascended gently in an arc, a reflected glow trailing as a pink ghost in the snow beneath. Then the necklace slowly descended to flick out in a sparkle of orange pinpoint explosions in the distant village and trees. Beneath in this weird setting of artificial moonlight and fireworks, we became aware with sympathy of the lonely, hunched-up groups of figures of the 6th HLI, and the 7th/9th Royal Scots dimly plodding their way towards the enemy and the unknown. Calls from our Jocks of 'Keep moving!' or 'Bash 'em Geordie' drew equally suitable or unsuitable response as each wave passed and vanished in snow. For a while the thunder of guns and waffle of shells in both directions joined the noise of the Bofors.

Once the attack had gone through we felt more secure in our isolated outpost. Very little sound of small-arms firing came back over the distance to tell us how things were progressing. There were a few distant explosions, and several flares of light, then we settled in to our vigil till dawn. Dawn almost invariably approached with a deeper hush in the stillness, and a brain-numbing intensity of cold; towards first light the silence was sometimes broken, but never the cold.

After 'stand down' early on the morning of 23 January 1945, all of us but a skeleton stag crowded into the dugouts to try to get warm, and get a bit of rest after our sleepless night. After poking carefully up the chimney of the stove to see if Jerry had left any explosive there to cook off in the heat, we lit the fire in Platoon HQ bunker and soon had it fed to a red heat without too much smoke from the chimney. On top a mess tin approached the boil for Compo tea, and the sizzle and scent of frying Spam and a few eggs from the farm filled the warming air. I had just got warm, curled up in a Jerry greatcoat in company with similarly thawing-out Jocks, and with the pleasant prospect of some food and sleep, when a runner called the awful words 'prepare to move' like a hand grenade slung among us from the door. Out into the cold again the cursing Jocks staggered, trailing equipment in one hand and gulping mess tins of rapidly cooling 'tea' in the other.

Pursuant on the policy of 'giving the enemy no respite', we were to pull out, and march back to Waldfeucht where we would concentrate in preparation for the attack on Heinsberg.

I walked back in the company column with Tommy Gray, still the only other platoon commander in B Coy since Colin had been wounded, and now due for LOB. I was surprised to see that Jerry must have been shelling one section of the road we had come up the night before, pretty heavily. Snow in the surrounding fields was spattered with earth and black blast marks. These must have fallen during the attack, but our attention was so concentrated forwards I don't think any of us were aware of 'noises off'. Just outside Waldfeucht we saw Ken Wilson with his platoon, and shouted greetings to him.

The column was moving slowly with the usual numerous unexplained stops and starts and lack of information on what was immediately happening – it was only gradually, usually through a process of deduction, that at the time we could piece together the bits of jigsaw on these moves which affected us so deeply. Here each move can be labelled in perspective; at the time it was all too often a move in the dark, interspersed with cold, lack of sleep, endless waiting, and odd biscuit meals.

We knew the reason for this and it seemed to have no easy cure. When an operation was thought up, months, weeks or hours of planning might go into the details of every aspect at the higher levels. As the time for the operation drew close this would have filtered with its local variations and application to Div. HQ. With time running out, it would be mulled over by the 'intellectuals' at Brigade before it was passed over to Battalion commanders and Company commanders, then with accelerated rush to Platoon commanders and NCOs, and finally the poor old Jock who had to actually do the job would get a rushed idea a couple of minutes or so after we had got it, and digested what he had gathered of it as he set off into action. There were, fortunately, notable exceptions to this course of events.

It was getting on into the late afternoon when we finally arrived at the 'Forming up point' in Waldfeucht. Here all the ammunition was checked, weapons and kit examined, and the automatic weapons tested out with a burst or two each into a shell crater in the ruins. The Jocks rested in doorways brewing 'char'. The roads were cluttered with all the Battalion vehicles; guns, carriers, Jeeps and so on. It always seemed amazing to me that such masses of weapons and equipment and men could set off into an attack, yet the farther one got towards the enemy, the thinner the evidence of accompaniment might become until finally in sight of the enemy there one was – rifle in hand, the enemy ahead, perhaps ten or less Jocks actually in sight at any one time, and almost as often as not one was the recipient of the artillery fire of both sides.

As time moved on we were pleased to see the numbers of tanks and self-propelled guns increase in the area. It seemed we would have good support. Also to cheer us up we were issued with a tin of self-heating soup each, the first and only one we ever had of these, and most effective too with a tube down the centre which burned like a firework as it heated the tin.

A call came for 'O' group, and I hurried to Company HQ established in a battered house. The plan for the attack was: first, to soften Heinsberg up with a concentrated barrage of heavy, medium and mountain artillery and the ever-present 25-pounders. While this was going on, B and C companies of the 4th KOSB, and the 7th/9th Royal Scots were to flank and surround the town on both sides, our Company, B, going to the left. Finally, at dawn, following a creeping barrage, the rest of the Battalion would clear the town from south to north. Our particular job would be to dig in and prevent the enemy filtering back into the town with reinforcements, and also to deal with any trying to break out of the town.

Heinsberg was a largish place lying on the edge of the valley of the rivers Wurm and Roer, and right under the heavy guns of the Siegfried Line, a fact which we grew to appreciate fully before the action was over. These, together with plentiful mortars, were to batter us as we had not been battered before in B Company for a solid thirty hours.

Eventually, freezing darkness descended, and with it came the order to move forward. It was the evening of the 23rd. The attack was not due to commence until 2 am the next morning,

24 January 1945, so we had the best part of the night ahead of us to march forward 10 miles over slippery ice and snow-caked roads.

It was as well we had had some chicken the day before yesterday, I thought, for breakfast due to the sudden move had been very sketchy. There had been no lunch, and tea and supper combined had consisted of quarter of a pint of soup and a block of bread. How fortunate we did not realise the next meal, and that only a scrap one, was not to come for more than thirty-five hours; nevertheless, our main worry was the steady cumulative effects of the lack of sleep. At least three chaps in the platoon, one an NCO, were very strung up and jumpy, and we were all steadily noticing the cold more.

As we filed out of Waldfeucht to the crunch of snow and clink of equipment, the searchlights of Monty's Moonlight glowed off the snowy scene, outlining our former billets, the 'Apotheek' and the school. I wondered if the farmer had got round to burying the schoolmistress yet; the ground ringing like iron underfoot was probably too hard for him to have worried.

So far the only sound, other than our scuffling along in the snow, was an occasional distant explosion somewhere towards the front; the guns had not yet started. For a while I talked with John Elliot as we walked in the company columns each side of the road, and discussed what we thought the ground would be like on the objective from the look of the map. I had attempted to memorise our part of the objective well enough to transfer it to paper as a test. I always tried to do this before an attack if we knew the objective, for there was usually little opportunity to refer to maps carefully once the attack was under way. On this occasion, too, we wanted to be quite sure because it had been arranged to bring down the creeping barrage to within 350 yards of our positions for the clearing companies. It would not do to go over the mark.

We were now making for Bocket, and Colin (Maj Colin Hogg) asked me to come up to the head of the column with him to help check the route off the map in the dark –; a difficult task over strange by-roads and tracks crossing snow-covered fields, and through dead villages. It was interesting to see Bocket, the village we should have attacked had the Germans not diverted us to Waldfeucht. It was difficult not to speculate on what different experiences would have been our lot here.

Through Bocket we cut across country over a small track at the head of which one of our Shermans had run onto a mine, blowing off a set of bogies and the right track. Trusting that the mines were all anti-tank ones and not sensitive enough to go off with a man's weight, we pushed on. Usually in these mines the firing mechanism could not come into operation until a pin of softish metal had been sheared through by the pressure of the victim, tank or man, according to which it had been designed for.

A mile more brought us onto a main tree-lined road throbbing with the traffic of vehicles, armour and other troops. The tanks were having a very tricky time on the frozen roads. Towards dawn we were to see many of them which were to have supported us later in the attack skid slowly and helplessly like heavy beetles into the ditch.

We were now thoroughly weary, cold and hungry, and, I must confess, somewhat depressed, each pre-occupied with the now all too familiar demands to be made on us in a few hours. I heard L/Cpl Wilson, who had already been wounded once, speaking with the authority of a connoisseur to a chap in his section on how he would like 'a nice Blighty wound in some soft spot to get out of it all' – a wish which was granted some weeks later.

In the long, straggling, snow-mantled village of Selsten CSM Frankie Pook came up to see how things were getting on at the head of the column. A very young and much-liked cheery chap with a strong Border accent, he talked and joked with the dark strings of Jocks by the wayside as he passed up and down the column. Some minutes earlier the skyline to our right and behind suddenly lit, shimmered and flashed with a continuous glare. A few instants later, coincident with the discharge of these numerous guns, the air overhead filled with a dismal orchestra of sounds from various calibres and speeds of shells. These ranged from the fierce bark and flitting red light of the Bofors directional tracer, to the scream, moan, sigh or crack of droves of others.

This weary icy walk seemed never ending, but the known trials always seem better than the unknown, and in the circumstances we were not exactly overkeen to reach the end of the road. In another deserted village, Laffeld, the column halted at about 1 am for a long unexplained halt. To keep warm, we broke into a small, damaged, suburban wayside house. It was, of course, empty and the same temperature as outside, though less draughty. Pte McKenzie lit a stove and made some Compo tea in the dark as he huddled, draped in curtains and civilian clothes. The rest of the platoon, likewise draped, were scattered about the house in groups similarly employed.

Outside, the drumming of the guns continued, merging with the throb of idling tank engines and the passing shells to rattle the frames of the windows. Every now and then these shook much more violently. Suddenly this increased enormously, and with it the shriek of approaching shells and the scattering of footfalls dashing for cover. They erupted astride the road. What little glass the house still boasted, crashed and tinkled. The Siegfried Line guns had got our range. We knew now that 'another stunt' had commenced for us.

Meanwhile, I had found and 'borrowed' a thermos flask to hold a reserve supply of tea, which I placed in my windproof top. Another disconcertingly accurate covey of Jerry shells screeched and blossomed about us outside, so we retired to the opposite side of the house and into the cellar for greater peace of mind while we waited. There was time enough to face them when we had to. Nearly all these German homes had big concrete floored cellars in which the household goods were stored. Every so often I went outside to see if there were any signs of a move. The shells had settled down to a routine now, arriving in batches at about five-minute intervals over the next three-quarters of an hour. It was a useful time to run over what information I had with the section commanders, and to let them look at the map, to pass this information on to the men more fully. When we reached the objective, if it proved to be a straightforward attack, each would know where to dig in in relation to the others, and what to expect – we hoped.

The booming revving of numerous tank engines outside gave us the cue to pile out into the cold, form up and once more trudge forward. The stimulus of danger had to some extent shaken the tiredness from us. I found myself trying to decide in my own mind just how much of our shivering in the biting early morning air was cold, and how much fear and excitement. I could not honestly answer, beyond deciding all three causes played their part. We had not gone far before L/Cpl Beal, now in charge of Cpl Finney's section, came up to me to report the absence of private Laurie, a regular. In view of the impending action we suspected a possible cause, but had not got to know him in well enough in a tight corner except to notice a tendency to 'bomb happiness'. His excuse on finally rejoining us after the battle was that he had gone to sleep in the cellar; yet strangely some of the Jocks were not too sure that they had not remembered him marching with them before he disappeared some time after we left the cellar. None could be definite enough for action to be taken.

A long trudge in the snow under the cold glow of artificial moonlight and the pink flicking light of the 40mm directional tracer low overhead brought us to the wrecked village of Aphoven. The racket of shells passing and explosions was terrific now. The front was anywhere from here onwards. As though to confirm this for all who passed, a furiously burning Churchill Crocodile flame-thrower and trailer lit the surrounding snow, houses and passing Jocks with a searing orange glare and smeared the sky with black, oily smoke. It had been hit alongside a house on the road. Neither the house nor the trailer was properly alight yet, so it must have just been hit. Small-arms ammunition cracked off inside as we passed the fierce radiation of its heat. If the crew had not got out within seconds, they must have been trapped.

Meanwhile, the barrage in both directions was steadily developing in noise and power, almost vibrating one's thoughts with the racket. A battery of unpleasantly heavy guns had started to drop shells ahead, to either side and among the column. Whether they were ours firing very short or the Siegfried guns we were not sure. From the direction of the approaching vicious screams they seemed to be our guns. Whichever side they belonged to, they were not getting the Jocks into any better frame of mind.

Repeatedly we dropped flat into the snow, a ditch or a doorway.

Of the six guns which fired in each salvo, the sixth shell was always the closest. Five shrieks overhead, then with less warning and far louder the sixth vomited a shower of earth about us, leaving a smoking black cavern in the snow. Shaking the snow off with equally explosive curses, the Jocks were on their feet going forward again. It was no place to stop and idle, which to that extent made the process of advancing easier.

By the wayside just mid-way through Aphoven we passed three more of our tanks, tracks churning helplessly as they skidded and bellied themselves in the ditch – three less to support us. The Jocks, to spur them to greater efforts, shouted such remarks as 'windy' or 'gie it a push' to the worried tank commanders poking out of the turrets.

Soon we were climbing out of Aphoven to the right up a track, and if anything the shells were falling more thickly on our route. One shell 'as near as dammit' eliminated a section who dropped at the fiendish screech and vanished in the eruption to reappear some seconds later coughing and staggering about like a group of doped flies. Ahead we were comforted by the lumbering shapes of a couple of Shermans, and a flail tank crashing its spinning chains in the snow to eliminate mines. The tanks did not show up too badly in the snow as they were whitewashed and adorned with white parachutes and German bedsheets.

As my platoon had the farthest to penetrate in the Company to keep contact with the Royal Scots, we were up ahead against the tanks, following in the tracks in case of mines on the borders of the path.

In the valley below we could now discern Heinsberg flecked with fires and belching explosions, silhouetting the spire of a large church or cathedral. The Bofors tracers still cracked past monotonously, curving slowly like a cascade of red pearls to twinkle their explosions over the distant countryside. A cutting coldness swept up from the ominous gloom of the valley but fortunately it had not brought with it the more cutting and lethal hail of small-arms fire I had rather expected as we crossed the skyline just after 2 am and started to wend our way down. We seemed so far not to have been spotted amid all the noise and flash of explosions. A new factor now, though, was the swish and crump of mortar bombs. This mortar fire did not necessarily mean we had been seen, but was probably defensive fire.

As we neared the main road leading into the town, Colin came up with me in front against the advancing tanks, to see 'the form', and dropped Tommy Gray's platoon (now under command of Sgt Dodd Oliver as Tommy was on his turn out of battle) at the crossroads. Next Don Urquart's platoon, also officerless and under Sgt Cowie, crept in against the town on the right while we with Company HQ followed on with the tanks.

Still we had encountered no other opposition than the DF task artillery and mortar fire. Ahead up a slope in the gloom as we crept round the western rim of the town, I could just make out a group of trees and a farm which I knew from the map I had memorised earlier was called Klosterhof. Next to it was another landmark, a little shrine. We had not far to go to get to the objective, and things were going very smoothly.

It was getting on for 2.30 am, and we were well up to time. It seemed we would be dug in on the objective as the second phase of the operation commenced with the creeping barrage alongside our positions. Ahead, the tanks ploughed cautiously through the snow, the 'flail' still leading and threshing the ground for mines as the turrets of the other two swung inquisitively like heads, training their guns on likely spots, ready to fire if trouble started and anxious meanwhile to retain the far more valuable weapon of silence and surprise. Though the tank engines made an enormous rumbling racket, it was well submerged in the fiendish noise of the artillery.

Just short of the farm, we were to branch off a track to the right and dig in on the edge of the town 300 yards away, while the tanks by-passed the farm and churned steadily on over the fields alongside the Royal Scots, just ahead of us, but somewhere out of sight. Colin was worried that it might not be the right track, but there was only the one on the map and this was right in relation to the shrine, so I took 10 platoon on ahead a bit.

Up with Cpl Allan in the leading section, we had got to within 100 yards of the drainage ditch on the edge of the town when I spotted some twenty or so figures moving towards us in the gloom. I waved the Jocks to drop in the snow beside the track. They evidently spotted us too, and stopped at about 70 yards, both parties faced with the same problems: friend or foe? We moved forward in groups a little closer, weapons trained on them as they did the same.

We were now about 20 yards apart in the leading section. If they were enemy, neither side would come off very well in the open once firing started, and this we were certainly not keen to get involved in as we were not yet on the objective in position for the rest of the Battalion's attack. I whispered to the section not to fire, and peered back to make out who they were. It was too dark for the binoculars to be of much use, but at least we had the advantage of the light over them with the searchlights behind us to the right.

Yes they were definitely Jerries. We could make out their tin hats and different rig-out. Neither side had yet challenged, and I realised as soon as this happened the battle would commence. I had just come to the conclusion, mind and heart racing swiftly as I sprawled in the snow with Cpl Allan, that while we still had the advantage of surprise we had better attack for all we were worth, though we would probably get hit hard in doing so for the Company was in line astern down the track behind. Just then Colin crawled up alongside. All this had taken only about a minute or two of thought-packed intensity so far. Colin decided, I supposed accurately appreciating the Germans predicament and fear of the likely response they would get to a challenge, that we should hold our fire a while longer to see if they would withdraw. This would suit us as in doing so they would coincide with our barrage which we knew within the next fifteen minutes should fall along the rim of the town. This would also enable us to get to our objectives and there dig in so that we might meet them on more favourable terms if they again tried to get clear of Heinsberg. Whatever Colin's reasoning had been in these few seconds, it proved a wise decision for almost immediately the Germans crawled in reverse back to the ditch and vanished towards some houses in the darkness.

Immediately, while they were still on the hop, we got up and moved forward out of the lane into the waste of snow to our left with the intention of digging in along the edge of some gardens bordering open country about 80 yards to the north.

We had covered half the distance out into the field and I was up in the lead with Cpl Beal's section, trying to see if I could locate the nearest section of the Royal Scots who should by now have been digging in 300 yards to our north. Suddenly a dark figure, a uniformed and helmeted German carrying a rifle, scrambled out of a ditch a few yards ahead of me and started to run frantically towards Klosterhof farm across our front. I called 'Halt!', which I had an idea meant the same thing in German and at the same time raised my rifle onto him. At this he swerved a bit more to the north and zig-zagged as he ran about 20 feet ahead of me. He was evidently one of the Germans who had withdrawn and who were now attempting to escape singly. I took aim in the middle of his back with a strong feeling of repugnance at having to fire at a man running away and in the back, when something seemed to tell him it was hopeless. To my intense relief he spun round, flinging his rifle into the snow and raising his hands in swift dramatic gesture. As he did so he called out a jumbled stream of broken English in a frightened voice. At first I was startled to hear what sounded like 'Don't shoot, Peter!' but which I eventually concluded must have been 'Don't shoot, please sir!'

As we closed in on him his fear seemed desperate and he almost screamed: 'Hitler no good . . . don't shoot . . . Kamerad, please!' At the same time he reached suddenly into his clothing, which nearly caused me to fire as I half expected a pistol or grenade to be pulled out. Instead, as though in the hope that if the denunciation of Hitler should prove of no avail he swung what turned out to be a gold pocket watch on a chain in my face as a peace offering. His isolation from his comrades seemed to have quite unnerved him. Had he been a fanatic and stopped to fire at us as we advanced over the snow from the cover of the ditch he could probably have accounted for quite a few of us.

We pushed on to the objective with the prisoner stumbling along too at the point of a Jock's rifle, still querulously pleading. I contacted the Royal Scots to establish where they were and let them know our positions, then we started to dig in the garden of a house on low ground overlooking the ditch towards Klosterhof farm. This was 250 yards to our west on higher ground and Company HQ was 95 yards south of us in some bushes over a fence. Our prisoner attempted to make a hole for himself as though anticipating trouble. We were now feeling very tired and cold and the Jocks had to be chased a bit to dig in to the iron-hard crust of the frozen, waterlogged bogland. Their shovels rang like steel to steel on the surface and when eventually after infinite labour we did get to softer peaty soil, we struck water only 14 inches down. Here we had been ordered to dig, so if trouble came we would have to make the most of it, lying full length in icy water, barely below the surface. Just then, when we were only partly dug in, a sudden fiendish volley of shells shrieked into eruption right among us. In the flashing light of explosion and confusion of the contrasting darkness, those of us who had a waterfilled hole to lie in did so wholeheartedly. As yet I had no hole, having used up time on contacting the Royal Scots and in fixing the positions, so I lay in a shallow scoop I had started against some earth Pte Neal had excavated beside me.

The whole position was blanketed with a haze of flashes, the most appalling noise, blast and smoke. It was our own 25-pounders putting down a concentrated barrage right onto us and about 350 yards short of the rim of the target on which they should have been falling. As fast as one salvo landed and the stunning concussion of the blast had rippled out, another batch of shells could be heard shrieking in on top. To know that these were our own shells put one's mind in a mental turmoil of desperate conflict, anger and amazement. Immediately between the crash and shriek of hurtling pandemonium came the new heart-rending sounds of groaning and piteous cries for stretcher bearers in agonised weakening voices. Glancing along the ground through the acrid smoke and pattering debris I wondered why Pte Neal was apparently not trying to take proper cover in his hole. Then I realised he was dead. He had been hit in the head by shrapnel from a shell which had cratered a shallow scoop in the frozen earth between us, carrying away part of the parapet he had been building round his hole. Beyond him another shell had crumpled and killed Pte Allaway in his first action after recently joining us as a replacement. Another couple of groaning men jerking and rolling in uncontrolled movement and injury I recognised to be Pte Mackay and Pte Barclay, who seemed desperately hit. The stretcher bearers had joined us, scrambling about frantically on hands and knees and throwing themselves flat as each salvo shrieked in. They were doing a wonderful job under terrifying conditions. Pte Barclay was rolled onto a stretcher and dragged back over the snow but unhappily did not survive the journey to the RAP.

Company HQ were also being shelled and one of their chaps was hit and died later. How long this hell lasted I could only guess but it seemed a good half hour before there was a pause. All this time I was staggered that Colin had apparently not been able to get contact with the artillery link on his radio to get the gunners to lift their range into the rim of the town. I have never yet found out exactly what happened as before I was to have a chance to see Colin again, Company HQ were themselves nearly wiped out. Surely, I wondered, these couldn't be enemy shells. The rapidity of their fire, the calibre and the direction from which they were arriving from the west all seemed to indicate our 25-pounders. Meanwhile, I became conscious of the deeper thudding of medium shells pounding the town to our rear. At the least pause we were digging in like madmen, but again a sudden approaching multiple shriek, this time it seemed from a slightly more northerly direction, heralded the arrival of more shells slap on us, along the line of the ditch bordering the edge of the town and up towards the Royal Scots.

We grovelled frantically, shivering with cold and fear while trying to mould our bodies deeper into the 4 inches of freezing water and mud and snow as hell blossomed about us again. Very few of us were properly below the surface of the waterlogged frozen bogland as to go deeper merely meant lying submerged in bone-numbing soup of ice, snow and water. A stunning blast of explosion on the opposite side of me from Neal's body revealed the unhurt but badly shaken and stunned forms of Ptes Learmonth and Wardale. They gazed towards me with a dazed, wide-eyed look of fright as their much-spattered beings appeared through the thinning smoke and pattering debris of a shell that had missed them by the length of a billiard cue. Wet and frozen though we were it was difficult to be sure that all the shivering was due to the cold alone. It was now getting light, a most depressing dawn. I was very grateful to have Sgt Dickinson back with me from his turn 'left out of battle' or LOB. He lay alongside in another scoop and we were both preoccupied all this while in carefully eyeing the line of the town and towards the village of Lieck on the other side. The enemy might appear from either direction. We dared not let up on this task in spite of the barrage for we both realised that should these shells prove not to be our own, the chances were that the barrage might herald an enemy counter-attack. I became aware with increasing amazement that it was possible to survive the blast of so many near hits and that if unhit by shrapnel one could get away with lying almost on the lip of a crater in bogland if the shell penetrated the frozen earth crust.

In spite of the worst the shells had been able to do, when there was a short interlude of peace it was revealed that one or two of my Jocks obviously had not had their appetites spoiled and were still contemplating breakfast. There was a shrapnel-ripped, blast-distorted hen house towards Company HQ about 20 yards away and one of my Jocks vanished into this. I expect he had visions not only of Spam and eggs, but perhaps boiled chicken later in the day when things eased off a bit. He was in for more than one surprise in this respect; and so were we.

Suddenly there were exclamations inside the hut and a rasping shout: 'Get out you ruddy b***! Schnell!' The door crashed open and a bedraggled, sallow-faced German stumbled out with his hands aloft, pricked onwards by a bayonet pressed into the seat of his pants, prodded by an eggless and chickenless Jock. This German, one of several found in our area as it grew lighter, was possibly one of those whom we had met on our entry and who had withdrawn to lie secreted all through the hell in our midst. I wondered what this Jerry thought of our gunners. He had been fortunate to have survived several pieces of shrapnel through the battered hut. The second surprise was not amusing and was slower to unfold. I had warned all my Jocks to be dug in by first light and to show no movement until we could see 'the form' – the whereabouts of the enemy. Unfortunately, a stupid few in both my Platoon and Company HQ did show themselves with unnecessary movement to our and their heavy cost.

Dawn found us lying miserably at full length, part submerged in shallow icy water. It was quieter, but the odd shell still screamed to crash close enough to keep our heads down. It was apparent that as light came we could expect to find enemy positions and stragglers on either side of us who might only reveal their presence to our sudden disadvantage. I was worried that our rifle bolts kept freezing solid, jammed if any water got on them and were very difficult indeed to free. If an attack came with them frozen we would have one shot each and a jammed and useless weapon. I hoped the automatic weapons were in better shape. Certainly we did not feel in great shape ourselves. Already we had been lying with chattering teeth for more than three hours under arctic midwinter conditions and with enforced immobility. We did not even have greatcoats to help stave off the biting cold that numbed our bodies to a degree which far surpassed any of our earlier experiences of cold. Our fear and tension did not help, nor did lack of sleep over the last two nights and lack of food. I could not visualise our being able to stick this for much longer. How blissfully ignorant we were then of what we would be forced to go through. We were to be pinned into freezing immobility for a further ten hours and with all this world could offer of hell and misery let loose about us almost continuously as cheerless daylight slowly replaced the glow from the burning town and the cold beams of Monty's Moonlight. We were able to make out the German-held villages of Lieck and Endebruch over a three-quarter-mile sweep of snow to our north-west.

About 800 yards away in this direction, in front of the Royal Scots positions, stood an isolated, stationary, white-draped Sherman tank, one of those which had originally advanced with us in the early hours. It had struck a mine, we realised as it grew lighter, and we could see the crew crouched against it trying to repair the blown-off track. The Battalion, if on time, I thought should just about be clearing the town now to our rear. I was therefore anxious to keep a sharp eye on any sign of the enemy trying either to break through our positions to escape towards Lieck, or to break in and reinforce the enemy in the town.

A lone heavy explosion, then another out towards the tank made me swing my binoculars back onto it. A black, tumbling pall of smoke was drifting over it while another and then another billowed, enveloping the tank from which three or so figures stumbled clear. They were clearly being sniped by an 88mm gun, probably a Tiger tank, in Lieck. One of the tank crew, evidently not knowing exactly where the enemy were, began to make his way in our direction. Then, hesitating, he swung up towards Klosterhof farm on higher ground overlooking us and past which we and he had moved earlier. When he was about 100 yards from the farm a couple of shots rang out, ploughing the earth and snow behind him. He turned and desperately ran back a few steps when there was another crackle of fire and he crumpled and rolled, skidding downhill in the snow, evidently badly hit. We watched sickened, puzzled and with racing hearts as he tried frantically to get up. Instantly a swift burst of what we recognised to be Spandau machine gun fire spun his overall-clad body, partly obscuring him in a spatter of snow spurts, and he lay still. Several Jocks, not thinking and understandably, had on the first shots got up and yelled, waving for him to come over. In so doing they fatally gave away our whereabouts to the enemy who had evidently not till then seen us. I was staggered to realise at that moment that the fire had obviously come from Klosterhof farm where either the enemy had been all the time or he had filtered back from Lieck village after the tanks had passed it. From then, about 6.45 am, right on until dusk, absolute hell with fiendish intensity lay in store for us. Klosterhof looked down right into our positions from its hill 250 yards away and we had seldom, if ever, been less able to dig in. Even so, it was only in stages that we began fully to appreciate what we were up against, and that not entirely until the place was eventually taken after two attacks 24 hours later. It was then found that a strong group of determined enemy were installed there with five Spandau machine guns, three 5cm mortars, a dozen or so rifles, loads of ammunition . . . and, perhaps worst of all, had been using the farm as an artillery observation post from which land lines ran back direct to the guns, including the heaviest, of the Siegfried Line.

Our two prisoners cowered in abject misery and mortification at their situation. For the rest of the day, with sniping, mortaring, machine gun and directed artillery fire for the most part under perfect visual observation, the enemy pinned our dark bodies down in the snow, where we all too clearly showed up, and set out to eliminate my Platoon and Company HQ at his leisure. When shots fell short or passed over, a word back to the guns corrected them. He had an oblique plan view of his mortar bursts among us. These commenced within a minute of the killing of the tank chap. We could painfully clearly hear the plop of their discharge and the black spatter of little craters rapidly diminished the virgin snow about us. Swiftly we realised that the least sign of movement, which signified a body was alive and not dead, drew a tornado of small-arms fire that crashed through our positions like the slash of fast-moving rake prongs scattering the earth and snow. Next our demoralised senses took in the swift, short scream of shells which our experienced ears told were coming right among us. These were mostly coming in from the north and north-west as opposed to the 25-pounders from the completely opposite direction. This seemed the end. The murderous intensity, accuracy and dominance of our position from above seemed to offer no shred of hope at survival. We crouched deep in the ice and water, soaked, freezing and numb, to try to hide our bodies from the hail of metal while peering anxiously between the snow and the tin hat rim to try to locate exactly where the Germans were firing from in the hope that we could snipe back and cut the accuracy of the artillery correction.

Cpl Beal had his section with McLaughlin in and near a bomb crater 25 yards ahead of me and the enemy seemed to be concentrating his main fury there first with the mortars, while keeping the rest of us down with his other weapons. The mortar with its vertical descent was the ideal weapon to get right into the crater. Once more I was amazed that one could survive so much blast from near-hits which seemed to rake one's lungs with pressure and set one's ears painfully ringing with the very core of noise. I was conscious of a detached, mad interest in noting that right in an explosion there is pressure rather than noise, pressure too heavy for the ear to interpret as noise. A shell about the equivalent of our 25-pounder landed in the 9 foot gap between Sgt

Dickinson's and my scoops, whacking my tin hat onto the bridge of my nose with numbing pain, as though a sandbag had dropped from a height onto my head, and the blast swept away part of a little mud wall I had scooped into the frozen, concrete-like barrier so that the main impact fortunately carried over my head.

Already I was staggered to grasp the fact that my little scoop in the earth was bracketed on three sides by the lips of craters and the parapet had been nicked by mortar fragments, shortly to be added to by bullets. One of these shells had been the one which killed Neal. It seemed weeks ago.

It was abundantly clear Jerry knew of our Platoon HQ positions already by the attention we had been getting, and so I told McKenzie, who lay alongside Brown in a scoop about 10 feet to the north of me, to try with the PIAT at some enemy who were putting on a daring stunt to tempt more of the Company to disclose their positions by drawing fire. We could clearly see several Jerries crossing and re-crossing an open barn door in the farm.

To reach the farm I told McKenzie to lob high angle at it, for the shot would be close on the limit of a PIAT's range. I had no great hopes of him doing any real damage other than possibly to their morale with the noise and the realisation that we had a heavy punch to hit back with, though it would only leave us five more bombs. All this time a Bren gunner and several chaps had been firing bursts back, but they had to be hurried, for the slightest raising of oneself above the level of the snow drew a tornado of fire within split seconds.

As McKenzie pushed out the PIAT to fire, he coincided with a 5cm mortar bomb which fell between us but much closer to Mac than myself, spattering his face with muck and flinging him backwards. For a moment he lay stunned. It had actually lifted the PIAT bomb up off the cradle of the projector but this had fallen in again, he said afterwards. I was greatly relieved to see that, though badly shaken, he was OK, and immediately fired a fine shot in anger which he could hardly have bettered with a rifle. It landed slap into the roof of the bar above the door, blasting chips of tiles down into the bar as shrapnel. 'Take that you ***s', he growled in vicious wrath.

I don't know whether it hit any Jerries fatally or not, but no more crossed the space of the door. Meanwhile, Sgt Dickinson and I were returning the sniping into each of the windows of the farm and into any other likely spot. Though we did not know exactly where the OP was, we hoped to minimise his accuracy with the artillery shoot and possibly the mortars too. Already the whole area of snow round us had been pock-marked and ploughed with explosions, blackened with blast and scattered earth, and that not yet touched was greyed with smoke blast. I felt it quite likely my hair was by now grey too. Each time either of us fired we had to show our head and shoulders for a short while, and this invariably drew a hail of fire. A rotting stump of a pollarded willow tree lying just ahead of Sgt Dickinson and myself seemed to act like a magnet to the bullets and was a Godsend to us as it was repeatedly chipped, nicked or drilled, covering my rifle with muck. The fearsome whine and twang of bullets ricocheting off it reminded me absurdly of a wild west film. I never imagined featuring in one of those. One great joy in firing a lot was a hot rifle to warm one's hands on!

The great difficulty in this shooting was to get enough of the Jocks to brave raising themselves at once to fire hard for a short while together, as by doing this one could regain the initiative to some extent, forcing the Jerries to take cover themselves, which, of course, they easily could in the safety of the building.

Quite early on, an astonishing thing happened in view of the very thin time the Company was having. One of the Jocks drew my attention to a Jerry, unarmed and with hands up running down towards our positions on the left where we had met the Germans in the lane. Whatever his reasons for doing this, he did not get far; before covering 50 yards he was shot dead by his former comrades in Klosterhof. Without a cry he pitched headlong into the snow, rolled, then lay still. I wondered about this a lot. Could he have been one of our chaps captured earlier who had managed somehow to get into a Jerry uniform to make escape easier? Perhaps he was a Frenchman or some other nationality press-ganged into the German army.

Again I made radio contact with Colin at Company HQ to ask him if he could get the artillery to blanket the observation post with smoke shells. It was difficult getting through on our 38 set; both the radio and its operator had suffered too much from blast and iced water. The thin metal mast of the aerial had also attracted more than the operator's fair share of misery as it poked up next to his chilled face. For a long time no response came to our appeal. The guns seemed to be occupied on more important targets. Some of my equipment had, I noticed, suffered by now on the edge of the parapet. An extra bandolier of .303 ammunition, which I had put up there to keep clear of the ice, had been cut about without exploding any of the rounds.

During quick looks while firing I could see the forward section was getting it badly. Gradually less and less life was evidenced there. I was sorry to see Cpl Beal lay dead on the rim of the crater, shot through the head. The only other Jock I could still occasionally see of the seven who should have been there was the ginger-haired very worried face of Pte McLaughlin. He kept glancing back appealingly towards us, making signs we could not interpret. Finally, I heard him shouting back above the noise: 'They're a' deed Surr, every yin, the section's feenished.' He then shouted back for permission and covering fire to attempt to join us. The crater was a death trap. Although large and deep unlike our miserable scoops, it was no protection from the vertical descent of the 5cm German mortar bombs. Despite attempts to dig foxholes within it, at least three bombs had fallen inside the crater and others had peppered the rim. I shouted to the Bren gunners, and as many of us as could, joined in with our rifles as soon as we saw McLaughlin stumble out of the hole and crouch, running a zig-zag course towards us as fast as he could painfully force his near-frozen limbs. His frantic appealing face was a picture of fear-driven painful effort. We managed to silence the Jerries momentarily, enough for him to get about half way with only four or five shots crackling and spurting the snow. Suddenly the vicious rip of a Spandau machine-gun raked and lifted the snow about him with a scythe-sweep of whining metal as Mac frantically threw himself headlong to crash into the ice and water of the drainage ditch a few feet ahead. When he had recovered himself and we had raised our heads again at the cessation of this lethal spray, Mac gasped back confirmation that the six others in the section had been killed. 'Jerry gaie near completed the *** job, did ye jus' see yon *** Spandau! Mon Ah feel deed as it is', he panted grimly.

Shortly after McLaughlin had joined us we became aware of a different type of shell approaching. A frightening, banshee-warbling shriek, thin oscillations of blood-chilling sound revealed themselves to be the spinning canisters of 25-pounder smoke shells which plumed prettily down, trailing billowing streams of acrid whitish smoke among us rather than the enemy. The fast moving canisters made a most morale-lowering sound and were quite a menace.

Cold, cramp, extreme exhaustion and a nagging suggestion of pessimistic fear, to a large extent induced by the appalling conditions and our complete inability to do anything to mitigate the situation until either an effective smokescreen or dusk still many hours away arrived, were becoming as much a menace to us as the wholesale efforts of the enemy. Already at least a third of the Platoon were written off and it was difficult to be sure there were not others hit. I contemplated the thought of an order coming for us to attack Klosterhof and realised that the Spandaus alone each firing at ten rounds per second would account for us within a couple of minutes at the most. To pull back, even if such an order should come, would have the same prospect. There was at least something to do which might ease one physical nag: hunger was gnawing heavily and those of us who had any biscuits or other rations left tried to make the most of what diversion these provided.

It seemed wise to shout across to the Bren gunners and riflemen to get an idea of the ammunition situation. I was shocked to discover that it was almost half gone just in hitting back as best we could to the murderous German fire. We had no news at all of the progress of the attack in the town, so could still expect an attack from that side too. In consequence, I decided we had better cut down on the fire we were returning. The direction the smoke shells had been coming from rather worried me. I could not be sure they were ours and fervently hoped that Jerry was not working up for a counter-attack, for we were not in very good shape to deal with one of any strength. We had no depth at all in defence, being only a thin wedge into enemy territory.

My limbs had become almost rigid in the mixture of water and floating ice chips. My feet and lower legs had no feeling at all. I glanced at them to still a gnawing mental suggestion that perhaps they had been blown off. The fingers of my hands alternated between numbness and the equivalent of violent toothache in each freezing finger joint. The gloves were wet and torn in working the rifle bolt and in keeping it and the ammunition clean. Suddenly an inspiration struck me: the tea in the thermos which I had tucked into my windproof what seemed a lifetime ago. I don't think I had ever felt such bitter disappointment as I did on hearing the swish and tinkle of broken glass and tea inside which was almost as cold as myself. I was foolish to have expected anything else. The blast and jolt of at least half a dozen of the nearer shells was more than enough to have done this. At each concussion as I lay, thermos down, the earth had kicked violently enough to put a pile driver to shame. In spite of this I drank the brew; rusty muck though it was, it at least tasted sweet. I had to use my teeth to sieve out the broken glass. I was later surprised to realise that under the circumstances the possibility of swallowing some had seemed of so little consequence. I could not recollect thinking of it.

In the thin film of smoke which partially screened us from Klosterhof we managed to get several more casualties evacuated to the house behind Coy HQ, which was being used as a Company aid post. In spite of the red-cross flags, armbands and painted tin hats the stretcher bearers wore, the Germans continued to fire at them whenever they were seen and in addition brought down another dose of heavy mortaring and shelling. Among this last batch of shells some far heavier long-range ones could be heard coming in like an approaching express train from a great altitude for an uncomfortably long time before they arrived: an awful, vibrant, crumping crash some way to our rear. Perhaps the Germans thought we were attacking through the smoke.

Cries of agony, groans and yells for stretcher bearers came from Company HQ, telling that they were being hit badly. I recognised one voice to be Capt John Elliot's but could not make out if he was in pain. 'Call on the 38 set for you to go to Company

HQ as quick as you can Surr', the radio operator croaked to me. My first instinct was that this was for an 'O' group, but I immediately realised something must have gone seriously wrong. Colin would never have ordered anyone to attempt crossing 95 yards of open snow and over a fence with no cover, except in extreme emergency. I knew, having watched McLaughlin run 25 yards that it was almost certain suicide with all those Spandaus so close, let alone the rifle fire. The film of smoke had unfortunately quite cleared. If I was to get even part way I knew it would be a miracle. That I would have to go was certain. I had been ordered. There was only one possible way. I prayed. I would put my trust in the one place the Spandaus could not reach, and make a start. What happened after that would have to be in the hands of God; no others or efforts of mine could help. I remember trying not to think that this was 'the end of the road'. It was with a queer unreal feeling that I prepared to go. Automatically I watched my hands take off all the surplus equipment, a difficult job lying flat in the scoop of a trench. I battled mentally to resist accepting that this was the last useful job they would do. My thinking seemed detached from my body as though I was watching the performance from outside. It was too difficult to get my tightly braced, frozen small pack off without sitting up, so I left it on. I decided to take my rifle too as I felt quite naked without it. I raised myself slightly to get a quick look at the best route to take to get through the wire and to locate just whereabouts in the bushes Company HQ had dug in, for we had dug in in the dark. I only had the haziest idea where to make for to get to the quickest cover at the other end. Having hardly focused my eyes to work a route out I had to drop flat again as a murderously accurate and violently loud crash of bullets ploughed into the snow and the log ahead. Sgt Dickinson gave me a look of sympathy along the ground as our eyes met. I said, 'You'd better take over till I get back', and in doing so surprised myself that I had included the return trip. He grinned, slightly with an effort, and said: 'Good luck Sir'. I think the obvious thought had crossed both our minds – that I had handed the Platoon over to him for the last time. I took my eyes off his cheery, plump, blue-chinned face, again much in need of a shave, and lay quietly for a few seconds gathering my thoughts.

Above I could hear the awful calico-ripping speed of fire of a Spandau giving a long burst somewhere overhead. I remember thinking, 'If I get up when that burst stops, he might have reached the end of a magazine and that will be one gun less.' With that thought, I was up and running, half crouched, as far as my numbed feet and legs could carry me, zig-zagging as I went to try to present a more difficult target. I had at first to make a slight detour to the rear to clear some slit trenches.

Almost immediately I was conscious, with the thought 'This is it' and a kind of prayer: the air all about me was quite alive with a terrifyingly loud, harsh, ripping, crackling noise and about my feet and on either side the snow and earth gave the appearance of peeling open, flicking like a series of giant zip-fasteners. A slender fruit tree beside me split, fluffed and toppled.

Whether my frozen limbs had let me down in trying to run too fast, or whether I had meant to, I do not know, but I found myself dropping into a slight depression in the snow which had unexpectedly presented itself. The cold of the snow on my face and hands and pounding heart and lungs told me with violence that I was still alive, intact. As I lay, panting wildly for breath, a few more bursts spun twirling clods of muck about me, raising a powdered haze of snow off the surface which blew and settled coldly on me like a chill morning mist. My small pack, I realised, must still be showing. The fire slacked off and just a few shots cracked overhead or clumped heavily short in the earth to my right. I decided to 'play possum' for a short while before doing anything else. I felt done in. The whole business had an odd quality of almost farcical unreality despite its grimness. Sgt Dickinson, I found later, really thought I had been hit. The Germans must have reached the same conclusion, which I could fully understand, for I lay in quietness now.

Another smoke shell splayed a merciful thin film of smoke between me and the OP, so I got up, crouching to complete the distance, finding it hard to have any faith at all that I should arrive, and so done physically and mentally as to feel far less interest in the whole thing than I kept reminding myself the occasion demanded. I got several yards in peace, then it started up again, crackling loudly, spinning black clods of earth in the snow. They seemed to be firing more wildly in the smoke tracery as I crashed painfully like a chased rabbit into the unexpected fence and fell heavily into the orchard at the back of the house. The firing was now spattering and twanging rows of gashes and brick dust off the wall. It seemed they had thought I was making for the house, for as I spotted the shambles of Coy HQ, thoroughly exhausted in every fibre of my being, the fire fell behind, then stopped.

The low bushes that surrounded the slit trenches of Company HQ had caused the mortars to burst in the air and spread down a lethal hail of metal. The scene which confronted me fully explained both why I had been summoned so urgently and why the message which had come from the Company HQ radio operator had been so nakedly direct and unorthodox in phrase.

L/Cpl Leitch the signaller was crumpled, grey in the face and sprinkled with debris over his 18 set radio, weakly, almost in a coma, calling the artillery for smoke shells. The lower half of his body was a mass of blood and torn clothing with one leg very nearly severed at the hip by a large piece of shrapnel. CSM Pook was hunched, groaning on his side, his face the same smoke-blasted pale shade as the snow and too weak to sit up. He had evidently been hit severely in the thigh or buttocks. Maj Colin Hogg had been hit equally badly, apparently in the chest and lungs, and like the other two was so weak with his wounds and concussive shock that he was on the verge of delirium. He seemed to be only keeping conscious by a painful effort but gave a slight sign of recognition as I crashed, gasping for breath, into the shallow, crumbling scoop in the earth in which they lay. I was very distressed to see Capt John Elliot lying flat, face in the earth of the trench, sprinkled with broken twigs and snow. Very faintly Colin croaked with agony: '. . . John . . . dead . . . poor . . .' but he could not manage any more and choked, coughing weakly as his voice tailed off. 'Pete . . . y'll . . . have . . . take over . . .' Colin managed to gasp and then crumpled up again after the effort 'Sorry . . . leave . . . you . . .', he croaked in a whisper I would have missed if our heads had not been so close as we lay side by side. My legs and feet, which had seemed to be devoid of sensation while I was running and almost uncontrollable, were beginning to feel awful as the circulation got going again. Colin crouched for a bit with his eyes screwed shut while I tried to find a stretcher bearer or any Jock to help evacuate Leitch, Pook and Colin. I was shocked to realise as I looked about among the craters that those of Company HQ left who had not been killed, wounded or previously evacuated were largely so stunned with the blast and shock or outright 'bomb happy' as to be useless. No matter how these individuals strove to pull themselves together, the repeated shock and blast on top of their lack of sleep and general exhaustion seemed to have destroyed all coordination between mind and body. One or two lay head down, quivering with cold and shock in their pathetic scoops, apparently quite deaf to my voice. It was difficult to tell, but for the shivering, which were still alive, which wounded and which hit mentally. How much of B Company was left to take over, I wondered, if 11 and 12 Platoons had had as rough a time as we and Company HQ had done? To try to find out would cost more men. There was only McLaughlin left of one section in my Platoon, at least three were dead in the section nearest me, but I could not make out what state the other section was in.

Pook had recovered a little now and I was able to convey the lack of available men to help in his and Colin's evacuation to him. He nodded slowly, wiping beads of cold sweat off his brow as he made an effort to get up with the aid of a tree stump. Somehow Pook and Colin, with my help for the first few yards, crawled and stumbled, trying to prop each other up, towards the rear, both near unconsciousness. If an enemy machine gunner saw us through the remnants of the bushes we were finished. I returned to Leitch to see if any more could be done for him while stretcher bearers were sought to evacuate him. I tightened the webbing tourniquet on his leg stump. It was so nearly severed as to be only held by skin and torn clothing yet he repeatedly gasped that he refused to be evacuated while he could still work the set. I think he realised as well as I did that for the moment there was no prospect of getting him out yet anyway and he was trying to make light of it. I found he was still through to the gunners, so I lay beside him, trying hard to recall all I could of my training with the artillery to give him corrections to the shells falling round Klosterhof, which he passed on to the guns. Unorthodox though these were I was delighted to see the shells bracket the enemy held farm. I hoped Colin and Pook got back to report on things to Bn HQ and was pleased to find one Jock fit to go back as a runner to catch them up, to help them and to ensure delivery of the news of our situation for I dared not radio back 'in the clear' to Battalion HQ. In the interval since I had been called for, the 38 set radio Leitch had used had been smashed by another bomb so we were out of direct touch with all Platoons. It was another three-quarters of an hour before I found another chap to help me lift Leitch clear of his set. He was nearly rigid with the cold and blue lipped. But for the fact that he was now too weak to argue against leaving his set and beginning to lose coherence, the two Jocks who had sufficiently pulled themselves together to carry him back to the house on a door would not have succeeded.

I could not lend a hand due to the need to stick to the command post and man the radio, while it lasted out, as our sole remaining means of communication. There were no NCOs left at Company HQ and, I realised suddenly, no other officers in the Company. Subsequently, on my recommendation Leitch got a well-earned award of the DCM, and Sgt Dickinson another notch nearer his MM. He earned this not for any one action, but for his solid, unshakable behaviour in a long succession of them. He had landed with, I think, the Green Howards on D-Day, to be eventually transferred to us as a replacement. He survived with sanity, efficiency and intactness almost every action until the war ended. All this while the mortaring and shelling continued unabated, though fortunately a little more of it was directed farther back. Evidently the enemy assumed we were more or less written off. He was, to appearances, almost correct.

So far the guns had been sending over smoke shells at Klosterhof and the HE shells I had asked for had not yet materialised. I gradually realised that the 18 set was giving way too under the accumulation of blast and perhaps low batteries. I hoped 11 and 12 Platoons had been able by now to contact other Companies or Battalion HQ direct for there were no runners to send and unless I managed to get back to use the 10 Platoon 38 set radio there was no way of getting in touch. Even had there been a runner he would not have got far unless the smokescreen got stoked up a bit. I resolved as soon as the smoke thickened a bit to attempt to get back to 10 Platoon to put Sgt Dickinson in the picture, to see if the radio was still working there, and also, with the realisation that I was now Company Commander, to get my Platoon back as soon as possible to fortify the house.

It was about three in the afternoon now and looking at my men who had been lying still in the wet icy misery after twelve hours of this process of elimination, I realised they would not stand much more exposure. Indeed, I was astonished that it was possible for men to survive such physical misery for so long, quite apart from the ample contributions of the enemy. If a counter-attack came at dusk they would be in a far stronger position in the house. I was worried, though, that unless I waited for cover of darkness to move them we might suffer further heavy loss.

As I lay there, alone now in the Command Post with the body of John Elliot and all around saw the evidence of the awful rain of explosives that had churned the twigs and earth to grey dust, I realised how very fortunate we had been in the Platoon to be clear of the bushes and in the open. Though we had all the while been fully visible to the enemy up the hill and, to judge by the mass of craters, had received close on three times the bombs and shells and machine gun fire, I think we had been able to survive largely because there had been no overhead branches to trigger down a hail of steel. Instead, each burst once it had penetrated the frozen ground crust had to some extent been absorbed by the boggy earth and crater rim.

I had looked at John when first I had arrived, but before I left again for 10 Platoon I crawled over once again to make quite sure that there was nothing that could be done. He was as before and quite cold, frozen. The only slightest sign of injury I could detect was a small new hole the size of a wheat grain in the middle of his leather jerkin in his back. John was a fine courteous chap who was very conscientious in everything he did. The Company would not seem the same without him. My thoughts kept going back to his wife and little girls at home and I felt quite numb and nauseated with the stupidity and waste of war. In normal life John was probably one of the least likely of any of us to have harmed a fellow being.

Another batch of smoke shells interrupted my thoughts, plummeting a spidery smoke filigree between our positions and those of the enemy. Seizing my opportunity, and this time with far greater confidence and less thought, I got up and ran fast in the direction of 10 Platoon. I hoped to complete the return trip after putting Dickinson in the picture and securing the radio under cover of the same flimsy smokescreen. I had almost reached my Platoon positions before some Jerry riflemen saw me and opened fire through the thinning smoke. The deafening whiplash crack of the bullets through the air informed me with unnerving persistence of their unpleasant closeness, but it seemed wisest to keep going. I was intrigued and even a bit elated to realise then, and a little later when more and heavier artillery crashed into our positions, that putting my trust in God on the first trip had, despite its ordeal, marked the overcoming of fear to a considerable extent and all sense of worry over the responsibility which had so suddenly descended on me in this action. In no time I found myself sprawling breathlessly back in my old mud scoop and feeling almost warm in spite of the icy water seeping through my clothes from the puddle in which I lay. I grinned back with relief at Dickinson's greeting as the fire overhead slackened off and stopped.

Sgt Dickinson was very depressed to hear of the blow which had almost obliterated Company HQ and was stunned into silence for a bit. He then told me that so far as he had been able to make out, there were no further wounded chaps left to try to evacuate from the Platoon positions, though more than 50 per cent of the Platoon had so far become casualties in equal proportions of killed and wounded. I was fed up to hear that our 38 set radio was now also out of action.

At this juncture it became apparent that the enemy, who had been unnaturally quiet for a spell, must have been made aware by my running that we were not all out of action yet. My exchange of information with Dickinson was cut short by our dropping our faces into the earth at the approaching shriek of yet another barrage of shells into our ploughed up patch of ground. I remember lying there and listening to these shells coming down from a great height with a queerly disinterested and detached feeling of unreality. So much had fallen and missed those of us who were left that it was almost beginning to seem that this could continue indefinitely. I concentrated as the earth vomited blackly about us, trying to rid myself of such thoughts as that if this was to be the end, might it be quick and total. Despite the furious concussion and fearful noise I became astonished to know that for the first time I was conscious of moments of complete freedom from fear. Partly I thought that this novel feeling might have been explained by having eluded death so often that day, but gradually as this new experience continued I became aware with elation that fear had met its match by my putting my trust in the one concept on which fear could not intrude. I was yet to find, however, that this wonderful state of mind had not been attained once and for all, but had to be fought for with varied degrees of success in each action, according to the balance with which one credited all power to God or shared this dominion with the clamour of fear and materiality. How hard I found it later to sufficiently remember this inspiration. Among the shells more were now falling behind us in the town. While waiting for more smoke to attempt my return to Company HQ, I instructed Dickinson to seize the first chance of either sufficient smoke or nightfall, still one and a half hours away, to withdraw the Platoon back to fortify the house. While talking, our attention was taken by slight movement from a distant, black-draped, nun-like figure kneeling in the orchard to the right of Klosterhof. Then just above this person we spotted a German uniformed figure in the fork of a tree, looking with binoculars down towards the Royal Scots positions. Dickinson took elaborate aim with his rifle and the figure in the tree toppled off and scrambled away so swiftly on his firing that if it did not actually hit him, it must have been very close. The 'nun' also scrambled away in a most unfeminine manner. Over towards the village of Lieck we saw more dark figures moving in front of the houses in our direction. A little while later seven Germans, armed and in single file, began to make their way towards the Royal Scots to our north. Between the houses of Lieck we saw the movement of a tank while looking at these chaps through the binoculars. It was difficult to make out if this was a Tiger or not, but clearly these chaps were part of a counter-attack by the Jerries, and as we were not personally involved we watched with interest to see what would happen.

The Jerries had got to within about 400 yards of the Royal Scots, whom they did not from the look of it seem to realise were there, when suddenly two of them dropped and lay writhing in the snow while the rest scattered and ran back in their tracks as fast as they could go. Coincidentally came the chatter of a couple of Bren guns, faintly over the distance. One by one four more crumpled and kicked on the ground, then lay still while the seventh, apparently wounded, rolled over a bank out of fire and crawled away. Probably more Germans had been involved in this attack beyond our view, but it seemed a very half-hearted affair, and for all our recent battering it was difficult not to feel sympathy for these fellow victims of circumstance. We were interested to see the confidence with which the German stretcher bearers appeared a few minutes later bearing numerous red-cross flags, arm bands, and painted tin hats and made their way out to pick up any wounded, knowing we would not shoot in spite of the fact that our own stretcher bearers had been deliberately sniped and mortared only that morning with flags, tin hats and arm bands showing at close on half the range.

As we watched, another scream of shells approached from the south-west, the sound of approaching 25-pounders immediately backed by the higher up flight of medium shells. We paused while taking cover, realising from the sound that though coming fairly close, they were not going to drop on us. To our delight we saw the face of Klosterhof farm erupt in plumes of black smoke, red brick dust, and rubble; split seconds later the line of the houses of the village of Lieck into which the Jerry stretcher bearers had only just disappeared disintegrated in a wall of flame and smoke. 'That'll serve the perishers!' McKenzie muttered spitefully. 'G'aan, paste the ***s.'

We were thankful to realise that the Royal Scots had evidently asked for this artillery support and must still be in touch with them by radio. Also, the quick response seemed to indicate that the attack in the town behind us must have been completed successfully for the guns had been free to respond as they had unfortunately not done when we had needed support so badly earlier.

As the guns were firing at right angles to us now, we sat up and watched with no fear of 'overs' or 'shorts' onto us, and little prospect that the Jerries would rake us with small-arms fire. We were astonished to see a group of Germans running to take cover from some forward positions in the farmyard which we had not previously located, and the Jocks, delighted with this change of fortune, helped speed the tripping Jerries by enthusiastically peppering them with rifle and Bren fire.

While the farm was still being shelled and we had the initiative I took advantage of this diversion to get back to Company HQ unscathed. In doing so I spotted with interest that one of our Crocodile flame-throwers was rumbling past on the road behind our positions and ran back to get it to burn out the farm which it easily had the range to do. Above the roar of the engine I managed to attract the attention of the sergeant tank commander whose head poked out of the turret. I expect he must have taken me for a grime-spattered Jock – I had no visible badges of rank and must have looked an awful sight – for he shouted as he roared swiftly past that he 'dare not do it without his officer's permission'. I felt really wild, but there was nothing I could do to stop him as he went out of earshot, short of firing a round past his ear with my rifle which would probably have only made him close the hatch.

Except for a few chaps, most of the survivors at Company HQ were so 'bomb happy' as to be useless, I found on my return; one chap shook violently and continuously. In addition, the 18 set was out of action, possibly due to being shaken by the last barrage, so we were out of touch with Battalion HQ and the guns; and as a result of 10 Platoon 38 set's damage we had no contact with the other two platoons.

Dusk was approaching and with it the most likely time for a German counter-attack, which we were not in very good shape to repel unless the Royal Scots informed the guns. To help a bit I made another attempt to contact the other two Platoons by runner, and made contact with Battalion HQ to give them our news. At the same time I withdrew the remains of Coy HQ a few yards back to the house to fortify it, and there we were rejoined by what was left of 10 Platoon. I was astonished to find that only one chap, Pte Ollerenshaw, had to be evacuated with partly frozen toes and trench foot as a result of lying in the cold and ice, half wet from before sunrise to after sunset.

I had not known the spirits of the Jocks so low with cold, lack of sleep and food and the reaction from the repeated shock both mental and physical; yet somehow we felt too tired and cold that night to eat more than the few biscuits some of us still had left. There was nothing else to eat in any case as the rations had not reached us. It struck me as I kept the chaps busy strengthening the house and on stag from doors and windows and trenches alongside, that the cockney seemed to shine most in taking sustained misery and punishment, and that the Jock seemed more in his element in the excitement of an attack. Though most of the chaps were Scots, some of our replacements, including Sgt Dickinson, were cockneys. I think they were an ideal mixture.

We were so out of touch with the rest of the Battalion that we did not know until afterwards that in the evening the carrier platoon had put in an attack on Klosterhof from due south, at right angles to us and screened from our view by the trees of the lane up which we had originally advanced. At last light we heard a lot of small-arms fire from our left front and some loud explosions, and the artillery fire of both sides suddenly came to life with renewed intensity. From this we guessed the Jerries might be either counter-attacking or being hit by some of our tanks. The attack was not a success, being met with heavy machine gun fire and the blast of *panzerfausts*. The Hon Charles Cavendish, one of the carrier officers, was hit in the thigh in the beginning of the attack. On the credit side was a fine MM won by Pte Lyons.

While this racket lasted we were caused a lot of uneasiness and all 'stood to', anxiously searching the half light for sight or sound of the enemy in the white stretch of snow and the dark of the trees beyond, our dead lying forward of us. I realised that it would be a good thing to get our dead back to the house as soon as it darkened a bit more and before the Jerries sent out any patrol to see if any information might be gathered from their pockets.

The last of our casualties had only been got back from the house a short while before we moved back into it. Among these I had been worried to find L/Cpl Alec Leitch, tended by a stretcher bearer as he lay on a shelf in the flooded ice covered cellar. It seemed that he had appeared too bad to move through the shelling at first. His leg still hung almost off at the thigh and he seemed only just conscious. Recognising me, he asked, very slowly and with effort, 'How are we doing Sir?'

When darkness was at last tinged with Monty's Moonlight, and an uneasy peace had again descended, I asked for volunteers from those few not on stag to come out with me and collect the dead, then realised they were all too bomb happy to attempt it without a bit of a rest to get a grip on themselves.

Meanwhile, Lt Harry Atkinson had arrived in the Company positions leading a listening patrol. He had been sent by the CO who had evidently gathered some idea of the situation from the casualties arriving back from our Company. His task was to try to penetrate towards Klosterhof under cover of the darkness to secure what information he could of the enemy following on the repulse of the carrier attack. I told Harry all I could of the enemy's whereabouts before he set off. He listened with puckered brows set above a tired, rugged face, then wishing him a safe trip I watched him lead his handful of dejected men forward through the bushes past the bodies of the dead lying around the Command post. I followed Harry's patrol out to collect the dead and their weapons with the only five chaps I could find who still seemed in a condition to do it. Three of them were part bomb happy with exhaustion and blast and shook with cold and fear, only coming forward with intense reluctance. First we made for the forward positions of my Platoon in the bomb crater, carrying a door we had broken from the house as a makeshift stretcher – Leitch had been carried to the rear on the last real one.

With nightfall it was freezing hard again so that the snow formed a crust which crunched underfoot with a noise which, to our taut ears, it seemed the enemy could not fail to hear, especially if he had sent forward a listening patrol to the position from which they had been driven by shellfire in the afternoon. We also felt very conspicuous with our dark shapes against the snow and stopped frequently to look and listen towards Klosterhof. We could clearly see the details of the building and realised it only needed a steady look in our direction by a German sentry to see us and trigger off another deluge of bullets and mortars. I realised, though, that if this did happen it would at least take attention off Harry's patrol 400 yards to our left and farther forward.

On the rim of the crater I found the body of Cpl Beal and below, as we crouched looking and listening in the semi-darkness of the snow, we saw the other five still, frost-covered forms. While four of us crept down to recover the bodies, the other two lay on the lip of the crater with a couple of Bren guns trained on Klosterhof to fire steadily back if trouble started. It was difficult to realise these frozen, frosted bundles were familiar, laughing, joking and swearing friends of a few hours before who had come through so much to get this far and to this end. I found my numbed mind just could not or would not think deeply about it as being real. The whole scene and setting seemed a cold, awful nightmare. The dead were frozen rigid in the positions in which they had been hit, with splayed limbs in part frozen into the shattered ice of the crater bottom; in consequence they were both difficult to free and to carry. Suddenly, an exclamation of astonishment came from one of the Jocks who was struggling to lift one of the bodies from the floor of the crater where it lay on its back in the ice. At the same moment, this figure, which was still but unfrozen like the others, uttered a queer weak cry followed faintly by the slow painful plea: 'Don't leave me.' We found this was Pte Middleton, who having been assessed as dead by McLaughlin when first he had been hit badly in the back, had lain on the ice in the crater bottom for about nine hours.

A couple of the chaps carried him back to the house as quickly as they could on the door and commenced to rub his near frozen limbs as hard as they could while plying him with rum to restore a little warmth. We had no blankets, so wrapped him in rags, paper and curtains. As he was carried back to the RAP he was still murmuring in a partial coma 'Don't leave me', evidently still thinking he was in the crater. McLaughlin was terribly distressed; indeed, we all reproached ourselves deeply for having left him [Middleton] unwittingly to this hideous experience. He must have been knocked out with the initial wound which together with the attitude in which he lay had convinced McLaughlin that he was dead. He had then been deserted to lie alone and helpless, freezing with the dead in the crater, still under fire, and must have been in agony of mind and body when conscious. Had we known his condition from the time McLaughlin had left him we would almost certainly have lost several more chaps in attempts to get him out before the light failed. That he had survived at all under such an ordeal was staggering. We heard rumours later that Middleton had survived and was making a recovery.

Syd Brown helped me carry in the body of Capt John Elliot whom we placed sadly in the company of all the other dark, silent, uniformed figures huddled in a snow-carpeted courtyard at the back of the Company HQ house. As though to soften the depression, Cpl Parry blurted out in his strong Glasgow-accented voice: 'They're awa' frae a' this . . . hell th'noo, Surr.' Then he added thoughtfully that if more of us were to go the same way, 'they' at least had been spared some of the trials of the queue. Prophetically, he was to reach the head of the queue himself in the spring after so many more ordeals.

The few of us left became more fully aware of our losses on checking the roll while reorganising to cope with stags for the night. I prayed that no further trouble would brew up in the long hours of brain-chilling cold still left ahead of us before dawn. The frost was increasing and a freezing draught eddied through the shattered windows and doors of our battered house. It was really beginning to seem that unless the men got a meal and a good rest soon, they would not be able to keep going for many more hours. Our last 'meal' had been that tin of soup the night before and a numbing reaction of mental and physical exhaustion had to be resisted constantly. Perhaps it was fortunate, though unappreciated, that the Germans provided some mental stimulus at intervals. This shrieked and crashed dismally about us on and off during the night, slung over by the Siegfried Line artillery. The prospect of enemy infantry activity at least in the form of patrolling, if no more, seemed so likely overnight that Dickinson and I dared not let up in our taking turns in visiting each Jock on duty at frequent intervals. We found them crouched and huddled behind their weapons which poked from some shattered window or door, each wrapped and draped in a motley collection of rags, curtains and carpets which they clutched to themselves in a vain attempt to generate some warmth. A weird and miserable crew they looked. Perhaps our very misery of cold and fatigue was an asset in dulling the thoughts of those with too active an imagination. Below and ahead of us in the pale snow light lay the stacked dead in the yard and beyond that the silver-and-black-laced scene of our day-long ordeal, topped by the brooding sombre mass of Klosterhof silhouetted on the skyline.

Capt David Colville formed our first direct contact with Battalion HQ since the start of the attack, apart from Harry's patrol, when he called just after midnight to see how we were getting on. I heard a little later that he was to take over the Company from me as a replacement Company Commander to Colin, but for the moment he returned to report at Battalion HQ.

At about 0300 hours, as no further trouble seemed to be afoot, I retired to the cellar with those off stag to try to get some sleep and get warm for a while. What a forlorn hope. I lay on the slippery, freezing floor for a painful two hours, only to gradually realise that I was wet from a pool of water which had formed where my body had touched the ice of the flooded cellar floor.

At dawn next day, 25 January, the peace was for a while shattered with unexpected and unexplained noises of violence from the direction of Klosterhof and the enemy. Then there was silence again. Such is the confusion of war that it was not till months afterwards that I learned that this final racket from the farm had been the overrunning of the enemy there in a successful attack which had been put in by the Royal Scots from the north.

Also in the morning David joined us to take over the Company. His batman carried a jar of rum sent by the CO, from which we were each given a double ration which for a while gave one the slight impression of warmth and took a little attention from our accumulating hunger. Information was negligible as to the movements of the enemy, but it seemed possible he had withdrawn a little overnight.

We learned that the Brigade and Battalion objectives had been successfully taken, our share of prisoners being 150 with many killed. C Coy had put in the final attack in clearing the town with bayonets at just before 1600 hours supported by tanks and flame-throwers. In this connection rather an interesting and unexpected incident had occurred on the start line just before C Coy put in their attack. A Crocodile flame-thrower, before moving in, gave a burst of flame down the street to be sure the equipment was in order. Almost immediately the best part of a Jerry platoon, hitherto unsuspected, walked out of the nearest building with hands in the air, and waving white flags. The effect of the fiendish screech and billowy roar of the flames on morale is terrific. Also, to our surprise we heard that 52 Lowland Div was, as a result of operation 'Blackcock', the first British division to fight in its entirety on German soil.

At about 8 in the morning the ration party at last reached us, and as things seemed pretty peaceful I decided to risk the smoke being seen in lighting the fire in the back room of our wrecked house to cook up some Spam and beans to go with our army biscuits and an unbelievably welcome cup of steaming tea. One could not help reflecting that the extra rations we were eating really belonged to the unreal, wax-like figures of the dead stacked outside the window in the yard; or that so easily any of the weary, grey-faced chaps clustered round the warm stove restoring their warmth and life might have been in that silent company outside instead. Life seemed to have so departed from known values as to be totally unreal. The thought kept coming to mind: how many minutes, hours or days might pass before yet more of these familiar faces flickering with humour, hopes and fears might pass away to be replaced, then replaced again by others, each perhaps equally hopeful of 'getting through' and believing that it was another who would 'get it'. To those of us who had managed to survive on this knife tip against the grindstone, the irresistible process of elimination seemed to suggest a future too heavily loaded against one to contemplate seriously.

At about 1000 hours the Padre arrived in a carrier with some stretcher bearers for the sad task of taking away our dead, those forms, faces and hands so familiar to us, yet now so different as to seem to have no connection at all with the hearty, lively friends we had come to know and like so well. As we said goodbye to them I think all our thoughts were on their families, still so happily in ignorance. As I took a last look at John's face I thought of the little girls who would see it no more, and my mind felt numb. It seemed to be failing to register things deeply any more.

By 1200 hours it seemed peaceful enough to risk going out forward into the snow to salvage what weapons and equipment we could. At that time we did not yet know of the final successful attack on Klosterhof, but Jerry had shown no reactions whatsoever to our movements, and so, not without a strong feeling of uneasiness, I took a couple of chaps out to the crater we had visited to get the dead overnight and the other positions along the ditch. The vividness of those terrible hours in the numbing cold came back with renewed force on seeing the stained, tattered equipment, the miserable grave-like scoops of foxholes with the surrounding snow blasted dark with explosives and earth, or here and there stained pink.

This job done I climbed into the roof of the house to search the villages to the north-west through the broken tiles with my binoculars for any signs of the enemy. All was still save for smudges of smoke from burning houses or vehicles in the distance. While up there I made a drawing of our positions with Klosterhof beyond.

The tension gradually eased from us as we picked our way round the house in the open and the half-expected reaction from sinister Klosterhof did not materialise. The peace and silence had a watchful, unreal element as we stood and walked in the snow where so recently one would hardly have dared to crawl. It was an experience, too, of intense interest and fascination to see our positions while we were standing up. Klosterhof seemed much closer now that the fighting had stopped. Our senses were saturated with leaden tiredness, but otherwise, physically, our crouching and lying all day in the bitter cold in about 9 inches of water and ice followed by the attempted sleep on the ice of the cellar, seemed to have left us not greatly the worse. The mental scars appeared to have left a deep mark, though, on most of the chaps and showed themselves in jumpiness, lack of resilience and brooding over the friends who were lost.

A SHORT REST AND
TURN IN RESERVE

Around midday I was at Battalion HQ trying to see if I could get any news concerning the progress of those who had been wounded, but there was very little yet. Colin and Pook had to my surprise actually arrived there more or less on their own after being wounded. While there I met the CO who told me that my new Company Commander, David Colville, had had to be evacuated with battle fatigue having worn himself to a standstill during the last action.

In the afternoon the order 'prepare to move' came, together with rumours that we were destined for a short rest at the completion of operation 'Blackcock' in the capture of Heinsberg, the final objective. We moved off at dusk in good spirits with the prospect of a night's sleep at the end of our march. Our direction was to the south-west back to Aphoven. We had just reached the outskirts of Heinsberg when the first of several very accurate salvos of German long-range shells screamed and erupted, straddling our marching column and we took hasty cover in some shattered buildings. I think no one was hurt beyond a bad shaking which stemmed as much from surprise as it did from the blast. It was disconcerting to realise that not only were we still in range of the enemy, but that unless this was an extraordinary coincidence he must still have had us under visual observation from an OP to the north, or have been tipped off as to our movements by radio. When the dust had settled and the Jocks had been chased back onto the road again from their various places of refuge, we stepped out more briskly to increase the range. We only had 4 km to go, but under the circumstances, our weight of equipment and the slippery road surface, the march seemed never ending. Several of the tanks which during the advance had skidded off the roads and bellied themselves in the ditches, were still stuck. As we passed some of these we met a group of miserable-looking, dejected and in some cases slightly wounded German prisoners wheeling little carts and perambulators loaded with their goods. Some of the obscene language the Jocks hurled at this luckless Crocodile as we passed would surely have shrivelled their ears up could they have understood.

At nightfall I established my HQ in the cellar of a small house in the frozen village of Laffeld. Next morning I heard that the CO was sending along yet another Company Commander to take over B Company from me: Capt Charles Marrow, from D Company. Charles, together with David and 'Smyg', had on occasion puzzled the enemy by blowing blasts on his hunting horn during an attack. He was a thinnish tall fellow with a strong sense of humour and was quite mad on horses. 'Pip' Powell returned at the same time as Charles, which caused a tricky situation. 10 Platoon, which I had trained with in Scotland and with which I had been since handing in the cannon, was also the last one 'Pip' had commanded and was the one he expected back, naturally enough. Charles, being new too, did not know the history, so he gave 10 to Pip and gave me 11 Platoon. There, as far as I was concerned, the matter stood, though I was very sorry to think of leaving those of my chaps who still survived and whom I knew so well. Unknown to me, however, a group of my chaps led by L/Cpl Parry and supported by Learmonth, Brown and McKenzie had worked out a petition signed by the Platoon asking for me back again which was delivered to Charles by Parry while 'Pip' and I were both in the Company office, and in view of this Charles had no alternative but to reverse his decision. 'Pip' always suspected, I think, that I had been at the back of this plot, but it was as much of a surprise to me as to himself, and made me feel that at any rate perhaps the Jocks did appreciate one's efforts.

How wonderful it was to be able to relax again properly that night, although lying on the hard floor of the cellar, and to no longer have to keep one ear tuned for approaching sounds of destruction.

With a reasonable sleep, breakfast and a wash and shave behind us, and wearing a change of clothes, we turned to the reorganisation necessary to replace the casualties to men (50 per cent) and equipment. I had lost eight killed, eight wounded, one with frozen toes and Pte Laurie, bomb happy, from the Platoon, though the latter had as sheepishly and mysteriously rejoined us after the action as he had disappappeared from us before it. He was doubly fortunate in that he was still unharmed, and that his NCO and all the witnesses to his disappearance in the rest of the section had been casualties. Strangely too he was one of the few regular soldiers in the company, and still seemed, outwardly at any rate, no less popular for his miserable performance. I think the average Jock was remarkably understanding in helping along or making allowances for those who cracked.

Nearly three days had now passed in this smashed, deserted and frozen village and supplies of ready fuel, including not a little smashed furniture, were getting scarce for the few roaring stoves when, with a jolt, the order 'prepare to move' reminded us – together with the occasional distant explosion – that the enemy and the ever-consuming front lay only a few miles at most over the desolate, winter-gripped landscape to our north.

On 28 January 1945 I climbed, with the rest of the advance party, into a small convoy of trucks in a swirling blizzard, and we threaded our way on sheet-iced roads, wondering towards what? Being an advance party, we guessed we were going to take over from some unit, and as the last operation had so recently ended it seemed we might be static, holding the line somewhere for a while as strength was gathered for the next spring forward.

This guess, backed by the usual rumours, was correct and with memories rekindled by familiar surroundings we bumped and skidded round the outskirts of Waldfeucht, glimpsed through the feathery scudding of the snow, and headed north-east again to pull up to the cries of 'De-bus' in another wrecked village. This village turned out to be Obspringen, the one on which we had watched the HLI and the Royal Scots put in their night attack on 22 January from our isolated snow-bound spinney.

The line here covered the River Roer, and extended through Echterheide, Haaserdreich, Dreich and Vinn. B Company being the one most cut about in Heinsberg were to be in reserve in Obspringen, where I took over our Company positions from a Canadian major in the 7th Cameronians. While waiting for the rest of the Battalion to arrive on foot, I selected a Platoon position in three small houses and had a stray cow roped in to be looked after by L/Cpl H – the wireless operator – so that we could augment the Platoon supplies with fresh milk. We kept the cow, Belinda, in a small shed in the back of Pln HQ and fed it lavishly, but in spite of the care its milk supply was never excessive, which we put down to its rather bomb-happy condition.

The German positions were almost following the line of the German–Dutch border with ourselves on the German side. D Company was dug in most uncomfortably in a wood – the same one, but a bit more to the north-east, as that in which we had first bumped the enemy at the commencement of Operation 'Blackcock' eleven days earlier.

Most of the civilian population had been evacuated from the villages, and so once the companies had settled down the scent of cooking chicken and roasting pork wafted furtively round the positions, telling that the Jocks were fully making up for those meals the Germans had caused them to miss recently. In addition, those who were able to get hold of mine detectors were busily employed in locating further delicacies buried by the German civilians – while, of course, 'testing for mines'. These included crated hams and bottled fruit and Charles Marrow was particularly peeved to see some artillery chaps unearth several crates of rather choice wines from the farmyard at Company HQ over which we had walked several times.

The weather was still terribly cold, particularly at night for those on stag peering out over the snow lit by a full moon. The forward companies were mostly occupied in patrolling at night, wearing white-hooded snow clothing. During our stay of seven days here, our only casualties were three men from A Coy under Lt Ian Scott who took out a strong fighting patrol to investigate the strength of the Germans in a village called Ende. To get there he had to pass through another village, Karken, which was supposed to be unoccupied, but in which the patrol came under heavy fire ahead, then sniping from behind, apparently from civilians. Under cover of a smokescreen after a sharp engagement, in which once again the Germans showed no respect for the red-cross flag in getting stretcher bearers to the wounded, one Jock managed to drag his badly wounded pal to a ditch in which they lay until darkness after the patrol had withdrawn. Later this Jock, Pte Lord, ordered two German civilians to rig up a stretcher and pull wounded Pte Proudfoot back to our own lines, but unfortunately he was so badly hit he died before reaching hospital.

Lt Col Melville summoned me up to Battalion HQ one day after David had passed on my report of L/Cpl Leitch's fine performance, and together we compiled the recommendation for an award. Col Melville was to get the DSO himself for his part in the last 'stunt'.

On the morning of 30 January, a visit was paid by a car-load of VIPs to look at the front – the GOC, CRA, Brigadier, CO and the GOC's ADC. This coincided with a high-flying formation of American bombers whose identity was just being discussed by these important people when the planes released several bomb-loads right round them and slap through the Coy and Battalion area in a volcanic sustained ripple of blasting explosions. One 500-pounder recorded a direct hit, fortunately without casualties, on one of my section billets, making an enormous crater. This accident resulted in a further drop in Belinda's milk supply and, we heard, profuse apologies from the air formation concerned to the 'brass hats' though no apologies reached to our level.

By now all the expert scroungers in the platoon had done their best in scouting round the village to drag in stoves and plentiful supplies of coke-nut fuel to install in the billets. We had found that a great drawback in taking over from a unit rich in transport (particularly the Americans) was that the stoves and fuel were often moved too.

To make up the strength of my platoon, several reinforcements arrived, all very young chaps around nineteen years and in one case, to the best of my belief, less. Among these were my future batman, Cupit, and young Evans, later to get a direct mortar hit in Afferden woods.

Being reserve Company at this time we had the job of digging alternative positions and working out what best to do if called in to stem a German counter-attack on any of several villages to the north. Reconnoitring the alternative positions involved much walking about on an area suspected to be mined. It gave one a queer, intensely alive, unreal feeling to tread gingerly about all day, marking out and digging new trenches not knowing if the next step might dissolve one wholly or partially. Ally Ross, Pioneer Officer, was busily employed with his men and detectors searching out these mines but was greatly hampered by the profusion of shrapnel chips scattered about the fields, each one of which produced a tell-tale whistle in the detector earphones. 'These b*** fields seem to be almost solid metal!', he exclaimed in exasperation.

While one of my sections was employed in digging a new position they unearthed a store of carefully wrapped and straw-covered linen and clothing in the earth under a little shed. The retreating German civilians had buried it. Much of it appeared to have been looted from the Dutch. Some chaps seemed to have an uncanny instinct where to look for these hidden caches, especially spirits which time and again I warned them not to touch, but one could not be everywhere and see all that went on at once, as I was later to find.

It was an even more persistent struggle for the NCOs and myself to keep the Jocks alert on stag, especially in a rear position, and on visits round sections during the night both Charles and I found several to be in a state of partial sleep. At night 11 Platoon would send a standing patrol out through our positions about 500 yards to the north-east to where the Germans had built a dugout under a partly hollowed-out haystack while we stood to in trenches round each of the section houses overlooking the fields on the edge of the village or poked our guns from fortified windows through whose glassless apertures an icy wind seemed to always be blowing off the frozen expanse of countryside.

The Germans had left a Spandau and an MG 34 in our billet in their hurried retreat from the village before the bayonets of the Royal Scots. These we used to bolster up our potential fire-power in case of an emergency, though it was not a good practice to use enemy weapons as a rule, for their distinctive noise could lead to confusion and battle accidents. The Spandau was put with the sentry on look-out duty, gazing over the snow to the ribbon of dark woods containing the enemy. Several false alarms were caused by the sharp, zip-like crackle of this weapon which the innocent sentry always claimed 'went off on its own'. Bomb-happy Pte L was the chief offender and it was, I think, the nearest he ever got to firing a weapon at the enemy. He could be heard crooning softly to himself in a plaintive falsetto voice during his spells of duty. Later, when some self-propelled 25-pounder guns moved in alongside the house in an orchard one could hear the clatter of his feet down the stairs to the cellar each time the guns fired, and there he would be found cowering, quite unnerved. Poor Belinda suffered from these guns too and not even the expert milking and attention of my former cow-hand radio operator could produce enough milk for Platoon HQ.

Slowly the Platoon was getting back to strength in men and equipment, and shovels were in great demand since our experience at Heinsberg. Nearly every man carried a full-sized shovel or pick now, some of which we had picked up from farms, together with two saws and an axe for felling trees to roof our slit-trenches.

Our leisure time was employed in writing home . . . still with the difficulty of not being able to mention our whereabouts or any experience more recent than a date about two weeks before. We rejoiced too in proper washing, shaving and tooth cleaning, whenever possible. L/Cpl Parry gave us many a pleasant hour on his mouth organ while we lazed or just slept on a heap of potatoes in the cellar for the sheer joy of this, at times, rather novel experience. Inwardly we were kept a little happier by large chunks of cooked bacon off a side found in 12 Platoon billet. Fortunately the enemy had been knocked so hard recently he was still busy licking his wounds and so on 2 February, without further incident other than the arrival of swarms of German civilians trundling their belongings from the direction of the enemy who had mercilessly demolished their homes, we had word that we were to move back from the line into Waldfeucht, again as Brigade reserve. It was revealing that the German villagers should have decided to come over and put themselves at our mercy in their hundreds even from as far off as Roermond rather than retreat into the Fatherland and other protection. It showed which way they expected the battle to roll in the future, if nothing else.

But for our move these civilians threatened to become a big problem as all had to be carefully looked over to be sure no Trojan horse act was in progress, after which they were shipped right to the rear in trucks. Both we and these civilians would have felt a lot less happy as we moved back over the frozen roads had we realised then that they had been mined, and that the mines had not yet claimed a victim in spite of the heavy traffic which had gone over them, including ourselves in the advance party trucks, because the frozen surface had taken and distributed the weight so as to render them harmless while the frost lasted. Within a couple of days the thaw did arrive sufficiently to blow up several trucks in the area. We heard some of the mines were of the ratchet type which let several vehicles pass, even when the thaw came, before going off.

As it was, our own movement back to smashed Waldfeucht on foot over the frozen, mud-rutted roads included a few moments of anxiety . . . and also visions of possible future roast beef, when some cows wandering along the roadside next to the marching column made their way towards about fifty Regal mines left scattered in the snow by the Jerries, and taped off by our chaps with mine tape. We paused breathlessly in our march, ready to dive flat as one cow threaded its way unconcernedly through the edge of the mines, not touching one.

To return to Waldfeucht again was a rather sad though interesting experience. Sad because we had lost so many friends since last we were there, and interesting because by some strange chance we as a Platoon were to find ourselves allotted the same corner café as a billet from which we had fought that eerie battle against the Tiger tank. How different it was to be able to walk about like a tourist, reconstructing each move of those haunting hours; to see the PIAT hit over the door where the Germans had stood, the hole in the wall from the shell which had carried through above us as we lay in the gutter, and the bullet chips and gashes in the alley. We took the billet over from another unit which had been in reserve there so it had been tidied up and 'organised' a bit. Though still in the range of the Siegfried guns, we were fortunately not shelled while there.

The company still needed a lot of reorganisation, and to complete this we were in for yet another change of Company Commander, making four since Colin was wounded. Alan Innes was promoted to Major and transferred to B Coy and Frank Coutts arrived as 2/ic from the A/Tank Platoon. Alan, known to all his fellow officers as 'Smyg' for a reason I never discovered, was tallish, big boned, wore glasses, and was usually rather quiet until amused when he had a most infectious, hearty, chuckling laugh which, with Frank Coutts' hearty roars of amusement, was to put new life into all who heard them on many later occasions that otherwise might not have been so bearable. Smyg, like Frank, was from the Border country, and farmed near Kelso. Frank, a massive ruddy-faced fellow with fairish hair, formerly of the London Police, but destined to make the army his career later, was a rugger international like Chris, our CO, and a merry spirit and booming sense of fun to match his size went with a first class knowledge of and enthusiasm for the job in hand.

Pip Powell and Tommy Gray were the other two subalterns in the Company. Pip, an ex-regular officer from the Buffs with a wife and child at home, was a great individualist, and a very likeable chap who was really in his element in livening up a party with thunderous shouts of 'Up my Beauty'. He was famed too for his habit of strolling about in an attack with only a walking stick in his hand, with a revolver to fall back on in an emergency in its holster. Tommy, more of a Scot in his accent than Frank or Smyg, was also an international footballer whom we were unfortunately not to see so much of as he was to be wounded in the coming attack.

It was pleasant to once again be able to visit one's friends scattered about the town in other companies in the few habitable houses left, and to meet them at a church service conducted by the Padre in a damaged hall. Alongside the hall in the rubble was a deep crater containing a dead horse, all that remained of a stable. Somehow it did not seem out of place in this strange, unreal life we were now leading that after the service we should test all the new and old automatic weapons to be sure they were in order, firing them into the crater. We also took the opportunity of trying a PIAT out, firing it at one of the wrecked Tiger tanks to test penetration from various angles as a guide to any future meetings with these enormous vehicles. Alongside one tank lay one or two large grey-green dud shells of a size we could not remember arriving during the shelling on our first entry into the town.

Much of our remaining time in Waldfeucht was spent hard at work in the wet which followed the thaw in strengthening the muddy roads that were giving way under the heavy supply traffic. To do this we moved rubble by the truckload from the ruins. While engaged in this one of the chaps, later killed at Haus Loo, got a bad gash in the head from a falling tile which knocked him out, and I carried him back to the RAP. I had come to be rather impressed with this chap, who though quiet and seemingly timid, was missed by us when he was gone because whatever the conditions he seemed always able to respond with a smile.

On 7 February 1945, our fifth day, the Americans arrived to take over from us, and we marched out of the town under the arch from which the Tiger had first blasted us on tumbling out of the Kangaroos and on towards Schilberg, busily speculating as to what we were in for next. Fuel was added to rumours that we might be moving up for another attack when we met and climbed aboard a long convoy of troop-carrying vehicles.

To our surprise, after crossing into Holland, we sped south-west to cross the Maas at Maastricht, and followed the river up into Belgium where our Company convoy pulled up in the town of Eisden beside the Maastricht canal, while the rest of the Battalion went on a short way to Stockheim. Here the Jocks were issued with a welcome change of clothes after a bath, and were billeted in a fine modern school with the officers in private houses over the road. It was a while before the thirsty Jocks had changed their Dutch currency for Belgian and could get a drink of beer.

To be surrounded by the friendly faces of Allies when going about made a nice change, and so when Pip and I took the Company on a longish route march for a bit of exercise and to keep their feet hard, we quite enjoyed ourselves, returning the greetings of passers-by and accompanied by the usual stray dog which soon attached itself to us and romped about, egged on by the Jocks. During a halt, Pip and I took the NCOs into a wayside *estaminet* for an awful cup of so-called tea in the village of Mechelen. We came back in a wide arc through some fir plantations, spotting the wreckage of one of our Typhoons ploughed into the trees.

On the evening of the second day, the order 'prepare to move' came, and early on the 10 February we climbed into the TCVs while it was still dark and bitterly cold, and moved north, bumping and speeding along as the wintry dawn spread mistily over the cheerless landscape. At times the route seemed astonishingly devious, probably due to cratered roads and blown bridges. We travelled through still sleeping Maeseyck and back into Holland over the Wessem canal at Grathem, then back over the canal on a creaking-squeaking Bailey bridge to Weert and across the Noorer canal to Nederweert following the Bois le Duc canal due north to Asten where we crossed it, increasingly puzzled as to what we were heading for. We began to note that from here on through Deurne and Ilsselsteijn the roads steadily deteriorated to just logs laid over seas of mud as the signs of recent heavy fighting multiplied. At Horst the convoy split and Bn HQ went on to Gunn. By this time we had all prepared ourselves to accept the fact that we were in for another 'stunt' very shortly.

The Battalion, we found, had been ordered to take over the line of the River Maas from the KSLI [King's Shropshire Light Infantry] and a unit of the Guards, while I had the unexpected pleasure of five days very welcome LOB in Horst in a house selected for me by 'Pipey' – Pipe Major Bunyan – on the advance party. The family had previously been bombed out by the RAF, and a son was missing as a slave labourer in Germany. Although they could unfortunately only speak Flemish, they were most kind to me. It was a treat to sit with them in their warm room with the children and surroundings of home life again, busily occupied though I was all the while censoring mountains of mail while blue-eyed, bullet-headed young Herman the baby, who had taken a great liking to these new strangers in khaki, spent his time in crawling all over me like a mountaineer. Due to malnutrition and having had to spend so much time recently in the cellars during air raids and then the fighting, most of the children were suffering from what they called 'Kellar' sores! In the absence of any civilian help, the parents were most grateful for the care of the stretcher bearers, who did what they could for these babies; a task which I think they rather enjoyed as a welcome interlude to their normally grim job. The family insisted on trying to persuade me to eat supper with them, which was quite embarrassing as they were so obviously short of food. The Germans, whom they variously referred to as the Mousse, or Moff, had cleaned their house of their radio, two cycles, their car, a clock, cutlery, a sewing machine, and even the babies' clothes which were sent by one thug to his own child at home, they said.

Down at the flooded river, the Battalion was spread very thinly over an unusually wide front, and for the most part in far from comfortable surroundings. During daylight quite a lot of enemy movement could be seen on the opposite side of the river, and no doubt they saw our chaps, for the mortar and small-arms fire of both sides was very active. At night numerous contact patrols had to stumble in the wet and blackness between our positions, and many successful shooting parties were staged by our chaps who quickly changed their positions after blazing off at night at the enemy, so that his return fire could be pinpointed for our mortars and artillery to 'stonk'. A Dutch company was stationed up on the river and they were of great value to the night patrols as they knew the country so well.

On the night of the 8th/9th the sky lit and flickered to the rumble of heavy artillery fire in the north, the beginning of what was later to be known as the battle of the Reichswald Forest. This necessitated preparations for a patrol from our Battalion to the enemy side of the river to find out the strength and formations opposite us. Lt Kendra, who had been briefed to take the patrol that evening, was flown over the area he would have to penetrate a few hours later. His orders were: 'Bring back a prisoner dead or alive for information purposes.' This was a most difficult job indeed, especially as with the attack the Germans had blown the Roer dams with the evident intention of slowing the advance and the river was steadily rising and widening to an angry torrent. Suddenly the patrol was cancelled . . . either the floods or the speed of advance had exceeded expectations. When, on the 15th, word came to move, and for the Americans to take over the positions, the flood probably had become acute. Supplies had to be taken up in amphibious vehicles, and our chaps had to move back from the river, wading, in places up to their chests in the icy, swirling water, following mine tape to keep direction – as one Jock put it: 'using Teller mines beneath the water as stepping stones in one place.' Meanwhile, Montgomery had, we heard, taken the Division under his wing. As a result of his aversion to two Battalions of the same Regiment being in the same Brigade, which resulted in one home district or town having disproportionate losses after any sticky action, he decided to swap the 5th KOSB, up till then with us in 155 Bde, with the 6th HLI from 157 Bde. To celebrate this parting of the Battalions, the pipes and drums of both units were brought up to play a massed retreat with the pipes and drums of other units of the Brigade in the town of Horst, to the delight of all, especially the children.

The kilts caused a tremendous sensation among the young women of the town, who tried very hard to keep a straight face to cloak the animation of their reactions in chatter, gestures and occasional suppressed giggles. The men looked frankly perplexed, but all obviously loved the novelty and pageantry of the occasion, and expressed their appreciation in spontaneous hearty clapping, and there were cries of approval at this picture book scene from the ranks of excited, large-eyed children.

OPERATION 'VERITABLE'

BETWEEN THE MAAS AND THE RHINE

Leaving the Americans to struggle with the floods, the Battalion embussed in TCVs and again moved to the north, keenly speculating on the sketchy shreds of news we had so far concerning the next attack. Montgomery's 1,000 guns, helped by the RAF, were crashing and drumming ahead of us and we had that tense, alive feeling coupled with the hopes and fears that went with waiting for the curtain to rise on another show and all that we knew that meant.

The Canadian army was engaged in a tremendous effort to burst through the enemy and reach the Rhine at Millingen, in preparation for the drive to the south and the clearing of the Reichswald forest, in itself an enormous task. This stretch of territory contained the Siegfried Line, of which we had heard so much, and the Germans – having for the moment almost drowned the American force which was to have crossed in the south to push up and join us, by blowing the Roer dams to raise the floodwaters – did not mean to let the battle be a walkover. With this temporary respite in the south the Germans hurled the equivalent of eleven divisions, including two armoured and four parachute, to meet the five British and Canadian divisions involved in the first phase of the attack (the 2nd and 3rd Canadian Divs, 15th Scottish, 53rd Welsh, and 51st Highland Divs). Meanwhile, the 3rd British Div, ourselves in the 52nd Lowland Div, and the 43rd Wessex Div together with all the remaining resources of 21st Army Group, were preparing for the follow through . . . though of course at that time at our level we so far knew almost nothing of what was going on.

As with our last operation the weather again took sides with the enemy, this time in the form of a wet, muddy thaw slowing down what should have been a fast thrust by a highly mechanised force to a mud begrimed crawl which quickly had the operation lagging behind the timetable.

Our convoy of trucks jerked to a stop late that night after a slow painful journey, and we jumped out into a driving drizzle at the divisional reserve area of Wanroi. Each section soon had itself installed in one of the wayside houses. I was settled in with Pln HQ with my small pack as a pillow and equipment scattered about on the dining-room floor of a bungalow. There was amazingly little furniture in the place, but the owners, who were just going to bed when we arrived and billeted ourselves there, were very pleasant. Next morning, still largely in the dark as to what was going on in this queer life of unexplained moves, we boarded the TCVs again after a few mouthfuls of biscuits, jam, and Compo tea; and said goodbye to our hosts who were as puzzled by our swift departure as they had been by our sudden appearance out of the dark and drizzle the evening before.

A quick run brought us to St Hubert, 20 miles south of Nijmegen, where we turned off the main road to hunt for billets in clusters of smallholding farms sprinkled over the rain-drenched fields. Even the carrier and Jeep were hard pressed to plough their way through the quagmire tracks.

Smyg had vanished on an 'O' Group for briefing at Bn HQ, and with this definite sign of a 'flap', the tempo of activity and tension increased. Ammunition, stores and equipment were checked quickly again, and, watched with interest by the farmer and his family, we fired a test burst into the mud with each automatic weapon, whirling black clots of muck back into our faces from each steaming bullet crater at our feet.

Later that evening, 16 February 1945, an 'O' Group was called in the Company HQ farm where we gathered seated round a map-covered table lit by a Tilley lamp in the farm parlour. Halfway through the briefing, we knocked off for the farmer's wife to serve us with an outsized plate of omelettes and pancakes. A sturdy Dutch woman, she sensed something important was afoot and was determined to make it an occasion.

The Germans, we heard, were living up to Montgomery's hope that they would stand and fight it out on this side of the Rhine, and our job under command of the Canadians was to wipe out as many as possible of the enemy as the British from the north and the Americans from the south forced them into a compression chamber between the two rivers. Monty had reckoned that once this had been done, the mauling of the enemy and his equipment would break the back of the Wehrmacht.

Cleve had been secured on 11 February, but since then the 51st Div had fought to a halt against fanatical resistance outside Goch from the German paratroopers. Our part was to cross the Maas at Mook, west of the Reichswald, and to work south with the divisional axis bordering the Maas, the Recce Regt to the right of us down to the river, and the 7th/9th Royal Scots, 6th HLI and Canadians on our left. The Canadians, we heard, had initially had very heavy fighting in the Reichswald Forest, probably the biggest wood-clearing battle ever fought, and had for the first time tried out the Sherman-mounted multiple rocket projectiles, up to 60 rockets per tank, each with the blast of a 5.5-inch shell. Our news of the results was that 1,000 Germans had been wiped out. Certainly the noise of these weapons, which we subsequently experienced at long range, put the German version, called the 'Moaning-Minnie' by us, to shame.

The Battalion had been ordered to move to a concentration area over the Maas, near Gennep, which had to be carried out during the hours of darkness. This meant that the operation would start for us at 2.30am the next morning, 17 February.

The 'O' Group over, I briefed the Platoon, and checked over all details with Sgt Dickinson and the other NCOs. I had borrowed one of Pip's Bren gunners for a while as a batman, but with this action impending I had to hand Murray back again, and took on a newcomer, Smith, a quiet, nervous chap, instead, partly because I sensed it might be as well to keep him close by for his first action. I felt a lot for these new chaps, tensed up to face the unknown and trying so hard not to show their feelings. I knew they would have two battles to face where we had one, and the first and by far the hardest would be the battle for mastery over themselves.

Before turning in for a short rest for a couple of hours, perhaps the last we would get for a long time to come, Tommy Gray, who shared a billet in another farm, and I sat for a while round the

Dutch stove with the farmer and his family. In this cosy warmth of family life adjusting our thoughts to all that the estimated month of the coming action's duration would involve, and reading the latest mail of the little mundane things that made up life at home, the future seemed a mad but inexorably approaching unpleasant dream, a needless farce which had to be gone through with because civilisation seemed to know of no better method of restoring freedom and sanity. Tommy discussed the chances of being hit in a month, and we tried to conjure up thoughts of what peacetime would be like again, but could not imagine it. We could not tell the farmer what we were up to, but had to say we would be departing in the early hours, in case we disturbed the family. He, with the distant reverberations of battle noises in the background to prompt his thoughts, I think guessed the rest, for he immediately became most insistent that victory should be toasted in cognac.

Two hours trying to keep warm in a little box bed passed all too soon, and tumbling out, fully clothed but for boots and gaiters, I was soon employed with Sgt Dickinson in chasing the Platoon out to queue in the dark with mess tins and mugs outside a barn for breakfast. It was a raw, freezing morning.

Inside the barn we could hear the roar of a 'Blower' and the voices of the cooks at work under 'Eccie' Douglas, their chief. They were the objects, no doubt, of considerable envy being LOB (left out of battle) on most operations together with members of the pipe band, particularly the pipers. At first the pipers had been normally employed in battle, but following almost irreplaceable losses, they were now usually kept with HQ Company in B Echelon.

With porridge, tinned bacon, bread, jam and tea safely inside, we moved off in file over the frosty, mud-ribbed track, towards the TCVs waiting for us on the main road. The only sounds were the drumming scuffle of feet on the iron-hard mud, the clink of metal, an undertone of occasional curses or wisecracks, punctuated by the yell of some exasperated NCO or officer. In the distance we could hear the whine of some fanatic TCV driver revving his engine madly to warm either it or himself.

The dim shapes of the Jocks looked more like Christmas trees than ever. It was an absurd weight to carry into action, yet every piece seemed indispensable: shovels stuck through cross straps, wire cutters, waterbottles, packs, entrenching tools, Bren guns, Bren wallets and magazine basic pouches, radio sets, PIAT and mortar bomb cases, bandoliers of 100 rounds .303 per man, and all the odds and ends such as Stens, Verey pistol and cartridges, gas cape, revolver, camouflage face veil as scarf, and perhaps an optimistic few with a kettle or pot to supplement the biscuit tins as cooking utensils when dealing with the occasional chicken.

The outlines of numerous TCVs bordered the road ahead, each only lit by a shaded tail light, and each engine purring out wisps of steamy exhaust to join our eddying breath in the crisp night air.

At last all were embussed and silent, chilled not only by the biting cold, but also by the realisation that another 'stunt' had commenced. The silence, however, was short lived for the dynamic melody of Parry's mouth organ soon burst forth, to be joined by the softer crooning of young Evans and Cupit. At first light next morning, young Evans was killed.

Before long the sounds of singing in the back of the truck were drowned as the convoy merged with the booming, squeaking and clattering of tanks, gun tractors and self-propelled guns threading their way with us on the long pontoon bridge over the still swirling floodwaters of the Maas at Mook.

The grey misty dawn gave way to a slight drizzle as we turned south on a broad, tree-lined concrete road bordering the river. A narrow gauge railway ran alongside, which the Germans had destroyed in places to prevent our using it for the carrying of ammunition and supplies. Occasionally the road was splashed with mortar craters, and the trees were gashed and chipped from the recent fighting. The density of destruction in smashed houses and vehicles as we progressed told us, as we noted all these signs of battle with a fairly practised eye, that our coming opponents had fought each inch of the way.

After passing through Riethorst and Middelaar we guessed the front was getting fairly close, for we de-bussed into the drizzle which had thawed the night frost and slushed the roads again. We continued squelching on, on foot and clad in gas capes.

The blackened shells of the smashed houses at St Agatha

showed our flamethrowers had been at work. All the contents of these houses: bedding, books and furniture seemed to have vomited out of the doors and windows, to be churned into the muck of the road, as though some civilians had made a desperate attempt to save some of their belongings amid the fury of battle; a scene we were to meet later in Germany.

On the walls of some houses the Germans had scrawled occasional threats and insults and swastika signs in chalk. Alongside these were chalked the famous sign, so we knew the 51st Highland Division was the one we were to take over from.

Passing through the town of Gennep, captured a few days earlier, the Germans had blown a bridge, now patched with a Bailey section, and there were all the signs of very heavy fighting. At the level-crossing of the Tilburg–Goch railway line we met battle-grimed sections of the Black Watch moving back past us, and the Jocks shouted greetings to each other.

Another mile and the column halted in the village of Heine, and fell out by the wayside amid rather noisy surroundings, for we were in the middle of a 25-pounder gun area. This meant the enemy were within a few thousand yards. Information so far at our level was almost nil. The halt might be for minutes or hours.

It became apparent the situation was in a confused flux at the front as the day wore on, but meanwhile the shivering Jocks of my platoon had lit a fire with the splintered woodwork and furniture of a house, and we sat round this trying to get a little warmer and drier. This halt, we began to gather, was in our concentration area.

Eventually the cooks' truck arrived, followed by Pip, whose TCV had broken down, and Smyg gave the order for them to get going on some tea making with the Blower to cheer and warm us up a bit. Almost at the same time Smyg was called to an 'O' Group at Battalion HQ, and after a long delay returned and proceeded to put Frank, Tommy, Pip and myself in the picture.

The plan was to carry out a two-phase attack in conjunction with the 7th/9th Royal Scots, through woods, and over 6 miles of country, with a Company objective of some houses on a crossroads at Siebengewald, next to a large seminary on the

Dutch–German border. In the first phase the Royal Scots were to clear Afferden woods, several miles in extent. We were to follow through, making our way across country via Molenhuis farm on the edge of the wood across an anti-tank ditch, over open fields via a group of houses called Kleine Horst and clearing several small woods, and a village of Kreftenheije, while the Royal Scots took Groote Horst village on our right. Finally, we had a customs house and another small wood to deal with before digging in. Our Platoon objective was the customs house.

In view of subsequent events, and the strength of the enemy, these objectives seemed wildly optimistic, especially as we were in the heart of the Siegfried Line defences. As a cross-country route march with all our kit and no enemy it would, as we were to see, have been physically exhausting.

Gathering my NCOs Sgt Dickinson, Cpl Allan, Cpl Hepburn, Cpl Parry, L/Cpls Wilson and McMichael I passed on what we were to do, which was greeted with pithy unprintable remarks as the full extent of the 'stunt' was appreciated from the map, and section commanders made off to brief their sections. Among the old hands still left on this operation were my friends Brown and McKenzie on the PIAT, Learmonth, Tarn, McLaughlin – who refused to take a stripe – and Cutter on trial as radio operator.

The Royal Scots and the 5th KOSB moved off on the first leg as we sat waiting and shivering in the already failing light after nine hours of uncertainty. I had found a quantity of novel German grenades, explosives and cartridges with small projectiles fitted at the back of the house, and spent my time examining these and hoping that a tin of soup I had in the fire would warm up before the word to move came.

Meanwhile, word came back that the attack had run into far fiercer resistance than had been bargained for halfway through the wood. This resulted in a hurried fresh set of 'O' Groups, and a drastic change of plan.

The new plan was to try to penetrate from the northern to the southern part of Afferden wood (it was in two main blocks) via Kasteel Blijenbeek, a moated castle in the central clearing, then skirt the eastern part of the southern block of woods along an anti-tank ditch, then penetrate to a group of houses called Koepel in this southern wood, and dig in there on high ground ready for any trouble before first light.

Again the distance was pretty heavy for an infantry foot-slogging attack, being not much less than the first one. At 18.30, just as I had started to open my tin of soup, word came for us to move, and with it that empty feeling in the stomach which I knew no soup could fill . . . this perhaps softened the blow of having to leave it!

In line with the plan we set off, not without personal misgivings concerning the distance, and the difficulties of fighting, let alone finding our way by night through these dense, hilly pine woods divided up into huge rectangular blocks split by sandy tracks, each stretch of wood and track looking much the same. This plan was shortly to prove grossly optimistic, if not suicidal, and I rather shuddered to think later what might have happened if Jerry had hidden in the wood and let several companies penetrate before showing himself.

We branched off the main road in Heinn near rather a nice English-looking church, taking a sandy log-reinforced track to the left towards the dark ominous sprawling mass of Broederbosch pine woods ahead. The guns on either side suddenly barked into life with a crack and flash like lightning, their night aiming posts showing faint, coloured pinpricks of light. The eerie, tapering, hollow sound of each salvo of shells ascended into the gathering darkness to crump-crump and echo dismally in the distance of the brooding woods, which seemed to breathe a heavy silence between each sound of violence.

A few hundred yards and we halted by the roadside. It was drizzling, and with the darkness came the cold. On we moved, then another unexplained halt, and each forlorn, gas-cape-clad figure again jettisoned its load of kit, ammunition and weapons to huddle by the roadside. At intervals the guns, now just behind us, sent their shells over our heads with a maddeningly awful series of ear splitting cracks. A steady stream of tanks, assault vehicles RE, carriers and occasionally ambulances, had started to move forward past us, each labouring with a complaining whine of gears and revving engine through the deep sand, adding to the noise of the whiplash-cracking shells. We were beginning to feel really cold and wet by now, tired and not a little depressed by our surroundings and the future, as well as hungry. Apart from a few biscuits and tea, we had had nothing since breakfast eighteen hours earlier.

Our path lay down a gradual slope, revealing the sandy rides with which the woods were split into rectangular blocks of about 500 x 250 yards apiece, each track being 40-60 feet wide. The engineers had cut the rides that were being used as the main axis into two sections divided by mine tape on poles and lit at intervals by coloured, shaded lamps facing back from the enemy one side for use by wheeled, and the other by tracked vehicles.

By about 2030 hours we were another mile or so further on into the drip and gloom of the trees when the column halted again, and in the comparative silence we could hear the cause – a doleful, muffled, crashing succession of thuds in the trees in front of us, marking the fall of German mortar bombs. We lay flat in the wet sand, waiting for the word to move on.

No information had reached us, but the whine of a labouring engine coming back down the track from the depths of the wood, followed by two more, each vehicle displaying in the silent eloquence of its red crosses as it passed, indicated that the head of the column had run into some trouble. This was confirmed by the distant stutter of automatic weapons at intervals.

The drizzle was getting heavier as our warmth evaporated into the wet sand. It was now about 2230 hours and a much louder drumming tattoo of crashes nearby was followed by the order to dig in by the roadside and wait. This we eagerly did as an opportunity to generate warmth, at the same time munching some Compo biscuits for supper.

Several hours' wait followed, huddled tight in a gas cape on the trench bottom, but nevertheless getting steadily wetter and colder for once again we were working without greatcoats.

At 3 in the morning on 18 February, sand spilling in on top of me as I tried to doze marked the arrival of a runner from Company HQ to call "'O' Group, Mr White Surr!' The enemy had been heavily resisting the 5th KOSB in their advance overnight with strong points and snipers cunningly sited in the dark maze forest sections, and had now been located in determined strength dug in in the vicinity of the Kasteel/Blijenbeek, and on the high ground dominating the space between the two blocks of forest.

The depth of penetration in the last plan had had to be modified again. A and C companies were to creep from the rim of our block of forest before first light and dig in just short of the anti-tank ditch, which was unexpectedly flooded on the right flank. At 0730 hours a heavy barrage was to come down on the enemy for a full hour before we in B company, followed at an interval by D company to leapfrog through, were to attack over 500 to 700 yards of low, open ground crossing the Afferden–Goch road, clearing the enemy from the sandy high ground and dig in there before full light. Churchill tanks and AVREs were to come up with us to bridge the anti-tank ditch with fascines for our crossing.

We fully realised now as we plodded on in the pitch dark and steady rainfall, which had replaced the drizzle, that we were trying to move into the heart of the Siegfried Line defences to attack a very determined enemy in prepared positions over ground he knew, and which we would not see until the attack commenced, and it said a lot for the Jock that he moved so philosophically forward in spite of this, and in spite of the cold, the wet, hunger and tiredness resulting from being almost continually on the go for the last thirty hours. There was a marked increase in bursts of swear words. None of us were in the best of spirits.

On our way towards the start line for the attack we traversed stretch after stretch of pine rides, occasionally changing direction and passing vehicles, including our Lloyd-carrier anti-tank gun tractors, having trouble in the deep soft sand. Gradually the darkness faded to grey, and the rain to a drizzle, then a damp mist.

There were no sounds of fighting ahead now, only the occasional revving of a tank engine or the squeak of its tracks faintly echoing in the wood somewhere behind us. The weight of our wet kit hung oppressively, cutting into our shoulders with the webbing, and we were glad when just before 7.30 word came to halt and dig in, covering an arc of low bogland in which our spades struck water a few inches below the surface. This was the start line for the attack, the Kasteel being in an open space somewhere through the next thin strip of wood on our left front.

We were to dig in in case of enemy retaliation during the barrage. Most of the chaps had got some shallow sort of hole started when from behind came the ominous increasing roar of the discharge of many guns, then swiftly, in rising volume and pitch, the shriek of droves of shells, which we could tell would land short, approximately in our positions. The barrage had started.

Those of us who were lucky enough to have a sand scoop to drop into, even if waterlogged, did so. As happened so often, the officers and NCOs, being engaged in 'O' Groups, had none and so we tried to mould ourselves to ruts in the track. For several minutes, until the guns had been corrected by radio to lift up over the trees by several hundred yards, the sand blossomed and cascaded about us, and trees toppled and splintered to the accompaniment of the most awful noise.

This carelessness on the part of our gunners drew searing, pithy comments from the Jocks to match the acid reek of cordite filling the air about us. Quite a lot of snow, which had not yet thawed, lay around and we could see from several gaping dark craters nearby, still steaming in the cold air, that we had been very fortunate not to have any hit.

The ammunition expended on this barrage must have been phenomenal. The sky overhead pulsated with a solid, continuous, moaning shriek of descending projectiles, while the muffled, vibrant drumming of explosions seemed to quite carpet the enemy positions. This display was to be surpassed by subsequent barrages shortly to follow. No wonder a captured German RSM asked in all seriousness later if he could be allowed to see our 'belt-fed 25-pounders'.

Meanwhile, in spite of this shaking and the continuing noise, I noticed several of the dogged or optimistic Jocks were occupied otherwise than just trying to take shelter. The odd wisp of steam here and there, and smell of Hexamine tablets proclaimed an effort by these few ever-hopeful chaps to coax some water to boil for the brewing of a 'fly cuppie' (tea) before the time came to go into the attack. This eternal pastime of trying to get 'char' going on such occasions, probably had some value in that it switched one's mind off the future to the present, and kept it occupied on a far saner pastime than the one looming ahead.

I decided to keep what little water I had left in my waterbottle to quench my thirst in that most thirsty of jobs likely to crop up in the near future: the digging of a slit trench with the stimulus of high explosive to speed the pace.

It was at this stage that No. 3 Section reported, not unexpectedly, that Pte Laurie had vanished again. As before, it seemed he had taken his departure somewhere on the approach march to the attack start line. However, there was a general feeling that he might have proved more of danger than use with us.

As the hour of the barrage drew to its close, and we were gathering our thoughts for the coming effort, the roar of powerful engines throbbed into life down a track on our right, and a Weasel carrier followed by three Churchill tanks, each carrying a large fascine of brushwood, came into view. These were to bridge the anti-tank ditch for us. At the same moment Smyg gave us the word in 10 Platoon to move forward after Tommy Gray's platoon, bordering the track towards the open, keeping within cover of the trees.

So far everything had gone according to plan in the approach. Although the two forward companies had had a very hurried task in getting dug in on their positions overlooking the anti-tank ditch before dawn, they had managed to probe for a few hundred yards with a couple of quick recce patrols. These had established that on the left the bridge was blown and that on the right the land was flooded. It would be the job of these two forward companies to give us covering fire as we attacked.

Hearts pounding and tummies aflutter we commenced advancing towards the rim of the wood and the waiting enemy, fixing bayonets as we went, cocking the weapons and pushing off the safety catches. Our armour, revving heavily in the thick sand and accompanied by the Observation Officer's artillery Weasel, was moving beside and ahead of us. As the fascine-carrying tanks lurched clear of the trees and into enemy view, the roar of their engines was overshadowed by a series of ear-splitting crashes from either two or three 88mm German anti-tank guns. As tongues of flame and darkly coiling smoke licked and billowed up from the stricken leading tanks, those high-velocity solid shots that had missed, scythed back with hideous crashing echoes deep in the woods to our rear, toppling and smashing the trees in their paths. At the same moment, to complete the dismal prospect the Germans opened up heavily with cascading mortars and field artillery on the forward rim of the woods through which we were crouching and dashing forward from cover to thinning cover towards what was beginning to look like a singularly unsavoury form of mass suicide. I could already feel my clothes were wet with my sweating, tense exertions and the empty feeling at the pit of one's stomach, which had seemed so insistent at the start line, was becoming freed by the excitement despite the prospect. The seemingly inevitable shambles that all battles appear to be had commenced.

I was moving with my Pln HQ on the track rim with about 30 yards to go to the edge of the wood. The head of this track was now luridly lit with towering sheets of petrol-, oil- and rubber-fed flame, darkening the surroundings with the smoke-pall: a heart tearing sight in its implications. The artillery Weasel was blazing furiously about 20 feet away, with ammunition starting to cook off inside. A smoking figure, we supposed the driver, tumbled out of this furnace and staggered to collapse in some bushes. It was not clear whether the rest of the crews of these vehicles had got out, but the crash of the shells cooking off inside the tanks told it was too late anyway. To add to the worries of the forward platoon, whose every effort to advance clear of the wood was driven back by intense machine gun fire and sniping, they and we waiting our turn now realised we would have to forfeit the support of the tanks both in their covering fire and in their bridging the ditch. This inferno of explosion, smoke and flame and the singing pelt of metal in the air induced the commander of the remaining unhit tank beside the Weasel to assess the odds as too heavy. He crashed noisily into reverse and churned frantically back to get out of sight of the German guns, flinging sand over us from his spinning tracks while two of my Jocks jumped clear as the hot-fumed monster ripped past scraping the bank and trees. Everything was happening at once in a noise only outrivalled by the confusion and smoke. Here and there Tommy Gray's men crouched ahead of us for bullet protection against the trees, peering towards the enemy seemingly uncertain as to what to do next. Then I saw Tommy himself, part of his left foot blown off by an 88 shell and being carried back to the RAP between two stretcher bearers. I was very sorry to see him go and realised his days with us were over. (Amazingly, after the war Tommy again played first-class rugby for Scotland, the empty part of his left boot stuffed with cotton-wool and sorbo rubber to deaden the pain.)

The slight whisper of a batch of descending 5cm mortar bombs, and a blast of explosion and twang of shrapnel beside me, obscured young Evans and Cupit for a moment in smoke. As it cleared I saw Cupit sprawling white faced, stunned, on the ground beside a hole the two had been scooping for protection. Evans lay on his back, his stomach ripped open and intestines spilt steaming in the cold about him. His left arm was missing at the shoulder, and his left leg off at the hip. He was still alive, but numb, and his eyes looked up queryingly though with recognition into mine as I knelt over him, to put a dressing on his leg stump to form a tourniquet, my mind sickened with the hopelessness of the sight, but yearning to help him more. Seeing the MO crossing the track, I called him over, but as I looked at Evans' eyes wildly staring, they fixed. He had got a direct hit, setting off his own load of small mortar bombs. This was their first action, and Cupit, looking sick, frightened and puzzled, started digging again beside the still form of his friend, spurred on by further bombs. Hepburn crouched, holding his face because of a small cut.

The most fiendish series of crashes, and splintering of wood showed the 88mm guns were still after the two intact tanks reversing down the track, and the German mortars and artillery were steadily pounding backwards and forwards searching for us in the trees. To my astonishment I spied Pip amid all, this strolling about in leisurely fashion with his walking stick, chatting with the chaps, for which I raised my tin hat to him. The attack had been 'temporarily called off', and to consolidate the advance so far, everyone was digging in fast to get below the level of the crack and hum of bullets and shrapnel spraying through the trees. Frank Coutts was just passing when the explosions of heavy mortars straddled our positions, and we both dived into my hole which somehow held us both. While it lasted Frank gave me what news he could, then as he climbed out he covered up Evans' body with a gas cape on his way to Smyg.

The crackle of passing bullets whenever anyone attempted to cross the track alongside us told that this was dominated by a concealed set of snipers ahead. It was now established that the Germans, well dug in on the high scrubland, overlooked and dominated our position with heavy fire power, and in the fortified Kasteel Blijenbeek, a prepared area of their choosing, meant to stand and fight it out. Already two attacks on the Kasteel by C Company had been repulsed with casualties. They alone lost more than forty men during the day. In the first attack a Platoon under Sgt Welsh using the mist as camouflage crossed a bridge, the only way in to the courtyard of the Kasteel, just as it was becoming light. The enemy did not show a sign of their presence until half the Platoon were inside, at which the main doors swung back and the Jerries opened fire with all they had at 10 yards range, hitting seven men, three fatally. With amazing presence of mind, and good fortune Sgt Welsh managed to withdraw the others swiftly into the mist, leaving the wounded. A short while later he volunteered to try to contact A Company on the right, but in the attempt was fatally wounded by a sniper who shot him in the head. Though he was evacuated to the UK within about 24 hours, he died soon afterwards.

Meanwhile, Capt Hill MC, the MO, together with Pte McBeth MM insisted on going to the Kasteel to attend to the wounded. At a later period arms were issued to the Doc as personal protection as the enemy showed so little respect for the red-cross flag, but on this occasion they were unarmed but for flags and arm bands, and in spite of being fired on, disappeared into the Kasteel. After half an hour, he strolled back with McBeth, bringing a wounded chap with them. He said while he lit his pipe, that he had had an interesting talk with the German MO while there.

It eventually took heavy artillery fire, rocket-firing Typhoons, then medium bombers to subdue the Kasteel Blijenbeek, whose sinister, disintegrating form began to take on legendary qualities as time wore on in the sombre Broederbosch woods.

'Wee Mac', Lt McColl of A Company, found himself pinned

Captain Peter White is in the centre row, second from left. In the pages that follow, words in quotation marks are White's own.

'Walcheren attack, heading for Uncle Beach, Flushing.' The Jocks mounted an assault on Flushing on 1 November 1944.

'Uncle Beach revisited three and a half years after our attack, [photograph] taken on the spot where our dead were temporarily buried. There were snipers in the cranes behind.'

Main picture: White found this marked German map in a strong point in Vlissingen (Flushing) and added the photographs and his own annotations. White's inset, top: Uncle Beach seen on the way over from Breskens. The cranes were occupied by snipers. White's inset, bottom: A German radar and wrecked British landing craft at Westkapelle.

White's copy of a mural from Vught barracks. 'These SS barracks struck us as delightful in their appearance and surroundings . . . only marred by harsh war-theme mural paintings. We had not, however, yet seen the whole camp. Vught we soon found included a notorious concentration camp.' Translated, the German script 'Wenn alle untreu werden . . .' means 'When (or If) everyone becomes disloyal . . .'. This probably refers to the SS motto 'Mein Ehre heisst Treue', which means 'My honour is loyalty'. Interpreted, this could mean that when all others have betrayed the cause of the Third Reich, only the SS could be relied upon to remain loyal.

'Cooking compo breakfast, Tripsrath Woods, Christmas 1944.'

'Waldfeucht, Operation "Blackcock", 1945. Sherman tank on right knocked out by the Tiger tank (left) & burnt. Tiger was then knocked out by 5th Bn KOSB A/tk guns. (Capt Hunter got MC).'

Counter attack by TIGER TANKS (10 tons Platzwaldfeucht. Spring '44)
STICK GRENADE

The 2 SPdr shell that went through the wall, a we lay.
myself, etc. behind x at x

a later light shot on the road wiped out some German infantry here

Counter-attack by Tiger tanks at Waldfeucht, 1945. 'We dashed back to the small alley which let at right angles on to the main road down which the Tiger would come and dropped into the gutter. The three of us lay side by side, McKenzie in the centre with the projector and Brown his no. 2, with spare bombs to reload on his other side. Our hearts were pounding furiously.'

Similar Arch the other side of the town in which the Tiger lodged.

Platoon HQ. in Apartment 70 ←

(Where we found the dead school master)

Some of my chaps dug in ↓

School ↗

"WALDFEUCHT S.E. GATE. Smoke rising out of the ruins the morning after

'Waldfeucht south-east gate, smoke rising from the ruins on the morning after the attack.'

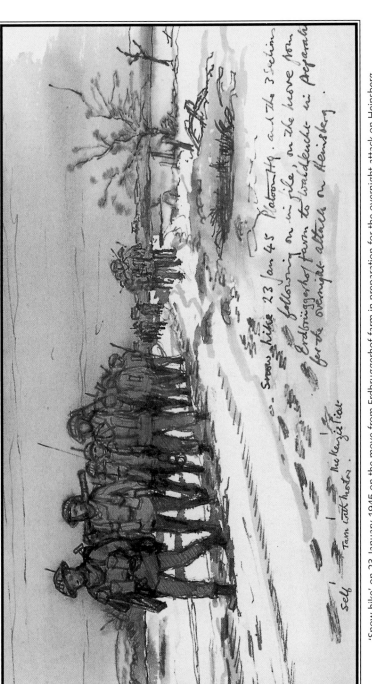

'Snow hike' on 23 January 1945 on the move from Erdbruggerhof farm in preparation for the overnight attack on Heinsberg.

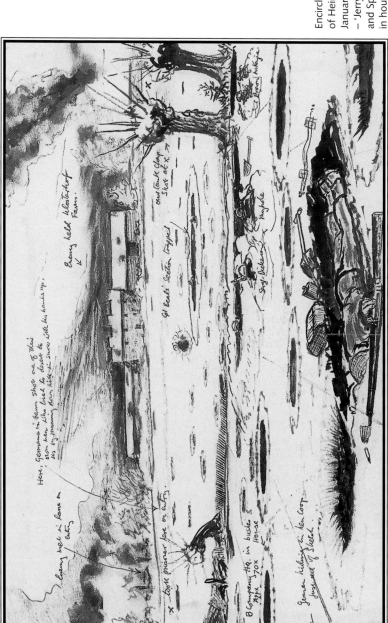

Encirclement of Heinsburg, January 1945 – 'Jerry OP and Spandaus in house'.

'Typhoon firing rockets at Germans in Kasteel Bleijembeek, sketched from my slit trench as the Typhoons were still at it.'

'Morning cuppa. Platoon HQ in Afferden Woods.'

Position dug for the artillery Forward Observation Officer on the rim of a wood between the Maas and the Rhine.

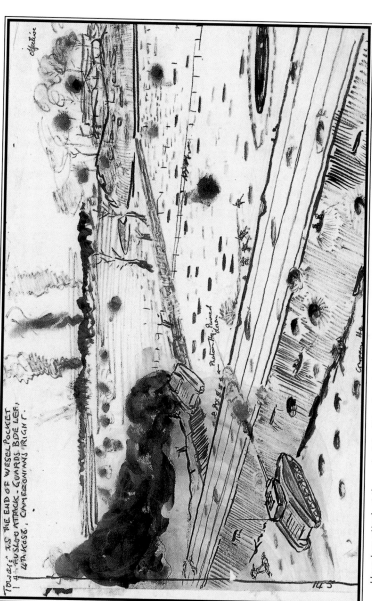

Haus Loo attack at the end of the Wesel Pocket with a guards brigade on the left, the 4th KOSB in the centre and the Cameronians on the right.

Pip's Position
2nd Section of Bridge
spit of land
Pebble & Sand bottom
Pip taking his platoon over 'our' Rhine bridge with the
few vehicles, to protect the far side while the
it and adjust the cables.
LMG. Pits, & Bofors guns at
each end.
'88' Shells landing about 500 to 800x

Crossing the Rhine.

70x Uniform → My Platoon HQ

Wesel →

← Strong current at fast walking Pace ←

B Company HQ

SUSSEX BRIDGE BUILT

Unit Signs →

Temporary B Coy HQ in Small Brick house under the tree ↑

CROSSING THE RHINE

'Company HQ. Cook Eckie Douglas getting ready for the expected German counter-barrage, his goats looking on.'

'Breakfast after the Rhine crossing.'

right under the noses of the enemy when daylight came, and as the day wore on, he was unable to evacuate the increasing casualties due to the Germans shooting up the stretcher bearers. When at last dusk came and he returned to Coy HQ, little more than the metalwork was left to his rifle which he produced saying, 'Look what the b***s have done to my rifle – but it still shoots!'

Meanwhile, as it was impossible under the circumstances to press the attack in its present form, there was the inevitable uncomfortable delay while hurried 'O' Groups were held at a higher level, and we crouched waiting. There was no roofing to our foxholes and the shrapnel was a menace, cascading down in a hail of steel when each bomb or shell exploded on touching the trees overhead. Young Smith, my batman, and the other new chaps, though tense, drawn and frightened, were standing the first loss well.

As time went on the tracks splitting the wood were becoming increasingly difficult to cross due to accurate sniping. Lt 'Jock' Beattie trying to cross one fast, tripped and fell, rolling into a tank rut and was accompanied by pursuing bullets. There he was stuck for a long while. He confessed to me later that while trapped there he had overcome with difficulty the idea of holding up an arm or leg to get an easy 'Blighty wound'.

Smyg, back from his 'Orders' Group at Battalion HQ in the next block of woods behind us, revealed that we were all, starting with my Platoon, to dig in over the track; however, I was to cross with him first to carry out a recce for the new Company positions south-west through the wood towards the village of Rempeld.

We both paused at the edge of the track before showing ourselves, to try to sense the rhythm of the snipers' activities, then with that same odd feeling of excitement experienced as a child in evading the haphazard blows of a pillow in 'Blind-man's buff', we both dashed for cover on the far side. The crackle of bullets into the bushes behind us confirmed we had been wise in our caution. A couple of hours later Capt David Colville, trying to get back to report to Battalion HQ, was fatally shot through the head and his sergeant was wounded when they chose the wrong moment for the same crossing; a very sad loss to the Battalion (of Colville's Steel family).

Once over, we both moved forward very carefully in case any enemy were still dug in there as we were moving on the extreme right flank of the Battalion area, with a gap between ourselves and the Recce Regt. As we moved we could hear the mortar bombs were pasting Bn HQ a bit back towards the track junction. We heard later that one of the Alsatian war dogs there had gone quite bomb happy, cowering whimpering in a hole and refusing to come out.

We quickly fixed rough layouts in our minds for the Platoon areas and Coy HQ, and were making our way back when we both paused in astonishment to listen, not quite trusting our ears that we were hearing correctly. About 50 yards ahead of us the wood finished on a road that ran along its rim, beyond which lay A Company pinned in full view of the enemy. Along this road from the right we could hear the sounds of an approaching convoy of 3-ton trucks which we knew from their distinctive revving whine were ours.

Whoever they were, they obviously did not realise they were placidly wandering right across the front line lengthwise, and in excellent view of at least two 88mm anti-tank guns and all that the enemy possessed in the way of small arms. That they had got as far as this from Afferden village and through Rempeld village unscathed seemed to be only due to the fact that the enemy must have been even more staggered at the sight than we were.

As Smyg and I crawled forward to peer down from a ridge of high ground in the wood to make out what was going on we heard voices of shouted warning from A Company.

The trucks, five 3-tonners, must either not have heard or not have understood for the drivers continued steadily on in convoy towards the smashed Weasel and burned-out tanks. As the vehicles drew level with us down a slight slope through the trees, the air overhead and in the trees about us crashed deafeningly to the bark of an 88mm gun's missiles and the numerous crackles of small-arms fire. Smyg and I dropped to the sandy pine-carpeted earth and crawled frantically backwards as fast as we could down the reverse slope to get out of line of the pelting hail of metal which cut ricocheting through the trees with an appalling, echoing racket. One by one the trucks crunched to a stop with engines still running. The drivers piled out and fled back through the wood past us to the right, crouching and tripping in their desperation to get clear, running like chased rabbits. Within seconds the first three trucks, then the other two, were burning furiously. The reason for their hurried retreat, we soon realised, was not just to get clear of the shooting. Frank had just joined us to see what was afoot when a series of indescribably devastating explosions occurred, each blast being followed by towering 60- to 100-foot sheets of flame and reddish-black smoke leaping and coiling high above the tree-tops. At each fresh explosion – and there seemed no end to them – the flames towered to greater heights. Pieces of the trucks, axles, wheels and bits of engines of all sizes buzzed and sizzled through the air at tremendous speed, then clattered and thudded heavily into the trees over a wide area. The three of us rushed for some cover more substantial than a tin hat and scrambled panting and puzzled into a German dugout. We could not think what it was the trucks contained to produce so vast and sustained a display of flame and explosion which continued for over half an hour. The answer was supplied later by a sheepish driver, almost unnerved by his experience, who stated that the trucks had been loaded with several tons of 5.5-inch shells and many hundreds of gallons of petrol and oil in jerrycans. These numerous containers instead of all exploding in one go, had cooked off steadily in batches in the increasing heat. We later heard that A Company had nearly been 'cooked' as their wet clothes steamed dry some yards distant. These trucks should have stopped far to the rear, but a military policeman had wrongly directed them. When the worst of the explosions and spinning debris had spent its fury, we scuttled back to the Company to bring them over the track to dig in. The double traversing of the track was accomplished in safety despite the still active snipers who were now also using a machine gun in short bursts.

Seeing our movements the enemy had obviously passed back information on our new positions to his heavier weapons. As we spread out through the pine woods in section groups to dig in, our self-congratulation at having cheated the snipers was cut short by the depressing whoosh-whoosh of ascending Moaning Minnie rocket projectiles in the distance. These, together with heavy mortars and later long-range artillery fire from the Siegfried guns to our south-east, increased, pounding dolefully backwards and forwards all about us in the woods as the day dragged by. The trees seemed to magnify the noise and echo of each missile's explosion. My Platoon, with positions laid out to cover all approaches, had just commenced digging in when the enemy, evidently hearing or seeing us through the trees from his hill, gave us as a Company all he had with his mortars. Several of us dived for cover into one of the few holes then available. Ironically, this was an old enemy mortar pit dug near the crest of our Platoon hill in a clearing. Being on the highest spot in that tract of wood was unfortunate. Jerry seemed to realise this would be our choice and the most intense concentrations of bombs blossomed everywhere around us for the duration of several minutes. About five mortars were firing by the sound of it. We could hear and count the faint tell-tale plopping of discharge from the enemy positions in any intervals when no bombs were bursting round the rim of the little hole where we sprawled in a tangled heap face down in the sand. It was a very shallow hole and in an attempt to keep below the level of the shrapnel which criss-crossed the air as thickly as swarming bees just above, we tried to wriggle our bodies deeper into the sand.

The worst of a mortar is its unexpectedness and vertical descent. Those bombs that touched surrounding treetops burst downwards in a hail of steel. It seemed merely a matter of time before a bomb came straight in. Several shuddered the sides of the pit, throwing sand over our backs, into our ears and down our necks. Young Pte Cutter, who was really quite unsuitable for such a pastime, gave way completely each time we listened with fascination to the plopping of the bombs' ascent from the enemy hill and lay quivering during the tantalizingly long wait for the whisper of their descent which sounded for a moment before our surroundings erupted to shattering crashes painful to the ear. As each climax came, the whimpering misery of Pte Cutter broke out in an uncontrollable stream of verbal pleading. He recovered enough in between to murmur 'I'm sorry, Sir' as he lay quivering beside me. Our hearts were going like ticking-over motorcycle engines. One's feelings at these times when apparently closest to a quick but foreseen end in which one could keep track of each sound and visualise the moves made by the enemy mortar crews in the process, seemed to clear one's mind to an intense aliveness and awareness of life. Thoughts raced as though boosted with a supercharger. The knowledge that at any instant this keen appreciation of life – the scent of roots rotting in the damp earth, the sight of C's tense ashen face alongside mine as we watched the sand trickling from the pit side loosed by each concussion and listened to the sigh of the wind in the pine-tops – that this thread and one's thought with it could be suddenly blasted into violent oblivion, seemed to hold a quality of dreamlike unreality about it more persistent even than the awful material evidence the explosives all too often produced. I felt a wealth of sympathy for Pte Cutter, but dared not show it for I felt he would just collapse the more. He had so lost control of himself by the time a pause arrived long enough for us to scamper out and continue digging that I told him to stop where he was until he had collected his wits. He was in such a state his condition might have put ideas into the heads of others. He grovelled in the sand moaning 'Oh God! Oh God, when will it stop . . . Sir . . . I, sorry . . . God! Oh stop it.' No one mocked him or made fun. We had all tasted too vividly of the ordeal ourselves to feel anything but great compassion.

It was fortunate the earth was so soft. It not only helped absorb the explosions and shrapnel, but also helped speed our digging in. As another batch of bombs plopped off, my Jocks sunk visibly out of sight in a fury of flying shovels and sand and obscene language until there was a scoop deep enough to drop into for shelter until the next pause. It was essential in a wood to provide a slit trench with some sort of roofing stout enough to withstand at least the smaller pieces of shrapnel from above, at the same time leaving one end open as a fire position for the two men who usually shared a trench. Quite a few casualties were needlessly suffered before this lesson was driven home.

About 200 yards behind us in the woods were some typical German dugouts constructed of interlocking heavy logs piled over with earth and the inside floored with straw. We made use of these portable materials once it became clear we might be stuck in these positions for some time. We also felled and cut small trees up into short lengths as roofing and stuffed a nest of straw into one end of each hole as insulation against the damp earth and the cold. During the afternoon while we were stripping materials from the Jerry dugouts, the enemy suddenly put down a short fierce artillery 'stonk' onto us so we took welcome cover in the dugouts he had so massively provided. As usual they were well furnished with stoves, easy chairs, tables and bedding looted from the Dutch. One bunker had been used as a stable. I was thankful Jerry had given us such solid shelter; we got some close hits.

In making our way back to the Platoon positions, we passed a group of shallow shell holes caused by the last batch to come over. Two of these had been duds, and I was interested to see that one could track the direction of the guns, and angle of descent of the shells, by the path each had cut and nicked in descending through the thick plantation of slender conifers to vanish in an oblong gash in the sand.

The thaw had set in, and though it was still very cold, the snow had vanished. Occasionally there were quite long periods of rather eerie silence but for distant rumblings, the drip of moisture off the trees and faint sounds of enemy vehicles or faraway shouts. Several times the Jocks had to be chased for making an awful din, shouting at each other or clattering shovels in these silences, with the result that nearly always the enemy would hear them and send five or ten bombs in the direction of the noise. Several chaps in 11 and 12 Platoons were killed this way during the evening.

Still there was no news of the renewal of our attack, and as the afternoon wore on our guns, which up till then had just been keeping themselves warm with the odd salvo, gradually built up a most concentrated and sustained barrage which we were only once again to hear equalled, so it seemed to me, at the Rhine crossing. So many guns were firing that the individual noise of each shot and explosion on arrival, combined with the incessant shriek of passing shells like droves of giant wildfowl in flight, made it impossible to identify any individual sound except short shells or enemy shells landing nearby. We almost felt sorry for the Germans as we listened to the appalling noise, crashing and echoing in a mind-vibrating continuous drumming of explosion, like a brace of heavy farm carts rumbling over cobblestones. This sound in its very penetrating persistence began to get on our nerves a bit as it continued almost without respite all the afternoon, overnight and part of the next day, and at odd intervals thereafter.

The 25-pounders firing low overhead made a thunderous crack, followed by an empty rolling sound as the air flowed back to fill the space thrust by the ascending shell. With all this noise we could get no warning when to drop flat for Jerry shells until it was too late.

Pip's platoon had been getting a very thin time during the afternoon and evening, and he himself had been evacuated with blood poisoning, of all things, again leaving me the only subaltern in the company, with Frank and Smyg at Coy HQ. Another officer, Ken Wilson, had also been evacuated with 'shell-shock', this was probably largely just lack of sleep, which as dusk approached once again began to be felt by us all. In the last 60 hours we had had 2 hours attempted sleep before crossing the Maas, then several hours freezing crouched in a hole on the approach march through the woods. The coming night did not seem too promising from the point of view of sleep either, though it was certainly beginning to look as though we were not due for any immediate continuation of the attack.

Our main worry now was to organise things for the night in case of a patrol or counter-attack, so I set off to Company HQ, taking cover for a while from some mortaring on the way. There was very little news when I arrived to crouch with Frank and Smyg in their dugout beside the radio operator, except that we were to improve the positions and hold the ground overnight. I was to get one section dug in forward on high ground as a listening post. A small patrol was to be sent out to see if Jerry had infiltrated back into the deserted part of the wood between ourselves and the Recce Regt on our right. A and C Companies were to remain forward in their old positions overnight and come back at dawn into reserve behind us in the wood.

The password for the night was challenge 'Morris' and answer 'Cowley', and there was to be a 100 per cent 'stand to' at dusk and dawn, with a 50 per cent 'stand to' overnight, two hours on and two off for the pairs of chaps in each hole. To back up A Company, Sgt Cowie's platoon would move forward for the night.

By the time I had got this news, my section commanders had collected their water and rations and a tot of rum to make up a bit for the lack of greatcoats, which were still back in B Echelon. None of us seemed to be particularly hungry, but I struggled through a cold tin of steak and kidney pudding and some tinned peaches to cover the missing meals of the day before, and also the combined breakfast, lunch, tea and supper of this day in arrears. I think we were all feeling too desperately tired to eat.

As we settled in for the night vigil, after 'stand down' at dusk, the chaps had all got their fox holes fairly well covered at one end following several hours' work in nipping out from cover between shelling and mortaring to cut down small trees with our two 'liberated' cross-cut saws taken from a farm. The shells, too, had by now saved us quite a bit of work in providing their own quota of felled trees.

I called over to see Pte Cutter, who was acting radio operator, to see how he had settled down. He was still very jumpy, but his thoughts were diverted a little by the irony, to him, of the BBC's news he could pick up very faintly on the 38 set. This had informed him that: 'Another quiet day has passed at the front.'

A German long-range gun which had been worrying us quite a bit during the afternoon, had now been joined by three more, together with the occasional whoop-whoop-whoop in an arc of sound, revealing the 'Moaning Minnie' rocket launchers were still intact. These, and clusters of mortar bombs at intervals, pounded our positions and stalked about with heavy tread in the wood all night, as though we were ants hidden in the ground under the churning heels of angry men. The rocket launchers seemed to be changing their positions after every salvo to avoid our artillery locating them. We heard after the battle that, in spite of our losses to mortars and machine guns, the enemy had had heavier casualties than ourselves as our guns had fired twelve shells to every one of theirs.

At intervals throughout the night Sgt Dickinson and I took turns in dragging our cold selves round the section positions to see all was well. We occupied different holes in case one got a direct hit in an attack or patrol. It was very difficult to see the positions in the dark among the trees and undergrowth. Creeping silently round them with an eye open for enemy patrols gave one the uncomfortable feeling a startled Jock on stag, just woken up from a furtive doze was quite likely to fire in panic before remembering to challenge. Lack of sleep made for jumpiness and carelessness. One could not dawdle going the rounds, as there were few intervals free from the crashing of mortars or shells.

In opening my biscuit ration, I was intrigued to find a little note pushed in by the packer reading 'If you are lonely, or feeling blue, write to Dorothy Charnock' with a Liverpool address enclosed. The Platoon were highly tickled with this, and never before had the biscuits been so popular as the Jocks sifted through them for further messages, but without success. This mental diversion from our surroundings provided new interest for the chaps, and with bright suggestions we had soon composed an interesting reply. In due course, and after much anticipation and speculation, the photograph requested of her arrived, was passed round for approval and several letters subsequently exchanged.

HALTED IN BROEDERBOSCH,
TYPHOON ATTACKS AND PATROLS

That was a restless, unsettled night with several false alarms of enemy patrolling to investigate and several bursts of jittery small arms firing by overtired chaps seeing or hearing things; so easily done in the circumstances, when tired eyes and taut senses convert a swaying bush or a snapping twig into the enemy.

After 'stand down', I propped my mess tin over three twigs and a pile of Hexamine tablets on the rim of my hole, feeling stiff, heavy eyed and thick headed, and cooked up some Spam and tea to eat with some biscuits for breakfast.

It was a crisp, cold morning and steam was soon wisping off the hot mess of the Compo tea mixture in which chips of Spam floated in the unrinsed mess-tin. Everyone once again looked worn, red eyed, greyish in the face with dirt and tiredness, and with quite a growth of beard. It was not much use attempting a shave or wash until we could get more than our precious pint or two a day of tea water. Our morning toilet was complete with a quick go on the toothbrush held in an icy hand, and a quick walk back a bit into the bushes hoping it would not coincide with yet another batch of projectiles from the enemy. How often one saw some desperate Jock diving for cover, tripping and trailing trousers half off.

In spite of the guns, a few birds gave an attempt at a dawn chorus to meet the first wintry rays of the sun. I thought how pleasant a scene it could have been in different circumstances; the crisp air, sunlight glinting on old dew-wet leaves stirring in a slight breeze which was dispersing the morning mist and carrying away the filmy breath from the muffled heads of a couple of my

Jocks poking out of the ground next to their weapons, the whole scene softly lit with a golden tracery of sunlight and shadow on the tree trunks and a carpet of pine needles in the white sand. The Germans, I thought, must have knocked off for breakfast.

The side of a ration box lay next to me. I had some chalks handy, so I took the opportunity of doing a sketch with which to decorate my hole. It took the form of an inn sign on which was pictured a pair of boots belonging to someone taking a header into a slit trench. Underneath was the legend: 'YE OLDE HEADER INN, Proprietor: I.B. WELL-UNDER'. This seemed to provide the Jocks with infinite mirth and the laughter helped put things in perspective again.

A little later the sound of aircraft engines overhead drew our eyes to follow the shapes of four of our Typhoons wheeling high over the Kasteel Blijenbeek like a group of vultures checking on their prey. One after the other they slipped swiftly sideways and down, the note of their engines roaring harshly up the scale with increasing volume. Already the first at full throttle seemed to be plummeting straight to destruction in the woods when a sudden formation of white wisps of smoke streaked forward of the plane, then a whoosh of discharge of these rockets reached us. At the same moment while the plane seemed almost into the trees, black streamers of smoke filmed back from the leading edge of the wings. We thought, with a catch in our throats, that he had been hit, as he vanished from sight among the tree tops. Instantly there was a tremendous blast of explosion. For an awful split second it seemed this was the sound of the plane gone straight into the earth, but instantly it reappeared, banking steeply, and soared fast out of small-arms range, making way for the next one shrieking down into the pall of reddish dust and smoke rising up from the Kasteel. The clatter of cannon fire explained the black smoke.

Several times they came again in sets of four to repeat their fascinating performance. They were a great morale raiser and a delight to the Jocks to watch, each one being greeted with a cheer echoing through the woods as it came and cries of unprintable approval. I took the opportunity of drawing my impression of the attack on a sheet of notepaper as the planes dived down. An army film unit took shots of these Typhoon attacks, during which several direct hits were scored, and an ammunition dump blown up. We later heard this had been shown in British news reels.

Despite this pasting, a recce patrol from D Company found the Germans still to be in occupation of the ruins, waiting for the attack by medium bombers which was eventually to knock them out, but not for a little while yet. Rumours had been reaching us that all along the front, and up to Calcar where the Canadians were, the fighting had been heavier and more bitter than expected, slowing up the programme of advance.

As another miserable day drew to its close, we were still in the same positions, with much the same activity by the guns and mortars of both sides. We had used the day to improve the positions, trying to sleep when the explosions were not too persistent, and in cleaning weapons or munching biscuits and the bitter, uninteresting chocolate from the ration box. We preferred the sweets usually. Towards last light I again made my way to Company HQ to be briefed for the night and collect rations, water, rum, the password, and make up any ammunition which had been spent during the day and previous night.

That evening Smyg asked me to take the Platoon forward after 'stand to' as soon as it was dark, and man the positions in the scrubby, sandy ground forward of our wood. At dusk we slunk from the trees and over the road past the few twisted bits of metal lying in a succession of shallow, smoke-blackened craters which marked all that was left of the five trucks.

It was a cold, clear, moonlit night, with a few scudding clouds, and occasional shelling by both sides. Our main object was to act as a listening post, to intercept patrols and to give early warning of any move the enemy might try in the dark. At midnight I was also to take out a small patrol to the German side of the clearing, and plot the extent of the flooding in the anti-tank ditch. We were to return and withdraw into the woods before first light.

At 2300 hours slight sounds behind us and the glinting of Smyg's spectacles announced his visit to see how we were getting on, and together we peered over the parapet towards the dark line of the hill occupied by the enemy, here a bit closer than on the left front opposite the Kasteel, and discussed landmarks ahead.

I was considerably worried by the brightness of the moonlight which gave good visibility up to about 75 yards. Beyond that one's eyes were strained to be sure of any but big or moving objects. In view of this I decided to take only two chaps with me to lessen the chances of detection and noise, for we knew that somewhere out there Jerry would also have a group of men listening and looking, who were quite probably between ourselves and the ditch we wanted to plot. L/Cpl Brown newly promoted, and I think the other was McKenzie, volunteered to join me.

Before leaving I held a section commanders 'O' Group to tell them what was afoot, and to arrange a password for our return. I handed the Platoon over to Sgt Dickinson in case we did not get back, and taking my revolver and two Stens with lots of ammunition, we set off. I decided not to clutter ourselves with grenades, as at our strength we wanted to avoid, rather than seek, trouble.

The ground ahead was about 500 yards of sandy soil planted with pine seedlings, then some rougher ground and pasture towards the silver streak where the flooded ditch was. Behind that rose the dark, clear shape of the hill and woods held by the enemy.

Waiting for a cloud to cover the bright moonlight, we crept one after the other over the parapet and down a slight slope towards scattered, stunted young seedlings, crouching as we went to present as small an object against the sky as possible to anyone on the ground ahead. Every few yards I paused, and the other two shunted to a halt behind me. In the silence we peered, listening intently, each with an arc to cover. I looked ahead and Brown to the left, McKenzie to the right.

After about 50 yards, during which our every move in the intense silence seemed to be making an appalling noise of crunching dry grass and being brilliantly lit by the moon, I decided we had better resort to crawling forward, and only then when in shadow. Very soon, in spite of the cold, keen night breeze, we were sweating with our exertions and the extreme tension of our taut senses analysing each dark shape ahead and each odd sound that at intervals broke the silvery, ghostly silence. We were now about 350 yards forward of the main Company positions, and about mid-way between our lines and the enemy. Looking back, our forward positions had already quite merged into the indistinct paleness of the grass and seedlings, rimmed with the dark line of our wood beyond.

In our pauses we could now hear occasional noises made by the enemy, a distant shout, probably well back in his rear areas, and intermittent hammering of what seemed to be a wooden post. The thickets and dry grass were getting denser as we painfully progressed, and the noise of crunching undergrowth and an occasional clink of metal, which we were unavoidably making, decided that from here on we would have to try to time our going any farther forward in swifter, shorter moves, whenever the occasional crash of artillery or mortars coincided with a cloud over the moon. From the clarity of the bank and line of trees looming darkly ahead it seemed certain that if the enemy forward night positions were approximately the same distance forward as ours, we were now well in range of his hearing and sight.

A bit more light had been added to the scene by some shells setting fire to a farm away on our left. Every now and then a shower of sparks and flame curled up adding a faint orange tint to the moonlight. A musical lonely clatter of tiles announced the collapse of the roof.

Our pauses were necessarily longer now, not only to let our breathing and bumping hearts quieten from the last exertion so that we might listen more intently, but also that I might check and analyse each shape ahead more carefully before going on. Quite apart from the possibility of running into his forward positions or a listening post, there was the likelihood of the enemy patrolling to keep alert to, on either side or even in the rear.

We were about 500 yards out, and in good view of our objective – the ditch – when strange scraping noises sounded loud and clear ahead, as though a trench were being silently dug about 20 yards off. We froze where we lay, checking and cocking our weapons as we strained our senses forward for clues on the exact direction and distance of the sounds. Beyond this sound, we could still hear posts being hammered – possibly wire being erected near the ditch. Further back came the sound of a truck revving in the woods, and faintly, distant German voices shouting to each other.

Telling Brown and Mac to cover me, I crawled painfully,

slowly forward on my own to investigate, carefully transferring the weight from each hand and knee gently in turn to cut noise. At intervals I signalled the other two to close the gap a bit. One being forward made less noise and also if anything happened, it gave a chance for Brown to report back as 'getaway man' while Mac gave covering fire.

For quite long periods, the sounds, now very much closer, had stopped, to restart, then stop again. Try as I might I could not locate the cause, or decide exactly how far off it was. My heart and breathing seemed to me to be making almost as much noise as the sound I was stalking, and I marvelled it had not itself been heard in the tenseness of the silence.

Suddenly, with a tingling spine, my eyes riveted on a round, head-like object moving in the shadow of a bush about 6 feet off amid newly scattered earth . . . not a German's head poking out of a trench, but of all things, a busy hedghog! He was happily at work on his home, perhaps disturbed from hibernation by the battle noises; I envied him his peace of mind, and sanity of purpose! It was amazing how loud his noises had sounded to our strained senses in the stillness, and no doubt the pauses were due to his having sensed some sounds we made in crawling. But for the enemy I think we would have laughed loud and long with the humour and relief of it. 'It's only a darned hedgehog!' I whispered back to the two others, and we continued a few more yards to the edge of the cover. From here I was pleased to find we could get a good look at the ditch and the extent of the flooding, the water shimmering silver except where it reflected the inky blackness of the wooded bank.

A faint glow of light on the dyke wall about 25 yards off suddenly stilled our whispers. A German having a sly smoke! Beyond him somewhere metal clinked. I wondered later if the extreme caution of our approach, due to the hedgehog, had saved us, for if a flare had gone up we were more or less certainly finished, which I realised would also be the case in all likelihood if we shot him.

Noticing the moon had moved a long way since we set out, I was astonished to find my watch showed it to be after 4 am and our patrol as well as the Platoon had to be back hidden in the woods before dawn. To get any closer, out of our cover, would certainly have put us in clear sight of the enemy, who also had a dark background, making it difficult to see where he was but for the momentary glow of the cigarette seen just the once.

Trusting the lenses of my binoculars did not glint in the moonlight, giving us away, I swung them along the line of the water again, trying to check the water against landmarks on the skyline. In places the reflection made the limits hard to define. Satisfied, I withdrew a bit, rejoining the others, then with infinite caution we crawled one at a time the first 75 yards or so, while the other two faced the enemy in turn.

As we neared our own lines again, we made our approach to within challenging range more and more openly without attempt at concealment, for as we had learned on an earlier patrol, this could be the most dangerous part of it if we were mistaken by a sleepy, frightened or just plain stupid Jock for the enemy. To be doubly sure I headed back to come in in front of the two Jocks who had wished us 'Good luck' on the way out.

We had got to within less than the length of a cricket pitch without a challenge. Puzzled, I gave the password myself, but still without a sound in reply. Quite loud repetition drew no response. Something seemed wrong, so I decided to reverse back a bit, and come in between two others to the right, beginning to wonder if a Jerry patrol had disposed of them silently in our absence. On coming in again the challenge was normal, and leaving Brown and Mac at Platoon HQ I made my way forward to the silent two, approaching them from behind.

Standing over their trench, all was silent, one figure slumped forward on the parapet, the other lying on the bottom of the hole. I pulled their weapons away before investigating further. I was still undecided as to what was wrong. Pte Griffiths, a small nervous chap of about nineteen, was the one slumped forwards who should have been on duty, while the other was supposed to be asleep. I shook him, still wondering, but now almost sure of what had happened. Griffiths jerked and staggered, as though stabbed in the back, standing on the chap below in the process. Possibly never have two sentries woken with such violent fright, and reached for weapons that were not there. The terror-stricken face and popping eyes of Griffiths printed clearly in my mind, like the photo of horror itself. Whimpering he looked up crying, 'Oh Christ . . . Oooooh help!'

In spite of the seriousness of this sleep, for which I suppose Griffiths and many others might have been shot in the First World War, it was not really so surprising; we had by now been on the go 95 hours, and few if any of us would have been fortunate enough to have totalled seven hours of odd attempts at sleep in that time. I had dropped off for a moment or two myself the night before as though heavily doped, although intending to keep very much awake. This was a difficult problem to overcome. What punishment can awe a chap whose occupation and future prospects, night and day, week in, week out, would from his perspective make a life sentence to hard labour seem heaven itself. The average chap seemed to respond best to being made to see he had left not only his own life open to a sticky end, but those of his friends, and their trust and respect too. This, perhaps backed with a few extra 'jobs' shortly afterwards, seemed to suffice and the same chap seldom gave trouble twice.

During the following day I took a section to dig a concealed position right on the very rim of the wood, giving a good view of the enemy frontage opposite. This was to provide cover for the FOO, or Forward (Artillery) Observation Officer, and his assistant. From there he kept watch all day and sometimes in the evening for signs of enemy movement so that he could direct the guns onto it via his 18 set radio and later a field telephone. It took a long time to dig and camouflage these positions, as we had been ordered to do it in daylight. To start with the chaps dug lying on their sides till the hole was deep enough to stand in. We supplied the FOO with a section of Jocks dug in, covering him from behind.

This was our third day in the woods, and things were for the most part slightly quieter, though shells, mortars and 'Minnies' were still coming over from time to time, with the usual far heavier reply from our weapons. Frank Coutts and I, carrying a rifle and pistol apiece, took the opportunity of this lull to make a recce patrol to the south-west corner of our wood, hitherto not visited by us, to see what lay there.

On our first evening when the attack bogged down, I had taken a quick patrol in the half light bordering the road in the rim of the wood but had not had occasion to investigate in the wood to any depth. We passed the old German positions from which we had taken materials and which were now much more battered by enemy shells, then down the slope through thinning trees beyond. In the distance we spotted more old enemy positions and spread apart to approach them carefully. This turned out to be a large underground, log-lined and earth-covered room, evidently used as a shellproof stable for Jerry horses. Not far beyond the wood ended beside a heather-clad, sandy ridge which we knew was held by the Recce Regt, though we could see no sign of them.

It was quite a treat, wandering through the trees on our way back, to relax my mind and try to recapture peacetime memories of woods. Perhaps it was a natural swing of the pendulum away from all the violence of recent days that the rare whistle of a few birds still about should give us so much pleasure. To look at the wood as a wood and not a military obstacle, and to note the purpling buds of approaching spring instead of the tactical value of the ground's undulation was a refreshing change. How upside down our values had become, I thought, that so much of our listening should be concentrated on the song of metal and death through the air, in preference to the singing of birds, or the wind in the treetops. All too soon this train of thought and the enjoyment of the stroll was terminated with the arrival of another squadron of Typhoons to scream down their loads of destruction, this time including some 500-pound bombs, onto the remains of the Kasteel.

That evening, on my visit to Company HQ Smyg asked me to take a contact patrol out to two positions of the Recce Regt on our right, to see that all was well in the gap in the front between our two units. We were to set out at 1 am.

When at last the time to depart came, I collected six men, a Bren gun, two Sten guns and three riflemen from the rear section, and handed the Platoon over to Sgt Dickinson. We followed the phone lines as far as Bn HQ to keep direction in the gloom of the trees, before turning westwards. Once out of the wood, it was quiet, cold and the air was crisply clear, with visibility about 70 yards. A lovely night. One could almost have forgotten the war were it not for the need to keep direction and be constantly alive to sight or sound of anything unusual. Travelling in single file, well spaced out, halting every 50 yards or so to look and listen about us, the only sound was the shuffle of soft footsteps behind me in the sand and short heather, and occasional distant explosions.

The brilliant disc of the moon hung haloed in the immensity and silence of the sky, bathing the scrubland about us in a soft silver, blue-shadowed luminosity. Never before had there seemed so many stars above. We were glad to be out of the sombre darkness of the woods at night.

By keeping to low ground and stooping at intervals it was easy to check surrounding objects against the sky, which would also be an advantage to us if we chanced into an enemy patrol. After several hundred yards, following verbal directions over ground new to us we should have been approaching the first Recce position. All our attention was now on listening intently for the challenge, possibly softly given, by the Recce chaps whom we sincerely hoped had been notified of our visit.

Suddenly, 'Halt, who goes there?' stopped us from a dark gash in the bank on our left. 'Friend'. 'Advance friend and give the password!' After a short chat, we moved on to find the next position, a small isolated house on the heather-clumped sandhills.

We got right up to this place without a challenge, so to be sure all was well L/Cpl Duncan and I went forward to investigate, covered by the rest of the patrol. The place seemed silent, quite deserted. We stood several seconds outside before noticing a faint chink of light glowing from under a blanket curtaining the doorway. A peep in disclosed the Recce chaps sprawled asleep in the candlelight of a small squalid room. The two chaps on duty were, we found, momentarily round the far side of the house. Had we been an enemy patrol we could have wiped out the lot. I gave the NCO in charge of the section a shake up in his ideas before starting on the return trip.

About two hours after the commencement of the patrol, we trudged back through Battalion HQ positions to reach our own, when to my surprise we were challenged from the trees by two chaps of my Platoon. As we neared them, I was more surprised to see standing between them a dark, pale-faced, very young,

German officer in jackboots, forage cap and leather jacket, and also a German private soldier. Parry's cheery voice cried: 'Huloo Surr, we've took twa b*** Jerries for ye!'

Though we had had no incidents to report from our patrol, in our absence the Platoon had been active in capturing an opposing patrol. Before being captured, these two had 'bumped' two of the Platoon section positions. On the first occasion the challenge had been given at too great a range, and in trying to escape the Germans had been seen by Pte McLaughlin peering from his Bren pit in another section as they flitted across a sandy ride in the gloom of the trees. He quickly informed Sgt Dickinson, who took out a section fast and cut them off before they reached the open, capturing them without resistance.

The German officer carried a map with his proposed route marked on it, which covered a circuit of the entire Battalion positions. They were to have estimated our strength, pinpointed our positions as far as possible and have found out, if they could do so, what trouble was likely to be expected from our sector in the near future. Quite a lot of useful information was secured from this officer, who turned out to be the native of a town the CO had visited for winter sports before the war.

Another day or two of this life on the forward slope passed with little incident other than the unwelcome arrival of some shells, far too close for comfort, before the HLI arrived to take over from us. We moved 30 yards behind them into the wood to back them up. This involved digging some more tree-covered slit trenches for the short duration of our stay. While we were there the Typhoons were once more hard at it trying to crack still further what was left of the Kasteel. I was sorry to hear that, among further casualties, Lt Kendra had been hit in the head the previous day, 22 February.

Greatcoats had at last come to comfort us a bit in a cold drizzle which had joined the enemy in making our positions uncomfortable. I think Jerry must have got wind of troop movements in the wood, for he pasted us heavily for a while with his mortars and artillery during the change over, and again a couple of days later when we moved out to trudge about 2 miles north into the wood to be held in Brigade reserve. This was a very slow, tiring walk, mostly in deep soft sand, for the first part following a wandering white mine tape for direction through the trees with mortars dropping about. However we were pleased to feel we might be due for a short rest and also to note the mortars being outranged.

Our destination turned out to be a dank, dripping block of woods spattered with rough earth trenches. We thankfully slung off the weight of our wet equipment, hung it on the trees as coat pegs and set about improving the miserable waterlogged holes which were to be our homes for an unknown period. A haystack was located in a field about a mile off, and large mounds of this were seen staggering in a trail of straw through the dark misty pinewoods, to end up as insulation against water and cold on the floor of our holes. Mine was quite cosy, with plenty of straw, and electric light from a torch bulb and an old radio battery. Sgt. Dickinson shared my luxury.

My Platoon was still under strength by a few men, and to make this up a really extraordinary chap was transferred to me from the anti-tank Platoon. At his own request he wanted to join a rifle company 'to get a bit more excitement'. Jones, already wounded once and an ex-paratrooper, was a tall keen-faced chap of great personality, and was later known in the Company as the 'One man army'. He had the closest approach to complete immunity from fear or nerves that I had so far met. He was as keen as mustard, and well worth watching at work either in cleaning his weapon, the Bren, stripped and polished down to the last item far in advance of the normal cleaning standards, or in preparing any scheme or thing needed to accelerate the despatch of the enemy. 'Any B*** Jerries I can go out and clean up Sir?' he asked, and meant it keenly. The rest of the Platoon looked on in amazement at the appetite, efficiency and system shown in his soldiering. Immediately on his arrival, he proceeded to organise the rest of his section as his unofficial batmen, and soon had a cosy straw-lined igloo rigged up with sticks, and a blanket he had scrounged from somewhere – he scorned the rest of us mortals dug into the ground. His use of those round him was done so naturally as to leave his 'batmen' ignorant of his influence.

Later I was to become familiar with his daily requests, asking if there was some patrol he could go out on, or some position or house to 'clean up', that is, rid of the enemy. He scorned a tin hat, wore a paratroop jerkin instead of a windproof blouse and gradually, until he was killed, became more and more unorthodox in the things he wore. In his general carry on Jones was as good as a music hall turn in our midst even at the most depressing times. For the latter reason alone I found his eccentricity was well worth tolerating. Smyg's summing up was: 'It seems he's a bit "fey".'

Though quite a few shells could be heard dropping with a lonely echoing crash in the woods, thus making the silence seem even more marked and everything more desolate than before, Jerry did not apparently have enough range quite to reach us, so we could relax properly and listen to them uselessly splintering the next wooded rectangle.

To celebrate Sunday, Col Melville called a Battalion parade for a Church service – the first time we had all been together in one group since the service in Kleit following the Walcheren Island attack. After the service he made use of the gathering to give us a talk on recent events, possible future events, and the 'bogeys' then much discussed and in need of some check: 'Battle exhaustion', 'Bomb Happiness' and desertion. In recent weeks, the number of cases answering to these descriptions had increased noticeably. The great problem being, he said, to tell the difference between the genuine cases and the 'phony' cases. We also discussed how this trouble might be avoided. More cheerfully, he then wound up in announcing a list of recent awards to members of the Battalion, which included the DCM for L/Cpl Leitch and his own DSO.

There were several new officers to chat with whom I had not met before and I had my only meeting with Lt Brown who was wounded in the next action. Some new men also arrived and the next morning as they sat in the sand enjoying the rare sun, going over the platoon weapons to see what they knew, I gave them a talk based on our experiences so far, which I would very much have valued myself coming new to action, in the hope that this would, at least for some, increase their chance of survival. Quite apart from trying to prevent their becoming needless casualties through not doing the right thing or not realising what was happening in certain circumstances on facing a live enemy and his weapons for the first time, there were many little tips we had learned through experience on how to look after ourselves in what comfort improvisation and scrounging could provide – tips on head cover, feeding in action, how best to preserve what warmth one could, and so on. Some of these chaps seemed to have a most hazy idea on such things as the priming of PIAT bombs, grenades, fuses, stripping automatic weapons, firing mortars, and one or two even weren't sure about how to deal with a rifle.

A ditch full of rainwater, which I discovered near my hole, provided me with an icy wash and shave, standing astride it, and an icy tooth clean. Then following in our turn, the Company marched back along the sandy tracks to the semi-civilisation of Gennep where a mobile bath unit had set up shop in a derelict building. Here, in an atmosphere of steam, Lifebuoy soap and swearing, we froze, soaped and spluttered in batches of pink, hopping nakedness, under a system of spraying and dribbling overhead pipes, to emerge at the far end glowing and fluffy headed in a change of clothes. It was sheer bliss to have had my boots off for the first time in eight days when the HLI took over from us, and now to feel the dryness and warmth of new underclothes and socks was a delight. After a reasonable sleep and a good feed we were new men.

Our 4-mile return march brought us back into the woods in better spirits, and feeling warmer than we had done for some time past. We had passed masses of vehicles of every type parked along the sandy rides, the air singing and cackling here and there in a signals truck or the radio of a tank or armoured car. I thoroughly enjoyed doing several sketches of the Jocks relaxing in the woods to send home.

With the arrival of the NAAFI rations, including the monthly bottle of gin or whisky for officers and sergeants, bolstered up with the rum ration, the woods echoed at night to haunting Border songs and merriment from gatherings held in various dugouts. Smyg held one of these parties by the light of a Tilley lamp in Company HQ's tarpaulin-covered, straw-lined hole, with Ally Ross, Jock Milne Home, Frank Coutts, Jock Beattie and the senior NCOs.

CONTACT LOST

One of our rare sights of the Brigadier, who paid a visit to Chris Melville, our CO, announced that something was afoot. Next day, I found myself detailed for another advance party. We boarded a small convoy of trucks, and made our way back through the woods towards Gennep, then at the main road, swung north-east towards Hommersum, a small deserted village just inside the German frontier 2 miles north of Broederbosch woods. It was a slow convoy on bad roads crumbling under heavy vehicles. The countryside, woods, houses and telephone poles were all smashed. How every wire on any poles that survived always managed to get shot away never failed to amaze me. It did not seem such a big target to get hit.

Before crossing the border we came on the wreckage of a Jeep which had blown up on a mine after pulling a few yards off the road into the stubble of a cornfield. Just next to it was a partly wrecked 3-tonner, half blocking the road. All that was left of the Jeep and driver were some widely scattered bits of metal round a shallow crater: just enough to recognise it had been a Jeep. There were part of the frame, a piece of tyre and steering wheel, the driver's foot in a boot, and a piece of the windscreen rim. All the rest seemed to have dissolved into shrapnel and dust. We had to pull a bit off the road to get past, hoping we did not hit another mine on the opposite verge.

Just then, as I was standing on the tailboard looking ahead to see what the hold up had been, my eye was attracted by a quick flash of orange flame and black smoke 600 yards up the road. As my eye focused on the smoke I saw a 3-ton truck rear up on its back wheels and drop down on its wheelless nose. It had driven onto another mine in a farmyard. As the bang reached our ears, distant figures ran up to the driver, who, as we entered the village, was lifted out of the cab, still alive, but with both legs off.

The place was lousy with mines on the verges and side tracks, and several more vehicles subsequently were lost. One could count on this same trouble with mines each time the Germans slowed our advance to a halt for a few days, or even hours.

Our job was to recce billets for the various companies in this small, almost totally wrecked place. It had started to rain quite heavily, and to reach the various farms and houses involved a great deal of walking about on tracks and small roads we knew were probably mined. We did this very gingerly, hoping there were no anti-personnel ones about. None of us, we supposed, was heavy enough to set off the anti-tank ones! Nevertheless, it gave one an odd feeling that perhaps the next step might see one translated into a puff of smoke drifting over the landscape. The church and churchyard had come in for some heavy shelling. About the ruins, umpteen craters were littered with broken tombstones, bones and coffin fragments, with scant respect for the occupants, who were tossed in all directions. A large vicarage-like house I picked for Company HQ had also been shelled a bit, exposing a hidden room walled in from part of another big room. I wondered if this had had an interesting history, with the Dutch frontier only 200 yards away. The smashed school, to judge from the straw-filled rooms, had recently been used as a billet for German troops. Another small house bore eloquent testimony to the speed with which the Germans had evacuated it. In the kitchen stood a table surrounded by tipped up chairs and abandoned German tin hats, bandoliers and other kit, while on the table were plates, knives, forks and partly consumed food and drink.

We on the advance party had just brewed up some tea and a few tins for lunch, when a despatch rider roared into the village with the news that the move was cancelled, and that we were to march back to the Battalion as fast as possible. To avoid a very long march round by road, we decided to cut cross country back to the woods. Two things rather worried us: first the possibility of more mines in this route, and secondly that we did not know where the nearest enemy were in this area or even if our proposed route would be clear.

As we squelched on the swampy tracks wandering over a flat landscape interspersed with drainage ditches and speckled with trees, farms and shell craters, we heartily cursed the 'organisation' (always a handy general term for pinning blame and our misfortune higher up among the 'Intellectuals'; the queer accented types the Jock liked to think dwelt and 'pattered' glibly about the 'Bigger Picture' at Brigade HQ and other levels beyond the range of gunfire).

We had brought all our kit with us, and this turned out to be a far more lengthy and tiring march than we had bargained for. Towards dusk we slunk along, perhaps a bit more furtively intent on cover as a blossoming series of black smudges, followed by the crump-crump of mortaring, drifted low over the cheerless, crater-blotched fields away on our left. Ours or theirs. We did not know, but this stimulated us sufficiently to divert a bit of attention from our cutting load of kit.

Long before we reached the anti-tank ditch separating us from the gloom of the wood we had been so pleased to think we had seen the last of, we could see the heads and shoulders of several figures dug in, watching us approach up the open track. We had taken it for granted they were our chaps and, as we neared them, sincerely hoped our judgment had been correct.

Fortunately they were our chaps, puzzled though they looked, for we found ourselves passing through positions sited and manned, pointing the way we had come. I have often wondered since, exactly where the enemy line was in this sector, for we had obviously wandered in from somewhere between the two forces! As the implications of the situation sunk in to one of our Jocks, he summed the situation up with their usual economy of words: 'Cor! Stone the crows!', and another, 'Struth'.

About 20 minutes more marching through deep sand in the darkening woods brought us to the old Battalion reserve positions. There we were surprised and fed up to find the Battalion had moved, and our march was not yet finished.

They were now holding a sector of the front to the south-east of the wood. The 'mess up', it appeared, had been caused by a CO in a unit to our right who, contrary to the Brigadier's intention, had committed his battalion to another attack in the woods. The

Brigade Commander, it seemed, had decided to attack again to the north of the woods in the Hommersum area, thus hoping to cut casualties after we had bogged down short of the Kasteel.

Lt Col Chris Melville was still there and held an 'O' Group in which we found our new positions were within a few yards of the road over the anti-tank ditch we had passed 20 minutes before. By now very tired, having had our kit on all day, and somewhat peeved with the war in general. We trudged back the way we had come to the edge of the wood. There I found Smyg taking over our new positions from the Welsh Guards. These consisted of a farm called Lakey, on the rim of the woods, with forward positions dug in to the edge of the anti-tank ditch. That the ditch and surrounding fields were flooded, seemed to indicate a possible reason for the odd name given the farm, the Jocks decided.

Meanwhile, on 27 February 1945 we heard rumours that the 6th HLI and B Coy of the 5th KOSB had attacked Groote Horst, one of the original objectives, though there was no definite indication, other than stray shells and mortars bursting away to our north-east, as to how far off the enemy line was ahead of us. By the expression 'line' we thought in terms of a strung out succession of strong points at various distances in farms, woods and odd buildings away in the darkness outside the wood.

The three Platoons in the Company drew lots for the forward positions, and also for manning the standing patrol 500 yards out during the hours of darkness. The remaining Platoon was to be held in reserve resting in the farm. I drew for the wall forward of Company HQ and Sgt Cowie for the standing patrol.

A cold wind was blowing from the direction of the enemy, and with it a slight drizzle, which promised another cheerless and sleepless night. It was quite dark as we groped our way forward and took over the positions from the tall figures of the Guards. Again, the directness of an 'aside' from a Jock reached my ears as the Guards departed; shorn of its Scots accent it was: 'Poor blighters, several more inches apiece to be hit!' and then another voice, 'Aye, and a bigger hole to dig too!'

A Jerry phone was laid on to my hole in the bank, which was handy in case of trouble. Being already soaked and fagged out was a bad start for the night which grew progressively colder and wetter as the hours dragged by.

I occupied the time in visiting the section positions at intervals, a tricky job crossing the flooded ditch on a 14-foot wobbly plank in the dark, or huddled under a sodden gas cape in the wet straw on the trench bottom.

From time to time I tested the line back to the sleepy operator in the farm, or answered a tinkle from Smyg or Frank. A door the Guards had torn out of the farm helped keep a little of the wind and rain off. I ate some chocolate and biscuits for supper, then was driven to dig again to try to generate warmth in my wet clothing. However, a stage of fatigue and cold seemed to have been reached at about 2.30 in the morning and onwards when I did not feel I had the energy left to either dig or even shiver to keep warm. I just sat curled up, with my nose breathing into the gas cape, keeping as still as possible to preserve this warm air in my clothes, peering out at the stray, unexplained flashes in the darkness and listening to the distant rumblings of guns.

At three in the morning Frank came out to pay a visit to ourselves and the standing patrol. They were relieved every two hours by another section squelching dimly past over the waterlogged fields. Frank stopped to chat a while. Looking towards a couple of fires glowing on the horizon, it seemed that the occasional salvo of our shells waffling their feathery way far overhead into the stillness was either pasting Jerry communications, or that the Germans were pulling back under cover of darkness following the success of the attack on Groote Horst. Very few shells were coming the wrong way. The rest of the Battalion was spread out to our south along the rim of the woods to the now ruined, smoking and at last 'Kaput' Kasteel.

At dawn C Company sent out a patrol and found the lifeless ruins tenanted only by the dead. Col Melville immediately went over to have a look at this sinister spot and established his HQ there. With the pale, chill arrival of dawn we pulled back from the forward positions for breakfast in the farm, and, we hoped, some sleep too. No sooner had we settled in snugly in wonderful relaxation-gathering warmth amid the hay in our wet clothes, than word came for us in B Company to advance. We were to penetrate beyond the Goghschen Dijk on the Kasteel road about 2,000 yards, and provided we met no enemy, wait there for further orders.

Smyg asked me to lead 10 Platoon at the head of the Company column as we trudged forward from the farm following a track beside the drainage ditch. There was no mortaring, shelling or any sign of life ahead. Just a brooding expectant silence which emphasised the sucking of the mud on our boots under foot. Two weeks of the estimated month's push had passed and the objectives of the original 5-hour advance still lay 2½ miles ahead over the cold wintry fields and battered landscape.

Our experience with mines the day before had made me very alert to this menace, and brought to my thoughts the words of a hymn by Mary Baker Eddy '. . . I will listen for thy voice lest my footsteps stray'. I found this very comforting in its reminder that the footsteps which really counted were the adherence in consciousness to that straight and narrow pathway of security which lies in the acknowledgment of a supreme power which is spiritual and not explosive, and that man 'created in the image and likeness' of that power is really in substance a spiritual expression too; guided not on a material path but on a spiritual one in true relationship to God.

It gradually became clear as we slowly penetrated forward, that contact had been lost with the enemy some time overnight, though it took some hours before we began to feel sure of this. How far he had pulled back we could only guess. Our life was occupied with the passing minute. What was happening in the 'bigger picture' talked about at higher levels we could only usually sift from rumours. In this case, though we were not to hear it for some time, the Americans had crossed the Roer and were hard after the Germans towards Cologne, as well as swinging north to meet us. For fourteen days the small British and Canadian force at our front had successfully put sufficient pressure to attract the best of the German troops between the Rhine and the Maas, thus giving the US forces a chance to get over the river. Once this had been done and the enemy back door levered open, the pressure had been drawn off our front to meet the new threat.

As I walked up the track ahead of the Company, picking our

path, my attention was divided between surveying the countryside for signs of the enemy, and the sand and grass of the track for the slightest sign of recent disturbance which would indicate mines. Suddenly my eye caught a series of faint cuts in the grass at right angles to the track and staggered at intervals. I only detected this when one step ahead, and stopped. The turf had been cut neatly on three sides of each rectangle to form a tight-fitting flap. I gently lifted the edge of one with my bayonet. There beneath, gleamed the metal of a 'Regal' mine. I detailed one of my Jocks to stop and warn the column past, then moved on with redoubled attention to the minutest sign of another trap, and thanking God for having been led to look in the right direction at the critical moment. I think from the appearance of the turf that these must have been laid as the light failed the previous evening, for otherwise the heavy rain earlier would have sealed the signs of disturbance. Until these mines were lifted the vehicles would have to wait until another route could be found.

At the road leading from the Kasteel, just ahead of us, I could see that the Germans had blown the bridge over the ditch and in addition felled several trees on top of this mess. Smyg came up the column, and said we would cross the road and take up positions near a small haystack on the far side, next to the ditch. To get there I picked my way carefully through the tangle of branches from the felled trees, followed in single file by the 120 men in the Company. Next day when repair work was started on this bridge, we were staggered to hear from the pioneers that the detectors had located 50 'S' type mines round these trees and the bridge – an anti-clearing precaution by the Jerries! The 'S' mine is a canister which is sunk into the ground, and usually has three pin-sized prongs protruding like a tuft of grass above the soil. If these are touched a small charge is fired which throws an inner canister into the air to about 4 feet 6 inches, when it explodes the main charge spreading a lethal hail of umpteen large ball bearings in all directions. That 240 feet had tramped their way through 50 of these without one going off seemed a miracle.

Against the haystack, which proved to be hollowed out, lay lots of largish black metal tubes. This seemed to indicate that we were on one of the sites from which the Germans had launched their

Moaning Minnies. We took up positions here and waited. In a little while fresh orders arrived that another company was coming up, and we were to advance about another three-quarters of a mile, and establish ourselves astride the Bergen–Groote Horst road near a house on the edge of the wood, this wood being the more southerly block of Broederbosch wood, a mile beyond the Kasteel.

Still there had been no sign of the enemy, but we were taking no chances. We had learned the Jerries' habit of suddenly disappearing, only to be met a short way back, dug into new positions and fighting as doggedly as before. Each time this cycle of events took place, variations of the same general pattern unfolded. Usually the first two or three vehicles suddenly went up in smoke on catching up with the enemy, next we put in an infantry attack with another batch of casualties, then, often when things seemed at their worst, we would gradually realise the enemy had melted away in the night once more, leaving a trail of mined roads and blown bridges.

Before we moved, Smyg sent Sgt Cowie out on a recce patrol to see if the house was clear of enemy. He was to take a section of men with him, and one of the only two 38 sets then still working to keep in touch. He was to work round in a dog's leg, coming in to the house at right angles from us so that if he ran into trouble we could give him heavy covering fire. At the angle of the leg of his route stood two small farms which he would have to clear too. Getting to the farms involved a lengthy stalk along the side of a waterfilled ditch called Ekklesen Beek. He wisely chose to keep off the track for fear of more mines, and reported the farms clear by radio as he passed them. As the distant figures of the patrol approached the house, we trained our weapons on it, and watched intently the quick jerky movements of the Jocks working their way towards it in bounds. They disappeared inside with no sounds of firing coming back. A couple of minutes later they reappeared, and we moved off to join them, dropping a Platoon off to dig in at each of the farms as we passed them.

Arriving eventually at the house, which turned out to be an inn, and still with no reaction from the enemy, Smyg decided to make this his HQ, taking over the cellar, while I dug my Platoon in to the high ground either side of the road. A horse at the back of the house had had a direct hit from a 25-pounder shell, cutting it neatly in two halves which lay several yards apart.

We were just inside the Dutch border by about a mile, and on a slight hill with a view down the road towards Groote Horst and open country ahead, while behind us the road disappeared into the forest. Beside the inn, or Gasthaus, a sandy ridge extended to the south-east bordering the forest, and I took a couple of chaps with me to explore these sand hills and select the Platoon positions. I was astonished to find this ridge was honeycombed with communication trenches and elaborate German dugouts lined with heavy timber, each fully furnished with stoves, bunks, lamps, coal, clocks, and even pictures and windows in some of them. This was the living quarters for a light anti-aircraft battery or rocket launchers it seemed, to judge from some nearby concrete platforms with ammunitions lockers.

After a quick but careful look over each bunker to make sure no Germans were lurking in them, or that they were not booby trapped, I selected one as my HQ then manned the positions at half strength to get the chaps some sleep in the dugouts before the night was upon us. Although it was very cold, the stoves could not be lit because of the smoke, sparks and chimney glow at night, though we eventually overcame this by slowly feeding on tiny chips of fuel.

All around the sandhills we kept finding small wooden Schu mine boxes of the type built by German children as their contribution to the war effort. Though these were empty of explosive, we trod everywhere with the utmost care in case there were any complete ones about.

In the late afternoon I took a patrol down to the bridge we had passed earlier to contact the ration and water-carrying party, and cover them and the CO back to our positions. Chris had a look round and a chat with Smyg before I escorted him back. Later a call came for Frank to go cross-country to an 'O' Group at the Kasteel. I called in to see Smyg before it got dark, in his cellar. There he and his HQ Jocks were resting like so many mummies laid out on the wine storage shelves, and Smyg in his white polo sweater was poring over a map by the light of a candle. He was a bit worried about some houses marked on the map in the woods to our rear, and also that for all we knew the mass of forest at our backdoor might contain any number of the enemy. Several Jerries had been captured after the main mass had vanished, and to feel more secure for the night Smyg asked me to take out a small recce patrol and check the woods and odd cottages in the nearest part of the 1¼ square miles of wood.

To do the job, Jones and two others volunteered. Jones was armed, of course, with his precious Bren gun and masses of ammunition normally carried by a second man. He scorned help, and with his heftiness easily coped with the extra weight. Two of us had rifles and the third a Sten gun and some 77 smoke grenades.

Smyg came along with us for the first few hundred yards. Jones, as usual, had to be held back in his keenness. He slunk along in the bushes, Bren at the hip like a Tommy gun, as though he were a large cat stalking something. His paratroop blouse flap hung at the back like a tail. On his head instead of the scorned tin hat, he wore a queer cap he had stitched himself out of some monkey fur. At the back of the cap he had draped his camouflage face veil, like Robinson Crusoe with a Foreign Legion neck flap. To complete this, his keen face was rapidly gathering another scruffy beginning of a beard, and on his feet, unorthodox to the last detail, were the clogs of a Belgian miner, part wooden, part leather, topped with anklets made from the felt lining of mortar bomb cases. These boots and anklets, he had explained to me when first my astonished gaze had fallen on them, were 'warmer than those provided by His Majesty'. He was undoubtedly 'a bit fey' as Smyg put it, but a great asset to the Platoon, and there seemed an unmentioned agreement to tolerate his taste in clothes, at least while 'at the front'.

Not long after setting out we sighted three figures approaching along the edge of the wood from the direction in which the enemy had withdrawn, they were carrying arms, and not taking a great deal of trouble over concealment. We lay in wait in their path, covering them as they approached, until we recognised them from their green berets to be Recce chaps. They were also on patrol, and reported the sandy rides to the east to be clear. We swapped information for a while, then wished them well and each continued our patrol. The first small wrecked cottage in a clearing in the wood was empty and without clues. Smyg had thought penetration to another one about 1,000 yards off beyond a big crater in the road towards Bergen would be too far, so we turned off to investigate a large block of woods in a circuit off the road eastwards, then back to our positions.

We advanced in diamond formation, myself at the front apex, and the chap with the Sten well back as 'getaway man' in case we met more trouble than we could extricate ourselves from ahead. Our progress was slow in the failing light and dense woods. Twenty-five yards at a move, then a pause to look round and listen. Our footsteps were softened in the pine needles, and there was an oppressive silence in the pine-resin-scented gloom. Once again I felt the oddly exhilarating, yet fear-tinged fascination of a patrol, in which one felt a queer kinship with the alert, quick witted movements of the squirrels and other wild animals, in realising the swiftness of our reactions and senses were the only things which could cut our losses if Jerry happened to be waiting with an automatic weapon. If Jerry saw us first, we realised having covered the Recce chaps as they approached, at worst we would not know what had hit us, and at best we would be extremely fortunate to lose no one.

So far our only indication that there was a war on had been some rough and recently occupied German slit trenches, littered about with ration tins, wrappings and cigarette packets. Footprints in the sand unmarked by the rain and the condition of an area used as a latrine told us the enemy had been here some time within the last fifteen hours or so.

We moved on more carefully, but were reassured by the chirping of a few birds going to roost somewhere ahead in the trees – it seemed unlikely they would do this if the Jerries were in the same area. Also we had been noting that the artillery fire which occasionally sounded was much more distant, seeming to indicate that if any Jerries were in the wood, they were most likely to be stragglers or cut off by our advance.

Jones was obviously revelling in every yard of it in keen anticipation of emptying a magazine into someone, despite his disappointment at being robbed of an opportunity when the three figures we had met earlier turned out to be our own troops. I reflected, not without comfort, that I was certainly glad this murderous apparition stalking the woods was on the right side!

A group of low, moss-covered earth mounds, which we knew from their peculiar shape to be German dugouts, caught our attention through the trees about 60 feet off. Listening intently we crouched in the gloom for a while, then slowly stalked them in turn. Kicking open the door to sling a stone in in lieu of a grenade to panic any occupants, but after the first we had a feeling they were empty. It took some time for our eyes to make out details inside in the dark, so it was just as well. As usual they were well equipped, but what interested us more was evidence of a hasty retreat in the form of black sausages, tinned meat and part of a hard, black loaf of bread left on the table in one, one of the tins being opened but untouched. Jones was for taking back a water bottle filled with something smelling strongly of cognac. He reluctantly left it, but only when ordered to do so.

The rest of the trip was uneventful, and we got back after dark with little to report. Smyg moved one of the Platoons from down the road in the farms, up to cover a gap in the wood at nightfall, thus giving us a better all-round defence. A quiet but rather eerie night was passed visiting the stags now and then in the long communication trenches winding on the crest of the windy hill and interspersed at intervals with bunkers, four of which were occupied by my chaps. It was odd to be using the Jerries' old positions after they had so recently cleared out, and to know that the trench wandering away over the ridges to our east linked up with further bunkers we had not yet had time to investigate. I resolved to do this in the morning. Once more the only indications of war in the darkness were distant fires, probably burning farms away to the north-east.

2 March 1945. Cpl Parry and Jones joined me in a recce of the meandering communication trenches, and system of bunkers next day. Parry as a private soldier had been a constant cause of trouble and anxiety to the officers of the Company during training in Scotland, due to his irrepressible, explosive high spirits and dynamic personality, which coupled with a very independent spirit and an upbringing in and accent of the Gorbals of Glasgow gave him quite a reputation for trouble, which often ended with him on a charge. A highly successful experiment in giving first one, then two stripes and the consequent responsibility had worked wonders in him once overseas, dubious though he was about accepting the promotion. He had been quite happy as a private. Now he and Jones made a wonderful pair. It had been some months before I had to a large extent mastered the interpretation of his amazing Gorbals accent. He was fond of muttering darkly towards the Jerries when things were a bit rough; 'Th'onny-guid-yin's-a-deed-yin!' This I eventually found meant, 'The only good one is a dead one'. Our outing took us about 500 yards along the sandy ridge, into several more deserted bunkers, and then to finding a watch tower. We quite enjoyed the change, and the interest of seeing more of the positions occupied by the enemy while we were stuck alongside the Kasteel.

Back at my HQ bunker a breakfast of soya sausages, tea and fried bread had been prepared over a stove carefully lit on charcoal to keep down smoke. As we were engaged in this the call came from Coy HQ 'prepare to move', and I made my way over to get the news.

To our amazement, the whine of carrier gears from the direction of Groote Horst disclosed Frank trundling along in the Bren carrier followed by a 15-cwt truck. We watched his approach with apprehension, but he drew up intact having traversed a track unchecked for mines.

The news was good. The Recce, scouting in their armoured cars, had lost contact with the enemy way ahead. We were to march a mile down the road to the 'Drie Angel' inn, and board TCVs there. The chase seemed to be properly on once more for the first time since the rush through France and Belgium the previous summer. As we heard this cheering news, the sound of trucks behind us from the woods disclosed a convoy held up by the crater in the road we had seen on our patrol the previous evening.

ON THE RUN

We marched a mile down the road, and halted to laze in the sun against the Drie Angel inn, listening to bursts of melody on Cpl Parry's mouth organ while awaiting the arrival of the TCVs. The first warmth of spring sunshine, the music, the good news and the knowledge that for the moment trouble was still several miles away made us feel at peace with the world.

As the various companies pulled slowly past in the Battalion column, the Jocks exchanged queries after friends, jokes or cheers. The driver of my Platoon HQ TCV was an amusing, walrus-whiskered, pipe-smoking fellow, who talked all the while of his life at home, his wife and his beloved garden. We were to see a lot of each other from time to time over miles of Germany, 'swanning' after the enemy until finally the truck got a direct hit.

In Groote Horst, the skeletons of German trucks and a petrol lorry beside some charred and still smoking buildings from which the glass had melted into the tar of the road marked a visit from our Typhoons. This spot was the start of a long journey over roundabout, cratered roads, everywhere scenes of death and destruction blighted the view; in the fields and by the roads were smashed vehicles, guns and houses.

At Siebengewald crossroads, our original objective, I peered through the smoke of my contented, pipe-puffing companion to gaze with interest at this much-thought-of objective. Heavily prepared defences had been rushed up by the Todt workers, several of whom, with German soldiers, were still sprawling untidily dead amid the stippled mess of artillery craters in the fields. How fortunate, I thought, that the attack had not reached this objective, for even if we had struggled this far with success, we would have found ourselves in the same impossible position as B Company had done at Heinsberg with the coming of daylight, for the seminary on higher ground over the River Kendel dominated it.

Turning right, we passed several miles of partly completed and often flooded defences. Jerry had certainly meant to hold us here, and it was most interesting to sit back in comfort and warmth, chatting with my companion and watching these now useless defences which might have caused us so much fighting, reeling swiftly past the windows.

Swinging north-east for a while, the country was less shattered by war, though here and there our long-range artillery had smashed up a village or crossroads. In addition, Jerry had left his own trail of destruction and delaying action in the form of blown bridges, felled trees and mines, which included some of the ratchet type that let several vehicles pass before claiming a victim.

Occasionally we passed a spattering of gashes and shallow craters in the roads, bordered by chipped telephone poles dangling their wires – a trail of destruction wrought by the cannon and rockets of Typhoons leading up to a group of burnt out German lorries or a staff car tipped in the ditch. Wayside graves marked those occupants not cremated in the vehicles.

Dead horses and cows, inflated, toy-balloon-like with legs sticking out sideways, were seen from time to time in the waterlogged pock-marked fields or lay roasted in neat rows in the ash of a cowshed, still chained in their places, silent witnesses to the madness of war. The owner, blank faced, raked for valuables in the wreckage.

Every hamlet boasting of a road junction or station was usually reduced to heaps of rubble sometimes still smoking. These, and many other scenes – sometimes of beauty, more often of horror – flitted in turn past the frame of the window. At times, probably because of these ruins, mines or blown bridges, we left the main roads to wander past fields and woods on bad secondary roads, or past trenches glinting zigzag mirrors of flood water. Once or twice the trucks slowed to twist between massive road blocks of tree trunks and earth. A large amount of this work was no doubt carried out while we were stuck in Broederbosch wood for two weeks. Sometimes, too, we glimpsed minefields bordered with massed barbed wire.

Gradually the surrounding countryside became more untouched and English looking, with gentle hills, woods and meadows. We travelled right on until dusk, and had covered only 7 miles as the crow flies, though many more by the route we had taken, when the convoy pulled up at the side of the road. We were to de-bus, leaving enough men to guard the convoy, and carry on on foot.

News was nil. Were we going into another attack? Where were the enemy who had for so long fought desperately for each inch of ground? I think perhaps the most tiring part of an infantryman's life is the lack of news, which is desperate at times, and the consequent needless drain on nerves for the Jock who hour-by-hour and day-by-day never knew at any moment if he would be called on to put forth the supreme effort, both mental and physical, which an attack demanded.

After about a mile of marching in section files each side of a tree-lined, dark avenue, the straggling crunch of marching feet coming the opposite way materialised as a column of about eighty German prisoners under escort. This added fuel to the Jocks' speculation that the enemy had turned to fight again somewhere a short distance ahead. In consequence some Jocks swore filthily at the luckless, shambling column of Hun to ease their feelings.

We were nearing the head of the convoy, which I knew from keeping track of things on my map was just short of the small town of Wemb, when gradually a deep droning of myriad aircraft engines filled the sky and spread overhead towards the enemy in the east. Almost immediately pencils of light stabbed up and swung about the sky from the direction of the Rhine, together with little orange and white twinkling pinpoints of bursting AA fire at a great height.

To judge by the immediate reaction of the enemy, he seemed to be pretty close. We judged it also to be a heavy raid from the time it took the planes to pass. It was a new and most interesting experience, having seen these raids set off so often in the past for a distant Germany, to be marching and watching from German soil as German prisoners passed alongside also watching and no doubt wondering if the bombs were destined for their homes as we had done when watching the rockets and buzz bombs streaking on their evil way from Holland.

At the head of the convoy we halted and took up defence positions, then watched the progress of the bombers indicated by the shifting searchlights and AA fire, as the wavering drone of their engines and the empty crump of the bursting shells faded into the wayside sounds of the night and the coughing clatter and undertone of the Jocks. 'One poor devil caught in the searchlights Sir, b*** glad I'm not up there!'

The dim gloom of a wood showed up on the right on a hill, while faintly, a short way off the road, I spotted the squat shape and dark loopholes of a concrete bunker. It seemed wise to inspect this as it quite dominated our position. I stalked it in company with Brown, but it was empty.

The CO, coming back on foot from the darkness, seemed to indicate something had held us up. He was followed shortly by the large form and Canadian twanging voice of the Intelligence Officer, Don Urquart, recently back from the wound he sustained while commanding my Platoon in Tripsrath woods and quite recovered. From Don I learned we had 'come up against a bridge, still unblown, but mined with several 500lb bombs each arranged with its nose cap against a Teller mine.' Fortunately the leading vehicle had been suspicious of the intactness of the bridge, and had pulled up in time to investigate. The delay in setting to work was that the REs suspected an anti-lifting device and were carefully examining things before clearing the explosives. Meanwhile, it was not considered that a column of men marching over in single file would have enough weight to touch things off, and Frank and Smyg, who had joined us at the head of the column, gave the order to proceed. Gingerly, in single file we picked our way past the still busy REs and breathed again on firm ground on the far side.

The dark, sprawling outlines of Wemb's houses and trees revealed themselves against the sky at the head of a whitish ribbon of road. Perhaps instinctively crouching a little, we hugged the grass verge to quieten our boots on the gravel, for we were at the head of the Battalion column and tensed with the suspense of wondering what reception would greet our entry into the town. Would it be silence or the crash of firing? Was the blowing up of the bridge by the first vehicle of the column in pursuit to have been a warning that we had caught up with the enemy? We knew that the next few minutes would provide the answer.

A hundred yards to go and there was still complete silence from ahead. A slight drizzle had commenced. Our boots rang out, making an awful noise as we reached the cobbles of the streets. Dampness filling the air had added an unreal mistiness and eerie quality to the scene which from our point of view already held sufficient dramatic content.

Now we were among the buildings, moving carefully in section groups from cover to cover against the walls, alarmed by the awful clatter of our steel-studded boots on the slippery cobbles. If there were any enemy, asleep even, in the place, they would by now have ample warning of our approach, yet nothing had happened. We had not yet seen a soul.

All the windows were shuttered. Here for the first time we met in quantity, and with surprise, the ghostly shapes of white sheets and pillow slips hung up as flags of peace, draped from almost every house and moving sluggishly in the night.

The mood of the civilian inhabitants was eloquently expressed by those flags. One both saw and sensed the occasional glimpse of white, scared faces, peering between the shutters or from the darkness of a window. The town seemed pretty well undamaged and rather a nice little place, quite English in appearance with, near the centre, trees in an avenue and on the right a bandstand set in a gravel square beside a totem-pole-shaped war memorial.

At some stage in our advance through the town, and at that time unknown to me, Jones, overcome by the wonderful opportunities offered by the surroundings and without the knowledge of his section commander, had flitted off in his grotesque rig-out on various excursions in and around neighbouring buildings. It was not till his death that the Platoon fully became aware that a mobile jewellers shop had been moving in their midst.

Suddenly, and amazingly, we found ourselves moving into the countryside at the far side of the town. Nothing had happened. It was of course possible, we speculated, that a recce patrol had penetrated the town ahead of us and radioed it was clear before we set off, but if so, we had as so often been told nothing.

Now at last there was some definite information. We were to dig in for the night astride the road and in a small wood alongside a farm round which Support Company were deploying their anti-tank guns. So ended our first day of what we later called 'swanning' after the enemy, and so also commenced yet another miserable night.

When we had prepared reasonable positions, we took turns by sections to file back to the barn in which the anti-tank chaps were sleeping peacefully in the dry straw and warmth to cook up some Spam and tea for supper. One section commander was still stupid enough after all his experience to let some of his men stroll back, leaving their weapons in their trenches, and had to be chased back.

It was far too cold and wet to contemplate any sleep in an ordinary slit trench when off duty, so partly to keep warm and occupied, Sgt Dickinson and I in turn built a really posh straw-lined dugout which was completed at 2 am. A misty drizzle kept up all night, but with the aid of our cosy hole we each secured two and a half hours partial sleep and warmth before first light. These apologies for sleep when on a 'stunt' seemed to accentuate rather than diminish our continual, and often desperate, feeling of tiredness.

After 'stand to' at dawn on 3 March the order 'prepare to move' arrived, and with it we scrambled to try to prepare some sort of a breakfast each as we sorted out our kit for the road. It was then that the odd noise of raucous crooning by a lone Jock, together with the most delightful scent and crackling of frying fat, drew our eyes to rivet with amazement on the most fantastic apparition squatting before a looted oil stove and cooking over it with a looted frying pan. It was, of course, Jones, but added to his usual unorthodox apparel, monkey fur cap and so on, his fingers sparkled with rings and shiny stones, and his windproof paratroop jacket glittered with gold watch chains ending in bulging pockets. A leg of sliced ham lay before him, and in the pan more of it was frying, punctuated with the shapes of eggs and onions. Beside him lay two dead ducks, presumably a reserve for dinner. Dashing off to answer a call for 'O' Group, and then to shake the sleepy drivers to life and load on the Jocks for the move put this scene out of my mind, and it was some time later that I got round to thinking about Jones. At that time the Jocks, none of whom seemed to have noticed him absent for a while in the town, seemed to think Jones must have got his hoard of trinkets in being fortunate enough to dig his slit trench on a cache hidden by some German householder.

There was very little news to be had at the 'O' Group other than the order of vehicles for another chase after the enemy of unknown distance and duration in the TCVs. The Platoon was carried in two 3-tonners, with the overflow in one of Company HQ trucks. As I was still the only subaltern in the Company since Pip went to hospital in the woods and Tommy was wounded, I took the front Platoon truck, while Sgt Dickinson took the last.

At the rear of the Company column was the 15cwt driven as usual by Hughes. Frank was in the Coy HQ TCV, and ahead Smyg's tam-o'-shanter bobbed in the carrier driven by lanky Brown.

We gathered the enemy were still some way ahead because the Brigadier passed up the column in his staff car, splashing over the wet roads in the drizzle. His nickname among the officers was Von Loompnek – a rather cruel hint that at times when things went badly, it was reckoned that he must be fighting for the wrong side!

Only a short distance from our starting point, the convoy pulled in to the side of the road and, for an unknown reason, halted. At intervals despatch riders clattered past in the wet, and several Recce Dingoes and armoured cars drove up the column.

Gradually the minutes of waiting ticked into hours, and the Jocks jumped out of the trucks to brew up tea by the wayside. With the aid of truck drivers and their petrol, quite efficient, long-burning fires blazed here and there from perforated tins filled with petrol-soaked sand. Round each fire a group of Jocks gathered, stamping their feet against the cold.

News eventually filtered down the column to us that a bit up the road was another bridge suspected of being mined with 500lb bombs, several of which lay alongside it.

Beyond this was a vast crater marking the site of a second bridge. We saw this when we passed the next day. It had been blown in an awkward place between two houses backed by anti-tank obstacles and a wood, making it necessary in the absence of an alternative route, to fill in this hole before proceeding. It was here, we heard later, that contact had first been made with the Americans in armoured cars on 4 March. Our two forces had at last linked up and the enemy was being forced back into a pocket towards the Rhine.

I had just succeeded in heating a tin of steak and kidney pudding on the exhaust manifold of the TCV engine revved a few minutes for the purpose, when it was decided to pull the vehicles off the road and into various farmyards to make ourselves more comfortable. A barn was found for the men to sleep in should we stay that long, and sentries positioned while the cooks got busy on the Compo rations for lunch. This consisted of knocking holes in the lids of each tin and standing them in hot water.

The farmyard presented quite a busy scene. Apart from the vehicles scattered about it, and the busy cooks with their roaring pressure stove, a group of Jocks were stripped to their vests, washing and shaving under the pump. The alert, hunted look of the hens told that other Jocks were not confining their attention to the eggs alone, while the rattle of chains and buckets in the cowshed confirmed we would have fresh milk for tea. A scuffle of boots on the cobbles and frantic, ear-splitting squeals from a Teutonic pig, revealed Jones lying on his stomach, recovering from an unsuccessful rugger tackle motivated by the idea of pork chops, from which his thoughts had to be diverted.

The farm was untouched by the war and carried a fine stock of cattle. We were rather intrigued to note that the electric light was still working, and that the farm did not generate its own supply. This was a most unusual state of affairs in our experience, and suggested the enemy had pulled back with great speed. Even when the power stations were still intact and the power lines not destroyed by fighting it was usual for the civil services to collapse at least temporarily on being overrun. Possibly the power was generated at Wemb or the larger town of Kevelaer still ahead of us. In this case it seemed not only that our Recce troops had passed this town, but that the nearest enemy were still some way off to the east. I failed to get any sense on the situation out of the ancient, gaunt, long-nosed and blue-eyed farmer.

Inside the farm, I found Smyg in his white polo sweater preparing for sleep on a couch with maps, equipment and the radio set beside him. I took the chance of doing a sketch of him before taking my own kit off for the first length of time since leaving Afferden woods and then following suit. We would, I think, have turned the old farmer out of bed to get a good sleep ourselves for the night, were it not that we hadn't the heart to turn the very old and not too well farmer's wife out too. The old farmer kept stalking in through our room to see her during the evening and then again out, to check up, no doubt, that his head of livestock still totalled the same.

Frank, Smyg and I took turns manning the 18 set with the operator during the night in case word came for us to move. In between these spells, I put a revolver in my trouser pocket, and using the small pack as a pillow, slept on the linoleum, enjoying the warmth of the fire and the comfort of a dry resting place for a change.

In the morning, although I had shaved the previous evening, I enjoyed the novelty of doing it again. Breakfast was wonderful: farm eggs, bacon, plenty of real milk in the tea, and bread, butter and jam. On such occasions, following a night of warmth which included some sleep, one could forget a lot.

The order 'prepare to move' had come with daylight, and after a quick kit check we were soon aboard the trucks rolling forwards again, past the mined then the blown bridges. A bulldozer had filled in a road of rubble traversing the crater. We were still not sure if these delaying tactics were to enable the enemy to turn and fight again on this side of the Rhine, or whether it was to gain time for the evacuation of what equipment he could salvage from the converging forces of the Canadians, British and Americans, now linked and hard in pursuit.

It was a crisp, cold morning with good visibility, and we were travelling with much greater speed than previously. We were struck by the fact that the wayside villagers were still in occupation and not evacuated by the enemy as on the other side of the Maas. Only the tiny tots waved us cheerfully past, as they would have done to any moving object, while the grown-ups stared with blank or sullen faces. Though signs of enthusiasm by adults at our arrival were not apparent, neither was open hostility; in fact some seemed to show relief that the tide of battle had swept past so painlessly. The most definite statement of feelings had unexpectedly come from one of the Battalion's most recent prisoners, who for reasons best known by himself, had burst forth with the words 'B*** Hitler!'

Our first halt was in a small village whose occupants had unwisely left ducks and hens wandering near the roadside. After about two minutes' desperate clucking and flapping, not another bird was seen for the duration of this stop; their fate was confirmed by delicious scents of cooking poultry when we pulled in to laager for the night. Steadily the miles and the hours rolled past as we relaxed, making the most of the change in our fortune in the last few days and taking in the details of German landscape, people, farms and houses with interest.

For quite some time the only sign of destruction had been the wreckage of one of our Typhoons which had been shot down, ploughing deeply into a field scattering pieces as it went. We passed it with sympathy. The main chunk of wreckage had stopped between two farms. By the roadside was a newly made grave, with a rough cross.

Shortly before dark, the convoy split into Company groups and fanned out over a given area containing many large, prosperous farms in which each selected billets for the night. Quickly the vehicles vanished inside the walled farmyards, to the accompaniment of fierce barking from the dogs which guarded each one. The worried and often frightened farmers and their families dashed hither and thither to satisfy each whim of the least Jock when this invasion out of the blue interrupted their suppers. The Jocks had quickly taken to the routine of this new life, and within no time each farm had become a guarded fortress with radio contact and supper, fires, beds or straw-filled rooms being organised within.

Our particular farm was the best billet we had yet had 'at the front'. A large room upstairs was selected for the Jocks and filled with straw. The farmer's wife, we suspected, was a bit of an actress, for to judge by the tremendous welcome she gave us, we were among the most honoured visitors ever to have graced the place. The house itself, as with so many German farms, contained the cattle stalls, the dairy, and the hay-filled loft all in the one unit. For a cold winter this seemed a very sensible arrangement, for we found the air inside the building warm and sweet, scented with the cattle and the hay. In front bordering the road was a walled and gated farmyard with outbuildings and at the back a fenced orchard under grass.

The family consisted of a silent, watchful farmer – a great contrast to his gushing wife – a son, his photo in a place of honour on the mantelpiece, missing in the Wehrmacht, and to the delight of the Jocks, a daughter, substantial, blooming, dark haired and twenty. In addition, there was a German cowhand of about fifty whom I sketched later. He struck us as probably the closest approach to the 'missing link' in existence. He did not appear to be able to speak, and grunted shambling about the place like a hideous Frankenstein monster. To help this chap look after the cattle, there were four slave-labourers: two square, inscrutable, Russian chaps, a Russian girl called Nina and a Belgian girl, Bertha.

Bertha was elected cook by the Jocks, and amid much giggling and gesticulation was set to work on preparing our supper. The farmer's wife still managed to maintain her smiles on the surface of simmering violence when relegated to the washing up in her own kitchen by the two slave girls whose faces glowed with delight not only at the novelty of this situation, but also in the gradually dawning awareness at their liberation.

Just before supper I decided it was time the Platoon had a proper weapons inspection. For this purpose Sgt Dickinson paraded the first section in the courtyard outside the kitchen windows, marched them down to the far end with booming orders and turned them in line, giving them the order 'For inspection, port arms'. As Sgt Dickinson marched smartly up to me and saluted, announcing the seven men lined up with weapons were at the alert awaiting inspection, I became aware of deathly silence in the kitchen and the faces of the family gazing in horror out of the windows. An obvious thought had crossed their minds: the chaps did look rather like a firing squad and to add fuel to the imagination of the Germans, I later found in talking to the Belgian girl that the retreating Jerries had fully primed them on the 'atrocities of the British'.

After supper, which included some very welcome farm-brewed potato soup, I retired with the NCOs to the drawing room, each armed with a mug of tea, and here we worked out the stags for the night in the warmth and comfort of a roaring fire. This, we decided, must be more like the good, old-fashioned wars when one packed up thoughts of fighting at night and made the most of things. I paid a quick visit to Company HQ in the next farm for any orders or news after seeing the sentries set in the slit trenches outside. Contact patrols were to keep touch between the farm billets during the night. In my absence the Jocks seemed also to have let their thoughts wander on the amenities of the place, for hearing giggles, shrieks and a general rough and tumble in process upstairs I sent up Sgt Dickinson to turn the three pink-faced, smiling and straw-wisped girls out of the men's billet. The girls, it seemed, regarded men as men no matter what uniform they wore, and unlike the adults in the farm did not think more deeply than this. Likewise, to the Jocks a girl was a girl the world over; language, politics and background were irrelevant.

For a while before turning in I sat with the NCOs by the fire in the drawing room, talking and enjoying the warmth. After a few minutes, soft knocking at the door revealed the wife and daughter, who asked if they could join us, which we allowed them to do. They seemed frightened and anxious to create a good impression. Their fright stemmed, I think, from a realisation that their little world had collapsed about them and that their former docile slaves might be contemplating revenge – situations we were later to meet, in which German farmers and their families were butchered in isolated farms by terrorising bands of revengeful and looting displaced persons. Later, the farmer's wife was shocked when the two girl slave workers boldly knocked at the door in their turn. Clearly this boldness was their new-found freedom at our presence beginning to assert itself.

I found sketching a great relaxation and had done a drawing of one of the NCOs. Nina and Bertha saw this, which seemed to delight them, and they implored me to do their drawings too. The light was not good, so I set a candle in the middle of a card table with the 'models' taking turns sitting opposite me, their faces lit by this flickering glow. Nina, quite an attractive girl, with a tanned face and hazel eyes, could talk no English or French, but sat grinning in silent delight beneath a rough scarf bound over her hair. Bertha was a more buxom, lively character, who confided to me in French that the farmer's wife was a 'cat' who had changed her tune since our arrival. She had had a billet full of German soldiers in only a few days before. Her chief sport had been to bully the Russian girl Nina. Bertha also informed me she was going to start walking back to Belgium in the morning. She could give no useful information as to where the enemy were at the moment and on this point we were quite in the dark. They might be in the next group of farms, or miles away. The German girl was my next customer, large eyed, silent and uncertain. Jones, who had strolled in, occupied himself in making improper suggestions to her. Not understanding a word, fortunately, she could only nervously say 'Ja' at intervals for politeness. To her consternation this had the NCOs in fits of laughter. To round off the evening, Jones, of course, had his 'phot'ey' done too.

When the time came to turn in, the Hausfrau lit a fire in my room, then offered me hot milk; this, with a proper bed and sheets seemed to me unheard of comfort. I declined the milk; with a son missing, it seemed just possible she had tampered with it, long chance though this seemed. I inspected the room and placed loose kit where it would fall or rattle if the door or window were moved. The bed was in full view of the unguarded window, and with this strange new life with which we were confronted, I debated with myself whether to evacuate the bed and sleep behind the door in case any monkey tricks were tried overnight. However, I decided I was too tired to worry, and taking off my boots and slipping my revolver into my belt I listened for a while to the cheerful crackle of the fire before falling asleep. Once or twice the lonely barking of a dog woke me, but the night passed without incident. The next night it would be my turn to go round sections at intervals, and Sgt Dickinson's turn for a good sleep.

THE BATTLE FOR HAUS LOO

At five in the morning I collected a group of NCOs from Company HQ and we made our way to report to another farm occupied by Battalion HQ, where we were to stand by for an advance party. It was a freezing dawn, and after hanging about outside for several hours getting very cold in the process and with no news to go on, we were eventually told the move was off. However, shortly afterwards it was on again and later that morning, 5 March 1945, we left Vossum and moved north-east through the terribly battered town of Geldern, and on through Tralen towards Issum. A few splodges of smoke on the horizon in front of us drew attention to the distant, dark specks of Typhoons and the Thunderbolts of the Americans, diving like swallows onto the Germans who were hemmed tightly against the banks of the Rhine and fighting fanatically to get as much equipment as possible over the river. Between ourselves and the Rhine lay 10 or 12 miles of countryside in which this desperate battle was being fought out, and which came to be known as the 'Wesel pocket'. Though at that time we were completely in the dark on the 'bigger picture' and our immediate future, our alert senses, primed by gathering experience and visual clues, told us that we were heading for another attack before long.

A short distance ahead of us we could now make out the rooftops of Issum, speckled and draped with slowly flapping, white, sheet-and-pillow-case flags. As our eyes took this in, our ears and the ominous tensing of our stomachs, responded to the growing rumble of guns. Another mile and we were passing them, bucking and bouncing in billowing smoke and dust as they belted their shells away.

Just outside Issum the convoy drew up and we de-bussed to

continue on foot. We were to select billets for the rest of the battalion when they arrived. Though the town was knocked about, it still contained most of its civilian population, as well as others from places worse hit nearby. The enemy was clearly in no condition to continue the evacuation of his civilian population to rear areas, as had been the case when first we had fought on German soil bordering the River Roer.

After picking our way clattering over tiles and phone wire into the town, we took over from units of the 53rd Welsh Div who had got in ahead of us. Company HQ was set up in a fine modern house already brimming over with quite a pleasant German family and the Platoons were put in fairly undamaged homes bordering the dirt road outside. I found great difficulty in understanding the Germans' docile acceptance of our presence, when matched against my thoughts on what reception our civilian population would undoubtedly have given invading Germans. Where were their Volksturm Home Guard? Why weren't we sniped at and vehicles sabotaged? One could only conclude the civilians had no heart for the whole stupid business; though whether this was only because the tide of war was rolling strongly against them was another matter. It seemed unlikely: there were repeated cries of 'Hitler no good!' during and immediately after the fall of France.

Word had spread like wildfire that there was a brewery in the town which had escaped destruction and to give the Jocks a treat, a truck was sent off to bring back a couple of small barrels which were tapped. The Jocks filed past to fill their mess tins with their first taste of German beer.

It turned out to be a fine sunny evening, and once the chaps had settled in, I went for a stroll round the town with Frank Coutts. There seemed to be a lot of activity round Brigade HQ which we passed, and with the Brigadier we noticed our CO Chris Melville, Bob Bearpark (Adjutant), John Henderson (Signals), Don Urquart (Intelligence), and Major Rae. Something was brewing. Chris mentioned there was a wrecked stationery shop along the road, and there I replenished my stocks of drawing and writing paper, digging out what could still be salvaged from a heap of rubble. It was pleasant to meet and chat with a Royal Scots officer, and hear how they had been getting on, before turning back. A German QM store for slave workers took our attention on the way. It was well stocked with French, Belgian, Dutch, British and Russian Army clothing.

As we arrived back at our billets, a battery of 5.5-inch gun-howitzers moved in to take the place of some noisy 25-pounders around our houses: an indication of the progress of the battle since our arrival, as the lighter guns had had to move forward to ensure adequate range for all targets.

The noise these medium guns made when they came into action a short while later was appalling. Just over the road from us in Company HQ one of these guns fired with the muzzle pointing over the roof of a small and ancient farmer's cottage, which was also one of my section billets. The first blast of flame and pressure took away the best part of the chimney of this little house, a lot of the tiles and some of the windows, smashing crockery inside. As the noise, dust and debris settled, the German family and chickens rushed panic stricken into the road, and the heads of the Jocks popped out of the windows. It was rather thoughtless of the gunners to position their gun so close. If the guns were called on for a barrage the place would rapidly crumble.

In the evening I sat with Smyg and Frank round a table lit by a paraffin pressure lamp in the parlour of our house, writing home and enclosing all my latest sketches. News had come that we were in for another 'stunt' next day, and it was quite a jolt after reading a little heap of letters from home which had just caught up with me to adjust my mind to the contemplation and acceptance of the morrow and the ever-pressing but unknown trials of the future.

We had been told that it was of the greatest importance to keep up maximum pressure on the enemy. The more he and his equipment could be mauled this side, the less he would turn to fight again the other side of the Rhine. Accordingly, we were to move forward on the 8th to take over positions from the Royal Scots Fusiliers in Alpen woods that evening, and the Battalion was to put in an attack at 0800 hours the following morning.

A warm, comparatively comfortable night was passed sleeping on the floor near the stove, with stags cut to a minimum because now the enemy had been caught up again and with troops ahead we knew where we were. In the morning, after breakfast and briefing, followed by a kit, weapons and ammunition check, we formed up in section files, and moved off to cover the 4½ miles to the 'FUP' (forming up point). As usual the rough plan on paper looked delightfully simple and free of snags: a feeling that was helped by one's normal wishful thinking – in this case that Jerry would have pulled back over the river by the time we arrived to do battle.

To add to the dejected look of the sections trudging, cluttered with kit up the road, it was a chilly raw day and rain began to fall and soak into our clothing. I wondered if a newspaper reporter would have described us as 'straining at the leash to be at the enemy, with morale at a new high', as seen through his spectacles, rose-tinted with tales of the heroics of war.

Once more to shut out a too vivid imagination, one's emotions had to be anaesthetised. The false bravado and showy keenness of the very few who said they wanted to 'rip the guts out of the so and sos' had long since vanished, if it ever really existed, from all but such chaps as Jones. In its place was silent resignation or perhaps pessimistic fatalism regarding a personal future, a realisation that the job had to be done by someone, that somehow that someone had turned out to be each one of us, and finally a realisation that the only possible solution to the situation, otherwise unalterable by us, was to push the grisly business to as swift and successful a conclusion as possible. In spite of some individuals' pessimism regarding a personal future, I don't think anyone doubted in the least the outcome of the struggle as a whole; that was taken for granted.

Though the future seemed to stretch away beyond speculation into the murky mists of doubt, lack of sleep, cold and marching draped with equipment, the thought persisted that some of these rugged, friendly faces round one would almost certainly see victory celebrated and know the feeling of peace once more. Others, and here one tried to turn a blind eye to the keen personal implication, would even more certainly not. Thoughts then assailed the mind in wondering how many of these sturdy forms bobbing along in the section columns would still be bobbing along to the next 'stunt' in two days' or a week's time. It was just not worth speculation, difficult though it was to keep one's mind off it at times. Each day and hour had to be dealt with in the best way possible as it came.

Our escapist mental meanderings were brought to earth with a jolt by the first material evidence of the troubles to come, and thoughts riveted again on the demands of the passing minute. Mortaring had been very heavy, pitting the roads and fields on either side and clipping the trees. Down on the left from the embankment of the road in a very mortared field of newly sprouting corn stood a Bren gun and some kit. Further on, more slashed equipment was scattered, and beside a mortar crater, a lone boot, a small pack and a trouser leg.

Glancing to the other side down the slope, the track-marks of two Bren carriers led up to their remains: one burnt out with loose equipment charred about it, the other thrown on its side beside a crater with bogies and tracks missing in the forlorn attitude of a tipped up, lifeless beetle. Scattered personal kit again told the occupants had been casualties. This scene was a warning notice of mines.

The cutting load we were carrying, soaked windproof, ill-fitting tin hat and cold, wet fingers gripping the rifle were suddenly forgotten. Just at the tree-lined crest of the hill were some German positions with two of our dead still clutching their weapons, crumpled forwards, separated by only a few feet from their objective. New sights and sounds chased each other through one's mind in rapid succession. We stumbled along in the mud, jumping clear from time to time as our tanks, later to support the attack, thundered past, spattering clots of trickling mud over us from their churning tracks. As each heavy monster roared by, the hot oily breath of its vibrant exhaust enveloped us. The crump of mortar fire sounded ahead, and one immediately grudged the tank crews their protective walls of steel. This thought was as quickly cancelled out by the sight of a blistered and smoke-blackened Sherman tank, still radiating heat. Its hatches were flung open, and ribboned with the ash of equipment, more of which was scattered about in the circle of heat-blackened earth on which it rested. Just over the road, the deep, spewed, muddy ruts of more tracks wandering off into an orchard led up to another two of our tanks bellied in the mud.

The guns of both drooped with the same expressive lifelessness of a dead hand. The throbbing power of all three had been silenced in full stride by some 88mm anti-tank gun ahead.

Beyond these smashed tanks, we passed through the new 25-pounder gun area with its attendant noise. Each group of guns scattered over the fields, flashing and recoiling in billowing smoke on bouncing wheels in turn with the mechanical little figures of the gun teams slamming in another shell before each gun had fully come to rest; then a flash, and it bounced anew. Once more the 'crack' and dismal, insistent, tapering shriek accompanied by the softer echoing sound which follows a clap of thunder trailed into the distance behind every ascending missile. We were nearing the front.

About 2 miles along, over the crest of the hill, the Company left the road, crossing a gravel track and trolley lines on the right, by a battered little house which was being used as a first aid post. A dark line of woods lay some 800 yards in front of us, and we hoped we were not again to be in for a wood-clearing battle. However, soon we turned back parallel to the road on a little mud track, passing yet another burnt out Sherman tank.

Not far past the tank Smyg established his HQ in a damaged farm and ordered me to dig in round another small farm building several hundred yards beyond. On our way there we came to realise the Royal Scots had had some bitter fighting between these two buildings to judge by the blood-stained webbing, some battered British rifles and automatic weapons, and several tin hats, one with a bullet hole through it, scattered along the mortar-pitted lane.

It was evident too that the Germans had some deadly anti-tank gunners, and that the battle had been recent, for we saw with sympathy for those tanks which were still intact and rumbling along the nearby road, that yet two more of our Shermans were burnt out on a track alongside our billet, and both were still very hot. It was impossible to tell if the crews had been trapped or not, as the ammunition had cooked off, wrecking and melting everything inside into a twisted, charred mess. The open hatches and a few bits of equipment beside one of them seemed to suggest someone had survived.

In the farm we took over from some pretty tired-looking chaps of the Royal Scots and, leaving the Jocks to improve the positions, I made my way back to Company HQ for further briefing, following a change of plan since the morning. Our objective was now to be the moated farm of Haus Loo. In our initial briefing before leaving Issum we were to have started the attack from the Xanten–Alpen railway line, clear Haus Loo, then, curving round in an arc from the left, clear some houses, first on the left, then some more on the right, check for enemy in a small wood, then dig in on the cross-roads at Bonning. Our attack was still to cover several thousand yards, much of it open country. As the night passed, however, it became increasingly uncertain whether our tanks had been able to reach the railway embankment. One thing was certain: the enemy were resisting even more fanatically than had been expected.

I had not long returned to the Platoon when an American private staggered up the track towards us from the right. It was evident he was not only partly bomb happy, but also the worse for drink. He took an instant and most embarrassing liking to me, and having established I was the 'Chief' of the 'Outfit' he became most insistent in wanting to join the Platoon. We got out of him that his Jeep had blown up on a mine. He stood swaying and bleary eyed, shaking his fist in the direction of the Rhine, streaming forth horrible swear words at the 'Krauts'. As the only way of getting rid of him, and to check he really was what he claimed to be, I chivvied, guided and pulled him back to Company HQ to be evacuated to the rear.

Down in the cellar, Smyg gave him a cup of tea to steady him a bit, as it was not too clear how much his condition was due to blast or to drink. He immediately took Smyg to be a man of great importance, and seemed as impressed as a chap in his state could be. He lurched forward, extending his hand to shake, with the slurred words 'Howd'y General!', spilling his tea as he swayed. Smyg decided he had better be sent to BHQ, so with great difficulty he was bundled into a Jeep and we set off in the dark. Several times he grabbed the steering wheel, nearly causing a pile-up, when he realised we were steering away from the 'Krauts' he was so determined to fight. By this time we had had quite enough of him and got rid of him at the first aid post so they could send him back with the group of casualties lying on the floor on stretchers in the dark. He could only be induced to stay when told he had been 'drafted' to this new 'Platoon'.

Back at Company HQ I rejoined Frank, Smyg and the senior NCOs for the final briefing. There were still no officer replacements and Sgt Cowie and Sgt Oliver attended. The extensive cellar, in which we gathered round a map spread on a packing case, was lined with dozens of bottles of preserved cherries, meat and other interesting concoctions which we made full use of to add variety to our meals.

We were to move off to the start line for the attack at 0445 hours the next morning, 9 March, crossing the Alpen road to a ridge overlooking the railway line which we would have to cross 1,500 yards away over open country, with the farm, our objective, about 700 yards beyond that. I studied the map for a long time to try to memorise it and visualise the lie of the land before returning to my Platoon. There the suffocating fumes of Hexamine tablets burning in a confined space told that supper was being prepared in the cellar.

Outside I was surprised to hear a few stray shells from the direction of the enemy whistle over and crump in the wood on our right front. After much labour the tea was at last made in a biscuit tin, but Pte Cutter, the radio operator, clattered down the steps following the arrival of the shells and tipped the precious, hot, messy liquid over the stairs with his boots. He was very nearly lynched. Pte Laurie, our regular soldier – and regular deserter – had long since vanished into the blue again; we had ceased to count him on our effective strength. A man you cannot rely on in an emergency is better not there.

I dug in one section over the road under L/Cpl McMichael, and we manned the trenches round the farm at last light, but with little fear that the enemy would be in any shape to bother us. Cold was still our chief worry, though several more shells whined over to crump hamlessly in the solitude of the wood during the hours of darkness. At 0345 hours next morning Sgt Dickinson joined me in rousing the Platoon to parade them in the dark, dispersed against the farm in section groups, and check the hundred and one details in preparation for the day's work; we also needed to go over things on the map with the NCOs one more. News had come that the Royal Scots had captured Alpen, which was short and to the right of our objective, and that the Cameronians were pushing on beyond. This was welcome information, but still the position of our forward tanks was confused. Conditions were misty, with visibility only 800 yards, and we heard after the battle that communication by radio, which was normally very good, had broken down between the CO and Brigade back at Issum and even with the artillery link for a while.

The damp mist made the morning very cold as we moved off on foot in the dark to join the other companies crunching along the road between the silent houses of a scattered hamlet on the hill crest after turning off the main road. Here the route was marked by white mine tape. Ammunition- and mortar-loaded carriers groaned and cracked with their tracks as they overtook us.

Groups of laden, push-cart tugging and dejected figures, clutching and comforting babies and children, walked out of the mist ahead – civilian refugees from the first objectives shelled in the valley below. We halted by a wayside heather patch. This was the start line. The first luminosity of the sky and a cold wisp of breeze swirling the mist foretold the dawn. The wonder and magic of the dawn's beauty, always exciting, somehow seemed more beautiful than ever, with the grouped silhouettes of the Jocks against it and the poignant realisation that for many of us it would be our last. Each moment seemed of sufficient value to drink in with all one's senses, even down to the pathetic, chirping attempt at a dawn chorus by a few explosive-stunned birds.

As we looked into the dark valley, a group of glowing rocket trails streaked up in an arc of sparks from the enemy positions on our left front; then came the dismal 'Moaning Minnie' of the discharge of these weapons. One could tell from the arc of flight whether they were coming near enough to worry us. They landed with a succession of crumps some way off among the Canadians on our left. Nevertheless, we readily responded to the resultant order to dig in in case another batch should be aimed at us while we were waiting; we were soon warm, and below the surface. Within minutes, wisps of steam coming up out of the heather about me gave away the positions of the tea brewers, as well as puffs of smoke from those who preferred a cigarette.

In a hollow over the track from us, Chris had established Battalion HQ and we could tell from the activity there shortly after A and D Companies set off, and from the distant but heavy sounds of enemy artillery, mortar, machine gun and rifle fire that things were not going quite according to plan. These two forward companies, through whom we were to leap frog later, were getting a very thin time.

Visibility gradually improved as it grew light. Medium tanks appeared on the hill behind us and several roared down along the skyline, then raced back up again. This puzzled us a bit at first, and with Frank I made my way forward under cover of some trees to get a better look at what was going on down in the valley. We could just make out the sprinkled figures of our two forward companies, tiny specks advancing slowly in line towards the railway embankment, half way to Haus Loo. Dirty black splodges of smoke blossomed among them and drifted off over the fields. Several of the figures lay still behind the advancing line. Just then the 88mm anti-tank guns opened up heavily, sending their stray shots ricocheting with a most frightening sound into the bank and over our heads. They were after the tanks advancing with the Jocks below, and I then realised that the odd activities of the cruiser tanks on the sky line had been a brave effort to distract these guns in drawing their fire from the advancing Shermans.

As we looked, two of our tanks below stopped; little dark shapes in the distance and eddying angry smoke started to curl up from them. We could not make out if any of the crews had got out as some smoke shells asked for by A and D Companies made seeing difficult. By now it was clear that the enemy still held the railway, which Brigade HQ had insisted had been reached by our tanks the night before. One of the leading Platoons was down to nine men let by Cpl Kirkhope, who was later awarded the MM. We heard with amusement after the battle that amid all this fury an immaculately dressed staff officer, complete with large map case and gloves, had appeared at D Company HQ, then temporarily in a small battered house, and had asked for Major Rae, of whom he demanded in a prim, accented voice: 'What is the position here? They tell me at Corps it's crumbling.' Major Rae replied above the noise that the only thing crumbling round there was the house, and that he had better come in and take cover fast. Any reply the staff officer may have attempted was drowned by the arrival of a batch of German rockets.

One of the Jocks had located some civilians in a hillside bunker just below us, and evacuated them to the rear with much weeping and wailing. The Nebelwerfer fired a few more rounds which detonated in a ripple of black puffs and blast quite a way off, and several shells blossomed fairly close, making us hug the earth for a while. Although we could quite probably be seen in our exposed positions near the skyline, Jerry evidently had plenty of targets to keep him otherwise occupied.

At last word came for us to move, 10 Platoon leading, followed by Advance Company HQ Rear. On our immediate left were the Guards, then the Canadians, and on our right the Cameronians, the Royal Scots and in the distance the Americans, all piling in to the 'Wesel Pocket'.

We scrambled down a steep, wooded hill to a mud track, making for a bridge to cross a water obstacle after passing a farm in which we spotted a few German civilians pottering about the yard. By the bridge was a large cream-coloured building which seemed both a pub and a farm to look at, in which the regimental aid post had been set up. At the roadside by a newly laid tank bridge, a white-faced casualty sat, while another blood-streaked, bandage-draped figure staggered with a limp back from the front as we trudged forwards, alert, tense and watchful.

A pattern of flashes and black plumes of smoke spattered across our path a short distance ahead, and as the crump of these mortars enveloped us Pte C took to his heels down the column, 'bomb happy'. Unfortunately he had taken our radio set with him, and short of shooting him as he ran, there was no way of stopping him. Shouts were of no avail. We plodded on, out into the open now, up a slight rise in a ploughed field and towards the two tanks we had seen knocked out earlier. I had made a mental note of these as a guide to keep direction. We still had about 1,000 yards to go to the railway track and the mortars were coming down around us, increasingly in batches of twelve.

We passed between the wrecked tanks, which were still radiating the heat of a furnace, on an oil- and smoke-blackened patch of earth scattered with a few pieces of charred equipment, but there was no sign of the crews, unless they were still inside, cooked.

My Platoon squeaked and clattered their way over and through a fence, Smyg just behind, with the Company spread out in arrowhead formation. Frank was somewhere out on the right. As the distance to the railway embankment narrowed, so the mortaring increased in its intensity. Some way ahead we could now make out the numerous scattered forms of A Company lying in and beside shallow mortar craters.

Our thoughts were interrupted here by a new factor – some very loud whiplash cracks from a sniper firing at us from the right. Just short of A Company Smyg ran over to consult with Maj Stewart on the situation before the next phase of the attack. Another much closer batch of mortaring blasted heavily just to our left and ahead, the smoke tasting pungently in our mouths and nostrils as it blew past. We took cover, and waited. I noticed with surprise as my eyes wandered over the figures of A Company about us that many of the sprawling figures were not taking cover, but lay in the attitudes and stillness of death, while others could be seen from their involuntary movements to be wounded. As we waited, the mortars continued to smudge black, oily-looking smoke puffs over the fields of short stubble, each emitting the familiar crump and shrapnel whine of decreasing note. There was something evilly decisive and disconcerting about this sound.

Smyg called me over to where he crouched in the stubble with Maj Stewart, and told me to take my chaps on up to the railway embankment and dig in there. Being the only one on my feet during this time, getting to and from Smyg was decidedly unhealthy, as the sniper gave me individual attention materialising in a series of deafening cracks from bullets passing near my head.

It was a tremendous job getting the chaps out of their craters and over the few extra yards to the railway track to dig in there. With the continued bursting of mortars and crack of snipers' bullets, the prospect of leaving what protection any shallow rut or crater the ground provided was not inviting.

I was astonished to see from my watch that although the attack had started at eight that morning, it was already midday! Where on earth had the time gone to? I had just started digging in when a call came for me to go to an 'O' Group along the embankment to where Alan, Maj Stewart and several others were congregated in a ground-hugging cluster beside a railway gangers' small concrete hut. The bank was just tall enough to afford protection from machine gun fire from the other side of it if one adopted a shuffling, half-crawling stoop.

The information was that the heavy reaction of the enemy in mortar, artillery and small-arms fire and his unexpected tenancy of the railway bank, from which he had now been driven, together with the casualties of the two leading companies in getting this far, meant that we in B Company, together with C, would have to give up all thought of penetrating to the cross-roads, but would have to attack the high ground of Haus Loo woods and the farm beyond to which the enemy had withdrawn. This advance would mean we had another 1,000 yards of open ground to cross. Our right flank was exposed because some factory buildings out there which were supposed to have been taken by the Cameronians had been established as one of the sources of the sniper and machine gun fire. The Company 18 set radio had been out of action from the start of the attack. Also, it was impossible in the early stages to call for artillery fire support as the gunners set had had a bullet through it. It was miraculous that this set again came to life later at a crucial moment when it was used to call down smoke shells to screen the digging in on the objective.

Smyg asked me to take my Platoon over the embankment immediately and work our way over to the left against it, then lie there until the other platoons were in position for the attack to go in. We were promised a smokescreen for the assault to give us some cover over the open ground. I arranged with Frank to fire two red Verey lights low across our front to let us know when the attack was going in. Haus Loo was to get a heavy 'stonk' from the artillery before we went forward.

I formed the Platoon up on the near side of the railway embankment and after a lot of vocal effort, they followed me over well in one wave. As we skipped across the metals of the tracks, the crackle and hum of snipers' bullets and machine gun fire spattered about exactly like a shower of hail. The sudden violence of this murderous fire as we crossed the skyline proved later to have temporarily unnerved the two new chaps carrying the 2-inch mortar and the PIAT, and in their frantic dive down the bank to get clear, they jettisoned their loads to speed their steps, including some mortar bombs – a disgraceful performance, which I did not get to hear about till the evening.

The sniping was now heavy, sustained and accurate. Behind us the bank absorbed the numerous missiles with a loud, heavy thumping which came simultaneously to the sharp crackle of their passage through the air, and we were dismayed to find as we dashed and crawled the 150 yards to the left to get to the attack position that there was next to no cover at all.

Jerry, seeing us scuttling along, realised another attack was forming up, and gave us all he had. To the crackle and clump of bullets, he added his artillery and mortar fire. Due to the noise, it was rapidly becoming impossible to exert control vocally over the Platoon which was spread out in section groups some distance along the bank. However, I was pleased to know section commanders had briefed each chap on the proceedings: the barrage, smoke shells, red Verey lights, then forward in line with bayonets fixed. All each should do now was to try to survive, ready to go forward at the red flares.

Several times I got up to satisfy myself on the layout of the Platoon, and how they were getting on, but I was only too pleased to drop flat again to elude the jet of bullets this attracted. There was not the slightest sign yet of any of the rest of the Company, and I began to wonder if the fire had become too heavy for them to get over the embankment to join us. As we waited I quickly realised our choice of position could hardly have been less fortunate in the circumstances. A cart track feathered with a few trees led from the farm objective to the railway line over which it crossed on our immediate left. The enemy had obviously registered this junction of the railway and the track as a defence fire task for his mortars and artillery. We were increasingly subjected, to mortaring especially, on a scale never previously met even at Heinsberg and which was never subsequently surpassed.

Jerry, in his desperate efforts to stem our advance and gain time for evacuation over the Rhine, was literally firing off all the stocks of mortar ammunition that he could not evacuate with him to get rid of it. This was supplemented heavily from time with Moaning Minnie multiple rocket mortars, 88mm anti-tank guns firing solid and high-explosive shot, and the occasional heavier long-range shell from the other side of the Rhine. By now I had the bulk of the Platoon lying in a meandering shallow gully in the field on my right and beside me along a shallow depression at the foot of the embankment. The snipers could obviously still see our small packs sticking up as we lay on our stomachs, watching forward between the rim of our tin hats and the ground, for whenever one moved a volley of bullets swept, ripping the grass ahead and spattering the bank behind.

So far the only casualties in the Platoon were Pte Blackwood, hit in the knee, and Pte Griffiths, the small nervous chap who had gone to sleep while on duty in Broederbosch Woods, who was wounded. Pte Fox, who lay near me in the ditch, was shaken but proud of two remarkable escapes from the snipers, which he showed me to pass the time. One bullet had drilled an oblong, neat gash through the metal of his shovel as it was held in his webbing straps, passing between it and his chest, while a second had nicked a line of neat holes through the folds of his windproof below his ribs; neither touched him. Unhappily he was finally hit and killed at the close of the day on the objective. How cruel this seemed. The third hit in a few hours, and once again a fraction of an inch would have saved him. My second Pte Jones, not the paratrooper, was also hit and died three days later.

Time was creeping on, but still there was no sign of the red Verey or the rest of the Company. A series of violent bangs just behind and the revving of tank engines informed us that several Shermans were firing from a hull-down position on the far side of the railway bank. This was unfortunate as it brought immediate, accurate and heavy 88mm anti-tank fire from a concealed enemy gun in the woods bordering Haus Loo. Pte Jones, the parachutist, was crawling towards a culvert 10 yards away to have a look through when a black flash enveloped it and hid him from view. Another, a solid shot, fell short at immense velocity ploughing into the earth ahead, stretching the whole surface of the ground on which we lay and, to our amazement, such was the force of the impact that the earth heaved sluggishly like jelly to and fro. Jones lay still a while as the smoke cleared, then to my relief he shook himself and continued towards the culvert. A third high-explosive shot smashed into the bank just above my head, close enough for me to feel a stunning hot force of the blast like a sudden cushioned weight jerked heavily on my back.

These tanks, we began to realise, had come up to support an attack being put in by the Guards on our immediate left. The earth of the green field ahead was rapidly becoming mutilated with a congested pattern of dark-rimmed craters. These were interconnected with ripped turf from shrapnel, bullets and solid-shot anti-tank shells, giving the impression that a madman had been at work with a monstrous plough.

At last the barrage of swiftly dropping shells erupted with shattering concussion on the smoke-hazed objective. The enemy, taking this as a sign that we were already moving forward to the attack, retaliated by heavily plastering the field ahead with mortars and wicked-looking cascades of phosphorous bombs from their Moaning Minnie rocket launchers. These spread a fiery yellow wall, a smoking inferno of pungent smoke and flame 150 yards ahead of us. A lifetime seemed to be passing in waiting for the red Verey to be fired which would signal our attack. Our present situation was so murderous I think we were almost praying for the appearance of these soaring red stars to release some of the pent-up misery in movement. I was getting really worried at this delay which had pinned us right on a German DF task target. We had no radio since Pte C's nerve had gone and he had run off with it. The Jocks were getting restive and near mutiny under the appalling blanket of continuous explosions and crackle of bullets embedding themselves into the railway bank and ripping the field. Over the track on our left heavy tank activity, small-arms firing, piteous cries from the wounded and shouts for stretcher bearers told that the Guards were having a thin time.

The clatter and squeak of tank tracks and the zoom of a Sherman's engine approached above the din from our left rear.

The armour was starting to move forward. Suddenly a loud explosion from an 88mm shell snuffed out this noise. In its stead, after a few seconds came agonised cries for help and for stretcher bearers. Black, billowing smoke and then towering tongues of licking petrol- and oil-fed flame spurted up from over the bank about 50 yards away. The cries swiftly grew louder and more agonised as the flaming tank heated up, and turned into shrieks of long, drawn-out, shrill and infinite agony above the roar of fuel-fed flames. There was something infinitely terrible about these cries from the trapped tank crew to which we, helplessly pinned down, had to listen. Violent, multiple, muffled detonations from the tank spurted the tumbling, flame-laced, black smoke pall up about 100 feet as the ammunition exploded, stilling the cries of the burning men. Now only the small-arms ammunition cracked off in an erratic continuous stream in the heat.

While the smoke still trailed a dirty pall into the sky, the roar of the engine of another tank drew our eyes to a second Sherman which lurched into view over the bank at the head of the track to the farm. There it halted, its guns viciously spitting shells and red tracer, swinging its turret as it raked the woods ahead in a solid hail of metal. Had I the authority I would have given that second tank commander a medal on the spot for pressing on in spite of seeing what a hideous end might overtake him at any moment.

The barrage was followed by smoke shells, but still no red Vereys soared to signal the attack. Had Frank been hit? I debated whether to advance without the signal. If we did so and the attack plans had for some reason, as so often before, been changed, we might find ourselves on the objective only to be attacked by our own troops' tanks and shells in error or to coincide with a continuation of the barrage. With no radio, there seemed only one solution. Telling Sgt Dickinson to take over for a few minutes, I crawled painfully along the ditch, then scrambled back over the railway track to clarify the position with Maj Stewart on the other side. I got over without being shot at, passing distressingly numerous casualties as I crawled through A Company positions on the far side of the bank towards Andrew. He was surprised to see me and said the rest of the company with Frank and Smyg had gone over the bank not long after we had done. Neither of us could fathom what had gone wrong. I began to feel pretty sure B Coy HQ must once again have been wiped out. Andrew advised a cautious advance to the objective. I crawled back to my men, picking up some weapons belonging to casualties on the way, and for the first time noticed that my trouser leg was ripped and my leg had been cut quite messily some time in the advance. Before we had set out from England, my preconceived idea of an infantryman's value on the battlefield had been largely dominated by visions of spectacular assaults, bayoneting and hand-to-hand combat playing quite a prominent part as in the films. I now realised from our experience so far that though these situations did arise, it was amazing how much of our lives, even in some attacks, consisted as in the game of chess or drafts in movement to the right positions on the board as a potential or actual threat, and the need to out-survive the enemy however adverse the circumstances seemed to be. If this were done, despite the frightening worst of the weapons involved, at the end of the 'day' when the smoke of battle cleared away, if one had reached the objective or managed to cling to it, our very presence as fragile puny human units motivated by the right spirit took us time after time with the sometimes gradual realisation that the battle had been won.

I was rather surprised as I scrambled down the embankment to rejoin the Platoon, again without further trouble from enemy snipers, to look down at their forms miraculously grouped in gullies of green grass almost like untouched oases in a ploughed field. There had been no further casualties. I sent a runner to sections with the order 'prepare to move', then forward we went in line over the marshy, long stretch of grass to the objective at a fast walk with weapons at the alert.

A line of mortar bombs fell heavily ahead and we moved on through the smoke still twirling and eddying as it blew back past us. How queer the seeming chances of their fall, and the thoughts that flitted through my mind. A surer hand than chance seemed to be guiding us, for had we moved off 30 seconds earlier the bombs would have coincided exactly with our stooping line of figures, hopping round craters and plodding forwards. Pte Blackwood, unable to keep up after his hit in the knee, gallantly limped along in the rear. A batch of Moaning Minnies and phosphorus shells followed the mortars, and a few more loud bangs back near the embankment helped persuade us we were no worse off in our present position of advance.

We were halfway there, and the expected hail of bullets when we were seen by the enemy had not come, to our amazement; nor had we seen any sign of the rest of the Company. If the enemy did open up with small arms, the chaps knew what to do. We would have to rush forwards a section at a time in short dashes under covering fire from the others and press on as fast as possible because we could not long survive in the open beneath the high ground of the objective.

We could see the trees and high ground of Haus Loo looming through the smoke of explosives hanging in a throat-drying fog above the grass. The low-lying ground was in part flooded. In this water and on the grass we were astonished and saddened to recognise the bodies of several of the chaps from the rest of the Company. More puzzled than ever we got through the water and climbed the sandy, wooded bank, which was seemingly deserted, working round to the right for more cover, and at the same time realising that in some queer way the attack had gone in without the red Verey signals, and in consequence without us. In view of this I had reluctantly accepted the conclusion that both Smyg and Frank must have become casualties.

A dead German lay near the crest, and ahead the ground dropped away to a waterfilled moat surrounding an island, with a glimpse of the farm beyond. The light was just beginning to fail in the late afternoon, and a flashing, twinkling through the trees followed by the crash of further bombs spurred us to advance fast round the rim of the moat between the trees to try to unravel the mystery of what had happened.

My astonishment was matched by my relief when I nearly skidded into a hole on the outer rim of the moat, and found Smyg and Frank digging there. They were both equally astonished, having written us off as casualties when we failed to arrive on the objective with them. After establishing that my Platoon was still largely intact, Smyg was just beginning to get rather annoyed, when I asked why the red Verey had not been fired: in the confused and shattering interval between my leaving them to advance over the railway bank, and the time of the attack, they had both forgotten to fire the Verey! In their advance far to the right of us in the smoke there was no chance of our having seen them move forward. Pte C, who had run off with our radio, was once again the recipient of hearty curses for the resultant shambles his thoughtless action might have led to, not to mention loss of life.

My chaps joined the rest of the Company in digging in as fast as they could in the explosives-tasting evening mist. They were just about dead beat. It was only the continuing fall of enemy projectiles round Haus Loo which prompted this additional burst of energy, for the day, which had started very early, had been a singularly demanding one.

The attack had attained its objective, but was even more confused than I had at first thought, as B and C Companies had been quite out of touch with each other during the advance due to radio failure, and also C Company had run into such fierce resistance initially that they had been driven back to the embankment, before eventually fighting their way forward to the farm buildings some time after B Company had seized their objective. The result of this was that when C Coy finally fought their way forwards under covering fire from the tanks, a serious battle accident was only averted by B Coy using yellow smoke flares to signal they were already in the position being attacked.

The Germans had fought fanatically in this action. A German sergeant taken in the farm buildings said their intention was to fight to the last man. One young German was overrun and despatched with a bayonet while still firing his Spandau with his jaw shot away. He was standing on the dead body of a comrade as he lay in the trench bottom to get a better firing position.

Frank Coutts shot his first personal kill with a rifle when he selected one of two Germans 'nattering to each other 50 yards off' on the objective. Another German, one of several bodies scattered about the objective, had died from his wounds when, lying on the stretcher, he was deserted by his comrades. Another batch of Germans had tried to stem the advance by firing off all their *panzerfaust* anti-tank projectiles at the advancing Jocks from point-blank range. In dealing with these Jerries, Cpl Wilson won an MM. Among other awards to result from this action, Maj Stewart and Maj Rae won MCs and Pte Finlayson, a stretcher bearer working with our Company, an MM. The cost had been one officer and eighty other ranks killed or wounded.

In the advance, one section had gone astray in the smoke and I sent out a patrol to search for these chaps, as well as to collect the mortar and PIAT now reported missing by their ashamed owners. It was fortunate this patrol went back so soon, for they were able to aid several other casualties hit and left for dead during the advance.

These casualties and others on the objective, some in agony with multiple and amputation wounds, were causing us much distress. We could only evacuate them very slowly and painfully two or three at a time, carried by men already worn out, stumbling well over a mile across the shattered unfamiliar and in places flooded landscape in inky blackness. The Germans were still doing their best to add what difficulties they could contribute right through till the next morning when Sgt Laidlaw was hit in guiding a party of stretcher bearers.

Two of the men in Company HQ, one of them Cpl McNaughton, were killed by a direct hit from a bomb in their slit trench, and when I made my way back to get orders for the night from Smyg, I found him busy burying these two. In the failing light another party of men were burying their friends of a few hours before in a sad little group out in the field. It was getting too dark, however, and this work was postponed until the morning. The horizon flickered and smouldered on two sides with battle fires like distant volcanoes.

A queer stillness had settled with the chill of night and to the accompaniment of occasional salvos of long-distance shells, mortars or 'Minnies', we hugged our gas capes tight about us and settled in for the long night vigil. The enemy had seemed so desperate, we had quite a feeling some form of counter-attack might be tried before dawn to knock any further advance off balance.

It somehow was quite in keeping with this mad, unreal existence that our mail should arrive last thing with the rations;

and that among the letters to cheer one Company Commander up at the end of his 'day's work', and so typical of the department concerned, was an income tax demand.

Towards dawn I clambered out of my hole on the crest of the wooded bank to make my way round the section positions to see all was well. It was frightfully cold and truly deathly still. I seemed quite alone on the hill, an island in a sea of gently moving mist covering the fields, with only the dark dim shapes of trees and hedges like jagged rocks poking out to the cold, starlit dawn sky. Suddenly I paused to listen intently. Yes there it was again, a faint despairing cry for help from somewhere towards the railway track beneath that clammy chill fog. It had to be a wounded chap either left for dead, but now recovered, or someone hit somewhere unnoticed, perhaps even a Jerry. I sent off a patrol with a stretcher to see what they could find, though it was still dark.

It was quite a long time before Cpl Parry, Jones and Cupit came puffing back up the bank carrying Pte Laidlaw, a lanky, amusing fellow, still in surprising spirits though near frozen and with a foot blown off at the ankle. Taking full advantage of a good swig at the treacly, warming black rum carried as a Platoon reserve in Sgt Dickinson's waterbottle, he even raised a smile and a joke, and thanked his bearers for the ride. He said he had called for help long and often during the night as he lay 500 yards short of the objective after a mortar had felled him in the advance, but it was many hours before the battle noises had died down sufficiently for him to be heard.

While Pte Laidlaw was being dealt with, a message had come via the 18 set – rather surprisingly, as a sniper had seemingly smashed it with a bullet during the advance – that the 'Dandy Boys' (our nickname for the 7th/9th Royal Scots) would be advancing through our positions at 0730 hours to keep up pressure on the enemy and would move up under cover of an artillery barrage.

Just on time the figures of the Royal Scots materialised in scattered groups picking their way through the mist, and between the trees of a shattered orchard beneath our bank, from which our Jocks encouraged them on as they poked their muffled heads and steaming mugs of tea from holes in the sandy slope. Though many of the bantering remarks were ribald, one knew they were far from unsympathetic, and the hunched up figures, weapons held across their bodies at the alert with both hands, bravely slung the banter back and plodded by as the shells shrieked in terribly close ahead. The barrage had been too close, as we had feared, and a couple of casualties were carried back on stretchers down the still advancing column up which they had walked intact themselves so short a time before.

The roar of an engine and the squeaking metallic clatter of its tracks announced the first of the supporting Churchill tanks ploughing and rolling sluggishly over the marshy ground in the eddying remnants of the mist, with pennant flying from its wireless mast. It had the same business-like power and majesty as a battleship at sea. The hunched, muffled, earphones-clad head and shoulders of the tank commander showed out of the turret. He was speaking into a microphone. I caught a blinding flash and black billow of smoke in the corner of my eye from the direction of the tank, and as I swung my head to look, it was enveloped in a ballooning pall of tumbling smoke and the explosion of a mine boomed in our ears. The tank revved once loudly and then there was silence, while the smoke drifted away.

As the tank took shape again out of the smoke we were relieved, and not a little surprised, to see the crew climb out unhurt to inspect the damage. Four links had been blown from the front of the right-hand track. The bogies and sprocket seemed intact. Within 2 hours we heard another roar of sound from the tank as it lurched forwards, repaired, and spinning clots of mud in its wake as it raced to catch up with the dwindling racket of the attack.

When these sounds had faded away, our eyes returned to the dismal scene about us and to reckoning up the toll we had suffered the day before. As a Company, however, we had been fortunate, and with this consolation we continued the burying of the dead lying in the marsh, carrying them to higher parts of the field to find a resting place. For each we fashioned a rough cross from the wood of the ration boxes, on which we wrote a name and number and hung a tin hat. The map reference of the graves was carefully recorded to be passed on to the War Graves

Commission, who would eventually move them to a military cemetery. It was difficult to read the familiar names of such hearty lively chaps on these crosses without an upsurge of queerly persistent unbelief to what we saw and were doing; that we would not see them again, nor they their loved ones at home. Was it but chance that any one of us should not be being buried by the ones to whom we had just said farewell? Indeed this feeling of unreality would often persist for quite a time; one would think, where's old so-and-so got to these days? Then one would remember but still only accept the thought with lingering reservations, for each lived on in one's thoughts in unfading youth with far more semblance of reality than that unreal morning scene. Among those we buried was the German Frank Coutts had shot.

While we were engaged in this task, Bren carriers were zig-zagging over the fields collecting other bodies and their weapons, especially those of the Guards who had put in a fine 'text book' attack on our left. In doing this they had suffered very heavily as we could see from the bodies still scattered over the fields. Reports reached us that one Guards platoon, after losing its officer and sergeant early in the attack, had been taken over by a corporal, who seeing two chaps in their first attack waver, then turn back under the mounting casualties, had shot them as an example to the others.

In the morning word came that Sgt Dickinson was to report to Battalion HQ for UK leave. What a queer life of contrasts, and how nearly he had missed it on so many occasions, not least in the activities of the day before. Grinning from ear to ear, he was off like a shot while the going was good.

Now that the Royal Scots attack had gone through, Smyg took his HQ and the other two Platoons on to the farm, a fine palatial red brick building coloured with a cream wash, but very battered from yesterday's battle. We in 10 Platoon were to spread out round the walls of the flooded moat, in which floated numerous dead ducks and branches blasted off the trees, and dig in there. I took a working party along to the farm to help in disposing of another sad task, the cattle. The large cowshed was full of these fine beasts, many terribly wounded, others unhurt but terrified and needing food and water. Many more were dead. The roof had been repeatedly hit by mortars and artillery which had spread down inside, and the walls had been punctured by high velocity tank shells. There was nothing for it but to shoot those animals that were in the worst state, while a group of German civilians, slave workers and a few Jocks dug a large pit out in the field. Next the carcasses were towed out to be buried with the help of a carrier.

The farm must have been a fine place and though every room was spattered with plaster, broken glass and smashed furniture, one could see it was once quite a manor house. Already the retreating Germans, the displaced persons and perhaps even a few of the Jocks had looted the farm from cellar to attic. Every drawer was pulled from its socket and the contents of material, clothes, papers, toys, photographs, books and myriad little things of family life were strewn ankle deep everywhere. Whoever's home it was, friend or enemy, it was a sad sight to see. I made my way right up into the roof to look through gaps in the tiles out over the landscape to the distant Rhine. Here and there columns of sluggish smoke hung in the sky above the last act in the battle for the 'Wesel Pocket'. With the binoculars I could occasionally make out signs of activity by vehicles and men, and with my ears, faint erratic sounds of battle. It seemed unlikely we would be called on to put in another attack this side of the Rhine. In the front of the house were one or two more dead Germans, and a few of their tin hats, gas mask containers and camouflaged ground sheets – three things they nearly always left behind. The Jocks had collected a heap of their weapons and were playing around with one of the anti-tank guns which had been such a menace to us, as we noted from the empty shell cases littered about.

During the attack, rumours had circulated that a large part, if not all, of the Cameronian company fighting on our right, had in some mysterious way been overrun and captured. I still do not know to what extent this report was true, but it seemed to explain why the buildings to our right still proved to be enemy occupied when we attacked. One constantly met such reports and rumours in action. This one seemed to have some substance, however, as we recaptured a lot of Cameronians among the troops at a POW camp we overran four weeks later. They had recently been taken and rumours had it that they were the same ones.

Tammy Youngson was acting OC C Company while Donald Hogg was taking his turn 'Left out of battle', and in the evening I visited him in the cellar of the farm where he had established his HQ. The place was partitioned off with blankets hung up as curtains and the floor covered with straw. In one corner a huddled and frightened group of German men, women and children were trying to prepare some food by the light of a candle. Whether these were the owners of the farm or not was hard to decide. The Jocks had unearthed a large barrel of beer somewhere, which Frank tapped to give the men a taste each in a mess-tin – after one of the NCOs had tried some out on a farm dog who lapped it up with relish, and still remained on his feet. This seemed to indicate the retreating Germans had not added any more deadly ingredients to it than those normally present.

I slept the night in a pile of straw in a stable, the former dormitory of the slave workers, going once round sections scattered on the rim of the moat in the early hours. Frank and 'Smyg' had settled in with Tammy down in the cellar, but it was far too stuffy down there. At daybreak next day the 25-pounders moved in round the farm, and were soon firing and disturbing our interval of peace. We gathered that the end of the 'Pocket', ('of nuisance value only') as the BBC had described it to the annoyance of the Jocks, must be very near, judging by the streams of prisoners trudging back down the main road.

This was the end of the last large-scale slogging 'set piece' battle which had cleared the western bank of the Rhine from Holland to Dusseldorf; though, as we were to find, it was not the last fight of all by any means. We came later to know how decisive the German defeat had been; they had lost the cream of eighteen divisions, and an estimated 100,000 killed, wounded and prisoners and their equipment.

SPRING AND THE BUILD-UP
FOR THE RHINE CROSSING

L ate in the morning, a call came to move about a mile to the farm occupied by Battalion HQ in preparation for another journey on an advance party. We passed scavenger teams still at work with carriers in the fields, collecting the debris of weapons and kit and a few more dead from the scene of the battle on either side of the railway track. The tanks had paid a pretty heavy toll in this advance, and we picked our way past several more burnt out Shermans and Churchill Crocodile flame-throwing tanks and trailers, each in its patch of scorched earth amid the sprinkled craters.

In the farmyard at Battalion HQ, I found the Sgt Cook, 'Tam' Beattie, preparing several ducks for lunch as a surprise for the CO. The news was that we were to move by road to the Marienbaum–Xanten area and find billets for the Battalion scattered along the main road about 3 miles back from the Rhine where we would be in Brigade reserve. 52nd Div would hold this stretch of the Rhine in company with 3rd Div in preparation for the build-up and assault crossing of the river.

Standing round the trucks waiting for the word to go, it was pleasant to see the officers and NCOs from the other Companies and chat with them again: John Henderson, Bob Bearpark, Jimmy Wannop, Ian Scott, Jock Beattie, 'Wee Mac' McColl and others. We were sorry to find that among the casualties Lt Brown had been wounded. It had been freezing hard overnight and the fields were still filmed with frost. Once the two trucks into which we crowded moved off, we rapidly became terribly cold. Our bed rolls were piled up in one end and we crowded, watching the passing landscape out of the back of the truck. The smaller roads were frozen and mud-ribbed, and the main ones crumbling under huge convoys of tanks, guns, armoured cars and supply vehicles freed by the end of the battle and already regrouping for the immense task of crossing the Rhine, and the build-up for the battles beyond. We were cheered to meet numerous truck-loads of prisoners coming back from the river.

To get to our destination some miles to the north-west, we passed through scenes indicating the heavy battles the Canadians had fought. This included forests shattered with explosives, the tops of the trees sheared off and all the usual dreary litter of armoured vehicles, dead cattle and smashed farms. Each group of scattered clues conjured to our minds the wealth of effort, misery, 'guts' and probable loss in some home of a loved one, which had been exacted yard by yard and crater by crater now so easily spinning past in our wake.

Outside one farm a group of Canadians had slaughtered several pigs which they had strung up to a beam while they gutted them to provide fresh meat. Between attacks, one developed the knack of relaxing to the utmost in enjoying such peace as the passing moment offered. This we were engaged in doing, standing in a tight group in the back of the truck, holding on to the canvas-covered bars of the roof as we swayed about. Next to me Sgt Brennan of B Company had a Sten gun slung from his shoulder, and in changing his hold for support in the roof of the truck the gun slipped butt downwards and hit the floor between us. At the best of times those early versions of the Sten gun were unsafe, for they only needed such a jolt to set them off by jerking the bolt back on its spring, which in returning would fire the gun. So it was that just as we arrived in Marienbaum, a deafening burst of five rounds sprayed between our tightly clustered heads revealing five splashes of daylight in a line along the canvas roof. Fortunately, at the fifth round, the gun, still upright on its butt, jammed and fell with a clatter over our boots.

With this unexpected firing, the truck crunched to a halt and the two in the front seats came round to see what was up. I still find it difficult to understand how no one was hit, especially as we were packed tight like passengers strap-hanging in a rush hour tube train. How different the story might have been if the gun had continued firing as it fell to the floor! The magazine should, of course, have not been left on. So accepted a part of life had closely passing missiles become, that apart from a few pointed remarks and wisecracks the incident was soon forgotten. Of recent weeks and months I had several times come to marvel at the aptness, yet infinitely delicate balance of that neat saying: 'A miss is as good as a mile.'

It was getting late when we arrived and we chose a large farm beside the road for the night, which next day when the Battalion arrived was allotted to D Company. It was a rather gloomy building, with large, 'Victorian', darkly furnished rooms. The subdued, frightened German family were informed of our plans, being greatly relieved to learn they would be allowed to remain in the cellar, at least for the night.

We chose the dining room as our resting place, got the fire going and barricaded the entrances so that we could settle in for a blessed sleep in comparative warmth and, we hoped, peace. Next day we selected a nice flat over a shop in Marienbaum for our HQ, with the Platoons in five battered houses bordering the gravelled war memorial square. Behind us the riddled steeple of the church contained an artillery observation post looking out over the Rhine. The rest of the Battalion had billets scattered either side of the fairly straight road towards Xanten in houses and farms. Brigade HQ was in a moated, red brick château beside two blown bridges patched up by the engineers with Bailey bridge sections.

Frank and Smyg were very pleased with our billet and we were delighted to find that a hot bath could be coaxed into being there. Smyg was also in a position to invite other company commanders to lunch at a table, sitting on chairs and eating off plates for a change!

We became aware that a shame-faced Pte C was again in our midst when we were busily engaged in getting the Platoons and their equipment re-organised. The truth was that he was just totally unsuitable for the work, and he was fortunate to get off with a series of prime rockets at various levels, and so could congratulate himself on having avoided the firing squad he would inevitably have faced had he been in an earlier war. Pte Jones also came in for a broadside for turning up on Company parade in the square in all the varied trappings of his highly irregular dress, in which he looked like a cross between a tramp and a bedouin sheik. He had failed to realise that the dress tolerated in action would not pass on an inspection parade. Our dress was becoming rather motley as it was, for replacements to casualties had not been provided with windproof, hooded smocks, but instead wore battledress.

Our task, we quickly learned, had two objectives: firstly, to be prepared to counter-attack any enemy who might cross the river and penetrate the 6th HLI positions bordering it, and secondly, to seal off completely our sector of the river frontage from all unauthorised persons without passes and of whatever glittering rank. This second job proved a most demanding and difficult one as sixteen posts had to be manned night and day for a fortnight, and an extraordinary number of high-ranking officers tried to bluster their way past adamant but highly uncomfortable Jocks at checkpoints, who demanded to see passes these exalted personages could not produce. On occasion even the CO had to come out to do his spell of stag to deal with more than usually persistent 'big-wigs'.

While all this careful sealing and screening was going on masses of interesting units and vehicles, including amphibious tanks and Buffaloes, bridging pontoons, hundreds of guns and mountains of ammunition, were piling into every available space. During daylight hours, more and more smoke generators and canisters tended by pioneers appeared over the countryside, pouring out coiling billows of bluish and yellow smoke screens to keep the enemy guessing on the date and place of the crossing.

One particular cross-roads just outside Marienbaum, which we had to staff with a check post, proved to be quite a dangerous spot. 88mm high-explosive shells arrived at frequent and odd intervals to blossom accurately all round and on it. These high velocity shells unfortunately arrived faster than sound, and so gave no warning. Because it was an important checkpoint on the main road those on duty always included an officer and a regimental policeman. One evening I had just completed a duty of two sets of four hours with an NCO, and we had strolled over the road to a tiny hut in which the next shift slept in the cellar to shout down the stairs for them to get ready for their stag, and were standing chatting just inside the doorway as there were no vehicles in sight, when the first shell to come over for some hours erupted with an awful racket, splashing the front of the hut with shrapnel. After a respectful pause to see if this was going to be followed by the rest of the salvo, four more crashes shook the little building from across the road, and alongside in the garden. When we again, and not too happily, stepped outside to deal with another vehicle, it gave me at least a queerly chilling shock which persisted for some time to see a new, shallow, grey, dust-rimmed crater within 3 feet of the border of the road on which spot we had stood for eight hours that day, and had just vacated three minutes before. These guns must have been firing at a range of not less than 4 miles, and probably 5, and were seldom far off target. I was amazed that an anti-aircraft gun could be so effective in a long-distance ground role.

The awareness that these guns had us so well registered made all subsequent stags on this spot singularly unsettling, and although, as far as I know, no further direct hits were scored exactly on the cross-roads, very many shells continued to crash their frightening sudden presence like a distant sinister dart player, all around the bull's eye in the days to come. The drivers of the various vehicles seemed also to appreciate the situation and were as reluctant as anyone to linger on the target longer than duty or necessity demanded. The general routine of firing worked out – with unpleasant variations – to a volley every 15 minutes for 2 hours, then a break. As time passed, more and more units were given passes and in consequence, our work, grew easier.

When they were not engaged on these checkpoints, there seemed plenty to occupy the Jocks; they wrote letters, painted vehicles and unit signs, overhauled equipment, and Brown, in common with most of the other company Jeep drivers, added refinements to the home-made side panels and windows of his vehicle. All our transport had to be dug in to withstand the heavy artillery retaliation we expected on 'R' Day when the crossing of the Rhine commenced. 'Eccie' Douglas, the cook, built a wonderful dugout for himself and his pet cat and goat. Another large one was started for the men of Company HQ, situated next to the monument in the town square, and we all worked in shifts on this.

We had arrived in Marienbaum on the evening of 11 March with the advance party, and within our first week there we became aware with pleasure that spring was awakening about us. Buds, spurred on by a warmer drier spell of weather, burst into soft mantles of fresh greenery on the hedgerows. The warmth of the sun which shone for several days out of a blue sky could be felt not only on our skin, but in the quickening of life and a lightness of heart, the more appreciated for its gentle strangeness which came peeping shyly from the dead skeletons of winter foliage. One became aware that the increasing song of the birds was being echoed subconsciously by the Jocks as they whistled in the same spirit about their work. In this lull between the storms, softened with the reawakening of nature and with the sight of lambs and calves wandering in the war-pitted fields, the thought of fighting and killing somehow seemed quite out of place and unreal, an ugly thing far more suited to the frosts, chill and misery of winter darkness. Even the muddy ground, for so long slushed with rain and snow or iron ribbed with ice, was drying to dust clouds under the wheels of countless vehicles.

Plenty of captured drink appeared from somewhere and several wild parties took place at various headquarters. One tremendous one at Battalion HQ with a large number of the officers present was just being brought to its close by the CO standing on a rickety chair at the head of the table to toast 'Victory'. At the crucial moment, the chair crunched to matchwood under the weight and zest of Chris Melville, who toppled backwards and disappeared from view with a crinkling clatter under the voluminous folds of a large wall map torn loose from its anchorage as he tumbled. At another party a nameless and no less illustrious officer was reported to have 'let off steam' towards the end of the evening by swinging like Tarzan from a chandelier while blazing away with his Luger pistol at objects which took his fancy round the room.

For a while we all seemed to be preoccupied with animals left by the civilians who had fled before the fighting, or had since been evacuated to maintain security. Any civilian or other person who could give no authority for being there was immediately arrested. All sheep, pigs, horses and cattle were driven back to collecting points to the rear to the accompaniment of many amusing, hectic and sometimes sad scenes. Maj Davidson and Maj Hogg, and other people who had farmed back in the Border country, joined in to play a valiant part with twirling of sticks, scuttering of hooves, clouds of dust and wild farmyard sounds. Many of the lesser animals and poultry were eaten. Out in a cratered field I found a skinny lamb tottering about which had lost its mother to a stray German shell and which was bleating piteously, and in so doing, to my mind expressing more vividly the misery of war in its symbolic simplicity than any of the horrors I had yet seen. I managed to catch it, and gave it to a Jock whom I knew was billeted in a farm which possessed a very lively nanny goat in good milking fettle, in the hope that this mischievous animal would consent to act as a foster mother. The Jock asserted that whether the goat consented or not, his section would see that the necessary milk was extracted at intervals to get the lamb in good running order again. This goat was a demon for charging one in the seat of the trousers with its butting horny head immediately one's back was turned. It was an interesting sight to see a section of determined and enthusiastic Jocks in their weapon-scattered billet, and in constrast to their normal occupation, intent on comforting and feeding this spindly-legged bleating mite. Even the CO had come by a fat dachshund as a pet, and was followed everywhere by this waddling German sausage.

This dog was christened Baron, and as far as I can recollect was given to the CO by an actual old and rather likeable baron who lived in a castle in the nearby wooded hills, and whom I later met while engaged in a recce with Frank. In honour of the dog, I attempted the composition of a poem, which the CO hung up in the mess:

> A certain hound lives in our mess
> Who's length is quite fantastic.
> His ancestors were pals of Hess,
> His crib of Vulcan plastic.

Came war upon his Jerry home
With noise and acts Teutonic,
So now his pals are under loam
And lack of meals 'is chronic'.

The countryside had quietened down
And khaki figures scurried,
Poor Baron's luck has 'come to town',
For meals he's now not worried.

The Colonel's pet of Fourth KOSBIE,
Is now our Baron's title,
He soon may have a family tree,
And Scottish bairns for Keitle.

In spite of the liberty taken in using KOSBIE, instead of KOSB which always makes borderers wild (apparently, as the Pipe Major confided in me, the former abbreviation has some hideous meaning in an Indian dialect), the CO seemed very taken with it.

One day I was detailed with Frank Coutts to recce temporary billets for some of the troops who would do the actual assault crossing of the Rhine. We were to visit every farm and building in a 1½–2-mile deep stretch of countryside bordering the railway line, and extending all the way between Marienbaum and Xanten, deciding how many men each house could hold.

Pip Powell had recently rejoined us after his sojourn in hospital with blood poisoning, and so was able to help out with the road checks while we were busy. Frank and I split the area between us, and I was astonished after two days of it to see the mileometer on the 15-cwt truck had notched up another 75 miles. For the most part our wanderings took us on by-roads and mud tracks or even over the fields, providing a wonderful change and relaxation in these pleasant country surroundings. There were, however, two unwelcome aspects. None of us knew to what extent this strip of fought-over countryside and its farm tracks and roads might have been mined by the retiring enemy. We could see from the state of the roads in places, and from the mud, that some of the tracks had not seen a vehicle for some little while, and these were traversed in a state of considerable unrest. From time to time we came upon particularly suspicious repair marks or signs and disturbance in the surface for which we could think of no reasonable explanation and braked hard to have a better look. Quite probably there might have been no mines within several miles, but one could only slip up once, and then, as we had seen, the results could be most disconcertingly decisive. Once or twice the driver was greatly relieved with my suggestion that on some more than usually uncertain looking tracks, we should proceed in reverse; thus hoping that if we did run over a mine it might be no bigger than a glass or Schu mine, and only remove the rear wheels. If there were any anti-tank ones about there would not be enough left to tell which way round the truck had been going.

The other fly in the ointment, and one which caused me much distress as well as ensuring that we entered every farm building we saw, was the shock of finding that though the farms were quite deserted of people, some of them still contained animals. On the first occasion we walked into one of these dark cow sheds, I was struck by the awful smell. We realised there were cows there from the warmth of the air, then the clanking of horns against metal and rattle of chains which greeted the sounds of our entry. Then gradually it dawned on my senses as my eyes got used to the light, firstly the remembrance that these farms were deserted of people, and then with a heartrending shock, the pitiful sight of the desperate animals, taut and hollowed hide stretched over visible skeletons. Some were near mad with pain, dairy cattle, unmilked for days on end. Some cows were better than others, and we supposed their water and food had lasted longer. Even more distressing were the calves, though they were in better condition – being unchained they had had more opportunity of scrounging what they could. We tried to drain the cows of some of their milk from hot distended udders, but they were wild, and we had little idea of milking and could not make out if all the milk had clotted, for we had little success and debated whether to shoot them. Instead, I opened the gates to the paddocks, hay and the water, and let them all loose with the calves, trusting that nature would find a solution as together they tottered painfully out into the fields and yard. In a corner pen on one of the farms, we found a gaunt but still massive blood-shot-eyed bull, foaming at the mouth and crashing at its chain; 'Understandably wild at the treatment of its family', the Jock driver thought. These animals may have been ten days or more like this. It was with considerable temerity that we loosed the fastenings of this wild brute, as we realised we would have to evade it somehow in crossing the yard to the truck. For a while it stood, still not realising it was free, and we retreated hastily, but we hoped not too obviously, towards the door. As we got outside, the clatter of the bull's hooves sounded, trotting towards us. Just in case, we loaded our rifles and grabbed a couple of wooden hurdles to divert this shambling, wild and steamy-nostrilled animal towards the fields. Fortunately, it did not seem to attach its ills to us and trotted off through the yard. Pausing, it saw the cows and with a surprising frolic of energy, the bull broke into a canter after them. We realised then that the farmer was likely to have his calving schedule upset. As so often, the Jock driver summed up the situation in a sentence of words as awful as they were both succinct and unprintable.

In many ways this short interlude of peace was one of the most pleasant we experienced on the continent, unexpected as it was and sandwiched between the bitter memories of the winter and the inevitable trials ahead. At night, when not writing home or on duty, we entertained or visited other officers in their messes, or sometimes sat at 'home' listening to the hauntingly sweet tinkle of 'Stille Nacht' on a musical box belonging to the house. It was a never ending wonder to me that our enemy had this other and so different side to his make-up. One of our visitors was a war correspondent who asked us a lot of questions. These made us realise at that time, so close against events, how difficult it was to relate our activities to him and to put them in their proper perspective.

While taking a spin round the area, enjoying a 'liberated' autocycle, I was struck anew at the rapidly massing material for the river crossing. Sometimes German fighter planes flew fast overhead at rooftop height to peep through the throat tickling smoke-screen which increasingly shrouded our side of the river, intent on seeing what we were up to. They skimmed like startled partridges flushed by beaters, hurtling over mist-shrouded thickets while numerous guns blasted at them. Several were brought down to add a splash of fire and a darker column of smoke to the fog. The enemy could have had no illusions as to our intentions. Guns and materials speckled the landscape as thickly as it had once been sprinkled with cattle. The hedgerows were lined and the barns bursting with supplies and ammunition. Other shell dumps were camouflaged as false haystacks. Every house and farm was becoming packed with troops, among them those of the 51st Highland Division and our sister Battalion 1st KOSB. The woods were bristling with tanks, normal, amphibious with Duplex drive and other weird types for special purposes. Massed in other areas were Buffaloes and DUKW amphibious vehicles and fantastic quantities of bridging materials. As time passed we were astonished to see even the Royal Navy involved. Enormous transporters lumbered by, with sailors and marines and assorted craft aboard, some as big as 45 feet long and 14 feet broad which had been hauled overland through Holland and Belgium.

If all these things had not impressed us sufficiently with the coming event's importance, we were certainly impressed on 'R' Day by the unexpected sight of Churchill, beaming and flourishing the V sign, and of Eisenhower. The latter had last been seen by us when he had inspected our unit in the wilds of Scotland. His interest on that occasion was reciprocated by the Jocks in their keen appreciation of his attractive lady driver. It was later reported that while Churchill was standing waving in a moving vehicle a trailing signal wire had brushed his hat off his head, to which he said: 'Better my hat than my head!'

As a final flourish, a 'personal message' from the C-in-C, Montgomery, was sent 'to be read out to all troops'. Monty was a great showman, but we had come to realise that his statements, brimming as they did with decisive optimism, were getting a reputation among the Jocks for reliability. As such they were a tonic to read. This one stated: 'On 7th February I told you we were going into the ring for the final and last round; there would be no time limit: we would continue fighting until our opponent was knocked out. The last round is going very well on both sides of the ring' (meaning the Russians too) '– and overhead. Events are moving rapidly. The complete and decisive defeat of the

Germans is certain; there is no possibility of doubt on this matter . . . 21 ARMY GROUP WILL NOW CROSS THE RHINE . . . and having crossed the RHINE, we will crack about the plains of northern Germany, chasing the enemy from pillar to post . . . Over the RHINE, then, let us go. And good hunting to you all on the other side . . .'

All these important people passed over the crossroads which had so attracted the enemy guns recently and at which they slung a few more shells later before being knocked out. This caused me to wonder if those concerned with the care of these 'VIPs' had been aware of the risks.

'OVER THE RHINE,
THEN, LET US GO'

About a week before 'R' Day, while I had been engaged in our billet in doing a large chalk drawing of our Pipe Major Bunyan complete with kilt and pipes, the artillery had started to warm up the guns with a few trial salvos like a boxer giving his opponent a few tentative jabs to measure reach and test reactions.

Suddenly, on Friday 23 March, the lovely spring evening was shattered with eruption after eruption of multiple gunfire which as it grew dark, lit the landscape like sheet-lightning glaring and flickering all along the river line. The thunder of innumerable guns steadily built up in volume and power as the gunners got into their stride of feeding their hungry guns with ton after ton of lethal food. Tomorrow, the 24th, was 'R' Day and these guns were concentrating first on the far bank of the Rhine and particularly those targets which had been pinpointed earlier. Special 'noise parties' on our side of the river had for some time previously done their level-best to tempt the enemy to fire and give away his gun locations and strong points.

Above the gunfire, at nightfall, came the skirl of pipes and the crunch of incessant marching feet as the Black Watch and other Battalions of 51st Division moved forwards through our positions towards the river bank from which the assault would commence in the early hours of the morning. Our task was not the assault, but to act as 'firm base' and to protect our bank and the bridges as they were built until it came to our turn to follow through and go 'swanning' after the enemy.

There was an electric feeling of excitement and confidence in the air symbolised by a throbbing stream of our bombers which had sailed over as a prelude to the guns to empty an avalanche of bombs which rumbled dust, smoke and thunder as the town of Wesel was obliterated on the far bank. All night men and vehicles streamed by road and cross-country in smoke-belching hordes and in infinite variety towards the five sections of effort from which the assaults would be made. Special cross-country routes had been laid and marked over the fields by means of mine tapes on posts and coloured shaded lights.

The forces involved no fewer than seventeen British and US infantry divisions, seven armoured divisions, two airborne divisions, a commando brigade and many other independent brigades and special units.

One felt a sense of privilege at being present as another milestone in history was heaved slowly and massively into position for its unveiling in the coming hours. With it, though, was a dragging sense of sadness at the realisation of the likely cost of its erection to both sides in lives athrob with youth and hope now, but which would be stilled at this time on the morrow; with ripples of grief lapping in silent widening circles to distant homes around the world and among the enemy too. That the outcome was now so evident even to a half-wit made the sacrifice and those that followed with time more and more difficult to accept – or to risk.

We had expected heavy enemy retaliation to our shattering gunfire which shuddered our billet violently all night and made our ears sing with the appalling racket. To our surprise – in one sense, but not in another – very little shelling did come back, though we had taken the precaution of moving our HQ down to the cramped quarters of our cellar. I for one had not realised then that the capture intact by the Americans of the Rhine bridge at Remagen on 7 March had to some extent drained the enemy from ahead of us while he attempted to seal this bridgehead.

At 9 pm the first assault troops, including the 1st Commando Brigade heading for Wesel, moved off over the 500 yards of dark muddy Rhine towards the enemy. At 1.55 am, waves of tightly packed Buffaloes roared, squeaking their way through gaps blown by the REs in the dyke wall to splash towards other objectives. The massed guns, lifting their range, fired on. It was a lovely dawn that greeted the tired eyes of the gunners and glinted its first light off a thousand hot, smoking gun barrels which had so out-thundered the mythical German Rhine gods. The noise of the guns passed all descriptions. Some heavies nearly dismantled our house with their blast. The sky was sprayed with Bofors tracer flicking after a streaking German recce plane soon after daybreak trying to locate the main threat. From the pilot's point of vantage the Rhine must have appeared to be alive with busy water beetles, running up and down the banks and churning through the water with repeated loads.

Ten o'clock approached and our fighter planes poised themselves, wheeling like eagles, ready to dive on any enemy AA guns which had survived the artillery. To replace the thunder of the guns the waves of sound from myriad booming aircraft engines gradually saturated the air. There behind us, surprisingly low and glinting in the sunlight of a clear spring day, was the wonderfully stirring sight of an immense air armada; patterned planes by the hundreds, migrating giants in the blue. They took an hour to pass. No attacking troops could have had a more encouraging sight to inspire their efforts and few defenders a more depressing one. Behind the lumbering Halifaxes, Lancasters and Dakotas, rolling and dipping on their tow threads, were the Horsa gliders. Having crewed 40mm and 20mm AA guns myself, I was appalled to realise what sitting birds these targets were to any determined enemy gunners still in action. I was also grateful that our own air-transportable days were over. We knew that if any of the gliders were hit, the men inside would have no parachutes and would probably be too low to use them if they had.

While the planes were still well back from the river line and coming up level with our billets, our hearts rose to our throats as tracer streamed up to meet them from the far side of the Rhine. White and black smoke-puffs burst, twinkling prettily to blossom like opening evil lily petals among dragonflies on a big blue pond. Beyond, short and around they burst, the smoke of close ones blowing back past these unhurried fragile intricacies of metal and life in the propeller slipstream while the plane slid rocking onwards. There must be few sensations worse than the heart-stilling tension and helplessness experienced in seeing such planes hit, stagger and spin down like dead autumn leaves, the tug-planes blazing or trailing smoke and the gliders plummeting with their living contents to disintegrate as funeral pyres in mockery of the spring greenery and of youth. Few in proportion though these fatalities were, they seemed to dominate the sky. One crashing glider almost smashed into the Adjutant's farm and a Dakota smoked down to lick in flames somewhere beyond it. Below this level the fighters dived to blast with cannon and rockets whenever they spotted the location of enemy AA guns still in action. The leading planes must by now have been unloading the paratroops in the blue distance, hazed with the smoke of battle, burning farms and here and there the darker oil-fed smoke of burning planes, tanks and vehicles.

Quite suddenly, it seemed, there was an odd silence after the hours of storm. With the paratroops down, gunfire had almost ceased for the moment and the last drone of air-engines murmured softly, receding on the rim of the sky. More intent listening made one realise though that the silence was only comparative between the few more obvious explosions. A muffled indefinite blanket of sound pulsated from the fighting, such as one might hear while dozing in the centre of a London park, listening to the restlessness of the rush-hour traffic throb.

This airborne drop was probably the most successful of its kind, and we later heard that the all-important link-up with the ground forces had taken place some time in the early afternoon. I was amazed that our airborne forces had been rebuilt up to such strength since the Arnhem losses in men and aircraft.

As soon as the 15th Division had established a secure bridgehead opposite our sector of the river, with a taxi-service of amphibious vehicles ferrying over supplies to the far bank of the Rhine, word came for D Company and ourselves in B Company to 'prepare to move'. We were to quit the comforts of our now homely billets, and make for the river bank on the evening of the 24th to give protection to the 2nd Army engineers, who were working at amazing speed in rushing over a class 40 pontoon bridge. This was one of ten, quickly projecting on bobbing floats towards the other bank to carry the enormous convoys of armour, supplies and men, piling up on our side: power to keep up pressure on the enemy night and day. Within twenty-four hours these bridges, each with a signposted name of a Thames bridge, were completed, and carrying nose to tail convoys of one-way traffic hour after hour. Besides these there were twelve ferries or rafts.

My new HQ was in a fine large and well-furnished farmhouse, complete with a well-stocked library and deer heads decorating the walls. It was set a few yards back from the Rhine, and before the light failed I made my way up into the roof to find a wonderful view out over the river and to the far bank.

Alongside the farm lay a long, narrow, petrol-driven canoe, which, according to an RE officer working on the bridge, had been used by 'a daft South African recce bloke' to patrol up and down the enemy bank the night before the crossing to select the most suitable spot for the landfall of the pontoon bridge. Our bridge, rapidly nearing completion, was built in two sections: first over to a spit of land jutting out from the far bank, then at an angle over a creek. There was continual zooming overhead as Spitfires patrolled as protection.

At each end of the bridge were groups of Bofors guns, and several times as we stood on watch listening to the squeak of the bridge straining against the 3½ knot stream, and the clatter of the REs working on it in the chill night air, these guns burst into deafening life, spitting fountains of red tracer. Above the guns we listened intently to the harsh scream of an Me109 diving past flat out, and dropped to brace ourselves for the expected bombs. These planes seemed, however, to be only on recce flights, and sometimes skimmed the water as low as 50 feet, when one caught the fleeting black streak of fuselage, blue exhaust stubs glowing in the nose. As the planes banked and climbed into the stars the lazy neon red tracers trailed in strings after them to sparkle out as orange pin pricks in the blue night.

Occasionally, to relieve the monotony I walked out over the bridge to see how things were getting on, and gazed into the dark waters strumming past the cables which anchored the pontoons into position on the pebble and sand bed of the river. It struck me as amazing that so far the enemy had made no real attempts to destroy our bridge. Just downstream a few hundred yards away, one of several of our searchlights shone low over the water towards the enemy to provide Monty's Moonlight for the front – now several miles off, we guessed. This particular light seemed to infuriate the enemy for some reason, and time and again shells crashed nearby. As often as not the shells, which appeared to be 88mm, splashed a brilliant silver cascade of spray short in the cold glare of the lamp, a lovely sight with its mirrored twin sparkling in the inky water. The only clues we had to the distance of the fighting came from a few faint fires and explosions which flared up on the rim of the night sky to the east.

At dawn, Company HQ moved up to join us, and the volume of traffic which streamed over the completed bridge spoke convincingly of the success of the attack. Pip took his men over the pontoon to guard the far end – armed with illustrated picture books from my library – and they whiled away the day sunbathing round their foxholes on the grass.

Company HQ made their home in a tiny house right on the dyke wall with its feet in the river. It contained a minute sitting room, bedroom and kitchen, strewn with the odds and ends of clothing and some pathetic bits of furniture of some poor German family who must once have lived here. Down in the cellar the Company HQ signaller squatted between a tinkling field telephone and a crackling 18 set radio.

I still found myself occupied with unabated interest in observing every detail of these German homes and countryside. Each village, each house and each room was a living museum teeming with fascination to me. Yet behind each scene and object lurked the sadness and stupidity of a war which a handful of madmen had unleashed on little people in meek, hard-won homes in so many countries. Where were the children who had once loved these broken toys? Or the housewife who had cooked for her family at the little stove, and no doubt been so proud of her modest home? Where was the father who had once filled these clothes? Was he one we would yet have to kill, or would he perhaps kill one of us?

For four days power had been flowing over the Rhine following the assault and building up in the 'lodgment' area like a coiling spring for the next effort – to fight forwards towards the Russians and the Elbe, and also to encircle the Ruhr. Once the Ruhr was cut off, the German monster would be fighting stomachless on the decreasing fat of an already gaunt carcass.

On the afternoon of 28 March I was detailed for another advance party under the comfy, bouncing figure of the 2i/c, Maj Horace Davidson. Boarding a handful of trucks, we swayed, clattering and squeaking, over the floating bridge into the devastated countryside beyond. So this was what the artillery had been steam-rollering so heavily. Everywhere were scenes of indescribable desolation: dead cattle, shattered orchards, houses, fields, farms, villages. Many buildings were still smouldering. The few civilians about wore dazed, vacant expressions as though they had not yet dared to face the implications of their broken surroundings.

So far we had seen no sign of any enemy dead, very few abandoned vehicles and little equipment to tell us how fierce a resistance our opponents had offered, which was puzzling. There were even premature bets and rumours that the enemy had cracked altogether. After about 5 miles slow bumping over cratered roads in failing light we approached the farming area of Bellinghoven, near Mehr, which was to be our Brigade concentration area, and very close against that in which the paratroop drop had taken place.

We had about an hour to find billets for our companies before the Battalion caught us up on foot. Horace hastily gave us each an area in which to search, and we spread out, stumbling along the farm tracks in the drizzle. Attracted by a faint glow in the velvety blackness, I picked my way with two NCOs over a slippery wet quarter mile of mud towards it. Dark patches in the wayside fields proved to be several trenches, German equipment and two dead Jerries who appeared to have been very recently killed. Much more warily we continued, recollecting we had not been told the 'form' hereabouts.

The glow, now accompanied by an all too familiar sour smell of burnt straw, timber and flesh, turned out to be a large, hot, smoking heap of rubble: all that remained of a German dairy farm. In the cattle stalls the cows, still chained in two long rows, lay charred and roasted hulks of steaming meat in the fiery embers. This destruction seemed to have been the fate of most buildings so far seen. Billeting would be difficult. Passing another much smaller and intact farm which would only hold about thirty men, we spied a large, dark shape looming on the wooded skyline about half a mile away. After a long stalk in which we nearly slipped into a water-filled shell crater in the track, this building turned out to be a formidable moated château. Inside, to our surprise, we could hear the muffled sounds of men's voices. Not knowing quite what to expect, we crept round the moat to the drawbridge and were there challenged by a crisp Scots voice from the dark and checked our dive to cover: it had struck us that these might have been Jerry stragglers. This challenge also had the effect of revealing Capt Tammy Youngson and Usher his batman who had crept out of the night behind us intent on the château too. We had been beaten to it by others, and turned back to make what we could of the smallholding and the burnt-out farm.

The small farm was locked and appeared deserted. I forced in the back door, to be met by the warm, sweet scent of cows. A distant glimmer of light showed from the cellar. There in this tiny, brick-lined hole in the earth which was almost completely filled by a double bed and household treasures, was a scared old man with one arm, a tight-lipped frightened girl of about fourteen, and a cluster of round-eyed smaller children. They were all blinking in the glow of a flickering oil lamp and were crowded together like trapped rabbits on the bed. This place with its loft and outhouses would somehow have to hold Company HQ and Pip's platoon. The burnt-out farm had had an outbuilding also and we returned to investigate it. There too in the cellar of the barn we found a frightened German and his family. When we burst in from the night to look down on them cowering in a straw-littered corner at the bottom of the ladder, they seemed quite unnerved by the violence of the destruction about them and seemed to fear the very worst of us. Gradually it dawned on the harrowed, sunken-eyed farmer that we meant no violence, and he quit standing between us and his hysterically sobbing wife amid her children on the floor – queerly reminiscent of a nest of animals at bay – and came hesitatingly up the ladder to us.

We gathered from this near desperate man that the smouldering mess had been his home, which Typhoons had wrecked because a 'Domkopf' Jerry major had insisted on using the farm as a base for his battery of rocket projectors. He blamed the mad major and not the RAF for his misery, and was pleased to relate that this officer together with fourteen of his men – two of whom we had earlier seen in the fields – had perished in the plane's attack. He showed us some steps to a cellar in the farm wreckage when he had grasped our requirements from the words 'Soldaten' and 'Slaapen', given with appropriate gestures by an NCO. We entered the cellar with him. It was surprisingly large and with a vaulted brick roof which still radiated great heat from the farm ruins overhead. This would hold two Platoons, I decided, and they were in for a centrally heated night beyond their wildest dreams.

Back on the road we had a long, cold wait for the rest of the Battalion to arrive. First came the vehicles, then a long time afterwards file after file of very weary, fed up and swearing Jocks. Swearing, I think, to offset their loads, the wet and the prospect of the days ahead. In the distance, some raucous blasts on a hunting horn heralded the approach of the large angular form of Smyg, who to my astonishment appeared at the head of the company column, tam-o'-shanter on the back of his head, a Bren gun over one shoulder, singing softly and chuckling to himself in a delighted way. His gait was not quite steady, and it was evident from the booming laughter of Frank's deep voice and the shriller merriment of slender Charles Marrow that the Rhine crossing had been well celebrated by these two also.

On arrival at the tiny farm, Smyg and CSM Pook, to the Jocks' disapproval, removed the now terrified family from the cellar and occupied its bed themselves. I settled down for the night with Platoon HQ: Sgt V. Godfrey (to replace Sgt Dickinson while on leave); L/Cpl Brown, 'Syd' to all; 'Taffy' our mature Welshman; dour heavily built Stein; sandy-haired, bony, red-faced, careful McKenzie – a typical Scot; Blackwood, back from the injury to his leg at Haus Loo, a small willing silent chap; and Tarn and Learmonth our two comics, remarkably similar in appearance, slim faced, slightly hooked noses and unruly hair. We were in the opposite half of the cellar to the German family, who seemed to find the snoring litter of Jocks about them in the straw a reassuring sight. Little by little the sobbing of the farmer's wife and the resultant whimpering of the children quietened. I noticed, too, from the chocolate-stained mouth of one child that some Jock had taken practical measures to quieten this dirty infant. Before going to sleep there were 'stags' to fix, then I tried talking for a while with the farmer to see what news this could produce. He was in no mood for this, though, understandably, and the language difficulty was almost impossible. However, I was cheered to learn the rocket projector had run out of ammunition after one salvo of twelve rounds and I hoped this was a sign of the times.

In the morning the delicious scent of roasting pork, a merry crackling from a large fire and the voices of appreciative Jocks led me to find Jones, his keen face alive with anticipation and helped by a rather disdainful Pte Byles, cutting juicy chops to add to those already sizzling on the fire from a young pig strung up to a tree and gutted. 'Roll up, roll up! They're lovely!' he cried, doing brisk business. Then spying the farmer, whose face was already beyond expressing further anguish, Jones selected a special piece for him and took it over: 'Cheer up Fritz, it may never happen; here have a bite. Lovely grub.'

In fairness, it should be said the pig had been an injured one. The Jocks were not the only ones guzzling themselves. In the ruins of the cowshed, a large bloated sow surrounded by squealing piglets fighting for milk was just nearing the close of a mammoth feast of roast beef in company with some furtive rats which were also digging holes into the hulks of still steaming burnt cattle and two horses. The sow waddled ponderously over to its shed, followed by the litter, and fell over into a heap of straw, quite overcome, to sleep it off; and there I sketched them. I could not get from my mind the horror of the scene which must have been enacted in the cowshed as it burned with all those chained animals.

Somewhere, overnight, two of the sergeants in the Company had located some bottles of spirits with which to celebrate the Rhine crossing. Having been used to drinking beer, and that in terms of pints at a time, they had seriously under-estimated the almost lethal power of their night's consumption. They were in an awful state.

In daylight, we were surprised to find another quite large farm nearby which had remained undetected in the dark, and into this A Company moved, among them Sgt Dickinson, posted to their strength after his leave, much to my sorrow, though it later probably saved his life as Sgt Godfrey who took his place was killed in our next action. Regrouping of our forces was still going on on the eastern bank of the river, and to our surprise we did not move immediately to contact the enemy, but were to remain there another couple of days. At the end of this wait, just before we moved, Maj Andrew Stewart located two German soldiers hidden in his farm, one armed and in civilian clothes. That they had remained hidden for so long in the same farm as 120 inquisitive Jocks was remarkable.

'Swanning' on the Other Side

News from the front during the wait, much of it pure rumour we suspected, was wildly encouraging. Certainly all sounds of fighting, but for one notable exception earlier on in our stay, had faded away into the distance. The exception had been a fierce attack, fortunately without casualties, by a Typhoon which had unleashed its load of rockets at the billet occupied by Battalion HQ of all places. Some pithy message must have awaited this luckless pilot on his return to base if Chris, our CO, was up to his usual form.

On the morning of 31 March, Smyg greeted me with 'Get your kit, Pete, you're off on another advance party.' We had come under command of the famous 'Desert Rats' 7th Armoured Divison, to team up with them as motorised infantry and go 'swanning' after the enemy. It was pleasant to be on the move again and away from our charred billet. Time went quickly with so much to see and the knowledge that at least for a day or so we were unlikely to be involved in another attack made for the greater sweetness of the passing minute. I was most interested to try to spot the airborne landing area, but this was surprisingly difficult. I think most of the landings, but for shot down planes and strays, must have been a bit to our south, although we did see a few black, whale-like hulks of glider fuselage broken in the fields and some torn shreds of coloured supply parachutes trailing in an orchard. While in the area of Bellinghoven, several reports had reached us of airborne chaps being found in the neighbourhood hanging by their harness from the trees and shot to bits.

At times we wandered among quite peaceful surroundings on country roads, but always blighted at intervals by scenes of gruesome destruction by artillery, rockets or bombs. We were heading towards the north-east at a fair speed whenever the road surface permitted, via Werth and Bocholt (bombed to pieces), Rhede, Kardingholt, Borkenwirthe, Weseke, Sudlohn and Stadtlohn. I have never before, or since, seen places bombed to such obliteration as the last named three towns. The engineers had bulldozed a new road through the powdered rubble and bricks. On either side lay acres of rubble and earth rimmed with crater upon crater, the lips of the holes overlapping in continuous pattern.

Towards dusk, when about 35 miles ahead of the Battalion, we pulled off the road in the village of Gros Burloo and turned in to a large countrified estate which seemed part hospital and part monastery. At the gates stood one of our Cruiser tanks with the hatches open. A tiny hole in the armour indicated a hit by a *panzerfaust*. Inside, when we found time to look, was a mess of cut equipment and blood. The Rhine lay way behind us and although we were still only about 6 miles from the Dutch border to our west, Montgomery's forecast about fast movement over the Rhine was so far encouragingly accurate and we had not yet caught up with the enemy.

Before the light quite failed, I joined Tammy Youngson on an extensive recce round the estate houses and farms to find billets for our respective Companies before the arrival of the Battalion which we expected at dawn. We had no news at all as to how recently the place had been taken or whether there might be still enemy stragglers lurking about, which made our numerous interviews with German farmers and householders, the more interesting. Tammy had a Sten and I a rifle, and we approached each farm, one covering the other. Tammy was the most unwarlike looking fellow: slender, gentle, rather 'intellectual' with a humorous twist to his mouth and twinkle in his eyes, and full of amusing tales which he elaborated by brandishing his Sten. We must have made a quaint pair of warriors in German eyes as we looked through their homes.

All the advance party – again under Horace Davidson – spent the night in blissful, though chilly, rest on white-painted iron beds in the austere clinical surroundings of a ward in this monastery hospital. At 0730 hours, the Battalion arrived in a stream of trucks, and were guided to their billets.

One of the three farms I had selected for B Company contained a massive 6 foot 6 inch German aged about thirty-five, with the belligerent look of an SS thug, but who claimed he was the farmer. The Jocks were for stripping him to look under his armpits to see if he had the SS tattoo marks reputed to be placed there. He had a very erect bearing and took a great interest in our weapons. I decided to try screening him. We had a smallish compact chap of German Jewish extraction in the Company with a foreign name the Jocks pronounced as 'Buzz-bomb', though he was as often referred to as 'The Jordan Highlander', but in a friendly way. It was amusing to see this quick-witted little 'Jock' firing rapid questions in fluent German at this enormous Jerry, who seemed taken aback by the unexpected onslaught. We could not 'trip him up'. It was from this time onwards though that we began to notice more and more sturdy young men of military age in farms and villages left by the retreating enemy, who had 'demobbed' themselves to civilian status overnight.

The Jocks were delighted with the billets: they contained several very pretty young girls, some being slave labourers. I could not but agree with the rather surprised remark of a Jock to me: 'Y'ken, Mr White Surr, some o'yon lassies gie a gae restful change t'a mon's eye! I never kenned these Jerry wummen'd interest me – they've a bonny bit shape t'them too – well built, ye ken.' Then after a wistful pause: 'Aye, yon's a bonny wench, yon; a bonny bit fluff: 'tis a hellish shame, non-fraternisation-Mr-White-Surr!' However, what the Jocks were deprived of here, they made up for in the other amenities of these very well-stocked dairy farms: eggs, milk, poultry, ham and bottled surprises. My own billet was with an old lady at the gatehouse, who had her mantelpiece decked with photos of her son draped with a black ribbon and an iron cross. The possession of this medal appeared to have fully compensated her for the loss of her son, who had been 'killed in action', she proudly said. Company HQ were in an annex to the hospital, on the main road. There Smyg had a room to himself; the others were full of patients, many, obviously, were German soldiers.

Next morning, Sunday 1 April 1945, Padre Findlay held an Easter Sunday service in the monastery. This seemed to be visiting day at the hospital, and when afterwards I settled down with Platoon HQ to roast a chicken for lunch over an open fire by the drive, we accumulated quite an audience of Germans. The villages round about all appeared to be very overcrowded due to the smashed towns nearby where my 'landlady' said thousands had been killed by the bombs.

Rumours reached us that there had been a major breakthrough by our armour which was racing ahead of us towards the Dortmund–Ems canal. There was a subdued spirit of excitement when we boarded the TCVs next morning to give chase. At first our progress was not fast. We rolled slowly forward for a while then came a long unexplained halt on a railway crossing. The fields were very pleasant in their spring freshness and the farms substantial, prosperous places bulging with the cream of the former occupied countries' cattle. I was delighted to find myself again with 'Walrus whiskers', my pipe-smoking, gardening, TCV driver friend, and we found plenty to talk about covering the period since last we had met. 'I wouldn't swap jobs with you poor blighters, for all the world', he said.

As we moved on again, a few mortar craters here and there told of some fighting, and near the road on the left we passed a group of farming folk gathered round an open grave, burying someone in an orchard, probably a German soldier or civilian.

Not far beyond, two more of our tanks stood knocked out; their movements frozen at the end of deep, splayed mud tracks. It was difficult to make out whether these were the victims of mines or anti-tank guns. One could read the method of advance of those tanks still pushing ahead from their messy trails straggling for the most part cross-country to make the chance of mining less probable. They usually kept about 50 to 200 yards from the road and occasionally crossed it for more favourable ground, leaving a mess of clay, just as though some giant destructive slugs had dragged themselves untidily over the landscape. The trails led unhesitatingly through such flimsy obstacles as hedges, walls, thickets, ditches and back yards. When a house or village came into view its walls were almost invariably punctured with shells or the bricks and plaster stippled with bullet craters shot by the tanks.

Each convoy of 'soft' vehicles fanning behind the armour, spreading like a drug of allied power through the arteries of a mortally wounded Germany, was arranged in such order that should any one section of it meet trouble from an enemy pocket by-passed by the tanks, that compact group would contain elements of all the essentials necessary to deal with it: infantry, artillery, armoured cars and command vehicles including radio trucks, petrol, ammunition and supplies, medical services and so on. To locate such threats and check for enemy movements in the gaps between the routes of advance spotter planes were constantly skimming overhead and zig-zagging at tree-top height to either side.

For the first time I found my mind, with almost guilty hesitancy, beginning to think furtively forwards along the tenuous delicate thread of our future, which seemed at last to be more robust; but I was frightened still to look too far for fear that one's personal thread, taughtened to the limit in this skein, which we knew now from its strength was tied to victory, might be snapped just a little way ahead and so near the end.

We had become conscious too of a swing in the thought of the German civilians we met, away from open hostility or dejected apathy, towards a feeling we suspected could be expressed in the words: 'Go ahead and put us out of our misery of war as quickly as possible.' We also met the first attempts at rebuilding or patching up homes immediately the fighting had passed, which indicated complete acceptance that the tide of war which had swept past their homes, was a one-way tide, decisive in its sweep.

As the hours and miles trailed by, so did the villages and towns, and an endless succession of scenes – interesting, sad, colourful, devastated and dead – occupied our attention. Whatever other emotions may have chased themselves through our thoughts, boredom was not one of them; that was kept at bay by the chill knife-edge of uncertainty which turned its keen blade in our subconscious – or stomachs from time to time between thoughts of hot meals, tea, sleep and warmth: the weather had again turned cold. Some optimists speculated hopefully that perhaps the fighting was 'all over bar the shouting'.

For a while we halted and a few Jocks piled out to get hot water for tea from a frightened, anxious farmer's wife and were followed out by sturdy, fair-haired children who gazed up at us with interest – then on we rolled again. Many of the villages were peaceful, with low gabled farms – cattle stalls, barn – and house built in one unit – surrounded by apple trees. Others just beyond would have holes blasted in them by our tanks or still smoked, burnt out. The cost of the advance was entered by the roadside as though in a ledger: one tank, three graves, one burnt-out 3-tonner, one grave. Each kilometre as it sped past tagged the memory with a scene here, an incident there.

Our route had carried us through Ahaus, Ahle, Nienborg, Metelen, Wettringen, Neuenkirchen, crossing the River Ems just beyond Mesum, where dusk turned the Battalion column off the main road to hunt shelter for the night. We took a dust road bordering a wood in which we were surprised to see what appeared to be the equipment of a German searchlight battalion in working order, dispersed, captured complete.

Again the column split into company convoys and finally we drew up in the dark outside a lonely farm in a forest and set about preparing supper and straw beds in the loft. The farm parlour, which had walls decorated with large photographs of forbidding Germans of farming stock in 'Victorian' dress, was turned into our mess for the night. After defence and emergency positions had been worked out, we retired to the musty warmth of this room to have our supper – of eggs from the farm – served by the hausfrau, as substantial and inscrutable as her ancestors glowering down at us from the walls. One could read nothing from her face, or that of the old grandpa farmer sitting silently hunched in the flicker of the firelight. There must have been a younger man, the farmer, somewhere; perhaps he had scuttled to hide when our invasion of vehicles had roared in from the night. If he was hidden in the straw of the loft, he must have had a trying night among all those Jocks sleeping, stumbling about and eating his farm produce. We had no news at all as to the whereabouts of the enemy, but we knew that stragglers might be anywhere and stags had to be kept on the alert. After supper and a chat with Smyg, Frank and Pip, and an attempt at getting information out of the two Germans, I climbed up into the loft to sleep among the tumbled Jocks snoring in the straw. Outside all was silent save for the distant barking of dogs, probably at another 'invaded' farm, and the thin sound of the wind sighing in the conifers and penetrating coldly through the cracks in the plank walls of the loft. It was a life of queerly gripping variety and interest, in spite of the moments of misery and fear, of excitement or horror. Each moment was lived with vivid intensity, the whole enriched with comradeship and humour to make it bearable; the presence of the friendly faces, voices and variously shaped forms of our companions, including all their little idiosyncracies – accents, jokes, strengths and failings – provided the friendly mental furnishings of our wandering 'home' amid our unfriendly foreign surroundings. I burrowed deeper into the straw in search of the warmth necessary for sleep, rejoicing in the comfort. This hayloft was in the roof of the house and somewhere below the German farm folk were lying in their beds. I wondered what their thoughts were. Outside it was raining heavily which made the straw seem cosier.

The barking of a dog nearby and noisy approach of a motorcycle awoke me after what seemed only a few minutes of bliss: the green luminous face of my watch showed 1 am. Almost immediately the CSM shouted the awful words 'prepare to move'. While section commanders chased and dug the cursing Jocks and their equipment out of the straw, Smyg held an 'O' Group by the light of a shaded torch. So far there was no information beyond the movement order, but coming at the time it did, we guessed something was brewing. The roll-call had to be checked extra carefully to ensure no sleeping men were left deep in the straw. Outside the loading up was done in the most depressing streaming rain and pitch-blackness.

To cloak our movements only pin-prick tail-lights were to be used, with the result that progress was painfully slow and dangerous on the twisting mud tracks. Several times we braked hard, just avoiding the tailboard of the truck ahead, and as often trucks slipped or drove into ditches to be laboriously winched out again.

Dawn found us still crawling along muddy by-lanes in the bitter cold, with the other company convoys joining us as we progressed. Harry Cartner, our MT officer, and the Adjutant were passed at the junction to the main road, checking and marshalling the vehicles as they reappeared from their night hideouts.

A mile or two on, in wet grey daylight, the convoy halted in a little village. It looked like being a long halt and the wet, shivering, equipment-trussed Jocks were given permission to de-bus and jump about to warm themselves. A few hopefuls got out their tea brewing equipment, others tried to continue their sleep on the floor of the TCVs. One or two were reading fresh Allied posters plastered on the walls of the village hall, laying down the law to German civilians for curfew and the handing in of weapons. I strolled over to a café to see if it was warmer inside and there found 'Body and Soul' – the Doctor and the Padre – busily engaged on patching up a despatch rider who had injured himself in a skid.

STABBED IN THE BACK
ON THE DORTMUND–EMS

It was the morning of 3 April 1945 and the first rumours of trouble ahead suggested, it turned out accurately, that a few miles to our north-east bordering the Dortmund–Ems canal, a fanatical stand was being made by a formation of SS battle school cadets from a training centre at Hanover.

The armour and leading infantry had been halted at the line of the canal. This was completely dominated by a very determined enemy led by the officer instructors, who were in possession of a high, wooded ridge bordering the canal, called the Teutoburgerwald. Our first task was going to be to hold the narrow bridgehead which the tanks had driven to a depth of a few hundred yards on the German bank.

Outside the trucks were starting up to shouts of 'Embus!' and tea brewers hastily handed in their steaming biscuit tins full of hot water which had been heating over piles of Hexamine tablets to complete the tea making on the move. The countryside was very attractive here with good roads and interesting old houses by the wayside. We were spinning along at good speed, strung out in a long, trailing necklace of khaki movement, and when we were about 5 miles from the canal the enemy-held hills showed up clearly. As the distance decreased we were completely puzzled as to why no attempt at all was made at a concealed approach. The traffic thickened and slowed, and the Battalion column swung into an avenue of beech trees off the main road to the left. We pulled up in front of an old farm manor house. It was drizzling again as we debussed and scrambled under the shelter afforded by the naked trees to eat a hurried lunch of sodden wet bread splashed with cold tinned beans.

At the 'O' Group which followed I learned that the reason for our bold approach had been that so far the enemy had disclosed only light mortars, machine guns, *panzerfausts* and other light infantry weapons, and did not appear to have any artillery backing. This was some comfort anyway. Smyg indicated he was going up ahead of the column with Frank to see the form, and asked me to bring on the rest after short interval.

It seemed we would come under range of the enemy small arms once we came in sight beyond Riesenbeck village, so we spread well out in file either side of the road. So far there had been hardly a rifleshot to tell we were anywhere near the enemy, and taking this as a good omen, we wended our way hopefully forward, laden to the teeth with wet equipment and clothes dragging heavily.

Pte Jones proclaimed his presence near me in the column with a jangling, clanking sound, as of an old-time knight in armour going forth to battle. His appearance, however, apart from a Bren gun over one shoulder and its ammunition had far more the look of a travelling tinker. A copper kettle, a pan and a cooking pot 'liberated' from a wayside house had joined the smoke-blackened half biscuit tin rattling from his bulging pack. He had evident hopes of cooking himself a good meal at nightfall. At his stubbled, determined chin, a tiny Alsatian puppy poked a bobbing cheeky face from its warm nest, tucked snugly in Jones's windproof jerkin. 'How do you feed it?' I asked. 'Bully, jam, biscuits, rum – the blighter'll eat a *** Jerry yet, if the war lasts long enough!' came the reply. His normal queer mode of dress was much the same, but for a strip of gay floral patterned curtain, a concession to spring, knotted round his neck as a scarf.

However, my attention was distracted at this juncture by the comments of the Jocks as we passed a tented field hospital in a shattered orchard, the receiving point, as we could see, of heavy casualties. 'The b*** butcher's shop's o'er busy yonder.' 'Aye, an' we're th'next *** batch for the knackers afore th'morn's morn if I'm noo mistaken.'

The side of the road squelched mud as we plodded on, passing a church and the first houses of the village. The remarks were fewer now and those uttered were of too high a swearing content to record. I supposed the Jocks had joined me in resigning themselves to the fact that we were 'off again', and despite our recent hopes, our coming ordeal did not look like being a walk-over. I was busy and a bit worried, trying to work out which direction the leading column had taken on the approaching fork road. I could see no sight of them, though I noted, not without misgivings, that we had come within clear view of the enemy-held hill 900 yards on our left. With stunning suddenness, as though it had arrived with my last thought, an awful crack-crump of explosion smacked our ears deafeningly. Tiles flew and clattered musically in a spurt of red-black smoke and brick dust off the far corner of the house as we were passing. Within seconds, the long files of Jocks tramping the roadsides had dived for cover in the ditch, into the houses and among the churchyard tombstones, the clatter of their boots joining that of the falling debris.

Tagged on to these sounds, the crunch and scream of tyres on the tarmac could be heard as two 3-ton lorries lurched into view through the dust, and slid to a halt alongside us – already minus their drivers, who had pulled on the handbrakes and baled out to take shelter while the trucks were still moving. These drivers now panted beside me in the doorway. 'Blinding b***s, they must have seen us', one said.

Seeing jerrycans in the back of the nearest truck, I asked: 'What's your load?' 'Petrol sir, my mate's got ammunition, mortar bombs, I think.' This led to a stream of blasphemy past my ear from a Jock directed at the drivers for placing an explosion of the first magnitude right among us should another shell touch off a load.

I had just started to advise these drivers that they would get their vehicles out of sight of the enemy if they drove only a few more yards past the church, when three more explosions straddled us at quick regular intervals, one into the garden opposite. Then came tense silence; not a sound or movement anywhere as the smoke thinned and blew lazily away.

At these additional shells, the drivers had disappeared back into the house and I decided we had better carry on while the going was good, for if a truck were hit, it would take twenty or more men with it. CSM Pook had evidently come to the same conclusion and joined me in chasing out the Jocks into file on the road. Pook was rather worried that this delay had caused us to lose contact with the head of the column.

Soon we were formed up again and walking fast, and I moved up to decide which of the roads the column should take at the junction. Just then, an armoured scout car slowed up beside me with the MO, Alan Hill, in it, puffing away peacefully at his pipe. 'Everything OK Peter?' he called – he had evidently seen the disturbance as he approached. 'Yes thanks, Doc', I replied, 'But you have pulled up on the bullseye. Have you any news?' 'No, not a clue; but they're stuck against maniacs ahead it seems', he called, driving off.

While talking with Alan, I had spotted a row of tiny figures moving on what appeared to be the embankment of the Dortmund–Ems canal half a mile ahead; evidently it was our leading Platoon. I shouted up to the front Jock in the file, eight men ahead of me, 'Take the right hand . . .' but here another 88 shell cut the rest of my sentence with a crash which chilled our stomachs anew and scattered earth and smoke from the grass verge of the road junction. At the same instant, as one man the Jocks instinctively dropped to a crouch and quickened their steps. In disbelief I watched six of the eight walk on as the other two continued to fold up and slumped into the roadway. One hit full with his face on the road and lay still, obviously killed, the second bloodstained bundle of khaki rolled and kicked slightly in silence beside the first, smearing stains on the metalled surface. The men next in file stepped between them, hurrying on. A 15-cwt truck coming back from the front materialised through the smoke and the driver with an expressionless face, apparently not realising what was going on, pulled up. 'There's a Field Ambulance down there on the left', I said, and we lifted the wounded chap up beside the still blank-faced driver. He drove on and we moved to lift the dead Jock off the road as another vehicle drew up, this time with two well-fed middle-aged 'Base Wallahs' in it. 'I say, what's the form old man? Anything up?' Then seeing the body and the mess 'Good Lord!' and they were off fast.

Unknown to us then, as we moved plodding on hard in the rain which had recommenced, Pte Cutter had been spotted by the RSM hiding in the churchyard where he had originally taken cover from the first shell. He was 'bomb happy' again, and so determined not to rejoin us with an attack in the offing that a fairly lengthy chase of hide-and-seek had ensued among the tombstones between this queerly contrasting pair – the small, dapper, alive 'cock-robin' form of RSM Beattie and the wilting, lanky, untidiness of the fugitive. In its grim setting, hardly likely to enhance the zeroed morale of Pte Cutter, this chase must have had the blended humour and tragedy of Shakespeare's works to onlookers. A column of dejected German prisoners had filed back past us from the direction of the canal at about this time and I wondered later if they had witnessed this farce.

At last we caught up the rest of the Company at the Bailey bridge over the canal. This waterway was very much narrower than I had expected and almost drained of water, probably due to the RAF smashing the dykes or lock gates somewhere. Down in the deep, muddy cutting a couple of lengthy Rhine barges were bedded in the muck. I met pale, compact, moustached Lt Ian Scott there and paused to chat a while and get an idea of the 'form' as the men moved over.

It was an extraordinary situation. I had expected the bridge to be swept with a hail of bullets, and heavily mortared. We were in full view of the enemy only a few hundred yards away on high ground, and there was complete, serene peace. Not a shot being fired. One could wander about at will without being shot at as long as no attempt was made to approach the woods, which suggested the enemy may have been conserving their ammunition. We were delighted to see that plenty of our tanks lay in hull-down positions along the far bank with their guns trained on the watching cadets. There was a complete stalemate so far. Our tanks could not get through the wooded hills, which were steep, slippery and overgrown, without exposing themselves to *panzerfaust* infantry anti-tank weapons at close range. The artillery could do little as the enemy were not relying on fixed, dug-in positions, but moved themselves fast when located. The two infantry attacks which had been put in had been allowed to penetrate by the enemy only to meet with deadly firing from an unseen foe ahead, behind and on either side of the trees. Casualties had been heavy. One could not but admire the desperate stand these SS were putting up and their method of doing it with such limited weapons and numbers. One estimate gave their strength as only 300. Perhaps there were more, but certainly they caused some of the most desperate fighting of the campaign and held up the bulk of two armoured divisions and supporting infantry for several days. They had learned their trade well.

It was 3 pm by the time we had climbed up the open slope towards the scattered holes occupied by the Somersets of the 53rd Division and took over from them. These chaps, lorried infantry, moved off with most of the tanks to make an encircling attack in a sweep to the south when nightfall came. I was pleased to find later, however, that a squadron or two of these tanks were to stop the night with us.

The waterlogged mud-slits we had inherited from the Somersets, in part shielded from the enemy by a 4-foot escarpment, were most uninviting, so while the light lasted we set about improving them, although we did not know whether we were to stop there the night, or be called to attack at dusk. Pte Jones, as usual well ahead of the rest of us in such ventures, had volunteered to scrounge for the Platoon while the others kept watch. Knowing what capable hands this job had been placed in, the Jocks waited with interest and anticipation to see what bounty Jones would re-appear with. The trust we had placed in him was well rewarded. Furious cries and the cracking of a whip sounded from a farm down the slope to our rear: 'Git up there! Gee up! Pull you German ***. Can't you understand English!' From this racket, we expected the arrival of something rather unorthodox, but the weird sight which finally did climb over the crest into our view was far beyond our hopes. First to appear was a swaying, colour-striped garden sunshade held in the drizzle, then gradually the weirdly dressed form of Jones perched in state with a yelping puppy beside him on a precariously loaded ramshackle farm cart.

Harnessed to it in a most Heath Robinson manner was a perplexed, straining horse. The cart was piled with straw, pillows, farm doors with which to roof slit trenches, bottled food, linoleum and a trussed bundle of squawking poultry. A bucket of fresh milk swung at the back and in the straw was a basket of eggs. An amazing collection for so short an absence. It seemed inconceivable that this carry on had escaped the attention of the enemy looking down on us from the trees, yet no attempt was made to shoot Jones from his carnival perch or to stir up the rejoicing throng from the Platoon who streamed out to greet him and secure trophies.

I was touched to be presented with the parasol later as protection against the wet: 'Have this for a dry night, sir. I've got a door to my boudoir!' Outside this straw-lined luxurious structure, I could see the puppy supping blissfully on milk-soaked bread and biscuits, and shredded farm ham.

A runner called me over to an 'O' Group at Company HQ just before dusk. I was to take out a listening patrol. The parasol would have to wait. Smyg instructed me to creep out when the light failed with a section and establish a listening post about 800 yards forward of our positions, near the foot of the enemy-held wooded slope. I made a recce a short way forward at dusk to memorise the layout of the land while it could still be clearly seen. Then, remembering our Koningsbosch experience of being taken for the enemy by our tanks, I contacted the tank troop commander whose vehicles lined our frontage and arranged recognition signals with him, carefully covering all likely emergencies. If I fired a green Verey light low across his front, it was us coming back. If a red one, the enemy were coming in greater strength than we could deal with, and he was free to open fire with all he had over our heads while we lay low until things sorted themselves out and we could climb out of our holes and scuttle back.

I had been loaned a Cpl Jones for a while and decided to take his section out with me, and hoped he was as resourceful as his namesake. We had a quick supper and inspection, then as soon as it was dark enough to screen our movements, picked our way silently forward in file. The ground had been sown for winter wheat, and a light and dark textured streak in the earth

I had noticed in daylight kept us on course. The darkness was intense, and the drizzle was giving way to a bitter cold wind. It was a while before we could make out the brooding, wooded hill towering ominous and silent against the skyline. When we did realise its presence, its closeness oppressed us. At the base lay the ghostly white hulk of a burnt-out farmhouse.

Eventually we halted and scattered to dig in, inch by inch with infinite care to avoid noise. The occasional rasping scrape of a shovel blade on a rock prickled our spines and froze our movement with apprehension. Our tense eyes and ears combed the hostile woods for a few long seconds, then digging recommenced.

The wind, the wet, the cold and the close proximity of an above-average enemy in such an isolated position combined to make the freezing hours of night vigil which followed very trying. I recollected too that the previous night had only provided us with two hours sleep. Two Jocks were in each slit trench, taking turns at two hours duty and two hours attempted sleep under a gas cape in the trench bottom. We had been warned to expect enemy patrolling and night infiltration, but although we did hear occasional unidentified noises from the trees and had our tired eyes playing tricks with us, the night passed uneventfully. Several clashes had taken place faintly on either side, however, distant staccato stuttering, stabbing the silence.

The first hint of dawn warned me to get the patrol back out of the flat open space before daylight made it untenable. Slowly we extricated ourselves from our holes with creaking, chilled limbs and frosted, wet weapons and windproofs, and crept back. We moved no less carefully as we approached our tanks, pausing frequently to ensure we did not miss the challenge and just in case I loaded the Verey pistol with a green cartridge – it would not do to put a red one in by mistake! Would the tank sentry remember us or panic as a first reaction to seeing our figures loom out of the misty half-light; an uneasy moment, but finally it came: 'Halt! – who goes there?'

I shook up the tank commander who was snoring under a tarpaulin draped from the tracks of the HQ tank to tell him we were safely in; then it was back to breakfast and scalding tea prepared by Pte Learmonth over a Primus from the Bren carrier. This meal consisted, as so often, of sandwiched slabs of bread and fried soya bean sausage – the fat congealing on our cold hands as we ate, while the hot metal of the tea mug scalded the fingers of the other hand and one's lips. Strolling about watching the sunrise with Sgt Godfrey while consuming this (there was nowhere to sit but on the wet mud), we spied the huddled bulky forms of Frank and Smyg wrapped in a tarpaulin – and blessed sleep; they lay in a shallow pit dug between the tracks of the carrier in oozing mud – for all the world '. . . like two slugs under a brick', as Sgt Godfrey, not disrespectfully, observed.

Godfrey, who looked very tired, as I suppose we all did, was a slight, oval-headed, soft-brown-eyed, rather birdlike chap, who had an 'old soldier's' grasp of his work and the short cuts. I think he still felt a bit under the weather from his celebration of the Rhine crossing with Sgt Cowie.

A couple of hundred yards away, a torn strip of earth ended in the twisted remains of one of two German Fw190 fighter planes, which had apparently been shot down while hedge-hopping the canal. Before turning in, I was tempted to go over and have a look at these, but thoughts of sleep won. In my absence out at the listening post, Pte Jones had made use of the sunshade for the night and I borrowed the mud-walled, straw-lined igloo nest he had built beneath it, while he cleaned his precious Bren gun at the door in preparation for the day's work.

I had been curled up there for about 35 minutes, getting warm, when suddenly the silence was ripped to shreds about us. Heavy droves of shells feathered their way high overhead and smashed dully, echoing along the wooded ridge among the enemy. At the same moment, the rows of tanks with turreted heads intent on the noisy scene, reacted just like a pack of dogs, barking viciously, jerking with the effort and spitting wicked, tracered streams of Besa fire into the smoking hill. Beyond this the slower chugging patter of Vickers guns poured their quota of fire at the woods. I had forgotten that a dawn attack was due by the 6th HLI and 7th/9th Royal Scots. Time was running out, we were scheduled to attack through them once they had secured the ridge. A runner squelched his way over towards where I stood watching outside my nest and pronounced the unexpected words 'prepare to move!' The usual pattern was unfolding: it was strange how our attacks seemed always prefixed by two or three nights' lost sleep and cold.

While the erratic, uneasy sounds of fighting clattered hollowly along the ridge – to each crash and crack its echo, gradually fading out over the crest – the Jocks were gathered from their holes, 'put in the picture', checked for equipment, inspected. At last word came and the long, spread-out strings of men filed slowly towards the looming hill and the future. The clay alone, I knew, could not quite explain the heaviness of our tread, nor the morning chill, a coldness inside inducing a slight shiver. The line up at the start, even of a race, can be unpleasant, I reflected.

The Battalion split up into two groups: A and B Companies, and C and D Companies. Battalion HQ would be with the right-hand group as that would be the main effort with tank support, penetrating the hill by a road valley. We on the left would have to penetrate the woods by a path and no tanks would be able to get through with us. Our task: to make a twin axis, 2,000-yard attack towards the town of Ibbenburen in the next valley. Our Company task, if all went well, was to secure a bridgehead over a stream just short of the town, which would form a springboard for the assault on the town itself. We would have artillery and medium machine gun support on the left, but it was doubtful if the 3-inch mortars could get through the trees with their carriers. 'H' Hour was fixed for 1700 hours. There was some doubt as to whether the ridge was quite clear of the enemy, whom it was reported had offered fanatical resistance to the dawn attacks – as we had suspected from the racket.

The woods of mixed deciduous and coniferous trees were quite silent above us when we climbed up into their dripping gloom, livened only by a few hopeful buds of spring and some hesitant bird chirps; unhappily all this was wasted on our senses which sought other signs with incessant restlessness. Behind, somewhere, a carrier laboured at the hill with whining engine and complaining gears.

Round the first climbing twist of the trail we were following we came upon three crumpled khaki figures scattered in pathetic grotesque postures by the side of the path, still grasping their weapons at the alert as they were hit by a concealed sniper on rounding the corner like ourselves. They were all about twenty years of age. One well-built youth, with tin hat knocked to the back of his head by the fall, looked up at us as we passed with unseeing blue eyes, a curled forelock of hair on his unfurrowed brow, an expression of mild surprise on his face, stilled without apparent pain. Five or six new chaps had joined the Platoon since our last fight to make up the numbers. This was to be their first, and in three cases last, action. I noticed a couple of these fellows steal tense, strained glances at the still wayside forms, reluctantly, yet as though mesmerised by the chill fascination of fear. Had they sensed that they would lie similarly still this time tomorrow? Higher up the casualties became depressingly numerous, and I hoped they were not all noticed by the Jocks, as they lay scattered in groups through the thick trees on either side.

It was difficult to decide, without feeling them for warmth, if these men had all been killed in the attack we had heard go in that morning or in the preceding attacks. I was surprised to see that in almost all cases the boots of these men had been removed by the enemy, who appeared to be suffering from lack of equipment on a scale obvious to us for the first time.

It was strange how one or two chaps in each section had so far managed to cling on doggedly unscathed, while new men were bowled over almost before one had got to know their names and faces. The Jocks were moving well, keeping widely spaced and watching intently outwards into the surrounding dense tree trunks and undergrowth, falling flat in all-round defence at each halt. Another group of dead showed up in a small clearing, this time Germans amongst them; very young, rather tall and badly dressed. One could tell from their harrowed features, pinched stubbled and now greyish, that they had driven themselves – or been driven by their officers – to the limit and beyond. One or two sounds of minor clashes had sounded very distantly from our right. The other column, we heard, had taken a few prisoners on the way through.

For a while we had been stalking along the flat crest and the path had opened up into a sandy, rutted cart track used by the woodsmen. Smyg and Andrew Stewart commanding A Company moved up ahead and signed us to halt. The trees were thinning into the blue air of a distant view out over the valley. A few shells waffled quietly and thinly, long-range ones at a great height overhead, then distantly: one-two, three-four-five, six, the crump of explosions came back to us and the distant palls of smoke drew our eyes to notice the faint pink sugar-grain houses of Ibbenburen scattered on the far slope of the valley. The artillery were registering a few trial rounds for range, the orchestra twiddling their instruments down in the pit before the curtain rose.

Smyg, Andrew and Frank crouched with the signallers and CSM Pook silhouetted against the distance ahead, Smyg and Andrew scanning the valley anxiously with their binoculars and talking together. Another bigger batch of shells trailed themselves lazily across the sky and erupted in columns of warm brick dust among the neat dwellings 1½ miles away. Murmurs of approval, 'G'aan paste the b***s', sounded from the forms lying about me. Frank came back and told me the plan was now for Pip's platoon, and not mine to secure the bridgehead. (Another murmur of approval from my Jocks in earshot.) We would have to clear a small wood instead, commanding the near bank which had been spotted with the binoculars.

So far there had been no sight or sound of the main enemy, but as he was not on the hill, we knew he must be somewhere in the stretch of farms, woods and fields spread out like an oblique map below us. 'Look! The blighters are throwing in the towel', someone murmured. Sure enough distant white bedsheets unfolded and waved sluggishly on the opposite hill from rooftops and windows, and a bit farther up the slope, there was a large red-cross flag. The appearance of these, which had been put up by civilians we realised, exactly coincided with the beginning of a barrage which, as we could tell from the colour of the dust arising, was scoring direct hits on the houses. One or two of the flags came down, sure sign of the presence of the SS and I shuddered to think of the fate the luckless householder must have suffered from his 'protectors' as we watched. No carriers or tanks had got through. We would have to go in without them.

Smyg and Andrew strolled back discussing together which

Company should go in to attack first, and decided to spin for it. A coin twinkled and plopped in the sand. We crowded in. 'Tails it is!', cried Frank in his deep resonant voice. So lightly are things decided which affect us deeply! Yet perhaps none of us realised then as we watched, some tense, others amused, at our 'Captains' tossing for positions before play commenced that this spinning, almost worthless disc of metal had seemingly decided by its fickle fall which of us should live and which die. Nor that in its lying, cooling face in the earth it had mutely mimed the future of some of the audience only a few minutes later and in the hours to come.

We lost (or won?) the toss and A Company moved off ahead of us down the track to form the first wave. The land over which we would have to advance came into view below as we followed: a broad 2,000-yard stretch of fenced and tree-dotted fields sprinkled here and there with a few farms and small woods. There was very little cover. In the distance a group of factory chimneys beside a small housing estate marked the first objective through which we would have to leapfrog in attack later.

The track curved sharply right down the side of the hill, then out straight again at the bottom towards Ibbenburen. We in B Company paused at the top curve, and leant against a sandy bank. We watched anxiously from our grandstand view in good visibility as the small, puppet-like figures of A Company reached the foot of the hill and spread well out over the fields and into the lane, walking in line with weapons at the alert. Still there was no sight or sound from the enemy. It was very quiet. Too quiet it seemed, to be natural.

A group of Manchesters had set up a couple of Vickers machine guns on the bank beside us to give covering fire over the heads of the advancing figures below into the houses and far woods. Suddenly the Vickers chugged into the steady monotony of their bullet-spitting fire, eating up their belts of ammunition like hungry Italians sucking in spaghetti.

I could make out Freddie Thurgar brandishing his weapon at the head of his men on the left, and 'Wee Mac' McColl plodding along nearer the lane on the right. They were 150 yards out now, and the leading men were scrambling through the fence wire into the second field. Still no sign of or reaction from the enemy.

The last two sections had just reached the fence when it happened: the fierce rip of a Spandau ahead dropped about eight of the figures in the field with the sweep of a scythe, leaving two hanging on the wire. The rest increased their speed of advance, a few running forward, crouching. The Vickers teams swung their fire onto the nearest barn and buildings. Several more of the scattered figures crumpled to another burst; some to lie still, presumably dead, others to roll slightly. Two of the fallen got up again and moved uncertainly forward.

One of the men who had fallen on the wire, slipped off and continued to move slightly for a while as though attempting to crawl back but was too badly hit to do so. Next I noticed with a pang of horror and disgust the reason for his efforts. At intervals the turf near his head was spattered darkly by a bullet, then he lay still – one by one the wounded were being picked off by a sniper who seemed to be concealed in a wood on our left front. We found later that most of these had been finished by a round through the head. Maddeningly, we could see what was happening and knowing it was our turn next, there seemed little we could do about it. The Vickers, now hissing steam with their sustained continuous fire and coiled about with spent ammunition belts, swung back onto the woods. I joined with a few others and a couple of Brens in firing at places we suspected to be the source of fire, but there was no tell-tale suggestion of smoke anywhere to give a clue.

Only a small handful of the left-hand Platoon were still on their feet and running forward over the open fields towards the still distant cover, and firing from the hip as they went at places likely to be concealing the enemy, of whom we had still not seen the faintest sign. Behind these pathetically few running figures, a scattered trail of casualties lay like bundles of corn in a newly harvested field. Freddie, shouting way head, was one of those still going, though I could see no sign of 'Mac', and hoped he was all right. A little group of men on the left, the mortar team paused, and fired a few rounds at the nearest houses, but they had not quite enough range. During this vital period radio contact with the guns had unfortunately become erratic, perhaps because of the hill, and much-needed artillery support was lost to us.

A Company HQ were nearing the small farm half-way down the track, and there they were pinned by a hail of fire. Freddie, on the left, was being driven back. Smyg decided we could wait no more, and with thumping hearts we hurried down the track to attempt pressing the attack beyond the tide limit of A Company, who were still far short of the factories.

10 Platoon were leading, and Smyg, who had come up with me into the forward section to sense the reception which would await us when we came into the level ground, decided that the field was as good as suicide and that we should infiltrate up what cover the lane offered. We had got about 20 yards up the lane apparently unnoticed when a series of loud sharp cracks sheared twigs off the hedges on either side. It was impossible to tell from which direction the fire was coming; perhaps even from concealed positions on the wooded hills behind us. To realise each crack was not just haphazard to upset us, but the skilled efforts of people with modern lethal weapons intent on finishing us with the least delay was, to say the least, unpleasant to think about. Fortunately, there did not seem much opportunity for thought. We completed the remaining distance towards Andrew in short rushes doubled on all fours or in frantic bursts of crawling when the crackling sounds were more than usually persistent about us. We were wet, plastered with mud and streaming with sweat, perhaps not all of it due to our exertions. Although we had moved off in the early morning, the greying of the countryside already heralded the approaching close of day – the last for a large slice of 'A' Company.

Somewhere away in the field to our left the voice of a wounded Jock was crying 'Stretcher bearers! Stretcher bearers! For God's sake where are you?'

I scattered my sections about the farm with a field of fire forward, while Smyg vanished into a dugout built into the bank by the farmer to consult with Maj Andrew Stewart who had established his HQ in there together with the Forward Observation Officer of the artillery. What was the next move to be?

Bullets were crackling and whining off the walls of the farm and trimming the green shoots off the hedges and trees all about us. Without tank or carrier support there seemed little prospect of any of us reaching the housing estate if we were ordered to press the attack the remaining 450 yards even to this objective. The enemy had been capable of cutting A Company about at a range of 1,000 yards.

Some cattle ahead of us in the fields had unhappily been hit as heavily as the Jocks. Those few still alive ran about in the distance crazed with fear and steaming at the nostrils.

Freddie Thurgar unexpectedly stumbled round a corner of the farm trailing a blood-soaked and apparently bullet-shattered arm at his side. Though haggard and almost grey in the face with fatigue and perhaps loss of blood, his countenance, pale blue eyes and thin, tired moustache belied the energy of a horrible stream of swearing which burst from him as he brandished a gun he still clutched and shook wildly in the direction of the enemy. He was followed by about eight dirty dishevelled men – all that was left of his Platoon still on their feet. It was difficult to tell which had been wounded, for most showed blood somewhere; either their own or from helping their comrades. They had rather the appearance of sleepwalkers – or nightmare-walkers.

The light was nearly gone when Smyg reappeared with an order over the radio from the CO, which, to our relief, was to consolidate for the night on the positions already won. The rest of the Battalion on our right had had an equally expensive and sticky advance: no tanks had been able to get through to support them either. Smyg and Andrew decided to withdraw the two Companies to a larger farm a couple of hundred yards down the track to our rear, and asked me to remain forward with my chaps in the small farmhouse as a standing patrol and listening post. We would have the company of the Forward Observation Artillery Officer for the night, who with his signallers could call down fire in the event of any counter-attack being attempted.

The front room of the farm had been converted into a first aid post and was crammed full of wounded and those who had died of wounds. The latter we wrapped in sheets after dark and laid at the back of the house out of sight of the wounded.

The building itself, a flimsy, half-timbered structure with one thickness of brick on the outside walls and plaster and lath on the inner walls, was not at all bullet proof. It consisted of a cellar, three small bedrooms and a hayloft upstairs. Downstairs there were three small rooms and a stable containing two cows, some pigs, two goats and their kids. At the rear was a small orchard. The farmer and his family had vanished, but all their furniture and effects were left, so they had possibly fled to the woods as the attack commenced. To be secure for the night, I dug one section to our rear in the T junction of a hedge with a field of fire all round. The two other sections I dug in with my HQ, round the farm, forwards of it and in it. The gunner officer and I settled down amid his signallers in a small back room.

I realised that if the enemy were still in the housing estate at dawn, all movements between the sections would be clearly seen and unless I did something about it during the darkness our position might become rapidly untenable in any counter-attack. To offset this I employed all men not on stag at quietly digging a set of communication trenches to link up the two forward sections, the house and the dugout in the lane. There were lots of bricks about with which we strengthened the walls of the trenches.

Although the Jocks were dead beat and had had no food since breakfast time, they saw the sense in this work and toiled throughout another sleepless night, taking their turns at stag as they came, with very little complaint. Worst hit were the men who had spent the previous night out on duty with me at the listening post: I think they felt as awful as I did. It was a pitch black night and we kept stumbling over the dead at the back of the house. None of us had the inclination or the energy to move them but finally this had to be done as I don't think it was improving morale. Whether it was the acute tiredness or not was difficult to decide, but I realised with an ashamed feeling of something being very wrong that my reactions of compassion and sorrow had during the last action been getting duller and duller. Was it sheer fatigue or was I getting callous, I wondered, for fear still seemed to retain its sting. I came to appreciate next day what it was. My mind was automatically refusing to register the tragedy deeply any more, perhaps driven by the subconscious fear that if each incident were still fully faced with the searing impact first experienced that these accumulating shocks would overwhelm me. Instead I strove increasingly for an anchorage of faith outside this mad material world.

At about 2200 hours Frank came forward to see how we were, and it was decided, as it seemed likely we would have to continue the attack in the morning, that it would be as well to try to tempt the enemy to return fire at us so that we could pinpoint his muzzle flash with cross bearings to give us some clues to use on the morrow. We still suspected the housing estate, but had no confirmation.

L/Cpl Duncan came forward with us a short way to a bend in the track, bringing his section's Bren gunners. Frank and I positioned ourselves to either side with our binoculars and compassed to position the flash of any return fire. The gun team were instructed to fire a short burst from each of several positions, moving each time to avoid retaliation. The sudden stutter of the gun echoed away into the fields, emphasizing the former silence of the night. There was no return fire. Nor did a second burst a few minutes later draw response. At the third attempt, after only three or four rounds, there was a faint twinkle of sparks from the base of some houses ahead, and a quick cry from the Bren gunner whose gun stopped firing. 'He's shot sir! Jerries got him clean through the head', No. 2 on the Bren shouted. This seemed uncanny. We fired a few bursts back at the position of the momentary stab of flame on our own account after trying to fix a compass bearing on the right spot. Surprisingly, the wounded chap, who had indeed been shot clean through the head, was still alive. We carried him back to the house, where he was wrapped in bedding then carried back to the other farm. We heard later reports that this Jock had not only lived, but recovered too. It was very much later that I met a possible explanation of this shooting; this was that towards the end of the war the enemy had been experimenting with infra-red equipment for night shooting by tanks and also by snipers.

For a while after Frank had gone back to the HQ farm, I sat in the back room with the gunner officer, ate a few biscuits I found in one of my pouches, exchanged a few words with the gunner, then tried to doze a while, curled up on the floor. Opposite me one of the signallers crouched over his radio which had its metal rod aerial poking up out of a broken window. Each time I jerked out of a doze, there he was intent on his hissing, crackling and singing box of tricks, from time to time giving a routine check back to HQ in the monotony of radio-ese double talk. It was comforting to feel we were in direct touch with the guns if things started happening, and for once to have the company of another officer in a forward position although we were both too worn out to say much to each other. In spite of the calm I felt restive about what might be going on outside and conscious of my new responsibility of providing protection to the FOO and his men, and so most of what little time was left to the night after the trenches had been finished, I spent around section positions and keeping watch forward.

A runner came from one of the forward sections at about 3 am to report sounds of movement out in the field towards the enemy. I went back with him. Certainly there was something going on about 200 yards in front, soft undefinable noises. The darkness was intense. I crawled out on the grass 50 yards forward of the trenches to silhouette what we suspected was an enemy patrol against the blue-blackness of the sky. It revealed nothing. Apart from these sounds, all was frost-crisp with the stillness of the early hours. One can see most clearly at night, I had found, by keeping one's eyes very wide open and looking around but not at the object one sought to see. After a while my tired eyes started to play tricks with me, but I was not keen to fire a Verey flare unless something definite materialised as this would draw attention to our whereabouts, about which the enemy might now be uncertain. Gradually I became aware with a prickling of the spine and a heart which broke into a trot that some dark shapes I had taken to be a hedge were very much closer and coming quietly and steadily towards me with scraping pauses. The grouping of the shape seemed to suggest about seven or eight men in clumps, and they were almost as close to me as the nearest section position was distant behind. I crept back as swiftly and quietly as I could, not daring to fire a flare until I had reached the edge of the field and some cover. 'Right, I've got them covered sir!' L/Cpl Duncan whispered, and bang went the flare as we crouched behind the Bren trained on the dark shapes, now about 30 yards off. As the white, fitful light soared hissing up just above the heads of the 'enemy', three dark cows reared with surprise and stampeded into the night! In spite of this alarm, the Germans did not react with fire. At this revelation, the hoarse whisper of Cpl Parry passed on the news to the other sections, '. . . *** this for a lark! 'Twas noo Jerry at a', onny *** coo-s.'

These cows were rather a menace. They continued to wander about restlessly, probably disturbed by the rest of the herd being dead. If any enemy did come, the Jocks would probably dismiss their approach as 'coo-s', so I kept watch until the sky paled to dawn.

Daylight revealed no trace of the enemy and no order to attack, so after checking things at the sections and struggling through one third of a tin of bully beef and some biscuits, I stood down 33 per cent of the Jocks to get some rest. The gunner officer was having a doze. Things looked very peaceful and more cheerful than the day before, and after finding there was no fresh news at Company HQ, I decided to get a bit of sleep. Sgt Godfrey, who had also been up most of the night, joined me in tumbling clothed with equipment as we stood onto a wrecked bed, which was situated in one of the two back rooms. Godfrey was snoring heavily almost as soon as his head hit the pillow.

After what must have been about 45 minutes blessed partial and complete oblivion, I awakened with a start to a sudden vicious crackling noise, and loud violent rattling on the walls of the house as though a giant were catapulting handfuls of large pebbles at it. For a moment my thoughts did not connect with where we were and I lay still with fright, puzzled and dopey.

Immediately a loud cry of blasphemy and pain came through the door of the room the gunners were in, and someone staggered noisily past. Amazingly, Sgt Godfrey was still asleep with a peaceful expression on his dirty, beard-stubbled face. He grunted to the jab I gave to wake him and sat up. I kicked open the door to the next room to be met by clouds of white dust as though someone had burst a bag of flour over the forms scampering over the floor on all fours and crawling in the mess of broken glass.

The gunner officer was flat on the floor and his radio operator under a table. The radio, I noticed, was smashed. Perhaps I was still part asleep, but I just could not make out what was going on. The expressions on the artillery chaps' faces quite apart from the shambles told me, if confirmation were needed, that it was something decidedly unpleasant.

At this juncture another burst of this quaint noise drew my astonished waking eyes to swift jets of dust and plaster cascading from a streak of jagged, fist-sized holes racing along the opposite wall of the room – a burst of machine gun fire passing clean through the thin lath walls!

It was a tiny, low-ceilinged room with a small door through which figures were frantically scampering and wriggling in a board-hugging cluster like a nest of disturbed weasels – but for the circumstances as comic a scene as I have met. I yelled 'Watch the front!' and slung my small pack with a crash and tinkle through the remnants of the window, meaning to get out that way to try to spot from which direction the attack threatened. I was on the floor too now. Somewhere outside someone shouted 'Jerries coming!' Another burst of fire smashed chips of woodwork off the door and splintered the window frame making me hurriedly change my plan of exit. From under a door a dull, roaring crackle and eddies of thick yellowish smoke came with soul tearing squeals of terror from the direction of the stable which had caught fire from tracer bullets.

All this had taken only a few seconds so far, and I crawled quite as frantically as my predecessors through the door in company with Godfrey, dragging my rifle. The house was well alight now, and I gave another yell into the cellar to make sure it was clear, at the same time thanking providence that we had completed our network of trenches during the night. It was vital to get out swiftly to take charge and meet the attack, but I resolved if it were humanly possible to fire a burst into the blazing cattle stalls and put the screaming animals out of their misery; they were chained and the place a sheet of flame.

Scampering through the hall, I came face to face with terrified Pte C and at that moment saw a trail of plaster film a white deafening streak along the scrim of C's tin hat – a round passing out of the lath just a shade above his head. Fortunately for his sanity he was unaware of this.

Outside the gunner officer was staggering, clutching his head in agony and stumbling towards the rear blindly. It transpired later that a piece had been smashed out of his skull. I think he survived.

For a few seconds there was ominous quiet. None of the Jocks could report the least sign of enemy movement in front. Another burst whining off the corner of the building seemed to suggest an attack from the side or back, and I scrambled to the communication trench to the rear of the building. The gun was firing a very rapid rate, but it was difficult to decide what type it was with the frightful racket the mutilated bullets made smashing off and through the flaming building. The fierce crackle of these bullets seemed to indicate that unless the fire was coming clean through the flimsy walls, the attack was from the flanks or rear, yet I could get no indication of its source. Seeing the plaster spraying off in a sweep along the side of the farm, I dropped hurriedly and just in time into the communication trench at the rear of the building, and scrambled on all fours along it. The farm had flared up as though petrol soaked, and was now a raging inferno, our former bedroom glowing, a shimmering furnace. An awful doubt raced chill-footed through my thoughts as I strove to recall if we had carried all the wounded back to the rear farm the previous evening. Were the last pitiful almost human shrieks coming from the far side of this roaring furnace being made by the cows, goats and pigs alone, or had any Jocks been trapped asleep in the cellar by the flames? None had answered my call, now it was too late; the interior of the building was groaning into a roar, towering sheets of flame and sparks high above.

There was still no visible source of the continuing murderous bursts of machine gun fire, so, spurred on by strips of flaming woodwork slipping down onto me from the skeleton of the roof, I crawled towards the corner where I knew a small ventilator opened onto the trench from the cellar. From this point I would also get a look at Ibbenburen and perhaps shoot any animals still alive.

I had just reached the next stretch of trench when a deafening crash, seemingly an 88mm shell, burst against the house dissolving my equipment and small pack outside the back room window – now a searing square of white hot light.

The noise was now, as so often in battle, swelling to proportions to beggar description, but in the hell which increasingly was enveloping us from some invisible source, I became aware the Jocks were being badly hit. Somewhere in a hole behind me I caught snatches of a voice which had changed beyond recognition, a badly wounded chap calling weakly to himself: 'Oh God . . . Oh God . . . finish it.' From elsewhere came sounds of involuntary moaning.

As I crawled round the building, further falls of burning timber and the leaning, hot wall forced me out of the trench towards a foxhole. Just then another high velocity shell enveloped me from behind with crushing hot violence sweeping me forward as I knelt scanning the fields from the edge of a waterlogged hole, my eye urgently seeking some sign of the enemy. The half-formed thought 'tank attack' was snuffed out with ear-singing, sparking blackness as I hit something headlong.

When awareness crept back upon me – I think probably about two minutes later – I became conscious first of a feeling of suffocation and great pressure on my back, bent stomach down; then with puzzled surprise I realised that my half-open mouth and teeth were clogged with cold gritty mud. I was face down, head first in a partially flooded trench, my head just held from the water by the painful forward tilt of my tin hat rim. All circulation seemed to have stopped in my arms which, I discovered on trying to wriggle free, were bent back on my chest. I had a creeping fear for a moment, unable to place or feel my lower legs and feet, probably because these were above me in the air and drained of blood.

The heavy weight in the middle of my back kneaded with movement as I struggled, giving an attempted yell which ended in a grunt due to the weight on my lungs. 'Is-thaat you surr, I thought you was Kaput!' a Scots voice said somewhere above: a Jock, one of two who had jumped in on top of what they had taken for a body in their desperation for cover. The end of his sentence was enveloped in another awful earth-shaking crash and twang of shrapnel very close above. There was pandemonium on my back, and part of the trench wall slid on my left shoulder.

It was then that the full realisation of the situation hit me too. The enemy must surely by now be on top of us, and here I was suffocating, pinned, helpless, upside-down with the trench caving in, and the burning building 8 feet away likely to collapse onto us, when I should have been on my feet sorting out the threads and controlling the Jocks who had been left. My persistent attempts at movement sufficiently distracted the Jock kneeling with spiky boots on my shoulders and back to divert his attention from the hell above so that he would try releasing me from his weight. By way of explanation for his using me as a doormat he said: 'I've got Bethune on top of me, Surr. He's in an awfu' mess. Hit bad.' I was distressed to hear this. Bethune was one of our recent replacements in his first action, a small, capable, cheerful chap with a pleasing Irish lilt to his speech. He had the promise of another 'character' in his make-up.

As I continued wriggling to right myself, I could tell from incoherent involuntary semi-animal sounds, groans and cries for stretcher bearers in weakening voices, that the wounded were in a very bad way. Suddenly hell commenced again and the knobbly, shivering bodies pressed down on me anew. The vicious concussion of three more almighty explosions very close at 5-second intervals crumbled the side of the hole. For a short while almost complete silence followed, broken into gradually by the decreased cries of the wounded.

At last I was upright again and trying to get enough feeling into my numbed fingers and arms to work a mud-caked rifle, looking anxiously round for sight of the enemy I felt certain must by now be upon us. I had from the start always feared an awful feeling that come what may, surrender was unthinkable, 'just not done' – a circumstance that therefore I had prayed might not arise – for despite myself I feared I should feel compelled to fight it out to a finish. It struck me then for the first time that if we were completely overrun it might require greater courage and level-headed judgment to acknowledge hopeless defeat and put oneself and one's men at the mercy of an enemy we had grown not to trust than to fight on, driven by the greater horror of being unable impartially to dissect the thought that in surrendering, one had perhaps succumbed to the ignominy of showing fear. The resultant determination to fight on whatever happened later comforted me with the only and surprise pleasure in this miserable day.

A quick look round at the horrifying change which had swept over our surroundings provided momentary relief at the complete astonishment of finding that enemy infantry and tanks were nowhere to be seen. A more detailed second look from a ground-hugging position in case the trouble started up again numbed me with its gradually realised nightmare implications.

In place of the farm was a 4-foot high heap of shimmering rubble ringed with smoking ash and steaming, heat-baked earth and trenches. The two Jocks with me in the hole were hardly recognisable smeared with caked mud, blood and ash. The uppermost, Pte Bethune, had been hit by shrapnel from a shell which had apparently been touched off by a bush – now a fluffed stump – at the edge of our hole. Among his injuries was a gaping hole in his throat through which he breathed bubbling, noisily frothing blood. He was quite conscious but stilled with shock and pain and lack of air. The pathetic forms of twenty-two other men were scattered about the farm and orchard, some quite still, others bloodstained mutilated bundles of messy khaki moving slightly with limbs missing, severed or broken. Some conscious, but in agony beyond their vocal control.

Beneath some white-gashed and bullet-drilled apple trees at the back of the house, I looked unbelievingly at the still form of Sgt Godfrey, shot through the centre of his forehead as he looked from his foxhole. Near him was the tall quiet form of Pte Storey, the 'father' of the platoon, a courteous, efficient regular soldier who consistently refused promotion. He too was killed. His sole desire had been to get back to his wife and home from which he had been parted for six years service in India before coming out with us. He had only seen her for a few days in the interval, and every day had faithfully written her a letter which he handed me to censor. To his right L/Cpl Duncan lay killed; another old stager, dour, thickset, blond Cpl Allan was wounded. Among the wounded on the other side lay L/Cpl Wilson, the 'Douglas

Fairbanks' of the Platoon, and I thought back to our night march towards the Heinsberg attack when he had blurted out how he looked forward to 'a nice Blighty wound in some soft spot to get out of it all'. I don't think he had meant this, but was very peeved with things at the time. His present wound, the second, looked neither nice nor in a soft spot.

I was startled to realise that as far as could be quickly seen only Pte Jones, myself and the Jock who had been immediately on top of me seemed to have survived intact of all of us who had piled out of the house or who had been in the nearest section.

I felt unsteady, with a head singing like a child's top I think from ear blast. Could all this be real? Perhaps the whole, swift, hideous thing had been a nightmare dream and I was still asleep in the little back room with Sgt Godfrey, with everything as it had been six to ten minutes before; I noticed with relief on glancing to the rear that the men dug in to the hedge junction were still there and grasping their weapons, but looking appalled by the awful scene ahead. They stood as though paralysed with the fear that if they came forward to help us they might coincide with another outburst of explosive fury. I tried to get up, mechanically brushing the mud off the bolt of my rifle and worried that it had jammed. To add to my queer, top heavy feeling I could still see no visible cause for our misery: the road to Ibbenburen was clear and peaceful, not a figure moved in the bushes and hedges, nor in the fields ahead.

Sounds of shouting and of running feet made me look behind again. What was that bright cadmium yellow smoke doing trailing off over the fields? I blinked with astonishment at the source of the shouting. Twelve or fourteen figures, Jocks, stretcher bearers, Smyg, Frank and Maj Stewart among them, were running towards us over the open fields from the rear farm. It was not strange that they should run to our help, but it was that they should do so in the light of the fury of the enemy less than a minute before, and completely disregard cover in their approach, with such apparent confidence that it would not recommence.

I was completely puzzled, and crawled to do what I could with a tourniquet of webbing on a youngster who had lost a leg. Nothing seemed to make sense, perhaps my mind was wandering.

Never before had the Platoon been smitten with such concentrated lethal fury in so short a space of time. Then my mind started to work, and I remembered the yellow smoke.

Just then Frank and Andrew ran up, and set to work on the wounded with the stretcher bearers. Frank spotted me; 'By God, Pete, I hadn't expected to see you again!' he said. Then Andrew came up and to my greater surprise and puzzlement said: 'I'm sorry I had to desert you Peter, but when I saw what it was I ran back to the other farm to put out a smoke flare.'

'What was it?' I asked, but with growing realisation.

'It was three of our own tanks Pete, worse luck; SP 17-pounders firing from back over those fields beyond our farm. The CO sent them round as soon as the armour got through. They took you for Jerries. They'd been told we'd been held up, but had the wrong buildings marked as enemy on their map: should have been the housing estate. The tank troop commander's in a bad way. He collapsed when he realised what he had done.' (He was killed, perhaps mercifully, on a mine a few hours later.)

I had not realised that Maj Stewart had been forward with us. He must have established himself in the mud-bank dugout when Godfrey and I had been asleep.

Looking back over the fields to the left of the rear farm, I saw the dark green, squat shape of one of the self-propelled 17-pounders still pointing in our direction from the position from which it had fired, only 350 yards away.

This incident, which had killed eleven and wounded twelve including most of the artillery party, had brought the total action casualties up to fifty-one killed and wounded. My Platoon, which had been undermanned since we started, was down from thirty-two to eleven. Four of my NCOs had been lost, and three killed had been new chaps in their first action. Just over half our casualties had been fatal.

We carried all the wounded back to the farm and laid them on stretchers in the barn. They were in a very bad way and neither the MO, the carrier, nor an ambulance had been able to get through to us yet.

Smyg had decided to evacuate the ruins and withdraw us to the rear farm for the time being, but I was worried that I could not tally my nominal roll with the casualties and stopped on, looking round the rubble and in the trenches to see if anyone had been overlooked. I was surprised to see that so heavy had the explosions been around the trenches that the sides of the holes had crumbled to shallow pits once we had crawled out of them. Walking along the trench past the rear corner of the mound of rubble, a muffled but heavy blast of explosion deep in the rubble threw me over off balance into the trench rut, where for a moment I lay still, feeling shaken in all senses and puzzled. Miraculously I was unhurt by the spray of red-hot brick fragments, and looking at the glowing gap blown in the smoking rubble, I realised what it must have been. The position of the explosion had been from the corner of the back room where I had dozed a while the previous evening. Beside me had been a case of PIAT bombs. These must have been crushed into the cellar when the roof collapsed, and had only just absorbed sufficient heat down there to 'cook off'. This gratuitous tailpiece, again provided by our own weapons and not those of the enemy, seemed about the last straw.

I collected what serviceable weapons I could find and carried them back with me to the rear farm where I was met by the decimated remnants of the Platoon still dug into the hedge, asking anxiously after their friends in the two forward sections and Platoon HQ.

Another check on the nominal roll against the men left and the casualties disclosed one Jock to be missing. I went back for a further look with the awful feeling that one of the chaps wounded or asleep must have been burnt alive in the blaze. It was not till next day that we found him, a blackened, charred, hardly recognisable body lying between the twisted metal frames of a stretcher where the front room had been; then someone remembered this shrivelled form had been a wounded chap carried in the previous evening but who had died of wounds.

Returning to the rear farm, I found one of the Jocks had made some very welcome tea, our first for quite a while. I took a mug of it along to Andrew Stewart who stood looking very tired beside the wounded, whom to our increasing distress we had not yet been able to evacuate. They were all too badly hit to take a sip, though one had a cigarette placed between part open trembling lips. We were tormented not only with the thought that the cause of this had been a battle accident, but that there seemed so little that we could do materially to aid them. I knelt beside Pte Bethune, still breathing with great difficulty through the hole in his throat, and loosened the clothing at his chest. His eyes were shut, but he seemed conscious. Outside our ears were suddenly attracted by the thin, sizzling approach of some long-range shells, the first to come the wrong way for some time. Each doleful concussion into the soggy earth about the farm seemed to hammer home our cold weariness of it all and draw attention to the chilled emptiness of our stomachs. Those who could, took cover, their movements seeming to emphasise the contrasting helpless stillness of the wounded on their stretchers in the barn. Only those least seared by pain betrayed recognition of these new sounds by the restlessness of their sunken eyes.

Pte Bethune's desperate efforts at breathing through the wound in his throat were getting weaker. The stretcher bearers had no morphia to still the pain of those worst hit but now some had lapsed into unconsciousness.

By a super-human feat Brown 'S' skidded into the yard unexpectedly in his carrier, having somehow negotiated the steep track through the woods on his own. With the aid of this vehicle we managed at last to evacuate the casualties to the doctor's armoured car some way to the rear. Unhappily Bethune and another of the wounded were found to have died on the way.

Meanwhile, Smyg had sent forward another platoon towards the burnt-out farm to keep a secure front. Through these Maj Stewart had sent one of his sergeants with a small patrol to recce the bridge in daylight to see if it was still intact and also to see if any sign could be detected of the strangely silent enemy infantry. All they met were some uncommunicative German civilians evacuating cattle from a burning farm. Someone fired a shot over their heads which sent them scattering. Andrew, taking advantage of the patrol's news, moved forward of us to the next group of houses.

All our platoon rations, some of our weapons, ammunition, 38 set radio, my own kit, though not my rifle and revolver, had gone up in the flames of the farm, so a hurried scrounge had to be done before the light failed to get at least partly reorganised with the remnants of the Platoon, equipping them with flotsam left after moving the casualties.

We moved the dead from the trenches working in pairs, lifting each heavy inert form gently and in silence. My thoughts alternated from numbness to a bursting conflict of emotion which almost overshadowed the desperate physical weariness as recognition came in each tattered bloodstained bundle of the friend of a few hours before. To each form memory triggered vivid pictures of outings in the past at home during training, or individual incidents and mutual trials in past actions, of being introduced to some relative, or of being proudly shown some photograph of a girlfriend, fiancée, or young family who were still not to know of tragedy perhaps for several days. Behind it all, recurring with a more nagging persistence to each action and yet still queerly unreal, was the thought that but for a seeming chance of time and place each body might so easily have been one's own.

The day was nearly spent. Misty dampness was rising up the valley with the approach of night. The orders I had been expecting all day to move forward to continue the advance had not come. We were to hold the positions won. No tanks other than the self-propelled guns which had shot us up had materialised, but the enemy seemed to have pulled back to Ibbenburen.

At nightfall additional comfort was added to the news of this respite when Smyg ordered the remnants of my platoon and myself to spend the night in reserve at the company HQ farm. Pip's platoon would be forward on standing patrol.

Despite the days, it seemed, since our last proper meal our real hunger was for the mental oblivion of sleep. Cold, tinned, soya-link sausage and biscuits and some bread found their way down a throat which seemed reluctant to receive them, then for that part of the night I was not on duty I subsided onto a wine storage shelf in the cellar to try and sleep. Next to me the 18 set radio and its operator, hissing, crackling and talking, gradually receded from my consciousness. Exhaustion eventually overcame the coldness of the slate slab and the vividness of the scenes and sounds of the last few hours, though at intervals until dawn the odd stray shell jolted me back to awareness of the increasing cold.

In the morning Frank and I picked our way past the warmth of the ruins of the forward farm from which smoke still filmed in thin blue spirals into the wintry sunlight. We had decided we ought to investigate a small barn about 100 yards to the right which we had not previously looked over. The dead still lay in a silent group on the grass near the ruins awaiting transport and they and the details of the scene of our ordeal now so peaceful in the morning light held my thoughts, try as I could to keep my mind on the present. A young goat kid, singed in its escape from the blazing farm and now wet with the dew and shivering and bleating piteously, was staggering about the hot ash's rim, crying for its mother who, being chained, had perished with the other animals in the fire.

As we neared the barn, if either of us had our minds on the job, our attention as always was more concentrated on the track for possible mines than on the surroundings. Suddenly a twig cracked in a bush beside us on the left. Our eyes and rifles swung towards it together just as a tall figure in grey-green wearing a forage cap over tousled fair hair stepped out right against us. His hands stretched higher in emphasis above his head as tired eyes, dulled with fatigue, anxiously searched Frank's and my face and our fingers on the triggers of our rifles for some human response which would quiet the tense fear of the worst his drawn, beard-stubbled face and quivering fingers betrayed. He was very young and I think very near breaking point and I couldn't help feeling sympathy for his desperation to decipher in those first few seconds whether this was to be the end of his book or the beginning of a new chapter in his youth. The young goat kid was bleating now having followed part way up the track behind us. The face of this youth was quite as eloquent in its pleading misery.

Frank and I were remarkably fortunate he had not shown himself as fanatical as some of his fellow SS officer cadets had shown themselves to be, for his presence was as sudden as it was unexpected. We promptly marched him back to the nearest section position. It was unfortunate for the German that the first man we met was Pte Jones, evidently still wild from witnessing A Company wounded being shot in the attack. Jones, of about equal build and height to the youth, immediately sprang forward and before we realised his intent landed the German a tremendous blow on the chin which floored him heavily on his back and flooded his tense ashen face with all its previous obvious fears. Jones had to be restrained from the evident intention of fulfilling the German's fears.

He was shaking like a leaf by now and despite another Jock offering him a cigarette as he was marched back towards company HQ, he kept looking anxiously behind him at the weapon in his back. I had to give Jones a ticking-off for taking unfavourable advantage of the prisoner's position. This he took with a subdued but contented smile as he nursed the knuckles of his right fist. Some little sounds from a bulge which moved a bit in the front of his windproof jerkin showed that the recent violent activity had upset Jones's puppy from his sleep.

The complaining sound of carrier gears from the rear heralded the arrival of two of Jimmy's Lloyd carriers which drew up alongside us. Onto these we loaded the dead with heavy hearts at saying farewell to these friends. We had to roll the charred body in a blanket.

It seems strange to look back on, but my next task was to try to catch the kid which kept following at a distance, to see if it could be persuaded to eat or drink something which might still its misery of bleating, but to no avail.

A few German civilians appeared from the direction of the enemy of whom we had had no sign for some time except for the occasional covey of long distance shells at lengthy intervals. A few of these landed close enough to jolt our peace of mind and inspire digging in when the realisation came that we would possibly be here for another night.

These Germans, for the most part sullen and dejected carrying precious bundles of belongings or pushing them in carts, some with children, were very reluctant to talk. We gathered, though, as the patrol had on the previous day, that the remnants of the SS had pulled back to Ibbenburen. I just could not fathom why there had been such a long delay in the attack being pushed on, though was personally thankful that we ourselves had been left in peace.

A cold drizzle which had persisted during the afternoon

increased towards nightfall, steaming and sizzling on the farm ruins beside which the remnants of my platoon were digging in for the night on orders from Smyg who was covering the track junction. Pip's and Sgt Oliver's platoons were dug in now astride the T junction 100 yards to the rear towards company HQ.

My platoon fire-power was now reduced to four rifles, a Bren and a Sten and my revolver which I lent to Taffy, our Welshman. At thirty he was a wise old bird at keeping out of harm's way and was one third or more older than some of the platoon.

Digging our holes for the night turned out to be a very wet, cold, muddy pastime. There was still no information at our level but we resolved to at least try and be comfortable if we could. We lined each hole with straw and bedding from the farms. I was sharing a 6 foot x 2 foot 6, 4 foot 6 deep hole with Pte Syd Brown as he had helped me construct it . . . and, cunningly, by the addition of another body to my hole for the night I had hoped it might be a little warmer. However, we were by now pretty well soaked to the skin with the drizzle and our teeth chattered increasingly as time passed.

Suddenly word came by runner to go to an orders group. With this news I struggled out past Brown through the wet straw and out into the dismal night, now lit again fitfully by the unpleasant suddenness of some more long-range 88mm shells exploding a quarter of a mile to the south. I was glad to be outside and with something to do again as a rather dismal reaction had set in among the chaps left to me now so many of their friends had gone. Their losses were only just beginning to sink in. At first one is just numb and this was wearing off. I think we must all have figured that, like musical chairs, the elimination process was only too obvious. Twice already my platoon had been whittled down by 75 per cent in one action and for those who had survived so far it seemed merely a matter of time, and not much time at that.

On the muddy lane back to Company HQ I was challenged twice by 11 Platoon. At the farm I stumbled down the dark cellar stairs and pushed aside the blackout blanket into the candlelight which flickered on the hunched weary forms of Alan and Frank resting on my former stone-slab bed and beside them the radio operator crouched over the scratchy singing of his 18 set. The news was that units of the 53rd (Welsh) Div, including the 1st Bn HLI would be passing through us during the evening to make an attack on Ibbenburen, with the support of tanks and flamethrowers.

With the fall of darkness came the clattering, squeaking rumble of approaching tanks from behind us, echoing back from the wooded hill. Each dark massive shape shook the earth of our fox-holes as it lumbered past towards the start line. With them in Indian file the dim forms of the infantry plodded forward like links in an enormous chain. There were no calls of greeting as they passed and the figures themselves were silent. Our silence was one of sympathy and theirs eloquent of their preoccupation, each with his mental Gethsemane, so often the worst part of an attack; though we suspected from the long silence ahead that the enemy were in no great heart themselves now.

The attack, silent for a change, was successful and the town fell with little fighting. It was typical of the lack of information at our level, though, that months should pass before we heard this. We could only gather from the lack of noise forward that this must have been the case.

As the sounds of the night reverted once more to the drip of the drizzle off the trees and the occasional cough or clink of metal from a Jock on stag, we settled down to the cold vigil till dawn, aware once again of the rest which comes with the easing of tension in the knowledge that troops, armour and space now lay between us and the enemy. I was interested to note, though, as the night wore on that now that danger, preoccupation with the enemy and consequently responsibility had subsided, one's mind thus freed found the physical difficulties of cold, wet, hunger and fatigue far more irksome.

'CRACKING ABOUT
THE PLAINS'

As the sky paled to the first sign of daylight, we, feeling sure a movement order would come soon, crept stiff-limbed from our holes. My small kit being destroyed, a beard was beginning to sprout on my face and I wondered how long it would be before I could secure another razor. Rubbing my hands on the wet grass and then on my face provided some sort of a wash to wake me up, while Brown coaxed some rather dirty-looking water to boil for tea over Hexamine tablets.

Soon enough the movement order came and A Company filed past us back towards the rear from the houses they had occupied overnight on the way to Ibbenburen. There they had incidentally found a slit trench against the wall of one of the houses scattered about with tell-tale cartridge cases which must have been occupied by one of the snipers who had done so much damage during our attack.

It seemed strange to line the platoon up on the road and find only enough men to march in one section file instead of the normal four files. With our backs at last on the farm we trudged off to rejoin the rest of the battalion and, we hoped, some transport on the main road.

On the way along the Ibbenburen side of the hill we passed the tracks in the lane and field of the self-propelled 17-pounder guns which had shot us up. Beside the tracks lay a significant pile of 17-pounder shell cases. The punch of a troop of these vehicles at close range together with their machine guns was the most terrifyingly violent slice of destruction the Platoon had yet met.

At the main road, which led through a neck in the hill back

towards the Dortmund–Ems canal, we once more began seeing the familiar faces of our friends in the other companies. To our surprise they were marching back towards the canal along the winding macadamised road with trees shrouded in wet mist on either side. What stunt were we on now, we wondered. Jocks called to each other to hear how their friends had fared in other companies and from the answers we soon gathered they had run into as sticky a time as we had. We passed about a dozen dead Germans on our side of the road as we wound over the hill, but as our dead had already been picked up it was still difficult to judge the losses relatively.

The march proved an unexpectedly long and tiring one on roads inches deep in slush on the edges where the tarmac had crumbled with the heavy vehicles of war. At the far end of the cutting through the wooded hill a shattered Jeep and carrier marked the spot where a recce party had run into a sticky end at the start of the operation. The newly dug graves lay alongside and included one with a civilian cap on it. A little further on the charred remnants of a crashed and burned out Fw190 fighter plane were splashed over a field.

About a mile farther on and the vehicles in both directions on inadequate roads had thickened into a traffic jam. Perhaps to lessen this, at a crossroads near the village of Segbert we turned left and cut across country. For ten minutes we enjoyed a rest at a farm which was minus quite a few eggs when we left.

Still there was no definite news of what we were up to. However, the column had now wound back onto another road under heavy traffic. Here at last were some positive clues for us to add to our deductions and rumours as to the military positions. As soon as we got on to this road we began to meet among traffic coming in the opposite direction, waves of motley, liberated personnel. They came, drunk from the joy of it . . . and sometimes just plain drunk . . . on foot, in looted cars and carts or by pushbike, cheering and saluting, Russian, Polish and French Displaced persons and Russian POWs.

For the next 50 to 100 miles this tide of fugitive humanity grew steadily into a torrent. They became the terror and in many cases the means of the sudden demise of wayside farmers and members of their families on whom they descended at nightfall for food, plunder and often rape.

The squarely built Russian soldiers, as heavy in their appearance as they seemed in their wits, saluted every Allied object that moved, apparently without fail, on roads nose to tail with army transport.

Finally, our battalion column, marching in section file on alternate sides of the busy road, got the order to halt and fall out by the roadside. In a flash the khaki figures dissolved off the road and filtered into the kitchens and yards of the wayside houses and smallholdings to the commencement of squawks from disturbed poultry, the rattle of milk pails in the cowsheds and the voluble 'patter' necessary to get farmers' wives organised in boiling water for tea.

Of my platoon, Jones, Tarn, Brown 'S', Byles and Taffy, finding their water not boiling swiftly enough, had to be restrained from adding the odd door or chest of drawers to an outside fire if not watched.

I found myself in a house seemingly deserted of civilians, in the company of Capt Tammy Youngson, Maj. Donald Hogg, Phil Carruthers (the Canadian loan officer), Smyg, and Usher, Tammy's batman. We soon had a fine fire going in the hearth with eggs found by Phil on the boil. A ramble by Tammy in the cellar produced enough wine for those addicted to it to get into 'Hellish good form', otherwise known as 'Fine fettle', in no time.

Gradually, from clues here and there we had deduced that while we had been engaged at Ibbenburen, the armour of the 'Desert Rats', outflanking this pocket of resistance, had forced a wedge way ahead of us towards the River Weser. Our job was now to catch them up with all haste to hold the wedge open. To this end we were to wait here for TCVs to carry us up to the north-east.

We were pleased to hear the TCVs draw up at last. Five trucks were allotted per company, the Jocks chased out from their various activities in the houses, then away the 1½-mile string of battalion vehicles moved.

It was pleasant to be on the move, rolling along in comparative comfort, munching what rations could be produced between us and watching the countryside, a never failing source of the most intense interest to me. On the left, away out over the rolling rich fields were wooded hills. On the right the land was flatter and studded with prosperous farms.

The only signs of fighting were occasional tank tracks churned in patterns of mud over the fields, a wall or farm with its brick face flecked with spraying machine-gun bullets and punched through here and there with an odd high-explosive or solid-shot tank shell. At a crossroads was the forlorn hulk of a wrecked Cromwell tank stopped in its stride by the retreating enemy.

After a long run at fair speed during which our warmth was torn from us by the eddying air of the open trucks, we suddenly slowed down and pulled in to the side for a reason which as so often remained unknown to us. Immediately the drivers, followed by a number of the Jocks, piled off to make the most of the halt. The drivers, from long experience, did not waste a moment. A perforated tin was produced and filled with sand. Into this petrol was poured and a match applied. On top went a billycan full of water. Tins of jam and Compo tea and wads of bread next appeared. This time the tea brewers were fortunate; the halt was just long enough to produce results.

The sound of engines starting up along the column spread towards us and hurriedly we clambered back into the trucks. Pulling sharp left we laboured up a long hill, revealing a fine view of villages and fields into the distance. The young spring greenery of the trees and sprouting corn in the fields were refreshing to our eyes. Down the far side of the hill we plunged, running fast. By the roadside lay the flame-bleached, twisted metal shell of a burned out 3-ton petrol lorry. All about it were scattered exploded and distorted jerrycans melted into the tar of the road.

For a while again the countryside seemed trim and untouched by war except for occasional heavy twin scars of tank tracks curving through the soft green film of the young corn-shoots, the tanks sinking so deeply in the rain-soaked earth that their bellies had scraped a smooth flat path between each track. At a road-junction another of our vehicles had met a violent end: this time a light tank, holed and fire-seared with blistered paint.

Still at our level we had very little idea of what the situation would be at the other end or of exactly where we were going. As the miles spun by, however, we realised each turn of the wheels was carrying us closer to whatever spot the enemy had chosen to turn and fight again and so, almost unawares, tension crept stealthily back until the unwelcome cold grip of its fingers twanged a string of nerves in our hearts and tummies from time to time.

For a while the country was open and flat, again gradually giving way to smaller pleasant hills not unlike so much of the English countryside. At lunch time the convoy stopped, this time, by good fortune, at some farms by the side of the road.

As each truck crunched to a halt the Jocks piled out to descend like a swarm of khaki locusts on the luckless farmers. In no time the cows were milked dry, the eggs, plus the 'fly' fowl (well hidden but given away by the scent) were on the boil. In numerous farm utensils adequately heated with liberal supplies of farm timber, thick brews of Compo tea were frothing to the boil.

Meanwhile, Alan, Frank, Pip and I sat in state in the farm lounge making the most of easy chairs with the farmer's wife to wait on us, it seemed quite willingly. Fried eggs, bread folded over greasy strings of tinned bacon and some char of strong brew cheered us inwardly. These short spells in the warmth of a house with a family still in it to make it homely, although German, were very welcome interludes.

After half an hour, just as we were wandering back to the trucks again, the noise of cannon fire in the sky attracted our attention to some of our Typhoon fighters diving down, attacking a streaking German jet plane which circled twice at high speed and dived onto some object hidden by the trees.

The drivers of the TCVs had by now almost become one with the Platoons. My own was, of course, the amusing old chap with a walrus moustache. He appeared to be aged about forty-five and as he puffed away at a battered briar pipe which was always in his mouth he resumed his talk about books, trees, gardening, his pals and their doings and his past experiences in Normandy. His truck, plus four others allotted to our company, was to stick with us for quite a while.

Hour after hour and mile after mile the convoy rolled onwards through the fading light of the afternoon into the dark. Our halt had provided us with no more information so at any time we expected to pull in for the night. Our journey had run off the edge of the only map I had of the area but still we rolled on.

The route we were taking in its tortuous twists and acute turns at times almost back in our tracks on secondary roads seemed to be governed by some reason, perhaps tactical, which was quite obscure to us. Whether we were trying to avoid pockets of resistance or blown bridges, or moving to keep more direct routes open for armour and supply vehicles we could not determine. The hands of my watch dragged themselves past midnight and then on into the early hours. It even seemed possible that we had got lost and that sooner or later we would find ourselves having gone too far, cut off in enemy-held territory.

Ghostly farms and little villages slid past in the night, each echoing back the whining labour of the TCVs engine. One imagined . . . and I think it was not always imagination . . . faces and forms peering out from the darkened windows of the houses at this invading ghost army in the dead of night.

The pearly light of dawn on 7 April found us still not having caught up with the enemy, picking our way along a lonely mist-wisped, low-lying stretch of secondary road. On either side of the road drainage ditches mirrored the strengthening light of the sky.

The first rays of the sun gave the mist a cheerful golden glow, obscuring the low-lying details of the landscape through which the trucks moved like a line of ships in a creamy sea. Being cramped in the trucks overnight had made us very cold and tired and gave one's legs an irritating restlessness.

While contemplating the possibilities of breakfast, we slowed and pulled into a pleasant small town called Diepholz, about 25 miles north-east of Osnabruck. Watched by a few of the townspeople, some in the streets and others looking from the houses, the battalion convoy split on the centre crossroads, the various companies turning each down one of the roads which radiated rather like the spokes of a wheel. BHQ turned to the left, B Company, ours, went straight on to pull up on a square and de-bus.

Alan Innes chose a fine undamaged hotel as his HQ. I chose a large well-kept private house over the road for 10 Platoon, with

Pip on the left and Sgt Cowie on the right farther up the road. Beside us the square contained some deserted German transport and a tandem motorcycle. The Jocks of S company took the tandem off the cycle and with a bit of petrol added ran around the district on it later. Lack of petrol, it appeared, had caused these vehicles to be abandoned by the retreating enemy.

There was still no concrete news of the situation so I set about trying to size up the form myself by attempting to pump a few of the silent bystanders who peered blankly at us. This had to be done in pidgin English and what little German had so far been learned. The information thus derived all seemed to indicate that enemy troops had left the previous night heading north.

Word came to dig in for all-round protection as it was not yet clear where the enemy or any pockets of them overlooked in armoured drive might be in relation to us. The possibilities to guard against appeared to be a counter-attack to isolate the armour ahead, or stragglers 'retiring' onto us to find their escape route cut.

The German civilians, as was usual in a town recently overrun, were still in the initial stage of relief at having survived the passing tide of war, fear that it might yet sweep back, shock at the fact that we were there at all, and a vague fear-tinged watchfulness of us as unknown factors to be matched against the brutal, atrocity-committing monsters depicted to them for so long by propaganda.

The lady of the house we were in was silent, tense and watchful, but very 'correct' in her attitude. I think her main fear was centred around her two pretty daughters of 18–20 years in a house teeming with rugged, battle-grimed soldiers. There were also two younger children, but no husband to be seen. As usual our first move was to search the house from the attic to the cellar for any hidden stragglers. I kept wondering if her seeming intense agitation while this was going on was due to either her husband being concealed somewhere, or the danger that any precious trinkets, which were always concealed if time permitted before our arrival, might be unearthed by the Jocks. Around the house in the garden groups of Jocks were busy digging fox-holes and clearing fields of fire of bits of hedge and shrub.

Tarn and Learmonth soon had the two elder girls well in hand in the palatial kitchen which we had taken over as platoon HQ, getting them to prepare a dish for us on the kitchen range. In no time the four of them, laughing, gesticulating and with a lot of banter from the Jocks, were settled in as a most efficient team of cooks to provide for our needs with some for them thrown in.

Quite soon the tall, thin, worried mother (if she was the mother, she might have been old enough to be grannie) asked if she could speak to me alone. She seemed so disturbed I began to wonder what some Jock might have been up to. However, I learned, partly in German and in French where that failed, that she was upset about possible damage the Jocks might do to her furniture, particularly the polish of the grand piano. It was indeed an exceptionally nice house, but seen against the endless trails of destruction her countrymen had left in the homes of other nations I was staggered and told her so: 'They are not Germans and will not wreck the place.'

Our house, being on a fork between two roads, presented quite a problem of defence with so few men left to me, so I was glad when one of Jimmy's anti-tank 6-pounders was dug in to cover one road while a scrounged PIAT looked after the other.

This new war of swift movement took some getting used to. The main problem seemed to be an almost complete and continuous lack of information at our level to put us into the picture about our relationship to the enemy, calls likely to be made on us or whether we were likely to be anywhere for a few minutes, hours or days. One could only judge these things on the facts one had been able to gather at any one moment, with ears and eyes restlessly alert to any possible clues or shreds of information of any sort. I have often wondered how far up the chain of command this failure lay when there was information to give. I suspect it was at Brigade HQ. For all I could learn, as so often, there may not have been any enemy straggler within miles . . . on the other hand the next village might be strongly held by enemy armour. Perhaps it was as well for the sake of alertness that one should always base one's defences on the latter assumption, tiring though it was in its drain on nerves and energy.

Once the defences were organised and a meal eaten, those who could settled down to catch up with sleep between turns on stag.

As dusk approached and there was still no definite news of the whereabouts, strength or intention of the enemy, Smyg decided to take a precaution or two. Instructions came to me to send out a standing patrol of section strength 800 yards down the road to give warning of any enemy's approach overnight. I took out Cpl Parry with a reduced section the required distance, sited the defences and settled them in and around a fine modern suburban house. The family, in spite of being Germans, were most helpful and very nice people. They even made beds for those Jocks not on stag in the slit trenches newly dug in their front garden. I was rather sorry to feel that circumstances would cause these beds to be occupied by Jocks in full kit and muddy boots.

Gradually a little news filtered down to us. The armour of the 'Desert Rats' and their accompanying infantry who had passed through the town ahead of us were doing splendidly 'swanning' somewhere well to the north. Meanwhile, the rest of our Division were pushing hard towards us from the direction of Rhine, with the possibility that some of the enemy they were dealing with might be pushed back in their retreat onto us.

With nightfall I was again approached by the lady of the house who led me to a fine big bedroom which she had prepared for me. This, I thought, was very nice of her and I thanked her for her trouble. For security and to keep a better check on things during the night I shared this with Platoon HQ L/Cpl Brown and I squashed onto the bed, boots, equipment, weapons and all when not on duty. Several times I checked round positions during the night. It was a fine night, no fires to be seen to the north which gave a clue that any enemy resistance to the armour must be some way off. A dog or two barked on and off as usual at the strange Scottish intruders. Inside the house it was quite still too but for the very soft crooning of some Jock on stag, heavy snoring from time to time, the leisurely ticking of a grandfather clock and a couple of times a glimpse of the mother moving about down a passage, most probably unable to sleep through worrying about the safety of her daughters. In the morning I learned they had slept in the next room to the one given me. I wonder if this juxtaposition had been carefully thought out by the good lady with the hope that there lay greater safety. She had not, I think, anticipated the amount of mysterious wandering about the house there seemed to be as the various Jocks made their way to and fro from stags out in the trenches. In the morning her face showed the terrible night of worry and perhaps terror she had spent, and I felt sorry for her.

In the morning I had a fine wash in the kitchen, the first for a fair time, and also a shave with a borrowed razor. This was followed by a tremendous breakfast of eggs. With all our dirt and whiskers off I think we must have looked much less fearsome. Perhaps, too, the night having passed off without the expected difficulties not unnaturally anticipated by the mother, everyone seemed in a wonderful humour. We were immensely cheered by the peaceful comfort of the night, the absence of the expected enemy and by the lack so far of an order to move again.

The daughters, who seemed to have spruced themselves up specially, were undergoing the usual leg-pulling and banter with great attention from L/Cpl Brown and handsome Jones. A smaller child was sitting on Taffy's knee eating Compo chocolate and sweets of which the Platoon had sickened owing to their lack of variety. It was well worth while watching the intense interest written on the faces of the family as we unpacked a box of Compo rations on the floor of the kitchen, the girls leaving their task of washing up which Jones had saddled on them as willing victims so that they could see the white bread, chocolates, tinned goods and so on too.

I never ceased to be surprised and puzzled by these Germans who seemed to take it almost as a normal procedure to have a crowd of Jocks, equipment, weapons and ammunition cluttering up their home. It could only seem that they had no real heart for the war or its cause for we met no obstruction or sabotage or hint of any activity from the Volksturm, or home guard, who if we were in England and the position reversed I am sure would at least have had a few burned trucks to show their spirit by the morning.

Suddenly the sky outside was seared with the zooming of a high speed aircraft in a dive and the heavy chatter of aircraft cannon fire. A look down the street just provided a glimpse of a streaking Jerry jet plane. A couple of explosions followed. Most probably this plane was attacking a bridge or convoy a mile or two to the north-west.

I was also surprised to see how full the streets were of German civilians again now that they had judged it safe to reappear in strength. Most of these people were carrying what looked like bundles of books and papers in their arms. Next I noticed where they were coming from. They were freely helping themselves to a stationer's shop which had sustained a damaged front from a tank shell. I think this looting was general and quite 'normal' wherever other shops were open or damaged. No policemen were in evidence and no citizens to uphold the law by word or deed – a strange moral kink which I thought might perhaps stem from the fact that what law there had been hitherto had been oppressive and therefore to evade it must have seemed in some respects a virtue. In any event their powers of responsibility and reasoning seemed sadly lacking.

Stepping over the road I visited Alan and Frank in their hotel HQ to see if any news had materialised. I found them in the lap of luxury. The manager couldn't do enough for them. They were reclining in a large double bed between white sheets, well contented, washed, shaved and fed, and had just retired from a session with the manager over his choicest wines, brought out for good effect. There was no more news, but several civilians who had proved difficult or had been suspected of being in contact with the enemy had been rounded up and I took these along to BHQ for questioning. It was an interesting walk through the town which had come to life again with many people about the streets in the spring sunshine. Some Germans were showing an active and open interest in the Jocks, their equipment, dress, rations and the British Army in general.

On my way back I met some of the company HQ Jocks grouped round a fire on the pavement, cooking up some Compo tea and some battered sausages and accepted an invitation to join them for some 'char and a wad with bangers' and a chat. After a while one of several Germans who had gathered on the rim of the Jocks to watch the proceedings and who spoke a bit of English came forward to ask about something which was puzzling the group a lot. 'How can you run your army and we do not see any officers?' The reply this brought obviously puzzled them even more. I was pointed out to them as an officer and Smyg as the company commander. Our dress was identical to the Jocks from boots to tin hat and over my shoulder was a rifle. To make things even more difficult for them to understand, due to our wearing no badges of rank in action to avoid sniping of leaders at close range, there was not even that clue.

Many times already it had been amusing to have my Jocks' claims that I was their officer doubted by civilians and now this same thought was expressed again, but I learned more of the reason for doubt. 'But how can you have any discipline, the mens for ze officer if you mix and are friend and make joke together as you are?' I could not get him to see that results are far better if given through mutual respect and understanding between friends with a common aim than if screwed out through fear and harshness by remote control by beings who set themselves up as of a different caste.

The Germans just could not fathom at all how discipline could possibly exist or survive between an officer and private soldiers talking and cracking jokes together and at each other while cooking battered bits of sausage in the smoke of the same fire. 'Ya, it werks', he agreed. 'But I chust can't understan'.'

These Germans' main concern now appeared to be not who was going to win the war, but rather, where the next meal was coming from. On the whole, apart from this interest in watching the Scots at close range, the vast majority wore an expressionless mask to cover any feelings. Some looked dazed, blank or miserable and a very few scowled or tried not to betray that they had noticed our presence there at all.

THE 'BOTTLED' ENEMY

By the 'fettle' and somewhat unsteady movements of the usual few Jocks known for their strong addiction to a 'wee droppie' it became obvious as the morning progressed that some 'Hooch' had been located and secreted, a punishable offence if caught on any scale. There was no sign of any enemy showing up and as the supply columns started to catch up with us again, the order came to prepare to move. The TCVs back from their refuelling rendezvous pulled up and we climbed aboard.

Apparently the 'swanning' armour was doing so well chasing the enemy up towards the River Weser, we would have quite a trek in catching up with them. A disturbance in the back of the truck followed by roars of hilarious mirth caused me to have a look.

Cohen, our stretcher bearer, was the unintentional cause of all the laughter. Known as 'The Field Marshal' in the platoon, he always appeared to know all about everything, particularly how to fight the war in its higher strategy. This he had been engaged in doing verbally and volubly, flourishing a bottle of drink which he had picked up to add emphasis to his argument. He had paused to refresh himself with the bottle and had promptly crumpled, mouth still open and eyes staring vacantly as though felled by a blow on the head from a sledge-hammer, his tongue stilled in full stride. The bottle most probably contained V2 propellant which kept him in a state of coma for the rest of the trip. With the astuteness of his race he had as a stretcher bearer painted several surplus red crosses on likely and unlikely parts of his person to ensure that in whatever position he might be seen by the enemy there would always be at least one red cross clearly visible. Now as he lay in the most grotesque posture on the floor of the truck he amply demonstrated that at least his theory about the positioning of his red crosses was well thought out.

A long trip followed – Stockheim, Bockhurst, Wesensted, Neuenkirchen, Sudwalde, where as the light failed we pulled in for the night covering a crossroads and T junction vital to the life of those units 'swanning' ahead. The platoon position was astride a main road and T junction. Just sufficient new men had been swapped over to me, including Sgt Oliver to replace temporarily the loss of Sgt Godfrey, to enable me to put three weak sections each in a farm down the road, with platoon HQ in a small house formerly occupied by another unit for a short while ahead of us.

Sgt Oliver, a small, dark, hatchet-faced, nimble-witted chap with a high-pitched border accented voice, gave a hand in getting the positions sited and dug to give all round defence as we had no information on the whereabouts or strength of the nearest enemy. We were to be prepared to deal with stray enemy units and stragglers who might blunder in from any direction as isolated enemy units were probably even more in the dark as to our whereabouts now than we were of theirs. The pace of the advance was staggering.

Still without a replacement to our radio destroyed at Ibbenburen, I was very grateful to come across a captured field telephone which put us in touch with company HQ in case of trouble during the hours of darkness.

Going round section positions later to see how they were organised I found Cpl Parry's section rejoicing in the farmyard over some spoils which the farmer had buried in the garden in a spot chosen for a slit trench. There were potatoes, sides of ham carefully wrapped up and bottled goods of various sorts. The farmer seemed really distraught, even terror stricken. Perhaps he thought we would take it out of him for having concealed this stuff. His wife was equally worked up and both were trying to explain the hidden store to Cpl Parry who was grinning appreciatively at a leg of ham in his hand. I let each section have some ham and to the astonishment of the old farmer, gave him back all the rest.

An hour or two later it became only too evident that another cache had been uncovered containing some potent gin and wine which had been drunk on the sly by about 40 per cent of the platoon. The silly asses, who were used to drinking beer by the pint at home, had tackled the find in the same manner. This swiftly rendered 35 per cent of them totally incapable. Some, like Jones, sprawled in rigid stupor on the floor or added their sounds of retching to the whimperings of the puppy which had crawled out of his windproof to get clear of the reeking alcoholic fumes. Indeed, in this section the puppy was the only object on its feet capable even of barking at any enemy who chose to wander that way. The scared farmer and his family had, it seemed, locked themselves in to a back room early on.

For the first time I felt really annoyed and ashamed of the Jocks. The whole battalion was incessantly faced with this problem of drink in which unfortunately some officers did not always show the example they should. What punishment could one awe a chap with to whom death and mutilation were constant companions in prospect or in fact week in, week out?

The section commanders had hardly been any better than the men on this occasion and were not all capable of taking in the prime rocket and my disappointment and disgust which I felt over the episode. Those whom it seemed might be rendered a little more serviceable by the treatment were doused in cold water to try to break the stupor. Had I not known the Jocks better, I would have thought the German view concerning discipline expressed the day before deserved a second look. Also, I knew enough from prisoners taken and the evidence of positions overrun to realise the problem was not unique to our side. Getting back to Platoon HQ I had to try to think out how, in view of this new situation, the large area we had to cover could be kept watch over all night. Clearly I would not be able to take much time for sleep myself.

The civilian occupants of the little house in which we were to spend the night were an old, wizened-faced man in bed who claimed he was ill (we gave him the benefit of the doubt and left him there) and a slim, blonde girl of about twenty-three who watched our every move with large, blue eyes set in a pale, drawn face. It was wistful with a quiet prettiness which in happier days one could imagine was radiant. In any event her presence was an obvious delight to the Jocks and I must admit intruded into my consciousness as a solace to eyes so used to men and scenes of discord. As dainty as a butterfly set off against a background of drab rocks. The Jocks soon had her organised in her kitchen cooking a fine supper under Brown's supervision. She could speak English well and claimed she was Dutch, though her accent and the frightened smile she seemed to squeeze for politeness at our presence fell short of the joy one might have expected to be expressed by one who, if Dutch, was now liberated. She also seemed reticent to a degree in talking about movements made by the enemy prior to our arrival.

Cohen, now just about able to get about again following his coma during the truck journey, was sent in his medical capacity to see if he could render any aid to the supposedly sick old man. I think, however, he was, of the two, in the worst shape. The Jocks, like moths round a flame, were now busy helping the girl wash the dishes and it seemed that to some extent despite herself she was coming to rather appreciate their attention.

A tinkle on the captured phone produced a call for me to go to an orders group at Company HQ. I handed over the platoon to Sgt Oliver and set off along the 'phone wire which would lead me to Frank and Smyg, whom I found well settled in a little brick home surrounded with a white wooden fence towards the centre of the village. They had a telephone switchboard set up and were in touch with the other platoons too.

There was no definite news of the enemy. Things were very much in a state of flux. Attention was mainly centred around getting the next morning's move by TCV organised for an early start. I related to Smyg the orgy of my Jocks whom I was slightly cheered to hear were not the only ones to be suffering from a swing of the pendulum after the recent fighting. Finally, I collected the password for the night. It was pleasant to rest and chat for a while before starting on the return trip and to relax in the knowledge that thus far we had covered so great an advance without being subjected to any more harrowing experiences or undue discomfort.

The moon was up lighting the silent village in its cold glow as I tramped back, treading in the dew-laden grass on the border of the road to deaden my steps and test the alertness of whoever was on stag at my HQ. The crisp challenge was pleasing to hear. However, inside I was disgusted to find that some more drink had appeared on the scene, this time produced by the girl in an apparent desire to appease the Jocks. I think she had done this out of nervousness to be on good terms with them for the night. Looked at from her angle the position must have been rather frightening. She was in a house full of strange foreign troops and with only an old, sick man as chaperone. This foolish action of hers was very nearly her undoing.

I told the culprits off roundly and sent them all off on extra stag to sober them. Leaving Brown and Learmonth to hold the fort and 'phone, I set out round section positions to see how alert they were and if time had sobered them a little.

On my return I could see no sign of the two Jocks I had left inside. Hearing a scuffle and sobbing in the dark of the living room, I swung the beam of my torch around until it lit on the wrestling forms and startled faces of these two, the slight shapely form of the terrified girl wriggling in their grasp. The girl had had, or had been given, too much to drink and now, hair tousled, face flushed, sobbing with fright and with her garments disarranged, these two were trying to take advantage of her pitiable predicament. For a moment they froze into a statuesque group in the glare of the light while three pairs of eyes blinked back at me like animals. Very fortunately for the girl and perhaps even more so for the drink-doped Jocks, temporarily bereft of their reason by the dual onslaught of alcohol and sex, things had not physically gone beyond a rough-and tumble.

I was really angry now in deep disappointment with the sum of the Jocks' activities during the day. The shameful though surly two, still held by a fierce animality almost stronger than discipline or reason, glared angrily at me, but slowly let the pale, now passive form of the girl slip free of their rough grasp in silence. She, eyes downcast and with colour mounting to her face in a surge of self-consciousness and shame, though not without a touch of pride perhaps in the self realisation of her evident beauty of form, hurriedly rearranged her garments and fled snivelling to hide her confusion in the sanctuary of the darkness. I wondered if the Jocks were entirely to blame. I think she had led them on, then having encouraged them too far had found herself in a situation getting out of control. I have never given two chaps such a wigging as these two, surprising myself at its fierceness.

Next morning provided a deeper insight into the episode, for in spite of what the girl had borne at the hands of the two culprits, she greeted them with a wan, flushed smile of confusion. The two Jocks grinned sheepishly back and at each other, their admiration evidently much increased. However, the passing of the main part of the night has yet to be related.

I settled to doze next to the phone at about midnight. At 0200 hours I awakened at the presence of excited breathing and a dark clumsy figure standing over me. My spine prickled. 'Someone bumped our section, Mr White, Surr!' This I recognised from the voice to be 'two' section, farthest down the road. 'A dark figure came over the fields towards us, Surr. He was challenged, Surr, but too far off and he ran back into the dark.'

'Keep a sharp look out!' I said, and sent him back again pleased at least with the information from him that the scare had sobered his section up a bit. I phoned Company HQ, then dozed again for about an hour, waking now and then to listen to the noises of the night. There were rather too many dogs barking at various distances for my peace of mind. The cause was quite possibly only our own chaps on duty about the farms, but I had not noticed so much barking earlier.

About an hour later another puffing runner crashed through the weapons and equipment on the floor in the dark and shook me urgently to report: 'Mr White Surr! There's *** Jerries about in the Platoon area. Seven or eight of the b***s went between our section, three section, and here. Hell! We couldn't fire Surr fur fear a'shootin up yin section and you Surr!'

'Get back quick', I said, knowing that he was probably one of the few properly sober chaps in his section if trouble started.

Rolling over I picked up the 'phone, gave it a wind and told Smyg what was going on. 'What's that? What's that?', a very sleepy voice, quite unimpressed with the news, said. 'Right-ho, keep me informed.'

In view of this and other movements reported and the shortage of men whom I felt would be 100 per cent sober and therefore not a menace to take with me, I decided to do a patrol round the area on my own to try to decide if these figures represented any more serious threat than enemy stragglers cut off by the swift advance and trying to filter back through us during the hours of darkness.

Taking my rifle and .38 and Verey with flares I set off. The night was cooler now towards dawn. It was still, with good visibility in the moonlight. I moved on the grass and in the shadow of the hedges whenever possible, pausing often to look and listen. It was really beautiful out. The moon had a double rainbow halo round it, its brilliance lighting my breath in the crisp air. How difficult it was to make out various dark shapes in the night in unfamiliar surroundings. Several times my spine tingled and heart broke into a brisk trot before the identification of cattle explained the sounds and movement.

My main apprehension lay in being shot up by some trigger-happy Jock in one of my own sections or another platoon who had his wits dulled by drink. None of then, except at my HQ, knew I was out. I met no sign of any enemy either in our area or in going 500 yards up towards company HQ road junction and beyond in the direction the Jerries had last been seen, so returned to try to get some more sleep before daylight. I managed to get warm, but Taffy, in off-stag, made too much noise on the other end of the bed which almost vibrated to his snoring.

Daylight soon followed, and with it a quick breakfast. 'Prepare to move' came over the phone and I paraded the platoon to tell them what I thought of the previous night's performance before we boarded the TCVs. They were a sorry-looking, shame-faced lot and the toll it had taken of them in vomiting, sleeplessness, the scare overnight (it transpired that two separate groups of enemy, possibly just stragglers, had passed through the company positions that night) and now their present hangover had almost been sufficient punishment. That they had regard for me I knew because of the petition they had drawn up and signed when I was given another platoon after Heinsberg and which secured my return to them. Later I was pleased to learn from Parry that my disgust with them and 'unsuspected energy' in displaying it had cut them deeply. I was rather shocked to realise afterwards that, quite contrary to regulations, so deep had my anger and disgust been I had been carried away to state that if I caught the ringleader of any future debauch I would undertake to 'personally knock hell out of him in front of the platoon with my fists'. This, I realised on reflection, was a dually rash statement in that first it might be reported higher up and second to knock hell out of some of the likely ringleaders would be a task of considerable hazard.

It was a lovely morning to be rolling forwards again in the TCVs and we were off on another long run through rather flatter country as we approached the Weser: Waseloh, Vilsen, Kleinenborstel, Martfeld, Bungelshnonen . . .

As the hours and miles dragged past we marvelled at the speed of the advance. Somewhere, very near now, surely, the enemy would have to turn and fight again to enable his forces to get over the river with what equipment they could. Excitement and tension was creeping back upon us. Bremen was quite close to our estimated position and speculation was voiced concerning what effect the loss of Bremen might have on the swifter termination of the war as the result of using its additional port facilities.

One or two wispy columns of smoke ahead told us we were almost in contact with the enemy again when the convoy slowed up and shunted together. We pulled up in the village of Hustedt just short of Holtum and Einste. Again we rolled on a few hundred yards to a position at which the Company trucks peeled off to allotted areas.

A wrecked Jeep, accident rather than enemy action by the look of it, lay at the roadside. Just beyond this Smyg called for an 'O' Group. Information about the whereabouts of the enemy was very confused. It was thought that Jerry was 800 to 1,000 yards up the track forking out of the village. Our assignment was to contain any attempt by the enemy to recross the river in strength, and if necessary 'mop up' any we could get at on our side.

The crackle of automatics and rifle fire sounded somewhere. We heard after that C Company had run into an ambush in getting to their positions. A brisk fight with casualties to both sides ensued before they got forward. The Battalion had a wide front to cover, so we would in consequence be spread pretty thinly. Our immediate task was to hold the village, hemming the enemy into a belt about a mile deep down to the River Weser, opposite the town of Verden.

The 'O' Group concluded, the Company de-bussed, rations were split from Compo-box to man-pack and greatcoats were piled in platoon bundles ready for quick delivery if needed. 'Good luck Sir!' my walrus-whiskered TCV driver called. Off we moved, warily, in section files dispersed on either side of a track leading towards the enemy. After 400 yards, half the possible distance separating us from the enemy, word came to halt and the Jocks got down on the ground covering the flanks. Another 'O' Group was called forward 500 yards, then 800 yards when a tentative stalk forward and standing up on the track tempted no reaction from the enemy which would give away his exact position. In a cluster on the ground Smyg issued an indication of the positions he wished us to take up astride the track. The Company was waved forward and we dug in along the line of two hedges bisecting the track at right angles.

This was low-lying marshland and meadow, and I soon found in digging myself a fox-hole that water was struck a few inches down. This meant excavating a mud parapet round the hole with grass-sodden sides as camouflage. We had long since learned that however peaceful the scene of the moment may be, hell could envelop one at a split second's notice and be sustained for hours. Once trouble had commenced it was usually too late for the improvident ones to make up for their laziness, and the penalties could be drastic. I was interested to notice that those few old-stagers who had survived so much with me were the most diligent in their care of excavation and choice of site.

At dusk the subdued whine of gears drew our attention to the cook's truck, an unexpected luxury. It was crawling forward up the track from the rear with some tea for us to sip with our cold Compo rations – cold because we were short of Hexamine fuel tablets and fires were out of the question. It was almost dark now. There were no sounds of nearby fighting and birds were chirping as they settled in to roost in the new greenery of the hedges which stood like dark walls above a dank mist rolling up with dusk from the river.

Somewhere ahead I became aware, with an increased pulse

rate, of a faint metallic squeaking accompanied by the soft whine of gears and the labouring of one or more powerful engines. This sound could mean only one thing. 'Tanks ahead Sir', a Jock up the track in a Bren pit yelled. 'Coming fast, too. Seems to be more than one!' 'Stand to!' The PIAT team hastily pulled their bombs out of their canisters, cocked their projector, put a bomb in the cradle and pushed their weapon through the hedge to cover a corner of the track 50 yards forward of where we lay with bated breath and romping hearts, intently waiting and listening to the leisurely clatter and squeak of the tracks and approaching engine zoom.

Unexpectedly soon, a light tank bucked and slithered round the bend into view. 'Hold everything, it's one of ours!' The tank commander's bereted and earphone-clad head poked out of the turret near the swaying and pennanted aerial rod. Two more of these 11th Hussar tanks followed. 'Meet any trouble?' I asked as he pulled up alongside. 'We brushed Jerry in the next village. He may put patrols out overnight. Getting too dark to stop forward in these any long. We'll pull in to laager for the night somewhere behind you.'

'Lucky you didn't pull back any later when it was too dark to recognise you or you would have tasted our PIAT! We had no idea you were swanning forward of us', I said.

After checking the Jocks' positions I climbed into my hole, wrapping my gas cape around and over me to settle in for the night vigil. The cold wetness of the lower part of my body soon informed me that I was resting full length in the water which had drained into the shallow scoop I had dug. The dew was settling heavily on the grass as the cold wet mist thickened. It was becoming difficult to make out even the nearest of the Jocks' trenches, peering hard into the night.

After several hours of steadily getting colder and wetter, which ruled out the risk of dozing off, I became conscious of a dark form moving uncertainly towards me. 'Mr White Surr' it called in a stage whisper, 'Listen Surr! . . . Can ye no' hear, behind, the fence wire Surr, it's moving, someyin getting through, likely.' Yes, sure enough there it was, the squeak and rattle of the barbed wire moving slightly in its staples somewhere towards the track in the white wall of mist behind us over the field.

Grasping my rifle I pulled my cramped cold joints into movement and commenced a long, wet stalk through the dew-laden, icy grass. There was definitely something going on where none of our company had dug in at nightfall. As I neared the road I could make out more movement of the fence wire and the occasional clink and scrape of metal. I decided that if anything happened I would be too conspicuous out in the field, so made my way gently back and round to the shelter of the dark hedge where I would have the cover of a ditch to work along beside the track towards the sound. Now I could hear the metallic clinking and rasping again and with it the soft murmur of voices speaking together. English or German? I could not yet make out any words. With infinite pains not to crack a twig or sound my boots dragging in the grass I crouched my way forward. Gradually I could make out the squat hulk of a vehicle standing out of the mist. There was no turret. Yes, it was a carrier! One of a section of carriers the CO, it turned out, had sent to back us up. They had dug a Lewis gun pit which was now finished, covering the track. Someone might have let us know.

Thankful at this discovery, I made my way back, taking the opportunity to call at each of my section positions to see all was well. This was always a touchy job knowing how readily some trigger-happy Jocks might be tempted to fire rather than challenge. Also some of them challenge in no more than a whisper to conceal their exact location from a likely enemy and should one chance into such a chap noisily, drowning his sounds of challenge one would have 'had it'.

The rest of the night was even colder than the first half. Slowly the violent shivering in wet clothes passed to numbness, aches and cramp. One felt that another puff of wind laden with the cold mist would carry off all the remaining warmth left in the body like the last speck of a candle stump snuffing out. Would dawn never come? Oh what would one give for a hot bath and a proper bed, and peace.

The birds stirring in the hedges were the first to realise the night was spent. Gradually the sky paled and the mist, thinning with the freshening breeze, revealed the miserable shivering heads of the windproof-hooded Jocks peeping out of their damp mud ruts.

A runner called for me to go to Smyg. There was a wood 500 yards on our right which had been preoccupying him and he asked me to take my platoon and comb it. Frank decided to come with me with the section of carriers to act as stop-butts at the end of the wood to fire at right angles onto any possible enemy we might winkle out. We arranged signals between us in case we met resistance. I spread the platoon out in line when we reached the start point – two sections up, platoon HQ and a section in reserve to follow behind. Soon after entering the wood we unexpectedly came upon a concealed house which did not appear on the map. A German farmer or woodsman was living there with his family and we paused to run through this place, watched anxiously by the chap and his wife. In reply to questioning I gathered the Jerries had been there but as far as he knew they had pulled back two days before.

I decided to make sure and joining the two forward sections we advanced slowly firing odd shots from the rifles and bursts from the Brens into the undergrowth ahead as we combed our way through. The shots echoed back sharply in the trees and foliage, drilling and nicking the stumps on their way. At the far end a shape broke from the bushes and fled over the fields, a small terrified deer! I was very glad we had not hit it.

Back at the Company area we stood down to 25 per cent manning. The very welcome sun came out and while my water was boiling in my mug propped over Hexamine on three twigs pushed into the mud with the thick Compo tea frothing inside, I had a wash in the water which had formed in the trench bottom. I had not had a change of socks for a long time since losing my small kit, so I took these off and rinsed them too to dry them again back on my feet.

Suddenly the peace of the morning was ripped violently apart by the pulsating roar of a German jet fighter plane flashing overhead at fantastic speed 50 to 100 feet up. It had gone in the same mental flash which took in the black crosses and swastikaed tail on the sleek, glinting, grey-green metal. I wondered if by chance there had been any connection between this visit and our firing in the wood. Our spent bullets must have peppered the line of the river and the village of Oiste where the tank chaps reckoned the enemy were.

It was pleasant to bask in the sun during the rest of the morning. At midday lunch arrived from the rear farm where the cooks had installed themselves. What a welcome treat to sniff the scent out of the steaming cans. We learned from the cooks that some mortaring and firing we had heard the evening before in the distance had been C Company in trouble again. There had been a sharp encounter. A patrol, part of which got cut off, had fought their way back and there had been two casualties on each side, one fatal in each case.

We also learned among other news of the battalion scattered around the villages of Varste and Blende to our north, that Chris Melville, DSO, our CO had left us for Div HQ where he had been appointed G1. We were very sad to hear this as he was much liked and had commanded us on all our stunts so far. Maj Horace Davidson our former 2i/c had taken over in his stead.

Every now and then a burst of distant violence or an oil-fed pall of dark smoke marking the end of some vehicle reminded us that the peace of the advancing afternoon was only local. Finally, Smyg decided that if we were to be stuck in the area for another night steps should be taken to try to avoid a repeat performance of the Company lying in icy puddles for another twelve hours. No immediate threat or call on us seemed forthcoming and the order was given for us to pull back a short way down the track to farms nearer the road.

Delighted, I picked three farms in line for the Platoon, taking one for my HQ. I instructed the farmer and his family that they would have half an hour to move themselves into one half of the farm while we took over the other. If the Germans were given longer, we had found too many items of home comfort were removed.

The chaps were now expert slit trench diggers and once the positions were laid out they were soon installed with all the refinements laid on: straw in the bottom and logs laid over with more straw, doors and earth as a roof to stop shrapnel. The positions were laid out to cover the main track and a smaller one in a broad arc, leaving 11 and 12 Platoons to cover the rear and the crossroads. After stags had been fixed I selected a fine bedroom and decided to concentrate on trying to make up on some lost sleep as I felt very low physically and I hoped that if I could generate a good lot of warmth I might get my still damp clothes dry at last. Crashing onto the bed in a shower of equipment and still with my boots on in case of emergency, I settled in to make the most of it, leaving Sgt Oliver on for the first half of the night's duty.

Almost immediately I became aware of a most persistent and vicious barking just outside the window of a dog belonging to the farm. For a long time I put up with it, hoping that either it would be quietened by the farmer or stop when it got used to the movements of the Jocks on duty. I could eventually stand it no longer and much as I like dogs I felt I must silence it by hook or by crook. I pulled out my revolver and telling the sentry at the back not to panic if some shooting developed I stalked out into the night. After a long and futile stalk in an attempt to get to closer range than about 25 yards and so make a clean job of it, I fired three shots rapidly at the fleeting phantom. I must have either hit it or so shaken it that it fled, for there was no further sound from it. That I had done this, worried me later.

After a shave in the morning and a decent farm breakfast I felt a new being. Outside in the yard the robust squeals from a pig of exceptional vocal power drew attention to Jones trying to catch it with energetic rugger tackles. Several times he seized a back leg but was dragged along the cobbles as though coupled to a locomotive. Eventually, however, much to my surprise, the noise of crackling fat and a lovely smell told of the success of this venture and the platoon tucked in to roast pork chops. Their first really solid meal for a very long time. I suppose one should have frowned on this activity. However, having seen the trails of slaughter, looting and destruction left by the enemy in the Low Countries and knowing that it put the Jocks into better shape to carry on, on balance and in moderation it struck me as a very small price for the farmer to pay when balanced against the hell and misery the Jocks had stood from his compatriots.

The farmer had earlier complained to me that the tank Hussars had taken a bucket from him to cook spuds. To this I had tried, with the barrier of language in the way, to tell him he was very fortunate. The German army did not confine its taking to buckets. Human beings were their loot for use as slave labour on farms such as his.

DIRECT HIT

I visited Company HQ to see if there was any more news. It was established in a pub over the road. Beside it there were two temporary graves of 11th Hussars chaps, just a couple of mounds of earth beside the road, with at the head two pieces of stick tied into a cross with string and on these hung their berets. At the corner was a third grave with a tin hat hung over a rifle pushed barrel first into the earth, the resting place of an infantryman, and scattered about it was some of his kit left where he had fallen.

The news was: 'prepare to move'. The squadron of the 11th Hussars would have to hold this position on their own while we made all haste towards Delmenhorst, just over the river from Bremen. There at a place called Sudweyhe the 1st/5th Queens who had been fighting down the bank of the Weser behind the armour were having a sticky time with some fresh troops from an SS training centre at Delmenhorst backed by the flak guns of Bremen only about 4 miles off, which were being used in a ground role.

Most of the above information we gathered, not at the 'O' Group but from first-hand experience as the day wore on. Greeting walrus whiskers, my TCV driver, I climbed in beside him, swapping news on our activities since last we had seen each other. It was a lovely warm spring day and an enjoyable first part of the journey along winding country and village roads often with sandy borders, the lower-lying parts rimmed with drainage ditches and climbing every now and then gently to higher land with woods and farms and fruit tree blossom to gladden the eye. At wayside farms life seemed often to be going on normally with the children running to look at us and sometimes wave and lambs frolicking in the rich spring grass of the meadows. We noticed here and there the name of a wayside hamlet or village: Schwarme, Godestorf, Osterholz, Okel. On a day like this with such peaceful surroundings it seemed mad to contemplate fighting.

The convoy was moving slowly and for a while it stopped. With the noise of the trucks stilled we immediately became aware of gunfire quite close and the Jocks sat up from their leisured postures to take notice. It was plain that lack of sleep and strain was telling on some and that our experiences at Ibbenburen had shaken many of the Platoon more than I had realised at the time. It was quite a shock to notice how drawn and haggard a few of them looked in peering out of the vehicles to try to get some clues on the noise and its possible implications.

Slowly the convoy resumed its forward trickle and soon we passed 25-pounders in the fields pointing to the north-west. Looking in the direction of their barrels and above the houses, farms and trees our eyes took in with reluctance and a quickened pulse the dismal sight of vast pillars of black and grey smoke suspended over the horizon in dirty smudges and coiling, black, oily billows tumbling its messy way into the blue.

There was a growing realisation now among the Jocks that the war might be very nearly over. A fear of looking too far ahead personally was replaced in the Jocks by an upsurging, fervent desire to live, to see the end, the unbelievable, seemingly impossible day when it would all be over. The possibility of being knocked over at the last ditch loomed like the all too familiar smoke and ominous rumbling ahead.

During one of our halts, Jones, as so often, seized the least opportunity of a scrounge. The truck pulled up with its tail-board next to the open window of a wayside farm at the entrance to a village. In one smooth movement Jones had hopped into the window, then reappeared with a large crate bulging with neatly packed eggs. We moved slowly on, passing a more built-up area before halting again.

Frank's large form climbed down from the truck ahead and he sauntered back to look in at my window. 'I'm going up into the carrier, Peter. Would you like to swap to my seat in the truck ahead?' For a moment I contemplated the move. Although the next truck forward did not contain my Platoon, I realised an officer should be in the leading truck; so for the first time in many weary miles and days of wandering I climbed out from the company of Walrus Whiskers. Before getting into the leading truck, I walked round to the back of my old one and told the Jocks there that if anyone wanted to ride in the comfort of the cab there was a vacant seat. To my surprise, no one took advantage of this usually coveted luxury and the trucks were beginning to move as I ran to climb into the seat Frank had vacated at the head of B Company TCVs. So it was that this seeming chance decision of Frank's to change seats undoubtedly saved me with a bare three minutes to spare from being smashed to pulp.

A few hundred yards on and more houses began to line the route as we approached Sudweyhe, a straggling village built in two separate parts. We entered the first section of the village, watched past by several of our Battalion standing at the corner of a T junction, so we guessed we were near our destination, which must have been the reason why Frank had moved. After another 300 yards or so we swung left in the second section of the village, following the carrier round another T junction. Just as the wheel spun straight in the driver's hands, three or four almighty explosions enveloped us in concussive succession. The last one, and the closest, seemed from the blast and racket to be a near hit from a 6-inch shell. I was conscious that this had carried away a wall just to the left and above the driving cab of our truck, pluming a black, tumbling cloud of acrid smoke which reddened with brick dust as it expanded in the clattering rubble that crashed heavily against the side of my new truck. Fortunately, the window was open and the blast, which was endways on to the windscreen, had apparently done no damage to us at least, though my head reeled with the concussion of it. My driver instinctively put his foot hard down on the accelerator and the truck bucked and engine screamed in his attempt to escape any more shells which might still be on the way to the same salvo.

A few hundred yards farther up we reached our new rear Company HQ position where we pulled in tight against the rear wall of a house to screen ourselves as far as possible from further shells. The chaps clambered out and took shelter round the side of the house as it appeared the shelling was coming from ahead. Looking back along the road I was surprised to realise the rest of the convoy was not with us. I was just asking the Jocks in the back of the truck where we had lost them, when I spied O'Connor from my Platoon HQ truck puffing wild-eyed and, despite the exercise, ashen in the face, towards us. 'Sir . . .', he gasped, 'Platoon HQ truck's hit Sir! . . . A direct hit from an 88.' He leant against the side of my new truck to regain breath. 'By God but you're lucky Sir . . . went clean through the seat you were in.' The full implication of this news only sunk in gradually. It had an air of peculiar unreality to it that I found difficult to assimilate. 'How are the chaps?' I asked. 'Hit bad I'm afraid, Sir . . . awful mess . . . Christ I feel done Sir!' he gasped, now doubled up and breathing heavily, his voice breaking in uncertain control and revealing for the first time just how physically and mentally shaky his condition was. I gathered he had been blown out of the back of the truck and had moved as fast as he could in his dazed condition to get clear of the road junction target which the guns had obviously got pretty well taped.

A short time later the lopsided shattered remains of my TCV was towed in by the last of my Platoon trucks to get it off the target before it was hit again. At the wheel, in the wreckage, scattered still with the glass from the windscreen but astonishingly apparently unharmed, I was pleased to see my pal, Walrus Whiskers. He was quite grey in the face and shaking. Seven large chunks of shrapnel had been splashed through the front of the truck's metal. All seven had passed in a compact pattern of gaping fist-sized holes through the back of the seat I had so recently evacuated, and then into the Jocks in the body of the truck. There I was saddened to find it had killed Jones, the paratroop chap, and seriously wounded five more, one of whom died later, and slightly wounded two others. One of these latter, Pte Cutter (my radio operator, the chap who had so often gone 'bomb happy') had astonishingly had his own life saved when one of these seven chunks of shrapnel had hit and embedded five of Cutter's own .303 rounds of ammunition from his bandolier into his back. Yet another of our radio sets had been written off in the process. The back of the truck was in a chaotic mess of tattered equipment, torn metal, glass, blood, broken eggs by the score . . . and valuables reminiscent of a jeweller's shop. Among this collection was Sgt Godfrey's GS watch which had been 'lifted' off him when he was killed at Ibbenburen. Poor old Jones. Had he finished the war at this rate of hoarding he would have retired a wealthy man. His perky little puppy, so loved by its fierce owner, was killed too. The loss of Jones, the 'one man army' as he was dubbed, was a very depressing blow on the Platoon, indeed the Company.

Walrus Whiskers seemed fascinated by his own and my escape. 'Another few minutes in there, Sir, and you would have had it in no uncertain manner', he said, looking at the cab. I had a light-headed feeling of unreality as I surveyed the mess and fingered the gaping holes in the backrest where my body should have been lying pulped through like a colander between the stomach, chest and throat. An incident of timing and seeming chance of this kind 'shakes one' more than a stray intangible bullet, however close in the open. 'So that's how it might have ended', I thought, with a strong sense of somehow having side-stepped my own funeral to instead be a spectator. That was the last time that I saw Walrus Whiskers. He was towed slowly away in the remnants of his truck, not sorry to get out of range of the 88s which all this while had continued to spatter the area. They arrived, not with the scream of a normal artillery shell, but travelling faster than sound their presence was felt and seen in the blossoming of hideous flame-centred, black-petalled flowers here there and everywhere as though seeking where we had got to. Those shells that smashed to the rear with flat trajectory passed with an ear-splitting crash which matched the almost instant explosion itself as it hit the first object in its path to the rear.

Shaking myself from this brooding and saddened by the loss, though profoundly thankful at having been so miraculously spared myself by Frank's suggestion, I looked about. As I did so I became queerly exhilarated with renewed appreciation of life in and around me which I had so taken for granted; I was bursting with a sense of gratitude. Sucking in the clear spring air I rejoiced in the scent and sight of a tree blossoming in the garden and in the warmth of the sun and the fanning of the breeze on my face. I looked at the hands of my watch. Only ten minutes had passed, thirteen in all since I swapped seats. It was strange to realise that had I not done so all the beauty and colour about me, which I had so taken for granted, would, despite the shelling, have been here just the same. All was going on just as it would have done. Even that cloud slowly changing shape in the blue would have been just there. Down in the dirt road a sparrow was picking at a mixture of egg and blood which had seeped from the wrecked truck, keeping another little life ticking over out of the remnants of death and the looted eggs Jones would not now need for his supper.

"O' Group, Mr White Surr!' a runner yelled towards me and my thoughts finally jumped back to the task in hand and this world we call reality.

Super-Sonic Barrage

The plan was to take over in daylight from the 1st/5th Queens in the forward positions. The exact location of the enemy SS was rather confused as they seemed to be moving about a lot to avoid being pinpointed. Kirchweyhe was on slightly higher ground than the likely enemy position down beyond a kidney shaped pond, a few copses and a group of houses standing on the low-lying marshland towards the river. These houses stood a quarter mile off. Beyond that and some more trees towards the skyline was the village of Drye 1 mile off and backing onto the River Weser. The left of the Company boundary was the main-line railway track which ran over a viaduct towards the enemy and which was the responsibility of C Company. On our right were A Company with one platoon slightly forward. Companies were about 600 yards apart officially, but our sector appeared to be between 800 to 1,000 yards. Since Ibbenburen my platoon had been made up to twenty-one, or two-thirds strength. Now, due to the 88 hit on the TCV, it was down to fourteen. Among these there still survived a few old hands: L/Cpl Brown, Cpl Parry, Learmonth and Tarn. After Ibbenburen I had managed to get McLaughlin to the Div rest centre as his nerves were beginning to give.

The problem of how to cover the enormous stretch of front given me with so few chaps was very worrying. A very weak Company HQ was 450 yards to our rear as our only depth for a counter-attack should a Jerry patrol or attack develop on our frontage. Our 38 set radio was again written off in the truck and with no 'phone our only means of contact would have to be by runner, thus depleting the platoon by one fourteenth. This was an unreliable and useless method for DF task or SOS artillery call in an emergency. In addition, the armour had pulled out with the Queens, leaving only four SP 17-pounders. The nearest other Battalion on our left were the 7th/9th Royal Scots about 4 miles off, thus leaving a large gap through which the enemy might filter and trouble us from the rear.

I split the platoon into two lots of four and two lots of three. The stronger sections I put on the flanks with the weaker one ahead of the three of us in Platoon HQ. Three section on the left were in a tiny house overlooking the lake and railway, two section in the centre in a large farm with a schoolhouse attached which from the straw strewn on the floor showed it had been used as a former German billet. One section were on the right in a smaller farm. All our HQs were in cellars except the left section and ourselves in Platoon HQ who had none. Jerry was flinging an incessant stream of 88 shells at us with disconcerting accuracy. These arrived in two main concentrations during our stay with something over 200 rounds in each effort.

I had never known the morale of the Platoon to be lower, and this was mostly the result of a lack of sleep, haphazard food and a steady drain on nerves due in no small part to lack of information which might have enabled them to rest more completely when the opportunities did occur. O'Connor had an almost complete breakdown after running into a batch of 88 shells. This was a most surprising event as I had thought him one of the steadiest and toughest in the bunch. In view of this I decided to keep those not on stag busy as the constant hellish crashing of shells pounding up and down the area made sleep impossible. Selecting a spot screened by the wall of a house from the likely line of the shells' approach we set to work on and off for the greater part of the night, digging a pit which we covered with a row of stout telegraph poles of which we had found a heap nearby. On top of this, our HQ, we heaped a layer of earth. Inside, a thick layer of straw provided odd moments of comfortable rest. We had to take cover from time to time. Twice the roof of our shelter was sprinkled with rubble from a near-miss. Another shell in the early hours shattered the windscreen of a TCV beside us.

One section was in a very bad way quite early on, having in the first couple of hours sustained four direct hits on the face of the farm from which they were looking out on stag. When I visited them I found them nearly demoralised. All four chaps were filmed over from head to foot in grey dust and plaster from the explosions. It appeared to have done no physical damage, but the blast and tension following their direct hit in the TCV earlier seemed to have reduced to water their will to carry on. On my visit to them I got outright complaints, for the first time even from NCOs, that they could not carry on or stick it any longer. O'Connor, a thickset, powerfully built chap of twenty-two with fair hair and blue eyes in a pleasant face had completely lost control of himself. He cowered, hunched in a corner of the front room, weeping profusely and openly while convulsed with violent shivering in his abject misery. I resolved to get him out before it spread to the other three. At my wit's end to know how to pull Cpl Jones together to carry on I cut him with my tongue to get him really angry. He was near to mutiny but the fire it had lit in him seemed to give him a spark which I hoped would smoulder at least until daylight came.

What made the situation even more difficult was that with so few men it was necessary to have '100 per cent manning' all night. Luckily, however, any activity by enemy patrols was narrowed on the centre of our front by the pond of about 50 yards across which would show up in silhouette any movement made.

Pulling and pushing O'Connor I made my way back to visit the centre farm where I risked lighting the stove to cook up some eggs and hot tea, primarily for O'Connor but ostensibly for Platoon HQ. This seemed to do the trick to a certain extent. He apologised to me and I persuaded him to take a grip of himself. Sending him to three section which was so far unmolested by a close hit, I swapped one of the chaps there back to make up one section.

For a while Smyg came forward to visit me and together we made our way to two section to try a pastime I attempted several times again before dawn: to see if we could pinpoint any of the gun-flash which would disclose the positions of the German weapons for our artillery to have a counter-battery shoot. On and off our 25-pounders, which we had passed in the fields on the way in, were firing, joined at one time by the mediums to paste

Bremen. These shells exploding together with several distant houses or factories on fire and odd unexplained twinkles of light helped make this task profitless. Once or twice flares soared up, reflecting in the water between us and the enemy who, it transpired, had patrolled energetically during the night. There had been several clashes in which quite a number of the SS recruits perished. But for the odd burst of fire from a Bren, the guns drowned all other noises.

For several hours in the early morning I kept up a constant patrol on my own, checking at and between the sections that all was well and working out an undercover route between section positions and Platoon HQ to be used when daylight came. It was obvious that all daylight movement of the Queens chaps had been pinpointed and registered for the guns for the shelling told they knew exactly where we were. To get this route organised I had to smash my way through fences, outhouses and vegetable gardens in the dark.

So often it seemed that perhaps at last the shelling had stopped, but then the awful suddenness of its crash-crump would start up again, the flash of explosion silhouetting the surrounding shapes of trees and houses. Once every so many shells there was the variety of tinkling glass or broken tiles clattering.

The lightening sky at last overcame the darkness. Perhaps it had been as well that I had had so few men, for the amazing increase in the damage to be seen about us bore testimony to the weight of metal and explosive which had drizzled on us all the miserable night. A crash and plume of smoke and brick dust in front of two section broke the short-lived silence. I made my way over. Just in front of the bulding I knew O'Brien had a Bren gun pit dug so that his weapon poked through a hedge commanding the lower ground. Almost sickened to look at what was left after the direct hit he must have sustained, I paused for a while looking at the remnants of the smoke and dust thinning as it blew through the skeleton of the hedge which was stripped of its leaves beside the stippled brickwork where the shrapnel had gashed redly as though into the flesh of the house. The eddying smoke dissipating in the morning air was all that moved beyond the dusty rim of the slit trench and seemed the last and swiftly vanishing symbol of the life that had dwelt in the pit a moment before. There in the gun pit was a huddled dust-covered heap of khaki with a Bren gun lying across it. It was moving a little. I wiped the cold sweat and dust off my face with my sleeve as I watched as though compelled and fascinated. My legs felt weak and my throat, which was where my stomach seemed to be, wanted to swallow, but could not. What could I do to be of any help?

To my amazement and relief this bundle turned over in the dust, revealing legs and arms which had seemed to be missing. A tin hat clattered off the erratically moving head which was shaking and spitting as though with a mouthful of dirt or smashed teeth and blood. For a moment the movement stopped except for the head which jerked rhythmically to the impetus of a pounding heart. 'O'Brien! . . . are you OK?' He looked round slowly and vaguely until he saw me from a face blackened with muck and dust and it seemed powdered grass or leaves. If his face had any expression it did not or could not show itself. If he was all right he obviously did not yet know it or for that matter what he had survived. He was all right but only just and I should think he was our nearest approach to a casualty that night. It seemed to take him several days to awake from either the shock or the memory of this experience . . . another result of the careless behaviour of the 53 Div chaps from whom we had taken over – they had walked quite openly about in the forward positions giving our exact location away.

On looking up at the chimney of No. 1 section's house I was almost as surprised to see that the stork which we had noticed perched up there on its nest the previous evening was still doggedly sitting there, despite the serious deterioration in the condition of the roof and walls of this structure overnight.

The Regiment of mediums which had taken to pounding Bremen were, it seemed, at last beginning to have the effect of cutting the enemy shelling of ourselves. I managed to have a solid breakfast of seven eggs, tinned bacon, bread and tea in comparative peace in No. 2 section billet. One of the Jocks had located a cow somewhere which in spite of the shelling was persuaded to give some milk. This was a welcome addition to the tea. The sun was out and things looked a little more settled and cheerful to us all, though our losses of the previous day, which had taken one-third of our already reduced number, hung heavily on our thoughts. The cheerful, dynamic, fearless presence of Pte Jones was particularly missed – his full-throated roars of laughter, his queer dress, the capers of his puppy and the confidence his casual devil-may-care attitude inspired in his fellow Jocks. He regarded the enemy and all his efforts with complete contempt. Each Jock seemed to have secured at least some small part of the choice hoard of jewellery he had amassed as a memento of this unforgettable character . . . pieces which, after later casualties, were to change hands again. Even in death his strong face retained a trace of its detached composure, with the suggestion of a smile set by the upward twisting corners of his half-open mouth.

WANDERING

After breakfast I called back at Company HQ to see what news there might be. At midnight it transpired we had come under command of 3 Div. I wondered what new stunt this might hold in store. The civilians of the town had proved unusually hostile to us in manner, quite a part of this possibly resulting from annoyance with our presence solely from the point of view of the number of shells thereby attracted onto them as well as ourselves. There was a report at Company HQ, the accuracy of which I never heard denied or confirmed, that a Jerry civilian had been found with a couple of hundred rifles hidden in his house. He had concealed and denied possession of these arms notwithstanding proclamations and loudspeaker instructions on their surrender. The report went that he had been taken out of the house which was burned and that he was subsequently shot. I was also surprised to learn that though our nearest troops on the left were over 4 miles away, we had had no one at all on our right flank overnight. How fortunate the enemy did not try a counter-attack, for with his own civilians to spy for him and with the odd radio left in our midst he must have known how stretched we were.

News had also come at dawn that the 2nd Battalion KSLI were coming along to relieve us and that we were to rejoin 155 Brigade who were having a rest at Nienberg. Our recce party had already left to go to Nienberg when, at about ten o'clock, we had orders to do an immediate handover and go with all haste to relieve enemy pressure on our friends the 11th Hussars. The enemy had been piling into them and they had been having a thin time to contain the Boche. Moveover, the illustrious persons at Div HQ seemed keenly to realise that if Jerry did break through, none of our troops stood between them and the enemy.

Our own part was to pull back to a couple of villages called Blender and Varste a little north of where I had tried to shoot the dog. We were then to go forward to Oiste, another village half a mile from the Weser opposite Verden, to put in an advance-to-contact and if necessary attack the enemy believed to be still in the village.

The shelling of our trucks on the way in had revealed how accurately the enemy had been informed of our movements, so it was decided not to run further risks in bringing the TCVs to meet us or to again pass the same fatal crossroads, for which I was profoundly grateful. This was a wise move as it turned out for as we stumbled our way 2 miles cross-country to the trucks across the cratered, ploughed fields and over by-roads, the sudden and awfully decisive sound of more bursting 88 shells dogged our steps. However, we gradually seemed to be getting near the rim of their range and the black bursts were falling safely behind us in the green cornshoots. This pleasant realisation was joined with an awareness of a wonderful easing of tension in all one's senses. It is only at such a moment that the joy of release from strain enables one to assess and marvel at the weight of the load just shed from consciousness.

We were shortly to find out that this feeling of safety was not quite so well founded as we had fondly imagined. At our level at that time we did not yet know anything of the detail of the foregoing plan, nor did we have maps of our present area from which to keep track of our immediate travels. We did know, though, that we were wanted in a hurry. The drivers, always keen on a bit of speeding, fortunately took advantage of their opportunity to the full. In no time the convoy was strung out in far greater intervals than would normally be the case. The light was beginning to fail and as we were driving with no lights it was rapidly becoming difficult to keep track of the speeding truck ahead. All my much diminished Platoon were in the truck with me and I missed the companionship of poor old Walrus Whiskers. After about an hour the pace steadily increased and I realised as we suddenly caught up two reversing trucks that our part of the convoy had begun to get off the right route. We turned and drove flat out to catch up the rest of the convoy.

Suddenly, close ahead there was the harsh roar of low, fast aircraft skimming the trees, the stutter of cannon fire, then the close explosion of four bombs. After half a mile we caught up with 'S' Company vehicles extricating themselves from the mess caused by this attack on the convoy by two German Fw190 fighter planes which had dive-bombed the trucks. Some vehicles had been hit, though not seriously, and a carrier and a motorcycle had been blown into a wayside field by bomb-blast. Those riding these vehicles had only sustained bruises!

As a result of this incident the convoy speed (always erratic if one is at the end) increased still more. The dim, swaying shape of the vehicle ahead drew steadily away though my driver blasphemed with his boot hard to the floor on the accelerator. Suddenly our TCV, overdriven, started to miss and backfire, then the engine cut out. Another Platoon vehicle behind towed us, fit-to-bust its engine too, for a mile before the twanging tow-rope snapped. This left us in rather a queer position. We were stranded in the dark on a by-road with no maps and no information other than that we were to put in an attack in the morning somewhere. The strange roads had no signposts. Even if we had had a map we would not have known where to make for. Nor did we have any information as to where any enemy pockets were which we might run into if we drove on, trusting to luck in the dark after repairing the tow-rope.

I ordered the trucks to be shunted to the side of the road and then looked round about to take stock. Beside us was a farm and farther up a crossroads and Y junction devoid of signposts. There was neither sight nor sound of further military traffic anywhere. I had fourteen of my own men, two drivers and fifteen men of another Platoon so we could give quite a good account of ourselves if we should brush any enemy before we managed to regain contact, but I was worried that unless this was done soon the attack in the morning would be cut by the extent of our strength.

I stationed a picket at each of the road junctions to stop any vehicles for bearings and help, then sent off Cpl Parry with a patrol of three men to investigate the most likely of the fork roads. Meanwhile, we pushed the two trucks into the farmyard.

Something dark was moving silently down the road. I ran out in time to stop two scared German civilians on cycles. I looked at their cards and told them they might get shot if they did not keep indoors during curfew, which they professed not to know about. I could get no sense from them on our position in relation to Riede which I knew must be somewhere near. It appeared we were closer to Marrtfeld if they were to be believed, but this did not help us. Eventually I let them mount their bikes and go.

I decided it was wisest not to move from our present position and get further lost or wander into enemy lines as, if the road junction was picketed, we would command the most likely route a search party would take in returning to look for us. I posted stags and pickets consisting of 50 per cent of the men, while the other half took their turn in resting in the farm. The occupants of the farm were two very old people, one the dithering old Burgomaster of five or six houses who showed every sign of the most intense fear. I soon guessed at the reason for this. In his dark hall there was a pile of old shotguns, swords and other antique weapons. He had heard that the penalty for not giving these up was now death, though he had diligently collected them to hand in to any Allied troops he might see; his obvious fear seemed to stem from the thought that we might not realise the purpose or intention of the pile of weapons. His gaunt, old wisp of a wife seemed even older than he was and not quite up to understanding, I think, that there was a war on at all. She seemed not to comprehend why we were there, nor why we spoke a strange language, nor why we had suddenly burst in on them for the night, taking possession of her home.

We searched the house and got the old lady organised in boiling some water for tea. It seemed there would be little to eat as we had very few rations between us. The old man put an oil lamp on the table which lit the sitting room dimly, while I rattled up the fire and piled more fuel on. Faced with this sudden invasion late at night neither of them seemed keen to risk going to bed and leaving us in charge of all that the house might contain. The old lady finally crept away into the dark and a key turned in a lock somewhere. The old man sat nervously opposite me at the other side of a table. If I could have talked German I might have set him at his ease a bit. I dozed for a while and looking up I saw he had crept away I suppose to bed. It was not a very comfy chair to sleep in, nor in the circumstances did I feel justified in attempting to sleep, but it was nice to be near a fire, in the dry and with no shells bursting around. At intervals I checked the stags. Besides the need to be on the alert for a search party or any other passing vehicle, for all I knew the enemy might be in the next house.

Shortly after daylight some shouting outside informed me of the arrival of Lt Frank Clark in a Jeep. He had passed the Y junction as I had hoped and been stopped by the picket. Using Frank's tow-rope to couple the two TCVs we set off to rejoin the rest of the Battalion. I soon realised that had we continued on our own the night before we would have gone in an entirely wrong direction. After many twists and turns we finally pulled up at a farm being used as Battalion HQ. I reported to Horace Davidson, the first time I had seen him in his new capacity of CO, to explain our absence overnight. He put me in the picture on where to find the Company. A long trudge followed which led us to the village of Oiste – the village in which we suspected Germans to be, so I was very interested to see the 'form' and hear what had transpired in our absence.

Soon I saw Jocks' heads poking out of slit trenches and from the windows and doorways of the village houses and located Alan. The Company had made a silent dawn approach to the village, expecting it might at any moment develop into an assault. They had got in without meeting any resistance to find that either the enemy had withdrawn over the river or had retired to another village or small group of houses we could see about a quarter of a mile to the north-east in a bend of the river.

Alan instructed me to site and dig my platoon in round a road junction and road block just south of the village where we had passed three graves of 11th Hussars chaps on our way in. Looking at the evidence left on and around the road one could deduce what had happened to them. The broad rubber tracks of an armoured car pressing heavily on the grass verge – a pile of spent cartridge cases, a couple of 2-pounder shell cases, some oil darkening the sand, some patches of blood-soaked earth and odd bits of webbing. They must have patrolled up to investigate the village within the last couple of days and been sniped by either a light anti-tank gun or a *panzerfaust*.

So far things had been quiet. The birds were singing in the warm sun and the Jocks settled down to a bit of sunbathing as they cleaned their weapons, resting on the edges of their slit-trenches. Only from time to time in the distance would one hear the sound of more sinister activity intruding on the peace of the countryside. Cpl Parry, lying on his back beside O'Connor, who seemed almost his old self again, was watching a skylark tumbling, hovering and joyously singing overhead in the blue. Some chaps were writing letters which would later be brought along to me to be censored, others were having morning tea and biscuits as they sprawled in the sand over their mess-tins, mugs and Hexamine fuel. For a while I lay there too with the warmth of the sun gradually penetrating my clothing. I can seldom remember a pleasanter respite. I ran the warm sand through my fingers as I lay, sucking in the scents of the surroundings as the gentle breeze wafted from this direction and that. Each scent seemed primed with memories of happier peacetime outings, manure, spring flowers and weeds in the hedge, crushed grass and hot sand and leaf-mould stirred up. A bee buzzed past, droning from flower to flower as I rolled over to watch its progress. In the distance cattle were mooing and over towards the church rooks were squabbling with their lazy harsh cries so full of memories of summer scenes. What glorious contrasts life can present so few hours apart.

Nevertheless, I glanced down the road and over the surrounding fields through the hedge to scan intently for sight or sound of anything unusual which might spell danger, and realised that though the physical relaxation was almost complete there was all the time an underlying tension of the mind if one contemplated more than a few minutes ahead, and this with its uncertainty, was always nagging in the background. My eyes were resting without focus as I daydreamed the precious minutes away. Distant firing brought them back to focus with a jerk. The whole situation now seemed summed up in the picture that took shape: a couple of my Jocks were sprawled, enjoying the bliss of the moment propped up against the graves of the Hussars: young chaps like themselves who had journeyed so far and endured so much to now lie so differently beside them. Yet of these two, one would lie similarly in only a matter of hours and the other would be wounded.

If the enemy were in the next village or over the river, I wondered what they might be up to. A pub was up the road, so I decided to climb up onto the roof and have a good look around from that vantage point. I had just got up there and was looking out through a hole where the roof was damaged when a series of wicked-looking black splodges of tumbling smoke burst into view and expanded towards the nearby church and over some trees opposite. As I took this in, the crash and blast shuddered the roof. Shots were all bursting about 60 to 80 feet up in the air – airburst 88mm shells. A few new holes from shrapnel had punctured the tiles, brightly spotlighting the disturbed dust dislodged about me in the attic by the blast. I wasted no time in clambering down at maximum speed.

Several more airburst shells darkly dotted the sky over the village in the next few minutes, looking almost as though black clots of mud or ink were being splashed onto an invisible sheet of glass overhead to slowly expand and blow away. Those Jocks who had not taken overmuch care in the digging of their slit trenches revealed their whereabouts as spadefuls of earth flung themselves up from the depths of some of the holes.

Meanwhile, Jimmy Wannop to my surprise turned up from the direction of the group of farms to which we guessed the enemy might have retired, and stated they were clear. Wherever Jerry was, he evidently had spotted that we had moved in to Oiste. Meanwhile, there had been some more sounds of not-too-distant small-arms firing, some mortaring, and either some shelling by our guns or more 88s within about a mile of us. As the minutes went by and no more violence made itself evident, some of the villagers began to peep and walk about outside their houses where other Jocks of the company were well established. They had kept to their cellars mostly so far, but seemed to have decided among themselves that Jerry was out for good and was not likely to try a counter-attack for they began to wander about the village street and the farmyards and had to be ordered in again. Partly because we did not want to have to deal with any needless casualties among them if more airburst arrived, but also we did not want any of them wandering on their bikes with useful information to any enemy still left in villages on our side of the river, or that they should block our field of fire if trouble did start.

A section of carriers had set out for the houses Jimmy said were clear and this patrol returned shortly, confirming this. News also came that two small attacks had been made by other companies of the battalion, restoring the situation which had been causing so much concern to the 11th Hussars and posing a threat to Div HQ. Perhaps this explained the odd 'noises off' which had crackled and crashed in the near distance earlier. Jimmy had dug one of his 6-pounder anti-tank guns into the garden of a tiny house in our area and it dominated the road to the south from this well-concealed position.

'Prepare to move!' a runner was yelling down the street at us. Almost at the same moment the geared whine and revving of engines of a column of TCVs rolled into the village in a cloud of dust. This triggered the comfortably settled Jocks to free volleys of vehement swearing, partly at moving from a now peaceful and pleasant locality towards the unknown and more trouble, and partly for having to abandon newly dug slit-trenches after so little a time. We were to hand over to our Recce chaps.

After the usual chasing around and checking of Jocks and their equipment to ensure none of either commodity was left behind, we were once again seated bumping and swaying as we rolled towards the future. It seemed evident that before we again caught up with the enemy it was most probable that the Weser would have to be crossed somewhere, unless there was a pocket of enemy resistance still to be mopped up south of the river.

These 'swanning' moves after the enemy in the TCVs had become quite a routine procedure to us by now. It seemed quite a long time since we had taken to being motorised infantry. The Jocks rather envied the drivers their 'cushy' jobs. Each time the Battalion was ordered into action, the trucks jettisoned us deep into the artillery zone, then trundled back to wait at wherever Brigade HQ was established until it was all over. They would then re-appear. The driver would look round at the faces of his truck-load to see which ones, if any, were missing, and then murmur,

'Bad luck, poor chap!' Then the cycle of events would re-commence. This time, however, I had a new truck and driver as poor old Walrus Whiskers for once had not needed to pose the question. As so often, from the news I could gather of him the experience had hit him more deeply than he or we had realised and I doubt if he drove much again.

For hour after hour the German countryside, mostly intact but for the odd patches of violence which had left its all too familiar marks, peeled past the trucks. From time to time we passed an old farmer – one seldom saw anything approaching a young one – working about his farm or trundling along the roads with a dog at the wake, as often as not in carts of rather quaint construction to our eyes – very long, with a narrow wheelbase. There were also dogs pulling small carts in some villages as life started hesitatingly to flow again. Very, very seldom did we see much in the way of mechanised transport or tractors. If there ever had been many, the retiring enemy must have pinched them to get away more speedily. There were not many German civilians about compared with the tide of displaced persons we again began to meet – sure sign always of an enemy pull back. One could almost judge the speed and distance and recentness of this withdrawal by taking careful note of all the clues this tide had to offer, not least of course by asking them how long they had been on the road, where they had come from, what shape Jerry was in when last seen, had he any 'panzers'; French was usually the most profitable language to get a clear picture, though we did not have many opportunities, except at the occasional halt, to learn much; also, lack of the right sheets of maps and unfamiliarity with the whereabouts of small German towns and villages was a major snag.

Often these displaced persons with their weird collections of improvised transport created difficulties for our advance and especially any essential two-way traffic. Their vehicles ranged from prams stacked with clothing, pots and pans, like miniature mobile hayricks, to broken-down old push carts or farm carts. Often there was the odd dog, child, cow or goat trailing wearily behind. I suppose the goat or cow represented the only reasonably sure supply of milk for a young family on the move in an otherwise uncertain and disorganised landscape. Sometimes one caught the glimpse of wayside picnics or bivouacs. Very occasionally we met liberated prisoners of war, usually the worse for drink, bowling merrily along in some ancient or abandoned civilian or army vehicle. How they got the fuel to drive those not propelled by producer gas was a mystery. Quite possibly these were sometimes propelled on spirits of various sorts from liquor stores they had broken into – half the fuel being consumed by the vehicle and the rest evidently by themselves. Perhaps, too, it may have been syphoned out of wrecked enemy or Allied vehicles which had come to grief but not been burned out. Quite possibly, too, they cadged some from good-natured Allied vehicle drivers.

At Hoya, a recently bombed town – or perhaps a shelled one – the rough, pitted and mess-strewn road was in parts bulldozed through a ploughland of little more than rubble where the buildings had once stood. Here we crossed the River Weser on a newly erected, creaking Bailey bridge, accompanied by the familiar rattle and clatter of wood boards and squeaking of metal joints. Gathering speed on the far side we soon left the smashed town behind and passed on through Hassel and the scented pinewoods of Forst Memsen, climbing out of the river valley onto small wooded hills. Since Hoya the roads had been speckled with another form of refugee going in the same direction as ourselves. This time German refugees with salvage they had gathered from the wreckage of their homes. The few men in evidence were well beyond army age. There were many middle-aged and elderly women in sombre clothes and some children. In contrast, the younger women and girls seemed to have put on the best clothes they could salvage from the rubble, perhaps taken from bombed shops. Again and again, whistles, cheers and jocular shouting heard ahead up the column revealed itself as our turn came to be caused by the figure of some young woman, sleek in her battered finery and trudging doggedly by the wayside.

The Jocks would, with alacrity, have given them a lift had they been free to do so. One could well imagine anger being expressed in reply to this cheery and admiring banter. The forlorn groups pushed all that was left of their worldly belongings in carts and prams before them and had left their dead behind under the rubble. However, on the whole they took it surprisingly well. A few even waved, smiling wearily back with tired eyes looking up at us from drawn pale faces. The majority, though, seemed so overcome with despair, grief or shock after their recent experiences that they appeared to be walking in a trance, their faces devoid of expression as though unaware of our presence and their steps a weary mechanical necessity.

As we drew away from the river, beyond the hills and into the plain, the occasional signs of war thinned out to be replaced by untouched dwellings and peaceful countryside again. There were violent exceptions, though, which formed one of the most common scenes all over the war zones whenever the enemy was forced to pull back fast. Typical of such scenes was one we passed during the afternoon on an open country road in otherwise peaceful surroundings. It began with a series of ruts and small craters gashed along the line of the road. These varied in size depending on the toughness of the road surface and by which weapon the soup-plate or washbasin-sized crater was produced – either by cannon or rocket. The peppered trail led up to a burned-out patch at the side of the road on which stood the bleached wreckage of a light German truck. A few yards beyond a German half track had ploughed into the ditch and turned on its back. This vehicle – also seared by fire and metal punctured and torn by explosive missiles – boasted only a few traces of the tight, gaudy-patterned, camouflaged paintwork so favoured by the Germans for their military vehicles.

Nearby on the grass verge someone had hurriedly heaped earth over the cremated bodies to form shallow temporary graves. These were surmounted by rifles pushed into the earth on the butts of which hung two of several scattered tin hats of German pattern and other equipment. This was the trademark of an attack by a rocket- and cannon-firing Typhoon. If one passed such wrecks again later the local civilians and farmers would by then have stripped the hulks clean of serviceable tyres, wheels, instruments and other accessories, just like the work of vultures on a carcass.

The railways were lifeless with only very rare exceptions, the shining metals dulling with rust. Locomotives were another favourite Typhoon target and an amazingly efficient job they made of so huge and lumbering a mass of metal left battered, torn and rusting with attendant trucks and carriages on and off the track.

Sometimes, though very seldom, we met single-cylinder tractors working on farms or on the roads, pulling trailers with a deep booming thump-thump-thump, the first of this type I had ever seen.

Gradually the dwellings by the wayside, each with its group of gossiping, staring householders watching us pass, got more numerous until they bordered the road in a straggling built-up area on each side. We became aware of a fair-sized town ahead. This turned out to be Nienberg, which was captured more or less intact.

Our arrival seemed to occasion great interest. At the centre of the town we were met by Frank who had gone on ahead on an advance party to recce the Company billets. We turned sharp left and motored out to the far north-west of the town where we pulled up outside an outdoor swimming pool. As the trucks crunched to a stop side by side on the gravel under chestnut trees showing their first feathery solidity of leaves, cries of 'De-bus' greeted us.

This was a pleasant surprise. Frank, wearing a white polo sweater, greeted us and led us with his group of NCPs to our billets. Some new chaps had been drafted into my platoon, thus making up its strength somewhat, but making the billeting more difficult as three-quarters of my platoon was supposed to have fitted into a tiny house. I went on another recce on my own to solve this and over a nearby stream found a miller's house beside a mill. There I installed two sections and kept the smallest with me and Platoon HQ in the wee house.

This proved a very comfy billet and the Jocks settled down in no time just as they would at home. The Hausfrau was a comfortable-looking woman of ample proportions with a slight, pink-faced, nervous husband, who spent his time fussing around to cater for every want and whim of the humblest Jock in order to get in on the right footing. (I realised later they had really expected us to turn them out of their house.)

There were several children of widely spaced ages and I gathered from looking round the walls that two sons had grown

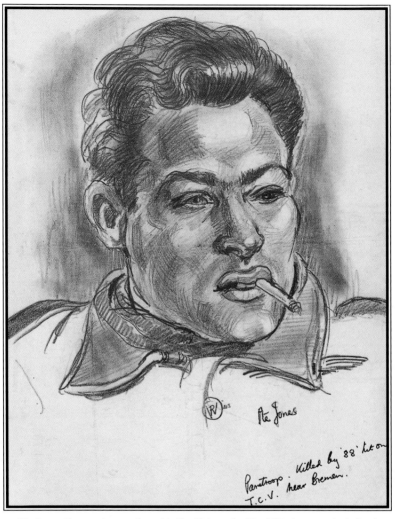

Pte Jones, the paratrooper famed in the Platoon for his ability to secure just about anything for the men. He was killed by an 88mm gun hit on a TCV near Bremen.

Pte McLaughlin — 'my best Bren gunner'.

'Pte Blackwood sleeping while waiting with the rest of the Platoon for word to start the Heinsberg attack. Wounded in the knee later in the Haus Loo (Wesel Pocket) attack.'

'(London docker) Platoon Sgt Dickinson MM, in my dugout in the Tripsrath Woods. Heavy mortaring outside.'

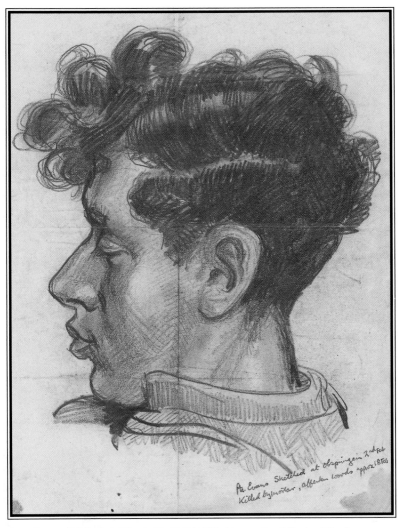

'Pte Evans, sketched at Obspringen, 2 Feb. Killed by mortar, Afferden Woods, approx. 18 Feb.'

'Major Innes, "Smyg", studying map on a night halt after breakthrough at Afferden Woods and subsequent TCV "swanning". Done in German farm, '45.'

'Pip Powell, Platoon Commander B Company, who liked to go into an attack armed with a walking stick and a revolver. Pip, a pre-war regular soldier with the Buffs, had been cashiered in peacetime for getting merry one night and bashing his CO through a plate-glass window. He was again commissioned during the war, surprisingly.'

'My one-time batman and later Bren gunner, Pte Bill Stein.'

'"Wee Mac" McColl, Platoon Commander A Company. After the war, Mac was killed in Ibetha [Ibiza?] in a car crash in the 1960s. He had a small hotel there.'

159

'"Pipey" – Pipe Major Bunyan, sketched while waiting to cross the Rhine during the build up.'

Pte G. Finlayson MM, Company HQ stretcher bearer at Marienbaum, before the Rhine crossing.

Platoon Sgt Cowie sleeping after the attack on Afferden Woods.

Mrs W.E. Storey
Pickering Road
April 20th/945. Thornton-le-Dale.
nr Pickering Yks.

Dear Sir,

I'm very sorry to bother you at this time. But I've just received information from the Record Office, that my Husband, Pte William Leonard Storey, No 4129350. 11 S.U. ... on the 5 of April. Can you please or someone give me fuller details of this lovely service over him. I will find it worrying on my mind so much. Myself I don't believe that it has happened to him. I'm sure it is a mistake. And he is still alive. I would like, and a letter gone for him coming back from India. And we had been —

— 2 —

that a ... together when he did come home. If only they had left him over there. He would have been far safer. He had none of his ... sent back to me as yet. If only this were a mistake or someone part Pte Storey? I should be. It's impossible for me to believe it was, when — He was on smiles, and wouldn't hurt anyone. All he was longing for was to come home to me. And now they say he will never come. If this it true, He has been killed, can't you please let me know how, and where they found him. I remain yours truly,

(Mrs) Marjorie Storey

Mrs Storey married Pte Rex Storey and had two weeks of married life and a 72 hour pass. Before he was posted to India for 6½ years and not seen again but for the 72 hour leave. She said in a second letter that she had managed to get a home of their own, a cottage a ... a surprise for when she saw him again, and could not realise to see the pleasure on his face like she saw it.

One of the many sad next of kin reply letters.

'One of the many sad next of kin reply letters.'

'"Poppa", the old Dutch miner, Stein, Maastricht, Xmas 1944.'

'"Nina", Russian slave worker, drawn by request after I had done Jones's sketch. (Done by the light of a candle on table between us in the farm.)'

'Russian slave worker Elizabeth or "Lizzy", Germany 1945.'

'Attack by Crocodile (Churchill) flame-thrower in village of Uphusen towards Bremen, infantry cooperation, 1945.'

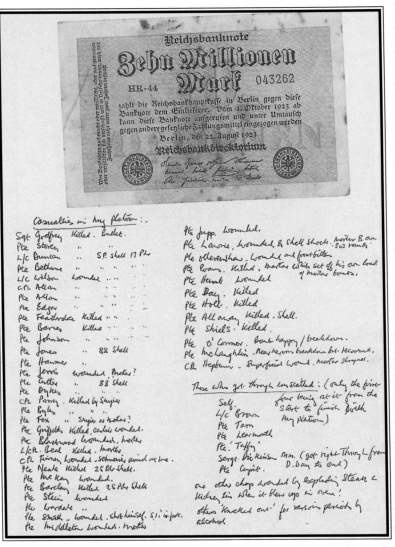

Top: A bank note issued in the inflationary period after the First World War and picked up by White in Bremen. Bottom: List of men in 10 Platoon, including details of who was killed, who was wounded and who survived – the latter by far the smallest number.

On leave in Blankenbergh, Belgium, 'the fighting finished'. Left to right: 'Wee Mac' McColl, John Henderson (signals), Peter White.

Left to right: Peter White, Pip Powell, Frank Coutts and Smyg Innes, with German children looking on. 'Maj Alan Innes giving the order to B Company in the town square at Oebisfelde-Kaltendorf in a takeover ceremony from the US troops. Subsequently the area was handed over to the Russians.'

'The pipers passing the town hall. German police chief, burgomeister in doorway and my secretary, Fraulein Schmidt, in white.' Peter White became chief of police in Oebisfelde-Kaltendorf when the British ran the military government in that part of Germany. He regarded his time there as the most rewarding he spent in the country.

The Jocks parading in Oebisfelde-Kaltendorf.

up and had entered the forces. There were pictures of little Hans and Wolfgang at play, then in the Hitler Youth, then solid and well fed, haughtily glaring out of the photos at us, one in the Luftwaffe and the other in Wehrmacht uniform. The next pictures were one with an iron cross on it (prisoner of war in Russia) and the other with a black band over one corner (shot down over England).

As a very welcome change and testimony to the speed with which the enemy had been pushed back, the electric light was working. The Hausfrau was busy, it seemed quite happily, beside a couple of my Jocks cooking our meals respectively over the same stove. After supper all grouped about in the same small room at the table, on the floor and on chairs, the rather uneasy atmosphere which had been underlying since our stay and which had been noticeable during the rather strange meal began to thaw in the warmth of the Dutch stove. The radio was put on by the nervous German, but as abruptly switched off with a decidedly uncomfortable fluster when he hit on a German voice seemingly dishing out a bit of pithy propaganda concerning Allied troops. It appeared this was coming from Bremen, so that station would probably soon go off the air.

The family seemed most anxious to be friendly. I suppose they were a fairly typical working-class to middle-class home and it was interesting to try to converse with them and to look about at all the little things which made up the contents of this home. The youngest child, aged about five, was taking an amazing interest in all our weapons and tried to handle them all during the evening. His especial favourites were the Bren guns. A Jock put an empty magazine on for him and cleared a gun. He sprawled on the floor, eyes ablaze with excited fervour and lips pulsating to a high-pitched do-do-do-do noise as he mowed down hoards of Jocks in his imagination. His mother joined the Jocks in great appreciation of the situation, but I think his pa was rather uneasy and distressed.

At bedtime we re-arranged all the kit and equipment to give us the maximum floor space for sleeping: PIAT bombs on the wireless, projector on the table, mortar and bombs on the kitchen sink, a Bren gun and a mountain of small packs and webbing and ammunition in a corner, and so on. We dismissed the Germans to the upstairs region. I think they were grateful to me for sparing them their beds when there were so many claimants for them, while we took over the lower floor.

The night was passed without incident, but the sanitary arrangements, as usual under invasion of so many, were rather getting out of hand. Heavy snoring in a confined space was my main memory of the night. The floor was hard, but it was a warm and secure rest. What, I wondered as I lay there listening to the sounds of the Jocks and the ticking of the clock, was the old chap thinking of upstairs, attempting to sleep with his family over a mass of strange soldiers who had just knocked on the door and suddenly taken over his home. I often found myself thinking of what it must have been like for these ordinary German families and I realised I had a deep sympathy for the situation, keeping in mind what it would have felt like if the boot had been on the other foot. I was therefore the more pleased on reflection to realise how outstandingly well, on the whole, the average Jock behaved as an ambassador for his country rather than a conqueror, once the fighting had stopped . . . and if steered clear of the fatal 'wee droppie'. He had a tremendous sense of humour, a wealth of kindness, especially to young children and old people which was very pleasant to see and he never seemed to retain anger or hate generated in the heat of a conflict. I was rather interested to notice as time went on that on learning the Jocks were from 'Schottland' the news appeared to act as a magic lubricant in our relationship to the inhabitants, with its usual crop of queries about doodlesacks and kilts.

Next morning there were frantic crowd scenes of washing and shaving and a queue outside a little outbuilding in the yard. Breakfast was much enjoyed, though I had come to appreciate its special attraction taken in the crisp early morning air after a rough night in the open.

Information came that the Battalion was to parade in half an hour in the grounds of the large swimming pool for a lecture on the war situation by Horace Davidson. His first talk to us as Battalion Commander and the first time for a long while that the Battalion was assembled together.

We learned that we were to again operate under command of

Gen Lyne and 7th Armoured Divison. Gen Lyne reckoned this next push would be the last lap and that he was intending to operate 'Flat out'. 'The larger picture' for our immediate future, parts of which only unfolded for us as the days passed, was that the 7th Armoured Division and ourselves in 155 Brigade were to drive for the Elbe across Luneburg Heath, whilst 53 Division with 4th Armoured Brigade pushed down the east bank of the River Aller to Verden and towards Bremen. As Horace talked to us, bouncing from one leg to the other, a heavily built though not overlarge man, inclined to portliness, he gave the appearance of being very light on his feet, almost like a ballet dancer. He talked with a breathy rather high-pitched voice. As he talked I feasted my eyes on the friendly familiar faces and forms of all those in the rest of the Battalion whom I recognised of old, but was disconcerted to realise how very high a number were new to me and how many of the faces I kept thinking of actually belonged to those no longer with us. Every now and then though I noticed with a kick of pleasure that some chap who had been wounded was back.

AMBUSHED

Later in the day the Company marched through the town under the interested gaze of the populace and with a few children and dogs following to a large chemical works in the northern outskirts. Here we queued in long, naked files wandering in clouds of soapy steam under the intermittent drizzling of hot water from a system of sprinkler pipes in the ceiling. The turbulence of noise and confusion was prodigious; puffing, blowing, laughter, the squelch of soap and loud slaps of hands on bare flesh. It was difficult to recognise who was who among dimly seen scrum of active pink and white bodies. This was our first approach to a bath for a very long time. Afterwards we collected a change of socks, shirts and underclothes, swapping the garments freely among ourselves until some semblance of a fit had been achieved by all but the oddest in size and proportion, who had to like it or lump it. Afterwards we marched back, getting a lift part way in a TCV. How different we felt in our being! How soft the clean clothes were after the matted mess of dirt, sweat and wool we had discarded.

In the afternoon I met Jimmy Wannop, OC anti-tank platoon, and strolled over to his section of the town to see a large, high-powered motorcycle he had captured and which was standing among his transport on a patch of grass in the park. We mounted this and had a high-speed run round the town before returning to our respective billets to brew up tea. I was interested to realise as we sped in and about the streets of the town banking steeply at the corners and accelerating the machine fit to bust it, that with our recent and likely future activities in mind, the prospect of a serious crash at speed seemed tame and of no consequence in comparison. To crash now and be broken up a bit . . . to carry on and be blown up or shot up a bit, or a lot, humanly who could say which might be the path beset by the least hazard. I wondered if Jimmy had thought along the same lines. What a queer jumble values seemed to have assumed. In any event, the outing was greatly enjoyed.

After tea there was a great deal to do to get the new chaps, weapons and equipment of the platoon sorted out, allotted and organised in the best way possible. This sojourn in so peaceful a spot could not, of course, last very long. In two days it was all too soon over. On 15 April 1945 we again climbed into the TCVs after parting from the now friendly German family. Pulling north-west through the town we turned in the direction of Rethem. At a crossroads on the outskirts we halted while a large convoy of the 7th Armoured Division tanks, to which we were attached, went by.

As usual we did not know how long the halt would be, but we crowded off the trucks and made our way into the nearest wayside house to brew up some tea and to heat up the various ration tins in hot water. The middle-aged lady of the house set-to with a will to get things organised. Cpl Parry, who was helping, was in his usual amazing spirits, shouting, singing, playing his mouth organ and passing wisecracks to various passing hausfraus and frauleins at the doorstep. The place we had picked on was a garage. The Jocks had located the lady's daughter somewhere and she was roped in to give a hand too. The spring weather or the rest in Nienburg seemed to have gone to Cpl Parry's head. I gave him instructions on splitting the rations for sections with the tea that had been prepared, which he disobeyed. Repeating the order I met insubordination for the first time from him or any other Jock and regretfully had no alternative, as it persisted, but to place him on a charge – the very first charge I had ever had to place a Jock on, and the last. As things worked out Parry was never to have this charge pressed, for, sadly, by nightfall his long, long trail was over and it seemed a mere fluke that I had escaped the same fate. Up the road I found Smyg had fixed his HQ in another house and an old couple were busily engaged in getting some water to boil for his tea. What a queer life this was.

Our resumed journey had not progressed far beyond the town

before we began to meet signs of the most intense mortaring everywhere. Just outside Rethem the roadside was gashed, as were the fields with their craters and with numerous slit trenches which from their condition and the scattered equipment evidenced very heavy fighting and casualties to match.

Just beyond, the convoy halted as our eyes turned to search the sky at the sound of angry aircraft engine at about 1,000 feet. It was a German plane floating serenely past a stipple of black, oily, bursting anti-aircraft shells. Suddenly another harsher engine drew our attention to a diving Typhoon hurtling towards the German plane from a greater height. We lost sight of the pair below the rooftops of Rethem as their engine notes merged then were out-noised by the stutter of cannon fire. Explosions and smoke already issuing from over the skyline confused the location of the funeral pyre of the German. Below this scene, over a thickly mortared field, a complete train load of 88mm guns was drawn up along a railway embankment leading to a road bridge under which we passed to enter Rethem. Some of the guns appeared intact. Others had their barrels split or peeled open like bananas' skins where they had been spiked. To see so many of these wicked weapons destroyed was a pleasant sight. The town of Rethem itself was in a really awful mess from bombing. Hardly a building was standing with four walls. Miserable, dazed civilians dejectedly turned over the rubble of their home, beachcomber fashion, as they hunted for any surviving valuables or clothes. They took no notice of our heavy military traffic winding bumpily past. At times the pattern of the streets had been so obliterated by craters and explosives that the engineers had bulldozed new roads straight through the powdered brick, glass, wood and mess.

This trail led us to the banks of the River Aller, where, beside the remains of Rethem church, we ran onto and swayed squeaking over the new pontoon bridge which had been floated over the Aller beside a wrecked road bridge. A little lower down river were the remains of a broken Bailey bridge which the engineers had constructed and which was then wrecked by an enemy plane. We later learned that the Germans had here lined up a batch of Welsh prisoners against a wall and had then mown them down with automatics. One of the Welshmen had the presence of mind to fall with the rest although he was not killed and then had the good fortune not to be finished off with those not quite dead by a pistol shot in the head, so that he was able to survive to reveal the foul crime, which the bodies confirmed.

At the far end of the bridge we rejoined the main road, only to find that the enemy had heavily mined and cratered it a short way up so that we had to make a several-mile detour over crumbling side roads. Even this was so heavily cratered in places that the engineers had had to construct wooden bridges on which we crossed. The surrounding fields were very low lying for a way and waterlogged. In consequence a few of our tanks which had earlier cut off the road to avoid mines had stuck like tortoises bellied in deep mud after ploughing for a way until the tracks did not grip. Some may also have been stopped by something less passive than mud.

We crawled past a village called Altenwahlingen where the wayside houses were spattered grey with drying mud from the tracks and wheels of innumerable vehicles, then at a crossroads shortly rejoined the main road. There, to the unsettlement of our stomachs we had our first real clue as to the likely proximity of the enemy in this sector when we noticed a few recently dug slit trenches covering this junction and from which the heads and weapons of some of our troops protruded.

I for one, and I am sure I was not alone, had hoped they might still be many miles away. Perhaps it was the likely proximity of the end of the war which was unsettling us. Also, I think as time went on it became more and more difficult to make the mental adjustments necessary to carry on into another 'stunt'. The utter futility of it all was beginning to become so apparent even to the Jocks. Surely Jerry had 'had it' by now. There was no chance of a comeback, yet the spasms before the end we knew could yet pack sufficient violence to cause us perhaps weeks of bitter localised mopping up of fanatics and all the misery and losses that would entail. A few hundred yards up on slightly higher wooded heathland the convoy stopped for an unknown cause. We hopped off into the trees to afford ourselves relief while as yet no metal was whistling about to make even this occupation full of unexpected hazard and to make ourselves a hurried meal. If trouble started, there might not be another opportunity. The liveliness had gone from the voices and eyes of the Jocks who munched for the most part each withdrawn into himself and in silence.

'Embus'. This was a surprise. We had expected to go on on foot until whatever we were in for started happening. Before we moved off we were to witness two cheering sights that helped dispel the darkness from our thoughts which was up till then creeping upon us as steadily as the approaching close of the day. Deep revving of engines and the loud clatter of tracks heralded another column of our tanks grinding their way past our trucks which were pulled onto the sandy scrub verge of the road. Just as these vehicles passed, another column, this time a weary and dejected grey-green shambles of shuffling humanity, started to stumble back past us along the road. It is strange how few prisoners one captured or saw with tin hats on rather than the peaked forage caps which gave each hunched figure a hangdog, vulture-like look. Some were carrying bundles, rucksacks or red hair-covered horse- or cow-skin bags of which they were so fond. We noted a few were wounded. This might have some bearing on the likely resistance or fanaticism of those left.

At last there was a little news just before we moved off. The position was that the armour was fanning out for all it was worth to force the pace and exploit the bridgehead. Another mile and we stopped again. 'De-bus' "O" group!' 'This is it', we thought.

The road at this point ran through thickly wooded small hills studded with conifers, a lot of it pine, and sprinkled with clearings and sand pits here and there in the heath and woods. About a mile and a half ahead was the village of Eilstorf. The battalion was to spread out right along the road in company blobs to protect this vital artery of the tanks and troops ahead. Our Company, B, were to protect the two road junctions between Altenwahlingen and Eilstorf, with the rest of the battalion covering to the larger village of Kirchboitzen about 2 miles beyond in more open country.

We immediately set about to dig in while the failing light lasted. A message came from the CO about an hour before last light to say that a German formation of some sort whose exact strength was not known was reported active in the woods to the left of the road. B Company were to investigate this report and clear the enemy if possible. Leaving Frank and Sgt Oliver to lay out our positions at dusk on the crossroads we formed up under Smyg and moved in section files alternate sides of the road about 800 yards through the woods in the direction of Eilstorf.

The coldness of the night had not yet come, but I was conscious of an inner coldness and tenseness; the border of fear which could only be dispelled by a fire, faith and hope within. We crept off the road and up a sand track in a wayside clearing. At the head of the track were two small woodsmen's cottages with air-raid shelters in their front gardens from which the heads of frightened civilians were peering apprehensively at us as we approached. We were moving well spread out now and automatically partly stooping to present a smaller target to anyone laying in wait in the rim of the brooding dark pine woods which flanked the cottage. The enemy might be bumped anywhere from here on.

Smyg called an 'O' Group. We huddled in the sand over a set of maps listening to his voice and the sing of the 18 set radio as we drank in the mould of the countryside we would have to cover while sufficient light remained to see. As we looked and listened, ever casting searching glances along the line of the trees, sounds of a disturbance towards Eilstorf told that some sort of mopping up was going on there.

'You take your Platoon ahead, Peter, spread out to provide a screen. Pip, your Platoon on the right to the rear. Sgt Cowie on the left rear. Company HQ, centre. We'll work right through this block of wood first, swinging up to cover the hill on the right before swinging over to this part of the wood on the left. Fix bayonets, check all magazines are loaded, put one up the spout, safety catches off. Keep well spread out, and see your chaps keep in line. Any questions?' 'Any supporting arms, sir?' 'No. Tanks would be no use in the wood. Artillery can't be used. We don't know just where the enemy are and there are some of our own chaps to the right. Watch your flanks, the light'll not last long. Right?'

We scurried back to brief our section commanders. Ever since our experience in Afferden woods we had developed a marked distaste for them in action which was reflected in the remarks of the section commanders and the Jocks. The only way to clear a wood without supporting arms was to move through like a line of beaters, two sections up and one back in each Platoon until we ran into trouble. There seemed no chance of surprise for the enemy had already been in action and knew where we were. If he had mortar support we would be in for a grim time indeed, for our experience was all too vivid of the downward hail of steel these weapons produced, bursting in the tree-tops. If we but knew where the enemy were we could then advance while firing to keep their heads down, I reflected.

'Right! Off you go, Pete. Let's get it over with', ordered Smyg. The only way to keep control visually and vocally was to walk forward between the two leading sections. The Jocks were treading warily and not too keenly with rifles at the port across their bodies, hunched to a stoop to compress themselves into as small a target as possible. There were only eleven of us in the first wave as we were not yet up to full strength. If and when we met the enemy, I realised with a tense dryness in my throat, the advantage lay entirely with him in choice of ground – concealment as against our open movement – and surprise. We would only know we had located him when some or all of us forward were suddenly fired on, perhaps from point-blank range. I wondered if all the Jocks realised this. 'If you are fired on, fire back for all you are worth even if you can't see the enemy, and get down fast', I called as we moved up past the cottages. 'Pass word down to the end chaps to keep watching the flanks'.

The civilians watched us with tense fearfulness as we passed a few feet away from their shelters. A mother clutched her children protectively. I supposed their prayers were for the men they knew to be lying in wait for us. I wondered if they knew where in the woods the German positions were situated.

Now we were among the trees. It was far darker under the canopy of the pines than I had expected. The pine-incensed, cathedral half-light and columns of the tall tree trunks receded into the gloom as far as the eye could penetrate, with here and there a tangle of dimly seen undergrowth. The woods seemed pregnant with an eerie oppressive silence but for the crunch and slither of our boots in the pine-needle carpet and sand underfoot.

High above a slight breeze whispered in soft waves of sound, combing through the swaying pine-tops with the sigh of distant surf and cold eddies penetrated the murk beneath to waft the clean scent of pine-resin freshly to our tense nostrils.

Every now and then a section commander's voice cut the silence to join my own in keeping the Jocks from bunching, in line and maintaining direction. There unfortunately seemed an almost constant need for these vocal corrections to control the chaps in the leading line to my extreme right and left. I was very loath to make too much noise, not only because these unavoidable sounds might enable the enemy to pinpoint our movements and so change their positions the better to ambush us, but also because each shout advertised which of us in the leading line was an officer or NCO. This was not the best form of health insurance. For this reason I was grateful to be carrying a rifle and not a Sten gun like Cpl Parry on my immediate left and the Jock on my right, a lanky nervous youth with wire-rimmed glasses. A rifle was at least some sort of disguise as to which of us was the leader. Little did I realise then just how accurate my thinking had been on these lines and how fortunate my choice of weapons.

As our eyes grew a little more used to the twilight of the trees, we could peer about us more easily to decipher each puzzling shape of tree-stump or undergrowth. A squirrel scrabbled up the far side of a tree, peeping round at us from various points of vantage. I wished I could have read its thoughts for wherever the enemy were, it must have known.

As we advanced I kept having to remind myself of the delicacy of the situation should the enemy open fire. Knowing what we would have done had the situation been reversed I felt sure that they would hold their fire until we were almost on top of them. In consequence I kept seeking the least gully and undulation ahead which might give a little cover and a momentary breathing space if we had to get down at any point. '*** this for a lark Surr! I'll no' be sorry t'ae gie awa' t'hell oot a these *** woods Surr, I tell ye!' cursed Cpl Parry. How I agreed with him. Yet all the time I was reminded of how pleasant a walk it could so easily have been in happier, saner days.

We moved down a dip, then up across a sand track with cart-wheel ruts recently ironed into it: probably the woodsmen. Some disturbed pigeons fluttered suddenly off the tree-tops in a flurry of wings which seemed to match the throb of our fear-boosted pulse rate. For a while we swung right up a hill, slipping in drifts of pine needles and soft sand. 'Pip, check that hill over will you!' Smyg's voice called.

I was relieved to have seen the squirrel and the pigeons as this seemed at least to indicate that the enemy were not in this particular part of the wood. The stage fright which had gripped us at the start of the performance had eased a little now as we warmed to the task. Our stomachs relaxed from their feeling of cold, weak emptiness and the fact that nothing drastic had happened so far cheered our thoughts a bit too. Perhaps the enemy had cleared out after all. The balance and feel of the rifle was comforting to my hands: my left hand round the stock, barrel across my chest, my right hand round the waist of the butt with index finger at home, reassured by the feel of the trigger. To be without a weapon, I reflected, would at such a time surely feel the equivalent to walking naked through a blizzard.

There was just such a wood as this near Ottershaw in Surrey through which I had played with my brothers when we were boys. I had painted a picture of it once at sunset with the warm colour of the trunks lit like coral fronds, pink and gold. The long trails and shafts of light ribboned the pine slopes with alternate stripes of indigo shadow and gold bars.

It was now almost twilight and the outside chaps in the forward line were becoming difficult to see at times through the trees. We came to a deep wooded dip, crossed it, then climbed towards a clearing at the crest of a small sandy hill. The idea of crossing the skyline at the crest before descending into the next block of wood did not appeal to me as we would present ideal targets to anyone on the far side.

Slowly, crouching, we made our way up to the crest, coming out of cover into the open with reluctance. If I had to pick a spot to ambush, this is the one I'd choose, I thought. I was conscious of an uneasy tension and that my heart was faster than the climb warranted. The only sound was the stubbing scuffle of our boots in the soil. We were nearly at the crest now and the ground was opening out into a sort of sand pit and quarry between us and the woods about 25 yards ahead. I was up with the left forward section. The tall, nervous, bespectacled Jock was on my immediate right, Cpl Parry on my immediate left, then another Jock and Pte Byles on his left. We were five of us slightly ahead of the rest of the line.

As we crossed the crest in line together, some very loud whiplash cracks of rifle bullets slashed the silence and the echo carried away into the surrounding woods. Cpl Parry fell like a log, shot through the head. Pte Byles pitched forwards grasping his stomach and lay perfectly still in a grotesque posture. About a fifth of a second passed before the implications had sunk in and the three of us still carrying forward on our feet dropped to cover as several more shots cut past us, one with a twanging, ear-searing whine as it cut up a spurt in the sand just ahead of me and to the left. There was no sign at all of any visible enemy ahead but I fired off a couple of rounds forward at random as I painfully crawled back off the skyline. The tall Jock was groaning, indicating the second volley had got him too. At first my reaction had been that the firing was some of the Jocks in the sections behind firing past our ears for some reason. My shovel and equipment kept digging in as I reversed back and it seemed an awfully long time before we reached the reverse slope.

The wounded chap was frightened to the extent of being temporarily unnerved by the pain of his wound which seemed to be affecting the muscles of his back. He lay writhing, moaning and imploring help, kicking hard with his heels into the soft sand. As time passed this sound subsided into a whimper and he seemed increasingly surprised to find he was still alive.

Locating Ptes Tarn and Learmonth I ordered them to put two HE mortar bombs over the crest at about 100 yards. As these plopped off and exploded, echoing in the woods ahead, Smyg and Pip Powell crawled up to see what the noise was about. As the bombs burst we used this diversion to crawl a little forward and shout to Byles to see if he was still alive. Parry was obviously finished. Poor old Parry. I thought of his wife and group of small children he had shown me proudly in a photograph of his little home in the Gorbals of Glasgow. He was only a child himself, full of irrepressible fun and humour, always at full blast like a human dynamo in whatever he did, whether playing on his mouth organ, singing or laughing. I had loathed being forced to put him on a charge during the afternoon and was glad that he had seemed to bear no grudge. Now if there was any consolation I was relieved to the extent that it could not be carried through.

Byles, a very young, slim youth with glossy fairish hair, lay quite still in the same position in which he had fallen. He was very retiring and quiet and seldom said anything unless spoken to, when his replies were always intelligent and responsive. I think he hated the army and since the loss of his hero and friend Jones, such a contrast from himself, he was if anything more silent than ever. Was there any possibility of his being still alive? His shovel, which stuck straight up from his equipment was quite still, indicating no sign of breathing. If we raised our heads or crawled forward to reach Byles we would be silhouetted on the skyline. Repeated calling brought no response. We did not know how strong the enemy were. Should we put in an attack? For anyone to crawl forward was obvious and certain death yet I could have kicked myself that I could not raise the madness or guts to make this suicidal gesture. On the radio Smyg, meanwhile, was talking back to Battalion HQ, reporting on the situation. As he talked and the moments of oppressive inactivity slipped by we watched Byles' body intently for the least sign which might indicate life, at each moment expecting the enemy might drill us through the forehead as we peeped over. What would the CO order? The woods stretched a mile or more ahead of us and with an enemy of unknown strength in failing light our isolated patrol might easily get into a situation from which it would be difficult to extricate ourselves. If we pushed on we would, it seemed, certainly lose more chaps and possibly achieve no good for the enemy could pull back in the gloom over ground he knew, sniping us as occasion served. As the light failed the sinister gloom of the surrounding dark forest with its unknown enemy content began to weigh more and more heavily on our senses. The Jocks were scattered round the base of the sand hill in a ground-hugging array, swearing softly to themselves as they watched outwards with fear-tinged tense alertness. The spectacled, wounded Jock had been attended to but his pain made him continually plead, almost whimper, for more attention until the tensed Jocks sprawled beside him remonstrated: 'For C*** sake shut up!'

Smyg crawled back from the radio having evidently got orders to pull back to the crossroads and dig in. Still there was the lingering doubt about Byles' condition and we spent several minutes more edging forwards to get a better look at him. To my apprehension Smyg raised himself up a foot or two for a quick look, his glasses glinting in the last light. At any moment it seemed he too might drop with a hole through his head. Byles had fallen on the opposite slope facing the enemy whom we judged from the lack of 'crack-thump' to the passing bullets must have been at point-blank range, perhaps as little as 25 yards. Even in the failing light any move forward in an attempt to drag the body back would have been seen immediately.

Pip, Smyg and I were in a group near the crest of the hill now. As our eyes met, there each of us read what was in our hearts: a dilemma which was one of the most awful moments of my life. The consciousness of what might have hung on it still haunts me. Each of us felt impelled to reach the body to be sure, yet we each as certainly knew that to attempt it would be fatal. In that moment of silence together we each must have realised that none of us could muster the madness or courage, whichever it should be called, to make this fatal gesture in cold blood and from a standing start. Smyg's voice in sudden decision cut the awful silence. 'Pull back. We'll have to put in a proper attack to clean Jerry out when we can see what we are doing in the morning.'

Taking a last look at the shovel sticking up from the body I tried unwillingly to persuade myself from its complete stillness, that he must be dead. 'Hell Surr! B*** the war. I never thought to wish yin o' our'n deed, but I hope we've no' left him there alive', one of the stretcher bearers said to me as he helped back the tall, wounded Jock. We reversed back into the blackness of the woods where the darkness in contrast to the openness and sand on the hill seemed almost unnerving in its tense silence. Had the enemy worked their way round behind us while we had been held on the hill? That long, gloomy walk back, continually searching among the tall pine trunks for sight or sound of the enemy, seemed never ending. Now that we had our backs to them, one's imagination kept prompting the thought that we were being followed. There could be no doubt, I thought, that my own morale at least had never felt lower. Several times then and later overnight I nearly approached Smyg for permission to take a patrol back when it was quite dark to bring back the two bodies. So dismal had been my memory of this experience and the sinister gloom of its setting, though, I was appalled to realise I just could not do it, voluntarily. The depression of my thoughts staggered me. For the first time I felt I was nearing saturation point in battle.

At last we reached the crossroads to tell Frank the sad news of Cpl Parry's and Byles's loss. He had heard the sounds of a skirmish but was not sure we had been involved. He led us in the dark to point out our positions for digging in overnight. We settled in to this task with heavy and angry hearts, angry as much with ourselves as with the enemy. I just could not visualise the platoon without Parry's cheerful presence. To think of him lying dead out in the clearing beside poor Byles seemed impossible. With Jones dead too, the very heart and dynamo of the Platoon seemed gone.

HITTING BACK

I had just completed my hole when a call came from Company HQ for me to go to an 'O' Group. I found Frank and Smyg beside a wood in a clearing over the road, sitting in the back of a hooded 15-cwt truck, poring over maps by the light of a candle. 'We are to put in an attack before breakfast at 0630 with tank and artillery support', said Smyg. 'Horace says that at this stage of the war he is all out to save lives.' For about half an hour Smyg, Frank, Pip, Sgt Cowie and I worked out the details together before dispersing for the night. A miserable icy night it proved, crouched in the bottom of the trench or on stag peering out into the dark and listening to the odd noises from time to time in the gloom of the trees. One could only guess whether enemy, animals or contraction in the cold was causing these noises. I found it quite impossible to get any sleep. Time and again my thoughts carried me back through the woods to Byles and Parry. If he had still been alive, the cold will have killed him by now, I thought.

Before dawn the depressed, frozen Jocks were chased out of their holes and briefed before we filed off up to the forming-up point to await the artillery's pre-'H' Hour barrage. 'Number ten platoon is again to lead, as we know the ground. Three Cromwell tanks are to work along the edge of the wood beside us, firing in at right angles. O'Connor, you keep them posted on our position by showing a yellow silk triangle level with our line of advance on the edge of the wood' (a job he was not at all keen on, making a sitting target for all and sundry with his dazzling triangle . . . but someone had to do it). No ammunition was to be spared. The tanks, in wireless touch, were to pour in all they had crosswise into the wood ahead while the Jocks themselves, each with an extra bandolier of ammunition, were to fire continuously from the hip at random as we advanced to keep the enemy's heads down. 'The cooks have promised you a fine breakfast when you get back.' 'If we get back', some Jock added. 'It'll no' do to' waste guid rations.'

We lay flat on the start line, shivering as the dawn spread. Once again I wondered how much of the shivering was caused by the cold, how much by excitement and how much by fear. If all went well it should be over in an hour and a half to two hours. It was difficult to keep off the speculation voiced by the Jocks concerning the breakfast. I looked about me at my men, loading the magazines to capacity and fixing their bayonets. Would we all get through this time or would yet some more friendly faces not return? Down the track near Frank were the stretcher bearers waiting to pick up the bodies of Byles and Cpl Parry as we advanced past them.

A heavy, vibrant succession of fierce, muffled crashes echoed in the wood ahead. The creeping barrage of 25-pounders and 5.5 medium artillery was pounding the crest where Byles and Parry lay and the woods beyond. Our signal for advance would be when the tanks started joining in, which should be at any minute. Faintly, above the drumming of the barrage we could hear the laboured revving of the tank engines as they pulled themselves sluggishly through the ploughland the other side of a narrow neck of woods which separated us.

Suddenly we heard the fierce rapid chatter of the tank Besas and the whiplash crack of their main armament. Some of the tanks HE shells were penetrating dangerously far in our direction before they hit a tree and exploded. 'Right! On with it. Fire in your own time and keep your magazines topped up. O'Connor get out to the rim of the wood as soon as you can, those tanks are firing more at us than at right angles. Keep your silk triangle tied to your back or you'll show up a mile off to Jerry.' 'Too right sir. B*** this for a game. I haven't a chance if I'm seen sir.' O'Connor had recovered control of himself quite well since being strafed by the 88s at Sudweyhe, but it took a lot of shouting at him to get him far enough to the edge of the wood for the tanks to see him as a marker to our position of advance. Poor chap. I felt for him, but he had more sense than a lot of the Jocks and was the best one for the job. More than once he had refused promotion.

After the usual initial coaxing and yelling the Jocks realised that there was nothing for it but to get up and walk forward, firing, praying perhaps and hoping for the best. It always seemed a little comfort to look along the line of Jocks stretching into the distance and feel that if Jerry did open up again as we went over the crest, one's own body was not the only target.

The volume of fire was extraordinarily heavy and sustained. The barrel of my own rifle was soon beginning to ooze grease through the wood stock joints as it grew really hot and the bandolier round my shoulder grew lighter. It was really comforting to listen to the incredible racket of shelling, tanks firing, automatics and rifles and to feel the repeated vicious kicking of the rifle on one's hands. How different to our previous gloomy stalk through the trees. Several times a sudden heavy explosion and tumbling blackness of smoke 50 to 100 yards ahead, followed by a crashing tree or two, marked the odd tank shell which had come far too far to the rear.

The trunks of the trees were increasingly chipped white, gashed and drilled by the solid hail of bullets. Had Jerry changed his position? Would he fire suddenly from some quite unexpected position on the left flank, perhaps? The German families in the two little cottages had again watched us set off. I wondered if they had been in touch with the enemy overnight and what they made of the present fantastic racket. I took care to always load the magazine of my rifle with two rounds in reserve in case I was caught out at a vital moment with it empty.

We were approaching the dip before the fatal hill, still nothing had been fired back at us. I was again up with the line of the forward two sections reinforced with the Bren guns of the third section and of Platoon HQ. Looking back it was reassuring to see the movement of 11 and 12 Platoons and Company HQ following us up, though they were not able to fire much except to the flanks for fear of hitting us.

Tension grew to its height as we started to climb the crest. I felt queerly alive as though living at twice normal speed. I could see the shapes of the tanks now ploughing along at the border of the wood. The racket of their shells crashing through the wood must, I reflected, be most depressing to any enemy, quite apart from the now intensifying stream of bullets from my chaps. The artillery had stopped. I hoped they had not smashed up the bodies of poor Byles and Parry during the barrage.

The next few steps would bring our heads out above the skyline and in view of the enemy. Sweat was running from under my tin hat and down my cheeks and nose. Subconsciously I tasted the salt of it as I bit my dry lips and swallowed. The next second or two would tell. Our firing was lifting spurts of yellow sand every now and then off the crest of the hill a few feet ahead.

Now we could see the trees beyond and our eyes raked the line of them for sight of the enemy with quite as much intensity as the hail of fire itself. I was conscious of the bodies of Byles and Parry lying in the sand a few feet apart to my left, seen from the corner of my eye, and that though the hill and beyond had been peppered with craters from the recent barrage, they had not been hit.

The tanks could no longer give us support as we moved down the reverse slope into the shattered trees again. 'Got the b***', O'Brien, a Bren-gunner yelled from the left. 'Gave the b*** a burst right across his face!' Near the rim of the wood were some newly evacuated slit trenches. There was more shouting and excessive firing from the left. Looking though the trees I caught a glimpse of scattered, grey-green clad bodies lying on the carpet of pine needles as the Jocks moved past them still firing for all they were worth from the hip.

Jerry had been caught on the hop. Overawed by the weight of fire as we came over the crest with the initiative firmly in our hands, the Boche had decided to pull back, but too late. Once out of the trenches he had had little chance down the smooth, long, pine carpeted slope among the slender pine trunks raked by a hail of continuous fire.

As we advanced we swung slightly left towards a sand track at the foot of the trees. The sand shone gold in the glare of warm sunlight out of the gloom of this block of wood. So far ten Germans lay dead in our wake. By the time we reached the track the number was increased to fifteen. Three of these lay beside the track. One had been killed by a bullet through the neck, the other two were victims of the barrage. One sprawled, blackened with blast in a broken heap on the rim of a 25-pounder crater. The other pathetic figure was in an awful mess from a direct hit from another shell which had taken his legs off with his trousers, exposing the bone stumps and torn flesh scattered with the sand which his fingers had clawed. His face bore an expression it was difficult to erase from my thoughts.

I could only feel deep pity and an overwhelming sense of the futility of war as we passed each body. There was no sense of achievement or elation that the chaps who had killed Byles and Parry had now been killed themselves, but rather a sense of depression and shame at having to have any part in so degrading a treatment of man to man in the middle of the twentieth century.

The Jocks had openly sworn at the start of the attack that to revenge the loss of their two friends of yesterday they would take no prisoners. Suddenly, just beyond this last group of dead Germans, another stepped out from the trees over the track ahead against the hot, smoking rifle barrels of three of these Jocks. For a moment I feared that before I could take any action the Jocks would shoot him down despite his having thrown his rifle at their feet and thrust his shaking hands high above his young, frightened, angular face. He was desperate with fear as his eyes pleadingly searched the grim, sweat-streaked faces advancing threateningly on him. His quivering mouth opened to plead, but no sound came. He swallowed heavily and his legs seemed to be sagging already as though in anticipation of the end. He could evidently think of no English expression of a request for mercy. Finally, in desperation as the barrel of the nearest Jock's rifle jabbed its bayonet towards his chest, he said 'Kamerad' quite softly and brokenly, in a voice, girlish in its pitch, like a young woman's and drained of all hope and vitality. I don't think the Jocks had ever meant to carry out their threat and as I came up with them to question the German there was obviously no need to order them not to kill him, for their fierce resolution visibly faded from them before this helpless, pleading youth as evidenced by the droop of indecision in the attitude of their rifles.

As the realisation that his prayers had been answered sunk in to our prisoner, the reaction from his strained tension of desperation seemed to have almost the same effect on him as though the Jocks had actually fired soundlessly. He swayed, staggering to regain his balance and his arms subsided as though all strength had ebbed from his limbs. Tears which had been brimming his eyes rolled slowly down, cleaning a track on the dirt of each cheek. He hurriedly scraped his sleeve at them in sudden awareness as he recovered and raised his arms again. He was quickly in control of himself again. I felt great sympathy for him in his momentary weakness. He obviously, like ourselves, was pretty whacked with lack of sleep and strain and I hoped I should have behaved no less well had our positions been reversed; though had this been the case, to judge by our news of the Germans shooting prisoners at Rethem, no mercy would have been shown.

So heavy had been the racket of our firing in the attack it had only just occurred to me to try to recall if there had been any evidence of the enemy firing back effectively enough to cause any casualties. No, all the Jocks were OK.

Our young prisoner could talk a little English. It seemed he had belonged either to his Company HQ or to a different section or platoon to the chaps who had caused us trouble on the hill the night before. He claimed that he was lost, and that the chaps he was with had withdrawn the previous night. Perhaps, though, he was just trying to dissociate himself from any personal involvement with the Jocks.

Before our return to the promised and much anticipated breakfast, we cleared a small wood the other side of the track, swinging back towards our positions and marching the young German with us. He looked an odd figure, walking through with the Jocks, a rifle barrel pushed into his back, hands clasped over his head and a cigarette a Jock had lit and given him poking from his lips. The cigarette's quivering betrayed the raggedness of his nerves and his red-rimmed eyes were pursed, half-closed to avoid the sting of the smoke.

As we moved back towards Company HQ rejoicing in the warmth of the sun and shuffling our boots in the sand of the track in relaxation at the relief which had followed the success of the attack, the acrid, faint blue haze of smoke from the firing and the shelling clung to the cavernous gloom under the trees. Its tang, mingled with the scent of the pine trees, wafted to our nostrils from time to time.

The birds, frightened into silence or scared away by the appalling racket, were resuming their cheery sounds of spring revelry in the heathland on our right and in the tree tops set dark against a lovely blue sky in which sailed snowy, sunlit clouds. In this peaceful setting Frank had returned with the stretcher bearers carrying the bodies of Byles and Cpl Parry wrapped in blankets. I was very distressed to hear from Frank that Byles must after all have lived for a short time at least as he had vomited from his stomach wound as he lay, though it seemed evident from his hit that he could not have lasted long. How I reproached myself and have done ever since that I did not manage to find within myself the guts or the madness to have attempted to get him back. Yet common sense told me that I would certainly have been killed too and perhaps have caused a chain of more casualties in attempted rescues for we knew now that the enemy slit trenches overlooked the bodies from slightly higher ground less than 20 yards away, and the bodies were silhouetted against the light-coloured sand which would have shown up the least movement, even in the half-light.

The two friends were buried side by side in rough graves, which in the beauty of the spring morning's fresh fragrance seemed a mockery of such a peaceful scene. I was suddenly aware with the sights and sounds and smells of the countryside and the heathland of a vivid picture in my mind of our last relaxation in the sunny sand and of Parry resting against the grave of the 11th Hussars chap beside the tall, spectacled Jock who had been wounded after Parry was killed the night before. The scene was almost the same and I felt an inner chill at its recollection. That similar day at Oiste so short a time ago now seemed separated from us by an age of time, yet it was well under a week. How many more weeks could this possibly last, or one last with it? Those of us from the original Platoon were very, very few, almost strangers among the new faces so steadily replacing the old ones who fell by the wayside.

As we lay in the open beside our slit trenches eating the much-looked-forward-to breakfast with what heart we could muster for it, and idly cleaning our weapons in the sun, their barrels still hot to the touch, one of our recce armoured cars pulled up beside us in the heather. Its radio was tuned to the BBC and a delightful tinkle of melody and rhythm floated towards us. I shall never forget the impact of those unexpected harmonious musical sounds. How fresh and gentle and strangely fascinating music sounds after the searing jarring rasp of war noises. It was as though I had heard music for the first time in all my life. It was so different. Yet the tune in itself was not an outstanding one or even classical. My mind went back to the memory of the Jock playing the piano after our ordeal in the snow at Waldfeucht when I had had a sense of the same feeling despite the grim setting in the dead of winter.

A small stream wandered through the heathland and sounds of laughter and splashing revealed some of the chaps having a wash and shave, while those not on stag were enjoying a doze lying on the heath and the sand of the track in the sun. In the distance down the track also lying in the sand and sun were the bodies of the three Germans we had last passed. Who would bury these chaps, I wondered, and those others in the wood if and when they were found?

Already the Platoon seemed adjusted to the latest losses both in jobs and mentally and life seemed to be going on much as before except for the realisation from time to time that the families of those lost were still in ignorance of it. Occasionally this was brought home even more poignantly when a letter or parcel arrived for a casualty, which would have to be sent back after a time lapse for the official news to get through. Some time too, I remembered, I would have to write a line to the next of kin of Byles and Parry. The large number of these letters I had had to compose seemed to make each more difficult rather than easier to write as time passed. The time and place of writing was often far from helpful in easing this task, which so often brought in its wake heartrending replies from parents, wives and sweethearts who just could bring themselves to accept news they were sure must be a mistake.

Word to 'prepare to move' came all to soon, and with it news that our armour had blasted its way out of the bridgehead and was starting to move really fast ahead. We boarded the TCVs near a small wrecked house on the crossroads and set off to rejoin the rest of the Battalion convoy near Kirchboitzen where we passed Bob Bearpark, Adjutant, Harry Cartner, MTO and Horace Davidson, the CO, standing by the roadside. The rest of the Battalion had struck lucky here with no casualties.

After quite a long move the convoy slowed down and halted for a while. We watched some of our guns during this interval belting heavy shells into another pocket of German resistance by the wayside which was being by-passed for later mopping up. On we moved again, then another halt. Frank borrowed a DR's motorcycle to run up to the head of the column and get the 'form'. During the wait in pleasant open country, a Jock spotted a deer about 1,000 yards off over a ploughed field sprouting new shoots of green corn. He raised his rifle and fired at this timid, distant form, immediately to receive a rocket from me and a healthy rebuke from numerous Jocks who slanged him viciously: 'B*** you, have ye no' seen enough killing you *** !' Fortunately he missed and the deer shied at a spurt of dust whipped up short of it and pranced away.

Fifteen miles of journeying brought us to the recently taken town of Walsrode where the streets were milling with thousands of displaced persons and Polish prisoners of war who had been liberated by the armour. They were busily engaged in breaking into wine stores and cellars and those not already so, were rapidly getting drunk to the evident dismay of a group of apprehensive German women watching the scene who evidently and accurately were appreciating the fact that once drunk the attention of the mob would next turn to them.

Passing through Walsrode we turned more towards the east into very nice countryside with not much to show that there was a war on except for a few faint pillars of oil smoke ahead, evidently the rim of our armour's penetration, and the occasional salvo from our wayside guns into an enemy pocket. It was getting towards evening and the convoy was lumbering slowly along, nose to tail. Again we halted amid a landscape of wide, rolling fields fringed and capped with ominous dark pine forests, each of which we viewed not in terms of so many trees but rather as so much cover for possible further German pockets of resistance who might have to be so painfully winkled out.

But for the damping presence of these woods on our spirits I became conscious from time to time of a rather elated feeling which I think was the general sentiment at the realisation of the speed of the breakthrough by the armour and the growing belief that some time soon we would link with the Russians, Germany would be cut in two, and the war's end would be in sight. As these thoughts grew, so did the dilemma of the desire to cut all possible risks of being winged at the last hedge.

We had some prisoners with us in my truck, four of them from the last wood clearing whom we had not yet had an opportunity to palm off onto some unit which could ferry them to the rear. They seemed nervous and three of them, all very young, were in evident terror that we would grow tired of their presence and dispose of them by the simple method of eliminating them. Such a solution was not remotely a possibility with us but from their carry on it struck me as more and more certain that that was their fear. Our own 'capture' was in another truck and I think by now trusted our intentions.

At last it was decided to halt for the night. Each company made use of wayside farms into which to pull their trucks so that the Jocks could sleep under cover in the barns and farmsteads. The three most frightened Germans had several times to be stopped from whispering together. As we stopped the Jocks jumped out of the back of the truck into the dark, pulling the prisoners with them. We found ourselves in a farmyard bordered on one side with pine trees about 10 yards away. Suddenly the three whispering Germans scattered into the dark running in their desperation of fear like scalded cats towards the trees. The older German seemed more content that we meant no harm to him and stood firm while Sgt Oliver sprayed a whole magazine from his Sten gun at the fleeing figures who were zig-zagging and tripping in their headlong flight through the trees. None apparently were hit at least fatally for we found no bodies on investigation. No one was particularly worried at their loss for it was obvious that they would do what so many of their compatriots were beginning to do when overrun: get civilian clothes and melt out of the army. In recent days we were becoming conscious of some most un-farmer-like toughs mooching about the farms and villages. Once they had side-stepped the war in this way they seemed to lose all interest in it and it would have been a job beyond our scope to try and sort out the deserters from the civilians.

I took my Platoon over a railway track to a barn for the night, there to find some artillery chaps already in occupation. We joined them. There was plenty of room for more forms to lose themselves in the straw. The German seemed quite content to topple over among the Jocks and go to sleep. I wondered where his three companions had got to and if any of them had been wounded.

We spent quite a reasonable and not too cold night buried in the straw and in the morning trooped along to the Company HQ farm for a quick breakfast of boiled eggs, tea and bread. Soon we were back in the TCVs again, gathering speed to the north-east, the trucks having as usual refuelled at some hastily erected petrol point rendezvous. It was amazing how enough petrol was always available to keep the masses of transport on the move, and how the rations and even the mail on occasions arrived at its appointed time or very near it.

After we had left the farm many miles in our wake, Sgt Oliver reported to me that his compass had been left behind in the barn. The loss of kit, arms and ammunition was an eternal problem in the Platoon. The chaps simply could not keep up to anything near their full scale of it unless chased continually to do so. Learmonth, my number one on the mortar, had even forgotten so obvious a thing as a 2-inch mortar when we had left our billet in Obspringen during the winter. Even the realisation that a weapon present and in good condition may mean the difference between life and death personally or for one's friends at almost any moment did not seem enough incentive for some of the Jocks.

STALAGS XIB AND 357

The day started to progress along the usual lines. Unexpected halts were seized as opportunities to attempt the brewing of cups of char if there was sufficient time for the water to boil over blazing petrol fires. Frequently the stop was not long enough and the tea brewer had to clamber hastily back over the tailboard of a moving truck, spilling his tepid brew of water of questionable origin from a battered biscuit tin.

Towards midday those who felt like it began to break into the tins of meat and vegetable hash and nibble bully beef, Compo chocolate and biscuits. It was a fine, warm, sunny day and as we could see little evidence of impending trouble ahead we settled in to relax to the utmost the opportunity offered.

Suddenly, at a halt a rumour began to buzz down the column that we were approaching a large prisoner of war camp near the town of Fallingbostel. In order to ensure that no reprisals were taken by retreating German fanatics against the prisoners, two companies, ours included, were to cut across country as fast as possible to the camp. We suddenly almost doubled back in our tracks, and ran round the edge of several fields of newly sprouting corn. Next we bumped along a farm track, all hoping that there were no mines about. This led us through a thick wood where one or two of the TCVs got stuck in the fine sandy mud and had to be towed out. Finally, we crossed a wide race-course-like ribbon of sand in two carriage ways 60 feet wide (our first sight of an autobahn, though still under construction), and pulled up under cover of a sand hill as tanks were sighted milling about ahead. They were obviously Shermans but to make sure all was well Smyg went on ahead in the company carrier escorted by a DR to find out the 'Form'. More rumour filtered down to us that this camp had been hit on at about ten the previous evening when our armour had overrun it, and that the rest of the Battalion was still at Walsrode restoring and keeping order over the drink-soaked displaced persons.

Gradually, we became conscious of a strange sound, at first faintly in the distance, as though from thousands of people wildly cheering in a distant football stadium. This startling sound led our eyes to discover a far away expanse of low wooden huts with tall, brick, grain-elevator-like buildings sprinkled among them. They were about 1,500 yards distant and their roofs appeared to be seething with humanity with a sea of movement swirling below round the huts, hemmed in by a faint silk tracery of thick barbed wire.

Argument and betting broke out among the Jocks as to which nationality the prisoner of war camp contained. Shortly the DR roared back, flinging up the dust to give the 'OK' and with engines revving loudly the convoy moved forward through the thick sand, gathering speed as we raced over the flat towards the wire and the commencement of about the most amazing 24 hours we were to ever be called upon to spend.

Two things that took our attention as we neared the camp were the seeming absence of any German guards and the fact that the figures pressing against the wire were dressed in khaki. We were later to learn that the prisoners had followed the news of our approach over a Heath Robinson home-made radio for five days before our arrival and that armed with this news and by sheer force of numbers and persuasion had taken over control from the German guards who were now prisoners in their own camp. The worst SS types among the guards had not risked waiting but had fled before the tanks of the 7th Armoured Division had arrived.

At last we reached the perimeter track round the wire to be greeted by a delirium of cheering, dancing, waving of arms and shouting by the prisoners which was returned equally heartily by the Jocks. The dress and shouting of the prisoners left no doubt whatever that in this part of the camp at any rate, the occupants were British.

A sudden surge of prisoners in one sector marked where the wire had given way before the pressure of thousands of bodies who flowed out in a frothing wave like a mass of khaki mud from a punctured dam wall. The surge was soon sweeping round the trucks, forced to a momentary halt while hands and voices thrust up their joyous and grateful greeting. A quick exchange of information was bandied back and forth in eager shouting: What regiment are you? What division? How are things going? How long have most of you been prisoners? Is it nearly over? What are conditions really like at home? When did Jerry leave? Did he have any tanks with him? Do you know if so-and-so is in the camp?

Cries of astonishment, greeting and cheering marked the recognition by the Jocks of one face among the prisoners as a member of our own company who was captured just short of Koningsbosch on the Dutch border during the winter and he had soon scrambled back among us. From him we learned that the chap captured with him was also there. The camp contained 20,000 prisoners of war, of whom 7,000 were either British or American. Most of the British prisoners had been taken at Arnhem and quite a number were from our own 7th Battalion. It was the RSM of the 7th together with the warrant officers and sergeants who had kept up the smartness and discipline of the English-speaking prisoners to an extent which appeared remarkable in contrast to the slovenly, smelly shambles which proclaimed the men of the other nationalities. It made one proud to be British.

After a short halt, the two companies split and filtered into various points in the camps, Stalags XIB and 357, to act as internal and external security as it was becoming obvious that without control things would rapidly get out of hand. Numerous figures of various nationalities were already stealing towards the large storage magazines and towards the town of Fallingbostel for food, loot, drink and, we were later to find when we had to send armed patrols out to restore order, for German women. We were to become familiar, all too familiar in the coming weeks as displaced persons and prisoners broke loose in a disintegrating Germany, with the pattern of behaviour; once the men had had a square meal, their thoughts, if not already there, turned from food to drink and from drink to women . . . then trouble.

The immediate and difficult task with so few men was to put a clamp down on any more stealing away from the camp and to put a stop to the wholesale looting of the food stores. All the prisoners were in varying stages of starvation which, added to the intoxication of their liberation, contributed to the frenzy of our near impossible task among the teeming thousands. If the food was all consumed in an immediate orgy it might be a long while before supplies could be brought up to fill the gap.

How to even start the task seemed near impossible to conceive. The handful of Jocks were like a few match sticks carried on a flood tide of milling humanity, reminiscent in numbers of Trafalgar Square or Piccadilly crowds on a state occasion. To make matters harder, all the crowd was in uniform of one sort or another too, much of it khaki, and insistent on waylaying one for information of some kind.

Only two platoons, mine and Sgt Oliver's, both still well under strength and close on dead beat from accumulated lack of sleep, were charged with maintaining order in our sector which included the storage magazines. For a while I stood with Smyg in the crowd, lost in the jostle and noise, bumped by figures fighting to get to the stores and by those laden with loot trying to fight and stagger their way clear. Shouting at the tops of our voices produced a sound barely audible to each other or to ourselves. Taffy was beside me with a Bren gun and seized with sudden inspiration, though somewhat fearful of the possible results of the action, I ordered him to fire a long burst into the air. The sound echoed deafeningly from the tall walls of the magazines. A sight followed that had to be seen to be believed. The source of firing was concealed to all but those of the sea of heads closest to us and as the echo carried away into the distance it seemed to carry all the noise away with it for an instant of startling silence, pregnant with a sudden surge of fear evident on the faces of all who had not noticed Taffy firing. 'Are the Germans back?' seemed to be written in everyone's expression. The silence only lasted about three seconds, to be followed by a different noise, the panicky scurrying of thousands of feet in all directions, clattering on the wide open stretch of tarmac. Only a few fugitive figures fumbled with their heavy loads of loot as they tripped and staggered away. Another burst from the Bren, added to with my rifle, soon had these figures clear too. I could not help feeling mean that we had had to resort to firing, although only into the air, to attain our ends, but I am sure it could have been done in no other way.

Now the task was to prevent a similar crowd from forming another attack on the stores. The furtive glimmer of promiscuous lights and isolated staccato noises told that some were still feverishly at work inside. To add to the immediate difficulty of the situation, one of the two available platoons had to be switched to another part of the camp. With this news came more: in addition I would have to find a guard from my already over-stretched Platoon to look after 350 German guards who had been rounded up in the camp. To these, just before dark, another 50 were added to my care.

I crammed these chaps into a large, barn-like, brick building with only one big door. Two men was the most I could muster to look after these Boche. If they got awkward the situation would be very difficult. These two would have to take it in turns to keep very much awake overnight. I stationed them, opposite the open door of the brick building, about 25 yards distant, with a Bren gun, a Sten and a heap of magazines for each gun. If the Germans did try a break-out overnight these two had instructions to fire at the door for all they were worth and keep firing.

Near the entrance to the door I noticed one of the Germans was an RSM, and found that he could talk English very well. I chatted with him for a while to try to sense his outlook and his thoughts on the treatment the Germans had meted out to the prisoners of war in the camp. I had found earlier in talking to Allied prisoners that most of those in the camp had been force marched right across Europe during the winter months, in threadbare clothes and with next to no food, many falling out to die by the wayside. As always happened with these conversations with Germans, I had to give up the talking in disgust. In defence of their treatment he blindly quoted the authority of the German leaders and those over him as though learned from a book. There was not the slightest sense of guilt or recognition of any responsibility whatever for the inhuman and barbarous treatment meted out to the unfortunate men placed in their power by the fortune of war. Many of the Allied prisoners resembled mobile skeletons. Others were too reduced to walk and the death rate among them was excessive.

I walked along to the perimeter wire to see how things were there. At this sector the camp changed over to POW of other nationalities and I was astounded to find that a two-way traffic had developed through a hole in the wire in the failing light. Men – and women – were passing in and out. The men were foraging for food and drink and bringing back to the camp with them slave-worker women of other nationalities they had found on the farms and also loose German women. The gap in the wire was plugged, but it could not be constantly patrolled and I was not surprised to find that before morning it had been breached again.

To add to my difficulties, I found on getting back to Platoon HQ that the inevitable had happened. Platoon Sgt Oliver and his pet cronies, L/Cpl Brown and Learmonth, had further reduced the infinitesimal strength of the Platoon by getting tight on some particularly vicious hooch. They were to pay for it that night and for a further three weeks in finding themselves constantly chased out on stag at all hours and running errands or being detailed for any of the less pleasant jobs that might come up. After a few days of this they began to put two and two together and though nothing further was said this was to prove more effective than the futility of a charge.

Tales of incredible stores in the magazines began to reach me from the Jocks, so I investigated. The tales were not without foundation. The place resembled a gargantuan Woolworth storehouse with rooms full of various rather cheaply made items. One, for instance, contained fountain pens which the looters had so messed about as to leave the floor ankle deep in them, many pens being squashed into the floor by trampling feet. In other sections of these big buildings there were combs, toothbrushes, petrol lighters, oil lamps, pressure lamps, radios; in fact truck-loads, it seemed, of every imaginable article covering acres of floor space. I wonder whether this was either a sort of German NAAFI store, or some of the prisoners had been employed in making these things.

Smyg had set up his Company HQ in a concrete store hut

nearby to my furniture-less wooden hut HQ and various NCOs and men kept gathering there from time to time to meet their friends, either from the battalion or from their home districts, who had been found in the POW cages. The CSM actually met his brother there whom he had not seen for four years. One or two of the RAF prisoners had been confined there since as far back as 4 September 1939, the day after war started!

The mystery of the complete disappearance of the Cameronian company on our right during the attack on the Wesel pocket was at least partly explained by our coming across some of these chaps as POW. I always regretted that I did not find time to talk to one of these men on what had actually happened to them during the battle for Haus Loo.

In talking to one prisoner I learned that 600 to 800 South African POW had been marched out of the camp by the Jerries to an unknown destination only two days before we arrived. Among these was a cousin of mine whom this prisoner had known and who was later released to stop and recuperate with my parents near Oxford before he sailed home. Back in South Africa he started a farm after getting married, but was killed by lightning beside one of his two small children inside the farm after so short a taste of his new life.

That night was a very busy one indeed, keeping the prisoners of war, both Jerry and British, in check. Needless to say, by far the greater problem was not the enemy but our own ex-POW. The camp was seething with a desire to break out for food and loot and I came in some measure to appreciate the problem and eternal headache a bunch of British POW must have been to any German guards. Some of the POW had used the utmost skill and ingenuity in building quite complicated mechanisms to make life in the camp more bearable. Some of these were constructed out of tins and odds and ends to heat water with bellows worked by an impeller, others were for cooking food, or just, it seemed, for the fun of making an elaborate lot of mechanism work together for no purpose whatever except, perhaps, to puzzle the German guards. Whenever a particularly unlikely piece of raw material was needed for a gadget – such as the radio valves for the Heath Robinson radio – the most likely of the German guards was worked on with a bit of bribery or blackmail or both.

When I saw my German POW in the morning light I was pleased that arrangements had been made for their disposal, for with only two men to guard them and keep them all the while in sight, sanitary arrangements had rapidly deteriorated well below zero, the whole entrance to their building for yards in either direction had become of necessity a very active latrine.

All these 400 Germans, plus some more who had since been unearthed about the camp, were loaded into twelve TCVs way beyond their capacity. With a handful of Jocks as guards and armed with a map-reference to make for I took this convoy to a temporary POW camp set up in a bleak, wired-off field where a host of grey-green clad, dejected humanity was already squatting in forlorn silent groups. The numbers of German POW being taken were becoming a real problem. During the first three weeks of April more than a million Germans were taken prisoner by the Allies. 325,000 of these, including 30 generals and a group of 21 divisions, had been unable to fight their way out of the Ruhr towns behind us. It was estimated that there were still some 50 divisions, including the 1st German Parachute Army, to be eliminated north of the central thrust across Germany.

There were still about seven German officers to be disposed of in the camp. Most of them, at least, to look at, appeared to be living specimens of cartoon characters depicting Prussian officers at their most typical. They had a pile of luggage packed ready for their move and among the bulging packs the Jocks soon discovered these Germans had actually had the neck to secrete a pile of food parcels for British POW, which prior to our arrival had been diverted for use in the German officers' mess.

The Jocks really 'saw red' at this and were all for polishing them off out of hand 'Come on, Surr, let's shoot the b***s', a Jock rasped with real violence in his voice, loudly clapping a magazine onto his Bren gun and enjoying the feel of swinging it across the unhappy, bloated, bullet-headed group of elderly and middle-aged Germans struggling to maintain their look of haughty arrogance while skating on the thin-ice fringe of fear, for the Jocks were neither meaning to act their fierceness, nor did they look as though they were.

The luggage of these officers was soon denuded of the food parcels and I suspect a few other choice items as well. Davidson, Smyg's batman, showed his indignation by collaring the fur-lined gloves belonging to the German POW commandant who only with difficulty succeeded in controlling his outraged fury.

I was intensely interested in talking to one of the two Jocks who had been captured during the winter on the Dutch border near Koningsbosch to learn how he had been led back to a German Battalion which had spent the night right beside and in ignorance of us, just as we had not realised they were there.

An enormous ammunition dump had been discovered while we were at Fallingbostel POW camps and during our second day there, Lt 'Wee Mac' McColl was sent with his Platoon to take this place over. Significantly, it contained approximately a million gas shells, among other things. 2nd Army showed great interest in this store and it seemed probable there were other items of even more interest there that we did not get to hear about. The Germans had made an attempt to move part of the dump but they had been stopped by the speed of advance of our tanks.

During the day the carrier platoon had had to put in an appearance in Fallingbostel to quell the looting and 'woman-handling' which had broken out among the roving displaced persons and prisoners of various nationalities who had got clear of the POW camp.

It was most depressing to walk about areas of the camp occupied by the non-English-speaking prisoners. It seemed that not only was the discipline and pride evident in our sector of the camp almost completely lacking in the filthy squalor, but also it struck me that the Germans had been far more severe in cutting rations supplies and clothes to such people as the Russians, Poles and French.

It was 17 April. The 7th/9th Royal Scots were having a difficult fight for the rail and road junction town of Soltau about 11 miles to our north-east about half-way between the rivers Weser and Elbe and word came for the Battalion, less Mac's platoon and one company, to move into reserve in a small village behind the Royal Scots called Mittelstendorf.

In quick time the TCVs were whining out of the gates one after the other in a steady stream with the Jocks cheering and being cheered by the POW who appeared, miraculously, to line the roads and the railway embankment on the way to Fallingbostel, to send us on our way. 'Good luck Geordie!' 'Put the lid on the b***s!', they called as we passed.

Fallingbostel was fairly quiet again after the disturbance of the day before as we passed through and over the River Bohme heading north-east towards Dorfmark through pleasant country of woods and fields and gentle hills. Not far beyond Dorfmark we became gradually aware of all the usual signs of trouble ahead.

INTO THE BLUE

News of exactly what was going on was pretty hazy at our level as usual. It was not for us to know the bigger picture, or exactly what shape the enemy were in for any further large-scale resistance. Indeed, the scale of overall resistance often made little immediate difference to the individual Jock, any more than if two individuals wrestling together would be involved more or be distracted by six other men or six million other men similarly engaged in the vicinity. One's immediate prospects and fate lay in dealing with the few men of any opposing formation with whom one was likely to come up against personally. In other words, even two tiny, well-armed formations fiercely clashing could provide for each of the men involved quite as much effort, struggle, turmoil, misery, fear and so on as might be one man's share on a D-Day Normandy landing, with quite as much vividness. It was the realisation of this often rubbed-in basic fact of life as an infantryman which now held our thoughts more and more. In its tantalizing and inescapable persistence in spite of the brightening overall picture it formed the more and more irksome dilemma of our immediate future.

How many more mopping up operations, attacks and so on would we be called upon to go through or could it humanly be thought reasonable to survive, with the pattern of past actions in mind, before the enemy accepted the obvious inevitability of ultimate defeat and threw in the towel to stop the contest?

The mood of the average German civilians had for a long time appeared to us to have passed the point of acceptance of defeat and to have realised with it that each day the struggle carried on made the prospects of the aftermath more and more grim.

Ahead of us we could now make out all the usual signs in the sky of destruction in progress on the ground. In addition to activity by our rocket-carrying fighter aircraft, the sky was smeared with dirty trails of smoke which varied in tint according to the materials burning. It seemed evident, though, that both houses and vehicles were on fire not very far ahead. Were we to be involved? 'Any news Surr?' 'No, not yet.'

Gradually scraps of information were put together and, added to visual observation of the unfolding scene, provided us with the knowledge that only that morning the Royal Scots and the Somersets in Kangaroo troop carriers had fought a fierce engagement to take Soltau. They had formed up and gone in behind a barrage of 5.5-inch guns and with the very active support of a bevy of flamethrowers. In consequence, as we followed, the road was pitted with craters while at the roadside frenzied civilians, distraught with hopelessness, tried desperately to quell their blazing homes with buckets, sacks and their bare hands, to stack what belongings could be saved clear of the flames. Stunned old people and dazed, frightened children were grouped beside the pathetic belongings, their future a nightmare blankness. At times the heat from houses burning each side of the road was so great as to make one wonder that no petrol tanks or canvas roof covers were touched off as our TCVs clattered and clinked and rolled, bumping through the rubble-strewn and crater-pitted streets.

The more recent state of combustion of the houses on the far side of the town told that the flamethrowers had not so long before been through. The armour was pushing forward as hard as it could go through Bohm Heide woods before fanning out across Luneberg Heath. The significance of the name of this heath we were not then to know.

The roadside was littered at intervals with the burnt-out or smouldering remains of German transport, sometimes with bodies in evidence and sometimes not. The situation seemed to be so much in a state of flux as to be bordering on the chaotic. To take advantage of the dazed condition of the enemy, of whom large groups were constantly being encountered who seemed to have no idea of what had hit them or what was going on but were generally agreeable to surrender, we were to leapfrog through the

Royal Scots and make for the town of Schneverdingen 8 miles to the north.

It was very fortunate that the enemy apparently did not seem to be coherent enough just then to appreciate how slender and overstretched our single axis of advance was or how easily it might have been cut. It was equally fortunate for our own peace of mind at our level that we were not in a position to be fully aware of this situation. It was only later that we learned that our own Battalion of about 850 men was stretched taut over some 40 miles of road and that our 'Shelldrake', Maj Ross, RA, was so far from his own guns that he could not contact them by radio. Fortunately, someone had had the foresight to attach a battery of guns to the Battalion column which would have helped in an emergency.

At the head of our column a typical example of the confusion of the situation was provided when Maj Rae, our 2i/c, in command of a recce party and his men swung round a corner near a village in their Jeeps to find themselves nearly impaled on the gun barrels of a couple of 88mm anti-tank guns. Fortunately, the German gun crews, equally startled by the situation were busily engaged in having breakfast. Before the amazed Germans had had time to take effective action, the Jeeps had vanished in the opposite direction even more swiftly than they had arrived.

As we pushed on north of Soltau into a countryside of wide, gently hilly openness with scattered woods and farms and small villages every few miles, we passed a wrecked German Mk IV tank, one of our Shermans burnt out, then a wrecked Dingo recce vehicle with a couple of our chaps lying killed in it. This last wreck bore all the signs of very recent occurrence and also gave us enough evidence to know that there were still elements among the Germans who were capable of causing us trouble. As we moved north the dark woods bordering the road gave way to wider horizons and smaller scattered woods which were more to our liking. There were some ominous, large areas of wood just to our east on the map and I sincerely hoped the enemy was not going to withdraw into such territory in a desperate bid to prolong the struggle.

Several times the Germans had blown the road in their

favourite kind of position – over a stream bed where the water would collect and make repair more difficult. At these points our bulldozers were busily at work repairing the holes. At one point the Germans had blown two craters together. Most of the farms appeared to be untouched, superficially at any rate, but others were reduced to heaps of smouldering ash, having been recently burnt by incendiary bullets from tanks or by a squirt from passing flamethrowers. On the whole the scene was very pleasant and almost English-looking – tough, somewhat sandy and flecked with pine, as in the New Forest.

Beyond the craters, in the village of Heber we turned off towards the north-west. As the evening approached we at last pulled up on a railway level-crossing just short of the pleasant and almost untouched town of Schneverdingen. This railway ran up towards Hamburg, not many miles to the north. We were, however, not to progress in that direction as things turned out.

After a short halt while a Company Commanders' 'O' Group was held, Smyg arrived back alongside the Company TCVs in his carrier. We were to move to the north-east sector of the town and take over from the 1st/5th Queens, who were motorised in Kangaroos and had taken the town without opposition only a couple of hours earlier. They were to chase after the armour heading towards Hamburg.

Gradually 200 prisoners were rounded up in the area of the town, but the chief trophy was a store of champagne which those with a taste for the stuff pronounced as excellent. It was found under a heap of peat, and I gathered that a large part of it was consumed at Battalion HQ.

The Company position, we found, covered two roads running out of the town at an acute angle down hill towards the railway track and the woods beyond. We were on a fine reverse-slope position on a gently inclined, sandy, ploughed field. I took over the slit trenches already dug and settled my Platoon HQ in a small house in which I shared a room with Sgt Oliver. The occupant of the house, a crinkled, bent, old lady, having established I was the officer, with nervous hesitancy presented me with an offering of wine which I refused with thanks. I found later, however, that the rest of the Platoon had lapped it up.

Just before dusk I took a section forward to the crest of the hill to dig in as a standing patrol in the shadow of a hedge, then continued forwards with a smaller patrol down the hill. This had a double purpose: to get familiar with the lie of the land while it was light enough to see it, in case trouble were to develop later, and also to check all the houses forward of us were clear of an enemy, who might literally be anywhere. While out, I took the opportunity of collecting a levy of eggs, a few from each of the houses, which the housewives gladly enough produced to the demand 'Habenzee Ajer'. However incorrect this may have sounded, it was most successful in producing eggs.

It was almost dark when I decided we had better return to 'stand to'. Just then a Jock spotted two dimly seen figures moving close together in the rim of trees beside the track. One of the Jocks casually raised his rifle to pick them off, as though out on an evening pigeon shoot. 'Hold it!' I called. An evening walk by a couple of young lovers, neither of them much over seventeen, strolling together in dark clothes was nearly brought to a tragic end. As we approached I was interested to see the amazement with which the tall, fair-haired youngster and trim, dark girl eyed us. Their mouths and eyes widened with disbelief and then apprehension as realisation dawned. Holding tightly to each other, knuckles whitening with the grip, they watched us come, each seeming to draw a little strength from the grip of the other. It seemed evident that this was the first inkling they had had that the town was occupied, and testified again to the speed of our advance. They had to be chased back to their houses over the railway after I had tried to explain to them that if figures were seen moving forward of us after dark, we would most probably open fire. As they flitted off, still holding each other as though to ensure mutual safety and looking back as they went, I thought how very nearly these two young people had come to being snuffed out, to lie staining the sand in each other's arms. Just then five more figures were seen in the distance down the track. The light was too bad to make out whether they were in uniform or not. Taking Pte Dodd with me and leaving the rest of the patrol near the railway, I stalked along the ditch to try to relocate the figures, which had now slipped into the murk of the wayside trees.

After stalking along for what seemed only a few minutes I was shocked to realise, looking back, that we had got nearly 1,000 yards forward of the Platoon positions on the hill. We had seen no further sign of the figures and I reflected that as they had slipped off the track, quite possibly they were enemy troops who had spotted us, in which case, by now it was not beyond possibility that we might turn out not to be the hunters, but at the ratio of two to five, rather the hunted. Here, I thought, was certainly a case of discretion being the better part of valour. How jolly apt these odd sayings are, I reflected, as, with this as an excuse, I guided our footsteps a little more promptly in the opposite direction, moving one at a time in bounds, each covering the other in turn. We arrived back just in time to see to it that the Platoon was alert on the 'stand to'.

With reinforcements the Platoon was two-thirds back to strength. The presence of so many new faces (though some of them were older hands from other Platoons in the Company) was a continual reminder of the loss of the old characters whose places they had taken. Among the NCOs, beside Sgt Oliver I now had Cpl Wilson MM, a fair-haired, hefty 6-footer, Cpl Dare, a wily alert chap of some experience and with a keen ruddy sharp-nosed face, and Cpl Jones, a thickset chap of slower action, though possibly not wits, than the other two.

The new chaps had settled in quickly, but those without experience in action seemed somehow to show their fear of the unknown demands yet to be made on them. Their unity with the older hands was almost complete and they seemed to draw confidence from watching how these older stagers set about things. Many of them were very young and would seem to have been better employed still at school.

During the evening I visited Smyg, Frank and CSM (Frankie) Pook in a fine modern home which they had taken over as their HQ. The German family who owned it had been given half an hour to clear out into the next house. With this time limit they had only been able to take essentials for their camp with the next-door family.

There was very little news to be gathered at this visit. No one seemed to have a clear idea of the strength of the enemy in the area or if he had any armour available. We suspected, however, that our own forces were flung out in a long, slender chain deep into enemy territory and that as night fell it was quite possible for the enemy to filter between the links of the chain – the small units holding towns, villages and crossroads along the axis of our advance. We knew we might expect trouble from all points of the compass, but particularly from the east and the west.

In the company area there was a small camp full of Italian POW who were so overjoyed to see us as to form a real embarrassment. There was evidence enough that a lot of the Jocks must have located more hooch in the company and though they were only mildly tipsy I realised that if the Italians did not keep from wandering about the positions in the dark we would have some corpses on our hands by the morning. German prisoners had continually been winkled out of hiding places in the town during the day and quite possibly there were still many more about who were only waiting for darkness to make a dash for it. It seemed unlikely to me that a Jock would show much concern if either an Italian or a German failed to answer a challenge properly but would shoot first to investigate afterwards.

Eventually I gave up the task of trying to explain to these Italians what was in my mind. They just would not keep to their camp and would just have to take their chance. The night was turning into a very cold one and perhaps this would drive them to bed before long.

I wondered if the standing patrol I had posted on the crest of the hill forward of us had any further sight of the suspected enemy we had observed at last light. I decided to pay them a visit after checking over the other sections and telling them I would be going forward and returning in about fifteen minutes. The last chap I spoke to as I made my way forwards was Pte Stein who was crouched in a hole in the ploughed field behind his Bren gun trained forward. 'Do you know the password, Stein?' 'Aye Surr!' he replied, repeating it. 'Right, I'll be back in a quarter of an hour from the forward position.'

I was pleased as I made my way forward to notice that we had one of Jimmy's anti-tank guns dug into the fence of a garden belonging to a small house in the Platoon area beside 3 Section HQ on the track to the east.

No sight or sound of the enemy had been noticed in the forward position, so I set out to return to Platoon HQ walking in the open down the line of the plough furrows to make sure my return was seen by those on stag behind. I was surprised to get almost on top of Pte Stein without a challenge. I stopped about 15 feet short of where I knew he must be to look harder for him. A clink of metal of a Bren being cocked very close by drew me to notice his dark form. In a flash I realised the gun was trained on me and I blurted out the password without waiting for his challenge. How fortunate I did! No challenge would have been forthcoming.

'By God! Is that you Surr!' he exclaimed in naïve amazement, as though I was the last person he had expected. 'You very nearly had it from the Bren, Surr!' he mumbled as though in apology. 'I had just cocked to fire Surr when you gave the password.'

'You clot Stein! It's your job to challenge. You knew I was forward and that I would be back in quarter of an hour. You can't expect people to walk all over the Platoon area constantly shouting the password to challenges they never get!' 'I'm verra sorry surr, I'll try and remember next time.' 'You'd jolly well better or there'll not be a next time for some poor blighter. You just can't go forgetting that sort of thing.' Poor old Stein. He meant awfully well and tried very hard but thinking seemed a most painful process to him. If instead he could put forth some sort of physical effort he always did take this line of, to him, least resistance. This, true to form, was what he had just in the nick of time been prevented from doing. If any Italians chanced his way during the night I realised we would certainly have a burial party to perform in the morning.

I retired to my little house for supper with the rest of Platoon HQ. The old lady had gone to bed and left the Jocks in charge of the lower floor. We had plenty of eggs, fresh milk and some vegetables which had been scrounged and it was nice to have the facilities of the kitchen to hand for the cooking. Several times I reminded myself during the night as I checked round positions to endeavour to guard against a repeat of the slip that had nearly occurred with Stein and his challenge. To think of the incident made the present seem queerly unreal. I was here, yet I might, it seemed, but for chance have been lying shattered from a point-blank burst from a Bren, rolled in a blanket awaiting my funeral on the morrow.

Though the cold night passed without incident but for the barking of dogs and in the early hours the sound of a truck which we supposed must belong to the enemy passing on its lonely way along a country road in the distance to the east of us, we were so aware of the isolation of our position that the need for alertness prevented us getting much sleep.

SCHULERN OASIS

At dawn I was confronted with an unexpected order for my Platoon to move immediately by truck to a small village 2½ miles to the south of Schneverdingen, called Schulern, as it seemed likely that German troops cut off by our rapid advance the day before might try to withdraw that way. I parked my chaps in two trucks outside BHQ while I went in to get my briefing from Horace.

'How many men have you got now?'

'Twenty sir!'

'Oh, well that'll have to do. I want you there to give us advance warning of any enemy coming up from the south', he said. 'Send the trucks back when you have unloaded.'

We had no 18 set radio or phone to keep in contact with Battalion HQ, so I asked Horace, if he could provide neither of these, could I have a motorcycle, which he promised to provide, but none materialised.

'Is the village clear of enemy at the moment sir?'

'I hope so.'

So did I. Just in case it was not, I put rather more than half the platoon in the second truck with instructions to follow us at an interval of 200–300 yards. This, I hoped, would give us greater scope for counter-measures should we in the front truck run into trouble.

The countryside might easily have been in England with woods, farms, green, rolling fields and cattle. It all looked very peaceful as we made our way quietly along at not too great a speed looking searchingly at everything as we went. About half way we slowed up to pass a crossroads beside a wood where a few houses and farms lay back from the road. All seemed well and on we went. We found the village to be smaller and more scattered than we had at first imagined. It was grouped loosely about a crossroads fed by three smaller tracks with three small woods and orchards with small farmsteads sprinkled about. We had a scare for a moment on noticing some German transport up a side track, but it was abandoned. We would have time to investigate later whether it was still in working condition. We certainly sadly needed some means of communication with Battalion HQ. I reflected as we jumped out of the trucks which turned and roared off back to Battalion HQ. If any enemy did materialise it would take a runner a little while to cover the 2½ miles and give warning. If too strong a force arrived for us to hold, or a tank, it struck me as rather ironical that if we could not hold them the enemy would get back to Schneverdingen long before a runner.

The immediate task was to dig in covering the crossroads. Once this was done we started to search in groups from house to house to make sure of what the village centre contained, before we started to patrol out to search the farms which lay within 500 to 700 yards of the centre. There were very few civilians in the houses in the middle of the village. Most of them seemed to have moved to the outer fringe as though they had sensed that the crossroads would be the trouble spot if a clash occurred.

'Stand to! A truck or something coming fast up the road, Surr.' In a flash the Jocks were off the road and into their slit trenches and the houses training their weapons towards the approaching sound. I looked hurriedly at the map. The vehicle was approaching from enemy-held territory to the west, but what puzzled me was that the very high revving of the engine sounded like a Bedford truck. Yes it was! The driver was piling on the speed as he approached the village. To him the place must have appeared deserted, but whatever the reason it was his evident intention to get through it as fast as possible.

Could it be a truck the Germans had captured and were putting through ahead of another formation to test whether the village was occupied? In any case he had to be stopped whoever was in it, so I stepped out into the middle of the road to wave him down, at the same time shouting to a Bren gunner in a slit trench at the side of the road: 'If there is any monkey business fire at the engine and tyres!'

Immediately the truck slammed on its brakes with dramatic effect in noise and dust as it swayed and crunched screaming to a stop at the edge of the road. The rather white, tense face of an RASC driver popped from behind the dazzle of the windscreen.

'Hell I'm glad to see you're here!' he gasped.

'What are you up to? Don't you know you are way off the axis. You've just come out of territory still held by Jerry!' I said. He blinked back and swallowed in silence. It transpired that he had taken a turn off the main route with his load of ammunition and had been wandering for some time, gradually realising that he was lost. As time passed he had become more and more aware that no British troops or transport or road markers were in evidence. He had seen German vehicles from time to time drawn up in villages, whether abandoned or not he could not say. He had not looked to see if any German troops were about the places, but with increasing panic he had been trying to cut his risks by going past any roadside dwellings and villages flat out while heading towards where he hoped our side might be.

In his strung-up state he could give no coherent indication of the route he had taken as we looked at my map, which might have provided valuable information for us. His hand quivered as he held the map and he released it to light up a cigarette and mop beads of sweat from his brow with an oily rag.

'For a moment I thought you were Jerries', he said. 'I saw that Jerry vehicle as I came in. B*** if I have ever been so glad to see khaki before!' We gave him his bearings and with a bad, crashing gear change, as ragged as his nerves, the truck rolled slowly away towards Schneverdingen.

'Ask where to go when you get there or you'll be in trouble again!' I called after him.

With this bit of excitement over, the sections, one covering each of the roads leading out of the village, settled in to cook breakfast. The rather odd sounds of another engine, this time behind, revealed a white-painted Volkswagen with red crosses on the sides. It spluttered to a stop beside me with Pte Lee at the wheel, lolling back in enjoyment.

'Found this old crate in the woods!' he said. 'There's a bit of fuel of some sort in and it seems to get along quite well, Sir.' He had also discovered an abandoned emergency German hospital in the woods while out scrounging eggs for his section. I was very pleased to have some form of transport on hand. 'Turn it towards Schneverdingen,' I said, 'and if trouble crops up be ready to get a message back to BHQ fast.' We could find no paint to paint out the red crosses, but some grease smeared on the side panels and then scattered with dirt did the job quite well. The presence of this vehicle made us feel far less isolated.

The day was turning into a very pleasant, warm, sunny one. The whole setting of the village, the spring and the birdsong made it difficult to realise that at any moment enemy troops, vehicles or even armour might suddenly swing into sight, touching off all the inevitable hell of battle in its wake. I had been pleased to find a few abandoned *panzerfausts* anti-tank projectors lying about, which if they worked would bolster up the PIAT.

We spent the day improving the positions and then checking over the neighbouring farms to make sure no Jerries were hiding in them. Each farm involved its own sort of controlled approach. The Jocks seemed to enjoy this. It certainly had a fear-brisked excitement and fascination about it in the continual uncertainty as to what we would find. This work had to be done slowly as I had not enough men to cordon off each house and I hoped to make the element of surprise offset our lack of numbers if we did meet any trouble. This very element of surprise added to the interest of the situation when startled farming folk suddenly became aware of our presence among them. I suppose we gave some of them quite a shock for we must have been the first British troops they had seen.

The closest to any 'enemy' we met was an old German farmer, much in need of a shave and dressed in part of his Volkssturm (Home Guard) uniform. He was obviously wearing this merely to save his own clothes while he was doing jobs about the farm. It was interesting to see the farm families 'at home' and search our way through their homes, taking passing note of their standard of life compared with farms at home. The furniture, pictures, decoration, equipment, dress, livestock and construction of the buildings never ceased to hold fascination for me. They were largely peasants really. Anything approaching the English gentleman farmer was, in my experience, quite a rarity. The rustic old men, the sturdy women and children and occasional younger men all seemed to have a tang of the earth about them akin to their livestock which was not altogether due to their lack of baths.

We did not return from these forays empty handed and the selective scrounging skill of the Platoon was brilliantly reflected in the variety of fresh produce which went to make up our meals while in the village. The time was passing wonderfully peacefully. We had finished tea and nothing untoward had happened to mar the day though one was ever conscious of the tension of the situation and our isolation from the rest of the Battalion. Just before the light failed our ears picked up the noise of engines more powerful than those of trucks approaching, this time from the east.

'Stand to!' There was a general flurry of activity at top speed. Brown and McKenzie lay back in a doorway in the shadow behind their PIAT covering the road from the east to fire at right angles at the side of any thick-skinned vehicle that passed their house. The chances were very much that they were our side as the main axis was 5 miles to our east.

'OK, they're ours!' several voices cried as three vehicles roared into view followed by a dust cloud: two armoured cars and a Recce Dingo. From each poked a bereted and earphone-clad head above which swayed pennanted aerial rods.

The Jocks popped out into view to join me in giving them a hearty greeting as they pulled up at the crossroads, their powerful engines rumbling hotly like enormous pots on the boil. How comforting their massive and business-like presence was. The singing and crackling of their radios made us feel back in contact with the throb and thrust of the advance again.

'Any trouble down there?' I called up at the troop commander.

'Not for a while. How have things been here?' We chatted for a bit and I told him of our truck which had pulled in from the west during the morning. 'We've been cruising about to protect the main axis from trouble from the flanks but I am getting these buses behind you foot-sloggers before dark comes. I don't relish stopping out if any *panzerfausts* are likely to be used,' he said. 'I tell you what, I'll recce this village of Sprengel a mile and a half down this southern road for you before I pull back.'

'Thanks, I'd like to know it's clear down there', I called. 'Good luck.'

Off he roared out of sight and earshot in the distance. After about 20 minutes we could hear him coming back, faster than they had gone out.

'Not too healthy!' He grinned cheerily. 'We got to the village, or nearly so, and some muck started coming back at us. Pinged off the sides. No damage done, didn't seem to have any heavy stuff!' This was disconcerting news, though it had far from damped this chap's interest in the village. 'Not to worry! Tell you what, we'll whip round the other side of the place and have a dekko at it from the rear.' And off he went into the now gathering dusk till the sounds of evening peace had resettled on our village. The brisk yet casual presence of the chap and his unruffled spirits were a pleasure to witness. After a long absence he eventually returned, to our surprise from the direction of the village of Sprengel: 'Quite OK some of our own chaps down there, the bone-heads took us for an enemy AFV.'

Just then there were sounds of shouting by a lone voice down a side road towards a village of Wieckhorst which lay over a small hill a mile to our east. A gaunt, startling figure was half staggering and half running towards us waving its arms and dressed in a Belsen-type, striped, pyjama-looking suit. He was pointing behind as he ran, shouting 'Deutsche Soldaten' excitedly. We eventually deciphered that two German SS types had held him up a few minutes before somewhere over the hill and had pinched a bundle of looted food from him. He pleaded for a gun to go back and shoot them and retrieve his precious food. He must have escaped from some concentration camp which had been overrun nearby. One of the Jocks produced a shotgun and some cartridges he had found somewhere and these were presented to the chap while the Dingo was turned round by the Recce chaps. Sgt Oliver, with my permission, jumped up in the front of the Dingo, pulling the Russian DP up after him, both as keen as mustard to get after the Jerries. The gaunt, pyjama-suited Russian and dapper, keen Sgt Oliver made a queer pair as the Dingo zoomed off, climbing out of sight over the crest of the hill.

Before very long a set of very disappointed men returned to say the two SS types were nowhere to be found. The armoured cars then departed in the direction of Schneverdingen. Later, a couple of hysterical German women came sobbing and wailing to me from over the hill to complain that the Russian had made up his food losses by holding them up in their farm pantry with the shotgun. So everything was square again, though I was very glad he had not used the gun on them and rather apprehensive as to what he might get up to if he unearthed some drink while still with the gun in his possession.

The point that intrigued me about this episode was how had these German women known that there were some troops of ours in our village of Schulern to whom they could appeal for help. No German civilians from our village had been allowed out up in that or any other direction. There appeared to be no telephones about. The only clue seemed that they had seen the Dingo go back towards Schulern and had chanced finding us. Among the unserviceable German Army transport in the village I had unearthed a motorcycle. To my surprise a few kicks had started the thing, so I decided to take a quick run back to BHQ to report and get any news there might be.

It was evident that the captured champagne had done much lubrication of the dry throats back at this HQ, for all were in 'great fettle' when I arrived and as I set off back on my cold lonely run in the half-light to Schulern I had been able to gather little information. Indeed, I wondered if my presence had really registered among the merriment. It was a bit tricky riding back in the dark with no lights at all on a strange bike and strange roads. I was quite pleased to splutter back into the village, though not to have a rifle jabbed into my chest as the bike pulled up while a familiar Scots voice said 'Halt! Who goes there! . . . Ock I'm sorry, Surr. I didn'a ken it was you.' I had ridden both ways pretty fast for though it seemed unlikely any enemy would have filtered back between our village and BHQ, there was nothing to have stopped this happening and I had hoped that a fast moving target would be harder for a wayside sniper to hit; in consequence I felt pretty cold.

Knowing that some of our troops were in the next village to the south gave us a greater feeling of security during the night, but I thought it wise not to relax our continual listening for anything coming into the village during our stay, particularly from the west where we had no idea of what was going on. I selected a room on the first floor of a house overlooking the crossroads and from time to time rested on a bed in full equipment, having pulled it beside an open window. From there I could check the sounds of the night for myself as an insurance against any of the Jocks on stag dozing off. Each night, according to the circumstances and state of emergency one had to try to draw a balance on how much sleep one dared to take for immediate security and how much sleep one dared to miss against the unknown demands on alertness and energy in the near future. One never could tell whether the next night or next several nights would bring circumstances which would rule out all possibility of rest.

Fortunately, no trouble at all cropped up during the night and shortly after first light our first sound of an engine since the armoured cars had departed materialised in the form of a Jeep coming from Schneverdingen with Frank Coutts at the wheel. Behind him were two TCVs, so, guessing the mission, I shouted down the street: 'prepare to move'.

'Morning Pete, we're off again.' The trucks turned and we piled in as we ate our breakfast. I would be quite sorry to leave our little village, I reflected. The isolation of it, as though cut off from the rest of the war, and our odd, unexpected visitors who had suddenly appeared from all points of the compass each with his own problem, the rural peace and the tension of the explosive possibilities had all given our stay a peculiar fascination. We also had fed very well!

TARGET SWITCHED

The two TCVS formed up behind Frank's jeep. At the rear Pte Lee lolled back in state with a few of his friends in the white-painted Volkswagen and off we went. We were just in time to join the Battalion column as it started to move. We were astonished to note that the convoy was pointing back along the road to the south, up which we had so recently advanced. 'What's up?' we asked each other.

Gradually the plan became apparent to us. We were having our target switched from Hamburg to Bremen. Our Brigade, 155, which had been attached to the 7th Armoured Division, the Desert Rats, was to return to 156 and 157 Brigades of 52nd Division who with 3rd Division and other elements of XXX Corps under Lieutenant-General B.G. Horrocks were to take Bremen and its approaches. 3 Div were to attack towards the left or west bank of the River Weser where lay one-third of the city which the river bisected. We in 52 Division were to attack the larger part of the city on the right bank.

The ride back down the axis made a long, weary day's slog in a not too fast convoy. The party enjoying comfortable motoring in the white-painted Volkswagen began to have trouble with their gearbox after we had got about half way. Loud and ominous sounds accompanied any change of gear and were followed by over-heating. Evidently there was no oil in the gearbox and sadly the proud owner had to drive the thing into the ditch and leave it. We passed through Soltau and Walsrode, then turned west towards Verden. A slice of the country between the two last-named places bore evidence of heavy fighting.

Verden turned out to be a very pleasant, small, riverside town overlooking the flats towards Bremen, beyond which were the hills of Vegesack in the distance. Information was very chaotic. We motored to the railway bridge the Bremen side of Verden and there the convoy stopped. Whether it was pure rumour or accurate information I am not sure, but word got about that to the north of us there were some woods which we were to clear in preparation for the build up for the attack on Bremen. We jumped out of the trucks into the hot sun and then walked in file either side of the road in a long, straggling, somewhat 'shambolic' Battalion string, turning right off the main road to the north-east.

Once out of the trucks we were all immediately aware of the dismal, blood-chilling sounds of plentiful activity from 88mm shells landing in the near distance and the awful shriek of Moaning Minnie multiple mortars, followed by the inevitable concentrated shuddering of the carpet of explosion from each batch. The adrenaline this added to our walk slightly pepped the weariness out of it as we trudged on for about three-quarters of an hour. Immediately the horizon of our future dropped down to zero. Our hearts and minds ticked over more speedily as once again life was accepted on a minute-by-minute basis. If I had figured things out correctly we seemed to be approaching a village called Scharnhorst, to the east of Halsmuhlen where we had left the main road.

Information, apart from rumour and guesswork, was, as usual at this stage, almost completely nil; nor was this through any lack of effort on the part of those at our level to gather what was afoot. We all assumed that we were going straight into an attack of some sort in connection with a wood-clearing operation.

Finally our company reached its dispersal area where we found a lot of chaps of the 7th Cameronians crouching in slit trenches, peering into some trees over a railway track. Still no information. 'Here goes another stunt', I thought to myself. The Company was lined up in a long field and a general re-sorting took place with the arrival of some new chaps to bring my Platoon up to something nearer its full strength of thirty to thirty-two men. Among those returned to me were cheeful, ruddy-faced, red-haired McLaughlin back from the Divisional rest camp. He had once held two stripes, but now refused to accept any as did several other of my privates including McKenzie. L/Cpl Brown had often refused to be put up for a second. The reason was always the same. They feared taking responsibility for their friends' lives in action. Also, I think the fact had well sunk in that the casualty rate among leaders was far heavier than those of private soldiers. I was surprised to have Pte Cutter back again from hospital so quickly after the five rounds embedded in his back at Sudweyhe had been pulled out. He was still very shaken and I think ought not to have come back so soon, if at all.

Among changes to the NCOs I was given two capable old stagers, Sgt Cockburn as Platoon sergeant and Cpl Carbarns as a section commander.

I established Ptes Tarn and Learmonth in a tiny farmer's cottage, already bursting at the seams with the farmer and his family, to prepare a very fine meal for the platoon. While they were engaged on this Sgt Cockburn checked over the ammunition and other equipment to bring it up to scale while I tested out the Bren guns, firing bursts into the railway embankment. This seemed a necessary precaution prior to any action for twice previously we had been let down by Brens firing only a single shot when they were badly needed. As usual, at the sign of imminent action various Jocks came to me to report the loss of kit, a broken extractor spring on a rifle, a sore leg, or other subtleties which came to the immediate forefront after having been concealed since the last action.

Just then a sudden reversal of orders came through. It appeared that we were no longer to be put into the woods to make a clearing attack, but to pull back to Halsmuhlen, near Verden, we suspected for another immediate attack on the approaches to Bremen. The only definite news we had had so far at our level in the Platoon was that the Hun was putting up some very stubborn resistance. This our ears could confirm as well as our eyes as we looked out over the river towards Bremen.

It was the evening of 19 April 1945. There were rumours that the delay was due to the fact that the armour, which had been switched from the drive north to the westerly one, was still some distance away from where it was wanted. We also gathered that the 51st Div and the 3rd were having a tricky time in the

Delmenhorst and Brinkum area as they got into position for the Bremen attack.

This news roused me from my comfortable, after-lunch siesta against the tracks of the Bren-carrier which rocked gently to the activities of Brown 'S', the driver. He was ferreting around it getting things shipshape to cope with the heavy demands likely to be made on it in the near future.

We marched back to a concentration area near BHQ where we found the TCVs waiting for us in a farmyard. The sun was out and with it a gentle drizzle settled to steam on our clothing as we climbed aboard. If we had been ancient Greeks I wondered whether some omen might have been construed from this. To me it seemed to suggest that though perhaps further misery was in store for us, this would at the same time be mitigated and made bearable by the sunshine of our growing understanding that the end could not be far off now. We did not know enough of the overall picture to hazard a guess of much accuracy, but it seemed to me from what we had observed and from the snatches of news we had so far heard, that only one or two major clashes could take place with the Ruhr out of action. Reserves of equipment and fuel would perhaps be too low in the diminishing territory still held by the enemy to do more than that. The unknown factor to my mind seemed whether after this stage, depending on how many fanatics there were left or the coherence of leadership and communications which would influence whether a ceasefire could be called, the mopping up of die-hards in difficult territory of mountains and forests might go on for a long time. My speculation could make no progress beyond the realisation that at least the winter was over and whatever struggles were left would surely be over before the summer was through.

Though the news did not seep down to us for some little while, the Americans were even then almost in contact with the Russians, and actually made contact on the morrow, 20 April, at Torgau, east of Leipzig.

As we again reached Halsmuhlen and turned towards the northern outskirts of Verden to de-bus, a few of the guns of 3 Div and 51 Div could be heard irregularly retaliating to the fire of the 88mm German guns and Moaning Minnies. We were pleased to realise that billeting was in operation. We were not in for an immediate attack after all. The Company sorted themselves out into a line of fourteen pleasant suburban houses on one side of the road and overlooking the river, giving us a distant view of Bremen. I was very interested to realise from the map that only 2½ miles or so over the river were the villages of Blender Varste, Einste and Hustedt which had held our attention only a shade over a week before. The shortness of time that had elapsed compared with the enormous amount that had happened to us since then seemed to me staggering. I never expect to have so packed a 7–10 days again.

Just over the road from us, some line of communication types were installed in tents hidden among the foliage of bushes and trees up a bank. I wondered what their job was. Once the Jocks were installed in their billets, two orders came: one that minimum stags were to be maintained to give the Jocks a good rest. This was welcome news. The second order was for Platoon commanders to report to Company HQ to draw pay for issue to the Jocks. Why this particular moment should have been chosen was interesting to speculate. Had the powers that be decided the war would so soon be over that the issue of the small, new, brightly coloured, green-blue mark notes would be used for shopping sprees by the Jocks in Bremen! The Jock would in that case have to be weaned from his present methods, whereby if he wanted anything, he just took it.

I had gone up in to the roof of my Platoon HQ billet to gaze with interest out over the low-lying flat fields either side of the river to get my first proper, though distant look at Bremen. The sun was getting low to the left of Bremen and tinting the mist forming as the air cooled along the line of river. The guns and Moaning Minnies were still at it and from time to time the sequin sparkle of their explosions and puffs of smoke showed where the missiles were landing in the distance, towards 3 Div positions over the river. Anything the enemy had so far sent in our direction had fallen quite a way short of us on other targets, though the 88mm guns had plenty of range to reach us if they desired.

Up in the roof I found all the bedding which the housewife had hidden some time prior to our arrival. I took enough of this downstairs to promise a night of reasonable comfort, among it a large, pink pillow of wonderful softness which I later added to my bedroll.

As so often, the Jocks had ransacked the houses in no time in their search for hidden treasure and had not bothered even to make a tidy job of it, leaving the contents of the drawers just scattered about on the floor. This was particularly difficult to stop. The downstairs part was in a bit of a mess anyway because of a few tank shells which had smashed the front, together with machine gun bullets, a few of which had ripped up the walls and gashed the furniture.

The Hausfrau, who had at first stoutly denied that there was any bedding in the house, could think of nothing really adequate to say when the Jocks made free use of the store of mattresses and so on, which I had located. I could well understand her reluctance to let the Jocks use it with their rough appearance, clothes and equipment, but the Jocks had had to put up with far more inconvenience from her countrymen. In the cellar another store of stuff was located. A photo of the lady's husband hung over a clock in the sitting room. It almost appeared that he was there, witnessing the occupation of his home. It was fortunate, perhaps, that he wasn't for he was a particularly nasty-looking piece of work in a Wehrmacht officer's rig-out.

At nightfall I visited Company HQ billet up a steep flight of stairs for a chat, tea and a warm up in front of the fire before turning in. It was our first 'stand down' sleep for a while. Much was to happen to us before we got another. I lay revelling in the relaxation of my mattress and particularly the soft pillow which was quite a contrast to the inside of the tin hat or my small pack which usually formed my nightly headrest. To sleep with one's boots off and with toes free to wiggle was an almost forgotten delight. The Jocks were sprawled thickly about me on the floor of the dining room, resting on and draped over with whatever they had managed to scrounge, from curtains to carpets. Some fresh, cool night air fanned my face as it eddied through a shellhole in the wall near my head, to some extent thinning the smell of sweat, boots and Jocks which otherwise filled the air. Fortunately, we were to have another bath in the morning.

Next morning a line of TCVs drew up, accompanied by cries of 'bath parade!' and we climbed aboard, armed with soap and towels. Our journey took us over the River Aller by way of a Bailey bridge which had been set up next to the destroyed road bridge and beside which there was a factory. Here a mobile bath unit had installed itself, evidently making use of the factory boiler for the heating of the water. The 'bath' itself assumed the usual ritual. There were a series of taps set in the ceiling of a large, hangar-like room, each dripping tepid water. We stripped our clothes off and formed up into shivering queues of nakedness as we edged our way slowly forward until wetted by the tap. This gave one the opportunity to apply a bit of soap. Under each tap the queues formed into circles slowly revolving to keep each of us wetted enough in turn. The slippery concrete floor felt very cold underfoot and few of us could have completed more than five or six 'revs' in the circle before it was necessary to fall out and rub oneself dry to generate some warmth. Then we edged forward in another queue to collect a change of underclothes. I felt very thankful we had not been subjected to this particular bath unit during the winter.

On my return to the TCV I found Taffy proudly installed with a big tin bath full of sugar which he had 'liberated' from somewhere and which would sweeten our tea for some time to come. We later found that nearly all the houses had tucked away somewhere what in England would had been regarded as perhaps several years' sugar rations. Perhaps there was a sugarbeet factory somewhere in the town from which the workers pilfered the sugar.

Preparations were well in hand for a tremendous lunch in my Platoon HQ billet when we got back and nothing could have been more welcome just then, short of the news that the war was over. The large dining room table was laid with a snowy tablecloth on which cutlery sparkled and plates gleamed. All the preparations had gone forward and accoutrements had been discovered and set out by the cooks under the scandalised eyes of the Hausfrau, who had only been tamed enough to prevent an explosion by being told that if she did not fall into line and enter into the spirit of the festive occasion she would have to quit the house forthwith. All of Platoon HQ sat down to enjoy the meal at the table. How they enjoyed it, quite apart from the food. Each Jock took up his table napkin (for some I think it was the first experience of such luxury and they seemed undecided on its correct use. Some tucked them in at the neck, others put them on their laps after looking to me for a clue). Each Jock poured himself out some water and set his glass down after a drink which was more a gesture towards the use of this novel equipment than a necessity. The array of 'eating irons' set at each place provided a lot of banter and amusement as the cooks arrived with steaming serving dishes which they set down to the proclamation: 'Choose your weapons!'

The only thing that marred the perfect enjoyment of the moment was the realisation of the likely immediate future, which was constantly being brought to our attention by the sight and noise of massing tanks and troops which we could see moving up on the road a few yards outside the shattered windows of the room in which we sat. To the passers-by we must have presented a scene of equal interest in its prim oddity.

RINGSIDE SEAT ON AN 800-BOMBER RAID

Remote glimpses of the plan for the attack on Bremen began to filter down to us. Various divisions were, if our information was correct, converging from all sides except the north and north-west. Delmenhorst, over the River Weser, was occupied by 3 Div, while 51st Div was also the other side of the river, but closer to us in Verden. Smyg had been called away to a Company Commander 'O' Group at Battalion HQ where he had already been a couple of hours. Also, we were aware of our guns firing to register on various targets on the approaches to Bremen as though they were tuning up in preparation for an imminent concert. Our mounting tension gave a restlessness to the waiting as we intently took note of each of the familiar signs of the gathering storm being moved into position. The weight of our armour and Crocodile flame-throwers suggested a sizeable clash but also gave us some measure of comfort. Before Bremen itself could be attacked, we would have to secure the string of suburbs between us and the final objective. Smyg suddenly re-appeared together with a call for 'O' group, which was held in Company HQ billet. It was nearly mid-morning on 21 April and I was glad we had got our lunch over free of interruption. 'Prepare to move.' We were to embus almost immediately and move down to the village of Langwedel near Etelsenn on the approaches to Bremen for the build up to the attack. An ultimatum had been fired and radioed into the city and what happened next would be dependent on the reply. We learned also that in case the ultimatum was rejected by the Germans (which it was), 'Bomber Harris' had an 800-bomber raid on the way, for which we would have a ringside seat.

Our journey was not a long one and our part of the convoy pulled up on a muddy, wet, traffic-churned road beside a T junction and a small wood in the village. Not knowing how long we might be in this location but long since having learnt our lesson, we based our plans on a long stop and getting settled in the maximum comfort possible. We piled off to explore the possibilities of the place and at the same moment became aware of the far closer explosions of 88s down the road towards Bremen. (We heard later that Brigade had meant to stop us farther to the rear as they reckoned the place 'unhealthy' as a concentration area, but the DR they had sent to stop us had not made contact with the 2i/c in time.)

I found a small hut in which to brew up tea and some more food. We could never tell when the next meal might be once action started. We had to use a sand and petrol fire and I hoped that the flames and smoke which issued from the hut in consequence did not attract the attention of the enemy gunners. Over the road was quite a comfortable loft in a small house to which I staked claim as a place for my Platoon to sleep should we stop in the village till nightfall. It was getting miserably wet and cold outside and a prospect of an unnecessary night in the open prior to any attack did not appeal to any of us at all. The village was jammed tight with troops, as so often in a concentration area before an attack, and this time our axis of advance for so large an objective was a very narrow one. The river cut down movement to the left where it squiggled parallel to the axis and at a distance ranging from a couple of hundred yards to a couple of miles. Hemmed in to the right at a much shorter distance was the railway track to Bremen, between a quarter and a half a mile away.

We were all beginning to notice the cold more, a sure sign of our tense state which was added to by lack of definite news. Were we to attack within the hour, at last light, overnight or at dawn? To have been able to fix one's mind on a definite time would have helped settle us. In any event we were grateful to throw off the load of wet equipment that after a few hours dragged, cutting with pain on the shoulders.

At 1415 hours the CO was called to Brigade. 'This is it!' we thought, with the usual butterflies in the tummy. At 1600 hours he gave out his order to Company Commanders, who shortly after passed them on to us, to be passed on in our turn in a section commanders', 'O' Group and to the men. The Germans had rejected the ultimatum, as we were sure they would, despite any wishes the poor civilians might have had to the contrary. Our initial objective was to be the small town of Uphusen, a suburb between ourselves and Bremen, the later objective. 'H' hour would be some time after midnight. The Jocks were to settle in and get what rest they could at short notice as from 2330 hours. Knowing the ultimatum had been rejected, we also knew that the 800 bombers might materialise at any time.

The light was already beginning to fail shortly before 1930 hours when our ears became conscious of a new sound above and beyond the splash and clatter of wheeled and tracked vehicles on the wet roads and the intermittent crump of spasmodic shelling by both sides. A distant, deep vibration almost like continuous thunder coming and going in waves of booming sound was gradually filling the heavens.

Visibility had cleared and as we swung our eyes back and forth overhead, we gradually became aware of a large, gnat-like cloud of small, thin shapes over the target and spreading over more of the sky in a dark, all-over pattern. They seemed, at a guess, to be above 8,000 feet. Very little flak was going up to meet them so far, just a few streams of tracer with twinkling sequins at their summit and some black and grey puffs of smoke.

An abrupt and terrifying wall of billowing black erupted and continued to spatter and spread over the south and south-east of the city as far as we could see from our point of vantage. Jocks and other troops were crowding out into the roads to watch and among them were one or two pale-faced civilians, no doubt with friends and relatives under the tons of explosives raining down from the skies. Bremen lay about 11 or 12 miles off and it was difficult to make out the buildings because the suburbs lay between. Seconds passed and still there was no sound other than the overwhelming vibration of the 3,200 aircraft engines saturating our senses and the excited cries of the Jocks at the spectacle. Suddenly the sound of the explosions reached us in an apparent pressure wave of crump-crump-crumping rumblings which swept round us like a rising tide. However one might have felt about the enemy, having seen blitzed cities in Britain, it was impossible not to feel pity for those being subjected to such a massively appalling spectacle, especially the children, women and animals who might be in the ruins, cellars and bunkers and who had no say in the matter of a surrender. The London blitzes I had been through bore no comparison in terms of the size of target and concentration of planes, yet they had seemed quite bad enough.

The planes were now overhead, coming from the direction of Bremen and turning in staggered formation to the south, as thick as migrating birds with ever more to take their places to keep the black, awful eruption of smoke, flame and thunder on the boil.

Very little flak had met the first wave, but now, beneath an enormous, dark, storm cloud of smoke and rubble-dust which towered into the sky, spreading widely over the countryside towards Delmenhorst, more flak of a white flash and puff variety started to pour up fast, showing up the more in contrast to the gloomy pall of the ever-spreading background. Here and there the smoke was rose tinted showing where fires were starting below. Most of the flak seemed to be 20mm and I wondered if this was because the Germans had been caught on the hop with their 88mm guns which they had been using so heavily in a ground role.

Another wave or two with about 100 planes or more each passed over and even this light flak died down, leaving the remainder of the raid to more or less stoke the wreckage at their leisure. One or two planes continued to wheel above the target after the last bombs had dropped rather like vultures over a carcass, possibly checking the damage. As they too droned off out of earshot, the artillery, hitherto just ticking over, took up the work left by the planes. As far as one could tell at their height, most of the planes in this raid had been Lancasters. Apparently none of our aircraft had been lost.

There was a strong rumour, which seemed to be backed up by those 'in the know', that before we went into attack another 1,000 planes would be available to give close support, and to soften up strong points of resistance. For some reason, probably the weather as at Flushing, this second raid never materialised. It was getting dark now and turning bitterly cold so we trooped back to stoke up our fire and brew more tea. We had less apprehension that the enemy would notice any glow from our little fire against the blaze the bombers had touched off in Bremen lighting the black, smoke-streaked sky with an angry red glow. It was difficult to keep from thinking about the human misery and loss and the desperate scenes this artificial sunset would go on lighting up throughout the rest of the night.

As night fell, the last artillery spotter plane, which had been directing the guns onto targets being softened for the coming attack, came flying back very low. It was drizzling and the small plane skimming over the treetops and fields seemed almost like a seagull gliding over green waves into a haze of mist in the darkening distance.

Now that it seemed reasonably certain that we would spend at least part of the night in the present location, I took a look round to see if the Jocks' billets might be bettered. However, all the houses off the main road were packed with chaps waiting for the attack. Many were members of tank crews and their massive vehicles were parked against the properties. In the roof of our farm I found a bottle of cherry brandy and having no use for it myself I gave it to Frank and Smyg. It was noticeable that everyone was a bit on edge as we all guessed that following the bombing it would not be long before things started to move. As so often, it appeared that the commencement would come at some unearthly hour of the night. Once the advance started it was more than likely that to keep up constant pressure on the enemy, we would be on the go night and day into the near future, perhaps for another ten days' battering. How unnecessary it all seemed when the outcome, perhaps only a few weeks, days or even hours away, was so obvious.

UP TO THE START LINE

(DETAILS OF THE ATTACK TAKEN FROM NOTES IN MY ORDERS BOOK AT TIME)

Frank Coutts and I took a short walk up and down the road in the hope of finding Bill Halliburton to get a bit of news out of him as he was the Battalion Intelligence Officer, but with no luck. At about 2130 hours a Company 'O' Group was held in the small, smoke-fumed room occupied by Frank and Smyg.

'Well, the show's on', said Smyg. 'The plan is to get the Battalion into this small town of Uphusen before first light and clear any pockets of resistance in the morning when we can see what we are doing. It is to be a two phase attack. First', continued Smyg, tapping his map with a large bony finger, 'A and C Companies are to move forward to an anti-aircraft site on the left here where one German wheeled gun was reported to have moved in earlier. C Company are to penetrate past some woods and huts north of the road. Their start line for the attack will be this road and track junction: 862919–858915.

'The second phase: as soon as C Company has the wood, we in B Company must move in. D are to move up on the left of the road while waiting for C to reach their objective, then pass through. Opposition so far has been mainly from self-propelled guns, but has only resulted in one casualty to two Battalions, against which 300 prisoners have been taken. A report reached Brigade that a Jerry officer is waiting to surrender Uphusen, but don't take this too seriously, it may not be a genuine report.

'In support we will have the 3-inch mortars with A Company medium machine guns, six Crocodile flame-throwers of the RAC. One troop of tanks of the Royal Scots Greys under command of our A/tk, to follow us up later. The Regimental aid post and Battalion HQ will be at Bierden, then at C Company position.

Zero hour will be at 0400 hours tomorrow morning. The artillery will fire H-15 to H, preliminary, H to H plus ten for A Company. This will consist of three field regiments, one medium and two batteries of heavy artillery. The forward observation officers will be with C and A Companies.

'The order of march in our company on de-bussing will be 12 Platoon, Tactical Company HQ, 11 Platoon, Company HQ, and 10 Platoon. Keep well dispersed. The "form" on the enemy's whereabouts is not too clear. Once C Company are cleared we may be able to penetrate up the main axis to the crossroads. If so, D Company will move at the same time on the left of the road. Keep your yellow smoke handy in case the guns, tanks or flame-throwers take you for the enemy, particularly if penetration is faster than it is expected.

'Tea will be brought forward at 0125 hours by 15cwt. All greatcoats are to be piled in Platoon bundles outside Company HQ. Each of you detail two of your Platoon to collect any prisoners who are taken forward until the objective is reached, then to Company HQ in an emergency you can call our SOS artillery task onto your own positions: Code word 'LUKE'.

'Let your chaps get what rest they can until 0100 hours. Check your TCV drivers are in the picture and that you know where they are to be found. At 0145 we will board the TCVs and move forwards to this crossroads here having picked up 6th HLI guides at map reference 885907. The 7th/9th Royal Scots, by the way, are at Verden, and the 6th HLI at Achim.

'The intention is that the other Battalions and Brigades of the Division will move forward along the divisional axis in a series of leapfrog attacks, keeping up constant pressure on the enemy. Each in turn will move up, attack, consolidate, then act as a firm base or springboard for the next chain of the leapfrog.' It was, it appeared, our turn to attack next.

'There are no more details now', continued Smyg, 'but I think we will have some good support when the time comes. Any questions? Right. Get back. Tell your section commanders. Put the Jocks in the picture and get some rest while you can. No one knows when we will get another chance.'

The likely future we could now fill in for ourselves by drawing on past experience: a shambles of an approach march in the dark; unexplained halts and waiting, getting wetter, colder and hungrier by the hour while under a turmoil of mental adjustment; the whole ordeal of the night being a conditioning prelude to the dawn attack over countryside we had not seen and into a town we could only guess at from the map. The Company Commanders had been slightly more fortunate in having had a glimpse of an aerial photo of the terrain to be covered on the morrow.

It was a change to have a Platoon not only up to strength at last, but well over it. They crowded round the light of my shaded torch in the attic to catch a glimpse of a map spread on the floor. I set out to pass on the information just given me and was thankful of the opportunity to impress on my memory this and the lie of the land in the map. As I talked I looked in turn at the faces lit by the lamp which threw a large dark pattern of moving shadows on the rafters and tiles of the roof. Each face carried so very much more than a chap one might have met in a street in peacetime. Each seemed older than its years with various hints in expression, line haggardness or nervousness or blankness telling of past ordeal and battles with self, won, drawn or in the process, as with Ptes Cutter and Smith, of being lost. The mental strain even at this early stage was visibly apparent and I decided to give these two the task of looking after any prisoners we might collect, to keep them occupied but not in the forefront of the attack.

The Platoon consisted of Sgt Cockburn, Cpl Carbarns, Cpl Dare, Cpl Jones, Cpl Gull (buckshee to strength and in place of a L/Cpl), Huntingford or Taffy, my batman and runner, L/Cpl Brown, L/Cpl McMichael (back from hospital) and Ptes. Learmonth, Tarn, McLaughlin, Cutter (radio operator, but I resolved to take him off it for this attack), Stein, McKenzie, O'Connor, O'Brien (both these latter still very shaken mentally from previous experiences), Denham, Blackwood (also back from hospital after his hit in the knee), Coupe, Minnet, Thompson, Newport, Bounds, Craze, Ross, Edge, Retcher, Lee (his hair streaked with the grey that had appeared there over the last couple of months), Hill, Blackshaw, Hignell, Fowles, Cupit, Harris, Tunstall, McOllom, Jubb, Egan, Didymus, Castle, Walton, Bolton,

Jenkins, Booth, Smith, and Griffiths (a very small chap with rather a hunched back, aged about eighteen or nineteen).

I was rather surprised to realise that by far the larger number of these chaps appeared to have very much the same quiet, reserved, serious approach to life, really almost timid except when worked up and then their performance could be surprising. On the whole they were quite alien to the nature of the work the Army was calling on them to do, but perhaps this sort of work was really alien to all of us. Only about three were over the age of twenty-five and most were about twenty.

Outside in the blackness and drizzle, spasmodic artillery fire thudded sullenly at various distances. In the road below a steady flow of tracked and wheeled vehicles splashed or shuddered past heavily, vibrating the building as a reminder of the build up and constant pressure being maintained on the enemy who were a few miles farther along the road. Most of the vehicles carried ammunition for the guns and mortars, or petrol and rations.

We had an hour and a half in which to rest. The chaps more or less subsided where they stood, to lie littering the floor of the barn attic so that they looked, in the beam of my torch, like bundles of sacking scattered about a warehouse. I found a wrecked settee which no one else had noticed and settled to rest on this with my small pack as a pillow, struggling to keep awake while the luminous hands of my watch all too quicky ate up the 90 minutes relative peace and comfort. A few Jocks were snoring. Once one cried out uneasily in his sleep. Rain was beating in waves on the roof and musically riveting along the gutter where it gurgled on the downpipe. I dropped off in to a doze for a short while, to awake with a start to some sound from a Jock coming in off stag. For a moment I lay perplexed, having forgotten my context in this queer life. Then I remembered reluctantly and with a jolt looked at my watch again. The moment had come to shake the shivering, cursing heaps of Jock into activity.

'Prepare to move! Wakey-wakey, come on get cracking.' Pte Tarn was informing McKenzie as they searched for their kit in the shambles on the floor: 'I tell ye, I'm noo takin' onny b*** unnecessary risks the morn's. The f*** war must be *** well nearly feenished the noo. I'm all for a quiet life, me; aye b*** the war!' A solid volley of obscenity broke out then because a torch wouldn't work. Next, McKenzie's voice: 'B*** it! It's *** well still raining.' 'Aye, an' if you'll listen it's noo f*** well all water coming down either! Those b*** 88s are still at it, *** it! . . . Whose took me *** small pack?'

Most Jocks could, in an almost uncanny manner, construct a sentence of abundantly clear meaning, which was built up almost entirely of the most outrageous swear words and filth imaginable; and so, most of what they said or shouted as they got ready for the road, defied recording. One got heartily sick of listening to this sort of conversation day after day.

Outside, the cry 'Tea truck's arrived' helped speed the Jocks downstairs and at last everyone had been pushed and chivvied clear of the attic, which I searched to make sure that no Jocks or equipment had been overlooked.

The section commanders had lined their men up against the TCVs in the road, and while they gulped their tea into which the rain was pattering, they checked once again over what each Jock was supposed to be carrying, particularly the weapons and ammunition, and inspected the barrels. With some Jocks, on a wet day a rifle barrel with a piece of paper screwed in the end provided a waterproof cigarette storage chamber, and it would not do in contact with the enemy to fire a volley which would shatter all the rifle barrels and scatter our frontage with shredded tobacco. The company already boasted one chap who, though he had not the neck to put a wound stripe up, had been wounded by an exploding tin of steak and kidney pudding he had been heating without a hole pierced in it.

The Company Jeep and carrier were ahead of the TCVs with the two 15-cwts behind in the convoy. At 0145 we were embussed and at 0200 hours the convoy together with those of the other companies started to move slowly forwards, nose-to-tail, with no lights. It was very cold and the drizzle was steadily increasing. The distance we were to cover was not great, about 7 miles, but going so slowly made the journey appear to be quite a long one. The revving engine in low gear and the rain beating on the windscreen in the blackness ahead helped to give this illusion. However, we were none of us keen that the journey should end too soon. It was an awful night for even a duck to be out.

Eventually, I judged we should be nearing the map reference at which the HLI guides should be waiting for us. Would they remember to be there? If not we would trundle on until we suddenly ran into the enemy a couple of miles down the road. Just short of a crossroads, we picked up the drenched guides in Usen village. We jumped stiffly into the muddy border of the road in the pelting rain. A dark arch of dripping elm trees overhung the road, with the houses of the village dark shapes beyond them.

We lined up and moved slowly forward in single file for nearly 2 miles, up to and through Achim, a small town about 8 miles short of the rim of Bremen and which the 6th HLI had taken a few hours before. We turned left in the town, our boots ringing, squelching and splashing amid cobbles, mud and puddles as we progressed. A few hundred yards down the side road, our guide realised he had led us wrongly and we retraced our steps in a long miserable Crocodile.

The rain had increased to an absolute downpour and we could not imagine ourselves more wet and miserable. It was pitch-black but for the flash of gunfire and an occasional spurt of flame from an exploding shell in the near distance. A flare or two glared at times and a lessening, inflamed redness stained the western horizon as the rain fought the fires following the raid on Bremen. At least the torrential rain was serving some purpose.

Again we turned left, this time onto a cinder track leading due west out of the town towards Bierden village. The next move? Somewhere in the miserable wet darkness, we were to find ourselves some form of shelter for the remainder of the night, or until such time as we should be called upon to attack. It was all unfolding as one might have expected it would. The volume of dejected grumbling and subdued swearing which had been issuing from the dark column of Jocks ever since we have set off was steadily increasing as the rain soaked through and through us, to run in rivulets down our necks and into our boots. With this wetness and the approach of the not too distant dawn we found the cold steadily more noticeable.

We were not slow to perceive that our gunflashes were now

flickering and flashing like sheet lightning some way behind us, followed at an interval by the moan and scream of the shells lobbing overhead. It seemed they were registering a few salvos onto likely targets in the coming attack. To reach my GS pocket watch and see what time it was seemed in the circumstances too much effort, but I guessed it could not be long before the pre-H hour barrage would suddenly light and sear the sky.

In spite of the persistent unpleasantness of the rain I am sure all our thoughts were more and more concentrated on the likely hell which we were powerless to prevent drawing nearer with each passing minute, as inexorable as the earth's rotation and dawn's approach. This was well summed up in remarks I had overheard earlier: 'Ah ken fine the noo Alick, what a condemned buddy has t'go through in his b*** heed on his last nicht!' 'Aye, and he onny has t'poot up wi' it the yince.'

It was getting on for four in the morning when we located and broke into a couple of farms, nearly frightening the occupants out of their wits. It appeared that we were the first British troops they had seen and even in peacetime, four in the morning is a bad time to pay a visit. 0400 hours was also the hour A Company was scheduled to cross the start line to commence our phase of the attack, to be followed 15 minutes later by C Company. No one had seen the ground over which the attack was to take place, though the Company Commanders had seen an air photograph.

The fiercely barking watchdog – one which ran along beneath a cable, tethered by a ring, making rather the sound of a trolley-bus as it approached scraping the wire – had to be silenced. To shoot it would mean the sound of a shot, and we had no idea where the nearest enemy were. I did not relish knifing it in cold blood. In fact, I don't think I could have done so. A pretty effective compromise was provided by the cord of a rifle wound and knotted round its muzzle. It was wild at not having buried its teeth into me, but now could only make fierce rumblings and whinings and had to curtail its activities through lack of breath.

We made our way through the cowstalls where the cattle clanked and breathed with restlessness at the sudden disturbance, and left the sweet-smelling warmth of this part of the building to enter the house. The commotion had the frenzied farming folk out of their rooms and onto the stairs in no time, from which point of vantage they blinked back at us like a row of wide-eyed owls clutching varied, and in one case inadequate, male and female night attire to themselves. Their fear and the evident awful dilemma of their position was painful to behold. The subtleties of it, however, were entirely wasted on the cold, dripping and swearing mass of steaming Jocks. Those not delegated to stag made their way straight up past the nearly unnerved family and sobbing womenfolk still standing at the head of the stairs, and piled seven or eight to a bed into the still warm nests, equipment, muddy boots and the lot, determined to make the most of what warmth and peace the night might still yield before the promised hell started at dawn.

I can only think – to my amazement and shame now, looking back – that I must have been in a mood not far removed from that of the Jocks, for I curled up on a sofa in the drawing room and covered myself with a carpet for warmth and to this day have no idea how the family spent the rest of the night robbed of their beds and unable to reach their clothes to dress. Perhaps they stoked up the fire in the kitchen for warmth and all sat there until the morning. They may even have had to settle down in the straw, pressed against the cattle to keep warm.

What peace there was was short lived. At 0345 hours the awful racket of the pre-H hour barrage butterflied our tummies with its implications and shuddered the windows in their frames, thereby, I should think, completing the misery of the German farm folk. At least they did not have to partake of our future and a few sheets and things could always be washed clean.

UPHUSEN: AN ATTACK
WITH FLAME-THROWERS

Fighting my desire to sleep as I lay on the sofa, I gazed at the map to memorise the town of Uphusen and its approaches well enough to transfer an enlarged copy of it into my note book. This done, I felt a little more at ease that the country over which we would have to attack would not be quite unknown to me when the time came. The luminous hand of my watch had crept past 4.20 am and I listened intently, wondering how the first two attacking coys were getting on. The sounds outside assumed added significance.

The sky was beginning to pale and the air blowing through a shattered window smelled crisp, clean and rain-washed after the storm. My mind felt too active and on edge to rest, tired though I was. The heavy wetness of my clothes chilled all comfort the well-furnished room might otherwise have seemed to offer.

I rose and resolved to find my way to the attic to puzzle out any snags in the lower-lying land towards Uphusen which we would soon have to penetrate. It was still too dark, however, to make out any detail of value so I climbed down and checked over the chaps on stag before returning to the drawing room. There I settled down next to the 18 set radio, beside which were Smyg, Frank Coutts, and the radio operator littered about with a shower of maps. We recognised the voice of C Company's signaller coming back from the attack, reporting to Battalion HQ; it appeared that they were a bit off course, too far to the left of the axis, but it was not yet clear whether this was due to enemy resistance or the darkness. For a while the voice faded out altogether.

As the minutes passed and we continued to listen for the Scots 'patter' amid the crackle and whistle of the set it gradually became clear that C Company had run into heavy sniping, sustaining several casualties. They appeared to be in part outflanked by an enemy attempt to surround them and repulsed repeated attempts by the Germans to blast them out of some shacks and houses, a few *panzerfausts* being fired from a mere 10 yards range. The radio was only kept in action through the hail of metal by the signaller ripping up the floorboards of the room he was in and lowering the set into the shelter of the hole. It was rapidly becoming obvious that the plan of attack would have to be modified. The CO had hoped to have phase II in operation before first light.

'Get your chaps organised, we'll be off soon' grunted Smyg as he crouched over his set. Giving word to Sgt. Cockburn to rouse the platoon, I climbed quickly up into the room again to look out in the stronger light. Banging the butt of my rifle through a tile for a better view revealed a landscape of heathland, stunted pine and heather through which ran ribbed sand hills building up in size on the right where the light-coloured sand contrasted strongly with the dark, tattered cloak of pine and heather attempting to clothe it.

Directly in front and below me at a distance of 150 yards I noticed an entrance to a German bunker, and at the same moment realised with a start what had drawn my eye to it. As I looked, the grey-green shapes of seven German soldiers clambered out into view and stealthily made their way over the sand to the right before vanishing over the brow of a small hill.

While the figures moved across the sand, each an ideal target jerkily passing unharmed along the sight of my rifle, I debated swiftly with myself whether to fire or not. I could certainly get a least three, possibly four of them before they got to cover, but restrained myself with the realisation that they obviously did not know that we were there. Our attack was to begin any minute and to fire would give our presence and position away. Their strength was unknown but our main strength might yet have to rely on the element of surprise. I rushed downstairs and round through some bushes in front of the house to try to follow their movements. I did not see them again. Evidently they had been called to help stem our two companies' attack on the right, unless they were stragglers.

I reported this activity to Smyg, who in turn gave out the modified plan of attack in which D Company were to assault on the right following another barrage and supported by one troop of Greys and one troop of Crocodiles. They were to attack through A Company, while we in B were to pass C Company on the left, by-passing the strong opposition they had drawn to themselves, if possible. We could not go too far to the left because of the river.

'Right! Sgt Cowie,' said Smyg, 'You take your chaps out about 800 yards to the first crest and dig in there to cover our approach and form up for the attack.' Slowly the remaining two platoons and Company HQ snaked out, following along a track through the sand hills and pine clusters towards 12 Platoon. With the memory that enemy soldiers had suddenly materialised out of the ground in this area a few minutes before, we moved with extreme alertness, watching carefully ahead and outwards on either side, with one eye eternally on the next bit of cover.

Suddenly on our right, about 25 yards away, we saw in a clearing in the trees a group of German tracked vehicles painted in a yellowish and green camouflage. They were probably ammunition carriers. A swift look revealed no enemy. They seemed to be abandoned, possibly through lack of petrol, and were the first of this type that we had seen. We hurried on and reaching Sgt. Cowie and his men, who had dug themselves in at the base of a small house on a heather-crested hill, threw ourselves down looking forward and to the flanks, to await our supporting armour.

'Keep down!' yelled Sgt Cowie. 'There are some *** snipers ahead!' His warning was confirmed as a couple of shots whiplashed through the air and heather like exclamation marks at the end of his sentence and Jocks rolled and ducked hurriedly from their vantage points on the crest. There was no sense in providing the enemy with target practice until one had to. These snipers were apparently in another house some few hundred yards beyond. '"O" Group!' a voice called and, crouching, we scuttled towards the rear of the small house where I could see the 18 set aerial sticking up.

As the immediate plan for the attack was unfolded to us in Smyg's unexcited voice, we were greatly cheered by the sound and sight of four Sherman tanks and three Crocodile flame-throwers which clanked and roared into position, noisily labouring through the churned sand and heather. These massive, rumbling monsters grouped themselves comfortably into a heather-bedded hollow behind us to await their instructions.

As Smyg gave out his orders for an advance to the first crossroads in Uphusen in an L shaped flanking movement, a couple of C Company casualties were carried back on stretchers from where they had been tended in the small house.

Scurrying back to the Platoon I set about detailing jobs. The sun was attempting to break through to cheer the chaps up a bit after the contemplation of the grey, agonised faces of the bandage-swathed casualties who had just been carried to the rear.

'Cutter, you bring back any prisoners we get', I said, realising that his nerves were already in such shape that he was likely to take to his heels any minute and only held himself in check by a painful and visible effort.

'You take point section, Cpl Carbarns, Cpl Dare, left, Cpl Jones, right. Platoon HQ centre. Each section will work with a tank in loose formation. Your job is to guard its flanks 'specially when we get into the built-up area, to keep off any enemy from having a go at them with *panzerfausts*. Watch the flame-throwers. Look where they are likely to squirt. They can't see you as easily as you can see them. The tanks are going to have a go at eliminating the snipers before we go over the crest. Our objective is the first crossroads you reach in Uphusen. Dig in as soon as you get there in the positions.' I pointed them out by means of a sketch in the sand. 'Keep your yellow smoke handy in case the tanks get confused.'

The first Churchill Crocodile flame-thrower revved up in a belch of hot, smelly exhaust and lurched, clanking, slowly towards the crest, towing its ponderous, beetle-like trailer of flame-throwing liquid. We rolled ourselves out of the way of its tracks as it passed to pause in a hulldown position on the skyline while the tank commander took stock of the view ahead.

Suddenly a spurt of angry flame streaked its feathery, black-edged way towards the farm inhabited by the snipers as we watched carefully to note the result. The cascade of devouring fire jetting from the tank issued with a sinister, crackling, whining roar. The farm was much closer than we had at first judged and as we prepared to move, fixing our bayonets, the other tanks joined in with lengthy bursts from their Besa machine guns into the farm and other buildings away on the left.

The fountain of fire cascaded in a red, yellow and black shower over the farm and heather ahead of it as the lethal hail of bullets ripped in their share of destruction. In a matter of moments, it seemed, the house was reduced from a flaming, torch-like inferno to a glowing skeleton. While we watched fascinated and appalled by the hideous nature of this weapon, a couple of snipers who had been burned out of the house got up out of the heather, itself licking with flames. They made a dash to get clear, but were almost instantly wiped out in a sheet of flame and smoke. I think that mercifully the bullets accounted for them an instant before the flame. They bowled over like burning rabbits in a heath fire. There can be few things so horrible as to see men being cooked alive by this weapon. The bounding, heavy, burning fuel penetrates and seeks out its victims from holes and crannies which would provide safety from bullets and shrapnel. Once splashed, men became flaming torches.

We had been so conscious of the activities about us which absorbed the attention of our eyes, that it was only now that we tuned our ears to listen for enemy retaliation by mortars, rockets or gunfire, and so became aware of our own barrage. The shells were falling somewhere not very far ahead, but their exact target was hidden from us by sand hills. The hills also screened a lot of the noise but for the shrieking passing overhead.

Time was getting on. The barrage had started at 0950. It was now nearly ten. Three more tanks were revving over the crest overtaking the Crocodile flame-thrower, 17-pounder gunned Shermans and 6-pounder Churchills. We ducked involuntarily as they commenced firing their guns beside us, the acrid tang of the black smoke eddying back to us as we lay in the heather, tense, dry throated and hearts pounding, waiting for the order to advance. Every now and then a hurried movement in the heather indicated a Jock rolling clear of the tank tracks. One had to watch carefully behind in all the noise to be sure one was not going to be crushed by another unexpected tank, or be caught in a burst from the guns or flame.

At 1000 hours the first section of 11 Platoon began to advance, each Jock adopting the usual crouching, slinking movement one automatically assumed in attempting to present as small and inconspicuous a target as possible to the waiting enemy. Now it was our turn. Down the gradual slope the Company spread, fanning out untidily and jerkily each side of the slow-moving tanks. Each section taking its turn in moving forward 50 yards, then lying panting and sweating in the heather covering the others in tactical bounds from ridge to ditch to a bend in the track or any other cover.

I smiled to myself – the tank chaps were taking no chances at this stage in the war either! The incessant, rapid, lethal chatter of the tracered Besas swept like a stabbing red spray of sparks, ripping any likely enemy hideout ahead. It was comforting to feel that for every red flash of a tracer flickering in front of us there were three or four non-tracer bullets we could not see. This racket was punctuated at long intervals by the whiplash crack of the tanks' main armament at a house or suspect shape in a distant hedge in case the enemy had any armour in wait. Once again I was interested to note the varied assessment placed by the Jocks as to whether being near a tank in an attack was a liability in that it attracted fire, especially from 88s, or an asset in that it could screen one from some small-arms fire or shell and mortar fragments to some extent.

After we had covered about 800 yards, a new sound made its presence felt – the feathery whisper of some high-flying German long-range shells, perhaps from naval guns in Bremen or beyond, which sizzled to crump vibrating the earth heavily in the sand hills on the right. These hills rose to a ridge about 600 yards away, with gullies between. The soft sand absorbed the shock and what smoke and dust the explosions made was lost in air already thick with the bitter tang of burning farms, heather, dust, cordite and flame-throwing activity. As a result we were uneasily unaware of exactly where the shells were landing. Mercifully the Moaning

Minnie rocket launchers and 88s seemed, so far, fully engaged on other targets.

On the left the ground sloped away slightly from the rough track we were using as our axis of advance, down to some fields, a few groups of houses, a church on the distant left front, and the river which here curved away from us for about 2 miles towards the village of Bollen. Opposite this village, indicated by the church, and 3 or 4 miles over the river was the fatal spot, Sudweyhe, where our TCV had got its direct hit, I reflected.

The ground underfoot was giving way to scrubby undergrowth which was slowing the advance a bit and offered better concealment for any waiting enemy. A large spurt of fire and billow of oily black smoke drew attention to the flame-throwers burning down a couple more farms about 350 yards to the left. Within two or three minutes the tiles were caving in to a white-hot inferno and in about 6 minutes the buildings had vanished but for the chimney stacks and flaming rubble. I found it difficult to keep my mind off the memory of the sounds of burning cattle in the stalls in the first few seconds.

Since the activity of the ill-fated snipers at the start of the advance, the enemy opposition in small-arms fire seemed to have been completely overawed by the weight of destruction which spread ahead of us like a rising tide. Suddenly, even as I saw them, a Jock yelled. 'Jerries ahead! *** the b***.' Some grey-green-clad figures materialised, moving towards us through the tangle of the shrub. As our eyes focused on them we were not altogether surprised to see that they had their hands up and were waving white rags as they advanced.

In case this was a ruse of some sort, the Company took to the ground and trained their weapons on them to cover them in, looking all the while for signs of any other activity for which this may have been a cloak. They were moving towards us from some burning barns on the left, and as they got closer we could readily see they were in no fit condition for taking any more punishment. They were dog-tired, sallow with fatigue and ill feeding and fright; they were bloodshot in the eyes and smelled of singeing, fire and smoke. Their uniforms were scruffy for the most part, and torn. One hobbled in evident agony, pretty badly wounded, too weak to hold his hands up and seeming desperate to keep up with his compatriots who were all too callous or worn out to offer him any aid. Eventually they had to be ordered to help him, and shambled dejectedly to the rear, escorted at the not too steady point of Pte Cutter's bayonet. He was almost as frightened as they were, it seemed, and it struck me that it was perhaps fortunate that none of them seemed physically capable of any swift movement which would cause their escort to let fly with his rifle.

Moving more warily we made our way forward once again until we reached another track, turning sharply to the right towards the outskirt houses of Uphusen which we could see were only a few hundred yards away. By now, after more than 3,000 yards of tense, laborious advance everyone was beginning to feel the pace a bit. The lack of serious opposition had surprised us, thanks to the armoured support, and Smyg called a hurried 'O' Group. As we had got so far Smyg decided to exploit the situation and push on towards the main crossroads, part way to our original objective which had been shelved when C Company had run into trouble.

'Peter, you take 10 Platoon forward to conform to the order of march', said Smyg. 'If you make it to the crossroads, dig in.'

As we neared Uphusen we had to leave cover, such as the shrub offered us, and did so with reluctance for now, if at all, the enemy were likely to try a stand. The tanks and flame-throwers added comfort to our advance to some extent as they laboured, revving deep throatedly, sluggish lozenges of ponderosity among the sprinkled sections of the Jocks. They seemed to exude power in every possible way open to them, from the massive note of their engines to their kicking guns and jets of liquid fire, all in action together now for all they were worth. The very ground we were walking over blazed smokily and little puddles of liquid fire laced the earth so that we streamed with sweat in the tension and heat, while our feet told us our boots were getting uncomfortably hot.

Despite Uphusen being an enemy village I felt sick at heart to see house after house blaze up in flame and towering sparks and smoke as the jets of trickling fire ate into them. Some had women and children in them too, as we could soon tell from the screaming and shrieking misery, piercing in pitch above all the hell of other noises of war. I dashed my Platoon quickly over the road to commence working along a ditch towards these houses, but there was no cover there. I found myself disinclined to believe the madness about me one moment then almost nauseated the next to feel one had to have any part in it. Was it really necessary? Events alone would tell in the next minute or two.

In the absence of cover there was nothing for it but to take the Platoon on as fast as our tired, sweat-drenched limbs could carry us at the double another 300 yards towards the remains of one of the first smouldering houses by a road block. Still no small-arms fire had come back at us. This, I realised, was almost certainly thanks to the incessant covering fire, flame, MG and shells from the tanks, keeping any Jerry heads down.

We all crashed onto the ground at the end of our long sprint, gasping for breath and taking stock of the shambles about us, ready for the next dash forward when the tanks, whom we had now outdistanced, had caught up with us. Meanwhile, glancing behind I noticed Smyg, with the rest of the Company deployed about him in various vantage points, signalling to me to come over to another 'O' Group. For some reason he must have decided to modify the plan again.

I ran over to him, 150 yards across a stubble field between two suburban houses, conscious as I ran that between the bursts of fire and hellish noise of the tanks, rifle shots were cutting past rather unpleasantly close. Some Jocks must have spotted a target for their attention, I thought, and hoped that as they seemed to be firing close past our own troops, they would not cut things too fine for our health. It was another minute before it sunk in that this fire was not directed past us at the enemy, but was rather the enemy firing at us.

Smyg had just started talking as Frank, Sgt Oliver, Sgt Cowie and I lay in the stubble around him when the lash of three very close bullets sliced between us to clump into and twang off the house behind, ricocheting loudly. We ducked and scattered farther apart, hugging the ground to present less of a target, while Smyg carried on at greater speed but in the same casual tone of voice. 'See that next road junction, 300 yards beyond the first objective,

Peter, get your chaps up there. Put your tank commander in the picture if you can. Right?'

The leading tank, which was working with us, was almost level with me on the road ripping fire into the houses ahead from whence the sniping seemed to be coming. I dashed over to it to try to attract the attention of the tank commander and get him to push on the remaining distance with us. I stood in front taking care to keep clear of the spitting Besa and crossed my arms, pointing up to the next crossroads. Shouting was almost useless above the appalling noise and zoom of the engine.

The searing of a bullet from the snipers off the armour of the tank fiercely reminded me that not all the fire was going in the right direction and I scuttled round the other side of the massive vehicle to see if it was any healthier there. Fortunately, the tank commander had seen me and despite the metal whistling about, pushed his shoulders and ear-phone-clad head out of the turret to pass me down his map to mark and write a message on. My stub of pencil had never moved so fast in completing this task for I had by now realised that wherever the enemy were, this side of the tank was as much in the line of fire as the other. I completed the note crouched against the flaming heat of the exhaust at the rear.

Scuttling forward again to rejoin the Platoon, I yelled for section commanders of the right and left sections and sent Taffy, my runner, forward to give the change of plan to Cpl Carbarns 50 yards up in the forward section where he was busily engaged firing at something. The road was getting more and more unhealthy with the lash of fire down its length. Just then the last of us threw ourselves from our knees to the earth as the tank behind, seemingly having lost sight of us in the smoke and confusion, spread a sudden hail of fire, sweeping over the front like a squirt from a hose and by a miracle hitting no one.

Crossing the road to Cpl Dare's section I dashed forward 200 yards with him. Our sweat-drenched clothes and grime-streaked faces were reddened by the glow of the burning houses alongside and our limbs ached with our exertions. 'Dare, take your chaps through Carbarns' section and dig in on the far side of the cross roads. Carbarns, give them covering fire', I shouted, then scuttled back over the road to see if I could locate the enemy who must have been well concealed in some house and were still splashing the road with their fire, which fortunately did not seem to be too accurate. Again, I felt sure this inaccuracy must have been due to the continuous covering fire from the tanks.

The road and surroundings had received quite a few of our shells and mortars and perhaps a few of the enemy's too. The craters these had made formed useful foxholes for one or two of the Bren-gunners to fire from at windows which might have contained snipers. Each of the roadside houses we passed had to be searched to make sure we did not get shot up from behind. This slowed us up, particularly as at times the street was too unhealthy to use and as far as possible we worked our way through the houses and over the backyards. Another hazard in the road was the free use the tank gunners were making of their weapons. Looking back at the nearest Crocodile flame-thrower about 50 yards to the rear and only just visible through the swirling smoke from two blazing houses opposite, we were just in time to get clear of a jet of flame aimed at the next house but one towards the crossroads.

This house was hit on the ground floor, the flames going through the windows and took fire with a bang as though of exploding gas. Immediately fearful female screams issued from within. A couple of seconds later several shrieking German women scrambled out of the thick, coiling, flame-licking smoke where the front door must have been, and fell in the road, partly draped in a billow of bedding. Two dashed back, distraught and wailing, I guessed to the cellar, either for someone who had not got out or for some precious article which had to be saved from the flames.

Meanwhile, the others sat and sprawled shrieking and wailing in the road oblivious of the pattering crackling of fire from both sides which was passing within feet of them. Finally, they picked themselves up and tumbled into a dugout at the side of the house.

All the while I felt torn between neglecting my duty of controlling the Platoon and of dashing in in desperation to try to save the two women. If they did not get out within the next few seconds their exit would be a sheet of flame when the doorposts took fire. Perhaps they had got out the side or back, I hoped, but I never saw them again.

Suddenly a tank opened up with its machine gun on a house three up on my side where movement had been seen in the shadow of a doorway. I was thankful that there were none of my chaps so far up on this side. Dare and his men were still almost opposite, Carbarns at the crossroads and the rest behind me on my side. I dashed up with Brown and McKenzie to see if this house contained the snipers. We almost hugged the walls as we went, popping into doorways to take stock before another dash.

The entrance of this house was shattered with bullets and the door was open as we crashed in, trying to adjust our eyes to the darker interior. Something was lying sprawled on the floor across the hall. It was an old man, on his back, dead. He was hit in the throat badly and almost the whole hall was covered in a large, spreading pool of blood, apparently buckets of it. It seemed impossible that so much had come from this pathetic old figure. From the door of the cellar under the stairs at his head, there issued sounds of crying and sobbing from the darkness, evidently the old man's family. He must have gone to peep fearfully from the door, realising the flame-throwers were firing the houses and anxious for his family. L/Cpl Brown stepped round the pool and went down the stairs.

Brown's voice was answered by guttural German exclamations mingled with the protesting sobbing of unnerved women from beneath. The thud of feet sounded, ascending the stairs and three dishevelled and hunted-looking Germans appeared, their hands held high and unarmed. Their worried, restless eyes played uneasily between the array of weapons pointing at them and the grim, congealing mess in which lay the body. When they recognised the pathetic corpse, their fear seemed redoubled.

These three, clustered at the head of the stairs and reluctant to put their feet in the blood which covered so much of the hall, were dressed in a mixture of civilian and military clothing. One had an overcoat partly concealing the uniform beneath. I guessed they must have been Volksturm, the equivalent of our Home Guard; otherwise they might have been deserters. As I questioned these miserable fellows as fiercely as I could to try to get a few clues on what other German troops there might be in Uphusen, I became aware of a child, a little girl of about three, who had appeared at the top of the cellar stairs. She stood transfixed, silent, with opening mouth and dilated eyes, looking at the body, I supposed of her grandfather, at her feet. Behind her the mother and I think grandmother climbed into view. The full horror of comprehension only crept into the child's expression at the shrieks of anguish with which the women greeted their recognition of the old man. The stark terror which resulted in the face of the child cut itself into my memory like a burn. From the way the women looked at us it was clear that they were convinced we had personally shot down the grandfather in cold blood.

The whole situation seemed a nightmare. A tank was firing again just outside the door so that cordite fumes joined the acid stench of smoke swirling in from the blazing homes over the road. We must press on with the attack, I realised, tearing more delicate human threads from the fabric of their families and homes; doing the very things that one would least want to do in all the world. I felt with all my soul the awful conflict of my desire to do something to comfort, explain and alleviate their suffering and my sense of guilt at having to have any part in such human misery. To stop and attempt this, I realised, would be to neglect my duty and responsibility to my own men.

I detailed a Jock to take the three prisoners back towards Company HQ from where they could be sent to BHQ for questioning. As the men marched off I realised I had unwittingly further increased the anguish of the women for the prisoners must have been either close relatives or their husbands; they sobbed and wailed in crazed and abandoned misery. The child was beginning to sob too and large tears rolled down its cheeks. This was too much. I picked it up to comfort it with a sodden, half-crushed bar of bitter ration chocolate from one of my basic pouches and patted its springy fair hair. I was pleased that this trembling, sobbing mite did not seem to connect me with the body beside which the women wept, held at bay by the dark congealing red lake. Brown and I turned, I think both equally upset by this incident, and realised that the kindest thing we could do was leave them.

For a moment we crouched at the door to sense some meaning in the shambles of noise and smoke and firing about us. '38 Set's out of action, Sir!' the radio operator reported. Some feet clattering the broken glass and tiles in the road behind us revealed Frank Coutts, 2i/c. I glanced at my watch. It was 1100 hours. For us the attack had been under way just one hour of eternity. 'How goes it Pete?' boomed Frank's voice. 'Smyg has decided to exploit the position still further while the going is good. This position is not too good a one to hold anyway, and C Company will soon be up.'

I think we were all feeling just about exhausted physically with all the running and crawling in the heat and smoke, and mentally too with the strain and tension of an attack. The Jocks who had started to dig in expressed their profound disgust at having to push on farther in volleys of filthy language.

It took about 6 hectic minutes for runners backed by my efforts to locate and pass on the information to section commanders, for naturally enough once an objective was reached, with sniping going on, the sections just seemed to melt out of sight into positions of concealment and cover.

The layout of Uphusen, smashed as it was, seemed to bear very little relation to the map which I had memorised over night. I recognised a mound-like hill on the right, however, which gave me my bearings. It was a terrible job trying to control a Platoon advancing through a strange area of crackling disintegrating houses, belching tank engines, spattering MG fire, flame, smoke and rubble, all the time with sniping to harry one from taking a steady, collected look around in the open. The tanks at this stage in the war were taking no chances, and seared any suspicious or moving object with a jet of flame with the least provocation. That we were likely to be mistaken as targets too, working forward of some of the flame-throwers in the smoke, gave one a continual uneasiness with earlier battle accidents in mind.

The plan now was to push right on while we held the initiative, over the main road, through a factory area beyond and dig in near the railway track bordering the open country looking to the north. As we began to move forwards again, scrambling from cover to cover against the walls of the houses and into doorways, we were aware of two disconcerting facts. First that the tanks and flame-throwers were not keeping up with us: for some reason they were holding back. Next we realised the reason; as we had advanced from the start of the attack we have been continually jolted by the concussion of the tanks firing their shells from right beside and behind us with all the awful noise that entailed. Now, although the tanks were some distance to our rear, similar violent explosions were jolting us, this time from German 88mm shells passing at high velocity the other way, to plume brick dust off the buildings and rubble behind us. We were nearing the northern rim of Uphusen and soon realised from the accuracy and sustained persistence of the shelling that the Germans had us under visual observation from somewhere in the open country.

The tank commander must have quickly realised this danger for when next I looked back our armour had vanished, I think to cover among some buildings up a road to our left. A direct 88mm hit would have been fatal, we realised, to a tank and fed up though we were at being left to go on alone, we had sympathy with the tank chaps' decision. It was indeed a wise one as from then onwards for the next thirty to thirty-six hours this hideous shelling got more and more active and accurate. Coming faster than sound and consequently with no warning they ploughed, each like a crashing express train, earthquaking the soil with solid shot or dud shells (we never knew which) or high-explosive ones violently exploding blotches of rubble and billowing black smoke here, there and everywhere. An occasional solid-shot shell ricocheted off a building to whine with a hellish noise way into the distance.

SITTING IN A TARGET

The Jocks were really 'browned off' by now and though short of breath with their exertions and weighed down with fatigue under their load of equipment, they still found time to grumble over the unnecessary slit trenches dug at the last objective and to curse and blind at the surrounding explosions.

For a Jock, at times like these, when full details of what is happening cannot be passed on in the shambles of the moment, life is full of moves and privations. Unlike the section commanders and myself they had not the incentive and diversion of responsibility to occupy their thoughts and could have had little sense of any plan or continuity in the series of shambles that constituted their lives. It was a never-ending wonder to me that they stuck it so well. The swearing really meant little. They would have sworn almost identically on an over tiresome route march. To a Jock life in action must have seemed a deliberate attempt by superiors to arrange for the minimum chance of rest and sleep or a proper meal coupled to a maximum drain on nerves and energy. To me at that moment things looked in much the same light.

At times it was very difficult to locate more than about four or five of the Platoon visually. How to keep the sections in some order of advance and at the same time not make oneself too obvious a target to snipers by moving about a lot between sections in the open was a dilemma with no solution. I was amazed that the snipers had not yet got me or, as far as I could make out, any other of my chaps. Radio communication had broken down between Company HQ and ourselves and also occasionally section commanders were showing an amazing lack of initiative and decision at the most ticklish times so that I had to adopt a constant, roving tour of each section, keeping Platoon HQ roughly central.

Looking back I could see that visual contact was also lost between ourselves and Company HQ, so that I was eventually much relieved to see the large, sweat-streaming form of Frank Coutts at my elbow. 'You had better dig in in the region of those houses on the far side of this cement yard looking over open country', he said. 'The rest of the company will be spread pretty thinly up to the main road in a semi-circle about 1,000 yards to the left with company HQ somewhere around where we are now.'

So far, except for the shelling and the two lots of enemy seen earlier, sustained sniping had been the only resistance we had met. Where the snipers were was a mystery. I began to wonder too if the bad shooting they had so far put up might be explained by the fact that some of the infantry immediately opposing us were Volksturm.

Carefully we worked our way through the cement works, past sheds and over railway sidings towards a fence and the open country. For the moment the snipers and the 88 gunners seemed to have lost track of our whereabouts and we had a period of comparative peace. To dig in on the objectives, I realised, we would have to expose ourselves a bit. All seemed well for about 7 minutes. We scrambled through the fence and scattered along the rim of open country. One section started to dig in in the railway yard, one just on the near side of the railway track, a bit forward, and the third in soft soil against one of several small houses on the rim of Uphusen. I put Platoon HQ centrally where, to my dismay, the surface of the ground was iron hard.

Our short-lived peace was soon explained. The German gunners to whom we must now have been in full view had evidently been spending their time working out our new range for the guns suddenly opened up again. The first intimation of renewed trouble miraculously did not kill anyone, for suddenly a pattern of explosions and black tumbling smoke blossomed about us with jagged, violent sound and whining shrapnel. The fatigued Jocks suddenly sped into activity and with the energy of desperation swore and hacked their way into and below the hard surface of the ground, each crashing salvo bringing a fresh spurt of energy in its wake.

As yet I could see no sign of Company HQ or of C Company to give us some depth of defence in the rear. Just then the angular bony frame of Smyg twanged through the wire of the fence beside me, spectacles glinting in the sun. He decided to move one of my sections a bit more to the left as we had a wide front to cover. As we could not make any impression on the hard ground I decided we could not long survive if we in Platoon HQ did not move too, so we joined 1 Section around the small house and garden overlooking the lower-lying land and railway, while 2 Section, similarly finding the ground in the rail yard too hard, I ordered to join 3 Section forward and in another small house and garden alongside us.

I decided to restrict movements on our front as far as possible for now we were sure the enemy had a clear view of our movements from some OP which was in touch with his guns, for we had not been moved more than a couple of minutes before the gunners had corrected their fire onto our new positions.

At 1140 hours we were dug in on our objective. Our phase of the attack had lasted exactly 1 hour and 40 minutes. Would the enemy try a counter-attack? I hoped not. We all felt worn to a standstill, very thirsty and hungry and very much on edge from the strain of the accurate and continued shelling. 'They must have mountains of ammunition', Pte Smith commented unhappily to me. We were peering through a hedge together where I had joined him in his slit trench while taking a look forward to see if any enemy movement could be located which might give us a clue on our immediate future.

Our view was over the railway and about a mile of fairly open country towards the enemy-held village of Oyten which I could see in the distance. We had a fine field of fire to cope with any infantry from that direction, I thought with relief. Our main problem, it seemed, was going to be the 88s. A distant embankment showed the position of what we later realised was an autobahn between ourselves and Oyten. I could see no enemy movement, but it was disconcerting to see his swift reaction to any movement made by us.

A few chaps were still digging painfully, trying to show themselves as little as possible in the forward positions and the guns were giving them special attention. So far no one had been hit, but I realised that to continue this operation in daylight would result in more casualties than we were likely to sustain in coping with a counter-attack from the houses alone, so I withdrew them to the shelter of the houses to await the cover of darkness before completing their task . . . if we were to stop there that long. Both these little houses were really smallholdings – a small barn attached and built as part of the timbered house and in each a little stable. We laid out fire positions for all the chaps in case of trouble before nightfall.

I was among the few left still digging outside at this period, having been engaged on other things thus far, and I was very relieved when my hole had got deep enough to give a little protection from some of the several very close shells that whiplashed past to explode about 25 yards behind me in the rail yard. The trajectory seemed very flat and more than likely the enemy were firing over open sights with some of the guns. Fortunately the high velocity seemed to be carrying most of the damage to the rear.

As the minutes, then hours, passed, I decided to work out an undercover route between sections, for Jocks were still showing themselves between the houses and the enemy response was very swift. To do this we cut our way through numerous fences 150 yards to the rear of the houses, making the round trip a deep V-shape of 400 yards to cover an actual distance of 25 yards. It was well worth it, though, as we soon realised for we had some longer intervals of peace when no one was to be seen. While engaged in this activity I found one of the sniper's nests which had caused us so much unpleasantness on the way in. It was a sniper's pit dug under some junk in the rail yard with three '14–18 war rifles lying in it. There was no sign of the men who had operated these weapons, though their footprints were to be seen round about in the sand and the pit itself was stocked with plenty of ammunition. I climbed in to see the view from inside and was a bit shaken to realise what a wonderful set of targets we must have provided to these chaps as we approached. That they had tried their luck at us we could tell from the recently fired empty cartridge cases scattered about and from the state of the barrels.

I think whoever the chaps were they must have been Volksturm men and clearly as we had approached them in our steady advance they had fortunately either got nervous or decided the odds were too heavy and pulled out. Their shooting had been so haphazard we had not realised we were so close on top of them. Both the little houses were still occupied by civilians and in our billet we found some discarded Volksturm clothes bundled into a cupboard. The farmer to whom they belonged looked ill at ease and very shifty in his gaze when I threw these onto the floor in front of him to see his reaction and I suspected that quite possibly he and the chaps in the next smallholding had been part of our recent 'enemy'. When we got close on top of them they must have decided they had more to lose by fighting it out and had scuttled back to their farms to change into civilian farming clothes for our arrival.

The family in our house – the man just mentioned of about sixty who had probably seen service in the last war, his smaller wife of similar age, a younger woman and a rather undernourished looking baby – seemed to be disposed peacefully enough towards us and we decided to let them remain living where they had taken up their abode in a bunker built into the foundations of the house on the enemy's side where if the enemy saw them, I reasoned, they might be more of an asset than otherwise in deterring fire. They had smoke already issuing from their chimney when we arrived so we felt more at our ease in starting another fire in the kitchen to cook up a tremendous feed for the chaps at teatime.

When first we had got into the house and before we discovered the civilians hiding in the bunker in front, we had each gone down to the cellar in turn to relax and eat some tinned rations for lunch.

Now that the civilians were moving about the house in full view of the enemy we felt a bit more secure from the prospect that the enemy would direct their fire at the building. However, it was very soon apparent that both we and the civilians had overestimated the humanitarian outlook of those we were fighting. During the afternoon the shells continued to crash past so close around the house that I felt the enemy must be very sure of their aim to cut the margin of a direct hit so fine as 4 or 5 feet to either side. Perhaps it was the smoke issuing from a second chimney, our tea cooking, which had tempted the enemy too far. It was plain he was out to get the house if he could, whoever was in it, for several solid-shot or dud shells smacked like a giant's fist into the bank holding the foundations of the house against the bunker housing the German family, and to our alarm the ground under the whole structure heaved slowly in the jelly fashion of an earthquake. That they did not hit us seemed to indicate the guns were sited at greater range than we had hitherto supposed.

At these shots the old lady and the young mother dashed in from the bunker in alarm. Wide-eyed and ashen in the face, the mother was so beside herself in fear for her child that she was quite oblivious to not having covered her bosom when she had been disturbed in breast-feeding the infant. She stood in near hysterics among the astonished Jocks with a screaming child in one arm groping to continue its disturbed feed while she leant with the other arm to support herself against the wall. Despite the strange, rough Jocks self-consciously about her, she seemed to derive steadiness from their presence, although we were supposed enemies.

One of the Jocks who had a young family himself at home, offered her some tea, but the elderly lady propelled the mother through to the back of the house to put a bit more bricks and mortar between themselves and the shelling; perhaps, too, to be removed from us, the cause of their present misery.

'B*** me, y'd no' think yon Jerries w'd shell their ane wummin!' said the Jock standing with his unaccepted mug of tea. 'Yons a scraggy bit'bairn tho'. Aufu' underfed, the lassie's no' giving as guid milk as yon Jerry coos', he added, indicating the couple of cows in the stalls beside us which had provided the milk for our tea. 'Poor wee b*** an' he'll grow into a Jerry too for our ane bairns te fight later likely.'

Plenty of eggs and milk made a fine tea for the famished Jocks. The shells were still crashing past or short of our little house as we clustered in the kitchen and the likelihood of one coming in through the flimsy wall which separated us from the enemy eyes marred the complete enjoyment of the meal. We were certainly lucky to be able to use a fire when so much in the enemy's view, but particularly close shells flashing past with a most appalling crash every now and then made us reconsider the wisdom of having smoke coming from two chimneys in the house.

Being without a radio to keep in touch with Company HQ was a nuisance. As the afternoon wore on I decided I had better pay a visit back to see Smyg and Frank and get any news. Part way on my 500-yard journey back I coincided with a salvo of 88mm shells which stippled the cement yard and sidings with splodges of smoke and twanging shrapnel and drove me to cover between two stacks of railway sleepers. I was comforted to feel the massive solidity of these balks of timber between myself and the enemy for a while, though I think the comfort was purely psychological for a high-velocity tank shell such as an '88' would have driven through them like an ice-axe through cardboard.

I moved a little more swiftly back the rest of the way to Company HQ as soon as there seemed promise of a lull in the shelling. The Bren carrier showing itself through a brick archway in the yard of a battered house revealed to me where Smyg had put his HQ. I moved through the archway and round the corner into the yard. Providence seemed to have just timed my movements to the split second for immediately another hideous series of explosions commenced to shudder my consciousness, one particularly violent whack of an HE shell splashed a jagged pattern on the brick gateway I had just passed through. I don't know quite which shook me more, the blast or the realisation that only three seconds before I had passed the point of a direct hit.

Another disquieting thought struck me as I looked about the yard in the thinning smoke and settling brickdust: someone had foolishly piled all the Company's reserve ammunition, PIAT, mortar and small arms on this, the enemy side, of the house where a stray shell could consign all of Company HQ to tumbling dust in the sky by touching it off.

The building was a school with a house attached. No doubt Jerry realised it was more than likely we would use it as a billet as he had done before our arrival. Inside I recognised Frank and

Smyg's voices. They were busily engaged on questioning the schoolmaster, most probably the head, who lived there and who spoke such excellent English as to invite interrogation. He turned out to be the local Hitler Youth leader, but apparently all men in his position had to be. There was very little information which could be classed as news other than that the Battalion as a whole had been dug in on the objectives by 1300 hours, and that the attack, after a sticky start, had been 100 per cent successful.

The door banged open and a Jock, almost like a chimney sweep in the grime of battle, stumped in holding a small boy of ten to thirteen firmly in his grasp by the scruff of the neck. 'He got in to our positions from the Jerry lines, Sir', the Jock announced. The schoolmaster and the Jock were dismissed while attention and interrogation switched to the fresh customer whose frightened, pinched face revealed the stress and ordeals of his recent past. His knapsack was taken from his grasp and tipped out on the table to reveal a crust of black bread as hard as a brick-chip, a bit of evil-looking sausage, some grubby string, a knife and a few dirty bandages. He was given some chocolate and some tea while being spoken to kindly, though probably he understood very little. We eventually gathered that he was trying to find his family, having walked from Bremen. This was interesting. 'Any Panzers in Bremen?' we asked (or hoped we had with the limited German at our disposal). We gathered that he had seen five panzers parked in a square in Bremen, pointing north. I was surprised that he knew a little English.

At that moment a particularly heavy dose of 88mm shells came over, forcing us all to take cover in the cellar where we crouched sipping our tea and hoping that all the ammunition stacked above us would not be touched off. The German child seemed past caring, being nearly overcome with fatigue and hunched in a drowsy heap in a corner.

Heavy earth concussion from time to time among the noise of exploding 88s began gradually to rattle us into awareness that somewhere Jerry had trained a naval or siege gun of exceptional calibre on us, most probably a 16-inch. An enormous crump on the crossroads we had passed earlier on fighting our way into the town left a crater of startling size with smoke or steam issuing from its depths. The explosion seemed equivalent in power to a 500lb bomb. The CO's poor batman had this shell all to himself. If the Germans had been aiming at the crossroads, which seemed more than probable, it was an amazing feat of accuracy to plant this missile within a matter of inches of dead centre from a probable range of 8 miles or more.

Just in case the German child had been sent over by the enemy to try to gather information about our strength, positions and intentions which he could scuttle back to report, we sent him off back to BHQ for an interpreter to pump more out of him.

As soon as the shelling allowed I returned to my platoon and was relieved to see that though the landscape and buildings had a marked increase in evidence of ripping and chipping from near misses, there had been no casualties. Perhaps this was partly due to the enemy firing quite a large proportion of shells which were either solid-shot anti-tank or dud HE.

Immediately the light began to fail we sneaked forward of the small farms to dig ourselves proper positions in case the enemy should try a counter-attack, then settled down to the long rest-robbing and cold vigil while the tired hours of the night dragged themselves endlessly past. One could not complain of boredom; the odd sounds, flashes, fires, imagination and batches of shells saw to that. At times long pauses made one begin to hope that perhaps the enemy had withdrawn his guns a bit, but at irregular intervals ear-splitting, whiplash cracks of super-sonic shells stabbed, cleaving the air overhead in flat trajectory to plough into Company or Battalion HQ farther back with muffled crashes.

Occasionally some fell shorter, unpleasantly earthquaking the house and its contents. The solid shot cut obliquely, jellying the boggy surface of the earth on which we lay like so many tensed, living seismographs, each time marvelling that our little homes, so constantly rocked, never sustained a direct hit.

As the light came and the morning mist lifted I glanced back at Company HQ. They had been less fortunate than ourselves for the shells that had missed us had bashed and pock-marked the walls and yard with ragged, ink-splash-patterned craters, ripping and leaving the tattered trees in a sorry state. No vehicles had been hit and the ammunition was intact.

We were rather shocked to learn that eighteen hours after the attack had gone in, a large number of Germans had materialised out of some buildings near the river on the left flank and to the rear of our advance as we had swung round to enter Uphusen. These enemy gave themselves up without resistance hours after we had passed them so close by. Had they opened fire on our flanks or rear after our tanks had gone past they might have caused us heavy casualties before we had time to realise what had hit us.

NIGHT ATTACK ON
BREMEN – FIRST PHASE

The date was 23 April 1945. What would it hold in store for us, I wondered as I looked about on the peaceful distant countryside which somewhere hid beneath its sunny smile of fields, trees and distant houses the eyes and quickly reacting sting of an alert enemy.

The sounds and scents of breakfast and morning washing under the farmyard pump were getting under way among the Jocks, while the German farm folk who owned our little house were pottering about on their side. Unlike ourselves they were in full view of the enemy. I still hoped that this might be a deterrent to a direct hit, which surely the enemy could have given us time and again by now as his nearest anti-tank 88mm guns must have had us under open sights from 2,000–3,000 yards range.

As the morning wore on into the afternoon, our guns and occasional rocket-firing Typhoons tried to eliminate these enemy weapons, but seemed to have little if any success in locating them. Occasionally heavy droves of our shells waffled overhead to spatter a series of black plumes in the woods and among an enemy-held housing estate about 1½–2 miles to our north. Meanwhile, we presumed that the spring was being recompressed on our side for the launching of the next phase of the attack. Would this involve us? That was the thought constantly in all our minds, and despite the now erratic shelling we rejoiced in the unexpected respite and pleasant weather.

We had gratuitous confirmation that the next town of Mahndorf, another mile up the main road towards Bremen, was still in enemy hands when a 'White' scout car, driven, I think, by UNRRA personnel, by mistake penetrated that far and so took the enemy by surprise that it was able to turn round and speed back again to safety. Subsequent events were to prove how fortunate they were . . . and suggested, too, that they may have been deliberately allowed to return unscathed.

156 Brigade had formed up to pass through us, their armour massing behind our little farm and to our surprise not drawing the response in enemy shelling that we had expected as they must certainly have been plainly visible. Just as darkness fell, they moved forward over the same road as the scout car. Leading Crocodile flame-throwers, a Churchill tank towing its flame-liquid trailer moved onto a buried aerial bomb in the road which was touched off by electrical remote control. The tank was completely wrecked and the crew killed. It was lifted into the air bodily and thrown onto its back like an enormous, tipped-up cockroach, with its turret gone and the trailer a roaring torch of flame and black smoke. A Lloyd carrier of the Royal Scots, containing a gun crew and a 6-pounder anti-tank gun, was blown to bits in similar circumstances a little farther up. Apparently the scout car, which had passed then returned over both these remote-controlled mines, had been considered too small a fry to blow up.

At the same time as this advance was under way, a troop of Bofors guns, in apparent ignorance of the devastating shelling with which the enemy had swept our frontage up until so short a time before, moved in forward of us and quickly brought their guns into action at nightfall, firing steadily with tracer into the approaches to Bremen's north-east suburbs. This we took from our past experience to indicate that most probably this was directional tracer to keep some of our attacking infantry on course in the dark.

The red pearls of these tracer shells were pretty to watch. Flicking in strings of four or five gems to burst to the winking of the gun's flaming white muzzle flash, they trailed a slow arc into the far night. Each exploded as a faint orange pinprick of light in the dark distant rim of trees, fields and houses. Now and then one of the shells soared up again, ricocheting among the stars like a spark from a fire. As we watched, we were poised, ready to dive for cover at the least distant enemy muzzle-flash, which would tell of the expected retaliation. Amazingly none came so we assumed that either the enemy were in the process of moving their guns farther back towards Vegesack, the other side of Bremen, or more likely they were too busy using them on the attacking troops.

While this activity twinkled in front of us, to our rear the tanks which had formed up in our area during the afternoon were still in the process of setting off for the attack. They ploughed heavily through the field towards the main road, backfiring, revving deafeningly and filling the night air with trails of exhaust lit by every gunflash. Each tank tore and spewed up the turf and earth in its wake like a ship at sea and vanished noisily into the angry, battle-inflamed night horizon towards Mahndorf.

So far most of our activity had been confined to sleeping, eating and routine patrolling. However, this was obviously too peaceful a state of affairs to last. The CO, who had been having his evening meal at Brigade, returned to announce that the next day the Battalion would assault Bremen. An immediate flurry of 'O' Groups was held to the accompaniment of noises and lighting effects 'off' as the Brigade wave before ours pressed the tidal rim of war up the narrow axis of advance along the main road to the west.

The unknown always seems worse than the known troubles and so although we had a fairly shell-free night, our coming ordeal weighed more and more heavily on us with each passing hour. I feel that in part this was because we each had almost dared to hope that the war might just conceivably burn itself out before another turn for us to attack came round. Meanwhile, until this happened we knew that the policy was to keep up maximum pressure on the enemy by day and by night, to give him no recuperative respite.

Next morning, 24 April 1945, we saddled ourselves, each with his dragging web harness dangling arms, equipment and ammunition, and trudged off in the dust up the road towards Mahndorf, watched with furtive relief by the family whose house we had occupied so much to their peril and mental misery. It was not a long march, about a mile and a half, but tedious in its stops and starts and the stomach-chilling tension of approaching combat. Our immediate task was to take over positions from some HLI who had dug themselves into an embankment and fortified some houses. Their positions bordered a branch of the railway track which curved away from the main Bremen–Verden line towards the autobahn and a village called Oyterdamm, where the enemy were on our completely exposed right flank.

The Highland Light Infantry had moved in there the night before. The company we were taking over from had almost got to these, their objectives, when suddenly they had been swept by a vicious hail of point-blank fire shot from a concealed set of quadruple-mounted 20mm anti-aircraft guns. These had opened fire at only 50 yards range and fourteen casualties were scythed down with explosive shells before the gun could be knocked out.

'Mind your ruddy heads over that *** bank!' was our warning on arrival that some enemy snipers were still peppering these positions with rifle and MG fire from the shelter of a housing estate about 1,000 yards to our north-west. Fortunately, the Germans seemed to have no mortars to lob down on us as we sheltered behind the railway embankment, for the Jocks always gave their positions away by instant retaliation when fired upon instead of sniping back from concealed positions when the enemy showed himself too.

Our billets were in three houses below the railway bank and our positions dug in the bank itself. Company HQ was farther back towards the Y junction, near the main Verden–Bremen railway track about 800 yards away, with 11 and 12 Platoons spread between. Being here was an unexpected but typical interlude following our contemplated entry straight in to an attack.

The day dragged on as we hung about these new positions waiting for some definite news concerning our future. A stray sniper's bullet from the enemy whined or cracked over the metals of the track to mark the passing time, to be punctuated by an occasional burst back from one of our Brens or the odd rifle fire.

By looking carefully with the binoculars from a spot picked against some foliage jutting higher than the metals of the track so that I was not sky-lined behind, I spent quite a lot of time watching the odd signs of enemy movement to try to pinpoint his exact forward and rear positions in my mind in case we might be called upon to attack in that direction. One peeped up infinitely slowly, shielding the lenses of the glasses from any possible glint and however long one lay in peace without a shot coming close, there was always a knife tip of uneasiness in one's stomach that perhaps somewhere out there a sniper might at just that moment have one lined up on his telescopic sights. I had the glasses lying still in my hand, resting on the hot metal of the rails in the sunlight. The air had the warmed-grease and sooty-dusty smell of railway tracks the world over and the ballast of the track edge poked its bumps into me. The material picture seemed so very real and solid that I found it difficult to conceive that if I moved suddenly or was spotted, I would be whipped into 'oblivion' at the flick of an eye and not even know it . . . or would one know it? It was difficult to picture, too, the trains that had run up and down here carrying very ordinary people about their jobs in life, and would some time, perhaps soon, do so again. It was odd, I thought, even now, how very hard I found it to believe that this madness of war was actually taking place at that moment, just as I had found that listening to my father talking about his 'war' sounded unreal. What we call reality has a dream quality at the passing moment of actuality which one finds it harder to think real at the time than later in retrospect. How often this had struck me during the war.

Suddenly the kicking of a Bren burst from a Jock in a pit a few yards to my left warned me to duck in time to miss the crackle of shots which lashed back overhead through the smoke blowing past.

At nightfall we 'stood to' in case of trouble at this most likely of times, then worked out stags for the night and cooked up some supper in a little house which we were sharing as platoon HQ. The two old German civilians there were hard put to it to know just what sort of attitude to take up towards us. I walked along in the dark before turning in, to see if I could collect any news from Company HQ. I felt rather restive about the security of our right flank if we were going to attack along the rim of the railway track into Bremen, with the enemy threatening our thin axis from ground he held just over the railway bank. The night proved quite a comfortable one, for I spent part of it in a proper bed in the little house. There were few sounds of close activity from the enemy. Those over the railway track seemed content to lick their wounds

and not seek fresh trouble. The civilians were grateful that we had
not ordered them out of their bedroom.

Just after breakfast, Smyg was called to a 'O' Group at
Battalion HQ. During the hours of darkness the tide of battle, to
judge by the spasmodic sounds and stray pall of smoke, had been
pushed a stage farther towards Bremen itself. With this call to 'O'
Group, came the order 'prepare to move', at about 1130. Almost
immediately a shot rang out from Cpl Carbarns' section. It
transpired that Pte Smith, who had earlier been my batman in
Afferden woods until Taffy Huntingford took over, had shot
himself through the foot. I found him sitting white faced on a bed
in the Section HQ house, his rifle and cleaning rag still in his
hands, looking with interest at the hole in his boot which was
staining the floor. 'I was jus' a-cleaning me gun Surr, an' I shot
meself in me perishing foot *** cor, it 'urts *** struth!' In view of
the circumstances of the forthcoming attack and his previous
difficulties in facing up to them, it seemed almost certainly a 'self-
inflicted wound' to by-pass the looming ordeal. We tied him up
and carried him off to Company HQ to have it attended to and
also to take a few statements from the rest of his section and one
from Smith too.

The Platoon turned out to move off and join the Company and
the rest of the Battalion. It was a fine sunny spring morning, 25
April, and the fresh greenery of the hedges and fields seemed to
suggest more the day for a route march or holiday than a fight.
Our section files were sprinkled on alternate sides of the busy
main road up which streamed all the machines and materials of
war in endless, dusty, noisy profusion. Ahead lay the suburb of
Arbergen about a mile away, and beyond that, Hastedt, a larger
place and the last suburb before Bremen itself. Exactly where the
enemy were resisting now was not known to us, but our final
objective was 6¼ miles away, so it seemed probable we would not
be called on to attack for a few hours more.

We had not gone far before the column halted and the
companies were ordered to fall out by the wayside. We had a big
barn alongside us on the corner of the road and made our way into
it and the farmyard, while Company HQ was established in a farm
over the road. Here we gathered more information on the coming

attack. Our objective had been changed in the early hours from the eastern end of the city to the centre. A large-scale map of Bremen, including the suburbs, was issued which was marked off in a long strip of squares in brown chalk, each square being a Battalion objective, leapfrogging Brigade through Brigade.

Bremen is split by the River Weser. Three-quarters of its mass lay on our bank to the north and the remaining quarter to the south over the river. This southern side had previously been plastered and by the time we drew level, although all the bridges were down, it should be occupied by 3rd Division, securing that flank. Of our right flank, the right-hand rim of which we would be attacking along, we had no news at all at our level of the enemy other than what we had been able to gather from our own experience. From this we knew it was quite open and that the enemy just over the rail track was alert and active. We had no clues on his strength in men or armour, but knew he had plenty of guns and ammunition.

Another 'O' Group was held in the small farm at about 1400 hours while outside the Jocks were getting the maximum enjoyment out of the company of a couple of flashy female slave workers who were employed on the farm and lazed in the sun amid the buzz of surrounding Jocks. Above the laughter and banter of the admiring troops there was all the while a subconscious background of intensive, drumming artillery. Except for the heavies with their deep, blast-like bark, the main gun positions were still forward of us, which was our chief clue to the likely distance of the rim of attack.

As each Battalion fought its way into its sector one became aware of a stepping up in the pulse of detonation, then the barrage lifted gently onto the next sector to tick over in a steady drumming there before building up to a frenzied climax for the next assault; then through the cycle of events again.

The state of buildings around us was that of a slightly 'blitzed' town, but we were to find that from Hastedt onwards the damage got steadily worse until within 1½ to 2 miles of the Bahnhof it appeared at its worst. Most of this damage appeared to have been done by bombers. Our 25-pounders were mainly firing airburst shells to keep the enemy heads down and off the streets. A 25-

pounder HE shell did not penetrate these large buildings deeply enough to be otherwise effective.

That the second 1,000-bomber raid, of which there had been rumours, did not materialise, was, we found, just as well for in places the cratering of the streets was so bad that it was decided to amend our method of entry into the city. We were originally to have advanced onto our objective in Kangaroos, there to de-bus, deploy and start clearing operations. The Kangaroos were then to have gone back in a ferry service to pick up the next assaulting Battalion while we consolidated and covered their attack. But it was to be a footslogging attack as far as the infantry were concerned.

We were not apparently due to attack our particular sector until the early hours of the morning, yet here we were moving off at 1430 hours on the approach march. It was going to be a nervy and tiring pastime from the look of it. The Company spread out and resumed the advance in long, staggered, double necklaces of sections each side of the road. Each Jock seemed to resemble, under his load of equipment, a shuffling, grumbling machine, moving forward in fits and starts in desolation, destruction, noise, smoke and dust.

Under a battered railway arch leading to Arbergen we passed a group of dead Germans and a few *panzerfausts* with which they had tried to hold up our tanks, draped and sprawled in and beside some hastily dug slit trenches in the railway bank. 'Poor blighters! They'll noo be mucked-aboot onny more the noo', a Jock remarked. Beyond, we moved, thoughts more active, along a tree-lined avenue. Each tree was ripped and slashed white and grey with shrapnel while the new spring leaves, already blasted off their twigs and churned to powder with the passing traffic, had had their short summer. A little way farther up we passed a deserted 88mm gun partly concealed and with a stack of ammunition alongside, still covering the railway arch. Each yard and wreck told with mute eloquence of the passing tidal rim of effort and misery and pain which was even now stalking its hideous path steadily ahead of us. Soon it would be our turn between the grinding stones of the mill to grind the opposing stone a bit, or in the attempt be ground down ourselves. At intervals harrowed-looking German civilians shuffled dejectedly past, pushing and pulling their small pram and wagon-loads of salvaged goods to the rear.

A sudden, unexpected crash of noise made us jump and swing our eyes to look at a group of self-propelled 25-pounder guns, bucking on their tracks behind a smudge of yellow smoke and flame. The pall of dust and smoke rising ahead from their targets and from burning buildings gave us for the first time a sure indication of just where the fighting was. It was not very far. These guns stood scattered thickly in the fields with no attempt at concealment, their gunflashes spattering whitely like raindrops in a pond. This lack of any attempt at concealment showed how complete and taken for granted was our assurance of mastery of the air over the German front.

Gradually, as we advanced we listened to the familiar change in the sound of the gunfire and the passing ascent of shells at differing distances from their gun barrels. For a while the column halted just forward of the medium guns and I rested the cutting weight of the webbing pack straps by leaning with my pack against the wall of a house. The whole structure shuddered violently to each discharging gun, which clattered the frames of the wrecked windows. Each ascending missile made a sudden, violent crack which mingled with an eerie noise as of rolling thunder tapering out of earshot into the distance.

Even ahead of the guns there was a steady flow of military vehicles passing towards the forward units, with a lesser stream coming back. Once again, any unusual number of red cross vehicles returning did not pass the eye of seasoned Jocks without attention for this was our gauge of resistance being offered by the enemy.

Again the column moved forward but with such jerky and gradual progress that soon the full operational load we were carrying had our shoulder and neck muscles aching. The surrounding shambles of battered Hastedt provided many a human scene of poignant misery and tragedy which, taken on its own and out of its context, could easily have overwhelmed one's sensitivity, sympathy and imagination. As it was, it served to make our own burdens and prospect seem less important. For the most part, except where recent shelling or flame-throwers had destroyed more houses, driving women, children and distraught old people to the surface, what living souls there still were in these ruins had taken to the cellars or large bunkers.

Beyond Hastedt and into the beginnings of Bremen, we came across more and more signs of very heavy bombing. Those buildings still standing were largely blackened shells, piled about with rubble and twisted girders, spiralling smoke and redly radiating intense heat from recent burning. Through a broken wooden fence in the backyard were the pathetic, torn bodies of a man and a woman civilian stripped and twisted by blast on the rim of a bomb crater, their pale limbs rivuleted by rainwashed ash. How many more were under the rubble? It seemed highly unlikely any proper defence services had survived for rescue work.

Over the road a short way beyond we came upon a crowd of rejoicing displaced persons noisily looting a liquor store in hilarious tipsy abandon. Bottles of mineral water spun out through the broken shop front and smashed into the street. A reeking, blood-shot-eyed chap in pale grey Yugoslav uniform tried to press an opened bottle of Vichy water into my hands. My throat felt so parched with the acrid smoky atmosphere that I took a swig but promptly spat out a filthy taste of some other vicious brew than was displayed on the innocent label.

At times enormous craters had to be negotiated in the road which would have to be filled up a bit to enable the supporting vehicles and tanks to get through. Falling tram wires, shot and blasted from their poles, trailed in profusion over our route and gathered thickly like brambles, entangling noisily in the clattering tracks of tanks and carriers. Another battered body, hardly recognisable as friend, foe or civilian, lay discarded, scattered with broken glass and dust down a side alley like an old sock. Scenes were getting more and more grim as dusk crept coldly on us and we worked our reluctant way forwards, closer and closer to the flame-seared, angry skyline and the enemy ahead. Here and there groups of houses were now still blazing fiercely on either side, suggesting the flame-throwers had very recently been at work. Pathetic, frantic figures and shouting drew attention to some old people and children staggering frenziedly about in the smoke-filmed, flame-lit half light in a snowstorm of swirling sparks. It made one's heart sick to see them attempting such a hopeless task of saving their homes from the flames with only pots and pans and buckets of water filled from the broken water main in a crater.

Over all was the sickly, acrid smell of gutted houses, shops, warehouses and burning rubber. The column halted again and we subsided where we stood, sitting in the jagged, darkening mess and smoking stench to seize a little rest amid the towering silhouettes of dark masonry. A kitten was mewing miserably somewhere in the ruins. The Jocks swore filthily, seemingly to derive some relief while listening to the shells now screaming in descent to explode with muffled thudding in the rubble not very far ahead. Our turn, it appeared, would not be long delayed. A clattering tramp of numerous feet tinkling the glass and tiles broke in on this racket and formed the only sound that marked the passing to our rear of an otherwise silent and dejected group of German prisoners – mixed shambles of infantry, marines, SS, AA and Volksturm troops under escort of a casual Jock, cigarette in mouth and tin hat right on the back of a filthy looking head. As it darkened we moved forward again, jerked into greater alertness and intensity by the sounds of much closer explosions and some small-arms fire somewhere farther off. I was astonished to notice two or three fairly heavy bombs which had been dropped during the raid we had watched our aircraft put in. They had crashed shallow craters into the thick concrete of the road and now lay unexploded, their metal cases split open with the impact and spilling out their sulphur yellow explosive contents.

About us at this point were a group of buildings which had just burned to the stage where all the roofs, floors and contents had been consumed by the flames while the masonry still glowed a dull red heat which almost matched the muddy, inflamed and smoke-canopied sky. In places the skyline ahead licked flame and soaring sparks from freshly fired buildings while above and beyond these tortured structural skeletons orange pinpoints of airbursting shells from our barrage twinkled. My watch read 2130 hours. No wonder we were feeling so tired and hungry!

A weird, towering structure materialised against the skyline not far ahead. We were astonished to see as we got closer that electric lights blazed at the entrance. Spilling out of this door into the light were an unexpected, shuffling mass of people. German civilians, they were percolating out to watch us pass like sugar trickling from a giant and punctured carton. This was our first sight of these enormously thick and squarish concrete air-raid shelters which so often had anti-aircraft guns mounted on top. The Germans watched us with silent intensity as we walked close by and I wondered what they were thinking. Their faces revealed nothing. I suspected they must have felt relief that the bombing and most probably the shelling was over as far as their war was concerned. Among the civilian clothes my eye detected a sprinkling of what looked like Wehrmacht uniforms, but which on closer inspection revealed themselves to be those of policemen. This structure certainly seemed to have fulfilled its purpose for all around it spread a sea of desolate rubble but for the odd ruin poking crazily out.

We swung right past the shelter, then left again beside the remains of a church to enter a broad road bisecting parkland which had been divided into allotments. At the end sprawled a large group of buildings which turned out to be a moderately undamaged block of flats. Bordering the road we marched past our anti-tank Platoon preparing their supper. 'G'aan, stuff your *** selves you lazy coots!' one of our Jocks called, and got jocund but unprintable reply. Someone had a 'squeeze-box' and was crushing out a lively tune which set our column whistling. Perhaps it was our whistling which tuned our ears more insistently towards the shells of the barrage, whispering and shuffling, and the occasional 'short' screaming close overhead to crump dismally somewhere not far beyond the wall of flats.

Some noisy, massive vehicles parked beside the road ahead with numerous powerful engines rumbling and belching blowlamps of exhaust flames. They revealed themselves to be a column of our tanks waiting for the next wave of attack, which it very much seemed was going to be our turn. Our tummies felt a bit more squeamish as the sections halted and shunted together like trucks on a goods train and we prepared our thoughts for what lay ahead. Our turn to halt came within the gloom of the flats on a crossroads. As the tramp of our feet ceased, so the dismal concussion of raining explosive sounded even closer ahead.

The clatter and zoom of a tank belting along at high speed towards us from the right took shape as one of our medium tanks. It ploughed dramatically, clanking and revving to a halt in a dusty spin-turn on the crossroads, reversed, spun to its right then roared off to halt somewhere ahead in the gloom.

NIGHT ATTACK ON
BREMEN – SECOND PHASE

Smyg walked back along the line of the Company: 'Get your chaps into the ground floor of these flats on the right for a short breather, while you come up to the first floor for an 'O' Group.' A stream of battle-grimed and equipment-laden men skidded and clattered their hobnailed progress into the polished, clean and well-furnished passages and apartments of the flats. We seemed to be breaking into another world of opulent peace. The owners or tenants of those flats that had not been selected for invasion, peered with timid interest at us from part-opened doors, each providing a cosy glimpse beyond of the trim furnishings, soft lighting, neat clothes and family life. It all seemed totally out of place and unreal compared with the acres of destruction, desolation and desperate scenes outside. Even the crash and scream of shells and rumble of tank activity sounded muffled and remote from within.

On securing an entry to a flat the clumping Jocks just slumped down amid a clatter of equipment to doze where they had subsided, for the most part with total disregard for the frightened and tense women, children and occasionally men of the family who stood looking on in uneasy bewilderment. One sensed each spectator was battling with a mental adjustment to a situation and its implications which they had probably worried about increasingly for some time as the sounds of battle had crept ever nearer. The occupants of the flat I had selected for Platoon HQ were a very well dressed, portly, red-faced man with a little moustache who was suffering from most obvious mental turmoil in trying to know what manner to adopt towards us. There was an interested, pimply teenaged son with a hatchet face whom we had met at the door and a pretty sister, his senior by a few years, who seemed washed out with fear or lack of sleep. The mother, like the daughter, had a trim, sleek elegance akin to a Dresden figure which was added to by expensive well-cut clothes in soft tasteful colours. In their startling contrast to the Jocks, they made the latter look like heaps of mud-smeared vegetables.

The father fussed about in a pathetic endeavour to make his uninvited, outlandish guests comfortable. He had evidently decided that the best line was to offer the utmost cooperation. He knew a little English and when he heard Platoon Sgt Cockburn address me as 'Sir', he dashed for a bottle of wine and some glasses and poured out two drinks tinkling the glass with his nervousness in rapid vibration. He seemed a bit abashed at my filthy, un-officer-like aspect and the similarity of my garb to the others and even more at a loss when I declined the drink with thanks and the explanation that I did not drink. Sgt Cockburn, however, was in fettle enough to do justice for us both. 'Go easy at it!' I warned him. 'The main troubles of the night are ahead of us yet.' I felt very sorry in a way for the father in his obvious fright. I wondered if, perhaps, he had threatened to give any invading troops a very different reception and was mentally turning on himself for not having done so. The daughter and the mother, who reflected the father's fears and who perhaps were the object of them, had taken refuge in each other's arms in a far corner of the room and there they clung to each other for mutual comfort, isolated by the sprawling men and tangle of equipment covering the thick-piled carpet. They were not to know the brief duration of our invasion and, happily for them, the men were too worn out to ferret about the place and get them busy in the kitchen, or even rise to the usual bait of 'pulling the leg' of the daughter, but dozed instead.

Leaving the Platoon, I set off to find Smyg for the 'O' Group in the back of the building on the next floor. Initially I had some difficulty in locating where he had got to and so made the frightened acquaintance of several more families in the flats before two teenaged, very likeable German youngsters, a boy and a girl, I should think brother and sister; took my arm and guided me to Smyg! Their complete lack of hostility, indeed friendliness, amazed me.

I found Smyg standing over a table spread with maps and his equipment and had arrived just as Sgt Cowie's eyes lit on a fine Leica camera in a light leather case, which he showed he intended to 'liberate' by placing it in his small pack. He was later very upset as he not only forgot to take the camera on leaving the flats, he left his small pack too, so that the German family gained the treasures already secreted therein.

'Right! are all the Platoon Commanders here?' said Smyg, with his interest still buried in the maps. 'This is our area "N" on the map. The area to be covered by the Battalion will be split into two strips. The division is this zig-zag moated area with the left of the axis the Weser and the railway on the right. Each strip will have a company up supported by another to pass through when necessary. B Company will lead on the right and D on the left. All west of the river should by now be in 51 or 3 Division hands. Do not at first clear buildings properly. Get to your objective as soon as possible. There will be one Crocodile per Company which is to be screened by an infantry section each side. These crocs will not be up at the start, but will be on call. If the crocs are up, forward sections must display a yellow silk triangle to show where they have got to and to avoid battle accidents. On call we will have AVREs, Petards and a recce party of REs in scout cars for mines; also a troop of SP 17-pounders. What reception awaits us is anyone's guess. The OC the German troops has threatened he is going to "fight to the last man". We shall see. Hamburg Strasse is the main axis to Verdner Friedrichstrasse, 11 Platoon up first on the right to Bahnhof Platz, then 10 Platoon is to take the lead.'

Smyg then proceeded to point out individual Platoon objectives and the likely position of Company HQ in consolidation. 'Artillery support will be H-25 to H, four field regiments, two medium regiments and four batteries of heavy artillery. The Barrage will end with two rounds of smoke and two rounds HE. The 38 set is to go on the carrier. Draw extra grenades. Watch the exposed right flank the whole way up and on consolidation. Take a good look at the Company objective on the map before you set off, as the buildings you are looking for may be down. Here it is:

the T junction between the library and museum. D Company will take the next crossroads on the left. If you see figures down there, do not shoot up D Company on consolidation. The moated island on the left of the Battalion position beside the river will be cleared by C Company after our objectives have been reached. Radio contact may be difficult. The trailing tram wires seem to be mucking it up, any questions?' After a couple relating to rations, prisoners and RAP, we hurried back to our Platoons to hold another 'O' Group.

As so often there seemed all too little oppotunity to pass the information down to the Jocks as 'O' Groups at higher levels had eaten up too much time. I made a hurried enlarged copy of the objective in my note-book and this laid out the section positions roughly on paper so that each Jock would have an idea of his position in relation to other sections when the spot was reached. From what we had so far seen of the devastation in the approaches to the city, it seemed that our main problem was likely to be recognising the landmarks and keeping to the route where buildings that might otherwise have helped us had been obliterated by the shells and bombs. 'Section Commanders, whatever you do, keep a tight control over your sections. Its likely to be rather dark, Bremen's quite a big place and as we get farther in it may be in even more of a shambles.' Outside, as the drumming of the artillery increased, I issued the order of march to my Platoon. The order 'prepare to move' came, then out we clattered into the flashing unfriendly darkness to fit ourselves into the Company order of march.

I located the Crocodile flame-thrower which was to advance with us and was greatly cheered to find that, in addition, we had two buckshee Churchill tanks which had materialised from somewhere and which raised morale noticeably. We split into section files and instinctively clung to the gloom in the shadow of the flats while waiting for the barrage to lift from its oppressive racket. It seemed impossible that we should see the two smoke and two HE shells which would signal us to advance.

11 Platoon were to lead us on the first few hundred yards and on finally getting the signal to advance over the tank radio they led off, moving jerkily from cover to cover. We followed at a

slight interval, clinging to the walls and moving carefully among the rubble to make ourselves as inconspicuous as possible in the dark. Any hope we might have entertained of our attack being accomplished as a silent penetration under cover of the night was suddenly shattered. The tanks, hitherto just rumbling to themselves with idling engines like a simmering volcano, burst forth with the most appalling roaring of engines and clatter and squeak of tracks crunching through the rubble. Their racket more than filled the quiet left by the artillery. Despite the usefulness of the tanks' presence, we heartily cursed their advertisement of our advance to any enemy who might be waiting in ambush far ahead among the forbidding gloom of the desolate rubble and acres of wrecked buildings. Any tell-tale sounds they might make, which could have warned of their presence and location, would be quite drowned, I realised gloomily.

Once the advance had commenced, aches, fatigue and hunger faded into second place in our thoughts. The fear-primed pumping of our hearts helped pep and wake us up a bit. Our hitherto empty-feeling stomachs now seemed fully occupied without their supper in getting adjusted to the future. Slowly, in fits and starts, we proceeded between tall, ominous shells of gutted buildings set with dark, gaping glassless windows which brooded cliff-like on either side. The surrounding silence to our oasis of noise and the unknown whereabouts and intention of the enemy or where he would make his stand, gave the experience a nervous tension, pregnant with lurking fears and danger to any of us who possessed too vivid an imagination. The possibilities of enemy mischief seemed endless in the circumstances if he was determined to fight it out. We were moving forward among these strange, confusing canyons of desolation as though on trust that we were not walking into an elaborately prepared ambush of the entire column from either side at point-blank range. To try to guard a little against this, at any halt I ordered part of each section to check quickly over the buildings alongside. At any crossroads we checked especially earnestly to try to detect any threat to the tanks from concealed 88mm guns. If any determined snipers did open fire, we realised locating them among the hundreds of gaping windows would be a terrible job.

At any open spaces, as well as the crossroads, we left the tanks waiting in the gloom and dashed flat out with a clatter and skidding of hobnailed boots towards any cover and shadow that could be found on the far side. Each time it came to our turn to take the lead, one felt as one madly dashed over that the fierce rip of Spandau bullets from some dark strong point might shatter our bodies at any moment. Each time, too, to get clear of the open, moonlit space and into shadow again seemed an awfully long and conspicuous run. At the far side we paused to regain breath while the tanks in their own way made a clattering, roaring dash to rejoin us. I suspected the tank crews must have felt quite as ill at ease as we did in contemplating just where and when we would run into the ambush that common sense told us must now lurk somewhere very close ahead.

We were several hundred yards beyond the limit reached in the attack of the previous Battalion and still no sign had been seen of the enemy to give any clue of his whereabouts, strength or intentions. The very quietness between our jerks of advance added fuel to our imaginations. What was Jerry up to? Had he prepared a last-ditch stand somewhere in the centre of the city? It would be quite possible, we realised, for several Battalions of enemy infantry to be concealed in the buildings already passed. The dangling tram wires trailing from the smashed posts and buildings caught up in clattering festoons on the tank and carrier tracks, filling the air with a twanging rasp as we got out of the residential districts towards the shops. I marvelled that the entangled metal did not bring these vehicles to a halt.

'The d*** radio's b*** well useless!' my 38 set operator grumbled to me. 'I did hear earlier though, Surr, that the BBC reckon things are going *** well here. I hope they are *** well right!' he added anxiously. Radio communication had also broken down between the various companies and the command post back in the luxury flats, though we were not to know this at our level till later. Communication was only kept open by means of a despatch rider ferrying backwards and forwards through the hazards of craters, wire and rubble.

Another open space materialised ahead: a large roundabout beside which stood a wrecked white tram and a shot-up, dark-painted bus over the road from it. The tanks again held back to let the forward sections clatter over the open space and establish themselves on the far side. The gloomy cavern of a road tunnel under the railway revealed itself to our right on our exposed flank. None of our troops were the other side of the track, so we treated the tunnel with the greatest respect, peering carefully through to try to make out if any anti-tank threat lay in its depths or at the other end.

'Hold it! Keep still, something moving in the tunnel!' I jerked out under my breath to the Jocks nearest me. Above the rumble of idling tank engines behind us, an echoing roar and a faint suggestion of light or its reflection issued from the blackness as we crouched, frozen, spines tingling and tensed in every fibre of our being. I cursed the racket of tank engines to our rear, for it was impossible to identify the sound in the tunnel. Whatever it was was coming fast.

With dramatic suddenness a dark swiftly moving shape formed and detached itself from the blackness and was on top of us as we recoiled, hearts hammering our ribs. We took the only action possible in the split seconds available and swung our rifles onto the dark shape to fire if needs be. As we did so there was just time to make out two figures almost on top of us, hunched on a motorcycle with a very dim light. We were still in the shadows as it banked to turn the corner towards the direction of our advance, and consequently had not yet been seen by the German riders. We stepped forward as one man to bar its path, fingers closing on the triggers as it seemed we would have to shoot to stop them. Instantly the riders saw us in the moonlight. They swerved violently. There was a momentary scream of rubber then an exclamation of pain as the bike stopped with the riders pressed right against the barrels of the two Jocks' rifles who were up with me in the leading section. Fortunately for the Germans neither Jock had fixed his bayonet. I had omitted to give the order. Otherwise the force of impact with the barrels into their bodies which made the Jocks stagger back, would have stuck both rider clean through like sausages on skewers. The motorcycle fell over so the two figures detached themselves from it as hurriedly as possible in their efforts to raise their hands before there was a chance of the Jocks deciding to shoot. Surprised exclamations in German, not unmixed with pain and fear continued as the Germans stood together, hands aloft. The driver appeared to be a D.R., though he may have been of higher rank for his badges were hidden under an overall. His peaked cap had fallen into the road with his goggles.

The pillion passenger was a lean slight man with a leather jacket over his uniform and had the look of an officer. He still muttered what I took to be curses, under his breath. Evidently German radio communication was giving trouble too. The Jocks frisked them both quickly for weapons (and watches), and they were marched back by one of the Jocks towards the rear to be whisked back for interrogation.

This diversion had let 11 Platoon get a little distance ahead of us and we set out to catch them up after running the motorcycle to the edge of the road. We had only covered a few more yards when the sudden violent shriek of a batch of shells enveloped us in an instant quadruple eruption of heavy explosions. We were only mid-way in our dive for cover as the flash, blast and shrapnel seared the street. Two landed in the road, bracketing us by 25 yards, one on the railway arch, and one on a building opposite. We had just smashed our way into a wayside door, when about five more shells arrived just as suddenly with the short vicious scream of a near direct hit. Some plaster and bricks fell about us and clattered our tin hats, but otherwise did no harm. These shells had the whack of about 5.5 inch calibre it seemed. The Jocks, coughing and patchy grey with spilled plaster, swore horribly and at great length. I did not voice my suspicions, later confirmed, that they were indeed 5.5' shells. They should have landed on the other end of the railway arch, and were evidently fired with the intention of keeping the enemy subdued on our exposed flanks. Before a message could be got back to correct this shelling, we subsequently heard that one of our supporting tanks had sustained a direct hit on the engine cover, which wrote it off, thought without injury to the crew. Another tank also suffered damage.

It was, as usual, a terrible job locating all the Jocks after such an incident. They just vanished and some, if inclined that way, remained 'vanished', thus evading the advance, to rejoin furtively later. Fortunately none tried this dodge and all reappeared. We soon regained contact with 11 Platoon and Smyg came up as we did so. All seemed too smooth to be true apart from the recent shelling incident. There was, nevertheless, an oppressive sense of lurking trouble. We were only 700 yards or so short of our objectives. The smoke from fires behind us no longer cut down the brightness of the moonlight. This gave a queer, cold light to the silent, deserted streets ahead. 'Bring your Platoon through to take the lead, Peter. This must be the big square short of our objectives. We'll cover you over', whispered Smyg. On our right was a large, solid building which I knew from the map detail to house the postal administration. It was surprisingly little damaged. (It was later used by our Battalion HQ, who fortunately evacuated it some time before it blew up from a German-planted time-bomb.)

Skirting the walls in the shadow, I led my men to the head of the square. I crouched to take stock of the surroundings before venturing on our long dash towards the cover of the museum. I was pleased to realise we were on course as I recognised the hangar-like steel skeleton of the Bahnhof and the station buildings on the right. A battered garage and hotel lay in ruins on the left. There was not a sign or sound of life ahead. The tanks had fallen a bit behind, and for the moment there was little sound of artillery and less of distant small-arms fire. It was queerly sinister and rather unnerving to contemplate the 300 yards of moonlit square confronting us, and the dark shells of the surrounding buildings, waiting, expectant, containing what? The cover was negligible. Cpl Dare's section (Point section) was in the lead. In groups of two, covered by the rest of us, they raced to a shelter out in the square. Still no enemy reaction. I dashed after him with Cpl Jones along the tram track to the tram shelter opposite the Bahnhof, followed by the rest of Platoon HQ. On the left Cpl Carbarns was filtering through the shadows along the rim of rubble, parallel to us on the other side of the road.

For a few moments I lay in the gutter, hidden in the shadow of the shelter, gulping breath for the next sprint and carefully running my eyes over the surrounding rim of buildings for any sign of a trap or impending trouble. 'Right Jones, take your section over to the museum and cover Dare over after you.' As he moved I joined him in the sprint. The loud clatter and skid of our boots echoed back frighteningly in the silvery sea of space which formed the square. Little did we realise then that a few feet beneath this deserted, lifeless scene were 1,500 to 2,000 squalidly crowded people living in air-raid shelters.

Reaching cover with relief at the far side I decided I had better let the other two Platoons and Company HQ catch us up a bit. I was considerably worried, too, that we had got at least 250 yards ahead of the nearest of our tanks. They would never be able to see our silk triangle of recognition in this light and with past experience in mind of twice before being fired on by our own tanks, we kept low and still so that they would not see figures ferreting so far ahead in the half-light. Smyg had soon worked up level with us over the road, joining Carbarns' section. Luckily the surroundings were recognisable in confirmation of the position of our objective, now only 100 yards ahead.

I was pleased to hear the roar and clatter of our armour over-hauling us again as we moved along on the last lap against the walls of the museum. There was still no sign of the enemy. I could not believe that the centre of Bremen had fallen to us without our having to fire a shot. The tanks swiftly deployed to cover the T junction and the square. Smyg, too, seemed puzzled and a bit worried that we had not yet located the enemy or fathomed what his game was. Surely Jerry must have some diabolical surprise yet to be unleashed on us for if he had not intended to make a fanatical stand surely he would have given in when the ultimatum was fired and saved so much loss and misery for the civilians. The museum itself was impractical as a section position and if Jerry had yet to reveal his hand we ought to get organised quickly to meet him on more favourable terms.

To cover the road junction I installed Cpl Dare and his men in the ground and first floors of the library at the corner, then doubled over beyond the museum to locate positions for the rest of the platoon towards what I recollected from the map to be a goods yard. This position should give us a field of fire forwards while still commanding the road junction and I hoped it would still be in visual contact with Dare.

I wondered what the time was. It must have been 2 or 3 in the morning. Quite suddenly I felt really tired. Together with Sgt Cockburn I broke through a gate into the rail yard then stopped. My spine tingled and heart raced as, tiredness forgotten, my eyes took in the sinister construction of a building immediately alongside us on the right. It had the top of a normal house, but the massive construction and unusual appearance of the bottom worried me. The ground floor was surely a concrete fort. Brooding, dark, blast-walled and steel shuttered windows eyed us. Taking Cpl Jones forward and to the left, we crawled under and in the shadow of some railway trucks to get a better look. There was no sign of life. If it was a block-house surely the enemy must have heard us busting through the rail yard gates. Perhaps he was waiting for more of us to show ourselves before he opened fire. 'Come on, Jones. If we want to find out more the safest place to be is probably right against it', I whispered. Together we dashed for the cover of its walls, conscious of the scattered form of Platoon HQ and two sections covering us in the shadows near the gate, their weapons trained on the windows and steel shutters. Yes, the walls were certainly concrete and from the inset windows, very thick.

A soft whirring sound attracted our attention and speeded our pulses at the location of the vent of an air extraction system blowing warmth through armour-plated slats. Though we still had not detected any sound of human beings inside, this seemed confirmation and was a very disconcerting discovery. It was puzzling too.

I crept along the wall towards the door, a solid forbidding slab of riveted grey steel. Together we gave it a push and stepped back on opposite sides of the entrance as it gave slowly and heavily. At the same time I pulled the pin of a 36 grenade and held on to the striker lever just in case. As the door smoothly continued to open with the weight of its own momentum, a broadening shaft of bright light shone out across the rail yard. A quick peep round the corner, kneeling to present my head at an unexpected level in case it should be fired at, revealed the surprising sight of a well-lit cream-coloured hall with a shiny floor and two more grey steel doors set one on either side. A flight of concrete stairs ascended on the right and continued downstairs. There was no sight or sound of occupation as we stood tense, listening for a few seconds at the doorway. I wished my heart was not making such a thumping. I felt sure it could be heard by anyone lying in wait.

'There's someone here Surr, I'm *** sure of it!' Jones whispered to me. I was sure too, but who, and what was the place? An army command post? If so, why was there no sentry to be seen? I looked about outside quickly in case we were being stalked from behind and this was some sort of trap. I waved Cpl Carbarns' section over. The two steel doors in the hall were locked. 'Search upstairs with your chaps, Carbarns. I'll look downstairs. Jones, watch the hall and these two doors.'

As the boots of Carbarns' section clattered up the concrete stairs, I suddenly detected voices coming up from below. German exclamations and the clang of another metal door down there. Those of us in the hall crept to the head of the stairs and I debated swiftly with myself whether to throw the grenade down, fire down a burst from a Sten gun, or chance the consequences of a quick look which itself might be met with a burst of fire up or a grenade. Something in the quality of the voices I could now hear more clearly below, just at the foot of the stairs by the sound of it, made me decide to risk a look with the grenade held ready to lob down. Perhaps I had detected fear in the voices. I was certainly glad I looked and so averted a tragedy. At the foot of the stairs were two elderly men in naval blue uniform, whose voices I had heard. Just behind them several women and children clutched each other in a huddle as they gazed up at us with stark, fear-dilated eyes. I pushed the pin back in the grenade and beckoned the men up to get them to unlock the two steel doors on the ground floor.

As the two reluctantly climbed up, searching our faces keenly and with fearful eyes to sense our intentions, one of the women moved forward a bit, sobbing softly and with a heart-pricking look of sheer misery and pleading brimming from her tear-filled eyes. What, I wonder, did she imagine we were going to do to their menfolk? Shoot them, or send them off to some distant POW camp? Her children moved forward to cling to their mother and started to whimper too, bringing the other women and children nearer to tears. I felt an utter cad, not knowing enough German to put them at their ease and seeing the anguish the least movement of one of the Jocks' weapons wrung from them. This sort of thing, I thought to myself, is one of the nastiest parts of an attack.

All this had taken only a few seconds in all, I suppose, but to all involved it must have seemed an eternity. I banged on the steel doors with the butt of my rifle to get the two old chaps to unlock them. At the same moment Cpl Carbarns' voice called from above, 'All clear up here Surr! Just living rooms, furnished but empty. A good field of fire though Surr.'

'Jones, take your section up and join Carbarns in keeping a sharp look out for any signs of a counter-attack. Look all round, but 'specially ahead and to the right flank', I ordered.

It was with surprise that I realised that although we had arrived at such an unearthly hour of the early morning, most of the grown ups in our billet had been dressed and only the children had been in their night clothes. It then dawned on me how painfully these families must have waited and how fearfully, as the tide of war had trickled towards them. I supposed they had debated whether to await our arrival dressed, at an open and lit entrance upstairs, or downstairs with the lights on and the front (and only) door unlocked. They must have realised the risk had they locked it of the place being exploded open or burned down for it must have been obvious that the sinister fortress-like appearance of the building was sure to attract particular attention. I never told them how close the course they had chosen had led them to a hair's breadth of the end they had most probably planned so hard to avoid. I have often marvelled with gratitude since that I did not throw the grenade down when we were so sure the place must have been a strong point of some sort. One of the Germans fumbled at the lock with the pressure of a rifle pushed into his back by an impatient Jock.

As the door of the room on the left opened I walked in behind one of the Germans to gaze in amazement about a well-lit, spacious control room. It was lined with panels of dials and switches, coloured lights, a master clock, and at the far end a clicking telephone exchange. There was also a desk with several phones on it and some two-tiered wooden bunks and another door leading off into an automatic exchange. Over the passage, investigation revealed washrooms and some WCs in working order.

Upstairs were the comfortable flats of the two men who seemed to control what I surmised to be the fortified railway telephone and perhaps signalling system. This would make an ideal HQ. What lay downstairs? I decided to look as soon as I had satisfied myself that the Platoon was established with fire positions laid out to repel any likely trouble. One section upstairs had a fine field of fire to command the right flank and forwards. The second was in an equally good position to deal with the left flank and the T junction of the main road.

I took a quick scout round outside to look and listen for any signs of trouble and to sense where Smyg had established his HQ. I could see no evidence of enemy activity, which strangely enough was rather worrying. To know the location of an enemy and his likely composition and strength settles one's mind a bit.

Returning to my new HQ, I set off downstairs to see what was there, but took no chances in case any enemy troops might still be secreted down there. There seemed the possibility, too, that it might have been connected with the Bahnhof bunker by a tunnel. My presence with Cpl Carbarns sent the women into another flap judging by the sound of their voices as our boots clattered down the concrete stairs. This, I guessed, evidently hinged on the fear that we would turn them out into the cold, hostile night and continued shelling which was now falling into the next sector for the troops shortly to leapfrog past us towards the docks and U-boat pens. The basement contained the families, personal effects and bedding of the two members of staff. It also contained the transformer rooms and main cable ends. I gathered that a large bunker, it seemed the one under the Bahnhof, ran a generator which charged the storage batteries and maintained the electric light, heating, water pumping, air conditioning and gave power for the exchange. I suddenly realised on kicking open the far door on the right that the women had been embarrassed at our sudden visit some while after our first entry into the place by more than the fear that I should turn them out. As the door crashed back I was quite as confounded by the embarrassing realisation that I had broken in on an intimate scene. Both women stood partly clothed, changing for a sleep they had evidently felt secure enough to take. I quickly withdrew after a momentary hesitation at the realisation that I did not know enough German to begin to express my apologies. I must have felt more flustered and confused than they as I left them, clutching bedding and clothing to themselves. If such scenes were likely to be repeated I resolved to put the basement out of bounds to the Jocks. On reflection another thought struck me too: surely these women were too young to be the wives of the two old chaps. Perhaps their husbands were in the forces and these were the in-laws. Anyway, I fled.

'Take over for a while, Sgt Cockburn', I said. 'I'm off to locate Company HQ and try to find out what's going on. Keep 100 per cent look out until we are sure the next Battalion has passed through.' Leaving my small pack and surplus equipment I crouched, flitting from shadow to shadow in search of Smyg and Frank in their new HQ. As I clattered my way I worried at trying to remember the password for the night before in case I got challenged, for I had left my orders book in my small pack. It was eerie to be out on one's own in this strange foreign city in the early hours under such circumstances; yet there was no denying a certain excitement. Anything or nothing might happen at any moment, it seemed, as I thought back over the variety of situations which had presented themselves over the last few hours.

I realised as I moved that though I could see no one, at least several Jocks and their weapons would be following my movements. There was every possibility that other less friendly eyes and weapons were trained on me from the tumbled, gaping ruins of the surrounding buildings which shone in the cold pale light of the moon like mounds of bleached bones and pensive, expectant skulls.

I was worried that the password still eluded my memory and that my progress over the hard, metalled surface and glass, scattered rubble in hobnailed boots should so advertise my movements. I was part way along the side of the museum moving towards the Bahnhof Platz when a figure detached itself from the opposite side of the road. I swung my rifle onto it as we faced each other and with inspiration I challenged: 'Corporal Dare?' It was. 'How are you getting on?' His chaps were well settled in, I found. Neither of us had any news. 'I think Company HQ is somewhere down there on the right', he said. 'Do you know the password, Dare?' I was pleased that he repeated it. I knew Smyg and Frank already had a good idea of our present location for a runner I had sent back to find them earlier had met them checking my defence layout.

A sentry outside what otherwise looked like a heap of rubble informed me I had located Company HQ. I penetrated into the bowels of this wreckage which, it transpired, was all that was left of a large hotel. The scene which unfolded was surprising as I got inside the basement. There, at a table covered with a trim cloth on which rested bottles and glasses of choice wines, sat Frank and Smyg, legs crossed and with an air of leisure in a benched alcove of a basement bar. Waiting on them in these surprisingly luxurious surroundings my astonished gaze fell on a neatly dressed obsequious hotelier who spoke excellent English. Both beamed at me in appreciation of my facial astonishment.

The Battalion was now on its objectives except for the clearing of the 'island', which it had been decided should be done at the coming of daylight. Where the German forces had got to was still a mystery. Sgt Oliver had routed between sixty and seventy armed German police from an enormous air-raid shelter under the Bahnhof. This massive concrete bunker was electrically lit, lined with bunks and teeming with civilians in thick, smelly air. A large pile of Luger pistols but little information was collected from these police.

While at Company HQ I got permission from Smyg to move Cpl Dare over from the library, which was now occupied by 11 Platoon, so that he and the others could join the rest of the Platoon, adding strength to our control house. I also learned that Sgt Dickinson had patrolled up to the dock area and had brought back some prisoners for A Company. There was still no sign or news of the 5th Bn KOSB, who we were still expecting to pass through. Radio contact continued to be very difficult, so I suggested to Frank that we patrol back to the tunnel beyond the postal building to secure the enemy motorcycle that had run into us to help communications. This we did, finding the machine still with its lights on, leaning against the wall where we had left it.

While we were out we stumbled over what at first I took to be a wounded chap rolled into the mess of the gutter. It turned out to be a reeking, drunken, displaced person who was fortunate not to have been churned flat under the tracks of some of our tanks which we could see from the powdered rubble had not missed ironing him out by many inches.

INTERLUDE

Imade my way back to the control room to see all was well with the Platoon, having learned that no further Battalions would pass through us until the approach of dawn as the rate of advance had been much more rapid than expected. This meant we would have several more hours to wait before we could relax a little with other troops ahead of us. Even then the ground on the exposed right flank just over the railway tracks that ran alongside our HQ would still be in enemy hands.

As there was only one entrance and to avoid being trapped if the place took fire during an enemy counter-attack I installed a strong point opposite the door and concealed in a shed. Two chaps were on duty there and two more at the entrance itself. In addition, I kept two contact patrols of a couple of chaps each roving round the area to link with Company HQ and the two other Platoons. Upstairs the remainder of the Platoon maintained a 100 per cent all-round watch while waiting for the 5th KOSB to pass through.

It was several days now since any of us had secured either a good sleep of more than an hour or two, or a proper meal and it was abundantly plain that we were all beginning to feel the effects pretty heavily.

Going downstairs I sat for a while in the warmth of the control room. A row of clocks whirred and clicked. At quarter-minute intervals there was the noise of the master-clock correcting the other clocks on the panel. The air purred with the sound of the air-conditioning plant. We surely could not have hit on a better billet in all Bremen. It had every modern convenience, including radio, central heating and WCs that flushed.

One of the Germans in what I now surmised to be railway

uniform came up into the control room where I was sitting, glanced at me and made his way over to his desk. He sat down and looked over to my side of the room with an expression of what I took to be puzzled interest. Suddenly a light showed green on his desk phone panel and the phone bell rang. As he reached to answer it my mind was working flat out to decide while I could still stop him, whether he should be allowed to do so or not. I did not know where the call was coming from, but it seemed evident from its coming at all that it was from some point not yet occupied by us. Neither did I know enough German to even begin to decipher what he might give away on our positions if he did answer. I swiftly realised that to stop him, the phone having already given the ringing tone, would also indicate something wrong at our end, that we were in possession of Bremen up to this point. As we had not yet made direct contact with the enemy, this might still be useful information, but to let him talk may have given away a lot more.

I jumped up and gave a loud yell of 'Achtung!', brandishing my revolver in his direction, hoping that this would have the desired effect in time, but resolved to put a bullet into the wall above his head if it failed. My meaning proved adequate, indeed he seemed merely to have been testing whether he could get away with it. As I made my way over to him, other lights winked and there were clicking and whirring sounds from the panel behind him. In English, French and what German I knew I set about trying to decipher from him just who was on, or likely to be on, the line and with what places he had still contact by phone. He said he had had a call from Hamburg just before we had got in and could still reach all places to the north of us. I called for Pte Lee, one of my chaps who had been a GPO worker, and together we went with the German into the circuit room where all the contacts were. There Pte Lee suggested we take out all the fuses to put the exchange temporarily out of commission. This, I hoped, would then give the impression to any future callers anxious to get information on our progress, that the line was either bombed or shelled.

We did not discover until two days later that this chap had a small locked room in the basement leading off the room into which I had inadvertently intruded while the two women were changing. Into this room the cable ends came and he could, and possibly did, tap in on these to communicate with the enemy.

I wondered whether the women had deliberately staged the embarrassing situation into which I had blundered when they had heard our boots on the stairs, with the purpose of flustering me from too close an inspection of this room. I think in any case the Germans living in the basement of our building were not really in a position to gather information which would have been of much use to the enemy. We had confined them to the basement and occasionally to the ground floor and from neither place could they have seen outside but for a glimpse of some railway trucks opposite the front door.

Eventually word came that the 5th KOSB were to pass through us early the next morning. We turned out to see them pass as they trudged towards the dock area. My Jocks egged the section files on with wit from the comfort and security of their positions, yelling such remarks as: 'Ye'll hae'nae bother the noo after th'hell we knocked oot a Jerry. Ye'll likely find we've feenished th' b***s for ye!' Meanwhile, C Company were busy completing the clearing of the island.

As daylight came the position began to clarify a little. Prisoners were constantly being winkled out as every building, bunker and ruin in the area was carefully searched. These prisoners were then marshalled by the RSM who buzzed round them like a cheeky little terrier. They were gone over for weapons, then marched off in batches of fifty. Gradually the motley haul mounted to the surprising total of 1,200. In addition to these, an SS police battalion was also rounded up. Their commandant insisted on being accorded the 'honour' of a formal surrender to our CO in the square, where before his assembled Battalion he handed over his dagger and pistol with Prussian precision, then his men piled arms. I marvelled that we had ever been able to percolate far from silently in a strange city by night through armed Germans who outnumbered us by about 2½ to one, with so far as I was aware not a shot being fired at us in resistance!

With these enemies 'in the bag' and a Battalion of our own past us towards the docks it became increasing difficult to keep the

Jocks alert. This was still very necessary, for we had strong reason to suspect the enemy still held all the area to our north just a few yards over the railway track. Certainly none of our own troops were yet there. Frank, who later had occasion to inspect the Bahnhof bunker, was staggered to find that despite unknown dangers from the enemy, fatigue, hunger and the inability to speak more than half a dozen words of German, two Jocks had actually installed themselves down there. They lay comfortably reclining on bunks in the shelter amid the teeming German civilians and a few still-armed police. As though this were not enough each had lying beside him his rifle . . . and a German fraulein. It was not clear whether fear or bribery with rations chocolate and cigarettes had induced these girls to submit to the Jocks.

As the sun rose, lighting up the grim ruins about us and the last wisps of smoke ascending from fires still smouldering in the rubble, thousands of displaced persons appeared from nowhere. Most of them, already merry with the intoxication of both liquor and liberation, seemed preoccupied with looting the city. In our area they at first concentrated on some wine stores and goods and food in transit in the railway warehouses. I stood in the square watching the scene from Company HQ as a group of French DPs broke out onto a balcony on the Bahnhof buildings, both men and women singing and clowning to the milling people in the square below. They busied themselves in trying to hoist an improvised tricolour. As they revelled, tanks and troops passed steadily up the main axis, interspersed with supply vehicles. Overhead our artillery shells trailed, moaning their dismal tune, pounding the far end of the dock area and into the park over the railway track. Suddenly there was a swift shriek of a short shell – unless it was a contribution from the enemy – about the calibre of a 25-pounder. Flame, smoke, plaster, brickwork and dust plumed, twanging outwards with shrapnel. It was a hit slap on the wall beside the revellers' balcony. For a few seconds after the crash of the explosion faded from the square, there was silence while the dust and smoke blew lazily away, lit with a warm, unreal light of spring sunshine. Remarkably, as the balcony again took shape out of the smoke, one or two of the stunned revellers could still be seen staggering sluggishly below the shrapnel-splashed brickwork of their battered perch. A violent stampede developed among the throng in the square below. I had intended seeing what could be done for the survivors when another incident distracted me. A report came that three other ranks from our Company, Cpl Cannon, Pte Connel and another private had found a civilian car into which they had climbed. Pushing the starter button had unexpectedly proved the vehicle to be in working order. Considering the fluidity of the enemy still at large, these three had very foolishly and contrary to orders set off for a spin round the area. Some firing had sounded fiercely through the road tunnel under the railway beside the Bahnhof, but its source or cause could not be seen from our side. At this stage these two separate incidents did not seem to have any connection. The Jocks had just disappeared. It was not until two days later when an attack was put in to clear north of the railway that the only survivor of this joy ride was recaptured from the German marines. His sorry tale was confirmed by the bullet-riddled and bloodstained car. I learned in talking to the survivor that as soon as their vehicle had emerged on the other side of the tunnel it had run into a patrol of marines who had fired, killing Cpl Cannon and Pte Connel outright. Being in the back, the third Jock had ducked down and survived to be captured. These were two of the most futile, unnecessary casualties, apart from battle accidents, that the company ever had.

During the day Smyg located and put a guard on the wine store which had been causing so much drunkenness among the displaced persons and to some extent among the Jocks. Increasing attempts were also made to stem the wholesale looting which was in progress. This produced bizarre scenes such as the sight of slave workers, like scavenging ants, dragging whole sides of beef through the rubble to consume in orgies in their miserable camps, cooked over splintered woodwork from the ruins.

Frank Coutts and I, accompanied by L/Cpl. Brown, had secured information from a hotel keeper that a chief of police was still to be found in the Bahnhof bunker and we set out to locate him. Our intention was to see what success he might have in stopping the German civilians who had joined the looters in strength. We would have moved less happily among the milling swarm of smelly shelter dwellers and quite a few German police who were still down there had we realised then that the shelter communicated under the station with the other side of the track, and that the marines who controlled that side had only a few minutes before shot up the Jocks in the car.

Before we eventually located the man we were after and fetched him out, we saw just about every facet of family life in the electrically lit caverns. Some of the occupants must have been living there for weeks, perhaps years, and now sanitation had practically broken down. There was no privacy and blowsy, doped-looking beings in varied apparel eyed us wearily from their bunks. Apart from some taking an interest in us as the first 'Ecosse' they had seen (revealed by Frank's tam-o'-shanter), the average German evidenced little expression. While on our search we were interested to locate the electric generator at work which powered our control room and lit the bunker. The mains for the rest of the city were, of course, out of action, as were all the other public services.

I was very sorry for the mothers struggling to carry on some sort of home life for the young children and babes in arms under these circumstances. Where they got any food from which was suitable for grown-ups, let alone children, was hard to imagine.

The German police chief confessed he would be unable to make any impression on his looting fellow countrymen without the authority of his Luger pistol to back him up, so we re-issued these weapons to some of the police.

I was considerably surprised during the day to meet some German stragglers being booed by German civilians.

It was decided that we should establish an observation post in the museum tower alongside our building, as it had a fine view of the line and marshalling yards almost as far as Vegesack. I climbed up with some of my chaps to investigate. Clambering out into the breeze on the roof provided a wonderful view and I had to remind the chaps not to show themselves too much.

I was surprised to notice that a locomotive standing about a mile down the track and pointing in our direction had wisps of steam escaping from the safety-valve. The area in which it stood was still enemy held and it struck me that to be letting off excess steam, it must have been stoked much more recently than our entry into the city. This was odd. Could the enemy have some scheme afoot of sending an explosives-packed train up the track to detonate in our midst, or perhaps they wanted to take a train-load of some special equipment out of the dock area before we overran it. In any event I decided I had better send a report on this activity to Smyg.

I poked my head out for a better view so that I could study the cab with my binoculars and the buildings round about for any signs of activity, but could see no movement. Returning down the stairs, I left two Jocks on duty up there in the OP. A couple of minutes later, as we stepped out of the museum and made our way over to the control house at its base, a brace of 88mm shells burst against the building. One shell hit just below the tower OP and badly shook the two Jocks in every respect. This showed that somewhere Jerry had an OP with an alert look-out who had spotted our slight movements on the roof. This incident was interesting too in that it was the first direct reaction the enemy had shown to our presence for some hours (apart from the marine shooting incident). It was pleasant to sit in what we hoped to be the shell-proof protection of the control room which the enemy had so comfortably provided for us, while his shells fell outside.

I had reported to Smyg on the communications system in our billet, and did so again, as despite our pulling of fuses there was still an occasional light winking and the clatter and buzz of the exchange working. I wished I had a complete and fluent command of German. The possibilities of pulling the leg of the enemy by ringing him up or answering incoming queries, or just chatting to him appealed to me in its novelty.

In an attempt to cut down looting and crowd scenes that might result in further casualties, a curfew was imposed restricting all civilians to their houses (except women, between 1000 and 1100 hours and 1500–1600 hours, when they were allowed out to scrounge food and water). A search was also instituted for the collection of all enemy weapons and ammunition. I acquired a police Luger, which I swapped for a camera from a Yank later at Oebisfelde. Lugers seemed to hold some fascination for the Americans. I was actually offered a Jeep in exchange too, a deal that would have aroused my interest if there had seemed the slightest chance that I would have been able to hold onto and use the vehicle personally.

It struck me that so far as I knew, no one had yet thought of searching the basement of the museum for any German stragglers, so I set out to do this. The top of the building was burned out, but I soon located the steps down beneath the tower. As I reached the foot of the stairs and stood adjusting my eyes to the darkness, I thought it wise to pull out my revolver. I also wondered if I was a bit rash to take on this job alone.

There was just sufficient light down there to distinguish, at times with the aid of touch, a pathway through a maze of weird and often large objects. Monstrous skeletons and carved figures kept confronting one out of the gloom. They must have been exhibits from the museum which had been brought down for safety and now in the gloom and the circumstances formed an outsized chamber of horrors. The eeriness of the experience of picking a path through this long, musty labyrinth had considerably heightened tension which was added to by the expectation of suddenly unearthing odd German troops who might still be in hiding. The thought was at the back of my mind, too, that any fanatic among such characters, with eyes better adjusted to the gloom, might in turn be stalking me as I was on my own. I paused at times, rather lost and not without a feeling of fear, to listen to sounds real or imagined which appeared to come from somewhere in the velvety, dusty forest of dark mystery. I hoped when I reached the far end that I would find an exit there after working down the length of the building. It was amazingly quiet. I could hear my own breathing, rather faster than usual, the tick of my G.S. pocket watch and my heart doing the rumba.

After a long search, all the while hoping that I did not find any difficult customers down there, I eventually reached a door at the far end of the vault. It opened onto a corridor, at the end of which was a dim glimmer of light. A little way up I met another door on the left. I pushed. It was not locked and opened silently to reveal a dank, dark, longish room. A glimmer of light filtered through a window partly obscured by an outside blast-wall. Peering more intently I made out an iron bed. Something lay on it, still and dark.

I tip-toed closer, half expecting to find the corpse of some forgotten soldier or civilian air-raid casualty. It was a body! That of a young, dark-haired woman of about nineteen. What on earth was she doing down here and how was she killed, I wondered. She lay on top of the bedclothes and in her clothes, but with her shoes off. I crept closer drawn to see if some evidence on her face might reveal some tell-tale expression as to her fate. The head lay rather unnaturally far back on the pillow, chin up. The oval mask of her face, with closed eyes, was framed by her dark hair on the pillow and bore a peaceful serenity I had not expected. Her arms, protruding from the short sleeves of a dark blouse, lay one beside her body and the other trailing towards the floor. Suddenly I became aware with a shock of the sounds of her slow deep breathing . . . she was sleeping the sleep of exhaustion. But why here in a bare dark dungeon of a room under the burnt wreckage of the museum and with no other soul about? Immediately I was fearful that she might awake and be scared out of her wits at seeing me there. I moved back out of the door and shut it as silently as I had opened it, greatly puzzled as to why she was there and who she was.

The answer provided itself unexpectedly a little farther down the passage. At the foot of another flight of stairs leading up to ground level, I froze in my steps on hearing German voices, among them one of a woman, talking in soft casual conversation. Moving towards a half-open door through which a lamp shone dimly, I peeped in and saw several German civilians resting or busy about a furnished room off which other rooms opened. This, I guessed, must be the flat of the museum caretaker or some other official. The mysterious 'sleeping beauty' I had found earlier must have been one of the family or a bombed-out friend who had been put up in an improvised bedroom separated from the rest of the flat. I had one scare before I climbed out into the ruins above. Distant voices and a torchlight were approaching and footsteps echoed along the corridor from the storage vault. It was with immense relief that I heard a volley of Scots swearing as a hidden obstacle was tripped over. I hoped they did not scare the girl. It was one of our search parties.

Our first night in the control room HQ was uneventful but for occasional shells and distant small-arms firing. I had a blissful four hours on one of the two-tiered bunks, but had the nagging realisation of the closeness of those enemy over the railway. Wondering what they might be up to ruled out complete rest.

By now two Battalions had passed through us to clear the suburb, factory and dock area to the north-west. The longer scream of shells before the crump of explosion told of the progress. The nearest enemy were, however, still only 250 yards away at the most, just over the railway track from us, so that this was now our main area to watch. If at any time during our advance through Bremen as a whole, the enemy had made a determined attack, even at only company strength and with one or two heavy tanks, he could easily have cut our supply lines and isolated us like a diver with his air pipe cut. Though this would not have affected the ultimate result, it would have disrupted the attack for a while and perhaps caused considerable mischief before they could have been cleared out. It was strange that so far as I know, the only chaps to penetrate our side of the track in our area were the two motorcyclists who had run into us on the way in, when apparently on their way to communicate with the cathedral and town hall.

During daylight I had taken the opportunity of 'standing down' as many men as I dared (50 per cent) so that they could catch up on sleep and prepare themselves proper meals so far as the rations allowed.

Pte Coupe, one of my chaps who had been out on the scrounge for a better radio than the one in our billet, reported to me that he had found a radio and also an armoury in a long steel and concrete bunker under the Reich Eisenbahn buildings. I decided this needed investigation, being the first I had heard of this particular bunker, and so returned with him to see it. We had to go round the side of the museum tower to get there. A Jeep with trailer attached was standing at the corner and we had just got level with this vehicle when our blood seemed to freeze within us. In a split second it was all over. We were still skidding for cover with ears singing from the blast of three really close shells which had burst, one in the road and two on the sides of the buildings of the alley in which we had been walking. Pte Coupe and I both crashed into the nearest doorway together and took cover there opposite the Jeep. As the smoke cleared, I was staggered to see that the Jeep and trailer were riddled with shrapnel and the vehicle's tyres were ripped in three places. 'Hell, Surr, we were only 4 feet away from yon Jeep when it was hit!' Pte Coupe muttered, half to himself, in awe-struck tones. As far as we were able to verify it, these shells were either 'shorts' or 'overs', 25-pounders fired by 43 Division from outside our divisional axis which should have landed the other side of the railway track. We completed the journey to the bunker feeling considerably shaken by the experience.

The bunker, electrically lit and of very thick concrete, was quite an extensive one. Furnished partly as some sort of office and storage place, it had already been well looted by the displaced people who had left a trail of scattered and damaged equipment, clothing and stores on the floor. There was a photographic developing room and a strong-room at the Bahnhof end with a massive 7-foot steel door of amazing thickness and weight. This door opened slowly with a long push to reveal cogs, other locking mechanisms and a combination lock. Beyond was a smallish steel- and concrete-lined room. We went in to look round, but came out with relief. If anyone had swung the door on us and turned the locking wheel we would have been in a desperate plight, even had someone known we were there. Back in the armoury I chose a .22 Mauser rifle with loading clip and ammunition as a memento, then smashed up the other weapons against a concrete post.

At dusk that evening, 27 April, while standing outside the control room, my eye was attracted by the glimpse of a figure moving in the half light about 400 yards forward of our positions. Whoever it was was picking his way between some trucks up the tracks of the railway siding. No Jock was immediately available to join me, so pulling out my revolver I stalked up along the line of goods trunks in what cover they provided, then, as the distance decreased, beneath them to see who this could be.

It turned out to be an old man who, bombed out, was living with his wife in squalor in a railway ganger's hut up there. I could get no information out of the old chap who peered sullenly at me in silence from a pair of watery eyes set in a blue-jowled, stubbly, dirty face. However, satisfied, I made my way back along a path beside the track in the open. I had got about half way when two shots from a rifle whiplashed loudly past my head, splintering and twanging off the woodwork of the trucks some distance forward. I dodged into the cover of a rail wagon, but could see no sign of whoever the sniper had been. My only clue had been the interval between the crack of the passing bullets then the much softer thumps of the rifle about 800 yards away towards Vegesack. So it could not have been what I had for a moment suspected: that the old chap had had a go at me with a Volksturm rifle, perhaps to get even for the loss of his home.

My sentries in the museum tower were subsequently sniped a dozen or so times, probably by the same chap, but with no success at the long range; the nicked stone parapet testified to some near misses, though. For a while we had to take greater care in our movements.

That night I called at Smyg's pub for a chat and a couple of gassy so-called orange drinks before returning with the password to fix stags for the night, pleased to hear that we would not move from our comfy hideout yet. Afterwards I sat in the control rooom with those of my Jocks who were off duty, listening to the radio we had scrounged that day. For interest's sake we tuned to a German-speaking station, partly because we had formed the impression that their musical programmes were better than the BBC. We were in for a surprise which had all the Jocks rolling in sarcastic laughter. During an interval between dance tunes, the old familiar voice of William Joyce, the traitor who was better known as 'Lord Haw-Haw', cut in with his nasal-rasping drone: 'Here are stations Bremen, Hamburg (and some other place), on a wavelength of . . .' Then followed a tale for consumption in England, evidently, and which amazed us. It concerned, among other things, the heavy losses which had been inflicted on us in our attack on the city; an attack which, it seemed, had failed. To be listening to this from the centre of the city from which the programme was supposed to be coming and two days after our entry struck the Jocks as rich. The broadcasting studios themselves were on the island we knew to be destroyed. Joyce's time was running out rapidly and soon hard facts would overhaul his eyewash and his career.

Though they had made up a lot of sleep, the Jocks were still very tired and a rather tricky period elapsed during the next twenty-four hours before the enemy were cleared from over the railway track. Our surroundings seemed for the most part peaceful and secure enough on the surface and it was difficult to convince the Jocks the enemy, who were in pistol shot if not stone's throw, might yet cause us trouble especially during darkness.

I came to really enjoy the sleeps provided by my bunk in the control room! It was some time since the switchboard had last given any sign of activity, but the leisured corrections to the master clock and the whirr of the extractor fan provided a measured lullaby I could not resist. During our short stay we had come to be on quite friendly terms with the railway families who lived in our basement. Several times I noticed the Jocks having a romp with one or other of the children and that the mouths of the toddlers were either stained with a circlet of melted Compo chocolate, or a small cheek bulged with one of the rationed boiled sweets. Our surplus 'dog biscuits' were also in demand. The Germans no doubt did not notice the word 'SPRATS' which these Army issue biscuits so tactlessly bore. One might have thought after the reputed pig-fat bullets of the Indian mutiny that the Army supply services would have learned a lesson in tact.

The next day we were suddenly startled by the heavy thundering of artillery smashing close by in the park area over the railway track. Several more stray shells carried over and smashed about our positions. This was 43 Division attacking to clear out the German marines. I had just been engaged in tracking down what I suspected to be a German straggler or OP.

While standing on the steps of Smyg's flat over his pub HQ and gazing up at the large, grey-green, camouflaged post office building, I had caught a glimpse of a uniformed figure furtively pushing out a telescope from a top storey window, head low down in a corner of the window. This looked suspicious so I took Pte. Schoolar, the Company runner and Frank's batman, along with me to investigate. After a long and quiet stalk up the several flights of stairs to what we judged to be the room in which they were, I kicked the door open as we three dashed in, prepared, we hoped, for anything. Two figures kneeling at the window spun round reaching for their weapons in startled amazement. We in our turn were equally amazed to recognise them as belonging to the Battalion 'I' or intelligence section. This was an OP they had established to try to detect signs of enemy activity.

As the thunder of the barrage increased over the track, I 'stood the Platoon to' 100 per cent in case any of the enemy retreated over the track onto us, then I hurried up into the museum tower OP to get a grandstand view of the attack. The scream of stray shells up there sounded awfully close at times. The scene was awe-inspiring. About 600 yards to our north a heavy drizzle of all calibres of shells and mortars was erupting beneath a towering wall of smoke and dust from the area of the park. They were arriving with a steady, echoing, drumming crumping in the trees and buildings: a most decisive and depressing racket. There was not a figure to be seen in the grey flame-flickering haze, nor could I yet see any sign of our attacking troops.

I was surprised to see, after the artillery had died down, how much was still standing in the way of trees and buildings among the ground haze of dusty smoke. The first sign of our own troops on the far side amazed me a lot. I caught glimpses of carriers and infantry passing at odd intervals between some buildings beyond the engine sheds, well ahead of the position we had expected to observe them. They must have moved very swiftly and right under the haze of the lifting artillery.

Later in the day BHQ and C and D Company took advantage of the park being clear and moved over there into better billets. At the same time the 28 American engineers were busy pushing their survey of the goods yards forward as the ground was cleared; they talked of having trains running again within three weeks.

Smyg decided that it was high time that strong guards clamped down on all the food and other stores in the station yard. Just beside our control room we had discovered that some of the rail trucks were loaded with potatoes, while in a building beside us was a food storage chamber. Both these places were seething with a horde of scrounging women, looting as hard as they could, filling sacks and pushing carts. If this were allowed to continue supplies of food might run out some time before normal supplies could be found to feed the stricken city. Struggling women had to be lifted bodily clear by the Jocks and myself when shouting our heads off proved of not the slightest avail, but they just fought their way back, struggling and wriggling through our grip like sinuous, smelly eels.

They seemed satisfied that unlike the German troops, we would not take any drastic reprisals. If they had taken only enough for immediate needs it would not have mattered so much. After a short free-for-all I decided there was nothing for it but to resort to the same wheeze which had had such quick results at Fallingbostel POW camp. Leaving Pte McKenzie battling with a buxom wench in his grasp, I pulled out my captured Luger and fired three quick shots into the air. The yard cleared as though swept by a giant invisible broom. Then commenced the task of repelling further attacks by shutting up the food sources as far as possible and putting extra guards on. A notice in English and German promising the death sentence to looters was posted up near the food store but vanished after a short time. Dingo armoured cars were constantly patrolling the streets, with Recce and military police personnel aboard to keep a watch on things.

That evening Smyg organised a tremendous evening dinner for the Company officers. Frank and I were still the only ones to keep Smyg company. It was held in the anteroom to the hotel bar under electric lighting specially rigged up from the bunker. 'George', the hotel manager, waited on us in tails as we sat round a spotless tablecloth on which silver and glasses glittered. Frank and Smyg had a high time with all the varied wines and unlimited supplies of champagne, schnapps, cherry brandy and so on with which they were plied. (MILGOV later clamped down on this and NAAFI sold the champagne at 16 shillings a bottle, having taken 100 per cent profit.) It was a queer experience, though, being served by a chap in tails to a wonderful meal in the cosy setting, while above us and all around were acres of rubble and rusting metal girders in a desolate, dead city centre. Our shabby, battle-grimed dress seemed very out of place. I marvelled at 'George's' composure as he moved expertly about, waiting on his uninvited guests who in addition would not pay. Admittedly most of the stuff we were eating consisted of disguised Army rations and he probably tucked into his share afterwards, but not a line of his inscrutable face or a flicker of his eyebrows betrayed anything but absorption in his task. Had he remotely considered substituting ground-glass for the sugar or putting arsenic in the coffee, I wondered? Perhaps he was pleased that the fighting was over and that the future was more likely to get better than worse. His hotel, but for a part of the basement, was reduced to a mountain of useless rubble. Perhaps his family had also suffered in the blitz. As with so many Germans as the days passed, I wondered what they really thought about the war, Hitler, concentration camps and ourselves. Hitler himself was disowned, at least on the surface, by everyone with the words 'Hitler no good!' Few, if any, would admit to being party members or to having supported him. He seemed to have got into power and waged a war without the consent or the support of the German people at all!

Whatever fighting was still taking place had swept by us now to the north-west towards the far end of the docks and in the direction of Vegesack. We rejoiced that so far we had been left to rest a bit and were only employed on protecting the axis with our presence, clearing things up and guarding certain points. On the evening of 28 April, Smyg decided to throw a party for the Jocks of the Company. It was held in a not too badly battered tavern in the corner of the Bahnhof Platz beside Smyg's HQ, and the owner and his wife slaved behind the bar counter to keep pace with the thirst of the Jocks for staggering quantities of wine which they were, to my alarm, consuming by the pint after pint after pint. Rather unwillingly I felt I ought to be there to be with the rest of my Platoon, and held a glass of *vin ordinaire* in my hand all the evening. This was gradually spilled out onto the floor as the evening progressed and my arm was jogged in the increasing revelries.

The party passed through all the usual stages in a thickening fog of cigarette smoke and increasing reek of drink. It began quietly enough with steady businesslike drinking. Gradually, various characters got up less and less steadily to sing tuneless songs, faces reddening and eyes glazing. There were interspersed with shaggy-dog stories and jokes. Sgt Maj 'Frankie' Pook, 'well on' and in 'hellish fettle', draped one arm around my shoulder and expressed embarrassingly complimentary sentiments to me in a confidential slur of words before he passed out, thereby doubly surprising me.

Dodd, Oliver, Cpl Arthurs, Cpl Neilson, Cpl Jones, Colour Sgt Jock Smith and all the usual ones slumped in turn to join the gathering groups of doped, sick and burbling figures lying over tables, on chairs and over the floor, each reacting to the varied ways drink hit them. Some of the Jocks were working themselves up into a frenzy which broke out into sprinkled fights, resounding with the crash of furniture and tinkle of glass. Above all rose the most frightful oaths directed at the German nation in general and threats to wreck the place.

The German couple behind the bar were beginning to look distinctly alarmed, but dared not refuse more drinks to those fierce Jocks still capable of asking for more, their fists rocking the structure on the bar counter. I found that, despite the wrongness of doing so, the only way to restrain some of the Jocks was to manhandle them, which in their drink sodden state was easily done. They were too far gone to listen to either reason or an order. Once again the consequences of Jocks, used to drinking perhaps eight or more pints of beer at a session and let loose with similar swallowing capacity on mixed spirits and wines, was becoming all too apparent. It was not immediately noticed that a few of the Jocks who had neither succumbed to drunken stupor, sickness or the effect of stepping out into the night air, had made their way over to the Bahnhof bunker to seek out 'German frauleins'. When it was realised what was happening, and only just in time before real mischief was caused, the section on duty joined me in sorting them out from varied stages of their amorous intent on terrified shelter dwellers, and trundled them back to bed. Once again it was amply proved that wines and Jocks just would not mix. How fortunate, I reflected, that the German marines had been cleared out before the party.

Next day, the fourth in the city, Frank Coutts and I went for a stroll, rifles slung, over to the 'island' business quarter of Bremen to have a look at the copper-green-spired cathedral, and the blown up and twisted rail and road bridges over the River Weser. In the cathedral, poking about in the dust in the half-light, we found a taciturn priest who showed us round, perhaps because he feared to refuse to do so. It was surprisingly little damaged considering the utter destruction all around it.

The surrounding buildings showed here as no more than a giant chess-board of rubble heaps and ploughed up roads, spattered with all the detailed, intimate debris of a blitz. Here and there gaunt rusting steel skeletons poked crazily out. As we walked we unwillingly smelled the tang of burnt goods and entombed bodies already beginning to make their presence felt. Apart from our troops and the occasional loot-laden, drink-soaked DP staggering past, the place was almost a dead city with an oppressive sense of gloomy desolation.

Later I made my way over to have a look at the Bahnhof itself, to see how sections of my Platoon posted to guard the place were getting on. Seldom could such wanton looting have taken place on such a scale before. To guard the remnants and wreckage was rather like shutting the stable door after the horse had bolted. The displaced persons and other odd people seemed not only intent on loot, particularly food and valuables, but they also proved to be intent on wrecking anything German they could lay their hands on. Wagon-loads of every conceivable item of stores, food parcels, clothes, instruments, Phillips radio valves and so on had been burst open. The contents of these vehicles were scattered ankle-deep among bicycles, bird cages and bottles and countless other items broken from storerooms in the station itself. The entire mess seemed to cover several acres. It was tantalising to walk and at each step crush some further package or item deeper into the mess. One foot was clotted with butter from a broken small tub and the other was flecked with sugar grains adhering to broken eggs. All the DPs in the city seemed to have been attracted here and were now held at bay by the Jocks who had constantly to thwart their attempts to creep back. DPs took evident advantage of the fact that they were assured of more humane treatment from the Jocks than would have been their fate under the Germans.

The strangest sidelight to this looting was my finding – in a storeroom in the subway which linked with the bunker near the electric generator – a station official in his uniform, looting feverishly side by side with DP. Once law and order wavered there was apparently no moral scruple to restrain even this chap to whom the goods had been entrusted.

The Jocks got great interest out of gathering round the radio to hear any references by the BBC to the Bremen front. Quite often they were stung to blasphemous anger by the news not matching up to our first-hand experience or the omission of credits to individual units in one instance and not in another. The Jocks were also annoyed by the trend of the radio and particularly any newspapers which reached us of beginning to dabble in petty political post-war worries as though the war was entirely over.

Our kitbags finally reached us when the B Echelon vehicles arrived. This enabled us to pull out our battledress and put it on for the first time in many weeks, discarding for the time being our filthy, battle-ripped, windproof smocks.

While we of 10 Platoon remained at our old billets, the rest of the Company moved over to the Eisenbahn buildings. The cookhouse was established in the bunker below and the bank was used as a dining hall. It was pleasant to once again see the Jocks in neat, clean battledress with the colour of their brigade bars and tartan shoulder flashes, with clean webbing and boots and with tam-o'-shanters on their heads. Their faces, too, looked strangely clean and newly shaved. The few Germans who had begun to appear took a surprising interest in us quite openly and gathered in handfuls about the Bahnhof Platz to watch us parade once again as a Company.

The Germans in our control-room billet also took a new interest in the changed beings who clattered in and out of their home. They were intrigued by the 'pips' on my shoulders and asked in puzzled amazement, 'Offitzier?' I would have been more flattered had they expressed slightly less surprise! The identical dress we had so far worn must have been puzzling, though. Once again, they like other Germans before them, expressed surprise to me on the closeness and ease of relations between officers and men in the British Army, compared to theirs.

Next came the familiar note of pleased surprise as the tam-o'-shanters and tartans were pointed to with the question 'Ecosse?'

Then another often followed it: they pointed to our trousers and with facial query mimed the wearing of a kilt. We then had to explain that in our Regiment only the pipers wore them and to put this over was quite a formidable task. Similar expressions of surprise from the Germans who had got to know us greeted the recognition of Frank, Smyg and Pip who had just rejoined us. I then realised we had hitherto been all classed as NCOs, if that, by our dress.

All who could rejoiced that day in eating and resting and looking forward to the promise of a good night's sleep with the comfort, a rare one indeed in action, of a blanket or two for the completion of bliss. Life did not seem half bad, I thought, lying on my bunk that evening with a full tummy of food and tea provided by the company cookhouse, some mail from home in my hands, pleasant music to listen to on the radio. There was no immediate foreseeable threat of a move to shatter our peace, the possibility that the war, to judge by the radio, would be over any moment, and the added feeling of peace of mind provided by the massive strength of the structure in which we rested should any fool, friend or enemy, shell us or shoot us up overnight. What a wonderful night's sleep that was. The very highlight of all the sleeping I had yet done or ever hoped to do. I not only had my boots off, I took my socks off too for real luxury. Next morning, how we lay and gloated over the prospect of breakfast with a pint mug of tea, all cooked for us; and other likely meals beyond it, then – was it too much to hope? – another similar night's sleep.

The sun rose with a flourish on our fifth day in Bremen. A Battalion parade was held in the Bahnhof Square, watched by an increased sprinkling of civilians, and Gen Hakewell-Smith came along to give us a congratulatory talk on the completion of the task of capturing the city. He gave orders for the mass of Jocks to break ranks and gather round. The day was then capped by the pipers, or 'Das Doodlesacken' as the Germans appeared to call them (or the pipes), coming on to play in the square. The skirl of the pipes in this strange setting acted as a magnet to German civilians and displaced people alike, drawing them out of the ruins from near and far to watch with intense interest.

Yet another day of peace passed for us in pottering around

Bremen and getting ourselves reorganised. I also found time to write home and censor the Jocks' mail. Then the whine of the TCVs heralded their arrival. 'Prepare to move!' 'Now what?' we all asked ourselves.

Leaving my wooden two-storey bed in the control room for the last time with a regretful glance about and a nod to the German family and a handful of sweets for the kids, I trudged with my Platoon to the trucks trying painfully hard to weigh up the likely remaining duration of this seemingly endless and mad war.

No Unnecessary Risks!

The only rumour circulating that seemed to contain a scent of reality suggested that we were to head about 20 miles to the north to take over an establishment from 43 Division. This apparently contained mental hospital or some such patients whom it appeared the enemy had been trying to eliminate. Whether this was true or not we were never to find out. Such a place did not materialise. The plan must have been changed while we were in transit. There were rumours, however, a short time afterwards that Belsen concentration camp was to have been the destination.

Rumour also suggested the enemy was still resisting on the high ground a short distance to the north-west of Bremen, and in the marsh and heathland to the north. One by one the convoy of TCVs rolled over the Bahnhof Platz and under the fatal railway arch chosen by the three Jocks for their joy-ride. On our right we passed some wrecked single-deck trams and on our left the shell-ripped trees and grass of the park and a towering concrete bunker which had been the former HQ of the last Germans to surrender in Bremen. A little farther on in Burgher Park, near the railway level-crossing, we were interested to see a POW hospital with some figures pottering about and watching us pass. Quite suddenly we were in open country, running along beside a small canal with water sparkling and ducks paddling in the fresh sunlight. Crossing the autobahn we kept on towards the north-east. It was a lovely spring day, 2 May if our reckoning was correct, and the Jocks, refreshed by the rest, were occupied as I was in watching the passing landscape with enjoyment. It was almost like bathing one's eyes free of the memory of rubble dust and of the destruction which lay behind us. We were not going too fast and enjoyed the detail of the village life and farm activities as we meandered through hamlets and countryside largely untouched by the war. The villages were rather scattered, straggling affairs, the homes mostly half-timbered peasant cottages and smallholdings set in low-lying marshland ribbed with silver-glittering drainage ditches in the green. This gradually gave way to more sandy and peaty soil pleasantly sprinkled with silver birch and heather.

After a long trip with one or two halts, the trucks whined off the road onto a sandy track, engaged four-wheel drive and with wheels spinning edged their way forward with noisy effort. Eventually we had to dismount as one by one the wheels bedded themselves in and the atmosphere became as murky with a blue haze of exhaust smoke as it did with obscene language from the drivers. With the Jocks walking they progressed a little more easily. The drivers eased off their swearing and the Jocks took over where they had left off. A 15cwt ditched itself and had to be pulled out by a Jeep and a carrier.

This proved to be an exceedingly long walk with the amount of equipment we were carrying. To our surprise, at the far end of the sandy track the order 'Embus' came and on the convoy rolled. Rumour was rife. At our level then, we had no real idea of the whereabouts or shape of the enemy. A few more miles and we reached a pleasant small town on slightly higher ground call Worpswede. This we felt sure must be our de-bussing-point but on we went again. We realised we had not far to go, however, as we had noticed the 7th/9th Royal Scots settling themselves in there. Another couple of miles and we branched off to the right over a small bridge, continued for ¾ of a mile, then at a Y junction, de-bussed on the left-hand fork. As we did so we realised that once again the Battalion was to be in contact with the enemy. Our reluctant ears and the uneasy lightness of our stomachs informed us immediately of sounds we hoped we would never hear again: the crump of erratic, stray shelling fairly close at hand and the very occasional burst of a more distant Spandau, reminiscent of someone jerkily ripping calico.

The enemy were still showing fight! 'Hell, Surr! Have yon Jerries no' had enough *** fighting yet? I tell ye, me, ma warr's feenished, I'm no takin' onny b*** unnecessary risks the noo; no me. I'll go gaie-canny 'til they're feenished, and b*** it. I'm fo' hame in yin piece me'sel an' I'll noo shoot another *** gun in ma life, noo again!' In these words Pte Tarn more or less summed up the sentiments of all of us.

As we formed up beside the trucks, preparing to march off, we searched our surroundings for any least clue as to what lay in store. All around us stretched vast rectangles of black soiled peat marsh on which flourished green grass. Each rectangle had its sandy tracked rim lined lengthwise with smallholding dairy farms set about 150 yards back from the road, in an intermittent straggle of birchwoods and orchard. Each cut their fuel from the peat bog at the rear of the house.

We were relieved to hear that it was our turn to reserve in B Company, with A Company 'up'. There was precious little definite news of the enemy and his exact location. He appeared to be somewhere over the marshland and heath a mile or so to our north and west. Our main task was apparently to locate and eliminate any stragglers we might find, who had been cut off by our advance, and to contain any attempts at patrolling which the enemy might make.

Each Company was sprinkled out along a line of farm billets. North-west of us lay D and C companies, D linking with A, while farther up the road were the mortar Platoon, BHQ and the anti-tank Platoon. We took over the positions from the 1st Bn the Worcesters, of 43 (Wessex) Division and they pulled out, I think as much in the dark on what the 'form' was as we were.

Not knowing what might be in store for us, we prepared for the worst and set about digging in for all round defence about each building, watched with variations of annoyance and interest by the farming folk who were still fully in occupation. We could not dig below 2 feet before the trenches became waterlogged. The buildings reminded me very much in their materials and design of the little farm at Ibbenburen out of which we had been shot-shelled-and-burned, and also of the one at Uphusen more recently where the 88 shells had made life so trying. I hoped fervently that we were in for a happier time here.

Four moderately peaceful days did pass in reserve, waiting and wondering. The Jocks got restive at being kept on the alert with so little news; waiting over the hours of darkness in their slit trenches, taking turns sleeping inside, then resting and eating all they could during the day. From time to time sudden violent sounds in the near distance told us that however illusive the enemy were, they were still reacting to any moves made by our forward companies. There was momentous tension and expectancy. The stolid German farming folk of our billet made occasional queries. Suddenly on the evening of 6 May, I heard the shout outside: '"O" Group at Company HQ, Mr White, Surr!' Lord! what's up now? I wondered. 'Coupe, keep your 38 set on for the BBC News. We don't want to miss the end of the war when it comes', Brown's voice called as I made my way over to the farm Smyg had occupied as his HQ.

The news from Company HQ, I realised in the first few words, would be a deep disappointment to Pte Tarn, to put it mildly. 'Well', said Smyg, 'at 0500 hours tomorrow morning, the company will parade ready to move forward through A Company to a position about 1½ miles beyond. There we will patrol and clear at Company strength, a 4 mile square piece of land. Its called an island by virtue of the fact that it is surrounded on the west by a river and on the north, south and east by a 15- to 25-foot canal-cum-stream. The information is that two days ago the Worcesters cleared this and captured a German platoon. They afterwards withdrew 1½ miles and it seems likely the enemy may have re-occupied the place. No support weapons can be brought forward to help as both the rail and road bridges are blown (there is a single track running north to south across the island). Also the 2i/c of the Worcesters blew himself up on a mine in his Jeep at the bridge while they were up there. Sgt Cowie, you will stop with your chaps as firm base to guard the southern end of our leg together with Company HQ Pip and Pete, you will lead in turn half way out in a clockwise direction, then on the return you will split forces and return separately down these two tracks to meet again at Company HQ. Keep in radio contact with me all the way.' Smyg then went on in detailing dress, rations and so on. We split up to put our chaps in the picture. I collected the Jocks of my Platoon from their two farms into the one and dished out the news, which was greeted with varied expressions of disgust.

Just before 3 am next morning, 7 May 1945, it was necessary

to start rousing the men to get some breakfast and get organised for the day's activities. It was inky-dark and chilly. The first sounds of cocks crowing came to us from other farms through the shrouds of mist which acted as a lighter background to the buildings and trees. I wondered if the lack of cocks crowing in the immediate farms in which we were living signified that the Jocks had already eaten them. Swearing was prolific as the muffled-hooded figures crashed about in the cold night air to the metallic rattle of mess-tins and weapons. However, their mood thawed somewhat with the later dawning of a fine spring day.

We paraded just before light. Men, weapons and ammunition were checked and I ran over likely methods of tackling the patrol, according to the cover we found on arrival, with the section commanders. We based our assumption on the countryside being very similar to that surrounding our present positions as far as one could guess from the appearance of the map.

Each one of us knew that the war might be over at literally any hour and all our experience and guile was pooled to ensure we completed the task within the framework of the orders given, while sparing no effort to minimise any possible foreseeable risk. I had never known such teamwork, yet under it all there was a nagging sense of reluctance in undertaking a daylight round trip of about 8 miles of patrol into territory containing an unknown enemy content, and no information at all on their likely whereabouts, if they were there, or what weapons they might be expected to have up their sleeves.

We understood we would have no artillery to call on if we met trouble, but as some precaution it was decided to make use of man-packed 3-inch mortars if close support were needed.

The Company cooks produced scalding tea and a sandwich to add to any other odds and ends we had been able to scrounge as a breakfast before we moved off at about 0400 hours on our 2¼ mile approach march to reach A, the forward Company. The blown bridge which was to mark the start of the patrol lay about a mile beyond their forward sections.

We marched up in file to A Company, then from thence we advanced as a patrol, with one platoon forward. At the line of trees, just short of the bridge, the column stopped and we waited for the Jeeps to come up to unload the mortar bombs and mortars. Two cases with three bombs in each were dished out to the men while the mortar crews carried their weapons. Sgt Cowie's Platoon had meanwhile gone 300 yards ahead to the bridge, where they took up positions to cover us in while we marched to join them in the positions they were to hold as firm base. The Jeep drivers were ordered to wait back under cover of the trees until our return in about four hours if all went well, and under no circumstances to come forward with their vehicles due to further suspected mines.

We reached the bridge, staggering under our load of mortar bombs as we walked along the grass verge, dumped our loads there, then picked our way carefully over the rubble lying in the water, to reach the far bank of the blown bridge. As we went, half our attention was taken in looking carefully for mines among the approaches and wreckage of the bridge, and half in a long careful survey of the landscape ahead to detect any signs of lurking trouble. 'Don't bunch, keep well spread out!'

A short distance to our right lay the blown rail bridge. The scene ahead was of peaceful heathland, heather, scrub, scattered young birch trees, a few houses of a village and sprinkled farms beyond. I took 10 Platoon over to the railway line and advanced carefully, using all possible cover, towards the country railway station in the distance. Pip took 11 Platoon on a parallel advance up the road 180 yards to our left, to cover the crossroads and search the village. Meanwhile, Smyg had decided to accompany us part way on the patrol rather than wait back listening in on the radio at the bridge and he followed with Company HQ a short distance behind me.

A movement 100 yards or so ahead of us in the tangle of young birch and heather drew my attention to a woman's figure sneaking away north towards the interior of the 'island' and looking back at us at intervals as she went. As she had seen us, we were not keen that she should be allowed to advance before us with this information over ground we were to cover, possibly alerting any enemy we might otherwise have surprised. I gave her a shout of 'Halt' and we waved her to come over, but she either did not understand or feared our intentions. She stopped, looked back, stopped again a few yards farther on, then hurried away, moving at a walk just short of a run when we repeated the call. 'Shall I wing her with my rifle Sir . . . get her in the legs and bring her down?' Pte Mckenzie suggested, though without enthusiasm. 'Noo . . . let her be mon, she'll likely no' bother us Surr', another Jock interjected to me. I had already considered the same idea and rejected it not only from dislike of shooting anyone or thing needlessly, especially a woman in the back, but I also realised ruefully that even the report of a 'shot across her bows' to halt her would defeat its own ends in warning any waiting enemy that a patrol was about. It would have been useful, perhaps, I thought, to have been able to question her in case she could be made to let slip any news of the enemy. Never before had we felt such an oppressive aversion to running the slightest unnecessary risks. A few Jocks muttered to each other on the chances of her tipping off the enemy. 'Hell, Surr! Have ye no' thought that mebee the warr's already feenished an' we've no' yet heard it?' 'How will any stray Jerries know when the war's over, Sir?' 'Concentrate on the job you're doing or you may miss the chance to see the end.' I myself was tantalised to think of the possibility of being ditched at the last fence, knowing that the patrol, only a routine one to supply a relatively unimportant piece of information at Brigade, might yet run into anything or nothing.

A short distance beyond, and 'O' Group was called by Smyg on the platform of the lonely country halt – just a platform and a little waiting room. Smyg informed us that he would keep his advance HQ in this area and stop here while Pip and I completed the patrol so that his radio would help bridge the gap to the mortars if we ran into trouble. It seemed to me that we would be out of mortar range for a large part of the patrol anyway. I suggested to Smyg that I marked his and my maps with a series of letters covering our proposed route which we would radio back as we passed them. In this way he would know to within about 500 yards, just where we were all the time. I also hoped this would double check any error of map reference passed over the radio if we did have to call for mortar support.

It was about six in the morning as we set off leaving Smyg at the cross tracks near the station. 'Good luck, watch your flanks and rear as you go!' Smyg called after us. The lack of cover forced us to advance in Indian file a lot of the time with myself at the head and I did not relish the thought that whatever trouble we ran into would more than likely be met by the leading section suddenly coming under fire. About 150 yards behind Pip followed with 11 Platoon. For a while we made use of what cover the houses of the village offered, leaving the railway to our right. The place at first glance seemed to be deserted, but a closer look into windows here and there rewarded one with a glimpse of movement of a face or figure within the gloom, watching. We could not search everywhere and had to trust to these being only civilians and that we would not be shot in the back.

Ahead of us now lay the road and near it the railway bordering a 1½ mile strip of dense thicket and woodland. I decided I had better remain with the leading section commander and leave Pln HQ third in the column, changing each section for a turn in the lead with me after every 1,000 yards. I kept Pte Coupe with his radio in the second section to be within hailing distance in case of trouble.

The complete lack of information and the tension of the queer circumstances of this patrol gave it a strain and a suspense which even the pumping of our fear-boosted hearts and the peculiar excitement of a patrol could not offset. Now there was just enough room to advance each section in arrowhead formation under cover. Already we were sweating with the labour of our progress up ditches, through brambles and covering short stretches of open ground, sprinting in blobs of two and three men at a time. Just on our left ran the road which circled the 'island's' rectangular shape. The job of the rear section was to check quickly over each farm and barn we passed to protect the rear. As we progressed so we got wetter and dirtier from the flooded, swamp-like ditches, dykes and farmyards which had to be negotiated. We must have presented a fearsome spectacle to the wayside farmers and their families, whom one after the other we nearly startled out of their wits as we burst from cover unexpectedly and searched their premises.

We had not gone many hundred yards when I spotted a lone figure pedalling down the road towards us. He had almost reached us when suddenly he noticed our figures sprinkled along the ditch and in the trees. I stepped out to stop him. He was surprised and intrigued with our uniform and not at all scared. He appeared, as far as we could tell, to be a Russian DP and in reply to our pidgin German questions I gathered that he thought the Germans had either pulled up to the north of the island, or out of it; but to interpret him was largely guesswork. He suddenly waxed excited and pointed up the road we were going and managed to communicate to us that 2km farther up, he knew of an SS officer who was hiding in a farm in civilian clothes. Here an inspiration struck me – if we could trust him – and I set out to get him to understand how he could help make the 'Wehrmacht Kaput'. He agreed to walk up the road ahead of the patrol, pushing his bike, on the look out for the enemy, while we slunk along in the bushes at an interval. If he saw anything he was to stop and look back. In this way we proceeded at greater speed and with a little more assurance that we would not be unexpectedly ambushed. A mongrel dog we had not hitherto noticed, joined forces with the Russian and sniffed about, running in and out of the bushes as our unorthodox patrol progressed, and so, to my mind, adding to the value of the pilot patrol proceeding us.

All was now going very smoothly, I gave word to Pte Coupe to radio back each letter marked on our route as we passed it to inform Smyg of our progress. Eventually we reached the house the Russian had intimated contained the SS officer. We spent ten minutes on thoroughly searching this with about fifteen men. None of the several terrified farm workers that the Jocks unceremoniously trundled out by the scruff of the neck for the Russian's scrutiny could be identified as this chap, to the intense disappointment of the Russian. He seemed immediately to lose interest in our patrol and mounted his bike to ride back towards 12 Platoon. I gave up the thought of making him continue to help with our task. To use any force on him might have rendered his services a doubtful asset.

Gradually we completed one leg of the rectangle and on reaching the northern rim of the island crossed the railway track, swinging to the east over 200 yards of open field towards another group of farms along the northern rim.

Suddenly one of the Jocks drew my attention to two distant figures dressed in blue-grey uniforms, moving near an outhouse of the farm we were heading towards. 'Jerries, Sir!' he pointed with anxious excitement. The Bren-gunner was already down on the ground commendably quickly, bolt back and sights on the Germans as I sprawled beside him to steady my elbows while I gave a quick look with my binoculars to size things up. How many were they? We were about 50 yards out in the field, the rest of the Platoon now sprawling in all-round defence positions. The Germans did not yet seem to have seen us. As I focused the glasses with tense speed on the figures, cursing my pounding heart and heavy breathing while trying to hold my arms dead still for a better look, two thoughts sprinted through my head: should we charge them, firing from where we were with 150 yards to cover in the open, or turn back to cover 50 yards behind, hoping that we would not be seen, and then stalk them from the shield of the trees?

'Hold it!' I heaved a profound sigh of relief. They were a couple of farm workers wearing forage caps and dressed in what were evidently Volksturm or Home Guard overalls! These gave them the identical appearance at this range to a couple of German soldiers moving about their positions. How nearly they had 'had it' from the Bren. The relief sent the spirits of the Jocks behind me soaring into jocund merriment which had to be silenced, for we were not yet half way through our task.

'Well, Sir, we may not have found that SS officer in that farm, but we'll have good supper with the thirty-five eggs we took instead', Cpl Dare ruminated to me as we got up and moved forwards again in higher spirits. 'Ye'll have a guid omelette an' noo doot Surr, we've no' got thirty-five eggs only, but nearer twa hundred'n feefty Surr!' another Jock interjected at my elbow, gently patting his windproof smock which I was amazed to see was bulging to capacity with them. They were held from falling out by the belt at his waist. 'It's a right guid job we had na' to crawl an' fight jus' now, Surr, or I'd be a walkin' omelette mesel' the noo!' Another Jock in the rear section we later found was carrying a large basket of them too, which were added to as the basket was passed to whichever section's turn it was to be last and to check over the farms.

Finally, we reached the extreme north-east limit of our patrol and the farthest distance from Company HQ. The railway track swung to the north while the road still remained beside us on our left as it turned to the east too. Another 1,000 yards to the east should bring us to the point where we could turn south again by a different route to Pip's platoon which was still following us at 250 yards. So far the only direct evidence of the enemy we had met was the encouraging sign of groups of recently occupied but now deserted slit trenches. I was beginning to feel very much more at ease in my mind that perhaps after all no more enemy had penetrated back on to the 'island'. There was no time to slack, though. It was very hard work all the time to keep the Jocks in their section order spread well out covering the wooded strips, and also keeping the following section commanders and Platoon HQ in their correct spacing behind. Neither the Jocks nor the NCOs seemed to try to think for themselves while there was someone else to do it. Even at this stage in the war fatigue was making them slack off when a job was nearing completion, which could, as we had seen in the car incident in Bremen, so easily and needlessly cost the lives of the wilful ones and those with them.

I noticed the last section at this point was lagging badly. On investigation I found several of them engaged on looting a farm, leaving themselves and the section ahead open to any attack. The ringleader appeared to be Pte Bill Stein, my batman while we were in Holland and the man who had so nearly wiped me out with his Bren.

Finally, the eastern leg was completed as we arrived at a Gusthaus or pub on the corner of a T junction in the sand track. The Platoon deployed to wait for Pip to come up with his chaps while I radioed back to Smyg to say 'We are coming down the home straight.'

Here my route with 10 Platoon cut south-west for 1½ to 2 miles of straight sand track forming the remaining side of the rectangle. Pip would continue for another ½ mile or so on our original course before turning down a track parallel to ours on the eastern rim of the 'island'. Before turning back and while waiting for Pip I had a good look through my binoculars out over the countryside beyond the limit of our patrol, but could see no sign of any enemy; nor did our presence moving on the rim of cover attract any reaction.

There was very little cover on the return leg, but we felt far happier that after all the place was clear of enemy. Then, about two-thirds of the way back, there was a momentary scare on seeing some movement of figures lying in the sand and heather covering the T junction at the foot of the track. This turned out to our intense relief to be Company HQ and was confirmed when about half a mile out I radioed a message of recognition to Smyg to ensure that no unthinking Jock down there assumed we were enemy, for they had not seen us for some hours.

On reaching Company HQ, I spread the Platoon in an arc, where they lay resting in the sun while I made my way to find and report to Smyg. We must have searched about thirty-five to forty farms or more on the route and covered quite a mileage so that now, with tension eased we felt really grateful for the rest of ¾ of an hour or so while waiting for Pip to get back. Some Jocks, still not satisfied with the large number of eggs we had so far got, came to ask my permission to collect more from the two farms beside us and I allowed one from each section to go.

Finally, Pip got in with nothing to report and we moved wearily back to the small station to collect the mortars and bombs which Smyg had ordered forward a bit to give added range in case of need. Moving back down the railway track in single file we eventually came within sight of the wrecked rail and road bridges. The two Jeeps waiting under cover 300 yards beyond saw us. Forgetting their orders entirely for some puzzling reason, and while still out of earshot, they raced forwards from the cover of the trees to meet us and load the mortars. The leading Jeep braked hard short of the bridge and turned. The following one, still out of vocal range, to our horror continued to drive fast right up to the bridge. As it slowed to stop a few yards short of it, an immediate, vivid splash of flame and tumbling smoke enveloped the Jeep. It lifted bodily in a three-quarter turn to the left in the air, disintegrating. Many feet above it small bits and pieces lazily spun back to earth to splash and clatter in the mud on either side of the embankment and on the road, as the blast of explosion hit us and swept past. There was something heart-stilling and horrible in watching the slowly tumbling bits and pieces and wondering which of the two familiar friendly forms of the drivers they represented. As the smoke cleared the Jeep was revealed as an almost complete wreck. The front two wheels had disappeared and the remains of the engine were bent back into the buckled body where the driver should have been. To our amazement, a shape, hitherto stationary and taken as part of the wreckage, detached itself erratically and staggered to collapse on the road as a bundle of crumpled khaki near the still smoking crater. Again all was as silent and still as before. As the nearest of the Jocks to scramble over the remains of the bridge ran up, the bundle moved a bit again to signify that whatever was left of the driver was at least still alive.

This conclusive proof that the approaches to the bridges were still mined, whether with anti-personnel weapons as well we did not yet know, certainly did not add to our ease of mind. We each anxiously picked our way over the rail bridge wreckage carrying a load of six 3-inch mortar bombs, then squelched across the meadow to the Jeep on the road. If one of us chanced on a mine carrying this load it would result in quite a bang. Reaching the Jeep, I was somewhat shocked to realise that the shallow crater beside the wrecked vehicle was situated exactly where we had walked earlier at the start of the patrol similarly bomb laden. I thanked God our weight had not proved quite enough to set off the explosion. How many more were still sown here, we wondered as we picked our way about with our hearts in our throats.

'He's alive, by God!' a Jock was calling as he knelt over the bundle, 'And in yin piece too!' The driver miraculously suffered from nothing worse than a deep gash in the head, a very severe shaking and shock. It was hard to imagine how he had escaped with his life as the engine's remains occupied what was left of the driving seat. Neither he nor the other driver seemed capable of saying anything.

The mine had been of the glass type which offered no reaction to a mine detector. It was of much less power than a Teller mine and left a crater only a couple of feet deep just next to the one that had so recently killed the 2i/c of the Worcesters.

It was not till that evening that the unbelievable news of the war's end filtered down to us and I subsequently wondered whether these drivers could have heard this over the radio a little earlier and have been so intoxicated with it that they had hurried forward with the glad tidings, completely forgetting the mines in their excitement.

The return march to the Company area seemed a very long one following our exhausting patrol. On the way I noticed what I had not done on the way out, that the fields around the main Y junction near A Company, who challenged our return, were plastered with what looked like shell craters of about 5.5-inch calibre.

That evening, just as we had completed the working out of stags for the night, the thud of running boots clumped hollowly towards us over the turf path outside, coming from the direction of Company HQ farm. An excited Jock's voice accompanied the thud of feet shouting 'Th' b*** war's feenished. Jerry's kaput. Hell is this no' a nicht' t' remember! It's no' a *** joke it's *** true I tell ye!' the voice urgently insisted to some sceptical Jock outside. 'Did I no' hear it mesel' at Company heedquarters? It's *** feenished!' Almost at the same moment the sky outside lit and flickered with red, green and white Verey lights and mortar parachute flares, brilliantly silhouetting the trees and farm buildings and lacing the ground with long, weird, moving shadows. To the plop of discharge of these flares were added a few distant shots and shouts as of a Wild West film celebration. It was short-lived rejoicing for within a few minutes a heavy 'rocket' arrived in reprimand from the Brigadier to put a swift lid on this jubilant lack of restraint and discipline shown by some nearby unit.

As the noise and the queries of the Jocks died down, I continued to stand at the door of the farm looking out into the night, listening to distant laughter and commotion. Could it be true? It must be. It was. Excited confirmation came from my own 38 set operator who had tuned to get the BBC faintly! I quite suddenly felt tremendously tired. It was not just the tiredness due to our long, nervy patrol. It seemed to be the tiredness of all the sleep we had lost over the last few months, yet curiously more of the mind than the body. With it, however, came a paradoxical feeling of lightness as though a heavy weight were slipping off one's consciousness, a weight so long a part of life that at times it was almost possible to imagine it had always been there. I hurried to Company HQ, queried by several Jocks on stag as I went, to make quite sure, still not trusting the news. This second confirmation made it no easier to believe.

If we found the news hard to believe, so did a German officer and about fourteen men who were reported to the left of A Company in the 7th/9th Royal Scots' area. They could not be convinced the war was over for a further forty-eight hours and repulsed with fire any attempt made to contact them. This seemed to demonstrate to just what extent the enemy communication and control had deteriorated. Our orders were, meanwhile, to carry on with normal stags and alertness just as though nothing had happened.

I had never pictured that the reception of this so long hoped for and magical news of the war's end would have been taken so quietly. Apart from the first boisterous announcement, no one had rushed about yelling the glad tidings. Two men in Sgt Cowie's platoon raised a cheer and in the evening Smyg issued a tot of rum to those who wanted it to celebrate. Later that night the sounds of a sing-song, no doubt helped by the rum issue, broke out from one platoon, but that was all. Life went on just as before. Perhaps those on stag talked a bit more freely than they normally did. Apart from the all-satisfying knowledge that so far as we knew no more attacks were to take place in Europe, our immediate future seemed to be almost as uncertain as before. For the first time a new topic, the chances of our being involved in attacks against the Japanese, was bandied about. Little did we realise how very near we were to this thought taking material shape a short while later.

The farmer, his wife and four school-aged, long-limbed youngsters were not so far 'in the picture' as to what was going on. As I made my way to turn in for the first part of the night before my spell of duty, I met the middle-aged couple standing at the door of the room I had let them keep. Behind, in the warm, flickering glow of lamplight I caught glimpses of the youngsters preparing for bed as I paused. I could sense the questions they so wanted to ask and which had been prompted by the unusual celebration of sing-song rum and fireworks which had broken the normal routine earlier. The farmer and his wife both looked much alike as they hesitantly regarded me from querying, china-blue eyes out of weather-beaten, sun-tanned faces like a couple of wrinkled walnuts. They seemed prematurely bent and greying after their hard life and in a way rather pathetic. They stood in their coarse, worn farm clothes, mole-like in their earthiness and scent, trying to think of some way of communicating a question I could guess at easily enough. The farmer stroked his stubbly chin for inspiration and making a sound in doing so as of sandpaper being rubbed together.

The elder son, running grubby hands through his tousled frizzy hair and with his shirt half off, came up to see if he could help. He was shortly joined by the daughter who may have been his twin. She looked rather like a sun-tanned angel in a much-patched, threadbare night-shirt. I, with limited knowledge of German, was equally stuck in trying to put over the news. We stood contemplating each other for some time. The girl was unplaiting long coils of blonde hair which fluttered almost like shimmering wings behind her head against the light as she worked with deft fingers.

'Der Krieg ist kaput, be-ended', I said in my pidgin German. 'Zo . . . allus kaput, allus kaput. Keine zieg, Hitler! Verdamt schwein!' The farmer muttered, or something to that phonetic effect, as he drew a deep breath in between pursed leathery lips, nodding his head in ponderous slow weariness. 'Zo . . . Engelandt keine zieg, Deutchland keine zieg . . . der verdamt Nazis.' He turned to put his arms round the shoulders of his wife and of his children, sighing thinly through straggly, decaying teeth. There were tears in the eyes of his wife and then in the eyes of the daughter. The frizzy haired son, looking puzzled, pulled his shirt on again. Behind him I caught a glimpse of the two smaller children, who, sensing something amiss, looked out from over the coverlet in which they were curled on some straw in a corner of the room. Their eyes shone brightly and wide in query like a couple of mice in torchlight. The farmer had moved slowly back with his wife to a table in the lamplight. She, bent and sobbing, had picked up something from the chimney-piece which I could not make out as she crouched over it at the table. Her distress was upsetting the others. The husband, himself looking strained and tired, tried to comfort her.

I felt very uncomfortable and puzzled that my news should have occasioned such a distressing scene. The tightly clenched bony hands of the woman jerked, trembling in their grasp of whatever it was she held, so that her knuckles showed white. A short strip of what looked like black velvet showed between her fists as she pressed the object in her hands to her breast, then, sobbing anew, dropped the thing onto the table and buried her head in her arms as it clattered. It was a black-banded photograph in quite a small frame of a young man in a Luftwaffe uniform. One of the woman's hands still fingered an iron cross which had become detached and its movements seemed the focus of the tear-staining eyes of the rest of the family whom I don't think were even aware of my presence any more as I gently closed the door.

Nothing could have so eloquently summed up the utter waste and stupidity of the war, and the futile tragedy it had brought to so many homes right round the world than this family at that moment. There were no real winners. Each country taking part had lost. Perhaps, though, there was a credit side; if matter and material forces had done all the losing, then the unseen credit balance must be on the side of materiality's opposite, a gain for the things of the spirit.

PUBLISHER'S EPILOGUE

VE Day, 8 May 1945, was not the end of the Jocks' war, but Peter White and a newly reinforced 10 Platoon spent it in the German countryside enjoying the spring sunshine, feeling secure and at ease for the first time for months. At last they could relax, meet friends, swap yarns and share a drink as the Battalion's pipers practised. However, fear was still the men's companion. They knew they might encounter SS fanatics who would rather fight on than accept defeat.

On 9 May, a trickle, then a constant stream of German soldiers from various units began to enter the Battalion area. The Allies were now faced with the substantial problem: what could or should be done with these men. Operation Eclipse was launched to disarm the German forces and collect their weapons. At the end of hostilities the enemy was concentrated in an area to the west of a line from Hamburg to Bremen, including Bremerhaven, Emden and the coastal area. The Jocks were under strict instructions to act properly towards their German charges – no more searching or looting of prisoners. Because there were too many men to intern, it was decided that each German unit, except SS, would remain under the command of its own officers who were subject to the direction of a local British divisional commander. A German liaison officer was attached to each battalion headquarters and it was through him that orders and requests for labour were given. 155 Brigade was ordered to clear an area to the north and east of Vegesack, north-west of Bremen. As part of the operation, 10 Platoon was charged with collecting and guarding arms and ammunition dumps, food and equipment.

German guides met the advance parties at Vegesack and provided safe conduct through their own fully armed troops to billeting areas for the British troops. Information was provided on the position of enemy mines which were to be lifted by German sappers. En route to Vegesack, 10 Platoon passed through Bremen, the scene of such recent and bloody fighting. White recorded how strange it was to enter territory where German forces outnumbered the British by 10:1.

Billets were found in Osterhalz-Scharmbeck and the Jocks made themselves at home. On the evening of the second day a powerful loud-speaker was rigged up in front of the town hall to relay Prime Minister Winston Churchill's victory speech. British forces and townspeople gathered to listen. Then the pipes and drums (the latter recently collected from the Duhamel's farm in Belgium where they had remained since the Jocks came ashore in October 1944) beat retreat for the first time in eight months. 'The whole ceremony's flourish was like a rich, ornamental seal being tagged on to the foot of our particular page in the war's history', White wrote.

But the page was not quite finished yet. The job of locating all arms, ammunition and equipment remained. White, Pip Powell and their Jocks visited villages, and with the help of local people, particularly children, White was able to compile a list of ammunition stores and dumps, 88mm guns and sites, small arms and military vehicles, together with their map references. Their next task was to collect as much of the material as possible, particularly the 88mm ammunition, some of which was in a dangerous condition.

Meanwhile, time was found to smarten up the men and their equipment and to repair vehicles. The Jocks' social life also began to look up: the village cinema put on a film for them and an ENSA show was held in Bremen. Much time was spent in writing letters home as straggling columns of badly dressed, undernourished, footsore German soldiers passed through on their way south.

Towards the end of May the Battalion set off for Sustedt. They believed and hoped they were destined for Norway but after about nine days' wait it became clear that they were to go to the American-held area of Germany near Magdeburg, next to the Russian sector. The Jocks' mission was to take over the military government, police force and administration of displaced persons and POW camps from the Americans, and to garrison the area.

Peter White was in the advance party that set off on the long journey across Germany. Battalion HQ was established in LetzLingen whilst A and B Companies drove on to Oebisfelde-Kaltendorf, which was full of American troops. During a five-day take-over, the Americans briefed the British, showing them vital points of interest (VPs), including a salt mine which had been converted into an underground factory where thousands of displaced persons had been forced to work. White became chief of police and Jan Duhamel acted as his interpreter. By the time the Battalion arrived, all systems were operating efficiently. No hostility was shown towards the Jocks and the townsfolk were generally well behaved and civil.

White felt that his time in Oebisfelde was the happiest spent in Germany. He was settled, at ease and enjoyed the work but not all the Jocks shared White's contentment. They resented the non-fraternisation rules that prevented them having local girlfriends, and they found the number of guard duties excessive. However, alcohol was plentiful, which proved some compensation.

The Jocks believed their wanderings were finally over, but suddenly one night, a warning order was received – 'prepare to move at short notice'. White was deeply disappointed to learn that the Battalion was to leave Oebisfelde, and soon found himself in the advance party heading back to Belgium. It was believed that the Battalion was to be reorganised along air transportable lines ready to be flown where needed as an Empire Strategic Reserve. The men were billeted in Moorsel village near Aalst – and the Jocks were delighted to learn that there was no non-fraternisation rule in Belgium. Billets were in local homes and those inhabited by young women were much in demand.

Now they waited again. White's life settled into a routine of marches, inspections of men and kit, and compiling aircraft loading tables. There were swimming galas and football matches. In the evenings, post-VE Day celebrations finally began in earnest. But all the while, rumours circulated about their future.

White took the opportunity to attend an instructor's course in art in Brussels for a fortnight which gave him a welcome break from duty, as did a ten-day leave spent in a hotel by the sea at Blankenbergh. He was also granted home leave which coincided with his brother John's break from serving in Italy.

Back on duty, there were yet more route marches, some lasting three days. Then on 5 August 1945, Peter White was off again in another advance party back to Germany. Still in the dark about the 'bigger picture', at least the Jocks now knew they were not joining the Empire Strategic Reserve. This time they were bound for Brackwede near Bielefeld in Westphalia where they were to take over administration and guard duties similar to their role in Oebisfelde. Here, guard duties were slightly less onerous for the Jocks as a Polish company was detailed to assist them.

The system of administration had become more official by now; new military government regulations were being enforced curtailing the freedom of action which White had enjoyed at Oebisfelde. However, living conditions were comfortable – the officers' mess was in a large house belonging to one of Rommel's former ADCs. The Jocks were relieved to hear the fraternisation rules had been relaxed since their last duties in Germany and got on very well with the local girls. White found it strange to watch them dancing together and to think back over recent events. The wheel of the Jocks' experience with the Germans seemed to have turned full circle. The contradictions and questions raised by the conflict continued to effect him, particularly in Bielefeld where he witnessed the devastation caused by Allied bombing. 'Perhaps in any future war the safest place might ironically be not at home, but as close as one could get to the opposing troops in the infantry', he said.

The end of Peter White's life with 4th Battalion KOSB was sudden. He was included in a group of officers and Jocks who were being transferred to the 1st Battalion, part of 3rd Division, to fill in vacancies left by those recently demobbed. It was rumoured that they were to take part in the war against Japan. This move was a great disappointment to White, who now felt a great affinity with 4th Battalion; the men had gone through so much together.

1st Battalion was stationed in Belgium, at Deynze near Ghent, in a part of the country that White knew well. It was intended that 3rd Division would go to Florida to be re-equipped by the US forces and trained in jungle warfare before being shipped over to the Pacific to take part in the assault on mainland Japan. However, before they left for Florida, Japan surrendered after atomic bombs were dropped on Hiroshima and Nagasaki: 'How we wished we had reached America before this happened. We might have had a lengthy holiday. The complete end of the war came as rather an anti-climax for now we knew it would be a year or more before we reached our turn for demob.'

White's final posting was with the 1st Battalion to Egypt, where it was deployed on peacekeeping operations in Palestine and Egypt's Canal Zone. White was promoted to Captain and appointed Education Officer. While in Egypt he typed up the notes he had made during the campaign in north-west Europe and sent them home to his father. They form the basis of his diary. He returned to England after his demob in 1946.

White went back to his studies at the Royal Academy from where he graduated in 1951. He found it difficult to settle down. For the next fifteen years he travelled widely, either by motorcycle or in a car pulling a caravan, and made his living writing, painting, illustrating geography text books and teaching English or French. He toured northern Europe, Spain, Portugal and southern France, and went overland to Yugoslavia and Greece. He also found time to tour the British Isles. White returned to England to settle down in 1966. He set up his own business accepting painting commissions, producing mainly portraits but landscapes too, and his work became well-known and respected on both sides of the Atlantic. He met Elizabeth, his future wife, at church and they married in November 1972. They lived very happily together in Aldeburgh, Suffolk until Peter died aged sixty-four from a heart attack in 1985 while restoring a picture.

Bill Allan, one of White's corporals, finished the war a sergeant and returned to his job as a joiner in Hawick. Later, he became Burgh Officer with Hawick Council. Captain Frank Coutts had a long and distinguished career in the Army, becoming a brigadier. He was Colonel of the KOSB from 1970 to 1980. Captain Alan Hill, RAMC, MC, returned to his medical practice outside Oban. Major Colin Hogg, who was mentioned in despatches, returned to his medical practice with Edinburgh Council and Major Donald Hogg, MC, went back to his farm in Kelso where he still enjoys the country life today. Major Alan 'Smyg' Innes, also mentioned in despatches, resumed his life as a farmer. Corporal Alec Leitch DCM was discharged from hospital where he had been treated for his wounds and returned to Musselburgh and his employment in the grocery trade.

The 4th Battalion KOSB remained in Germany after VE Day as part of the British Army of the Rhine, except for a brief period spent in Belgium on stand-by for duty in Palestine. Demobilisation began in August 1945 and the process was complete by the beginning of 1946 when the battalion was placed in 'suspended animation' – effectively disbanded. It was reformed in May 1947. In March 1961, the 4th and 5th Battalions were amalgamated to form the 4th/5th Battalion the KOSB as part of the reorganisation of the Territorial Army. In March 1967, the 4th/5th Battalion the KOSB disbanded but the Regiment still thrives. It won battle honours in Korea, Malaya, Aden and in the Gulf War. At the end of the twentieth century the 1st Battalion saw duty in Northern Ireland and as *With the Jocks* went to print the men of the KOSB had just returned to the UK from service in Cyprus.

INDEX

Note: Major entries for people are in chronological order. Peter White is abbreviated to PW